T0287308

The Nauvoo Endowment Companies, 1845–1846

THE NAUVOO ENDOWMENT COMPANIES

1845–1846

A DOCUMENTARY HISTORY

Edited by
DEVERY S. ANDERSON
GARY JAMES BERGERA
Foreword by
RICHARD S. VAN WAGONER

Signature Books • Salt Lake City • 2005
A Smith-Pettit Foundation Book

Jacket design by JSK Design

© 2005 The Smith-Pettit Foundation. Published by arrangement with the copyright holder. All rights reserved. Signature Books is a registered trademark of Signature Books Publishing, LLC.

www.signaturebooks.com

The Nauvoo Endowment Companies, 1845-1846:A Documentary History was printed on acid-free paper and was composed, printed, and bound in the United States of America.

2018 2017 2016 2015 2014 7 6 5 4 3

LIBRARY OF CONGRESS CATALOGING-IN-PUBLICATION DATA
The Nauvoo endowment companies, 1845-1846 : a documentary history / edited by Devery S. Anderson and Gary James Bergera ; foreword by Richard S. Van Wagoner.
p. cm.
"A Smith-Pettit Foundation book."
Includes bibliographical references and index.
ISBN 10: 1-56085-187-2
ISBN 13: 978-1-56085-187-5
1. Nauvoo Temple (Nauvoo, Ill. : 1841-1850) 2. Temple endowments (Mormon Church)—Illinois—Nauvoo—History—19th century. I Anderson, Devery S. II. Bergera, Gary James.

BX8685.N3N38 2005
289.3'77343—dc22

2005042885

In memory of

Gregory Clare Anderson

and

Ella Almeda Larsen Turner

CONTENTS

FOREWORD

Richard S. Van Wagoner

FROM MY EARLIEST YEARS I HAVE BEEN BLESSED WITH AN INQUIRING mind. Exploring new frontiers of thought has been a life-long passion. Reading, in particular, has been high adventure. It occurred to me long ago that men and women of sufficient curiosity and intensity of thought can make valuable, even undreamed of discoveries. I believe this is especially true in the field of Mormon studies.

Ironically, in a culture for which "the Glory of God is Intelligence," such intellectual endeavors as asking important questions and sharing new ways of thinking have not always been appreciated or encouraged. In fact, many elements of our Mormon past cry out for more attention. Buried treasures remain hidden, spectral voices demand amplification, veils need parting. Mormon history should not be a mystery.

Devery S. Anderson and Gary James Bergera, in this absorbing book, reveal a crucial chapter of the Mormon past which has been, for the most part, concealed from view. Their intensive and seemingly exhaustive research is revelatory, a veritable treasure trove of information respecting the activities of the endowment companies of the Nauvoo, Illinois, temple. Readers will find insightful commentary as well as chronological entries embodying every available primary source listing members of the endowment companies and related activities of the Nauvoo temple from December 11, 1845, to February 8, 1846.

Nauvoo Mormons were compelled to receive their temple endowments as quickly as possible pending exodus from the city. Life beyond the horizon was a vision of uncertainty. The Saints, once again forced to abandon their proclaimed Zion, hungered for the promised spiritual power and protection of the temple endowment. Abundant faith assured them they could endure the trials ahead as they bid adieu to their homes and beautiful city to start anew elsewhere.

Genealogists will find a wealth of demographic information in this book respecting family members who were officiators and/or participants in the Nauvoo endowments and other temple ordinances. The general LDS reader will be aroused to thought and dialogue, both compelling reasons why we unsettled, curious souls will read and appreciate good books like this one.

EDITORS' INTRODUCTION

The Mormon sojourn in Nauvoo, Illinois, which lasted from 1839 to 1846, is important for many reasons. Among others, it marked the end of the Joseph Smith era in Latter-day Saint history, thus elevating the significance of the doctrines and practices established there. Besides plural marriage, which the prophet introduced to a select group of followers, he also revealed the temple ordinances to various men and women between 1842 and his death on June 27, 1844.

The relevance of these temple rites was made clear in October 1840 when a general conference of the church approved plans to build a temple in Nauvoo. Three months later, a revelation to Joseph Smith, which historian Glen M. Leonard calls "the Prophet's most significant recorded [revelation] in nearly three years," gave further sanction to the new edifice.[1] Building upon earlier revelations of sacred ordinances performed in the church's "House of the Lord" in Kirtland, Ohio, it declared:

> [V]erily I say unto you, how shall your washings be acceptable unto me, except ye perform them in a house which you have built to my name? For, for this cause I commanded Moses that he should build a tabernacle, that they should bear it with them in the wilderness, and to build a house in the land of promise, that those ordinances might be revealed which had been hid from before the world was. Therefore, verily I say unto you, that your anointings, and your washings, and your baptisms

1. Glen M. Leonard, *Nauvoo: A Place of Peace, A People of Promise* (Salt Lake City: Deseret Book Co., 2002), 235.

for the dead, and your solemn assemblies, and your memorials for your sacrifices by the sons of Levi, and for your oracles in your most holy places wherein you receive conversations, and your statutes and judgments, for the beginning of the revelations and foundation of Zion, and for the glory, honor, and endowment of all her municipals, are ordained by the ordinance of my holy house, which my people are always commanded to build unto my holy name. And verily I say unto you, let this house be built unto my name, that I may reveal mine ordinances therein unto my people; For I deign to reveal unto my church things which have been kept hid from before the foundation of the world, things that pertain to the dispensation of the fullness of times. (D&C 124:37-41)

The design of the new temple was soon drafted by William Weeks, a young architect trained in New England.[2] Weeks's plans revealed a temple that tripled the size of its Kirtland predecessor, which was dedicated in 1836 and abandoned in 1838. To oversee the project, Joseph Smith organized a Temple Committee consisting of Reynolds Cahoon, Alpheus Cutler, and Elias Higbee, who managed construction and costs until the temple's completion in 1846.[3]

In February 1841, actual construction of the temple began with excavating space for a basement and, the next month, laying the foundation stones. On April 6, 1841, Joseph Smith, with the Nauvoo Legion in attendance, presided over the cornerstone ceremony.[4] Seven months later, the first ordinances were performed in the basement—baptisms for the dead, a ritual Smith had broached publicly in Nauvoo in August 1840—in a temporary font dedicated in November 1841.[5]

2. See J. Earl Arrington, "William Weeks, Architect of the Nauvoo Temple," *BYU Studies* 19 (Spring 1979): 337-59.

3. Leonard, *Nauvoo,* 245.

4. Ibid., 233-36.

5. The ordinance of baptisms for the dead underwent at least two stages. Beginning in September 1840, members performed proxy baptisms in the Mississippi River. In October 1841, Joseph Smith announced that such baptisms would be suspended until they could be performed in the temple. The following month, a temporary font was constructed and dedicated in the temple basement, and ordinance work resumed. At least 11,500 proxy baptisms were performed between 1840 and 1845. See M. Guy Bishop, "'What Has Become of Our Fathers?' Baptism for the Dead at Nauvoo," *Dialogue: A Journal of Mormon Thought* 23 (Summer 1990): 85-97. See also Alexander L. Baugh, "'For This Ordinance Belongeth to My Temple': The Practice of Baptism for the Dead Outside the Nauvoo Temple," *Mormon Historical Studies* 3 (Spring 2002): 47-58.

Six months later, on May 5, 1842, as construction continued, the prophet began for the first time to introduce washings, anointings, and the endowment ceremony to trusted associates on the second floor of his Red Brick Store, thereby forming the foundations of the Quorum of the Anointed. It was this ceremony, with some alterations, that would be performed in the Nauvoo and subsequent LDS temples. The next year, on September 28, 1843, during a meeting of the Anointed Quorum, Joseph Smith "was by common consent and unanimous voice chosen President of the quorum and anointed and ord[ained] to the highest and holiest order of the priesthood (and companion)." Smith's companion was his first wife, Emma Hale Smith.[6] This ordinance, called the second anointing (also the "fullness of the priesthood"),[7] was first performed on this occasion and marked the admission of women into the Anointed Quorum. The sixty-six men and women who received these ordinances during Smith's lifetime met numerous times from 1842 to 1844 in the Red Brick Store and other locations around Nauvoo. After Smith's death, the Anointed Quorum—joined by new initiates—continued to meet under the leadership of Brigham Young until the temple opened in December 1845. Young increased quorum membership by some twenty-four members during the eighteen-month period preceding completion of the attic level of the temple.[8]

When Joseph and Hyrum Smith were murdered in mid-1844, construction of the temple was halted for almost two weeks. But despite the shock and sorrow, construction resumed on July 8, 1844. However, other issues occupied the attention of church leaders. With Joseph Smith's death, they faced the issue of presidential succession, primarily the assumption of Sidney Rigdon, who had been Smith's first counselor in the First Presidency, that he was the "guardian" of the church. The majority of Saints accepted instead the leadership of the Twelve Apostles, Brigham Young asserting *de facto* supremacy because of his status as president of the quorum. On August 18, forty-three-year-old Young addressed the church and admonished members:

---

6. Joseph Smith, Diary, Sept. 28, 1843.

7. For a discussion of this ordinance, see David John Buerger, "'The Fulness of the Priesthood': The Second Anointing in Latter-day Saint Theology and Practice," *Dialogue: A Journal of Mormon Thought* 16 (Spring 1983): 10-44.

8. For more on the Quorum of the Anointed, see the editors' introduction to Devery S. Anderson and Gary James Bergera, eds., *Joseph Smith's Quorum of the Anointed, 1842-1845: A Documentary History* (Salt Lake City: Signature Books, 2005).

> I discover a disposition of the sheep to scatter, now the shepherd is taken away. I do not say that it will never be right for this people to go from here or scatter abroad; but I do say wait until the time comes, or until you are counseled to do so ... I wish you to distinctly understand that the counsel of the Twelve is for every family that does not belong to the [Wisconsin] Pine company to stay here in Nauvoo, and build up the Temple and get your endowments; do not scatter; "united we stand; divided we fall." ... If we do not carry out the plan Joseph has laid down and the pattern he has given for us to work by, we cannot get any further endowment—I want this to sink deep into your hearts that you may remember it. If you stir up the flame of dissension, will you get an endowment? No![9]

Construction on the temple progressed steadily and Brigham Young easily foresaw the day when the Saints would benefit from it. His mention of the "Pine Company" referred to a committee, headed by Mormon bishop George Miller, established in 1841 to harvest Wisconsin timber for the temple. By 1844, they had processed over 1.5 million feet of lumber. Young presided over the capstone ceremony at the temple site on May 24, 1845. The following October, with the lower floor enclosed but still unfinished, the Saints held their first meeting in the building.[10]

Interestingly enough, the rooms that would receive the most attention were located on the upper, or attic, level. The architect's design designated the attic story as office space with a large room called the Council Chamber in the center, but Young had decided as early as January 1845 that temple ordinances would be performed there.[11] After the roof was finished in September 1845, members of the Anointed Quorum, which for the previous three and a half years had performed the ordinances out-

9. Qtd. in *History of the Church of Jesus Christ of Latter-day Saints, Period II: From the Manuscript History of Brigham Young and Other Original Documents,* ed. B. H. Roberts (Salt Lake City: Deseret Book, 1932), 254-55 (This is the seventh volume of Roberts's *History of the Church* series). The term "endowment" was used generically by Latter-day Saints to refer to a pentecostal outpouring, or gift, of God's spirit. For instance, members were promised, and indeed experienced, an "endowment from on high" (D&C 105:34) at the inaugural worship service in the Kirtland temple in 1836, without any of the rituals now associated with the more specific use of the word "endowment." Few in the audience on this occasion, when Brigham Young spoke, knew that such a ritual existed; so Young's argument would not have been persuasive if he had not been able to draw on the broader definition.

10. Leonard, *Nauvoo,* 252-53.

11. Ibid., 253.

side of the temple, held their first meeting in the building on November 29. "[W]e did not Clothe ourselves [in temple robes]," wrote Apostle Heber C. Kimball, "as others wished to be with us the first time in the Lords Hous[e] when we should offer up the the sign[s] of the Holy Preasthood."[12] The next day, Young dedicated the attic for the administration of endowments.[13]

The attic story included twelve offices, six on the north side, six on the south. Each was 14 feet square, except for two rooms located at the west entrance which were slightly smaller.[14] Each room was numbered, those on the north side given even, and those on the south side odd. In the center of the floor, the Council Chamber measured 88 feet 2 inches long and 28 feet 8 inches wide. According to Nauvoo temple historian Lisle G Brown, "The Council Chamber was fully carpeted, painted white, and heated by two iron stoves."[15]

After the November 30 dedication of the attic, preparations were made to fashion the Council Chamber into separate departments for administering the various stages of the endowment. As temporary rooms, each department was separated by canvas curtains hung from the ceiling. This material was purchased by Elder Orson Hyde the previous June and was intended to be used in erecting a large tent, or tabernacle, in Nauvoo, which was never realized.[16] On December 2, Heber C. Kimball and son William brought potted plants to dress the department designated as the Garden of Eden. Tubs for washings and anointings were donated by Brigham Young and Heber C. Kimball. The Celestial Room, representing the highest heaven, was decorated with donated and borrowed furnishings. Church bishop Newel K. Whitney brought the veil to the temple on the morning of December 4, which Brigham Young hung on the

---

12. "Brigham Young allowed an unendowed person to see them performing signs of the priesthood," writes historian D. Michael Quinn (*The Mormon Hierarchy: Origins of Power* [Salt Lake City: Signature Books in association with Smith Research Associates, 1994], 514), "but not to see them dressed in their endowment robes."

13. Leonard, *Nauvoo,* 253.

14. See Lisle G Brown, "The Sacred Departments for Temple Work in Nauvoo: The Assembly Room and the Council Chamber," *BYU Studies* 19 (Summer 1979): 368.

15. Ibid., 367-68.

16. Ibid., 370. Hyde had purchased over 4,000 yards of canvas for $1,056.56, later used for tents and wagon covers when the Saints began their trek west. See Elden J. Watson, "The Nauvoo Tabernacle," *BYU Studies* 19 (Spring 1979): 420.

The Nauvoo Temple, or House of the Lord, was located on the east side of Wells Street between Mulholland and Knight Streets. The three-story edifice was constructed of gray limestone and white pine lumber, modeled somewhat after the Saints' House of the Lord in Kirtland, Ohio, but reflecting Greek Revival styling. Some 128 feet long, 88 feet wide, and rising nearly 160 feet to the top of an angel-decorated weather vane, the temple cost approximately one million dollars to complete. The plaque located on the third story above the main entrance read: "The House of the Lord, Built by the Church of Jesus Christ of Latter Day Saints. Commenced April. 6, 1841. Holiness to the Lord." The third-floor attic was dedicated on November 30, 1845, the temple proper on April 30, 1846, and again over the next few days.

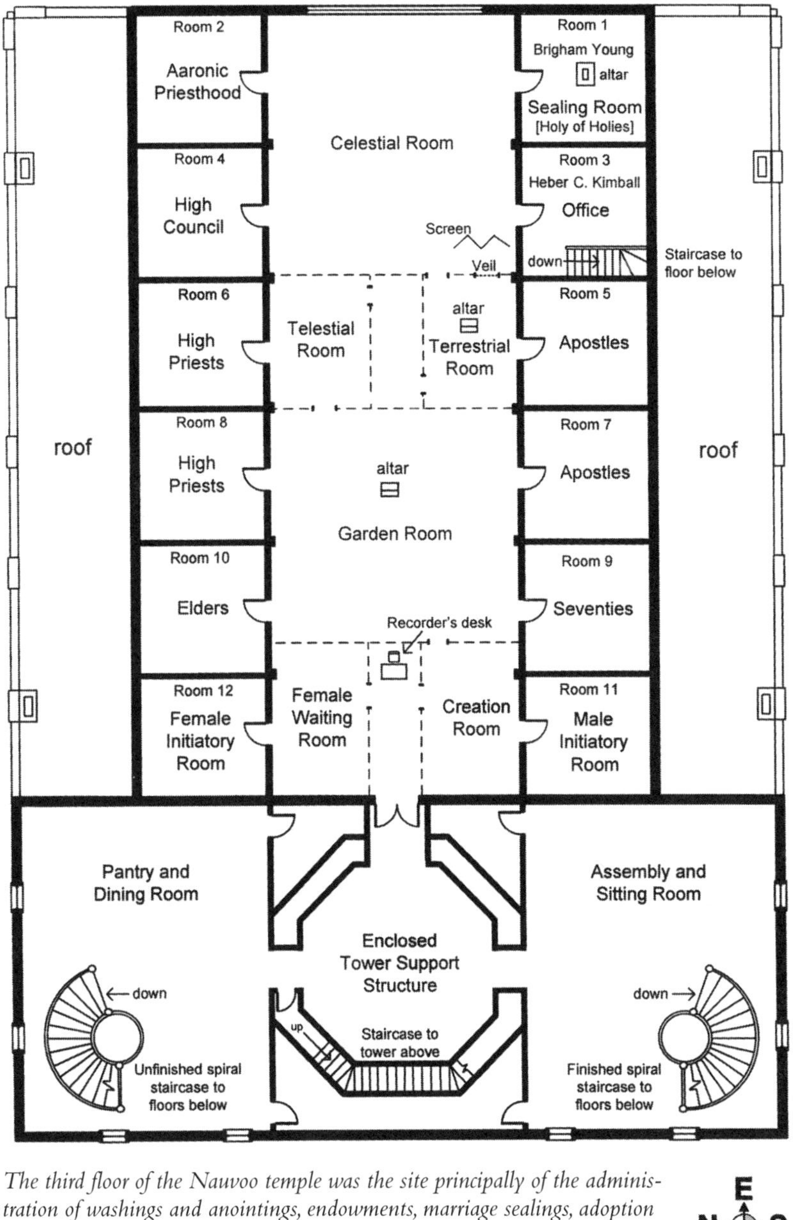

The third floor of the Nauvoo temple was the site principally of the administration of washings and anointings, endowments, marriage sealings, adoption sealings, and second anointings. It also housed the offices of the church's presiding authorities and quorums. Drawing by Lisle G Brown; original in private possession; used by permission.

10th between the terrestrial and celestial compartments. Women were instructed on how to sew ceremonial temple clothing. When everything was ready, Young, Kimball, and Apostle Willard Richards "entered the celestial room for prayer" on December 10.[17] Later that day, several members of the Anointed Quorum were washed and anointed, then re-endowed, being the first to receive the sacred ordinances in the Nauvoo temple. Ceremonies for previously endowed members continued until 3:30 a.m. Brigham Young and others spent the night in the temple, sleeping only one and a half hours before beginning the first day of introducing the endowment to new initiates.

As the process of endowing the general adult membership of the church began on December 12, it greatly increased what had already become an intense, time-consuming endeavor. William Clayton commented on the demanding schedule from December 10 through 12: "During the whole of the three days already spent in the endowment, President Brigham Young presided and dictated the ordinances and also took an active part in nearly every instance except when entirely overcome by fatigue through his constant labors to forward the work."[18]

Over the next two months, the administration of endowments and other temple rituals occurred almost every day, and the number of initiates grew rapidly. The reason for the urgency was because the Saints were being threatened by outsiders and were preparing to leave their city and begin the trek west. As an indication of the increased resentment toward the Mormons throughout Illinois, the Nauvoo city charter was repealed in January 1845. With that action, the Saints realized their time in Nauvoo was limited. In fact, scouting parties were sent to begin exploring areas for possible future settlement, including the region of the Great Salt Lake. Mob violence the following fall added to the urgency to consider a new home, and preparations to leave Nauvoo began in earnest. After talks to sell their property (including the temple) failed, a committee was empowered to dispose of the church's and members' properties after the main body of Saints had left.[19]

Prior to their departure in early 1846, over 5,000 men and women

---

17. Brown, 370-71.

18. William Clayton, Diary, Dec. 13, 1845.

19. Roberts, *History of the Church,* 565, 569. See also Lisle G Brown, "'A Perfect Estopel': Selling the Nauvoo Temple," *Mormon Historical Studies* 3 (Fall 2003): 61-85.

received their endowments between the temple's preliminary opening on December 10, 1845, and its closing two months later on February 8, 1846. This was an exhausting task accomplished during a turbulent time, and the large number of people endowed demonstrates the sense of purpose and urgency church leaders felt.

In summarizing the endowment and its place in the spiritual lives of the Latter-day Saints, Glen Leonard explains: "It [i.e., the endowment] consisted of the ordinances of washing and anointing, followed by instructions and covenants setting forth a pattern or figurative model for life."[20] Perhaps the most helpful—and LDS church-sanctioned—description of the endowment, as performed later in Utah, was provided to, and by, nineteenth-century American historian Hubert Howe Bancroft in his history of Utah, subsequently reprinted in Salt Lake City by LDS publisher Bookcraft. "The ceremony of Endowment, or as it is termed, going through the endowment house," explained Bancroft,

> occupies usually about eight hours. It has been described at length by several persons who have experienced it, and I give herewith a condensation of the most reliable accounts. Minor changes have been introduced since the days of Joseph Smith, but, in the main, the rites are as they were in the beginning. Certain days in each week, throughout the year, are set apart, upon which candidates present themselves at the endowment house, as early as seven o'clock A.M. Each is required to bring a bottle of the best olive-oil, and supposed to bring his robes also, although it is common to borrow the latter from friends, for the first appearance, after which every good Mormon possesses his own. These garments are described as follows: The temple robe, alike for both sexes, is a long, loose, flowing garment, made of white linen or bleached muslin, and reaching to the ankle. It is gathered to a band sufficiently long to pass around the body from the right shoulder underneath the left arm, thus leaving the latter free. A linen belt holds it in place. The women wear a head covering made of a large square of Swiss muslin, gathered in one corner so as to form a sort of cap to fit the head, the reminder falling down as a veil. For the men, a round piece of linen, drawn up with a string and a bow in front, something after the fashion of a Scotch cap, is used. The under garment, which is also alike for both sexes, is a sort of jacket and trousers together, something like the night-dresses made for children; and is worn night and day. When

20. Leonard, *Nauvoo,* 258.

changed, only an arm or a leg must be removed at once, the fresh garment being thus put on as the other is taken off. This garment protects from disease, and even death, for the bullet of an enemy will not penetrate it. The prophet Joseph [Smith] carelessly left off this garment on the day of his death, and had he not done so, he would have escaped unharmed. Over the inner garment the men wear an ordinary shirt, and the women a white skirt. White stockings and a pair of white linen slippers complete the costume. Entering the building, the candidate's own name and age are registered, and also the names of the parents. The candidates hand in their oil, remove their shoes, and pass with their bundles of clothing into a bath-room divided down the middle by a heavy curtain which separates the sexes. Here the ceremony of purification is performed, the women being washed by women, and the men by men. The person washed is informed that he or she is now cleansed from the blood of this generation, and if faithful, shall never be subject to the plagues and miseries which are about to come upon the earth. Next follows the anointing. The oil is poured from a large horn into the hand of the person officiating, and applied to the crown of the head, eyes, ears, mouth, and feet of the candidate. The eyes are touched, that they may be quick to see; the ears, that the hearing may be sharp; the mouth, to bestow wisdom upon speech; and the feet, that they be swift to run in the ways of the Lord. Then a new name, which is rarely to be mentioned, is whispered into the ear, and all are marched into room No. 2, where they are seated, the sexes on opposite sides of the room, and facing each other. Here they are told by a priest that any person not strong enough to proceed may retire; but if any portion of the ceremony is disclosed, the throat of the person so offending will be cut from ear to ear. Those faltering, if any, having retired, the remainder are taken into room No. 3, where a representation of the creation, the temptation, and fall is given. Each candidate then puts on over his robe an apron of white linen, upon which are sewn pieces of green silk representing fig-leaves, and also the cap or veil. All good Mormons are buried in their endowment robes, and the veil worn by the women covers their faces when they are consigned to the grave. In the morning of the resurrection, this veil is to be lifted by the husband; otherwise no woman can see the face of the almighty in the next world. This ends the first degree; and the initiated are now driven out of Eden into room No. 4, which represents the world, where they encounter many temptations, the chief of which is the false gospel preached by methodists, baptists, etc. Finally St James and St John appear and proclaim the true gospel of Mormonism, which all gladly embrace. After

> this they receive certain grips and pass-words, and all are arranged in a circle, kneel, and the women lower their veils. Then, with the right hand uplifted, an oath is taken to avenge the death of Joseph Smith, jun., upon the gentiles who had caused his murder, to teach the children of the church to do likewise, to obey implicitly and without murmur or question all commands of the priesthood, to refrain from adultery, and finally, eternal secrecy concerning all that transpired in the endowment house is promised. Then comes an address, after which another room is entered, leading from which is a door with a hole in it, covered with a piece of muslin. The men approach this door in turn and ask to enter. Then a person behind the door reaches through the opening, and with knife in hand cuts a certain mark on the left breast of the shirt, another over the abdomen, and one over the right knee, which marks are faithfully copied by the women in their own garments after returning to their homes. The man then mentions his new name, gives the grip of the third degree, and is permitted to pass in. This is called going behind the veil. When the men are all in, each woman is passed through by her husband, or having none, by one of the brethren. This concludes the ceremony[.][21]

The majority of Saints who received their endowment in Nauvoo viewed the experience as a source of spiritual strength and comfort.

---

21. Hubert Howe Bancroft, *History of Utah, 1540-1886* (Salt Lake City: Bookcraft, 1964; 1st ed. 1889, vol. 26 in Bancroft's *History of the Pacific States of North America* Series), 357-58 n. 17. The First Presidency of the LDS church issued the following endorsement of Bancroft's project in 1884:

> We call your special attention to a subject of import to this community. Mr. Hubert H. Bancroft, the celebrated historian, is publishing an extensive work entitled *History of the Pacific States.* It is a work of much more than ordinary value and is the result of many years arduous labor, and the expenditure of large sums of money. The collection of original manuscripts and books and documents of reference constitute an immense library of themselves.
>
> From this mass of data Mr. Bancroft has, by the aid of many able writers, under his personal supervision, condensed into presentable form the history of all the states and territories on the Pacific slope including Mexico. The work, when completed by his own hands, will form a succinct yet comprehensive history of the western part of the American continent. It will, no doubt, find its way into all the chief libraries of the civilized world, and will be a standing monument to the author's genius.
>
> Utah is to receive special attention: one whole volume will be devoted to this territory, and the people and church which have founded and established it. This volume it is confidently expected will be authentic and calculated to extend a knowledge of the true condition of our affairs. We there-

Those who had been endowed under Joseph Smith recognized, and were not disturbed by, modifications in the ceremony administered under Brigham Young: "I and my wife received our Endowment having formerly received it in the Days of Joseph and Hyram," wrote Joseph Fielding in his journal, "but it is now given in a more perfect Manner because of better Convenience, the 12 are very strict in attending to the true and proper form." In fact, Smith had charged Young with making alterations as needed. L. John Nuttall, Young's secretary, recorded Young's 1877 reminiscence:

> Bro[ther] Joseph [Smith] turned to me [Brigham Young] and said: "Brother Brigham this is not arranged right, but we have done the best we could under the circumstances in which we are placed, and I wish you to take this mat[t]er in hand and organize and systematize all these ceremonies with the signs, tokens, penalties and key words." I did so and each time I got something more; so that when we went through the Temple at Nauvoo, I understood and knew how to place them there. We had our ceremonies pretty correct.[22]

As reconstructed from the available first-person accounts, church members experienced the Nauvoo endowment ceremony as follows: First, they were invited to appear at the temple at a specific time by a man appointed as a messenger. This usually occurred the night before. Prospective initiates were also instructed to cleanse their bodies before arriving at the temple. Upon entering at the designated time, they climbed the stairs to the attic story. Men and women separated and were taken into examination areas to be questioned regarding their worthiness and character. They were then escorted to rooms for the initiatory ordinances: the women to the northwest room, the men opposite the main hall to the southwest room. There they disrobed and waited to receive the ordi-

---

> fore, commend the work to your support and patronage. (John Taylor and George Q. Cannon, Letter to Presidents of Stakes and Bishops, Nov. 1, 1884, LDS Archives.)

According to Elder Franklin D. Richards, LDS officials subsequently "decided to purchase 1000 copies [of Bancroft's *History of Utah*] for distribution by the Church —James Dwyer to canvass for the work in & throughout Utah and ... an agency be established here for the sale of the work outside of Utah" (Franklin D. Richards, Diary, May 9, 1889).

22. L. John Nuttall, Diary, Feb. 7, 1877, L. Tom Perry Special Collections, Harold B. Lee Library, Brigham Young University, Provo, Utah.

nances of washing and anointing. When called upon, they passed through a canvas curtain and entered a tub where they were washed from head to foot. Those performing the ordinance spoke words of blessing as part of the ceremony. Then they were anointed with consecrated olive oil poured over their heads from a horn. This was usually done by another officiator, and similar words were repeated. Men performed these rites for men, women for women (see appendix 1). As part of this ceremony, initiates were given a new name and an undergarment, on which special markings were cut into the fabric. Prior to leaving this room, initiates were ordained to become kings and queens in eternity. Their names, birth dates, and places of birth were also recorded.

After the washing and anointing, initiates dressed, and the men were guided into a room representing the Creation. Each man took on the role of Adam in the ensuing drama. According to Leonard, "The teachings began with a recital of the creation of the earth and its preparation to host life. The story carried the familiar ring of the Genesis account, echoed as well in Joseph Smith's revealed book of Moses and book of Abraham."[23] Evidently unlike Joseph Smith's endowment ceremony, the Nauvoo temple account of the Creation was narrated by three heavenly beings: Eloh(e)im, Jehovah, and Michael conversed over the six days of the Creation process from behind a curtain. Up to the formation of Adam, the women waited in a room across from the Creation Room. They joined the men at the point in the drama when woman was created from Adam's rib, the women thus assuming the role of Eve.

From the Creation Room, the entire company entered the Garden Room, which was adorned with plants, trees, shrubs, and flowers in a setting representing the Garden of Eden. According to William Clayton: "In this apartment is also an altar. Here the man and woman are placed and commandments given to them in addition to what is given in the creation."[24] Next a serpent, as portrayed in the Book of Genesis, entered the room to tempt Adam and Eve, encouraging them to partake of the forbidden fruit (in most endowment sessions, William W. Phelps played this role). Clayton added, "Here also after the man and woman has eaten the forbidden fruit is given to them a charge at the Alt[a]r and the first and second tokens of the Aaronic Priesthood."[25] The serpent is cursed and

23. Leonard, *Nauvoo,* 258.
24. Clayton, Diary, Dec. 11, 1845.
25. Ibid.

leaves the room, slithering on its stomach. The men and women are banished from the Garden for their disobedience.

From the Garden Room, the company entered the Telestial Kingdom, which represented a post-Edenic world. According to Clayton: "In the telestial kingdom, after the man has proved himself faithful[,] he receives the first signs and tokens of the Melchizedek priesthood and an additional charge. Here also he vouches for the conduct of his companion. They are then left to prove themselves faithful."[26] Leonard expanded on this topic: "The disobedience and expulsion of Adam and Eve from the Garden of Eden set the stage for an explanation of Christ's atonement for that original transgression and for the sins of the entire human family. Also included was a recital of mankind's tendency to stray from the truth through apostasy and the need for apostolic authority to administer authoritative ordinances and teach true gospel principles."[27] Then, Clayton continues, "they are admitted into the terrestrial kingdom, where at the alt[a]r they receive an additional charge and the second token of the Melchizedek Priesthood and also the key word on the five points of fellowship."[28]

The apostolic authority Leonard alluded to was portrayed dramatically in the ceremony and reflected important developments incorporated under Brigham Young. On the day the general church membership began attending the temple, December 12, 1845, Young and others added the roles of New Testament apostles Peter, James, and John to the drama. "Eloheem gives the charge to Adam in the Garden and thrusts them into the telestial kingdom or the world," wrote Clayton. "Then Peter assisted by James and John conducts them through the Telestial and Terrestrial kingdom administering the charges and tokens in each."[29]

In summarizing these charges and instructions, Leonard has written:

> Participants were reminded that in addition to the Savior's redemptive gift they must be obedient to God's commandments to obtain a celestial glory. Within the context of these gospel instructions, the initiates made covenants of personal virtue and benevolence and of commitment to the church. They agreed to devote their talents and means to spread the gospel, to strengthen the church, and to prepare the earth for

26. Ibid.
27. Leonard, *Nauvoo,* 258.
28. Clayton, Diary, Dec. 11, 1845.
29. Ibid.

the return of Jesus Christ. Through personal promises to their Heavenly Father made in the Nauvoo Temple, the Saints expanded the meaning of being a covenant people.[30]

In concluding the endowment, according to Clayton, "after [they have] received all the tokens and words and signs[,] they are led to the veil where they give each to Eloheem through the veil and are then admitted into the Celestial Room." A prompter at the veil assisted each member by helping them repeat these words and gestures. After entering the room representing the Celestial Kingdom, the newly endowed Saints were greeted with a beautifully decorated room representing the highest heaven. This room was adorned with mirrors, paintings and portraits—most of them of church leaders and other prominent Nauvoo Saints—maps of the world, of the United States, and of Nauvoo. Against one of the walls was a brass clock. "In the centre and body of the Celestial Room are two splendid tables and four splendid sofas," wrote Clayton. "Also a small table opposite the large Window on the East end of the room on which stands the Celestial and terrestrial Globes."[31]

The length of time required for an endowment session varied, depending in part on the number of people going through at any one time. Companies could be as small as a dozen or fewer people, but before the temple closed in February 1846, some companies had more than quadrupled in size. One, on February 6, 1846, numbered over eighty-five. Sessions could be as short as one and a half hours or as long as five or more hours, depending on the size of the group.

Such large numbers receiving their endowments just prior to the temple closure was explained by Brigham Young on February 4, 1846. Young had met with the apostles and other leaders the day before and had decided "that it was imperatively necessary to start as soon as possible" for the west, and he therefore decided to close the temple.[32] However:

> Notwithstanding I gave out word that we would not attend to these [temple] matters [anymore]—yet the House was thronged all the day. The anxiety are so great that the Brethren would have us stay here & continue the endowments until our way will be Hedged up & our enemies intercept us—but I tell you Brethren that it will not do—this is

30. Leonard, *Nauvoo*, 259.
31. Clayton, Diary, Dec. 11, 1845.
32. Roberts, *History of the Church*, 578.

> not the last Temple that we will build—in this house we have been payed well if we were to receive no more—& I tell [you] that there will be double the anxiety manifest to build the next[,] that there was to Ericte [erect] this—then be satisfied— I am going to load up my waggon & be away from this place immediately— I walked off some little distance from the Temple soposing the crowd would disperse—but on returning to the Temple again—I found the House thronged to overflowing[.] [L]ooking upon the multitude & knowing the anxiety of the Brethren—that were thirsting & hungering for the word—we commenced sealing & anointing & continued & continued [sic] also the washings Night & Day—putting through from 2[00] to 300 Persons within 24 hours & spent the night.[33]

On just a single day alone (February 6, 1846), 512 people in eight different companies received their endowments. The next day, "upwards of six hundred received the ordinance of first anointment of the Priesthood, this being the last day for administering them, for the present."[34]

In addition to administering endowments, much of the activity in the temple during its two months of operation focused on other equally important ordinances. On January 8, 1846, the second anointing was administered for the first time since the days of Joseph Smith. As with the administration of the first endowments a month earlier, those who first received the second anointing in the Nauvoo temple had received it previously from Joseph Smith or under his direction. Leonard described this higher blessing as a "crowning ordinance" and "a promise of kingly powers and of endless lives. It was the confirmation of promises that worthy men could become kings and priests and that women could become queens and priestesses in the eternal worlds."[35] During the ordinance, explained LDS historian Lyndon W. Cook, a husband was "ordained a priest and anointed a king unto God," while wives were "anointed priestesses and queens unto their husband."[36] "In actual practice the second anointing as performed for couples by an officiator was the first of two parts comprising the fulness of the priesthood ceremony," wrote David John Buerger in his study of the ordinance. "The second part was private,

33. Brigham Young, Diary, Feb. 3, 1846.

34. George A. Smith, "History of George Albert Smith," Feb. 7, 1846.

35. Leonard, *Nauvoo,* 260-61.

36. Lyndon W. Cook, *Joseph C. Kingsbury: A Biography* (Provo, UT: Grandin Book, 1985), 94.

without witnesses, and involved only the husband and wife. Its significance related to the resurrection of the dead ... In this part of the ordinance, the wife symbolically prepared her husband for his death and resurrection, a ceremony that gave the wife a claim on her husband for herself in the resurrection."[37]

Several diaries and reminiscences elaborated on the second portion of the second anointing, such as the following recital from Lewis Dunbar: "At the temple at Nauvoo she [i.e., Nancy Wilson] received her washings and anointings even to become a queen and a priestess, after which time she attended to one other ordinance which was to wash the feet of her husband [i.e., Lewis Dunbar] and anoint him to be her king and priest and Savior, that she might have claim on him at the resurrection[.]"[38]

Over the course of a month, at least 594 people—172 men and 422 women—received their second anointing, including nine men by proxy. Unlike its administration by Joseph Smith, this higher ordinance now extended to plural wives. Based on a tabulation using original and derivative temple records, eternal marriage sealings performed during the years 1842 to 1846 for both the living (monogamous and plural) and by proxy (again, monogamous and plural) totaled 1,303, of which 206 were by proxy, while adoptions (children sealed to their parents, and men, with their families, sealed to senior church leaders) numbered 294, of which 202 were of the latter type. The total number of endowments performed during the same period reached 5,583.[39] (See table 1, p. xxviii.)

The daily record William Clayton kept for Heber C. Kimball made clear that plural marriage was an important part of the temple and played a role in the endowment ceremony itself. When taken through the veil into the Celestial Room, the men were received by Eloh(e)im, the women by their husbands. Single women, who did not have a husband to receive them, were brought through the veil by a male volunteer. But a closer look at these instances where men received a woman of a different surname through the veil reveals that the men were often, in fact, receiv-

37. Buerger, "'The Fulness of the Priesthood,'" 26.

38. "Record of Lewis Dunbar Sr. and Nancy Ann Wilson," entry dated Jan. 21, 1846, LDS Archives.

39. *Nauvoo Sealings, Adoptions, and Anointings: A Comprehensive Register of Persons Receiving LDS Temple Ordinances, 1841-1846* (Salt Lake City: The Smith-Pettit Foundation, 2005), Appendix I. For different totals, see Richard O. Cowan, *Temple Building Ancient and Modern* (Provo, UT: Brigham Young University Press, 1971), 29.

TABLE 1. Temple ordinances, 1842-46

Baptisms		Endowments	
Living	0	Living	5,583
Dead	15,626	Dead	0
Total	15,626	Total	5,583
Wives sealed		**Second anointings**	
Living	1,097	Living	594
Dead	206	Dead	9
Total	1,303	Total	603
Adoptions (children sealed to parents)		**Adoptions (adults sealed to adults)**	
Living	92	Living	202
Dead	0	Dead	0
Total	92	Total	202
Cumulative totals			
Including baptisms		*Excluding baptisms*	
Living	7,568	Living	7,568
Dead	15,841	Dead	215
Total	23,409	Total	7,783

ing their plural or prospective plural wives. On December 16, 1845, as an example, Heber C. Kimball received sisters Abigail and Laura Pitkin through the veil. He married them in the temple a short time later, on January 7 and February 3, 1846, respectively. John Parker, who took Sophia Roundy through the veil that same day, married her as a plural wife on February 3.[40] The next day, Orson Hyde received Martha R. Browett and Mary Ann Price through the veil, women he had already married polygamously in 1843. He was sealed to them in the temple on January 11, 1846.[41] On December 29, 1845, Brigham Young received four plural wives through the veil; Kimball, three; Parley P. Pratt, one; George A. Smith, three; and William Clayton, one. These women were all members of the same endowment company,[42] and the men were sealed to them in

40. Clayton, Diary, Dec. 16, 1845; George D. Smith, "Nauvoo Roots of Mormon Polygamy, 1841-46: A Preliminary Demographic Report," *Dialogue: A Journal of Mormon Thought* 27 (Spring 1994): 50, 54.

41. Clayton, Diary, Dec. 17, 1845; Smith, "Nauvoo Roots of Mormon Polygamy," 48.

42. Clayton, Diary, Dec. 29, 1845. For a fuller record of known polygamous marriages and sealings in Nauvoo, see Smith, "Nauvoo Roots of Mormon Polygamy," 37-69.

January and February. Husbands and prospective husbands continued to receive women through the veil and to participate in polygamous sealings until the temple closed.

The administration of endowments, sealings, second anointings, and adoptions was fatiguing, but fulfilling, to those officiating in the ceremonies. Yet occasional obstacles could be frustrating as temple officiators sought to continue the work. For example, on December 19, 1845, less than ten days after the work began, Brigham Young complained that "we have been thronged to that extent that it was almost impossible to move without running against some fifteen or twenty persons who were gawking round where they had no buissness & lauling [lolling?] & breaking down Mahogany chairs worth $5[.]00 and tearing open the curtains & gazing in where they had no right."[43] On January 23, 1846, a non-Mormon named Milburn, who had helped to construct the temple, attempted to receive his endowments. He did this, according to John D. Lee, "in order as he told a confidential friend to find out what was going on there, that he might reveal it to the world. Of course he did not get admission."[44] However, at least five recipients of the Nauvoo endowment did publish exposés of the temple ceremonies after their departure from Mormonism.

More disruptive occurrences, however, involved officers of the law who came to the temple in search of church leaders. On one occasion, marshals arrived to arrest the Twelve on charges of counterfeiting. In the daily record kept for the Seventy, John D. Lee recorded on December 23, 1845:

> Some 8 or 10 officers came in with writs from Springfield [Illinois] for the Twelve [apostles] & many others[.] they denied having any rits[,] but in order to attempt [to divulge] their corruption Pres[ident] Young sent down a man in disguise with a cloke on verry much like his own (B[righam]. Y[oung].) Pres[ident] J[edediah]. M. Grant—who acompanyed the man in disguise to the carriage [which] stood near the Temple [and] that was expected to convey Pres[ident] Young away[, said that] on reaching the carriage [he,] pres Grant[,] said to Br[other] W[illia]m Miller who was the man in disguise. ["]Pres[ident] Young the weather is growing colder["]—at this the officers surrounded the

43. "General Record of the Seventies, Book B," Dec. 19, 1845, photocopy in editors' possession, original in LDS Archives.

44. Ibid., Jan. 23, 1846.

> carriage & drew out a writ & read [it] & said ["]Mr Young you are my prisoner[."] the Prisoner[,] apparently unconcerned[,] invited them to get into the carriage[,] or some of them, which some 2 or 3 did & Drove to the Mansion & finally started to Carthage [Illinois] being elated to the highest glory in immagination. still they are gone & we hope all will be well— & that they will soon find out their mistake[.] we intended that they should have found out their blunder before they left the city but in this we have been mistaken[.] they may take him to Springfield before they discern the prank.[45]

Miller was released and returned to Nauvoo the next day. Three days later, however, on December 27, another attempt was made to arrest Brigham Young. According to William Clayton's notes for December 27, 1845:

> At 15 minutes past 10 o'clock the United States Deputy Marshall, from Springfield, by the name of Roberts, came to the Temple in company with Almon W. Babbitt, — He was freely admitted to every part of the Temple; to which he desired access. He went into the tower, on the roof, and into the Attic Story, passed through the various departments into the east room, where he very intently examined the portraits, and made enquiries as to whose they were, severally[,] but obtained no correct information on the subject. He was requested to take off his boots in the preparation room, which request he complied with.
>
> After remaining about half an hour he departed — At about 2 o'clock he returned in company with Sheriff [Jacob] Backenstos, and a gentleman whom the Marshall introduced as from New Orleans — They visited the Middle room and the tower, and departed after about half an hour.[46]

The following day Heber C. Kimball, speaking of attempts to capture the Twelve, worried that the marshals might even kill them. In return, "we dont want to kill them," Kimball insisted, "but if they attempt this we will not say to the Boys hold still—but go your length[.]"[47] With tensions still high the next day, John D. Lee recorded that "an alarm though false reached the Sacred apartments that the governors People were below at

45. Ibid., Dec. 23, 1845.

46. Clayton, Diary, kept for Heber C. Kimball, Dec. 27, 1845. See also "General Record of the Seventies," Dec. 27, 1845.

47. "General Record of the Seventies," Dec. 28, 1845.

the outer Door, & had expresed a determination to enter in Search of the hogs that were said to have been stolen, the evening previous[,] from Mr. Hibbard[,] one of his Apostate citizens[.]" This occurred during the presentation of an endowment ceremony. According to Lee:

> Brigham Young said[, "]Bro. Lee[,] come go down quickly & see that they do not enter[,"] furnishing me with a six shooter well loaded[.] at the Same time I ran downstairs to the outer door where I met the Porter Tho[ma]s Woolsey ... who informed me & those that were with me that the alarm was false in part[.] I then gave the tyler [door monitor] instructions to let no officer pass that Night at the peril of his Life[.] I returned and corrected the rumor[.][48]

By January 14, Lee noted, "public prejudice is so great against us, and the excitement is so alarming that we may not be able to continue giving the endowment more than three weeks longer; therefore it is determined that we continue night and day in the administration of the ordinances of endowment."[49]

The work of performing endowments at such a hurried pace, while priesthood leaders conducted church business in their respective rooms in the temple's attic story—all the while evading arrest by law enforcement officers—meant that there was a great need for some kind of relaxation, especially after all but the temple officiators had gone home for the night. John D. Lee reported that on December 17, 1845, "Bro[ther] H C Egerson ... who was an excellent Fidler came in by permission & animated our feelings with melodious notes on his violin[.] We all rejoiced & Praised the Lord in the dance[.]"[50] On December 30, Clayton recorded a similar scene:

> The labors of the day having been brought to a close at so early an hour viz; half past 8. it was thought proper to have a little season of recreation. accordingly, Brother [Hans] Hanson was invited to produce his violin— He did so, and played several lively airs, among the rest some very good lively dancing tunes. This was too much for the gravity of Bro[ther]. Joseph Young, who indulged in a hornpipe, and was soon joined by several others, and before the dance was over several French fours were indulged in. The first was opened by Pres[i-

48. Ibid., Dec. 29, 1845.
49. Ibid., Jan. 14, 1846.
50. Ibid., Dec. 17, 1845.

> dent] B[righam]. Young with Sister [Elizabeth Ann] Whitney and Elder H[eber]. C. Kimball with Sister ~~Whitney~~ ^[Catherine] Lewis^[.] The spirit of dancing increased until the whole floor was covered with dancers[.] After this had continued about an hour, several excellent songs were sung, in which several of the brethren and sisters joined— The Upper California was sung by Erastus Snow. After which Sister Whitney being invited by Pres[ident]. Young, stood up and invoking the gift of tongues, sung one of the most beautiful songs in tongues, that ever was heard. The interpretation was given by her husband, Bishop Whitney, it related to our efforts to build this House, and to the privilege we now have of meeting together in it, — of our departure shortly to the country of the Lamanites, and their rejoicing when they hear the gospel. and of the ingathering of Israel. Altogether, it was one of the most touching and beautiful exhibitions of the power of the Spirit in the gift of tongues which was ever seen—(So it appeared to the writer of this)[.] After a little conversation of a general nature, the exercises of the evening were closed by prayer by Pres[ident]. B[righam]. Young—and soon after most of the persons present left the Temple for their homes.[51]

Although perhaps unusual by today's practices, Brigham Young set the context for these joyous moments in the temple:

> Pres[ident]. Young called the attention of the whole company, and then gave them a message, of this import, ~~that~~ viz; that this Temple was a Holy place, and that when we danced we danced unto the Lord, and that no person would be allowed to come on to this floor, and afterwards mingle with the wicked, He said the wicked had no right to dance, that dancing and music belonged to the Saints— and he strongly impressed upon the mind of those present the impropriety of mingling again with the wicked after having come in here, and taken upon them the covenants which they had— He spoke pointedly to his daughter Vilate and told her that if she should do so after this, she might expect to meet the frowns of a father who held the keys of the Priesthood— He was followed by L[ucien]. R. Foster, who concurred in the remarks of Pres[ident]. Young, and said he would like to have the question put,

51. Clayton, Diary, kept for Heber C. Kimball, Dec. 30, 1845. The song, "The Upper California," was sung to the melody of "The Rose That All Are Praising" with variant lyrics penned by Apostle John Taylor (Michael Hicks, "Poetic Borrowing in Early Mormonism," *Dialogue: A Journal of Mormon Thought* 18 [Spring 1985]: 136-37, 141).

> that it might be known how many of those present were willing to make a covenant to this effect, that they would not mingle with the wicked any more in their amusement, Elder H[eber]. C. Kimball said before the question was put he wished to say a few words. He felt thankful that Pres[ident] Young had touched this subject, & also that we had this opportunity of meeting together in this manner— said that those who were parents had become responsible for the conduct of their children, and for his part he should not be willing that his children should meet with the wicked, or have any thing to do with their amusements— He said to his own children, that they had covenanted here this evening, that they would receive the instruction, and listen to the counsel of their father & mother—and he hoped they would remember it.[52]

Through such entertainments, Mormons enjoyed themselves while still shunning the influences of the outside world. With the Saints' enemies increasing in numbers, the temple represented a place of refuge and safety. Even though the temple could not be completely shut off from outsiders, as noted above, it at least presented a psychological, if not real, line of defense.

After ordinance work effectively ceased on February 8, 1846, and the temple closed to most activities, the rooms making up the sacred departments were eventually dismantled, the furnishings returned to their owners or used for other purposes. According to one account, people "could be seen ... busily engaged removing articles of furniture, stoves, carpets, pictures and other furnishings."[53] During this time, from about February 11 through June 20, 1846, small groups of men—totaling some fifty-three—continued to meet periodically and hold prayer circles in the temple (see appendix 2).

Although soon to be abandoned, the temple was dedicated privately by Joseph Young with a few individuals on April 30, 1846. By then most of the Saints, including Brigham Young, had started west. The next day, May 1, those still in Nauvoo attended a public dedication presided over by Orson Hyde. "Holy and Everlasting Father," Hyde prayed,

> before Thee this morning we present ourselves and acknowledge Thy

52. Ibid., Jan. 1, 1846.

53. Journal History of the Church of Jesus Christ of Latter-day Saints, Feb. 3, 1846, qtd. in Brown, "Sacred Departments," 374.

> mercy that has been extended to us since we have been on Thy footstool, and for this opportunity of dedicating this house. We thank Thee that Thou has given us strength to accomplish the charges delivered by Thee. Forgive us our sins and the sins of Thy people. Thou hast seen our labors and exertions to accomplish this purpose. By the Authority of the Holy Priesthood now we offer this building as a sanctuary to Thy Worthy Name. We ask Thee to take the guardianship into Thy hands and grant that Thy Spirit shall dwell here and may all feel a sacred influence on their hearts that His Hand has helped this work. Accept of our offering this morning[;] and that soul that blesses this temple[,] let blessings rest on his posterity to the latest generation, and that soul that shall practice evil against this temple and Thy House, set Thy face against him and let evil take the portion of his inheritance. Administer to Thy people and let Thy honor and glory fall on our heads, not in the eyes of men but in the day when the world shall become Thy dominion. May we have the honor to tune the lyre[,] that Thou hast redeemed us from every nation and made us holy and pure and that we have washed our robes and made them white in the blood of the Lamb. [If i]t must needs be that offenses come, we offer it as the fruit of our labors and may the oppression under which they [we] groaned be to our good. We ask that the angel of mercy may be round about this temple and that light may descend upon us and let us pass to the courts of the heavenly [realm]. Let Thy Spirit rest upon those who have contributed to the building of this temple, the laborers on it that they may come forth to receive kingdoms and dominions and glory and immortal power. Accept of us we pray Thee, inspire every bosom to do Thy will, cause that truth may lead them for the glorious coming of the Son of God when you come in the name of the King [and] the Lord of Hosts shall be the King. Gather us in Thy Kingdom through Jesus Christ, our Lord, Amen.[54]

The ceremony was repeated over the next two days. Workmen continued their labors to complete the still unfinished rooms of the lower floors. Any remnant of the sacred departments of December 1845 to February 1846 was already gone when a visitor toured the attic in September 1847, long after the bulk of Saints had left Nauvoo. "The chamber itself is de-

---

54. Qtd. in *LDS Temple Dedicatory Prayers, 1836-1996* (N.p: N.p, ca. 1997), 8; cf. transcript of minutes by Thomas Bullock in "Dedication of the Nauvoo Temple," *Nick Literski's Latter-day Saint Temple Homepage* (www.keithhdavis.com/Mormon/nicksl/nauvoo.html). Nearly three months earlier, on February 8, 1846, Brigham Young had conducted a very private dedication ceremony.

void of ornament," he wrote, "and I was unable to ascertain whether it was intended to have any, if it should have been completed."[55]

For most Saints, the endowment represented spiritual power and protection to endure the trials ahead as they left their homes and started anew. Their perspective was thus somewhat different from the current experience of LDS church members receiving the endowment, and it is interesting to consider the original context. The urgency that emanates from all the historical sources helps to explain how the temple became such a defining achievement in Nauvoo and how that legacy impacted subsequent generations of Latter-day Saints.

The entries that follow are arranged chronologically. They include virtually every available primary source regarding the endowment companies and related activities surrounding the Nauvoo temple rituals from December 11, 1845, to February 8, 1846. Every effort has been made to be as faithful as possible to the original documents, although there are certainly unavoidable misreadings. For example, the spelling of the names of men and women was particularly problematic. Generally, we tended to reproduce the names as we deciphered them from the records we consulted. Occasionally, however, we inserted bracketed corrections or clarifications. While we do not presume to have satisfied every reader's wishes, we hope we struck a reasonable balance between readability and fidelity to the original texts.[56] Finally, some excerpts appear landscaped on pages so as to accommodate the longer lengths of certain lines of text. In these instances, bracketed editorial insertions appear rarely, if at all, thereby providing readers a better appreciation for the complexities of the original sources.

The documents that follow chronicle the Saints' determination to bestow spiritual knowledge and power through a process first envisioned by Joseph Smith. Hopefully, this compilation will help to generate further explorations of this aspect of Latter-day Saint history and devotion. For a documentary history of the endowment prior to the Nauvoo temple, readers are urged to consult the companion compilation, *Joseph Smith's Quorum of the Anointed, 1842-1845: A Documentary History,* especially its introduction, annotations, and biographies of endowment initiates.

---

55. *Palmyra Courier,* qtd. in Brown, "Sacred Departments," 374.

56. For an atempt to reconcile and standardize these names, see *Nauvoo Sealings, Anointings, and Adoptions*.

APPENDIX 1. Known Nauvoo temple officiators

Men's department

Washers

Randolph Alexander
Cyrus A. Allred
Isaac Allred
Milo Andrus
Israel Barlow
Edson Barney
Royal Barney
Alonzo Barrow
Ezra T. Benson
Charles Bird
Alfred Brown
James Brown
Harrison Burgess
William F. Cahoon
Welcome Chapman
Benjamin L. Clapp
Lorenzo Clark
Jonathan Crosby
William Crosby
Hiram Dayton
Simeon A. Dunn
Edward P. Duzette
George P. Dykes
Lorin Farr
Burr Frost
David Fulmer
Jacob Gates
Stephen H. Goddard
George Grant
Madison D. Hamilton
Levi W. Hancock
Jesse P. Harmon
Peter Haws
Henry Herriman
Chandler Holbrook
Joseph Holbrook
Joseph Horn
Joseph G. Hovey
Daniel D. Hunt
William Huntington
Orson Hyde
William Hyde
Dana Jacobs
Aaron Johnson
Joseph W. Johnson
John Kay
Heber C. Kimball
Andrew L. Lamoreau
Alonzo LeBaron
Amasa Lyman
Leslie Lyman
Andrew Lytle
John Lytle
Alexander McRae
Cyrus A. Mead
Albert Merrill
George Miller
Benjamin Mitchell
Andrew Moore
Samuel Moore
Levi Nickerson
Horace Owens
Parley P. Pratt
Charles C. Rich
Samuel W. Richards
George C. Riser
Noah Rogers
Moses M. Sanders
Lucius N. Scovil
Perrigrine G. Sessions
Ranson Shepard
George A. Smith
Abraham O. Smoot
Willard Snow
William Snow
Leslie Syme
John Taylor
Chauncy G. Webb
Edward M. Webb
Alexander Whiteside
Newel K. Whitney
Brigham Young
Joseph Young
Leslie L. Young
Phineas H. Young

Anointers

Randolph Alexander
Isaac Allred
Milo Andrus
Israel Barlow
Edson Barney
Ezra T. Benson
Samuel Bent
Charles Bird
Alfred Brown
James Brown
Harrison Burgess
William F. Cahoon
Dominicus Carter
Welcome Chapman
Darwin Chase
John M. Chitister
Benjamin L. Clapp
William O. Clark
William Crosby
Hiram Dayton
Simeon A. Dunn
Edward P. Duzette
George P. Dykes
Wilber J. Earl
Elisha Edwards
John Eldridge
Bradford Elliot

APPENDIX 1. *(Anointers—continued)*

Lorin Farr
Jacob Gates
Jackson Goodale
Jedediah M. Grant
Zenos H. Gurley
Madison D. Hamilton
Levi W. Hancock
Jesse P. Harmon
Peter Haws
Chandler Holbrook
Joseph G. Hovey
Orson Hyde
William Hyde
Dana Jacobs
Aaron Johnson
John Kay
Heber C. Kimball
Andrew L. Lamoreau
John D. Lee
Amasa Lyman
Andrew Lytle
John Lytle
Albert Merrill
George Miller
Andrew Moore
Samuel Moore
Isaac Morley
Samuel Mulliner
John Murdock
John Pack
William Pitt
Parley P. Pratt
David P. Rainey
Charles C. Rich
Franklin D. Richards
Samuel W. Richards
Albert P. Rockwood
Noah Rogers
Moses M. Sanders
Perrigrine G. Sessions
Ranson Shepard
Luman A. Shirtliff
George A. Smith
Abraham O. Smoot
Willard Snow
William Snow
Levi Stewart
John Taylor
James Townsend
Theodore Turley
Newel K. Whitney
Brigham Young
Joseph Young
Leslie Lyme Young
Phineas H. Young

Women's department

Washers

Elizabeth Barlow
Jane Blevin
Diantha Billings
Ruth Bovier
Sophia M. Burgess
Tirza Cahoon
Lydia Carter
Phebe Chase
Mary Clapp
Augusta Cobb
Sarah Crosby
Lois Cutler
Elizabeth Durfee
Dorcas Dykes
Olive Farr
Anna B. Fordham
Mary Gates
Lydia Granger
Caroline E. Grover
Clarissa Hancock
Sophrona M. Harmon
Clarissa Herriman
Rebecca W. Holman
Hezekiah Hunter
Polly Z. Johnson
Vilate Kimball
Pamela Lott
Maria L. Lyman
Hannah Lytle
Mary C. Miller
Phebe Miller
Rhoda A. Miller
Mary A. Noble
Julia Pack
Sally Phelps
Mary Ann Pratt
Sarah D. Rich
Jane Richards
Nancy H. Rockwood
Amanda Rogers
Patty Sessions
Jane J. Sherwood
Agness M. Smith
Bathsheba W. Smith
Lovina C. Smith
Mary Smith
Sarah Smith
Margaret T. Smoot
Artemisia Snow
Malvina Snow
Catherine C. Spencer
Julia Stone
Leonora A. Taylor
Mercy R. Thompson
Eliza Jane Webb
Elizabeth Ann Whitney
Nancy Winchester
Phebe Woodworth
Mary Ann Young

APPENDIX 1. *(Women's department—continued)*

Anointers

Elizabeth Barlow
Pamela A. Benson
Diantha Billings
Sophia M. Burgess
Thirza Cahoon
Phebe Chase
Mary Clapp
Lois Cutler
Elizabeth Durfee
Olive Farr
Mary Gates
Julia Granger
Lydia Granger
Caroline E. Grover
Clarissa Hancock
Clarissa Herriman
Rebecca W. Holman
Vilate Kimball
Pamela Lott
Maria L. Lyman
Mary C. Miller
Samuel Moore
Mary A. Noble
Julia Pack
Mary Ann Pratt
Sarah D. Rich
Nancy H. Rockwood
Patty Sessions
Sarah Smith
Caroline O. Spencer
Catherine C. Spencer
Agness M. Smith
Bathsheba W. Smith
Mary Smith
Margaret T. Smoot
Artemisia Snow
Leonora A. Taylor
Mercy R. Thompson
Elizabeth Ann Whitney
Nancy Winchester
Phebe Woodworth
Jane Young
Mary Ann Young

Unspecified duties

Abigail Abbot
Myrza Alexander
Lucinda Allen
Phebe Angell
Lettice Barney
Sarah B. Barney
Caroline Bird
Mary Ann Bird
Maria Bond
Hester A. E. Brown
Mary M. Cahoon
Nancy Cahoon
Mary Carpenter
Susan A. Chapman
Clarissa Chase
Beulah Ann Clark
Louisa Clark
Mary J. Codey
Mary Coltrin
Elizabeth Coolidge
Caroline Crosby
Almira Dailey
Margaret Dana
Sarah Davis
Permelia Dayton
Mary Deforest
Rumanah B. Derby
Mariah E. Edwards
Cynthia Ann Eldridge
Sarah Jane Everett
Martha Jane Farnham
Mary M. Felshaw
Eliza Ann Felt
Maria Fosdick
Mary E. Frost
Zeruah Goddard
Mary D. Grant
Jane Ann Green
Susan Green
Clemicia Hamilton
Anna Harmon
Sophrona M. Harmon
Lucinda Harris
Mary E. Harris
Lucy Hatfield
Martha S. Haven
Mary Henderson
Eunice Holbrook
Mary I. Horn
Sarah D. Horr
Caroline Huntington
Elizabeth Caroline Hutchins
Zilpha Jacobs
Merilla Johnson
Sarah M. Johnson
Ellen Kay
Philinda C. Keeler
Sarah Kerr
Sarah M. Kimball
Sally Ann King
Sophia Lance
Julia P. Martin
Jemima C. Mead
Margaret Ann Merrill
Phebe Miller
Lovina Mitchell
Catherine Mulliner
Mary Ann Nickerson
Peggy Patten
Margaret M. Rainey
Jan F. Rea

APPENDIX 1. *(Unspecified duties—continued)*

Hannah Repsher	Jane Rogers	Agness Taylor
Roxanna Repsher	Mary J. Sanderson	Elvira Teeples
Jane Richards	Lucina Sessions	Susan Townsend
Mary H. Parker Richards	Altamira Shirtliff	Almira Tufts
Pamela M. Robinson	Julia Ann Shumway	Diometia Walker
Ellen A. Rockwood	Sarah Smith	Alvira Wheeler
Eda Rogers	Julia Stone	Electa Whiteside
		Hannah Wood
	Upper department actors	
Eloheim		
Horace Burgess	John D. Lee	George A. Smith
Benjamin L. Clapp	Orson Pratt	Orson Spencer
Jedediah M. Grant	Parley P. Pratt	John Taylor
Orson Hyde	Charles C. Rich	Brigham Young
Heber C. Kimball	Lucius N. Scovil	Joseph Young
Jehovah		
Benjamin L. Clapp	George Miller	Noah Rogers
Jedediah M. Grant	John Pack	Lucius N. Scovil
Levi W. Hancock	Orson Pratt	George A. Smith
Orson Hyde	Parley P. Pratt	Erastus Snow
Heber C. Kimball	Charles C. Rich	Orson Spencer
John D. Lee	Franklin D. Richards	John Taylor
Amasa Lyman	Albert P. Rockwood	Joseph Young
Michael		
Harrison Burgess	Orson Hyde	Franklin D. Richards
Benjamin L. Clapp	Aaron Johnson	Albert P. Rockwood
Simeon A. Dunn	Heber C. Kimball	John Scott
George P. Dykes	Amasa Lyman	Lucius N. Scovil
Jacob Gates	George Miller	George A. Smith
Jedediah M. Grant	John Pack	Abraham O. Smoot
Levi W. Hancock	Parley P. Pratt	Erastus Snow
Henry Herriman	Charles C. Rich	Willard Snow
		John Taylor
	Middle and lower department actors	
Peter		
Benjamin L. Clapp	William Hyde	Parley P. Pratt
Jedediah M. Grant	Aaron Johnson	Charles C. Rich
Orson Hyde	Orson Pratt	Lucius N. Scovil

APPENDIX 1. *(Middle and lower department actors: Peter—continued)*

George A. Smith
Erastus Snow
Willard Snow
William Snow
Orson Spencer
John Taylor
Joseph Young

James

Richard Ballantyne
Israel Barlow
Ezra T. Benson
Samuel Bent
Daniel Carter
Benjamin L. Clapp
Alpheus Cutler
George P. Dykes
Jedediah M. Grant
Levi W. Hancock
Jesse P. Harmon
Henry Herriman
Aaron Johnson
Amasa Lyman
Joseph B. Noble
John Pack
William W. Phelps
Parley P. Pratt
Charles C. Rich
Franklin D. Richards
Albert P. Rockwood
John Scott
Lucius N. Scovil
Luman A. Shirtliff
Abraham O. Smoot
Erastus Snow
Lorenzo Snow
William Snow
Orson Spencer
Hosea Stout
Joseph Young

John

Israel Barlow
Ezra T. Benson
Daniel Carn
Benjamin L. Clapp
Jacob Gates
George D. Grant
Levi W. Hancock
Jesse P. Harmon
Henry Herriman
Joseph Horn
Jesse D. Hunter
Aaron Johnson
Heber C. Kimball
John D. Lee
William Miller
Joseph B. Noble
John Pack
Morris Phelps
Orson Pratt
Parley P. Pratt
Charles C. Rich
Franklin D. Richards
Albert P. Rockwood
William A. Sanger
John Scott
Lucius N. Scovil
Henry G. Sherwood
George A. Smith
Abraham O. Smoot
Erastus Snow
Lorenzo Snow
Willard Snow
William Snow
Levi Stewart
John Taylor
Theodore Turley

Serpent

David Candland
Wilber J. Earl
Levi W. Hancock
William Hyde
John D. Lee
William W. Phelps
Erastus Snow
Newel K. Whitney
Lucian Woodworth

Other officiators

Prompter

Isaac Allred
Pamela A. Benson
William Burton
David Candland
William L. Cutler
George P. Dykes
Jacob Gates
Jedediah M. Grant
Levi W. Hancock
Orson Hyde
Joseph A. Kelting
Heber C. Kimball
Vilate Kimball
Aaron Johnson
John D. Lee

APPENDIX 1. *(Prompter—continued)*

George Miller
Isaac Morley
John Pack
Julia Pack
Orson Pratt
Parley P. Pratt
Franklin D. Richards
Albert P. Rockwood
Lucius N. Scovil
George A. Smith
Abraham O. Smoot
Artemisia Snow
Erastus Snow
Lorenzo Snow
Catherine C. Spencer
Orson Spencer
Hosea Stout
Mercy R. Thompson
Elizabeth Ann Whitney
Brigham Young
Joseph Young
Phineas H. Young

Tyler
Elijah Averett
John D. Lee
William W. Phelps
Lewis Robbins

Messenger
George P. Dykes
Aaron Johnson
Alexander McRae
Erastus Snow

Marshal
Henry G. Sherwood

Clerk
David Candland
Lucian R. Foster
Henry Herriman
John D. Lee
Charles Waddell

Wardrobe
Daniel Carn

Fire Tender
Elisha Averett
John L. Butler
Jesse. D. Hunter
Andrew Lytle
John Scott
Hosea Stout

APPENDIX 2. Known members of Nauvoo temple prayer circles

February 11-June 20, 1846

Randolf Alexander
William Anderson
Truman O. Angell
Amos Babcock
Ormus E. Bates
Ichabod Beach
Wilmer B. Benson
John M. Bernhisel
Curtis E. Bolton
Benjamin Brown
Thomas Bullock
William Burton
Benjamin L. Clapp
Graham Coltran
John Coltran
Zebedee Coltrin
Jonathan Crosby
Samuel Eggleston
Addison Everett
William Felshaw
John S. Fulmer
Levi Gifford
Stephen H. Goddard
John L. Heywood
Isaac Higbee
John Houston
Daniel D. Hunt
John Kempton
Abel Lamb
Tarleton Lewis
John Loveless
Leslie Lyme
Wandel Mace
Stephen Markham
Cyrus A. Mead
Jesse K. Nicol
Charles W. Patten
William W. Phelps
Franklin D. Richards
Levi Richards
Phineas Richards
Samuel W. Richards
Thomas B. Richards
George C. Riser
Moses M. Saunders
Ranson Shepard
Erastus Snow
Phares Wells
Melvin Wilbur
Carmichael William
John Young
Joseph Young
Phineas H. Young

ABBREVIATIONS FOR FREQUENTLY CITED SOURCES

"Book of Adoptions and Sealings"	"Book of Adoptions & Sealings of Parents & Children," January 11-February 4, 1846. Excerpts and summaries in D. Michael Quinn Papers, Special Collections, Beinecke Library, Yale University, New Haven, Connecticut; in Stanley H. Ivins Papers, Utah State Historical Society, Salt Lake City; and in editors' possession; original in LDS Archives. This is a record of adoptive sealings between parent and child (biological and other) performed in the Nauvoo temple.
"Book of Anointings"	"Book of Anointings—Wives to Husbands," January 8-February 7, 1846. Excerpts, photocopies, and summaries in editors' possession; original in LDS Archives. This is a record of second anointings performed in the Nauvoo temple.
Book of Living Sealings	"Book of Sealings (Living)—Wives to Husbands," January 7-February 8, 1846. Excerpts and summaries in D. Michael Quinn Papers, Special Collections, Beinecke Library, Yale University, New Haven, Connecticut; in

	Stanley H. Ivins Papers, Utah State Historical Society, Salt Lake City; and in editors' possession; original in LDS Archives. This is a record of sealings of wives to husbands, both of whom are living, performed in the Nauvoo temple. Bracketed text, giving variant spellings of names, is reproduced as it appears in the various sources in editors' possession.
Book of Proxy Sealings	"Book of Proxey—Wives to Husbands," January 7-February 5, 1846. Photocopy in editors' possession; excerpts and summaries in D. Michael Quinn Papers, Special Collections, Beinecke Library, Yale University, New Haven, Connecticut; and in Stanley H. Ivins Papers, Utah State Historical Society, Salt Lake City; original in LDS Archives. This is a record of sealings of wives to husbands, one of whom is dead, performed in the Nauvoo temple.
Brigham Young, Diary	The diary of Brigham Young, LDS Archives. Scribes include William Clayton, Evan Greene, John D. Lee, Willard Richards, and Brigham Young.
Franklin D. Richards, Diary	The diary of Franklin D. Richards, LDS Archives; also in *Selected Collections from the Archives of The Church of Jesus Christ of Latter-day Saints* (Provo, UT: Brigham Young University Press, 2002).
Heber C. Kimball, Diary	The diary of Heber C. Kimball, published, in part, in *On the Potter's Wheel: The Diaries of Heber C. Kimball*, edited by Stanley B. Kimball (Salt Lake City: Signature Books in association with Smith Research Associates, 1987). The original is housed in LDS Archives.
History of the Church	*History of the Church of Jesus Christ of Latter-day Saints. Period I. History of Joseph Smith,*

	the Prophet by Himself, 6 vols., edited by B. H. Roberts (Salt Lake City: Published by the Church/Deseret Book, 1902-12); a seventh volume, *Period 2: Apostolic Interregnum,* was published in 1932; see *Selected Collections from the Archives of The Church of Jesus Christ of Latter-day Saints* (Provo, UT: Brigham Young University Press, 2002). The original manuscript is housed in LDS Archives.
"History of George Albert Smith"	George A. Smith, "The History of George Albert Smith," LDS Archives; also in *Selected Collections from the Archives of The Church of Jesus Christ of Latter-day Saints* (Provo, Utah: Brigham Young University Press, 2002).
John D. Lee, Diary	The diary of John D. Lee, excerpts in D. Michael Quinn Papers, Special Collections, Beinecke Library, Yale University, New Haven, Connecticut. The original is housed in LDS Archives.
John Taylor, Diary	The Nauvoo, Illinois, diary of John Taylor (George Q. Cannon, scribe), published in "The John Taylor Nauvoo Journal, January 1845-September 1845," edited by Dean C. Jessee, *BYU Studies* 23 (Summer 1983): 1-96.
LDS Archives	Archives, Church of Jesus Christ of Latter-day Saints, Salt Lake City, Utah.
Manuscript History of Brigham Young	*Manuscript History of Brigham Young, 1846-1847*, edited by Elden J. Watson (Salt Lake City: Elden J. Watson, 1971); the original is housed in LDS Archives; also in *Selected Collections from the Archives of The Church of Jesus Christ of Latter-day Saints* (Provo, UT: Brigham Young University Press, 2002).
Nauvoo Temple Endowment Register	*Nauvoo Temple Endowment Register: 10 December 1845 to 8 February 1846*, compiled by

	the Church of Jesus Christ of Latter-day Saints Temple Records Index Bureau (Salt Lake City: N.p., 1974). Forward slashes (/), indicating compound names, maiden names, middle names, variant spellings, etc., are retained as they appear in the *Register.* This is a chronological listing, compiled from a variety of manuscript sources, of all men and women known to have been washed, anointed, and endowed in the Nauvoo temple.
"Sealings and Adoptions"	"Sealings and Adoptions," compiled by Joseph F. Smith (ca. 1869-70) from "Book of Adoptions," "Book of Anointings," "Book of [Living] Sealings," "Book of Proxey [Sealings]," and other records. Photocopies, excerpts, and summaries in editors' possession; original in LDS Archives.
Seventies Record, Book B	"General Record of the Seventies. Book B." John D. Lee, principal scribe. Photocopy in editors' possession; original in LDS Archives.
Thomas Bullock, Diary	The Nauvoo, Illinois, diary of Thomas Bullock, published in *Thomas Bullock Nauvoo Journal,* edited by Greg R. Knight (Orem, UT: Grandin Book, 1994).
Willard Richards, Diary	The diary of Willard Richards, LDS Archives; also in *Selected Collections from the Archives of The Church of Jesus Christ of Latter-day Saints* (Provo, UT: Brigham Young University Press, 2002).
William Clayton, Diary	The Nauvoo diary of William Clayton, published in part in *An Intimate Chronicle: The Journals of William Clayton,* edited by George D. Smith (Salt Lake City: Signature Books and Smith Research Associates, 1991). Additional excerpts in D. Michael Quinn Papers, Beinecke Library, Yale University, New Ha-

ven, Connecticut. The original is in possession of the LDS Church.

William Clayton, Diary, kept for Heber C. Kimball	The Nauvoo diary of William Clayton, kept for Heber C. Kimball, published in part in *An Intimate Chronicle: The Journals of William Clayton,* edited by George D. Smith (Salt Lake City: Signature Books and Smith Research Associates, 1991), 199-258. Portions of this diary contain Nauvoo temple ordinance data. Photocopy in editors' possession; the original is in LDS Archives.

I.

Early December

1845

WASHINGS AND ANOINTINGS

Thursday, December 11, 1845

This morning I [Brigham Young] came early to the [Nauvoo] Temple[,] went and took breakfast with bro[ther] Joseph Kingsbury[,] returned to the Temple [and] found several of the brethren there,[1] ... spent some time acting as Eathloheim [Eloheim] [after] having ~~joined~~ been occupied with bro[ther] H[eber]. C. K[imball] until 3. O[clock]. PM. in anointing[.] [T]he brethren in the [Holy Order] met in council[2] and [I] laid before the brethren S[amuel]. Brannons letter[3] & other matters[.] staid in the Temple this night[.]

—Brigham Young, Diary.

---

1. For the past twelve days, the Quorum of the Anointed, or Holy Order (those who had been previously washed, anointed, and endowed), had been readying the attic level of the temple for the general church membership, which began arriving the next day (see our *Joseph Smith's Quorum of the Anointed, 1842-1845: A Documentary History;* also note that the present volume repeats the last dated entry of the previous volume—that of December 11, 1845—for context and continuity).

2. In the Nauvoo temple endowment drama, church members portrayed characters—Eloh(e)im, Jehovah, and Michael—drawn from the Bible and Book of Abraham and introduced into the Creation/Garden of Eden stories, including the role of the serpent or tempter.

3. Samuel Brannan (1819-89) migrated to Kirtland, Ohio, in 1833 and worked

I [William Clayton] will now give a description of the way the attic Story is finished. The main room is 88 feet 2 inches long and 28 feet 8 inches wide It is arched over, and the arch is divided into six spaces by cross beams to support the roof[.] There are 6 small rooms on each side the main room about 14 feet square each. The last one on the West end on each side is a little smaller. The first room on the South side beginning on the East end is President Brigham [Young']s Room the second E[lde]r H[eber]. C. Kimball, the third ~~George A Smith and others of the Twelve~~ ^P[arley]. P. Pratt and Orson Pratt^[4] the fourth John Taylor, ~~and others of the Twelve~~, ^Amasa Lyman, J[ohn]. E. Page & G[eorge] A. Smith^ the fifth Joseph Young and presidents of Seventies. The sixth is a preparation room for the male Members.

On the North side, the first from the East end is for Bishop Whitney & the lesser Priesthood; the second for the High Council. The third and fourth president George Miller and the High Priests quorum[,] The fifth the Elders Quorum and the sixth the female preparation Room.

The main room is divided into apartments for the ceremonies of the endowment. Beginning from the door at the West end is an alley about 5 feet wide extending to about 3 feet beyond the first Beam of the arch[.] on each side of the Alley is a small room partitioned of where the saints receive the first part of the ceremony or where the man is created and a help mate given to him. From these rooms too the third partition in the Arch is planted the garden, which is nicely decorated and set off with shrubs and trees in pots & Boxes to represent the Garden of Eden. In this apartment is also an alter. Here the man and woman are placed & commandments given to them in addition to what is given in the creation. Here also after the man & woman have eaten the forbidden fruit is given to them a charge at the Alter and the first and second tokens of the Aaronic Priesthood, They are then thrust out into a room which is dark being the one on the North side between the fourth and fifth division of

---

as a printer. He presided over the Saints in the eastern states (1845–46) and then led a group from New York to San Francisco by ship (1846–47). In June 1847, Brannan met Brigham Young near Ft. Bridger and tried to convince him to settle in California rather than Utah. Failing, Brannan returned to the Bay Area. He was excommunicated in 1851. Although he went on to become a successful entrepreneur and California's first millionaire, he lost most of his property by the time of his death. He also published the first newspaper in San Francisco, the *California Star.* For more on Brannan's letter, see the entry of William Clayton on page 6, note 12.

4. As used throughout this book, carets (^ ^) refer to text added interlinearly.

the arch which represents the telestial kingdom or the world. Opposite to this is another apartment of the same size representing the terrestrial kingdom and between these two is an alley about 4 feet wide. In the telestial kingdom, after the man has proved himself faithful he receives the first signs & tokens of the Melchizedek priesthood and an additional charge. Here also he vouches for the conduct of his companion. They are then left to prove themselves faithful, after which they are admitted into the terrestrial kingdom, where at the alter they receive an additional charge and the second token of the Melchizedek Priesthood and also the key word on the five points of fellowship.

There are words given with every token and the new name is given in the preparation room when they receive their washing and annointing.

After [they have] received all the tokens and words and signs they are led to the vail where they give each to Eloheem through the vail and are then admitted into the Celestial Room.

The Celestial room occupies the remainder of the main room being the space between two divisions of the Arch. This is adorned with a number of splendid mirrors, paintings and portraits. On the East wall are the following Portraits viz. in the centre Pres[ident]. B[righam]. Young and next to the left H[eber]. C. Kimball, Orson Hyde. To the right, Willard Richards John Taylor and George A. Smith.

On the East side of the first division of the Arch in the centre is the portrait of L[ucius]. N. Scovil,[5] next to the right is George A. Smith, next John Smith the Patriarch To the left is Barsheba [Bathsheba] Smith, and Mother Lucy [Mack] Smith.

On the West side of this partition in the centre is the portrait of[,] to the left[,] H[eber]. C. Kimball & Caroline Smith[6] To the right W[illia]m Cottier[7] John L. Smith.

---

5. According to art historian Jill Major: "Because of the scant time the first Nauvoo Temple was open for sacred ordinances, portraits of prominent Nauvoo citizens were borrowed to adorn the temple walls." Scovil's portrait may have been hung because of its availability but also to recognize his work on the committee that oversaw construction of the Nauvoo Masonic Lodge and for helping prepare Joseph Smith's Red Brick Store for the endowment. For more on the temple portraits, see Jill C. Major, "Artworks in the Celestial Room of the First Nauvoo Temple," *BYU Studies* 41 (2002), 2:47-69.

6. Caroline Amelia Grant Smith (1814-45) was the wife of apostle and Church Patriarch William Smith and sister-in-law of Joseph Smith.

7. William Cottier (1820-?) was one of the Nauvoo temple's stone cutters. He

On the East side of the second division in the centre stands a brass clock over which there is a splendid portrait of the late Hyrum Smith and next to the right C[harles]. C. Rich, George Miller & Clarissa Smith. To the left sister [Sarah] Rich, next Mary Catherine Miller and last Leonora A. Taylor.

There are also a number of maps. A large map of the world hangs on the North side wall, and three maps of the United States and a plot of the City of Nauvoo hangs on the West partition. On the South wall hangs another large map of the United States. besides a number of large mirrors and paintings.

In the centre and body of the Celestial Room are two splendid tables and four splendid sofas. Also a small table opposite the large Window on the East end of the room on which stands the Celestial and terrestrial Globes.

All the rooms are nicely carpeted and has a very splendid and comfortable appearance. There are a number of handsome chairs in it.

~~This morning~~ B[righam]. Young & wife, H[eber]. C. Kimball and G[eorge]. A. Smith, also sister Mary Smith, Mercy R. Thompson, W[illiam]. W. Phelps and his wife tarried in the Temple all night, We only obtained about an hour and a half sleep. In the morning sister Young and the other sisters went home. B[righam]. Young and myself went to Joseph C Kingsburys and eat breakfast. We there had an interview with Willard Snow who has just returned from his Mission to Boston. From thence we returned back to the Temple and found several of the brethren had come in with the expect[at]ions of receiving their anointings These following viz. Alpheus Cutler Reynolds Cahoon, Orson Spencer, Joseph Young, Isaac Morley, and Wm Clayton also Lucy Morley, Lois Cutler, Tirzah Cahoon, Catherine C. Spencer, Ruth Clayton, and Permelia Lott, each received their washings and anointings. We commenced a little before one o clock. George A. Smith and myself[8] washed the brethren and B[righam]. Young and Amasa Lyman anointed them assisted by George Miller. Sister Vilate Kimball and Elizabeth Ann Whitney attended to washing the females. At 2 o clock they also washed and anointed Mercy R. Thompson[.]

At 1 o clock E[lde]r Orson Pratt came up into the room while we

received his endowment in December 1845. He later joined the followers of Mormon dissident Sidney Rigdon.

8. William Clayton probably means Heber C. Kimball.

were attending to washing and anointing. He has just returned from his mission to the East and brought with him $400 worth of six shooters.

See 4 pages back. The men were washed by G[eorge]. A. Smith & John Taylor, and anointed by myself[9] and B[righam]. Young. The sisters were washed and anointed by sister Whitney Mary Ann Young and ~~Mary Smith~~ ———————— Elizabeth Ann Whitney.

About half past 1 o clock mother Lucy [Mack] Smith arrived. The weather is cold and some inclined to snow.

A Little before three Sister Elizebeth Ann Whitney and My wife[10] got through washing the sisters about half past 3 [and] the following were taken through all the ordinance & ceremony viz

Alpheas Cutler & Lois Cutler
Reynolds Cahoon & Tirzah Cahoon
Isaac Morley & Lucy Morley
Orson Spencer & Catherine C. Spencer
William Clayton & Ruth Clayton
Cornelius P. Lott & Permelia Lott

also mother Lucy [Mack] Smith and John Smith with her as proxy ^Also John M. Bernhisel^ Mercy R. Thompson with whom brother John Taylor acted as a proxy[.] President Young officiated as Eloheem P[arley]. P. Pratt as Jehovah and George A. Smith as Michael[.]

The first charge was given in the garden by President Young, the other two charges by H[eber]. C. Kimball, who also received most of them through the vail and Amasa Lyman received the remainder.

Immediately after all these were taken through, myself[11] and George A. Smith washed and anointed David Candland and John D. Lee. Sisters Elizabeth Ann Whitney and Mary Smith washed and anointed their wives whose names are Aggatha Ann Lee and Mary Ann Candland. They were assisted by Vilate Kimball. It was about 5 o clock PM, when they commenced washing and anointing these.

A little before six we commenced taking them through the ceremonies Heber C. Kimball acting as Eloheem George A. Smith as Jehovah Orson Hyde as Michael W[illiam]. W. Phelps as the serpent[.] We were also assisted by P[arley]. P. Pratt.

President [Young] having gone out some time ago returned while we

9. Probably Heber C. Kimball.
10. Probably Heber C. Kimball's wife, Vilate.
11. Probably Heber C. Kimball.

were in the garden. The signs & tokens were all given by H[eber]. C. Kimball. He also received them through the vail. It was about half past seven when we got through Those last who were taken through were then instructed farther regarding the signs by E[lde]r Orson Hyde.

The President then called all those who were present into the Celestial room. We formed a circle, offered up the signs, and then offered up prayers for the sick; for our families and that the Lord would frustrate the plans of our enemies. E[lde]r John E. Page being mouth.

After we got through president Young called the following persons into Hebers Room viz. H[eber]. C. Kimball, P[arley]. P. Pratt, J[ohn]. Taylor, O[rson]. Hyde, John E. Page, George A. Smith, Amasa Lyman, Newel K. Whitney, George Miller and W[illia]m. Clayton. The President then stated that he had received a letter from Samuel Brannan saying that he had been at Washington[12] and had learned that the Secretary of War[13] and the heads of the government were laying plans and were determined to prevent our moving West, alleging that it is against the Law for an armed body of men to go from the United States to any other government. They say it will not do to let the Mormons go to California nor Oregon, neither will it do to let them tarry in the States and they must be exterminated from the face of the earth.[14]

We offered up the signs of the Holy priesthood and prayed that the Lord would defeat and frustrate all the plans of our enemies and inasmuch as they make plots and lay plans to exterminate this people and destroy the priesthood from off the earth that the curse of God may come upon them even all the evil which they design to bring upon this people. And that the Lord would preserve the lives of his servants and lead us out of this ungodly nation in peace.

After we got through there was a unanimous feeling that the Lord would answer our prayers and defeat our enemies. Pres[iden]t. Young said we should go away from here in peace in spite of our enemies.

---

12. At the time he wrote the above mentioned letter to Young, Brannan was in Washington, D.C., hoping to obtain money to finance his expedition to California. Neither Brannan's letter nor Young's response survives. See Will Bagley, ed., *Scoundrel's Tale: The Samuel Brannan Papers* (Spokane: Arthur H. Clark, 1999), 108, 117.

13. This was William L. Marcy (1786-1857), who served under U.S. President James K. Polk from 1845 to 1849. He would later direct the Mexican War and serve as Secretary of State under U.S. President Franklin Pierce.

14. LDS church leaders had asked for support in securing U.S. government contracts to construct blockhouses or to carry mail on the Oregon Trail.

It was now a little after 9 o'clock and we soon after retired to our homes. President Young and Amasa Lyman tarried in the Temple all the night.

—William Clayton, Diary, kept for Heber C. Kimball.

....

A.M. went to the [Nauvoo] Temple around 9 o clock. Pres[iden]t. [Brigham] Young and H[eber]. C. Kimball were going out to breakfast. They continued to work untill half past 3 o clock this morning. After I [William Clayton] left they took the following through President Brigham Young & Mary Ann Young, William W. Phelps & Sally Phelps, Parley P. Pratt & Mary Ann Pratt, Amasa Lyman & Mariah Loisa Lyman, George Miller & Mary Catherine Miller, John Taylor & Leonora Taylor, Lucian Woodworth & Phebe Woodworth, John E. Page & Mary Page, Joseph C. Kingsbury, Mary Smith, widow of Hyrum Smith, Agness Smith, widow of Don Carlos.

I spent the forenoon writing the history of these proceedings in E[lde]r Kimballs Journal also gave a description of the upper room. At 12 Pres[iden]t. Young said I could go and fetch my wife [Ruth] if I had a mind to. I immediately went down and returned with her at 1 o clock. I then went into the preparation room and was washed by E[lde]r H[eber]. C. Kimball & George A. Smith, and then anointed a priest and a king unto the most High God by Pres[iden]t. Young and Amasa Lyman and pronounced clean from the blood of this generation.

Those who were anointed at the same time were Alpheus Cutler, Isaac Morley, Orson Spencer, Reynolds Cahoon, myself and Joseph Young. Amongst the females were Lucy Morley, Lois Cutler, Thirzah Cahoon, Catherine C. Spencer, Ruth Clayton and Permelia Lott. Brother [Cornelius P.] Lott was washed and anointed last evening. Sister Jane Young is sick and unable to attend. After washing and anointing we all passed through the ceremonies together with Mother [Lucy Mack] Smith, Mercy R. Thompson and brother Lott. It was about half past seven when we got through. Afterwards those present offered up the signs of the Holy Priesthood and had prayers John E. Page being mouth.

Pres[iden]t. Young then called the following persons into brother Kimballs room viz. H[eber]. C. Kimball, P[arley]. P. Pratt, O[rson]. Hyde, John Taylor, Amasa Lyman, George A. Smith John E. Page, N[ewel]. K. Whitney, George Miller and myself. The Pres[iden]t. stated that he had received a letter from brother Samuel Brannan stating that he had been at

Washington [D.C.] and had learned th[at] the Post Master General[15] and Secretary of War were making preparations to prevent our going West, alleging that it is against the Law for an armed body of men to go from the States to another government. They say the Mormons must not be suffered to remain in the State and neither will it do to let us go to California and there is no other way but to exterminate them and obliterate them from the face of the earth. We offered up the signs and asked our heavenly father to overrule them and inasmuch as the heads of this government are plotting the utter destruction of this people that he will curse them and let all the evil which they design to bring upon us come upon themselves.

Pres[iden]t. Young said we shall go out from this place in spite of them. All the brethren felt agreed that God will deliver us from the grasp of this ungodly and mobocratic nation.

At 9 o clock me and my wife went home thankful for the blessings and privileges of the day.

Before we had prayers however John D. Lee, Aggatha Ann Lee, David Candland & Mary Ann Candland were washed and anointed and taken through the vail.

—William Clayton, Diary.

....

The following are the Records of the washings and Anointings of the Seventies begining with the first Presidency (of the Seventies)[:]

Thursday 1 o'clock, P.M. President Jos[eph]. Young was washed by George A. Smith and anointed by President Brigham Young & Amasa Lyman — And Jane Young his Wife was washed and anointed by Eliza[beth] A. Whitney. ...

—Seventies Record, Book B.

....

[A]t 5 PM ... myself [John D. Lee] and wife received our washing & anointing. we being [having been] previously notified by Pres[ident] B[righam] Young to go home[,] When I was first engaged in the Temple or rather at the close of the same, & [to] purify our hearts by fasting & prayer & clense our bodies by washing in clean water. After passing through the sacred ordinances of the House of the Lord Pres[ident]

15. This is Cave Johnson (1793-1866), who served under U.S. President James K. Polk from 1845 to 1849. He introduced the use of postage stamps into the U.S. postal system.

B[righam] Young then informed me that my services was needed all the while here in the Temple during the time of giving Endowments[.] I accordingly returned home about 10 at night with feelings of gladness & joyful acclamations of Praise to the Giver of All Good.

—John D. Lee, Diary.

....

Elder Heber C. Kimball and I [Brigham Young] went to Joseph Kingsbury's and ate breakfast and returned to the [Nauvoo] Temple. ...

I officiated in the Temple with the brethren of the Twelve [apostles]. We administered the ordinances of endowment to:

Isaac Morley and his wife, Lucy;
Orson Spencer and Catharine C.;
Joseph Young;
Alpheus Cutler and Lois;
Reynolds Cahoon and Thirza;
William Clayton and Ruth;
Cornelius P. Lott and Permelia;
Mother Lucy [Mack] Smith and Mercy R[achel]. Thompson.

At eight p.m., we assembled for prayer. Elder John E. Page was mouth. After which I called the Twelve [apostles] and bishops together and informed them that I had received a letter from Brother Samuel Brannan, stating that he had been at Washington [D.C.] and had learned that the secretary of war and other members of the cabinet were laying plans and were determined to prevent our moving west; alleging that it is against the law for an armed body of men to go from the United States to any other government.

They say it will not do to let the Mormons go to California nor Oregon, neither will it do to let them tarry in the states, and they must be obliterated from the face of the earth.

We prayed that the Lord would defeat and frustrate all the plans of our enemies, and inasmuch as they lay plans to exterminate this people and destroy the priesthood from off the earth, that the curse of God may come upon them, and all the evil which they design to bring upon us, may befall themselves; and that the Lord would preserve the lives of his servants and lead us out of this ungodly nation in peace.

I said we should go out from this place in spite of them all, and the brethren all felt that God would deliver us from the grasp of this ungodly and mobocratic nation.

Brother Amasa Lyman and I tarried in the Temple all night.

—"Manuscript History of Brigham Young," in *History of the Church,* 7:543-44.

....

In the order of Endowment, a list is made out the day previous, of those who wish to take their endowments. Every person is required to wash himself clean, from head to foot. Also to prepare and bring a good supply of food, of the best quality, for themselves and those who labor in the house of the Lord. In the latter about twenty-five persons are required in the different departments to attend to the washing, anointing, blessing, ordaining, and sealing. From twenty-five to fifty persons are passed through in twenty-four hours.

I was among the first to receive my washings and anointings [on December 11, 1845], and even received my second anointing [on January 14, 1846], which made me an equal in the order of the Priesthood, with the right and authority to build up the kingdom in all the earth, and power to fill any vacancy that might occur. I have officiated in all the different branches, from the highest to the lowest. There were about forty men who attained to that order in the Priesthood, including the twelve Apostles and the first presidency, and to them was intrusted the keeping of the records. I was the head clerk; Franklin D. Richards was my assistant clerk. My office was in room number one, at President [Brigham] Young's apartments.

I kept a record of all the sealings, anointings, marriages and adoptions.

I was the second one adopted to Brigham Young. I should have been his first adopted son, being the first that proposed it to him, but always ready to give preference to those in authority, I placed A[lbert]. P. Rockwood's name first on the list. I also had my children adopted to me in the Temple. Brigham Young had his children adopted to himself, and we were the only ones, to my knowledge, that had our children so adopted at the Temple at Nauvoo [Illinois]. As time would not permit attending to all the people, the business was rushed through day and night.

—John D. Lee, *Mormonism Unveiled; or The Life and Confessions of the Late Mormon Bishop, John D. Lee* (St. Louis, Missouri: Bryan, Brand & Company, 1877), pp. 169-70.

....

Nauvoo temple endowments performed on this date:

First Company: Alpheus Cutler, Lois Cutler, Reynolds Cahoon, Thirza Cahoon, Isaac Morley, Lucy Morley, Orson Spencer, Catherine Spencer, William Clayton, Ruth Clayton, Cornelius P. Lott, Permelia Lott, Lucy Mack Smith, and Mercy R. Thompson.

Second Company: David Candland, Mary Ann Candland, John D. Lee, and Aggatha Ann Lee.

—*Nauvoo Temple Endowment Register: 10 December 1845 to 8 February 1846,* compiled by the Temple Index Bureau of the Church of Jesus Christ of Latter-day Saints, 1974, under date.

Friday, December 12, 1845

This morning bro[ther]. H[eber] C. K[imball]. & I [Brigham Young] anointed b[r]o[ther] Joseph Young had a council at 12. O[clock]. I acted as E[l]ohiem[.] took dinner at bro[ther]. J[oseph]. Kingsbury's[.] returned to the Temple[.] officited at the vail[16] ~~at about~~ 20[.]

—Brigham Young, Diary.

....

This morning I again went up to the Temple with my wife.[17] The morning is very fine but cold. We arrived at a quarter to 10 and found several of the brethren all ready arrived and preparing for the washings of others who have been notified to attend. At quarter after 10 A.M. we again commenced the washings and anointings to the presidents of the seventies and their wives and also to Elder Orson Pratt and his wife. The names of those washed and anointed this morning are as follows.

Levi W. Hancock, Henry Herriman, Zerah Pulsipher, Jedidiah M. Grant, Albert P. Rockwood, Benjamin L. Clapp. These were washed by George A. Smith & P[arley]. P. Pratt and anointed by B[righam]. Young and H[eber]. C. Kimball.

The names of the females are as follows

Jane Young washed and anointed by Elizabeth A. Whitney
Clarissa Hancock do do [ditto] by V[ilate]. Kimball
Clarissa Herriman do do [ditto] by Mary Smith
Caroline Grant do do [ditto] E[lizabeth]. A[nn]. Whitney
Nancy H. Rockwood do do [ditto] V[ilate]. Kimball
Mary Clapp do do [ditto] Mary Smith

---

16. Those officiating at the veil were also called prompters. Their role was to ensure that each person repeated the phrases and performed the gestures correctly prior to entering the Celestial Room.

17. It is not clear if "I" refers to Heber C. Kimball or William Clayton or if "my wife" refers to Vilate Kimball or Ruth Clayton.

Sister Pulsipher is sick and unable to attend. After these were all washed and anointed E[lde]r Orson Pratt and Sarah Marinda Pratt came in. He was washed and anointed by George A. Smith and Amasa Lyman who did the washing and Pres[iden]t. Young and H[eber]. C. Kimball attended to anointing.

Sarah Marinda Pratt was washed and anointed by V[ilate]. Kimball.

[A]t half past 12 o clock all things being prepared to take these through the remaining ceremonies they commenced Pres[iden]t. Young acting as Elohee [Elohim], P[arley]. P. Pratt as Jehovah Orson Hyde as Michael W[illia]m W. Phelps as the serpent H[eber]. C. Kimball assisted through the whole. President Young gave all the charges and received Orson Pratt through the Vail. The remainder of the men were received through by O[rson]. Hyde the females by their husbands.

The names are as follows who are now admitted through the vail. Orson Pratt & Sally [Sarah] M. Pratt

Joseph Young & Jane Young
Levi W. Hancock & Clarissa Hancock
Henry Herriman & Clarissa Herriman
Zerah Pulsipher.
Jedidiah M. Grant & Caroline Grant.
Albert P. Rockwood & Nancy H. Rockwood
Benjamin L. Clapp & Mary Clapp

At a quarter after 3 P.M. Pres[iden]t. Young H[eber]. C. Kimball, N[ewel]. K. Whitney & Vilate Kimball went to J[oseph]. C. Kingsburys to dinner[.]

About 2 o clock the following were washed and anointed, viz James Allred, Charles C. Rich, William Felshaw, George W. Harris, William Meeks, Truman O. Angel. The washing and anointing of these was done by Newel K. Whitney, George Miller, Amasa Lyman, George A. Smith & John Taylor[.] About the same time the wives of the foregoing were washed and anointed as follows Elizabeth Allred by E[lizabeth]. A[nn]. Whitney

Lucinda Harris by Mary Smith
Polly Angel by Lois Cutler
Sarah D. Rich by Mary Smith
Mary H. Felshaw by Lois Cutler
Caroline Meeks by Lois Cutler.

Hannah Fielding was also washed and anointed at the same time by Mary Smith but her husband is not yet washed and anointed[.]

At 20 minutes past 3 P.M. all things being ready the ceremonies were commenced to take the above through in the following order.

John Taylor acting as Eloheem
George A. Smith " Jehovah
George Miller " Michael
W[illia]m W. Phelps " the Serpent

All the charges were given by E[lde]r John Taylor. He also received the brethren through the vail and they each received their wives through[.]

At 20 minutes to 5 the following were admitted to pass the vail being those who were washed and anointed at 2 oclock. E[lde]r Taylor officiating at the Vail and John M. Bernhisel first was blessed through [?] to correct his memory[.]

James Allred & Elizabeth Allred
Charles C. Rich & Sarah D. Rich
William Felshaw & Mary H. Felshaw
George W. Harris & Lucinda Harris
William Meeks & Caroline Meeks
Truman O. Angell & Polly Angell

At 5 o clock Pres[iden]t. Young, H[eber]. C. Kimball N[ewel]. K. Whitney, Vilate Kimball and Elizabeth Ann Whitney returned. At a quarter after 4 the following men were washed and anointed viz Joseph Fielding — Noah Packard

William Snow — Samuel Rolfe
Norton Jacobs — Willard Snow
Erastus Snow — William W. Player
Aaron Johnson

These were washed by George Miller and Orson Hyde and anointed by Amasa Lyman and Parley P. Pratt. At the same time the wives of the foregoing were washed and anointed in the following order Polly Zariah Johnson by Mary Smith

Lidia Snow by Mary Smith
Sophia Packard by Lois Cutler
Malvina Snow by Lois Cutler
Emily Jacobs by Lois Cutler
Zillah Player by Phebe Woodworth
Elizabeth Rolfe by Phebe Woodworth
~~Artimenia~~ ^Artimetia^ ^Artimesia^ Snow by Loisa M. Lyman

At 16 minutes after six oclock P.M. all things being prepared the foregoing persons together with Hannah Fielding were taken through the ceremonies of the endowment. The following persons officiating

Orson Hyde as Eloheem
Orson Spencer as Jehovah
George A Smith as Michael and

W[illia]m W. Phelps as the Serpent. All the charges were given to them by Elder O[rson]. Hyde together with much good instruction. They were received through the vail commencing at 14 minutes after 8 o'clock by President B[righam]. Young. (see next page [i.e., next manuscript page].)

At half past 6 o clock Pres[iden]t. B[righam]. Young H[eber]. C. Kimball and Newel K. Whitney retired to the Bishops room and consecrated for the endowment 14 bottles of oil which had previously been prepared by Bishop Whitney. They returned and undressed at 20 minutes to seven.

At 5 minutes to 7 P.M. the following persons were washed and anointed viz.

William Huntington Sen[io]r. ~~& Lydia Huntington~~ Henry G. Sherwood ~~& Jane I Sherwood~~ William Crosby — Lucian R. Foster and Miles Romney. These were washed by George Miller and Charles C. Rich and anointed by Amasa Lyman and Isaac Morley assisted by Benjamin L. Clapp. At the same time the wives of the foregoing were washed and anointed as follows.

Jane I. Sherwood by Loisa M. Lyman
Sally Crosby by Loisa M. Lyman
Ann Mariah Foster by Loisa M. Lyman
Elizabeth Romney by Loisa M. Lyman

Lidia Huntington was washed and anointed by Tirzah Cahoon and blessed by all the sisters present.

At 14 minutes after 8 o clock [we] ^commenced receiving^ the following ~~were received~~ through the vail being those who were washed at a quarter after 4 this afternoon, viz

Joseph Fielding & Hannah Fielding.
Noah Packard & Sophia Packard.
William Snow & Lidia Snow.
Samuel Rolfe & Elizabeth Rolfe.
Norton Jacobs & Emily Jacobs.
Willard Snow & Malvina Snow.
Erastus Snow & Artemesia Snow.
William W. Player & Zillah Player.
Aaron Johnson & ^Polly^ Zeriah Johnson.

President Young received Noah Packard through who is quite sick. Joseph Fielding, William Snow, and Erastus Snow were received through by E[lde]r H[eber]. C. Kimball and the remainder by E[lde]r Orson Spencer. Each man receiving his own wife through after he himself was admitted.

At about 25 minutes to 11 o clock the last one of these were received through the vail.

E[lde]r Orson Pratt acted as prompter while President Young and H[eber]. C. Kimball officiated at the vail, and Isaac Morley acted as prompter while Orson Spencer officiated. At 25 minutes after 9 o clock every thing being prepared[,] the ceremony of receiving those who were lately washed was commenced in the following order. Pres[iden]t. B[righam]. Young as Eloheem

H[eber]. C. Kimball as Jehovah
Orson Hyde as Michael
W[illiam]. W. Phelps as the Serpent

They were also assisted by E[lde]r P[arley]. P. Pratt[.] Pres[iden]t. Young gave the first charge in the garden & E[lde]r P[arley]. P. Pratt the second in the Telestial Kingdom. E[lde]r Pratt also continued and gave the charge in the Terrestrial Kingdom.

At 10 minutes after 11 o'clock [we] commenced receiving the following through the vail[,] being those last washed & anointed[;] Their names are as follows, viz.

William Huntington Sen[io]r. & Lidia Huntington
Henry G. Sherwood & Jane J. Sherwood
William Crosby & Sally Crosby
Lucian R. Foster & Ann Mariah Foster
Miles Romney & Elizabeth Romney.

President B[righam]. Young received L[ucian]. R. Foster, and W[illia]m Huntington through. E[lde]r H[eber]. C. Kimball received W[illia]m. Crosby through and Joseph Young recei[ve]d Henry G. Sherwood & Miles Romney. each man receive[d] his own wife after he himself was admitted. At a quarter past 1 o clock the last one was admitted all the brethren being much fatigued by the labors of the day.

At half past 10 o clock Elder H[eber]. C. Kimball made a selection of brethren to assist in the endowment tomorrow. He made a selection of those who were willing to volunteer freely whose names are

Charles C. Rich	Benjamin L. Clapp
Jedidiah M. Grant	Orson Spencer

Isaac Morley — Erastus Snow
W[illia]m. W. Phelps — Willard Snow
Aaron Johnson — Joseph Young

These are selected in addition to the members of the quorum of the Twelve apostles.

At a quarter after 1 o clock President B[righam]. Young, A[masa]. Lyman, G[eorge]. A. Smith, C[harles]. C. Rich, W[illiam]. W. Phelps, J[ohn]. D. Lee, P[arley]. P. Pratt, O[rson]. Pratt, & O[rson]. Hyde clothed and offered up the signs and prayers, E[lde]r George A. Smith being mouth. After prayers the following took their blankets and lay down to rest on the floor of the Temple where they tarried over night, viz.

Pres[iden]t. B[righam]. Young. — Amasa Lyman
George A. Smith — W[illia]m W. Phelps
Charles C. Rich — John D. Lee
David Candland

E[lde]r Joseph Young and his wife tarried in his own room over night.

During the whole of the three days already spent in the endowment, President Brigham Young presided and dictated the ordinances and also took an active part in nearly every instance except when entirely overcome by fatigue through his constant labors to forward the work.

Perfect peace and harmony prevail during the whole time, except in one case which happened this afternoon, wherein Phebe Woodworth interfered with business which did not belong to her, and in the presence of those who are higher in authority than her, and undertook to dictate and control those who were legally and righteously appointed to superintend and administer the ordinance of washing and anointing of the females.

—William Clayton, Diary, kept for Heber C. Kimball.

....

Pres[iden]t. [Brigham] Young presides and controls the whole business [of temple work] and take[s] a very active part himself.

—William Clayton, Diary.

....

A condensed Table form for Record Keeping

[See page 17 for excerpted portion.]

—Seventies Record, Book B, under entry dated December 11, 1846.

[Washings and anointings for Friday, December 12, 1845]

No.	*Members*	*by washed*	*and by whom Anointed*		*Age*	*Month day year*
Name	Pres Jos Young	George A Smith	Pres B Young & A. Lyman		47	April 17 1844
2nd	Levi W Hancock	"	P. P. Pratt H C Kimball		41	" " "
3rd	Henry Herriman	"	" "			June 9th 1845
4th	Zerah Pulsipher	"	" "		56	6th " "
5th	Albert P. Rockwood	"	" "		34	9th " "
6th	Benjamin L. Clapp	"	" "		31	Aug 19th " "
7th	Jedediah M Grant	"	" "		29	Feb 21. " "

All except [illegible] was washed & anointed Fri 10 A.M. Dec 12th 1845.

& Thurs P.M.	John D. Lee	Heber Kimball		Heber C Kimball	33	Sept 6th 45
and	David Candland	"	G A Smith	" " "		

Female Department

Date			
Dec 12th	Jane Young	Eliza A. Whitney	by the same
[illegible]	Clarisa Hancock	Vilate Kimble	V. Kimble
	Clarisa Herriman	Mary Smith	Mary Smith
	Nancy Rockwood	V. Kimble	& do R. do
	Mary Clapp	Mary Smith	[illegible]
	Caroline Grant	E. A. Whitney	E. A. W.
	[illegible]	[illegible]	[illegible]

—Seventies Record, Book B, oversized portion,
under entry dated December 11, 1845.

[A]bout 4 AM I [John D. Lee] entered the Temple & in connection with several others cleaned up the rooms in the different departments & prepared for the endowment at half past 9 morning[.] the 12 [Apostles] having come in they commenced opperations[.] I will mention here that I had for several days to be door keeper[18] as well as chief cook & bottle washer. I do not mean in giving the endowments but to see that all things were in readiness & kept straight in the preparation time[.] Pres[ident] B[righam] Young as soon as circumstances would advise organized & placed help in the different departments & I was set apart for a clerk to keep the records of the Saints. I was truly thankful that I was thus favored as I had much writing in the rear to do[.] through the day and part of the night some 53 persons were washed and anointed under the hands of Pres[ident]. Joseph Young [Henry] Harriman pres[idents] B[enjamin] L Clapp G[eorge] M Grant Samuel Bent Isaac Moorley C[harles] C Rich & Phineas Young.

—John D. Lee, Diary.

[T]he 12th [of December] I [Joseph Fielding] and my Wife [Hannah] received our Endowment having formerly received it in the Days of Joseph and Hyram [Smith] but it is now given in a more perfect Manner because of better Convenience, the 12 are very strict in attending to the true and proper form[.]

—Joseph Fielding, Diary, LDS Archives.

W[illia]m. Weeks came to me [Norton Jacob] and said he wanted me to go home and prepare myself and wife and come to the temple at 12 o'clock a.m. ready to receive our endowments. We most joyfully complied with this request and at about 5 o'clock p.m. we were washed and anointed in the House of the Lord. It was the most interesting scene of all my life and one that afforded the most peace and joy that we had ever experienced since we were married, which has been over fifteen years. Brethren W[illia]m. Weeks, Truman O. Angel, Charles C. Rich, George W. Harris, James Allred and W[illia]m. Felshaw were the first that received their endowment in this House of the Lord, which took place on this day, the time before having been occupied in the washing and anoint-

18. The doorkeeper guarded the temple entrance. Not only did he protect the temple and ensure that the endowment ritual could be performed uninterrupted, he also protected Brigham Young and other church leaders, who were wanted on charges of counterfeiting.

ing those that had before received endowments under the hands of Joseph Smith the Prophet, which he conferred upon them one year ago last winter. After those six went in with their wives, Amos Fielding, Noah Packard, Samuel Rolf, Aaron Johnson, W[illia]m. Snow, Willard Snow, Erastus Snow, [William] Player, and myself with our wives were called in and all passed through the endowment at the same time.

—"Life of Norton Jacob," typescript, L. Tom Perry Special Collections, Harold B. Lee Library, Brigham Young University, Provo, Utah.

....

[A]t about half past 4 oclock P.M. brother G[eorge]. D. Grant notified me [Franklin D. Richards] to appear at the Temple the next morning at 8 oclock with my wife which we did[.]

—Franklin D. Richards, Diary.

....

On the 12th December Myself [Erastus Snow] and wife Artimesia received the first ordin[an]ces in the temple and were called to labour & administer in the temple from that time forth and I departed not from the Temple day or night but continued in the labours and duties thereof with the Twelve [apostles] and others selected for the purpose; about six weeks[.] Mrs Snow continued in the female department about a month[.]

—Erastus Snow, Diary, LDS Archives.

....

In company with my [Brigham Young's] brethren of the Twelve [apostles] I officiated in the Temple until midnight.

Orson Pratt and his wife, Sarah Marinda, the First Presidency of the Seventy and their wives and others numbering in all twenty-eight males and twenty-seven females received the ordinances of endowment.

Several tarried in the Temple all night.

—"Manuscript History of Brigham Young," in *History of the Church,* 7:544.

....

Nauvoo temple endowments performed on this date for:

First Company: Orson Pratt, Sally [Sarah] M. Pratt, Joseph Young, Jane Young, Levi W. Hancock, Clarissa Hancock, Henry Herriman, Clarissa Herriman, Zerah Pulsipher, Jedediah M. Grant, Caroline Grant, Albert P. Rockwood, Nancy H. Rockwood, Benjamin L. Clapp, and Mary Clapp.

Second Company: James Allred, Elizabeth Allred, Charles C. Rich, Sarah D. Rich, William Felshaw, Mary H. Felshaw, George W. Harris, Lucinda Harris, William Weeks, Caroline Weeks, Truman Angell, and Polly Angell.

Third Company: Joseph Fielding, Hannah Fielding, Noah Packard, Sophia Packard, William Snow, Lydia Snow, Samuel Rolfe, Elizabeth Rolfe, Norton Jacobs, Emily Jacobs, Willard Snow, Malvina Snow, Erastus Snow, Artemisia Snow, William W. Player, Zillah Player, Aaron Johnson, and Polly Zeruiah Johnson.

Fourth Company: William Huntington Senior, Lydia Huntington, Henry G. Sherwood, Jane J. Sherwood, William Crosby, Sally Crosby, Lucian R. Foster, Ann Mariah Foster, Miles Romney, and Elizabeth Romney.

—Summary of information compiled by the Temple
Index Bureau, *Nauvoo Temple Endowment Register:*
10 December 1845 to 8 February 1846.

Saturday, December 13, 1845

Rules of order drawn. up— In the evening went out with bro[ther] A[masa]. Lyman returned about 10. O.[clock]— the bret[hren]. assembled. about 12½. O.[clock] I [Brigham Young] accted as Elohiem.

—Brigham Young, Diary.

....

This morning Pres[iden]t. [Brigham] Young and E[lde]r [Amasa] Lyman left the Temple for a little season and returned about a quarter after 10 a number of the brethren being already assembled and preparing to continue the ordinances. About the same time E[lde]r H[eber]. C. Kimball and Vilate Kimball arrived and soon after P[arley]. P. Pratt, O[rson]. Hyde, O[rson]. Pratt, N[ewel]. K. Whitney, sister Whitney and others.

At 15 minutes after 11 o clock [we] commenced washing and anointing the following, viz.

Samuel Bent	George D. Grant
Daniel Spencer	William L. Cutler,
Philo Dibble	Franklin D. Richards,
William Miller	Phineas H. Young,
Thomas Burdick —	

Elders Benjamin L. Clap & Henry Herriman administering the washing and Isaac Morley & Joseph Young attending to the anointing. They finished these at 10 minutes after 12 o clock.

About the same time the following who are the wives of the foregoing were washed and anointed as follows, viz.

Lettie Bent washed by Mary Smith and anointed by ~~Elizabeth Ann Whitney~~ ^Vilate Kimball[,]^ Elizabeth Grant washed by Mary Miller and anointed by Elizabeth Ann Whitney. Mary Spencer ~~washed~~ washed by Mary Miller & anointed by Vilate Kimball. Hannah A. Dibble washed by Mary Smith and anointed by Elizabeth Ann Whitney Jane S. Richards washed by Mary Miller and anointed by Elizabeth Ann Whitney. Phebe Miller washed by Mary Miller and anointed by Vilate Kimball Anna Burdick washed by Mary Miller and anointed by Elizabeth A. Whitney.

At 20 minutes after 12 [we] commenced receiving the above through the ceremonies[.] the officers officiating were as follows. President B[righam]. Young as Eloheem

John Taylor as Jehovah
H[eber]. C. Kimball as Michael
W[illiam]. W. Phelps as the Serpent
P[arley]. P. Pratt as Peter
Amasa Lyman as James
Orson Pratt as John

Last evening an arrangement was made establishing better order in conducting the endowment. Under this order it is the province of Eloheem, Jehovah and Michael to create the world, plant the Garden and create the man and give his help meet. Eloheem gives the charge to Adam in the Garden and thrusts them into the telestial kingdom or the world. Then Peter assisted by James and John conducts them through the Telestial and Terrestrial kingdom administering the charges and tokens in each and conducts them to the vail where they are received by the Eloheem and after talking with him by words and tokens are admitted by him into the Celestial kingdom.

At 5 minutes before 2 o clock P.M. President Young commenced receiving the following into the upper department[19] being those who were washed & anointed at 15 minutes after 11 o clock viz.

Daniel Spencer and Mary Spencer
Phineas H. Young
Samuel Bent and Lettice Bent.

---

19. The upper department was the Celestial Room, the final stage of the endowment ceremony where members were received through the veil and symbolically into the Celestial Kingdom.

At half past 2 o clock President Young retired to his room, being weary and E[lde]r John Taylor continued to receive the following viz.

Franklin D. Richards & Jane S. Richards
William Miller & Phebe Miller

At 3 o clock E[lde]r John Taylor retired and Joseph Young received into the upper department

Thomas Burdick & Anna Burdick
Philo Dibble & Hannah Ann Dibble.
George D. Grant & Elizabeth Grant.
William L. Cutler

The last one being admitted into the upper department at 4 o clock[.]

At 20 minutes after 1 o clock P.M. [we] commenced washing the following

Peter Haws Lucius N. Scovil
Titus Billings Newel Knight
Elijah Averitt, Albert Carrington, Joseph Knight
Sen[io]r., Samuel Whitney ~~Sen~~ and Lorenzo Young

Elders Benjamin L. Clap and Henry Herriman attending to the washings and Isaac Morley and Joseph Young to the anointing assisted by E[lde]r Charles C. Rich.

They finished the ordinance of washing and anointing to the above at 32 minutes after 2 o clock.

About the same time these brethren were administered to. their wives ~~were wives~~ were also washed and anointed in the following order, viz.

Charlotte Haws washed by Ma[r]y C. Miller and anointed by Eliz[abe]th A[nn]. Whitney[.]

Lucy Scovil washed by Sarah D. Rich and anointed by Vilate Kimball[.]

Diantha Billings washed by Barsheba [Bathsheba] Smith and anointed by Elizabeth A[nn]. Whitney[.]

Lydia Knight washed by Sarah D. Rich and anointed by Vilate Kimball[.]

Cherrizade Averett washed by Ma[r]y C Miller and anointed by Bathsheba Smith[.]

Rhoda Mariah Carrington washed by Ma[r]y C Miller and anointed by Bathsheba Smith.

Phebe Knight washed by Sarah D. Rich and anointed by Vilate Kimball.

At half after 3 o clock P.M. [we] commenced receiving the foregoing through the ceremonies, the following persons officiating viz.

In the upper department
P[arley]. P. Pratt as No 1[20]
Orson Hyde as No 2
John Taylor as No 3
In the middle department[21]
John Taylor as No 1
Charles C. Rich as No 2
Orson Pratt as No 3
W[illia]m W. Phelps as No 4

At 5 minutes after 5 o clock [we] commenced receiving the following through into the upper department in the following order.

Samuel Whitney born April 18, 1772 received by Elder John Taylor.
Joseph Knight Sen[io]r. born November 3, 1772. received by E[lde]r P[arley]. P. Pratt.
Phebe Knight born March 21, 1800 received by her husband assisted by P[arley]. P. Pratt[.]
Titus Billings born March 25, 1795 by Elder P[arley]. P. Pratt.
Diantha Billings born August 23, 1795 by her husband & P[arley]. P. Pratt[.]
Lucius N. Scovil born March 18 1806 by E[lde]r P[arley]. P. Pratt[.]
Lucy Scovil born March 11 1807 by L[ucius]. N. Scovil & P[arley]. P. Pratt[.]
Peter Haws born February 17 1795 by L[ucius]. N. Scovil.
Charlotte Haws born April 8th 1798 by Peter Haws & L[ucius]. N. Scovil[.]
Elijah Averitt born December 12 1810 by L[ucius]. N. Scovil[.]
Cherizade Averett born June 27 1812 by Elijah Averett & L[ucius]. N. Scovil[.]
Newel Knight born September 13 1800 by L[ucius]. N. Scovil[.]

20. The numbers identify the parts played by the actors. In the upper department: 1 = Elohim, 2 = Jehovah, and 3 = Michael; in the lower and middle departments, 1 = Peter, 2 = James, 3 = John, 4 = the serpent or tempter, and 5 = prompter.

21. The middle department refers to the Garden, Telestial, and Terrestrial Rooms. The lower department was the Creation Room.

Lydia Knight born June 9 1812 by Newell Knight & L[ucius]. N. Scovil[.]

Albert Carrington born January 8 1813 by L[ucius]. N. Scovil[.]

Rhoda Mariah Carrington born March 22 1822 by Albert Carrington & L[ucius]. N. Scovil[.]

Lorenzo Young born Octob[e]r 19 1807 by John Taylor—he was received one of the first in this list.

At a quarter after 7 o clock the last of the foregoing was admitted to the upper department. Erastus Snow & Joseph Young acting as prompters.

At 14 minutes before 5 o clock P.M. the brethren commenced washing the following, viz.

John Lytle	born	August 18 1803
John Mills	"	January 14 1816
Isaac Chase	"	December 12 1791
Hans C. Hanson	"	November 23 1806
Peter C. Hanson	"	June 11 1818
Andrew Lytle	"	December 25 1812
Elisha Averett	"	December 12 1810.

These were washed by Levi W. Hancock and Benjamin L. Clapp and anointed by Isaac Morley and Albert P. Rockwood. They finished the washing and anointing to the foregoing at 20 minutes before 6 o clock P.M.

About 5 o clock the sisters commenced washing and anointing the following, in the following order.

Christiana Lytle born February 16 1806 washed by Agness Smith, An[ointe]d. by Bathsheba W. Smith[.]

Elizabeth Mills born November 14 1916 Washed by Leonora ~~A~~ Taylor and anointed by Sarah D. Rich[.]

Phebe Chase born December 7 1794 washed by Mary C. Miller and anointed by Bathsheba W. Smith[.]

Hannah Lytle born June 4, 1801, Washed by Mercy R. Thompson and anointed by Leonora ~~A~~ Taylor.

They finished these ordinances to the above at half after 5 o clock P.M.

At 15 minutes after 6 o clock [we] commenced receiving the foregoing through the ceremonies, the following persons officiating, viz.

In the Upper department

John Taylor as No 1

Amasa Lyman as No 2

George A. Smith as No 3

In the lower department

Orson Pratt as No 1
Joseph Young as No 2
Levi W. Hancock as No 3
W[illiam]. W. Phelps as No. 4
and Orson Spencer as prompter[.]

At a quarter to 7 o clock P.M. the foregoing were received into the upper department in the following order.

Isaac Chase by H[eber]. C. Kimball[.]
Phebe Chase by I[saac] Chase & H[eber]. C. Kimball.
John Mills by H[eber]. C. Kimball Elizabeth Mills by John Mills & H[eber]. C. Kimball[.]
John Lytle by L[ucius]. N. Scovil and Christiana Lytle by John Lytle and L[ucius]. N. Scovil[.]
Andrew Lytle by L[ucius]. N. Scovil;
Hannah Lytle by Andrew Lytle and L[ucius]. N. Scovil[.]
Elisha Averett by Lucius N. Scovil.
Hans C. Hanson by Lucius N. Scovil.
Peter O. Hanson by Lucius N. Scovil.

The last one being received at 20 minutes after 9 o clock.

About this hour the following persons were washed and anointed as follows, viz.

Augusta Cobb born December 7 1802 washed by Nancy H. Rockwood and anointed by Elizabeth A[nn]. Whitney.
Ellen Rockwood born March 23 1829 washed by Nancy H. Rockwood and anointed by Elizabeth A[nn]. Whitney.

At 7 o clock the following High Priests met in the High Councils room duly clothed, viz.

George Miller, Peter Haws, Charles C. Rich, Aaron Johnson, Willard Snow, Levi Richards and Joseph C. Kingsbury. These offered up the signs of the Holy Priesthood and then had prayers. George Miller being mouth.

About 7 o clock a report came up that a person just from Springfield [Illinois] states that Lucian B. Adams, son of the late Judge Adams has effected a complete revolution in the minds of the inhabitants of Springfield, so much so that Judge Pope is convinced that E[lde]r [Theodore] Turley is imprisoned through persecution and says he shall discharge him the moment he arrives at Springfield.[22]

---

22. Theodore Turley had been arrested at Alton, Illinois, on charges of counter-

President Young has superintended the days business, himself generally taking an active part in the ceremonies. The following of the Twelve [apostles] were also present and assisting in the ordinances, viz. Heber C. Kimball, Parley P. Pratt, John Taylor, Orson Hyde, George A. Smith, Amasa Lyman, Orson Pratt. Also N[ewel]. K. Whitney, George Miller, W[illiam]. W. Phelps, Isaac Morley, Joseph Young, Charles C. Rich, Jedidiah M. Grant, Albert P. Rockwood, Henry Herriman, John D. Lee, David Candland, Erastus Snow, and others.

In the female department sisters Elizabeth Ann Whitney, Vilate Kimball, Mary C. Miller, Agness M. Smith, Barsheba [Bathsheba] W. Smith, Mary Smith, Mercy R. Thompson, Leonora ~~A~~ Taylor, Sara D. Rich and others.

Perfect peace, harmony and good feeling prevailed through the day.

About 10 o clock most of the brethren and sisters retired home except the following who slept in the Temple over night viz. W[illia]m. W. Phelps, Erastus Snow, David Candland, Henry G. Sherwood, Benjamin L. Clapp, Henry Harriman and Aaron Johnson.

After the brethren had mostly left the Room, W[illiam]. W. Phelps draughted the following to be observed in this House under the dictation of the President.

Rules of Order

Rule 1st. No person allowed to enter these apartments without changing or cleansing shoes in the Vestry.

Rule 2nd. No person allowed to wear his hat or cap, while in these rooms.

Rule 3rd. No person allowed to enter further than the reception or washing and anointing rooms till he or she has been washed and anointed.

Rule 4th[.] No person allowed to pass from one room to another while receiving the ordinances without being conducted by a superintendant.

Rules for those who have received the ordinances.

Rule 1st[.] No person allowed in the rooms without an invitation while in the hours of labor, excepting at the hour of prayer.

Rule 2nd. All persons who are invited are requested to remain in their rooms during the hours of labor.

---

feiting and was jailed in Quincy. He was released on a $250 bail in mid-December 1845.

Rule 3rd. At the ringing of the bell, all walking about, and loud talking, must cease.

Rule 4th. No person allowed to remove things from one room to another without permission of the owner, and to be returned immediately when done with.

—William Clayton, Diary, kept for Heber C. Kimball.

....

[W]e with br[other]s S[amuel]. Bent. P[hineas]. H. Young W[illia]m Miller, George D. Grant, and a few others, Daniel Spencer, W[illia]m L. Cutler, Philo Dibble and wives received our washing & annointing in the "House of the Lord" in the attic story. I [Franklin D. Richards] pray thee my Heavenly Father in the name of Jesus Christ thy son to impart unto me from henceforth that portion of thy good spirit which shall enable me to keep inviolate all those sacred obligations which I am placed under by virtue of the endowment this day conferred upon me for I feel myself blessed beyond measure in being called upon so soon to enter in while many of my brethren who perhaps are more worthy than I am are delayed[.] help me my Father I pray thee to be as forward to do good to my fellowmen especially those who are of the household of faith as thou hast been to bestow upon me these precious blessings of thy "holy House" and may they have the savory effect upon my vessel to sanctify it and make it a vessel of honor fit for my Masters use yea O God may I be faithful unto the attaining to the fulness of these two Priesthoods and have the power therof unto the renewing of my body and may my companion also be sanctified by the same means and each of ^us^ understand and perform our duties to each other well that the bond of union may become perfect and never be broken[.] may we both keep close mouths, faithful spirits, and observe all things pertaining to the Oath of the priesthood and be found faithful therein and never fall but rise in intelligence until we become fit for the presence of our Father in Heaven, all which blessings we ask in the name of Jesus Christ[.]

—Franklin D. Richards, Diary.

....

We continued officiating in the Temple; twenty-five males and twenty females were administered unto.

I [Brigham Young] drafted rules for the preservation of order in the House of the Lord.

News arrived from Springfield [Illinois] that Lucien B. Adams, son of the late Judge [James] Adams, has effected a complete revolution in the minds of the inhabitants of Springfield, so much so, that Judge Pope is convinced that Elder [Theodore] Turley is imprisoned through persecution and says he shall discharge him when he arrives at Springfield.

"Manuscript History of Brigham Young," in *History of the Church,* 7:544-45.

....

Nauvoo temple endowments performed on this date for:

First Company: Daniel Spencer, Mary Spencer, Phineas H. Young, Samuel Bent, Lettice Bent, Franklin D. Richards, Jane S. Richards, William Miller, Phebe Miller, Thomas Burdick, Anna Burdick, Philo Dibble, Hannah Ann Dibble, George D. Grant, Elizabeth Grant, and William L. Cutler.

Second Company: Samuel Whitney, Joseph Knight, Senior, Phebe Knight, Titus Billings, Diantha Billings, Lucius N. Scovil, Lucy Scovil, Peter Haws, Charlotte Haws, Elijah Averitt, Cherizade Averitt, Newel Knight, Lydia Knight, Albert Carrington, Rhoda Mariah Carrington, and Lorenzo Young.

Third Company: Isaac Chase, Phebe Chase, John Mills, Elizabeth Mills, John Lytle, Christiana Lytle, Andrew Lytle, Hannah Lytle, Elisha Averett, Hans C. Hanson, and Peter O. Hanson.

—Summary of information compiled by the Temple Index Bureau, *Nauvoo Temple Endowment Register: 10 December 1845 to 8 February 1846.*

Sunday, December 14, 1845

4. O.[clock] A.M. rec[eive]d. news that Lucian Adams, son of Judge A[dams]. had wrought quite a revelation in the minds of the people of Springfield [Illinois] relative to bro[ther]. [Theodore] Turley. I [Brigham Young] spent the day in superintending the work[.] about 11. O.[clock] the bret[hren]— met for sevell [several hours?] & I presented the rules of order after singing & pray[er]s accepted. We then partook of the sacrament spent the rest of the day with the brethren in giving them instruction and offering prayer's to the most high: at 2. o.[clock] met in my room with H[eber]. C. Kimball & others[.] deputed W[illiam]. W. Phelps & P[arley]. P. Pratt to address the people which they did and Bro[ther] [John] Taylor dismissed with a blessing[.] we then read some letters and [a

news article on the] J[acob]. B. Backenstos trial [and] went into the lower room [and] gave some instruction relative to the pulpits.

—Brigham Young, Diary.

The following brethren and sisters assembled in the Attic story of the Temple according to appointment, viz.

Pres[ident]. Brigham Young & Mary Ann Young.
Heber C. Kimball & Vilate Kimball.
Parley P. Pratt & Mary Ann Pratt
Orson Hyde
Orson Pratt & Nancy M. Pratt
George A. Smith & Bathsheba W. Smith
Amasa Lyman & Loisa M. Lyman.
John Taylor & Leonora ~~A~~ Taylor.
John Smith & Clarissa Smith.
Newel K. Whitney & Elizabeth A[nn]. Whitney.
George Miller & Mary C. Miller.
Alpheus Cutler
Isaac Morley & Lucy Morley.
W[illia]m W. Phelps & Sally Phelps.
John M. Bernhisel.
William Clayton.
Joseph C. Kingsbury.
Franklin D. Richards.
Samuel Bent & Lettice Bent.
Agness M. Smith & Mary Smith.
Mercy R. Thompson & Tirzah Cahoon.
Lucian Woodworth & Phebe Woodworth.
Orson Spencer & Catherine C. Spencer.
Cornelius P. Lott & Joseph Fielding. Joseph Young.

Soon after 11 o'clock those who were present were ordered by the president to cloth themselves, which being done and seated at 20 minutes after 11 o clock sang, "Adam Ondi Ahman" &c. After which we bowed before the Lord and president Young offered up prayers. We next sung "Glorious things of thee are spoken" &c. When bread and wine [were produced,] having been provided by Bishop N[ewel]. K. Whitney[,] Elders Isaac Morley and Charles C. Rich were called upon to administer the sacrament. They broke the bread which was then blessed by Isaac Morley and passed round by Charles C. Rich, who also blessed the wine and passed it round likewise.

We then sang, "O happy souls who pray &c" and "Come all ye sons of Zion." After which President Young introduced the subject of having rules of order to govern all who come here and to regulate our works, printed. He wished to know the minds of the quorum whether they thought it best. It was voted unanimously that we think it wisdom to have some rules printed for that purpose.

It was also unanimously voted that President Young introduce the rules.

He then explained that he had some rules draughted last evening, but they were now at the office to be printed ready for tomorrow, he however explained the majority of them explaining also the order he wished carried out, and then took a vote whether this quorum will sustain him in this regulation.

The vote was unanimous in the affirmative.

He then observed that he should henceforth have all the cloth, which was intended for robes, garments and aprons, brought and either cut or made in this Temple under the superintendance of those who know how to do it right. There are now scarcly two Aprons alike nor two garments cut or marked right, and it is necessary to observe perfect order in this thing and it never can be done unless we take this course.[23]

A conversation then ensued on the distinction of office or power, between a president of Seventies, and a member of the High Council or a High Priest. It arose in consequence of some of the High Council having been washed and anointed by some of the presidents of Seventies & inasmuch as their had been some considerable difference in the views of the brethren in regard to the difference of authority between the High Council and Seventies, President Young concluded it would be wisdom to have the subject understood at this early stage of business so as to prevent any feelings or dispute arising on the subject hereafter.

He stated that the Seventies are ordained Apostles, and when they go forth into the ministry, they are sent with power to build up the Kingdom in all the world, and consequently they have power to ordain High Priests, and also to ordain and organize a High Council.

---

23. Those who received their washing and anointing were given an undergarment to be worn on a permanent basis. Robes and aprons were worn only during the endowment ceremony and were removed prior to leaving the temple. The

Some of the High Priests have been ready to quarrel on the subject, supposing they had power and authority above the seventies, and some in their zeal for power, have abused and trampled on the feelings of some of the Seventies.

There is too much covetousness in the Church and too much disposition amongst the brethren to seek after power and has been from the beginning, but this feeling is diminishing and the brethren begin to know better. In consequence of such feelings Joseph [Smith] left the people in the dark on many subjects of importance and they still remain in the dark. We have got to rid such principles from our hearts.

He then referred to the manner in which the corner stones of this Temple were laid as published in the Times and Seasons[24] and then stated that the perfect order would have been for the presidency of the Stake to lay the first or South East corner. The High Council the 2nd or South West corner. The Bishops the North West corner and the priests the North East corner, but added the High Priests laid the South West corner, but they had no right to do it.

He then introduced the subject of the brethren making objections to any person being permitted to receive the ordinances, and added that when objections were made he should feel bound to determine whether the person making the objections was a responsible person, if he was not he should do as he pleased about listening to the objections, but if he was a responsible person he should then listen to the objections.

To make a man a responsible man he must have the power and ability not only to save himself but to save others, but there are those who are not capable of saving themselves and will have to be saved if they are saved at all by those who are capable of doing it. An objection from such would have no weight on his mind.

When a man objects to another receiving the ordinances he becomes responsible to answer to God for that mans salvation. And who knows but if he received the ordinances he would be saved, but if we refuse to give him the means he cannot be saved and we are responsible for it.

There is no law to prevent any man from obtaining all the blessings of

---

aprons represented the leaves worn by Adam and Eve in the Garden of Eden.

24. The *Times and Seasons* was published in Nauvoo, Illinois, from 1839 to 1846 as the church's journalistic voice. It was initially a monthly publication, but came to be issued semi-monthly after the first year. Throughout its six-year run, it was edited by Gustavus Hills, Ebenezer Robinson, Don Carlos Smith, Joseph Smith, Robert B. Thompson, and John Taylor.

the priesthood if he will walk according to the commandments ^pay his tithes^ and seeks after salvation, but he may deprive himself of them.

After much important instruction from the president the signs of the Holy Priesthood were offered up and prayers, Elder Orson Hyde being mouth after which the company were dismissed till next Sunday with strict orders to be here and dressed precisely at 11 o'clock.

At 2 o'clock P.M. agreeable to appointment nearly all those new members who have received the ordinances the past week assembled in the upper department to receive instructions in regard to the ordinances and their duty to be observed henceforth and forever.

At the same hour Pres[iden]t. Young, H[eber]. C. Kimball, P[arley]. Pratt, O[rson]. Pratt, O[rson]. Hyde, J[ohn]. Taylor, G[eorge]. A. Smith, A[masa]. Lyman, N[ewel]. K. Whitney, G[eorge]. Miller, W[illiam]. W. Phelps, W[illia]m. Clayton and P[hineas]. H. Young retired into president Youngs Room. The President appointed W[illiam]. W. Phelps and P[arley]. P. Pratt to instruct the brethren and sisters now waiting, which was done and much good instruction given by them. They were especially instructed more fully into the nature and importance of the blessings and powers of the Holy Priesthood which they have received, and it was enjoined upon them not to talk out of doors, but to be wise and prudent in all things.

They were also informed that no one will be admitted into these rooms during the time we are to work except those who are called to assist, unless they are invited by those who have authority.

At a quarter to 5 they were dismissed by blessing from E[lde]r Taylor.

At the same time this was going on those who were in president Youngs room were listening to a number of letters which were read together with the report of the trial of J[acob]. B. Backenstos as published in the Peoria Register.

About 5 o clock nearly all the company having left the house president Young and others of the Twelve [apostles] went down to the lower story of the Temple to council together on the arrangements of the Pulpits. The following persons remained and slept in the Temple over night, viz. Pres[iden]t. Young, A[lbert]. P. Rockwood, J[ohn]. D. Lee & David Candland.

—William Clayton, Diary, kept for Heber C. Kimball.

....

At the Temple all day. Quite a number of the quorum assembled in the Temple and clothed at 11 o clock. After singing and prayer the sacrament was administered by Isaac Morley and Charles C. Rich. President [Brigham] Young instructed the quorum concerning a number of items and proved that the office of seventies are higher than the office of High Priests or high Council. At half after one we offered up the signs and prayers Elder Orson Hyde being mouth. ...

At 2 o clock P.M. was called into the Presidents room with the President, H[eber]. C. Kimball, Parley P. Pratt, Orson Pratt, Orson Hyde, John Taylor, George A. Smith, Amasa Lyman, Newel K. Whitney, George Miller, W[illia]m W. Phelps and Phineas H. Young where I read a number of letters from different individuals to Prest. Young on various subjects ...

At 2 o clock also, those new members who have been received into the quorum last week met in the Celestial room where they were instructed more fully into the Order of the Priesthood and their duty by W[illiam]. W. Phelps & Parley P. Pratt.

—William Clayton, Diary.

....

[F]or the first time I [Franklin D. Richards] partook of the sacrament of the Lords supper in the righteousness of the Saints ^in the Lords House^ and again attended meeting in the afternoon at 2 oclock with those who were not prepared with white [clothing.] a rich time to my soul[.]

[B]y invitation of Pres[iden]t [Brigham] Young I spent the week in the Temple every day and several nights in helping to bestow that which I also have received upon others[.] Jane [Richards] also spent 4 or 5 days with me there in assisting to sew &c— a precious week to us both[.]

—Franklin D. Richards, Diary.

....

The Twelve [apostles] and others with our wives met in the attic story of the Temple.

After prayer and singing, Elders Isaac Morley and Charles C. Rich administered, and we partook of the sacrament.

I [Brigham Young] introduced the subject of establishing rules for the preservation of order in the House of the Lord which were agreed to and ordered to be printed.

A conversation ensued on the distinction of office or power between a president of the Seventies and a member of the High Council or a High Priest. It arose in consequence of some of the High Council having been washed and annointed by some of the presidents of Seventies and inasmuch as the views of the brethren differed, Pres[ident] Young considered it would be wisdom to have the subject understood at this early stage of business, so as to prevent feelings arising later.

Pres[ident]. Brigham Young stated that the Seventies were ordained Apostles, and when they went forth into the ministry they were sent with power to build up the kingdom in all the world, and consequently, they had power to ordain High Priests and also to ordain and organize a High Council. Pres[ident]. Young said: "Some of the High Preists have been ready to quarrel on the subject, supposing they had power and authority above the Seventies and some in their zeal for power have abused and trampled on the feelings of some of the Seventies. There is too much covetousness in the church, and too much disposition amongst the brethren to seek after power and has been from the beginning, but this feeling is diminishing and the brethren begin to know better. In consequence of such feelings Joseph [Smith] left the people in the dark on many subjects of importance and they still remain in the dark. We have got to rid such principles from our hearts.["][25]

I [Brigham Young] referred to the manner in which the corner stones of this Temple were laid as published in the *Times and Seasons,* and said that the perfect order would have been for the presidency of the stake to lay the first or southeast corner; the high council the second or southwest corner; the bishops the northeast corner; but the high priests laid the southwest corner, though they had no right to do it.

I spoke of the brethren making objections to persons being permitted to receive the ordinances, and added, that when objections were made I should feel bound to determine whether the person making the objections was a responsible person, and if he is not, I should do as I pleased about listening to the objections; but if he was a responsible person I should listen to them.

To constitute a man responsible he must have the power and ability not only to save himself but to save others; but there are those who are not capable of saving themselves and will have to be saved by others.

When a man objects to another receiving the ordinances he becomes responsible to answer to God for that man's salvation; and who can tell but if he received the ordinances he would be saved, but if we refuse to give

25. The above two paragraphs are taken from the Journal History (LDS Archives) account of this day's events.

him the means he cannot be saved and we are responsible for it.

There is no law to prevent any man from obtaining all the blessings of the priesthood if he will walk according to the commandments, pay his tithes and seek after salvation, but he may [also] deprive himself of them.

After much profitable instruction we united in prayer, Orson Hyde being mouth.

Meeting adjourned for one week.

Two p.m., many of those who had received their ordinances the past week met and received instructions from Elders Parley P. Pratt and William W. Phelps.

The Twelve met and read some letters, also an account of Sheriff [Jacob B.] Backenstos' travel from the *Peoria Register.*

We went down to the lower room and counseled on the arrangement of the pulpits.

I remained in the Temple all night.

—"Manuscript History of Brigham Young," in *History of the Church,* 7:545-46; and Journal History of the Church, LDS Archives.

Monday, December 15, 1845

At 5 minutes to 9 o clock A.M. [we] commenced washing and anointing the following, viz.

Thomas Grover	born	July 22nd 1807
David Fullmer	"	July 7, 1803
Simeon Carter	"	June 7 1794
Phineas Richards	"	November 15, 1788
Lewis D. Wilson	"	June 2 1805
Stephen Chase	"	April 11 1799
Ezra T. Benson	"	February 22 1811
Freeman Nickerson	"	February 5 1779
Asahel Smith	"	May 21 1773

These were washed by Aaron Johnson and Lucius N. Scovil. And anointed by Amasa Lyman and George A. Smith. They finished at 25 minutes after 9 o clock.

At half after 9 o clock [we] commenced washing and anointing the following in the female department, viz.

Caroline E. Grover	born	June 25 1808
Rhoda Ann Fullmer	"	February 12 1813

Lydia Carter	"	December 11 1801
Wealthy V. Richards	"	September 6 1786
Nancy Wilson	"	July 1811
Orry Anna Chase	"	June 1 1784
Cornelia A. Benson	"	October 21 1809
Huldah Nickerson	"	August 19 1780
Elizabeth Smith	"	December 1 1785
Huldah Butler	"	August 16 1786

These were washed by Mary Ann Pratt and Nancy H. Rockwood and anointed by Vilate Kimball, Sarah D. Rich, and Diantha Billings. They finished at half after 10 o clock[.]

At a quarter to 10 o clock the president [Brigham Young] called the brethren together who had Volunteered to assist in administering the ordinances this day and made the following appointments Amasa Lyman—Orson Hyde, George A. Smith—Lucius N. Scovil Erastus Snow and Franklin D. Richards to administer in the upper and middle department W[illiam]. W. Phelps to officiate as the tempter. Also Joseph Young and Jedidiah M. Grant to anoint the seventies. Samuel Bent and Isaac Morley to anoint the members of the High Council & High Priests. Benjamin L. Clapp and Henry Herriman to wash the members of seventies. And Charles C. Rich and Phineas H. Young to wash the members of the ^members of the^ High Council & High Priests John D. Lee and David Candland as clerks to attend to fires in the rooms and upper apartment &c. Aaron Johnson, Benjamin L. Clapp, Elijah Averett and Henry Herriman to attend to fires in the washing rooms, also heating and carrying in water and assisting when needed in the washings.

At a quarter to 11 o clock the bell was rung and [we] commenced receiving those washed and anointed this morning through the lower and middle departments. the following persons officiating, viz.

In the upper department
John Taylor as Number 1
Amasa Lyman as number 2
Erastus Snow as number 3
In the middle department
Orson Hyde as number 1
Franklin D. Richards as number 2
Lucius N Scovil as Number 3
W[illiam]. W. Phelps as number 4
and George A. Smith as prompter.

At half after 12 the foregoing were received into the upper department in the following order, viz.

Stephen Chase by H[eber]. C. Kimball.
Amy Ana Chase by S[tephen]. Chase & H[eber]. C. Kimball.
Asahel Smith by H[eber]. C. Kimball.
Elizabeth Smith by A[sahel]. Smith & H[eber]. C. Kimball.
Freeman Nickerson by Amasa Lyman[.]
Huldah Nickerson by F[reeman]. Nickerson & Erastus Snow[.]
Ezra T. Benson by Erastus Snow.
Lydia Carter by S[tephen]. Carter & E[rastus]. Snow.
Caroline E. Grover by T[homas]. Grover & E[rastus]. Snow.
Lewis D. Wilson by Erastus Snow.
Nancy Wilson by L[ewis]. D. Wilson & A[masa]. Lyman[.]
Phineas Richards by Amasa Lyman[.]
Wealthy V. Richards by P[hineas]. Richards & A[masa]. Lyman.
David Fullmer by Amasa Lyman[.]
Rhoda Ann Fullmer by D[avid]. Fullmer & A[masa]. Lyman[.]

Finished receiving these into the upper department at 15 minutes to 3 oclock P.M. Phineas H. Young and Erastus Snow acting as prompters.

At 20 minutes to 12 o clock [we] commenced washing and anointing the following High Priests viz,

Jesse D. Hunter	born	July 5 1806
Ruben Miller	"	September 4 1811
Daniel Carn	"	December 13 1802

These were washed by Charles C. Rich and Phineas Young and anointed by Isaac Morley & Charles C. Rich.

[A]t 10 minutes to 12 o clock [we] commenced washing and anointing the following members of the Seventies, viz.

Jacob Gates	born	March 9 1811
Hosea Stout	"	September 18 1810
Harrison Burgess	"	September 3 1814
Lyman O. Littlefield	"	Novemb[e]r 21 1819
William Redfield	"	October 14 1810

These were washed by Henry Herriman and Benjamin L. Clapp and anointed by Joseph Young and J[edediah]. M. Grant. Finished in the washing and anointing of these at 12 o clock M. At 12 o'clock we commenced washing and anointing the following in the female department, in the following order, viz.

Mary M. Gates born July 30, 1813 washed by Mary A. Pratt & anointed by Jane Young[.]

Louisa Stout born October 19 1819 washed by Diantha Billings & anointed by Jane Young[.]

Kissiah Hunter born 1810 washed by Mary A. Pratt & anointed by Leonora A. Taylor.

Sophia M. Burgess born April 12, 1810 washed by Mary Ann Pratt & anointed by Jane Young[.]

Mary Ann Redfield born March 8 1814 washed by M[ary]. A[nn]. Pratt & anointed by Leonora A. Taylor[.]

Rhoda Ann Miller born November 25 1814 washed by Diantha Billings & anointed by L[eonora]. A. Taylor.

Margaret Carn born September 27 1806 washed by D[iantha]. Billings & anointed by L[eonora]. A. Taylor.

Finished washing and anointing these at 20 minutes to 1 P.M.

At 1 o clock P.M. the bell was rung and [we] commenced receiving those washed at 12 o clock into the lower and middle department. the following persons officiating, viz

In the upper department

Orson Hyde as number 1
Lucius N. Scovil as number 2
Franklin D. Richards number 3

In the middle department

John Taylor as number 1
Amasa Lyman as number 2
George A. Smith as number 3
W[illiam]. W. Phelps as No. 4
and P[arley]. P. Pratt as prompter.

At 20 minutes after 3 o'clock P.M. [we] commenced receiving the following into the upper department in the following order.

Reuben Miller by Heber C. Kimball[.]

Rhoda Ann Miller by R[euben]. Miller & H[eber]. C. Kimball[.]

William Redfield by Heber C. Kimball[.]

Mary Ann Redfield by W[illiam]. Redfield & H[eber] C. Kimball[.]

Daniel Carn by Heber C. Kimball[.]

Margaret Carn by D[aniel]. Carn & H[eber]. C. Kimball[.]

Jacob Gates by Lucius N. Scovil[.]

Mary M. Gates by J[acob]. Gates & L[ucius]. N. Scovil[.]
Hosea Stout by Lucius N. Scovil[.]
Louisa Stout by H[osea]. Stout & L[ucius]. N. Scovil[.]
Harrison Burgess by L[ucius]. N. Scovil[.]
Sophia M. Burgess by H[arrison]. Burgess & L[ucius]. N. Scovil[.]
Jesse D. Hunter by L[ucius]. N. Scovil[.]
Kissiah Hunter by J[esse]. D. Hunter & L[ucius]. N. Scovil[.]
Lyman O. Littlefield by L[ucius]. N. Scovil.

Finished receiving these at 5 o clock P.M. Phineas H. Young and Erastus Snow acting as prompters.

At half after 2 o clock [we] commenced washing and anointing in the male department the following High Priests viz

Elias Smith	born	September 6, 1804
Edward Hunter	"	June 22 1793
Peter Fullmer	"	February 22 1772
John Herrington	"	February 26 1764
Jesse Baker	"	January 2 1778
Samuel Williams	"	March 22 1798
John S. Fullmer	"	July 21 1807
John Murdock	"	July 15 1792

These were washed by Charles C. Rich and Phineas Young and anointed by Isaac Morley and Samuel Bent.

Of the quorum of Seventies.

Thadeus Cutler born June 18 1809 washed anointed by Henry Herriman and Benjamin L. Clapp, finished 3 o clock

At 3 o clock [we] commenced washing and anointing the following in the female department in the following order viz

Lucy Smith born January 4 1821 washed by Mary A[nn]. Pratt & anointed by D[iantha]. Billings[.]
Ann Hunter born February 16 1803 washed by Mercy R. Thompson & anointed by L[eonora]. A. Taylor[.]
Susannah Fullmer born [blank] washed by Mary A. Pratt & anointed by L[eonora]. A. Taylor[.]
Mary Ann Fullmer born September 15 1818 washed by M[ercy]. R. Thompson & anointed by D[iantha]. Billings[.]
Sarah Baker born May 22 1782 washed by Nancy H. Rockwood & anointed by L[eonora]. A. Taylor[.]

Lemirah Cutler born September 21 1811 washed by N[ancy]. H. Rockwood & anointed by L[eonora]. A. Taylor[.]

Ruth Williams born October 26 1786 washed by M[ercy]. R. Thompson & anointed by B[athsheba]. W. Smith[.]

Martha Herrington born November 17 1779 washed by N[ancy]. H. Rockwood & anointed by D[iantha]. Billings[.]

At 5 minutes after 4 oclock P. M. the bell was rung and [we] commenced receiving those washed at half after two oclock, into the lower and middle department, the following persons officiating, viz.

For the upper department

John Taylor as No 1
Amasa Lyman as No 2
George A. Smith as No 3

In the middle department

Erastus Snow No 1
Franklin D. Richards No 2
John D. Lee as No 3
W[illiam]. W. Phelps as No 4
Orson Spencer as prompter

At 6 o clock P.M. [we] commenced receiving the following into the upper department in the following order, viz (being those washed and anointed at half after 2.)

Jesse Baker by Lucius N. Scovil[.]
Sarah Baker by J[esse]. Baker & L[ucius]. N. Scovil.
Peter Fullmer by L[ucius]. N. Scovil.
Susannah Fullmer by P[eter]. Fullmer & L[ucius]. N. Scovil
John Herrington by Lucius N. Scovil[.]
Martha Herrington by J[ohn]. Herrington & L[ucius]. N. Scovil.
Edward Hunter by L[ucius]. N. Scovil.
Ann Hunter by E[dward]. Hunter & L[ucius]. N. Scovil.
Samuel Williams by Lucius N. Scovil[.]
Ruth Williams by S[amuel]. Williams and L[ucius]. N. Scovil[.]
John S. Fullmer by Lucius N. Scovil.
Mary Ann Fullmer by J[ohn]. S. Fullmer & L[ucius]. N. Scovil[.]
Elias Smith by Lucius N. Scovil.
Lucy Smith by E[lias]. Smith & L[ucius]. N. Scovil.
Thadeus Cutler by Lucius N. Scovil[.]
Lemirah Cutler by T[hadeus]. Cutler & L[ucius]. N. Scovil.

At [blank] minutes after [blank] o clock finished receiving the above into the upper department. Erastus Snow and Franklin D. Richards officiated as prompters.

At 5 o clock P.M. [we] commenced washing and anointing in the male department the following High Priests viz.

George P. Dykes	born	December 24 1814
Joseph B. Nobles	"	January 14 1810
Isaac Chase	"	February 4 1796
Winslow Farr	"	January 12 1794

These were washed by Charles C. Rich & P[hineas]. H. Young & anointed by Isaac Morley & Sam[ue]l. Bent.

Of the quorum of Seventies

John L. Butler	born	April 8th 1808
Robert T. Burton	"	October 25 1821

Washed by Benjamin L. Clapp and Henry Herriman and anointed by Joseph Young and Jedidiah M. Grant.

Finished at 25 minutes after 5.

^[A]t half after^ At half after 5 o clock P.M. [we] commenced washing and anointing the following in the female department, viz.

Dorcas Dykes born November 30 1811 washed by D[iantha]. Billings & anointed by L[eonora]. A. Taylor.

Mary A. Nobles born October 19 1810 washed by Mercy R. Thompson and anointed by L[eonora]. A. Taylor[.]

Tirzah Chase born July 29 1796 washed by N[ancy]. H. Rockwood & anointed by D[iantha]. Billings[.]

Olive F. Farr born June 23 1800 washed by Diantha Billings and anointed by L[eonora]. A. Taylor.

Abigail E. Chase born October 4 1820 washed by M[ercy]. R. Thompson & anointed by L[eonora]. A. Taylor[.]

Charlotte Chase born May 11 1825 washed by Mary A[nn]. Pratt & anointed by D[iantha]. Billings[.]

Diana Chase born July 25 1827 washed by Nancy H. Rockwood & anointed by D[iantha]. Billings[.]

Finished washing and anointing these at half after 6 o clock P.M.

At 23 minutes to 7 o clock P.M. the bell was rung and [we] commenced receiving the above, into the lower and middle department, the following persons officiating, viz.

In the upper department

George A. Smith as No 1

Amasa Lyman as No 2

Erastus Snow as No 3
In the middle department
Orson Hyde as No 1
Charles C. Rich as No 2
Henry G. Sherwood as No 3
W[illia]m. W. Phelps as No 4
Orson Pratt as prompter.

At 22 minutes after 7 o clock P.M. [we] commenced receiving the following into the upper department being those who were washed and anointed at 5 o clock in the following order. viz,

Ezra Chase by Heber C. Kimball[.]
Tirzah Chase by E[zra]. Chase & H[eber]. C. Kimball
Charlotte Chase by Heber C. Kimball.
Diana Chase by President B[righam]. Young.
Abigail Eliza Chase by W[illia]m L. Cutler.
Winslow Farr by Pres[ident]. B[righam]. Young[.]
Olive F. Farr by W[inslow] Farr & B[righam]. Young[.]
John T. Butler by L[ucius]. N. Scovil[.]
George P. Dykes by L[ucius]. N. Scovil.
Dorcas Dykes by G[eorge]. P. Dykes & L[ucius]. N. Scovil[.]
Joseph B. Nobles by Lucius N. Scovil[.]
Robert T. Burton by Lucius N. Scovil[.]
Mary A. Nobles by J[oseph]. B[ates]. Nobles & L[ucius]. N. Scovil.

Finished receiving the above through at a quarter to 10 o clock. Phineas Richards and Erastus Snow acting as prompters.

About half after 8 o clock the president made a selection of men to assist in the ordinances tomorrow and also a list of brethren to be here on Wednesday to receive their endowment.

At 20 minutes to 10 President B[righam]. Young, Heber C. Kimball, Orson Hyde, Orson Pratt, John Taylor, Amasa Lyman, George Miller, George A. Smith, John D. Lee and Franklin D. Richards retired to President Young's room being clothed and[,] having offered up the signs of the Holy Priesthood[,] offered up prayers[,] Pres[iden]t. Young being mouth. At 5 minutes after 10 o clock they dismissed[,] part retiring to their homes and the following tarried and slept in the rooms viz. W[illia]m W. Phelps, W[illia]m L. Cutler, Elisha Averett, Hans C. Hans[on], Peter O. Hanson, Franklin D. Richards, Joseph Young, Jane Young, Agnes M. Smith and David Candland.

As on the days previous the most perfect harmony and good feeling prevailed. President Young superintended and directed all the movements of the day also selected those who should come on Wednesday assisted by E[lde]r Kimball.

The names of those selected to work tomorrow are as follows. P[arley]. P. Pratt, O[rson]. Pratt, J[ohn]. Taylor, O[rson]. Hyde, A[masa]. Lyman, G[eorge]. A. Smith, O[rson]. Spencer, L[ucius]. N. Scovil, F[ranklin]. D. Richards and Aaron Johnson for the upper department[,] W[illiam]. W. Phelps as Tempter.

P[hineas]. H. Young & C[harles]. C. Rich to wash the High Priests, S[amuel]. Bent & J[ohn]. Murdock to anoint the High Priests, B[enjamin]. L. Clapp & H[enry]. Herriman to wash the seventies J[oseph]. Young and J[edediah]. M. Grant to anoint the Seventies Elijah Averett, Jesse D. Hunter & H[osea]. Stout to carry in water & keep fires in wash rooms Elisha Averett door Keeper & D[avid]. Candland & J[ohn]. D. Lee clerks &c.

—William Clayton, Diary, kept for Heber C. Kimball.

....

Temple of the Lord in Nauvoo the City of Jos[eph].

[See page 44 for excerpted portion.]

Monday night 10 clock the services closed for the day[,] making that [final for all who] received their washings and anointings to day & I [John D. Lee] for one [have] not been out of the House of the Lord more than once in a day. Jos[eph] Young Pres[iden]t & his lady spent the night in the Temple.

—Seventies Record, Book B.

....

I [Harrison Burgess] was notified to appear at the Temple at 8 o clock Am with my wife to receive our Endowments, We were there at the hour, appointed and about 9 o clock we received our washing and anointings preparatory to the fulness of the priesthood with the signs and tokens belonging to the same. Mon[day] the 22 [of December] I was called upon by Pres[ident] Joseph Young to go [to] the Temple and assist in the work of Endowment with a request: that I would help him clear through untill the work was done; which I did. Thurs[day] 25 of Dec[ember] I was requested to go home and get my wife to assist in the Female department[.] she also continued to labor there till the work was done[.] Jan[uary] 22 [1846] at 7 o clock PM myself and wife received the ordinance of sealing

[Washings and anointings for Monday, December 15]

Date 45	Members	by whom washed	by whom Anointed		day Mo year
AM					
December 15	Pres Hosea Stout	Henry Herriman & Benj L. Clapp	Jos Young J. M. Grant	35	Sept 18th 1845
"	Harrison Burgess	" " "	" " "	31	[illegible] 3c̈
"	Pres Jacob Gates	" " "	" " "	34	Mar 9 "
"	Lyman O. Littlefield	" " "	" " "	26	Nov 21 "
"	William Redfield	" " "	" " "	35	Oct 1st "
	Louisa Stout	Sister D Billings	Sister Jane A Young	36	" "
	Sophiah M Burgess	" Mary A. Pratt	" " "	35	Apr 12 "
	Mary M. Gates	" Mary A. Pratt	Jane A. Young	32	Jul 30 "
	Maryann Redfield	" " " "	Leonora Taylor	31	Mar 6th "
	Lemirah Cutler	" Nancy Rockwood	" " "	34	Sept 11
Thurs.					
Dec 15th 5 P.M.	Aggathann Lee	" E. A. Whitney	" Nancy Rockwood & Taylor	31	Jan 18th "
	Maryann Candland	" " "	" " "		
Dec 15th 45	John L. Butler	16 Henry Harriman B L C	Jos Young J M Grant		
	Robt. T. Burton	17 H. Herriman & B. L. Clapp			April 8th 1845

—Seventies Record, Book B, oversized portion,
December 15, 1845.

by Pres[ident] Brigham Young. The morning at 10 oclock we received the ordinance of second anointing by Pres[ident] H[eber]. C. Kimbal.

—Harrison Burgess, "Autobiography," LDS Archives.

Went to the Temple in the morning with my wife Wealthy D. Richards, and received my washing and Anointing and passed on from the creation to the garden, telestial, terestrial, and Celestial [rooms] within the vail.

—Phineas Richards, Diary, LDS Archives.

This morning at 8 o'clock I [Hosea Stout] went with my wife [Louisa Stout] to the Temple to recieve our endowment and was there until near noon before we commenced recieving it & was engaged until evening in recieving it.

—Hosea Stout, Diary, in *On the Mormon Frontier: The Diary of Hosea Stout, 1844-1861,* edited by Juanita Brooks (Salt Lake City: University of Utah Press/Utah State Historical Society, 1964).

The ordinances of endowment were administered to sixty-four brethren and sisters. The Twelve [apostles] and others officiated.

—"Manuscript History of Brigham Young," in *History of the Church,* 7:547.

Nauvoo temple endowments performed on this date for:

First Company: Stephen Chase, Orryanna Chase, Asahel Smith, Elizabeth Smith, Freeman Nickerson, Huldah Nickerson, Ezra T. Benson, Cornelia A. Benson, Simeon Carter, Lydia Carter, Huldah Butler, Thomas Grover, Caroline E. Grover, Lewis D. Wilson, Nancy Wilson, Phineas Richards, Wealthy V. Richards, David Fullmer, and Rhoda Ann Fullmer.

Second Company: Reuben Miller, Rhoda Ann Miller, William Redfield, Mary Ann Redfield, Daniel Carn, Margaret Carn, Jacob Gates, Mary M. Gates, Hosea Stout, Louisa Stout, Harrison Burgess, Sophia M. Burgess, Jesse D. Hunter, Kissiah Butler, and Lyman O. Littlefield.

Third Company: Jesse Baker, Sarah Baker, Peter Fullmer, Susannah Fullmer, John Herrington, Martha Herrington, Edward Hunter, Ann Hunter, Samuel Williams, Ruth Williams, John S. Fullmer, Mary Ann Fullmer, Elias Smith, Lucy Smith, Thadeus Cutler, and Lemirah Cutler.

Fourth Company: Ezra Chase, Tirzah Chase, Charlotte Chase, Diana Chase, Abigail Eliza Chase, Winslow Farr, Olive F. Farr, John L. Butler, George P. Dykes, Dorcas Dykes, Joseph B. Noble, Robert T. Burton, and Mary A. Noble.

—Summary of information compiled by the Temple Index Bureau, *Nauvoo Temple Endowment Register: 10 December 1845 to 8 February 1846.* Editors' note: According to the register, John Murdock was washed and anointed on this date and was therefore also probably endowed.

Tuesday, December 16, 1845

8 o clock being the hour appointed for meeting[,] president [Brigham] Young, H[eber]. C. Kimball, George A. Smith and some others were here at the time appointed the morning being very fine but cold.

At a quarter after 8 o clock A.M. [we] commenced washing the following High Priests in the male department, viz.

Elam Ludington	born	November 23 1806
Morris Phelps	"	December 20 1805
Isaac Higbee	"	December 23 1797

These were washed by Charles C. Rich and Phineas H. Young and anointed by Samuel Bent and John Murdock. Also at the same time [we] commenced washing and anointing members of the quorum of Seventies, viz.

Howard Egan	born	June 15 1815
John Brown	"	October 23 1820
James Harmon	"	September 29 1801
Jesse P. Harmon	"	August 11 1795
Appleton M. Harmon	born	May 29 1820

These were washed by Benjamin L. Clapp and Henry Herriman & anointed by Joseph Young and Jedidiah M. Grant and finished at 10 minutes to 9 o clock.

At 25 minutes after 8 o clock A.M. [we] commenced washing and anointing in the female department as follows viz,

Mary E. Ludington born July 24 1824 washed by Sally Crosby and anointed by Lois Cutler.

Sarah Phelps born March 20th 1820 washed & anointed by Lois Cutler[.]

Charlotte Higbee born May 20th 1814 washed by Jane J. Sherwood & anointed by Lois Cutler.

Tamson Egan born July 27th 1824 washed by Lois Cutler & anointed by the same[.]

Elizabeth Brown born December [blank] 1822 washed by J[ane]. J. Sherwood & anointed by Mary C. Miller[.]

Jane Blevan born August 27 1804 washed by Jane J. Sherwood & anointed by Lois Cutler.

Anna Harmon born March 4 1798 washed by Sally Crosby & anointed by Bathsheba W. Smith.

Sophronia M. Harmon born April 5 1824 washed by Sally Crosby & anointed by B[athsheba]. W. Smith[.]

Finished washing and anointing these at 10 minutes after 10 o clock.

At 9 o clock President Brigham Young, Heber C. Kimball, Orson Pratt, George A. Smith, [and] Amasa Lyman, retired to President Youngs Room, and without dressing consecrated & dedicated a new horn which has been prepared for the anointing, praying that we may be permitted to use it for this purpose and for many years to come and that the spirit and power of God may attend it whenever it shall be used.[26]

At 20 minutes after 10 oclock A.M. President [Brigham] Young, Heber C. Kimball, Orson Hyde, Orson Pratt, ^George Miller^ Amasa Lyman and George A. Smith clothed themselves and retired to President Youngs room and consecrated 13 bottles of Oil which had been prepared and perfumed by Bishops [Newel] Whitney and [George] Miller. After consecrating the Oil a letter which had been written by E[lde]r Hyde was dedicated to God with prayer that the desired object may be accomplished by it. At half after 10 they got through and undressed.

At 25 minutes to 11 o clock the bell was rung and [we] commenced receiving those washed and anointed this morning into the lower and middle departments, the following persons officiating, viz.

In the upper department.

George A. Smith as No 1

Amasa Lyman as No 2

Orson Pratt as No 3

In the middle department.

Orson Hyde as No 1

Orson Spencer as No 2

Lucius N. Scovil as No 3

26. The horn contained enough oil to pour onto the head and other parts of the body of the initiate during the anointing ceremony.

W[illia]m. W. Phelps as No 4
Aaron Johnson officiated as prompter.

At 7 minutes after 12 o clock [we] commenced receiving those washed and anointed this morning into the upper department in the following order, viz.

Morris Phelps by Heber C. Kimball.
Sarah Phelps by M[orris]. Phelps & H[eber]. C. Kimball [.]
Elam Ludington by Heber C. Kimball[.]
Mary E. Ludington by E[lam]. Ludington & H[eber]. C. Kimball[.]
Jesse P. Harmon by Lucius N. Scovil[.]
Anna Harmon by J[esse]. P. Harmon & L[ucius]. N. Scovil[.]
Howard Egan by Lucius N. Scovil[.]
Tamson Egan by Howard Egan[.]
James Harmon by L[ucius]. N. Scovil[.]
Isaac Higbee by Lucius N. Scovil[.]
Charlotte Higbee by I[saac]. Higbee & L[ucius]. N. Scovil[.]
Appleton M. Harmon by L[ucius]. N. Scovil[.]
Sophronia M. Harmon by A[ppleton]. M Harmon & L[ucius]. N. Scovil[.]
John Brown by Lucius N. Scovil[.]
Elizabeth Brown by John Brown & L[ucius]. N. Scovil[.]
Ellen A. Rockwood by President B[righam]. Young[.]

Finished receiving these through at 3 minutes to 2 o clock. President [Young?] prompted the first 3 and Phineas H. Young the remainder.

At a quarter after 11 o clock A.M. [we] commenced washing and anointing the following members of the quorum of the seventies in the male department, viz

John Scott	born	May 6 1811
Israel Barlow	"	September 13 1806
John Pack	"	May 20 1809
Perrigrine Sessions	"	June 15 1814
William Burton	"	October 3 1809
Chauncey G. Webb	"	October 24 1811
William Mathews	"	January 28 1808.

Washed by Benjamin L. Clapp and ~~anointed by~~ Henry Herriman and anointed by Joseph Young and Jedidiah M. Grant.

Also the following High Priests, viz,

David Sessions	born	April 4 1789

Clark L. Whitney " May 6 1808
Joseph W. Coolidge " May 31 1814
Lorin Farr " July 27 1820

Washed by Charles C. Rich and Phineas H. Young, and anointed by Samuel Bent & John Murdock and finished at 25 minutes to 1 o clock P.M.

At half past 11 o clock [we] commenced again the washings and anointings in the female department as follows, viz.

Phylote Pack born May 20th 1774 washed by Sally Crosby & anointed by V[ilate]. Kimball

Patty Sessions born February 4 1795 washed by Sally Crosby & anointed by V[ilate]. Kimball.

Sylvia P. Lyons born July 31st 1818 washed by S[ally]. Crosby & anointed by V[ilate]. Kimball.

Elizabeth Scott born September 10 1815 washed by J[ane]. J. Sherwood & anointed by V[ilate]. Kimball.

Elizabeth Burton born April 11 1804 washed by J[ane]. J. Sherwood & anointed by V[ilate]. C. Kimball

Lucine Sesions born September 29 1817 washed by J[ane]. J. Sherwood & anointed by M[ary]. C. Miller.

Elizabeth Barlow born December 28 1811 washed by N[ancy]. H. Rockwood & anointed by V[ilate]. Kimball[.]

Eliza J. Webb born May 4 1817 washed by Nancy H. Rockwood & anointed by J[ane]. Young.

Rhoda Ann Whitney born June 10 1822 washed by J[ane]. J. Sherwood & anointed by Jane Young.

Elizabeth Coolidge born July 1 1815 washed by J[ane]. J. Sherwood & anointed by M[ary]. C. Miller.

Elizabeth A. Mathews born August 10 1807 washed by S[ally]. Crosby & anointed by M[ary]. C. Miller[.]

Julia Pack born March 8 1817 washed by Nancy H. Rockwood & anointed by J[ane]. Young[.]

Nancy Farr born January 27 1823 washed by J[ane]. J. Sherwood & anointed by M[ary]. C. Miller.

Finished washing and anointing these at 3 minutes after 1 o clock.

At half after 1 o clock P.M. the Bell rung and [we] commenced receiving those washed and anointed at a quarter to 11 into the lower and middle departments the following persons officiating. viz,

In the Upper department

Orson Pratt as No 1

Franklin D. Richards as No 2
Amasa Lyman as No 3
In the middle department.
Orson Spencer as No 1
George D. Grant as No. 3
Charles C. Rich as No 2
W[illiam]. W Phelps as No 4
Aaron Johnson officiating as prompter.

At 4 minutes to 3 o clock [we] commenced receiving the foregoing into the upper department in the following order, viz.

Perrigrine Sessions by Lucius N. Scovil[.]
Lucine Sessions by P[errigrine]. Sessions & L[ucius]. N. Scovil[.]
William Mathews by Lucius N. Scovil[.]
Elizabeth A. Mathews by W[illiam]. Mathews & L[ucius]. N. Scovil[.]
Chancy G. Webb by Lucius N. Scovil[.]
Eliza J. Webb by C[hauncey]. G. Webb & L[ucius]. N. Scovil[.]
David Sessions by Lucius N. Scovil[.]
Patty Sessions by D[avid]. Sessions & L[ucius]. N. Scovil[.]
Israel Barlow by John Taylor[.]
Elizabeth Barlow by I[srael]. Barlow & J[ohn]. Taylor[.]
John Pack by John Taylor.
Julia Pack by Jo[h]n Pack & J[ohn]. Taylor[.]
Clark L. Whitney by John Taylor[.]
Rhoda Ann Whitney by C[lark]. L. Whitney & H[eber]. C. Kimball[.]
Sylvia P. Lyons by H[eber]. C. Kimball[.]
Lorin Farr by John Taylor[.]
Nancy Farr by L[orin]. Farr & J[ohn]. Taylor.
Phylote Pack by John Taylor[.]
Joseph W Coolidge by John Taylor[.]
Elizabeth Coolidge by J[oseph]. W. Coolidge & L[ucius]. N. Scovil[.]
John Scott by L[ucius]. N. Scovil & H[eber]. C. Kimball[.]
Elizabeth Scott by John Scott and H[eber]. C. Kimball[.]
William Burton by H[eber]. C. Kimball[.]
Elizabeth Burton by W[illiam]. Burton & H[eber]. C. Kimball[.]
Augusta Cobb by President Young & H[eber]. C. K[imball].

Finished receiving the foregoing at 25 minutes after 5[,] Orson Spencer, Phineas H. Young & W[illia]m L. Cutler officiating as prompters.

This morning Father James Taylor was ^again^ baptized by E[lde]r John Taylor at 8 o clock, ~~and~~ confirmed in the Temple by E[lde]r John Taylor about 2 o clock P.M. and ordained a High Priest at a quarter after 2 o clock by George Miller, John Taylor and Samuel Bent.

Also William Whiteing Markham was ordained at half after 2 o'clock P.M. into the Seventies under the hands of Benjamin L. Clapp and Elder John Taylor.

At 15 minutes after 2 o clock [we] commenced washing ^and anointing^ the following members of the quorums of seventies in the male department as follows, viz.

Thomas Moore	born	June 15th 1801
John Kay	"	October 6 1817
Charles W. Hubbard	"	February 7 1810
Joseph G. Hovey	"	November 17 1812
Charles Shumway	"	August 1 1808
Warren Markham	"	July 30 1824
William Whiteing Markham	"	January 3 1829

Washed by Benjamin L. Clapp and Levi W. Hancock and anointed by Joseph Young, Jedidiah M. Grant and Benjamin L. Clapp.

Also the following High Priests, viz.

George W. Pitkin	born	May 17 1801
James Taylor	"	June 21 1783
John D. Parker	"	November 22 1799
Noah Hubbard	"	October 20 1778
Stephen Markham	"	February 9 1800

Finished washing and anointing these at 10 minutes after 3 P.M.

At a quarter to 3 o clock P.M. [we] commenced washing and anointing in the female department in the following order, viz.

Hannah Markham born April 1 1803 washed by Sally Crosby & anointed by M[ary]. C. Miller[.]

Eliza R. Snow born January 21 1804 washed by Rhoda A. Miller & anointed by M[ary]. C. Miller[.]

Catherine A. Markham born August 17 1826 washed by S[ally]. Crosby & anointed by L[eonora]. A. Taylor[.]

Almedia S. Roundy, born March 7 1829 washed by J[ane]. J. Sherwood & anointed by M[ary]. C. Miller[.]

Martha Ann Hovey born December 24 1814 washed by Sally

Crosby & anointed by Mary C. Miller[.]

Julia Ann Shumway born November 28 1807 washed by Rhoda A. Miller & anointed by E[lizabeth]. A[nn]. Whitney[.]

Ellen Kay born February 14 1814 washed by Sally Crosby & anointed by M[ary]. C. Miller[.]

Abigail Pitkin born July 17 1797 washed by Sarah D. Rich & anointed by Vilate Kimball[.]

Laura Pitkin born September 10 1790 washed by S[arah]. D. Rich & anointed by V[ilate]. Kimball[.]

Mary Ann Hubbard born August 12 1816 washed by S[ally]. Crosby & anointed by V[ilate]. Kimball[.]

Amanda Pitkin born February 11 1805 washed by S[arah]. D. Rich & anointed by V[ilate]. Kimball[.]

Mahala D. Moore born February 28 1806 washed by S[ally]. Crosby & anointed by E[lizabeth]. A[nn]. Whitney[.]

Dorcas A. Moore born January 26 1828 washed by Sally Crosby & anointed by M[ary]. C. Miller[.]

Elizabeth M. Moore born September 13 1826 washed by Rhoda A. Miller & anointed by E[lizabeth]. A[nn]. Whitney[.]

Agness Taylor born August 22nd 1787 washed by S[ally]. Crosby & anointed by L[eonora]. A. Taylor[.]

Cynthia Hubbard born October 22 1785 washed by J[ane]. J. Sherwood & anointed by V[ilate]. Kimball.

Sarah E. Hubbard born June 9th 1825 washed by S[ally]. Crosby and anointed by M[ary]. C. Miller[.]

Finished washing and anointing in this department at 3 minutes after 4 o'clock P.M.

At 26 minutes after 4 o clock P.M. [we] commenced receiving those washed and anointed at a quarter to 3 o clock into the lower and middle departments[,] the following persons officiating, viz.

In the upper department

Orson Pratt as No 1

George A. Smith as No 2

Amasa Lyman as No 3

In the ^lower^ department president Young prompted

In the middle department

John Taylor as No 1

Samuel Bent as No 2

Daniel Carn as No 3

W[illia]m W. Phelps as No 4
Orson Spencer officiated as prompter.

At 7 minutes after 6 o clock [we] commenced receiving those who were washed and anointed at a quarter after 2 o clock into the upper department in the following order, viz:

George W. Pitkin by Heber C. Kimball[.]
Amanda Pitkin by G[eorge]. W. Pitkin & H[eber]. C. Kimball[.]
Laura Pitkin by H[eber]. C. Kimball[.]
Abigail Pitkin by H[eber]. C. Kimball[.]
Eliza R. Snow by Pres[iden]t. B[righam]. Young[.]
James Taylor by John Taylor.
Angess Taylor by James Taylor & John Taylor[.]
Noah Hubbard by Orson Spencer[.]
Cynthia Hubbard by N[oah]. Hubbard & O[rson]. Spencer[.]
Charles Shumway by Orson Spencer.
Sarah E. Hubbard by H[eber]. C. Kimball[.]
Julia Shumway by Orson Spencer.
Charles W. Hubbard by Orson Spencer[.]
Mary Ann Hubbard by C[harles]. W. Hubbard & O[rson]. Spencer[.]
John Kay by Orson Spencer.
Ellen Kay by John Kay and O[rson]. Spencer[.]
Joseph G. Hovey by Lucius N. Scovil[.]
Martha Ann Hovey by J[oseph]. G. Hovey & L[ucius]. N. Scovil[.]
Thomas Moore by Lucius N. Scovil[.]
Mahala D. Moore by T[homas]. Moore & John Taylor[.]
Dorcas A. Moore by T[homas]. Moore & L[ucius]. N. Scovil[.]
Elizabeth M. Moore by T[homas]. Moore & L[ucius]. N. Scovil.
Stephen Markham by John Taylor.
Hannah Markham by S[tephen]. Markham & J[ohn]. Taylor[.]
John D. Parker by John Taylor[.]
Sophia A. Roundy by John D. Parker & J[ohn]. Taylor[.]
Catherine A. Markham by S[tephen]. Markham & J[ohn]. Taylor[.]
Warren Markham by J[ohn]. D. Lee[.]
William N. Markham by John Taylor.

Finished receiving these into the upper department at 9 o clock. Orson Pratt, Franklin D. Richards & John D. Lee officiating as prompters.

During the day the 29th quorum of Seventies brought in 44 bottles of Oil for the anointing which was delivered into the care of Bishop Whitney.

President Young has been very busy through the day, dictating the order of business, appointing men to work in the various offices and giving much important and beneficial instruction, at different intervals, in connection with Elder H[eber]. C. Kimball who has also taken a very active part in conducting matters.

At half past 6 o'clock Pres[ident] Young made a selection of the following persons to officiate tomorrow, viz;

C[harles]. C. Rich }
F[ranklin]. D. Richards } In the upper department
L[ucius]. N. Scovil. }

Orson Pratt, Orson Spencer, George A. Smith and Lucian Woodworth in the lower and middle department.

Samuel Bent and Aaron Johnson to anoint the High Priests— Phineas H. Young and David Fullmer to Wash the High Priests

President Joseph Young takes charge of selecting men to wash and anoint the Seventies—Elijah Averett —Jesse P. Harm[on] —John Scott and Hosea Stout, to keep fires in the washing department. also carry in the water. — Elijah Averett to be Door Keeper[,] H[enry]. G. Sherwood [to be] Marshall[.]

At a quarter after 6 o'clock the following High Priests, viz. George Miller, William Huntington Sen[io]r., Lucian Woodworth, Joseph C. Kingsbury, met in the High Priests Room and having clothed themselves offered up prayer according to the order of the Holy Priesthood, Lucian Woodworth being mouth[.]

Sisters Whitney and Kimball have been very busy through the day overseeing the washings and anointings in the female department—and instructing the Sisters in cutting and making robes and garments[.]

Pres[ident]. Young retired at 5 minutes past 7, and Elder Kimball at 17 M[inutes]. past 7.

—William Clayton, Diary, kept for Heber C. Kimball.

....

The morning is warm and pleasant the Snow is about 3 inches in depth making pleasant under foot as well as over head — this morning at

8 o clock I [John D. Lee] am keeping the time of coming & going in the House of the Lord.

At ½ past 8 AM the washing & anointing comenced — the first washed by Pres[ident] H[enry] Herriman & B[enjamin]. L. Clapp and was anointed by Pres[ident] Jos[eph] Young (the candidate Howard Egan) born June 15 1815
[Marginal notation: "Tues[day] morning Dec[ember]. 16. [18]45 9 oclock morning"]

[See pages 56-57 for excerpted portion.]

43 bottles of oil were furnished by the 29th Quorum of Seventies[,] Augustus A. Farnham Senior President of Said Quorum —

—Seventies Record, Book B.

....

[A]bout 4 oclock in the morning I [John D. Lee] entered the Poarch in the lower court where I met the Porter who admitted me in through the door which led to the foot or nearly so of a great flight of Stairs which by ascending led me to the door of the outer court which I found tyled [guarded] within by an officer[.] I having the proper implements of that degree gained admittance through the outer and inner courts which opened and led to the sacred departments.[27] The titles of these apartments are not lawful for me to give at present[.] Having entered I found myself alone with the Tyler that kept the inner courts[.] [I] set about and soon got fires up in the different rooms and [began] setting things in order for the day[.] at about 9 oclock in the morning the washing and anointing commenced, in both departments some more than 50 persons received their washings and anointings through the day and night under the hands of the above persons referred to[.] I have been closely engaged all the day both in writing and assisting as prompter at the veil etc. opperations of the day closed about 1 oclock in the morning[.] Pres[ident] B[righam] Young A[lbert] P Rockwood and myself tarried over night in the Temple[.]

—John D. Lee, Diary.

---

27. Here John D. Lee uses Masonic terminology in reference to temple activities. A tiler, or tyler, closed the building in and kept the lodge's interior hidden from outside view. As the guardian of the entrance to the lodge, the guard "tiled," or protected, the building. In Masonry, "degrees" were stages of progression. The word comes from the Latin *gradus* from which are derived *grade, gradual, graduation,* etc., meaning a step, or set of steps. When united with the prefix *da-,* meaning "down," it becomes *degradus* and refers to steps, degrees, or progress by marked stages.

[Washings andanointings for Tuesday, December 16, 1845]

Jane Egan	18	washed & Anointed by Sister L. Cutler		July 27. 1824
John Brown	19	~~washed by Sister L. Cutler an by~~	born	Oct 23rd 1820
James Harmon	20		born	Sept 28 1811
Jesse P. Harrison	21		" "	Aug 11th 1795
Appleton M. Harmon	22		" "	May 28th 1820

The above Persons were washed by President Herriman & B. L. Clapp And anointed by Pres Jos Young & J. M. Grant. [Marginal notation: "At the same time"] Ana Harmon & Sophronia was washed by [blank] and was anointed by [blank]

John Scott	washed by Herriman & Clapp & anointed by Jos. Young & [illegible]	born	May 6th 1828 [?]
John Pack 24	" " " " " " " " " " " "	"	Feb 1809 [?]
Perrigrine Sessions 25	" " " " " " " " " "	"	June 15 1821 [?]
[illegible] 26	" " " " " " " " " " " "	"	[illegible]
[illegible] 28	" " " " " " " " " " " "	"	[illegible]

Date Members Name No by whom Washed & by whom anointed Age Mo year

No. of Female =

Tues [illegible] A.M. Wm Mathews was washed by Herriman & Clapp & anointed by Pres Jos Young & J M Grant born Jan 28 1815

Dec 16 [illegible]	*Sisters*	
Elizabeth Brown	[illegible] Shearwood A by M. Miller	Dec 1822
Elizabeth Scott	V. Kimble	Sep 10 1815
" Burton	Nancy Rockwood "	Dec 27 1811
Eliza Webb	" " by Jane Young	May 4 1817

15 past [?] P.M. Thomas Moore Jr 29 was washed Pres Herriman & Clapp Pres J. Young & J. M. Grant June 15 1801
John [illegible] 30 " " " " " " " Oct 6 1817
Charles W. Hubbard 31 " " " " " " " Feb 5 1810
J. R. G. Moore 32 " " " " " " " Nov 17 1812
Chars Shumway 33 " " " " " " " Aug 18 1808
Warren Markham 34 " " " " " " " July 30 1824
Wm W. Markham 35 " " " " " " " Jan 30 1829

Sisters

15 minutes of 3 P.M. Catherine Markham washed by Sister Crosby Anointed by Sister Taylor Aug 17 1825
" Martha Hovey[?] " " " " " " M Miller Dec 24 1824
" Julia Ann Shumway " " " [illegible] Miller & Sis Whitley Nov 28 1809
" Ellen Kay " " Sister Crosby & M. Miller Feb 24 1814
" Mary Ann Hubbard " " " " & V. Kimble Aug 12 1846
" Mahala D. Moore " " " " " S Whitney Feb 26 1806
½ past 11 A.M. Elizabeth Burton " " S Rockwood A. V Kimble Dec 28 1811
" Mathews " Sister Crosby A M Miller Aug 10 1808
P Sessions " J. Shearwood A M Miller Sept 29 1817
Julia Pack " by Nancy Rockwood & J Young Mar 8 1817

—Seventies Record, Book B, oversized portion,
December 16, 1845.

I [Brigham Young] have been busy in the Temple dictating the order of business, appointing brethren to officiate in the various departments, and giving much instruction at different intervals; Elder [Heber C.] Kimball assisted me. Sixty-nine brethren and sisters received their ordinances.

—"Manuscript History of Brigham Young," in *History of the Church,* 7:547.

....

Nauvoo temple endowments performed on this date for:

First Company: Morris Phelps, Sarah Phelps, Elan Ludington, Mary E. Ludington, Jesse P. Harmon, Anna Harmon, Howard Egan, Tamson Egan, James Harmon, Isaac Higbee, Charlotte Higbee, Appleton M. Harmon, John Brown, Sophronia M. Harmon, Elizabeth Brown, and Ellen Rockwood.

Second Company: Perrigrine Sessions, Lucina Sessions, William Mathews, Elizabeth A. Mathews, Chancy G. Webb, Eliza J. Webb, David Sessions, Patty Sessions, Israel Barlow, Elizabeth Barlow, John Pack, Julia Pack, Clark L. Whitney, Rhoda Ann Whitney, Sylvia P. Lyons, Lorin Farr, Nancy Farr, Phylote Pack, Joseph W. Coolidge, Elizabeth Coolidge, John Scott, Elizabeth Scott, William Burton, Elizabeth Burton, and Augusta Cobb.

Third Company: George W. Pitkin, Amanda Pitkin, Laura Pitkin, Abigail Pitkin, Eliza R. Snow, James Taylor, Agness Taylor, Noah Hubbard, Cynthia Hubbard, Charles Shumway, Sarah E. Hubbard, Julia Shumway, Charles W. Hubbard, Mary Ann Hubbard, John Kay, Ellen Kay, Joseph G. Hovey, Martha Ann Hovey, Thomas Moore, Mahala D. Moore, Dorcas A. Moore, Elizabeth M. Moore, Stephen Markham, Hannah Markham, John D. Parker, Sophia A. Roundy, Catherine A. Markham, Warren Markham, and William W. Markham.

—Summary of information compiled by the Temple Index Bureau, *Nauvoo Temple Endowment Register: 10 December 1845 to 8 February 1846.* Editors' note: According to the register, Jane Blevin was washed and anointed on this date and was therefore also probably endowed.

II.

Mid-December

1845

PRAISING THE LORD IN DANCE

Wednesday, December 17, 1845

At 35 m[inutes]. past 7. Pres[ident]. B[righam]. Young came in, and at 9, appointed each man his particular duty for the day.

At 9, [we] commenced washing, and anointing the following High Priests in the male department

Levi Jackman	born	July 28. 1797
Samuel Heath	"	May 3. 1754
Asahel Perry	"	Feb[ruar]y 26. 1784
Elijah Fordham	"	April 12. 1798
A[ma]sa Lyman	"	Nov[embe]r. 26. 1785
Tarleton Lewis	"	May 18. 1805
Jonathan Beckelhymn	"	Dec[ember]. 31. 1787
Elizer G. Terrill	"	Mar[ch] 13. 1804
Ezekiel Peck	"	Sept[ember] 2 1785
Thomas Gates Senr.	"	May 7. 1776.

These were washed by David Fullmer and Phineas H. Young and anointed by Samuel Bent and Aaron Johnson[.]

George W. Langley born Sept[ember] 20. 1818 of the quorum of Seventies, was also washed by Phineas H. Young and anointed by Pres[i-dent]. Joseph Young[.] these were all finished at 10 o'clock.

[We] Commenced washing & anointing in the Female department also at 9 o'clock, as follows—

Angeline Jackman born April 17. 1789. washed by M[ary]. C. Miller anointed by B[athsheba]. W. Smith[.]

Polly Perry, born June 24. 1789. W[ashed]. by A[ugusta]. Cobb. A[nointed]. by B[athsheba]. Smith;

~~Jane Heath. B. June 24. 1789 W. by A. Cobb A. by B. Smith~~

Jane Heath. B[orn] Dec[ember]. 1793 W[ashed] by P[atty]. Sessions A[nointed]. By B[athsheba]. Smith[.]

Mary Langley, B[orn] Nov[ember]. 22. 1826 W[ashed]. by M[ary]. Miller A[nointed]. by M[ary]. [Ann] Pratt[.]

Susanna Beckelhymn born June 12 1790. washed by Patty Sessions & anointed by Diantha Billings[.]

Melinda Lewis born March 27. 1811 Washed by Patty Sessions. anointed by Mary Ann Pratt[.]

Electa Peck born July 1. 1779 Washed by Patty Session anointed by Mary Ann Pratt[.]

Anna B. Fordham, born March 24. 1811. Washed by Mary C. Miller, anointed by Bathsheba W. Smith[.]

Susannah Bigler, born Oct[ober] 11. 1785 Washed by Mary C. Miller, anointed by Bath[sheb]a. W. Smith[.]

Sarah R. Lyman born March 10. 1786 Washed by Mary C. Miller, anointed by Mary Ann Pratt[.]

Martha R. Browitt born June 22. 1819 washed by Patty Sessions, anointed by Mary Ann Pratt.

Mary Ann Price born June 5. 1816 Washed by Mary C. Miller, anointed by B[athsheba]. W. Smith[.]

Margaret Moon, born Jan[uar]y 14. 1820 Washed by Patty Sessions anointed by Mary Ann Pratt.

Finished washing & anointing these at 10 m[inutes]. after 10.

At 5 minutes before 10, the bell rung, and [we] commenced receiving those washed and anointed this morning into the lower & middle departments, the following persons officiating—viz—

In the upper department

Charles C. Rich	as	No.	1
Franklin D. Richards	"	"	2
Lucius N. Scovil	"	"	3

In the middle department

Orson Spencer	as	No.	1

W[illiam]. W. Phelps	"	"	2
L[ucius]. N. Scovil	"	"	3
Lucian Woodworth	"	"	4

Orson Hyde officiated as prompter—

[A]t 45 minutes past 9, Lucian R. Foster, entered the east room and commenced recording the proceedings—in place of W[illia]m Clayton, who was wanted for other duties, at the Temple Office.

At 11¼ commenced washing and anointing the following High Priests, viz,;

~~Edmund Bosley born June 25. 1776~~
~~John Benbow —— April 1. 1800~~
~~William Moss —— Sept. 27 1796~~
~~Hezekiah Peck —— Jany 19. 1702~~

these were washed by David Fullmer and Phineas H. Young and anointed by Isaac Morley and Samuel Bent —— finished at 25 m. past 11.

At 20 M. after 11. commenced washing & anointing in the female department, the following persons, viz.

~~Martha Peck, born March 13. 1788 washed by Patty Sessions, anointed by Diantha Billings~~

~~Jane Benbow, born Jany. 12. 1792 washed by Hannah Lytle, anointed by Diantha Billings~~

~~Elizabeth Moss, born Jany. 30. 1803 washed by Patty Sessions, anointed by B. W. Smith~~

~~Ann Bosley born Oct. 29. 1779 washed by Diantha Billings, anointed by B. W. Smith.~~

~~finished at 10 minutes before 12.~~

~~At 25 m. past 12. Stephen H. Goddard, born Augt. 23. 1810, was washed by Henry Herriman & Benj. L. Clapp & anointed by Joseph Young and Jedidiah M. Grant — also Charles W. Patten, H. P. born Novr. 4. 1811. washed by P. H. Young and David Fullmer. anointed by S. Bent & Isaac Morley~~

At 25 minutes past 11 o'clock [we] commenced receiving into the upper department those who were washed & anointed this morning, in the following order, viz.—

Martha R. Browitt by Orson Hyde[.]
Mary Ann Price by Orson Hyde[.]
Margaret Moon by W[illia]m Clayton[.]
Asahel Perry by C[harles]. C. Rich[.]
Polly Perry by A[sahel]. Perry and C[harles]. C. Rich[.]

Susannah Bigler by C[harles]. C. Rich[.]
Asa Lyman by C[harles]. C. Rich[.]
Sally Lyman by A[masa]. Lyman & C[harles]. C. Rich[.]
Thomas Gates Sen[io]r. by C[harles]. C. Rich[.]
Jonathan Beckelhymn by C[harles]. C. Rich[.]
Susanna Beckelhymn by J[onathan]. B[eckelhymn]. & C[harles]. C R[ich.]
Elizer G. Terrill by C[harles]. C. Rich[.]
Ezekiel Peck by C[harles]. C. Rich[.]
Electa Peck by Ezekiel Peck & C[harles]. C. Rich[.]
Tarleton Lewis by C[harles]. C. Rich[.]
Melinda Lewis by T[arleton]. Lewis & C[harles]. C. Rich[.]
Samuel Heath by C[harles]. C. Rich[.]
Jane Heath by S[amuel]. Heath & C[harles]. C. Rich[.]
Levi Jackman by C[harles]. C. Rich[.]
Anjeline Jackman — L[evi]. Jackman and C[harles]. C. R[ich].
George W. Langley by C[harles]. C. Rich[.]
Mary Langley by G[eorge]. W. Langley & C[harles]. C. R[ich].
Elijah Fordham by C[harles]. C. Rich.
Anna B. Fordham by E[lijah]. Forham and C[harles]. C. Rich[.]

^Franklin D. Richards officiated as prompter to most of these—^ Finished at 35 m[inutes]. past 1.— W[illiam]. L. Cutler and Aaron Johnson Prompters.

At a quarter after 11 [we] commenced washing and anointing the following High Priests in the male department, in the following order, viz.

Hezekiah Peck,	born	January 19. 1782
Lewis Abbott	"	December 18. 1795
Chandler Rogers	"	January 27. 1795
Charles W. Patten	"	Nov[embe]r. 4. 1811
Edmund Bosley	"	June 25. 1776
John Benbow	"	April 1. 1800
William Moss	"	Sept[ember] 27. 1796.

These were washed by David Fuller & P[hineas]. H. Young and anointed by Samuel Bent & Isaac Morley.

The following persons, belonging to the quorum of Seventy, were also washed, by Henry Herriman, and John Lytle, and anointed by Joseph Young and J[edediah]. M. Grant. viz.

Noble Rogers	born	August 10. 1799
Stephen H. Goddard	"	August 23 1810

~~Stephen H. Goddard~~ ^Nobell Rogers^ having previously been ordained to the quorum of Seventies by Joseph Young and H[eber]. C. Kimball.

At 20 m[inutes]. after 11, [we] commenced washing and anointing in the female department, as follows, viz;

Martha Peck. born March 13. 1788 washed by Patty Sessions, anointed by Diantha Billings[.]

Jane Benbow. born January 12. 1792 washed by Hannah Lytle, anointed by Diantha Billings[.]

Elizabeth Moss born Jan[uar]y. 30. 1803 washed by Patty Sessions. anointed by B[athsheba]. W. Smith[.]

Ann Bosley born Oct[ober]. 29. 1779 washed by Diantha Billings. anointed by B[athsheba]. W. Smith[.]

Peggy Patten, born Dec[embe]r. 11. 1812 washed by Patty Sessions, anointed by D[iantha]. Billings[.]

Amanda Rogers, born May 18. 1797 Washed by Sarah D. Rich, anointed by Patty Sessions[.]

Mary Rogers, born Feb[ruar]y. 23. 1811 Washed by Patty Sessions, an[ointe]d by Mary Ann Pratt[.]

Ann Abbott born June 19. 1799 washed by Patty Sessions, anointed by D[iantha]. Billings[.]

Finished at 3 minutes after 1 o'clock.

At 10, minutes past 1. the bell rung, and [we] commenced receiving the foregoing persons into the lower and middle departments, the following persons officiating, viz.

In the upper department

Orson Hyde	as	No.	1.
F[ranklin]. D. Richards	"	"	2
L[ucius]. N. Scovil	"	"	3

In the middle department

Orson Spencer	as	No	1
Lucius N. Scovil	"	"	2
Charles C. Rich	"	"	3
W[illiam]. W. Phelps	"	"	4.
John D. Lee	Prompter		

At 20 minutes past 2 o'clock, P.M. Bishop [George] Miller perfumed 45 Bottles of Oil after which the following brethren, viz. Heber C. Kimball, Orson Pratt, Amasa Lyman, George A. Smith, W[illiam]. W. Phelps, and Joseph Young clothed themselves and retired to Elder Kimball['s] room, Where after offering up the signs of the Holy Priesthood they dedicated & consecrated the whole for the anointing in the following order, viz; the first 6 Bottles,

Eld[er]. H[eber].C. Kimball being mouth
2d, 6 Bottles Elder Orson Pratt being mouth
3d, 6 bottles G[eorge]. A. Smith mouth
4th 6 bottles W[illiam]. W. Phelps mouth
5th 6 bottles Elder Amasa Lyman Mouth
6th 6 Bottles Elder Joseph Young mouth
7th 6 Bottles H[eber]. C. Kimball mouth

[R]emaining 3 Bottles Elder Orson Pratt mouth, after which they consecrated 2 Bottles to the healing of the sick.

They then offered up prayers for the sick and other subjects, according to our daily custom, Geo[rge]. A. Smith being mouth, at 3 o'clock they undressed.

At half past 2 o'clock [we] commenced receiving into the upper department, those who were washed at a quarter after 11. o'clock viz.

Hezekiah Peck by Lucius N. Scovil[.]
Martha Peck by Hezekiah Peck & L[ucius]. N. Scovil[.]

Chandler Rogers	by	Lucius N. Scovil[.]
Amanda Rogers	"	Chandler Rogers & L[ucius]. N. Scovil[.]
Edmund Bosley	"	Lucius N. Scovil[.]
Ann Bosley	"	E[dmund]. Bosley & L[ucius]. N. Scovil[.]
William Moss	"	Aaron Johnson[.]
Elizabeth Moss	"	W[illia]m. Moss & Aaron Johnson[.]
John Benbow	"	Aaron Johnson
Jane Benbow	"	John Benbow & A[aron]. Johnson[.]
Lewis Abbott	"	Aaron Johnson[.]
Ann Abbott	"	L[ewis]. Abbott & A[aron]. Johnson[.]
Charles W. Patten	"	Aaron Johnson[.]
Peggy Patten	"	C[harles]. W. Patten & A[aron]. Johnson[.]
Noble Rogers	"	Aaron Johnson[.]

Mary Rogers by Noble Rogers & A[aron]. Johnson.

Finished receiving these at 6 minutes past 4. John D. Lee and William Burton officiating as prompters.

At half past One o'clock ^P.M.^ [we] commenced washing and anointing, in the male department, the following High Priests, viz;

Calvin C. Pendleton	born	Oct[ober]. 25. 1811
James Whitehead	"	April 12, 1813

Albert Petty	"	August 10. 1795
John Fidoe	"	[blank] 1796
William Kay	"	April 11. 1811
Almon W. Sherman	"	May 9. 1803

These were washed by Phineas H. Young and David Fullmer and anointed by Isaac Morley & Samuel Bent.

Finished washing & anointing these at half past 2 P.M.

Also at 25 minutes past 2 in the male department [we] commenced washing washing [sic] & anointing the following members of the quorum of the Seventies, viz;

William Pitt	born	August 16. 1813
Daniel Hill	"	April 2. 1807

[W]ashed by Benj[ami]n. L. Clapp & John Lytle, anointed by Benj[ami]n. L. Clapp and Jedediah M. Grant. Finished at 15 m[inutes]. before 3.

At a quarter after One, P.M. [we] commenced washing and anointing in the female department, as follows—viz.

Elizabeth Hill born [blank] Washed by Patty Sessions, anointed by D[iantha]. Billings[.]

Lois H. Sherman. born March 2. 1811 washed by Patty Sessions, anointed by D[iantha]. Billings[.]

Jane Whitehead born Jan[uar]y 20. 1810. washed by Patty Sessions, anointed by D[iantha]. Billings[.]

Mary Ann Kay born Aug[us]t 26. 1819 washed by Patty Sessions, anointed [by] Thir[z]a Cahoon[.]

Sally Ann Pendleton born, Oct[ober] 10. 1816 washed by Anna B. Fordham, anointed by Mary Ann Pratt.

Catharine Petty born Feb[ruar]y. 16. 1803 washed by Anna B. Fordham, anointed by Diantha Billings[.]

Lydia Fidoe born June 28. 1813 Washed by Patty Sessions, anointed by Thirza Cahoon[.]

Cornelia M. Pitt born Dec. 25. 1824 washed by Anna B. Fordham, anointed by Mary Ann Pratt.

At 25 minutes past 3, the bell rung, and [we] commenced receiving in to the lower & middle departments the foregoing persons, who were washed & anointed at half past one. the following persons officiating—

In the upper department—

Orson Pratt as	No.	1
Charles C. Rich as	"	2
L[ucius]. N. Scovil as	"	3

In the middle department

Orson Spencer as	No.	1
C[harles]. C. Rich as	"	2
L[ucius]. N. Scovil as	"	3
W[illiam]. W. Phelps as	"	4
Phineas H. Young Prompter		

At 35 minutes past 4 [we] commenced receiv[in]g into the upper department, those washed & anointed at half past one. in the following order—viz;

William Pitt by Lucius N. Scovil[.]
Cornelia M. Pitt by W[illiam]. Pitt & L[ucius]. N. Scovil[.]
James Whitehead " L[ucius]. N. Scovil[.]
Jane Whitehead " James W[hitehead]. & L[ucius]. N. S[covil].
Daniel Hill by L[ucius]. N. Scovil[.]
Elizabeth Hill by D[aniel]. Hill & L[ucius]. N. Scovil[.]
William Kay by L[ucius]. N. Scovil[.]
Mary Ann Kay by W[illiam]. Kay & L[ucius]. N. Scovil[.]
John Fidoe " ~~L. N. Scovil~~ Aaron Johnson[.]
Lydia Fidoe by John Fidoe & A[aron]. Johnson[.]
Albert Petty by Aaron Johnson[.]
Catharine Petty by A[lbert]. Petty & A[aron]. Johnson[.]
Almon W. Sherman by A[aron] Johnson[.]
Lois H. Sherman by A[lmon]. W. Sherman & A[aron]. Johnson[.]
Calvin C. Pendleton by A[aron]. Johnson[.]
Sally Ann Pendleton by C[alvin]. C. P[endleton]. & A[aron]. J[ohnson].

Finished receiving these at 10 m[inutes]. past 6. John D. Lee and William Burton officiating as prompters.

At 5 o'clock [we] commenced washing and anointing in the Male department the following persons of the quorum of Seventys.

William F. Cahoon	born	Nov[embe]r. 7 1813
Archibald Hill	"	Aug[us]t. 22. 1816
John Hill	"	January 22. 1814
Edson Barney	"	June 30. 1806
Bradford W. Elliott	"	Jan[uar]y 12. 1824
John A. Whiteside	"	May 19. 1811
Lewis Robbins	"	Sept[ember] 8. 1811
Elijah Newman	born	Sept[ember]. 17 1798

These were washed by Benjamin L. Clapp and John Lytle and anointed by Joseph Young, Albert P. Rockwood and Jedediah M. Grant, B[enjamin]. L. Clapp and John Lytle Finished at 8 minutes before 6.

At 4 minutes past 5, [we] commenced in the female department, ~~the following~~ washing & anointing the following persons, viz.

Nancy M. Cahoon, born July 17. 1817 washed by Patty Sessions, anointed by D[iantha]. Billings.

Lillis Barney, born April 20. 1805. washed by Jane Bliven, anointed by Mary Ann Pratt[.]

Electa Whiteside, born May 5. 1816 Washed by Patty Sessions, anointed by Mary Ann Pratt[.]

Ann Eliza Elliott born Nov[embe]r. 1. 1820 washed by Jane Bliven, anointed by Mary Ann Pratt[.]

Isabella Hill, born July 8. 1821 Washed by Patty Sessions, anointed by Diantha Billings[.]

Margaret Hill, born Dec[embe]r. 16. 1816 Washed by Jane Bliven, anointed by D[iantha]. Billings[.]

Losana Newman born April 4, 1813 Washed by Patty Sessions, anointed by D[iantha]. Billings.

Finished at 8 minutes past 6.

At ½ past 6 [we] commenced receiving into the lower & middle departments, the foregoing persons[,] the following persons officiating—viz—

In the upper department.

Joseph Young	as	No.	1
Benj[ami]n L. Clapp	as	"	2
J[edediah]. M. Grant	"	"	3

In the middle department

Orson Pratt	as	No	1
Albert P. Rockwood	"	"	2
Henry Herriman	"	"	3
John D. Lee	"	"	4

W[illiam]. L. Cutler Prompter

At 12 minutes past 8 [we] commenced receiving the foregoing persons into the upper department, in the following order. viz;

William F. Cahoon by Benj[amin]. L. Clapp.

Nancy M. Cahoon by W[illiam]. F. Cahoon & Jos[eph]. Young[.]

Elijah Newman by Joseph Young[.]

Losana Newman by E[lijah]. Newman & Jos[eph]. Young[.]

John A. Whiteside by Joseph Young[.]

Electa Whiteside by J[ohn]. A. W[hiteside]. & J[oseph]. Young[.]
John Hill by B[enjamin]. L. Clapp[.]
Margaret Hill by J[ohn]. Hill & B[enjamin]. L. Clapp[.]
Edson Barney by B[enjamin]. L. Clapp[.]
Lillis Barney and E[dson]. Barney & B[enjamin]. L. Clapp[.]

Archibald Hill	by	B. L.	Clapp[.]	
Isabella Hill	"	"	"	& A[rchibald]. Hill[.]
Bradford W. Elliott	"	"	"	
Ann Eliza Elliott	"	"	"	& B[radford]. W. Elliott[.]
Lewis Robbins	"	"	"	

Finished receiving these at 20 minutes to 10. W. L. Cutler and John D. Lee acting as prompters[.]

About 6 o'clock, P.M. Pres[ident]. Young selected the following persons to work on Thursday and notified them to be present, viz; C[harles]. C. Rich

L[ucius]. N. Scovil	W[illia]m Crosby
Franklin D. Richards	Elijah Averett
John J. Butler	Jesse D. Hunter
Isaac Morley	Henry Herriman
Samuel Bent	Phineas H. Young
Aaron Johnson	Jedediah M. Grant
W[illia]m L. Cutler	Daniel Carn
Hosea Stout	Benjamin L. Clapp
Peter Haws	

He also selected a list of names of persons to be present on Friday to receive their washing and anointing, and put the list into the hands of John Pack to give notice to the individuals[.] About 20 minutes past 10, about 16 or 18 persons assembled in the east room and sung a hymn—and joined in prayer with Pres[ident]. Young[.] He slept in the Temple, also his son Joseph and 10 or 12 other persons.

—William Clayton, Diary, kept for Heber C. Kimball.

Brother Lucian R. Foster is now appointed to keep the Records of the endowment. Margaret [Moon] came with me to the Temple this morning and received her washing and anointing. She was washed by sister Patty Sessions and anointed by sister Mary Ann Pratt wife of E[lde]r Parley P. Pratt one of the Twelve [apostles]. I conducted her through the remaining ceremonies and also received her through into the upper or

Celestial department. I feel grateful for this privilege and for all the blessings I receive from day to day[,] for the mercies of the Lord to me are great and many of them. I instructed brother Foster in regard to keeping the Record and in the evening assisted E[lde]r [Brigham] Young and [Heber C.] Kimball to collect a list of brethren to come here on saturday.

—William Clayton, Diary.

....

At 6 o.clock A.M. the Saints commenced gathering in compliance with the order of the day. The following are the Names of those that spent the ^Night^ in the House of the Lord. viz. Pres[ident]. Jos[eph] & Lady Amasa Lyman John D Lee David Candland H[ans]. C. Hanson & Peter Hanson — on the Day previous W[illia]m W. Markham was ordained into the [illegible] Seventies under the hands of President Jos[eph] Young and Henry Herriman, he was born Jan[uary]. 30th 1829 [?] 74 Persons appear on the list of candidates this morning who are to receive their washings and anointings to day & out of that No. only one Seventy apears on the list with his Family — leaving about 30 High Priest & their wives this is done to [illegible] age. the H[igh]. P[riests]. being generally aged men in the cause as well as in years. At 9 O.clock A.M. the washing comenced in both departments [illegible]

[See page 70 for excerpted portion.]

It is now ½ Past ten at night, the business of the day have just come to a close, the Spirit of the ^Lord^ has been with his saints in the performance of his ordinances — Br[other] C[hristian]. H. Hanson ^(Hans Christian Hansen)^ brought in his violin and made Melody unto the Lord which cheered the hearts of his People and while under the power of animation Pres[ident] Brigham & [his brother] Jos[eph] Young J[edediah]. M. Grant B[enjamin]. L. Clapp J[ohn]. D. Lee & John Lytle danced before the Lord [with] Pres[ident] B[righam]. Young & the Brethren and Sisters that were presant. in connection with the above refered to were Elish[a] Averett F[ranklin]. D Richards Orson Hyde L[ucian]. R. Foster & little Jos[eph] Young (B[righam] Y[oung's] son) Sisters Mary An[n] Pratt Mercy Thompson & Eliza R. Snow. retired to the East room or uper department where we celebrated the Praise of God by singing & Prayer, we then returned to rest[,] the watchm[e]n who stand in turns through the Night — excepted.

—Seventies Record, Book B.

[Washings and anointings for Wednesday, December 17, 1845]

Date	*Members Names No.*	*By whom washed & by whom Anointed*	*No. Age year born*
Dec 16			
PM			
George W Langley 36		Pres H Herriman & B L Clapp & A Pratt J Young J M	Sept 20th 1818
Noble Rodger 37		" " " " "	46 years

Br Rodgers was ordained of the Seventies under the hands of Heber C Kimble & Pres Jos. Young —

Sisters Department

3 P.M	Mary Langley	M Miller & Maryanne Pratt	Nov 22 1826
3 P.M.	Mary Rogers	P Sessions & " "	June 19 1811
	Camelia M Pitt	" " D Billings	Dec 25 18
	Elizabeth Hill	Anna Fordham Maryan Pratt	
5 PM	Wm L Cahoon	Pres Herriman & B L Clapp Pres Young J M Grant	Nov 7 1813
"	Archibald Hill 39	" " " " "	Aug 22 1816
"	John Hill 40	" " " " "	Jan 29. 1819
"	Edson Barney 41	" " " " "	June 30 1806
"	Brad. W Elliott 42	" " " " "	" 12 1829
"	Lewis Robbins 43	" " " " "	Sept 8 1811
"	John A Whitesides 44	" " " " "	May 19 1811
"	William Pitt 45	" " " " "	" 16 1813
"	Daniel Hill 45	" " " " "	Aug 2 1808

—Seventies Record, Book B, oversized portion, December 17, 1845.

[A]bout now I [John D. Lee] got up with my writing & had some considerable time to spend in officiating[.] I through the day acted as prompter for nearly 40 persons to take through the veil[.] I also acted as Tempter while in the garden[.] This evening B[righam] Young gave permission for the seventies to take a company through extra after the services of the day closed which was done and a continuation of this permission will be kept up each day incessantly[.] at 10 oclock the work of the day stoped[.] Bro[ther] H C Egerson [Hansen] ——— the Tyler at the door of the outer court who was an excellent Fidler came in by permission & animated our feelings with melodious notes on his violin[.] We all rejoiced & Praised the Lord in the dance[.] Pres[ident] B[righam] Young & Joseph his brother Bro[ther] [Benjamin L.] Clapp or Chapp J[edediah] M Grant J[ohn] D Lee John L Butler & John Lyttle all participated in the dance[,] after which Pres[ident] B[righam] Young said that we would retire into the East room and again celebrate the praise of God by singing and prayer which[,] when we had done[,] we retired to rest[,] all but the guards who stood in turn 2 hours each till day when all was up and at work in order to get things ready for the day[.] at 9 in the morning the washing and anointing commenced in both departments[.] It went well through the day [and] a good part of the day was occupied as usual[.] I this day acted as prompter through the day or rather the veil[.] about 6 oclock I went home to attend to some business [but] I [first] here obtained permission from B[righam] Young to Bring my family in and let them pass through the ordinance of the endowment[, which] I [announced to them] this evening[.] while at home I had application by Pres[ident] H[orace] B Owens & lady to be adopted into my family and take upon them my Name which I consented to do[.][1]

—John D. Lee, Diary.

....

We continued our labors in the Temple, administered the ordinances of endowment to sixty-nine brethren and sisters.

Ten twenty-five p.m., eighteen persons assembled in my [Brigham Young's] room and joined with me in prayer.

---

1. Under the "Law of Adoption," individuals could be sealed to prominent church leaders. The practice began in the Nauvoo temple and continued in Utah until 1894. See Gordon Irving, "The Law of Adoption: One Phase of the Development of the Mormon Concept of Salvation, 1830-1900," *BYU Studies* 14 (Spring 1974): 291-314.

My son, Joseph A. [Young], remained with me in the Temple all night.

Letters were written to Stephen A. Douglas, M.C.,[2] J. P. Hoge, M.C.,[3] W[illia]m. S. Marcy, Secretary of War, John Wentworth, M.C.,[4] and John Chapman in relation to our movement to the west, in consequence of learning that attempts were made to induce [the] government to prevent our removal.

—"Manuscript History of Brigham Young,"
in *History of the Church*, 7: 547.

Nauvoo temple endowments performed on this date:

First Company: Martha R. Browitt, Mary Ann Price, Margaret Moon, Asahel Perry, Polly Perry, Susannah Bigler, A[ma]sa Lyman, Sally Lyman, Thomas Gates Sr., Jonathan Beckelhymer, Susanna Beckelhymer, Elizur G. Terrill, Ezekiel Peck, Electa Peck, Tarleton Lewis, Melinda Lewis, Samuel Heath, Jane Heath, Levi Jackman, Angeline Jackman, George W. Langley, Mary Langley, Elijah Fordham, and Anna B. Fordham.

Second Company: Hezekiah Peck, Martha Peck, Chandler Rogers, Amanda Rogers, Edmund Bosley, Ann Bosley, William Moss, Elizabeth Moss, John Benbow, Jane Benbow, Lewis Abbott, Ann Abbott, Charles W. Patten, Peggy Patten, Noble Rogers, and Mary Rogers.

Third Company: William Pitt, Cornelia M. Pitt, James Whitehead, Jane Whitehead, Daniel Hill, Elizabeth Hill, William Kay, Mary Ann Kay, John Fidoe, Lydia Fidoe, Albert Petty, Catharine Petty, Almon W. Sherman, Lois H. Sherman, Calvin C. Pendleton, and Sally Ann Pendleton.

---

2. Stephen A. Douglas (1813-61) settled in Illinois and was admitted to the bar in 1834. He held several local offices and was appointed a state supreme court judge in 1841. Serving in the U.S. Senate from 1847-61, he became known as author of the Kansas-Nebraska Act. He was defeated by Abraham Lincoln for the U.S. presidency in 1861 and died of typhoid fever later that year after an exhausting speaking tour defending the Union. In this entry, the letters "M.C." designate a Master in Chancery (officer in a civil court), but President Young seems to use them here as an honorific title.

3. Joseph Pendleton Hoge (1810-91) was elected to the Illinois 6th Congressional District, which included Nauvoo, and served from 1843-47. He also served as an Illinois State Court judge. He later moved to California and was a delegate to the Democratic National Convention in 1876.

4. John Wentworth (1815-88) edited the *Chicago Democrat* and served as a U.S. Representative from Illinois from 1843-51, 1853-55, and 1865-67. Between his last two terms in Congress, he was elected mayor of Chicago from 1857-58 and 1860-61. The next year he became a delegate to the Illinois State Constitutional Convention.

Fourth Company: William F. Cahoon, Nancy M. Cahoon, Elijah Newman, Losana Newman, John A. Whiteside, Electa Whiteside, John Hill, Margaret Hill, Edson Barney, Lillis Barney, Archibald Hill, Isabella Hill, Bradford W. Elliott, Ann Eliza Elliott, and Lewis Robbins.

—*Nauvoo Temple Endowment Register: 10 December 1845 to 8 February 1846,* compiled by the Temple Index Bureau of the Church of Jesus Christ of Latter-day Saints, 1974, under date.

Thursday, December 18, 1845

At 14 minutes past 9 o'clock [we] commenced washing and anointing, in the male department the following persons of the quorum of Seventies, viz;

Wilbur J. Earl	born	March 29. 1817
Daniel S. Jackson	"	December 4. 1814
William A. Sanger	"	August 19, 1810

These were washed by John Lytle and John Brown and anointed by Joseph Young and Benj[ami]n. L. Clapp. Finished at 9 o'c[loc]k. 25 m.

Also, the following persons, of the quorum of High Priests were washed and anointed—viz;

Jacob Zundell	born	Aug[us]t 26. 1796
George Lyman	"	Nov[embe]r. 17. 1799
Abraham O. Smoot	"	Feb[ruar]y 17 1815
Charles Hulet	"	March 3. 1790
Sylvester Hulet	"	March 1 1800
~~William A. Langes~~	~~"~~	~~August 19 1810~~
Solomon Chamberlain	"	July 30. 1788

These men washed by William Crosby and John Lytle, and anointed by Samuel Bent and Peter Haws. Finished at 12 m[inutes]. past 9 o'clock.

At 20 minutes to 9 o'clock [we] commenced in the Female department, the washing & anointing of the following persons, viz;

Loisa Sanger, born March 26, 1812 washed by Mercy R. Thompson, anointed by Bathsheba W. Smith[.]

Rosina Lyman, born March 29. 1818 Washed by Jane Sherwood, anointed by Mary Ann Pratt.

Mary Sanger born April 17. 1812 washed by Mercy R. Thompson, anointed by B[athsheba]. W. Smith[.]

Margaret T. Smoot, born April 16. 1809 washed by Sophronia ^M^ Harmon, anointed by Leonora Taylor.

Emeline Waterman born Oct[obe]r. 6. 1805 washed by Jane Sherwood, anointed by Leonora Taylor[.]
Sarah Zundall born January 8. 1809 Washed by Sophronia ^M^ Harmon, anointed by Leonora Taylor
Harriet Earl, born April 15 1828 washed by Jane Sherwood, anointed by B[athsheba]. W. Smith[.]
Orice Burnham, born Nov[embe]r. 20, 1813 washed by Sophronia ^M^ Harmon, anointed by Mary Ann Pratt[.]
Margaret Hulet, born April 19. 1794 washed by S[ophronia]. M. Harmon anointed by Leonora Taylor[.]

Finished at 20 min[utes] to 10.

At 10 O'clock the bell rung, and operations commenced in the lower and middle departments[,] the following persons Officiating, viz;

John Taylor	as	No.	1. }	
P[arley]. P. Pratt	"	"	2. }	in upper dep[artmen]t
J[edediah]. M. Grant	"	"	3 }	

In the Middle department the following,

Aaron Johnson	as	No.	1
Hosea Stout	"	"	2
Jesse D. Hunter	"	"	3.
W[illiam]. W. Phelps	"	"	4

George A. Smith, as prompter.

At half past 11 o'clock [we] commenced receiving into the upper department the foregoing persons, in the following order—viz—

William A. Sanger by Heber C. Kimball[.]
Mary Sanger by W[illiam]. A. S[anger]. and " " [.]
Abraham O. Smoot by H[eber]. C. Kimball[.]
Margaret T. Smoot by her husband & H[eber]. C. K[imball].
Mary Amanda Utley by John Taylor[.]
Loisa Sanger by Reuben Miller & J[ohn]. Taylor[.]
Jacob Zundall by W[illiam]. L. Cutler[.]
Sarah Zundall by her husband & [William] Cutler[.]
Solomon Chamberlain by W[illiam]. L. Cutler[.]
Emeline Waterman by S[olomon]. Chamberlain & [William] Cutler[.]
Orice Burnham by Reuben Miller[.]
Charles Hulet by W[illiam]. L. Cutler[.]
Margaret Hulet by Cha[rle]s. Hulet and [William] Cutler[.]
Wilbur J. Earl by Lucius N. Scovil[.]

Harriet Earl by W[ilbur]. J. Earl & L[ucius]. N. Scovil[.]
George Lyman by L[ucius]. N. Scovil[.]
Daniel Jackson by L[ucius]. N. Scovil[.]
Sylvester Hulet by L[ucius]. N. Scovil[.]
Rosina Lyman by George Lyman & L[ucius]. N. Scovil[.]

Finished at a quarter past 1 o'clock Aaron Johnson and John D. Lee officiating as prompters.

At 2 m[inutes]. before 11 O'clock [we] commenced in the male department washing and anointing the following High Priests.

William Parks	born	March 21. 1787
Alphonso Young	"	Sept[ember] 23. 1805
Lyman Stoddard	"	February 8. 1795
Benjamin F. Johnson	"	July 28. 1818
Ormond Butler	"	March 9. 1775
John Stiles	"	Nov[embe]r. 16. 1791

[T]hese were washed by William Crosby and John Brown — anointed by Isaac Morley and Samuel Bent— Finished at 11-24[.]

Also the following of the Seventies quorum, viz;

Alexander McRae,	born	Sept[ember] 7. 1807
David D. Yearsley	"	March 3. 1808

[W]ashed by Benjamin L. Clapp & John Lytle, anointed by Joseph Young & B[enjamin]. L. Clapp.

Also the following Elders, viz;

Nahum Curtis	born	July 7. 1784
Thomas Travis	"	April 1. 1790

These were washed by William Crosby and John Brown & anointed by Isaac Morley and Samuel Bent.

Finished at 13 min[utes]. past 11 o'clock.

At 17 minutes before 11, [we] commenced in the female department, washing and anointing the following persons, viz;

Mary Ann Yearsly, born Jan[uar]y. 8. 1811 W[ashed]. by Jane Sherwood, anointed by Mary Ann Pratt[.]

Mary Pew born Dec[embe]r. 10. 1821 W[ashed]. by Patty Sessions, anointed by Leonora Taylor[.]

Delia Curtis, born December 4, 1789 W[ashed]. by Patty Sessions, anointed by Leonora Taylor[.]

Marinda Bennett born Aug[us]t 26. 1826 W[ashed]. by Sophronia M. Harmon, anointed by B[athsheba]. W. Smith[.]

Millesant Parks, born Dec[embe]r. 29, 1805 W[ashed]. by Sophronia M. Harmon, anointed by B[athsheba]. W. Smith[.]

Nancy Young born May 13, 1805 W[ashed]. by Jane Sherwood anointed by Leonora Taylor[.]

Melissa Johnson, born Jan[uar]y. 23. 1820 W[ashed]. by S[ophronia]. W. Harmon, anointed by B[athsheba]. W. Smith[.]

Mary Travis born May 12, 1784 W[ashed]. by Patty Sessions, anointed by Mary Ann Pratt.

Persis Stiles, born Nov[embe]r. 7, 1797 W[ashed]. by Jane Sherwood, anointed by Leonora Taylor[.]

Ruth Stoddard, born Oct[ober]. 13, 1804 W[ashed]. by Patty Sessions, anointed by Mary Ann Pratt.

Finished at half past 11 o'clock.

At 15 minutes past 12 the bell rung and operations commenced to receive into the lower and middle departments, those who have been washed since 2 m[inutes]. before 11. the following persons officiating, viz;

Orson Pratt	as	No.	1	}
P[arley]. P. Pratt	"	"	2	} upper department
C[harles]. C. Rich	"	"	3	}
G[eorge]. A. Smith	as Prompter			}
P[arley]. P. Pratt,	as	No.	1	}
C[harles]. C. Rich	"	"	2	} middle dep[artmen]t
Aaron Johnson	"	"	3	}
W[illiam]. W. Phelps	"	"	4	}

Geo[rge] A. Smith, Prompter

At half past one o'clock [we] commenced receiving into the upper department, those whose washing and anointing commenced at 2 m[inutes]. before 11, in the following order, viz,

Alexander McRae by Lucius N. Scovil[.]

Marinda Bennett by Hosea Stout & L[ucius]. N. Scovil[.]

Mary Pew by John Scott & L[ucius]. N. Scovil[.]

Benjamin F. Johnson by L[ucius]. N. Scovil[.]

Melissa Johnson by B[enjamin]. F. Johnson & [Lucius N.] Scovil[.]

Alphonzo Young by L[ucius]. N. Scovil[.]

Nancy Young by A[lphonzo]. Young & [Lucius N.] Scovil[.]

William Parks by W[illiam]. L. Cutler[.]

Millesant Parks by W[illiam]. Parks and W[illiam]. L. Cutler[.]

Lyman Stoddard by W[illiam]. L. Cutler[.]

Ruth Stoddard by L[yman]. Stoddard & [William] Cutler[.]

John Stiles by W[illiam]. L. Cutler[.]
Persis Stiles by John Stiles & [William] Cutler[.]
David D. Yearsley by W[illiam]. L. Cutler[.]
Mary Ann Yearsley by D[avid]. D. Y[earsley]. & [William] Cutler[.]
Nahum Curtis by L[ucius]. N. Scovil[.]
Delia Curtis by N[ahum]. Curtis & [Lucius] Scovil[.]
Thomas Travis by L[ucius]. N. Scovil.
Mary Travis by Th[omas]. Travis & [Lucius] Scovil[.]
Ormond Butler by John D. Lee[.]

The above passed in to the upper dep[artmen]t. and finished at about half past 3. John D. Lee and Aaron Johnson acting as prompters[.]

At 25 min[utes] past one o'clock [we] commenced in the male department, washing & anointing the following high priests, viz;

Robert Pierce, born April 11. 1797
Saber Durfee born Dec[embe]r. 28. 1791.
Stephen Winchester May 8. 1795
Elijah Malin Feb[ruar]y 1. 1773

[W]ashed by William Crosby and John Brown anointed by Isaac Morley and Samuel Bent.

Jacob Weiler born March 14. 1808
Elis M. Sanders " Dec[embe]r. 5. 1808

[W]ashed by William Crosby and John Brown anointed by Isaac Morley and Samuel Bent.

Also the following persons, members of the quorum of Seventies—

Stephen Winchester Jun[io]r. born Sep[tember]. 21 1820
Charles Price born 1800

[W]ashed by John Lytle and John Brown anointed by Joseph Young & J[edediah]. M. Grant[.]

Finished at 26 m[inutes]. before 2 o'clock.

Ellis M. Sanders was ordained a High Priest, in the Washing & anointing Room, before being washed, under the hands of Samuel Bent & Isaac Morley. at half past 1 o clock[.]

At 20 min[utes]. past 1 o'clock [we] commenced in the Female department washing & anointing the following persons, viz;

Catharine Malin born Jan[uar]y 31. 1779 W[ashed]. by Mercy R. Thompson an[ointed]. by Patty Sessions[.]
Sarah Malin [born] January 10. 1804 W[ashed]. by Jane Sherwood, anointed by Leonora Taylor[.]

Eliza Ann Mialin born March 24. 1823 W[ashed]. by Mercy R. Thompson. an[ointed]. by Patty Sessions[.]
Nancy Winchester born May 21. 1795 W[ashed]. by S[ophronia]. M. Harmon anointed by B[athsheba]. W. Smith[.]
Jane Price born [blank] 1813 W[ashed]. by S[ophronia]. M. Harmon anointed by Leonora Taylor[.]
Esther Ann Gheen born Dec[ember] 24. 1801 W[ashed]. by Jane Sherwood anointed by B[athsheba]. W. Smith[.]
Maria Weiler born March 28. 1802 W[ashed]. by S[ophronia]. M. Harmon an[ointed]. by Leonora Taylor[.]
Hannah Pierce, born June 4. 1802 W[ashed]. by M[ercy]. R. Thompson an[ointed]. by Patty Sessions[.]
Amanda S. Gheen Born Jan[uar]y 18. 1830 W[ashed]. by Jane Sherwood an[ointed]. by Leonora Taylor[.]
Ann Alice Gheen born Dec[embe]r 20. 1828 W[ashed]. by Jane Sherwood an[ointe]d. by B[athsheba]. W. Smith[.]
Rachel Sanders born Sept[ember] 14. 1807 W[ashed]. by S[ophronia]. M. Harmon an[ointe]d. by Leonora Taylor[.]
Mary H. Pierce born Nov[embe]r. 29. 1821 W[ashed]. by M[ercy]. R. Thompson an[ointe]d. by B[athsheba]. W. Smith[.]
Margaret P. Whiteside born April 19. 1823 W[ashed]. by M[ercy]. R. Thompson, an[ointe]d. by Leonora Taylor[.]
Nancy Maria Winchester, B[orn]. Aug[ust] 10. 1828 W[ashed]. by M[ercy]. R. Thompson an[ointe]d. by B[athsheba]. W. Smith[.]

Finished at half past 2.

[A]t half past 2 o'clock [we] commenced receiving into the lower and middle departments those whose names are recorded on the two foregoing pages—whose washing commenced at 20 m[inutes] past one o'clock.

The following persons officiated in the upper department. viz;

John Taylor	as	No.	1.
P[arley]. P. Pratt	"	"	2
C[harles]. C. Rich	"	"	3

In the middle department. as follows

Orson Hyde	as	No	1
B[enjamin]. L. Clapp	"	"	2
F[ranklin]. D. Richards	"	"	3
W[illiam]. W. Phelps	"	"	4

George A. Smith " prompter—

At a quarter past 6 o'clock Pres[ident]. [Brigham] Young left the Temple for the purpose of going a short distance to marry a couple.

The Weather this day has been very cold, it being very difficult to keep comfortably warm in the Temple, the wind blowing very strong from the North West all day.

At half past 4 o'clock [we] commenced the business of receiving into the upper department those whose washing commenced at 20 minutes past 1. in the following order, vis;

Stephen Winchester by H[eber]. C. Kimball[.]
Nancy Winchester by her husband & H[eber]. C. K[imball].
Nancy Maria Winchester by H[eber]. C. Kimball[.]
Esther Ann Gheen by H[eber]. C. Kimball[.]
Ann Alice Gheen " H[eber]. C. Kimball[.]
Amanda S. Gheen " H[eber]. C. Kimball[.]
Saber Durfee " H[eber]. C. Kimball[.]
Elijah Malin " H[eber]. C. K[imball].
Catharine Malin " H[eber]. C. K[imball]. & her husband.
Robert Pierce " Pres[ident]. B[righam]. Young[.]
Hannah Pierce " Robert Pierce & B[righam]. Young[.]
Sarah Malin " Brigham Young[.]
Eliza Ann Malin " Brigham Young[.]
Mary H. Pierce " Brigham Young[.]
Margaret P. Whitesides " " " [.]
Ellis M. Sanders " " " [.]
Rachel Sanders; " " " [and] her husband[.]
Charles Price " Benj[amin]. F. Clapp[.]
Jane Price " " " " [and] C[harles]. Price[.]
Jacob Weiler " " " " [.]
Maria Weiler " " " " & J[acob]. Weiler[.]
Stephen Winchester Jr " H[eber]. C. Kimball[.]

These were passed through at half past 6. Franklin D. Richards officiated as prompter.

[A]t 6 o'clock a report came to Pres[ident]. Young that Theodore Turley had arrived in town, being liberated on bail of 250 dollars for his appearance at court next term; provided a bill of indictment should be found. report brought by Henry W. Miller.

In the Male department the following persons were washed and anointed, commencing at 20 minutes before 5 o'clock, vis; H[igh]. Priests

David Pettigrew,	born	July 29, 1791
Caleb Baldwin	"	Sept[ember] 2, 1791

These were washed by William Crosby and John Brown, and anointed by Isaac Morley and Samuel Bent.

Of the quorum of Seventies,

Thomas M. Pearson born Aug[us]t. 29. 1827

[W]ashed by John Lytle and John Brown, and anointed by Jedediah M. Grant.

Finished at 4 m[inutes]. before 5.

In the female department commencing at 20 minutes past 5, the following persons were washed and anointed—viz;

Elizabeth Pettigrew born Oct[ober]. 14. 1791 W[ashed]. by M[ercy]. R. Thompson, anointed by Leonora Taylor[.]

Nancy Baldwin born Sept[ember] 14. 1798 W[ashed]. by M[ercy]. R. Thompson, an[ointed]. by Bathsheba W. Smith[.]

Finished at half past 5.

At 10 minutes before 6, [we] commenced receiving into the lower and middle departments the above mentioned five persons[,] the following persons officiating, viz. in the upper department, John Taylor as No. 1. P[arley]. P. Pratt as No. 2 L[ucius]. N. Scovil as No. 3.

In the middle department as follows, viz C[harles]. C. Rich No. 1. Erastus Snow No. 2. Aaron Johnson No. 3, W[illiam]. W. Phelps No. 4 George A. Smith as prompter—

[A]t 10 minutes past 7 [we] commenced receiving the foregoing persons into the upper department in the following order. viz;

David Pettigrew,	by	John Taylor[.]
Elizabeth Pettigrew	"	John Taylor & D[avid]. Pettigrew[.]
Caleb Baldwin	"	John Taylor[.]
Nancy Baldwin	"	" " & C[aleb]. Baldwin[.]
Thomas M. Pearson	"	John Taylor[.]

Finished at 23 minutes before 8. Erastus Snow officiated as prompter.

Pres[ident]. Young returned at 10 minutes before 8 o'clock.

The exercises of the day being over, Pres[ident]. Young retired to bed about 12 o'clock.

In consequence of the great pressure of business during the week past it has been decided to devote Saturday to the purpose of washing the robes and other garments, which had been used in the business of initiating those who had come in through the vail—but there being a general desire in the minds of all those who had officiated in the ordinances particularly the Sisters, that the work should not cease, it was afterwards determined that the clothes should be washed this night, and it was accordingly done, by the labors of several sisters, taking up the greater part of the night.

—William Clayton, Diary, kept for Heber C. Kimball.

This morning is remarkably windy and blustery, as much as any day this winter before — Notwithstanding it is ~~y~~ quite comfortable in the Temple. at 5 A.M. fires were up in the preparation and washing rooms ready for operation but owing to the inclemency of the weather the candidates were not on hand as soon usual. The following were selected to officiate for the day. Namely Isaac Morley Samuel Bent Phineas Young W[illiam] Crosby Daniel S. Carns Jesse D. Hunter Aaron Johnson & Lady H[enry]. G. Sherwood & Lady C[harles] C Rich & Lady L[ucius]. N. Scovil[,] High Priest[s,] and Hosea Stout [illegible] W[illia]m Pitt Louis Robbins John L. Butler Seventis. The Twelve & their Clerks were considered to be on hands all the while, also Pres[ident] Jos[eph] Young Henry Harriman B[enjamin] L Clapp J[edediah]. M. Grant & J[ohn]. D Lee[, who] has been on hand all the time & will likely be — the whole arrangement as matter of course is conducted by the direction [of] Pres[iden]t Brigham Young.

25 M[inutes] P[ast]. 9 AM	Wilber J. Earl 46	March 29 1817
	David S. Jackson 47	Dec 4 1814
	John Brown 48 through mistake	
50 M[inutes] P[ast]. 1.00	Stephen Winchester	Sept. 21 1820
	Cha[rle]s Price	/ 1800

The 4 men above written were washed and anointed by Pres[ident]. J[oseph] Young [and] Henry Herriman[;] (~~Anointed by~~) John Lytle & [illegible] ~~by~~ the 2 latter officiated in washing —

[At] 12 M[inutes]. to 5 Thomas M Pearson ^49^ was washed & anointed by the Persons above refered too. five Seventies with their Wives only were take[n] through to day. The extra company that we intended to take through to night was omited on accounted of the extreme whistling [?] of the weather. we however have in contemplation a company for the evening on the Morrow. Pres[ident] J[oseph] Young Returned home. Pres[ident] J[edediah]. M. Grant spent the Night here [and] the remainder of the [seventies] & Twelve also went home with the exception of Pres[ident] B[righam]. Young John Robbins John L Butter David Candland Daniel Carns to midnight & J[ohn]. D. Lee — who tarried over the Night in the Temple. Some of the Sisters remained until [they finished the] washing some of the garments preparatory for the morrow. It is now ten o clock at Night & we are [illegible] with intense interest at the reading of [illegible; see below.]

—Seventies Record, Book B.

[O]n my [John D. Lee's] return to the temple I called in at Br[other] J Beans & notified Nancy his daughter to cleanse her body by washing in clear water purify her heart by humbling her self in fasting and Prayer & come up to the Temple and receive her anointing and washing[.] She manifested some dissatisfaction and said that she chose to wait a little longer until her mind should be reconciled[.] after laying the order of the Kingdom before her I told her to do as she pleased but that my garments should be cleansed from her sins & left them[.] I returned to the House of the Lord where I found Pres[ident] B[righam] Young Joseph Young J[edediah] M Grant John L Butler David Candlin ——— Lewis Robbins & some few of the Sisters who spent the night in the Temple[.] It was 2 PM when I entered the temple[.] Perhaps 2 hours were spent in reading and listening to a California pamphlet that have a pleasing description of the situation and locality of the country[.][5] At ½ past 12 we retired to rest.

—John D. Lee, Diary.

On Saturday the 18th of Dec[ember] 1845, having been called on by the Council of the Twelve Apostles I [Abraham Owen Smoot] went to the Temple in Nauvoo to receive my endowments, at the hour of 8 o'clock in the morning I was received into the preparation rooms, with several others of my brethren, and I was there prepared to be conducted into the washing and anointing room, where I received my washings in clean and pure water, preparatory to my anointing, which I received under the hands of Samuel Bent, President of the High Council. I was then presented with a garment, b[e]aring the marks of Priesthood, which I was in-

5. This is probably Lansford W. Hastings's *Emigrants' Guide to Oregon and California* (Cincinnati, 1845), which was used by the Donner Party in 1846.

structed to wear as a prevenation from evil. I was now prepared for the reception of further ordinances in the House of the Lord which were to me Sublime, great and glorious, making on my mind endurable impressions, or as the prophet said "engraving upon the heart & writ[t]en upon its inner parts &c." After I passed through these sublime ordinances I was then conducted by Elder John Taylor to his private room and invited to spend the evening with him in company of my wife [Margaret T. Smoot], which we did with pleasure. During the afternoon I was called upon by the Secretary of the Temple to return next morning to the Temple, to assist them in the labor in the holy place, with which request I gladly complied.

—Abraham Owen Smoot, Diary, LDS Archives.

....

Sixty-six persons were administered to in the Temple. I [Brigham Young] retired to bed about midnight.

In consequence of the great pressure of business during the past week, it had been decided to devote Saturday [December 20] to the purpose of washing robes and garments used, but there being a general desire in the minds of all those officiating in the ordinances that the work should not cease, it was determined that the clothes should be washed during the night.

—"Manuscript History of Brigham Young,"
in *History of the Church,* 7:547.

....

Nauvoo temple endowments performed on this date for:

First Company: William A. Sanger, Mary Sanger, Abraham O. Smoot, Margaret T. Smoot, Mary Amanda Utley, Loisa Sanger, Jacob Zundell, Sarah Zundell, Solomon Chamberlain, Emeline Waterman, Orice Burnham, Charles Hulet, Margaret Hulet, Wilber J. Earl, Harriet Earl, George Lyman, Daniel S. Jackson, Sylvester Hulet, and Rosina Hyman.

Second Company: Alexander McRae, Marinda Bennett, Mary Pew, Benjamin F. Johnson, Melissa Johnson, Alphonzo Young, Nancy Young, William Parks, Millesant Parks, Lyman Stoddard, Ruth Stoddard, John Stiles, Persis Stiles, David D. Yearsley, Mary Ann Yearsley, Naham Curtis, Delia Curtis, Thomas Travis, Mary Travis, and Ormond Butler.

Third Company: Stephen Winchester, Nancy Winchester, Nancy/Maria Winchester, Esther Ann Gheen, Ann Alice Gheen, Amanda S. Gheen, Jabez Durfee, Elijah Malin, Catharine Malin, Robert Pierce, Hannah Pierce, Sarah Malin, Eliza Ann Malin, Mary H. Pierce, Margaret P. Whiteside, Ellis M. Sanders, Rachel Sanders, Charles Price, Jane Price, Jacob Weiler, Maria Weiler, and Stephen Winchester Jr.

Fourth Company: David Pettigrew, Elizabeth Pettigrew, Caleb Baldwin, Nancy Baldwin, and Thomas M. Pearson.

—Summary of information compiled by the Temple Index Bureau, *Nauvoo Temple Endowment Register: 10 December 1845 to 8 February 1846.*

Friday, December 19, 1845

Pres[ident]. [Brigham] Young having slept in the Temple was present at the appointed time for commencing operations—and soon afterwards proceeded to appoint men to the various stations— The following persons reported themselves ready for duty, and received their appointment

Brigham Young — H[eber]. C. Kimball
George A. Smith
Amasa Lyman — Orson Hyde
Joseph Young No. 1 Middle dep[artmen]t / anointing
Orson Pratt
George Miller
John Smith, Patr[iarch]., Phineas H. Young

Jedediah M. Grant	as No. 1	}	also anointing
L[ucius]. N. Scovil	" " 2	}	upper department
John Scott	" " 3	}	
Aaron Johnson	" " 2	}	
C[harles]. C. Rich anointing &	" " 3	}	middle departmen[t]
W[illiam]. W. Phelps	" " 4	}	
H[enry]. G. Sherwood	Marshall		
Daniel Carn	to remove garments		
John L. Butler	to tend to fires		
Hosea Stout	Waterman		
Jesse D. Hunt	Waterman		
William Crosby }			
John Brown }	washing		
A[braham]. O. Smoot	anointing		
Alexander McRae	messenger		
Erastus Snow	messenger		
Benj[ami]n. L. Clapp			

Jesse P. Harmon Washer
F[ranklin]. D. Richards Prompter

At 15 minutes before 9 o'clock [we] commenced in the male department, washing & anointing and the following High Priests were administered unto viz;

Caleb Haight.	born	Aug[us]t. 28. 1778
Harvey Green	"	Dec[embe]r. 4. 1806
Lorenzo Snow	"	April 3. 1814
~~washing by~~ also		
Elder John Pea,	born	July 11. 1783

Washed by William Crosby & John Brown anointed by C[harles]. C. Rich and Abraham O. Smoot.

Also, the quorum of the Seventies

Isaac C. Haight,	born	May 27. 1813
William Anderson	"	March 29. 1809
Vernon H. Bruce	"	August 18. 1815
Hector C. Haight	"	January 17, 1810

Washed by Jesse P. Harmon & John Brown[;] Anointed by Joseph Young & J[edediah]. M. Grant.

Finished at 25 minutes past 9—

In the female department washing & anointing commenced at half past 8 o'clock, as follows, viz;

Lydia Moon, born March 17. 1783 W[ashed]. by M[ercy]. R[achel]. Thompson. An[ointed]. by Bathsheba W. Smith[.]

Elizabeth Pea born May 17. 1783. W[ashed]. by Patty Sessions. An[ointed]. by Sarah D. Rich.

Jane F. Pea, born Nov[embe]r. 17. 1820. W[ashed]. by Patty Sessions — An[ointed]. by Patty Sessions[.]

Eliza Ann Haight born Oct[ober] 22. 1815. W[ashed]. by Patty Sessions. An[ointed]. by B[athsheba]. W. Smith[.]

Julia Ann Van Orden born Oct[ober] 6. 1805 W[ashed]. By M[ercy]. R[achel]. Thompson An[ointed]. by B[athsheba]. W. Smith[.]

Mercy Ann Bruce born April 27. 1813 W[ashed]. by Mercy R. Thompson. An[ointed]. by Sarah D. Rich[.]

Emeline T. Anderson born Sept[ember] 25. 1812 W[ashed]. by M[ercy]. R[achel]. Thompson An[ointed]. by B[athsheba]. W. Smith[.]

Julia Haight — born January 19. 1810 W[ashed]. by M[ercy].

R[achel]. Thompson. An[ointed]. by Sarah D. Rich[.]

Jane Ann Green born November 13. 1813 W[ashed]. by Patty Sessions An[ointed]. by B[athsheba]. W. Smith[.]

Sarah M. Johnson born Mar[ch]. 17. 1824 Wa[shed]. by M[ercy]. R[achel]. Thompson An[ointed] by B[athsheba]. W. Smith[.]

Alice ~~Walwerk~~ ^Hurst^ born Feb[ruar]y 18. 1809— W[ashed]. by Patty Sessions. An[ointed]. by Patty Sessions.

Finished at 33. min[utes] past 9.

Bell rung at 5 minutes past 10, and [we] commenced receiving into the lower & middle departments the persons who have been washed & anointed this morning—the following persons officiating, viz;

Jedediah M. Grant.	as No. 1	}	
L[ucius]. N. Scovil.	" " 2	}	upper dep[artmen]t
John Scott	" " 3	}	
Joseph Young	as No. 1	}	
Aaron Johnson	" " 2	}	middle dep[artmen]t
C[harles]. C. Rich	" " 3	}	
W[illiam]. W. Phelps	" " 4	}	
F[ranklin]. D. Richards	prompter.}		

Pres[ident]. [Brigham] Young left the Temple a short time at 12 m[inutes]. past 11. in company with Bishop George Miller, and Reuben Miller, the latter intending to return to his home in the Eastern part of the State on special business— He soon after took his departure.

At 20 m[inutes]. before 12 [we] commenced receiving into the upper department, in the following order, viz;

Lorenzo Snow	by	L[ucius]. N. Scovil[.]
Alice ~~Walwerk / Hurst~~	"	" " [.]
Sarah M. Johnson	"	Aaron Johnson.
John Pea	"	Charles C. Rich[.]
Jane F. Pea	"	~~John Pea &~~ L[ucius]. N. Scovil[.]
Elizabeth Pea	"	C[harles]. C. Rich & John Pea[.]
Harvey Green	"	L[ucius]. N. Scovil[.]
Jane Ann Green	"	Harvey Green & [Lucius N.] Scovil[.]
William Anderson	"	Orson Spencer[.]
Emeline T. Anderson	"	" " & W[illiam]. Anderson[.]
Caleb Haight	"	O[rson]. Spencer[.]
Vernon H. Bruce	"	" " [.]
Mercy Ann Bruce	"	" " & Vernon H. [Bruce.]

Hector C. Haight	"	"	"	"	[.]
Julia Haight	"	"	"	& H[eber]. C. K[imball].	
Isaac C. Haight	"	"	"	[.]	
Elisa Ann Haight	"	"	"	& Isaac Haight[.]	
Julia Ann Van Orden	"	"	"	[.]	
Lydia Moon	"	"	"	[.]	

Finished at half past 1 o'clock—F[ranklin]. D. Richards and William Burton officiating as prompters—

Washing and Anointing in the male department commenced again at 26 m[inutes]. before 12. William Crosby and John Brown washed and Abraham O. Smoot and Peter Haws anointed the following High Priests, viz;

Robert Stone,	born	June 7. 1777
Wandel Mace	"	Feb[ruar]y. 19 1808

also the following named Elder

Edward Miller	born	Nov[ember]. 22. 1816,

also High Priest

Addison Everett,	born	Oct[ober]. 10, 1805

The following named persons of [the] quorum of Seventies were washed by Jesse P. Harmon and John Kay—and anointed by B[enjamin]. L. Clapp and J[edediah]. M. Grant—viz;

George W. Brayton	born	Sept[ember]. 3, 1814
Zimri H. Baxter	"	Feb[ruar]y 16. 1807
Alvin Winegar	"	May 13. 1816
William Carmichael	"	Aug[us]t 15. 1804
Stephen M. Farnsworth	"	Oct[obe]r. 8. 1809
Joseph S. Scofield	"	August 2. 1809
William Gray	"	December 30. 1811
W. Waterman Phelps	"	January 23. 1823

Finished at 21 m[inutes]. past 12.

In the department, Female, washing and anointing commenced at 3 m[inutes]. past 11, and the following persons were washed and anointed.

Marcia Abbott born Nov[embe]r 26. 1811 W[ashed]. by Patty Sessions. An[ointed]. by B[athsheba]. W. Smith[.]

Martha Bowker born Jan[uar]y 22. 1824 W[ashed]. by Mercy R[achel]. Thompson. An[ointed]. by Leonora Taylor[.]

Julia Stone. born March 27. 1803 W[ashed]. by M[ercy]. R[achel]. Thompson, An[ointed]. by Patty Sessions[.]

Sarah Jane Witte born Feb[ruar]y 1. 1821 W[ashed]. by Patty

Sessions, An[ointed]. by B[athsheba]. W. Smith[.]

Martha Knight born March 17. 18[blank] W[ashed]. by M[ercy]. R[achel]. Thompson An[ointed]. by B[athsheba]. W. Smith[.]

Sarah M. Cleveland born Oct[ober]. 20. 1788 W[ashed]. by M[ercy]. R[achel]. Thompson An[ointed] [by] B[athsheba]. W. Smith[.]

Phebe Graves born Oct[ober]. 29, 1788 W[ashed]. by Patty Sessions anointed by Leonora Taylor[.]

Mary P. Brayton born Sept[ember] 13 1818 W[ashed]. by Patty Sessions an[ointed]. by Leonora Taylor[.]

Margaret Riding born May 13. 1819 W[ashed]. by M[ercy]. R[achel]. Thompson An[ointed]. by Leonora Taylor[.]

Margaret Mace born Oct[ober]. 23. 1811 W[ashed]. by M[ercy]. R[achel]. Thompson An[ointed]. by Leonora Taylor[.]

Mary Ann Carmichael, born Oct[ober] 29. 1808 W[ashed]. by M[ercy]. R[achel]. Thompson an[ointed]. by B[athsheba]. W. Smith[.]

Julia Ann Farnsworth born May 1. 1819 W[ashed]. by Patty Sessions an[ointed]. by Leonora Taylor[.]

Margaret Ann Clapp born Aug[ust]. 13 1775 W[ashed]. by M[ercy]. R[achel]. Thompson, An[ointe]d. by B[athsheba]. W. Smith[.]

Eunice Baxter born March 1. 1811. W[ashed]. by Patty Sessions An[ointed]. by Leonora Taylor[.]

Orpha M. Everett born March 25. 1814 W[ashed]. by M[ercy]. R[achel]. Thompson An[ointed]. by B[athsheba]. W. Smith[.]

Mary Winegar born July 6. 1818 W[ashed]. by M[ercy]. R[achel]. Thompson An[ointed]. by Leonora Taylor[.]

Lydia C. Phelps born Jan[uar]y 14, 1827 W[ashed]. by Patty Sessions, an[ointed]. by B[athsheba]. W. Smith[.]

Clarissa A. Scofield born Nov[embe]r. 9. 1820 W[ashed]. by M[ercy]. R[achel]. Thompson. An[ointed]. by Patty Sessions[.]

Clarissa Miller b[orn]. Sept[ember] 12. 1817 W[ashed]. by Patty Sessions. An[ointed]. by Leonora Taylor[.]

Finished at 25 minutes before 1.

At 15 minutes past one, [we] commenced receiving into the lower and middle departments those who were last washed and anointed. the following persons officiating, viz;

Joseph Young	as	No.	1. }	
B[enjamin]. L. Clapp	"	"	2. }	in the upper dep[artmen]t
L[ucius]. N. Scovil	"	"	3. }	
J[edediah]. M. Grant	"	"	1 }	
John Scott	"	"	2 }	in the middle dep[artment].
Aaron Johnson	"	"	3 }	
W[illiam]. W. Phelps	"	"	4 }	
Franklin D. Richards	prompter—			

At 3 o'clock [we] commenced receiving into the upper department the company last washed and anointed, in the following order, viz

George W. Brayton by John Taylor[.]
Mary P. Brayton, by her husband & J[ohn]. Taylor[.]
Stephen M. Farnsworth by John Taylor[.]
Julia Ann Farnsworth by S[tephen]. M. F[arnsworth]. & J[ohn]. Taylor[.]
Margaret Ann Clapp by B[enjamin]. L. Clapp[.]
Joseph S. Scofield by John Taylor[.]
Clarissa A. Scofield by her husband & J[ohn]. Taylor[.]
Robert Stone by John Taylor[.]
Julia Stone by R[obert]. Stone & J[ohn]. Taylor[.]
Martha Knight by H[eber]. C. Kimball[.]
W[illiam]. Waterman Phelps by H[eber]. C. Kimball[.]
Alvin Winegar by H[eber]. C. Kimball[.]
Lydia C. Phelps by H[eber]. C. Kimball & W[illiam]. W. P[helps].
Marcia Abbott by H[enry]. G. Sherwood[.]
William Gray by B[enjamin]. L. Clapp[.]
Mary Winegar by Alvin Winegar & [Benjamin] Clapp [.]
[blank] by B[enjamin]. L. Clapp[.]
Addison Everett by C[harles]. C. Rich[.]
Orpha M. Everett by A[ddison]. Everett & C[harles]. C. R[ich].
Zimri H. Baxter by C[harles]. C. Rich[.]
Eunice Baxter by Zimri Baxter & C[harles]. C. R[ich].
Sarah Jane Witte by C[harles]. C. Rich[.]
Phebe Graves by Samuel Bent.
Sarah M. Cleveland. by C[harles]. C. Rich[.]
William Carmichael by C[harles]. C. Rich[.]

Mary Ann Carmichael by W[illiam]. Carm[ichael]. & C[harles]. C. Rich[.]
Edward Miller by C[harles]. C. Rich[.]
Clarissa Miller by E[dward]. Miller and C[harles]. C. Rich[.]
Wandel Mace by C[harles]. C. Rich[.]
Margaret Mace by W[andel]. Mace & C[harles]. C. Rich[.]
Martha Bowker by Brigham Young.

At 27 m[inutes]. past 2 [we] commenced washing in the male department, and the following High Priests were washed by William Crosby and John Brown, and were anointed by Abraham O. Smoot and Peter Haws, viz;

David H. Redfield	born	Aug[ust] 31. 1807
Stephen Longstroth.	"	June 29 1787
Henry Wilson	"	May 16. 1803

Also the following of the quorum of Seventies, were washed by Jesse P. Harmon and Alexander McRae

Jonathan Crosby	born	July 20. 1807
Jeremiah Robey	"	April 19. 1809
William Symons	"	April 25 1797.

[T]hese were anointed by Joseph Young and B[enjamin]. L. Clapp

Isaac Allred	born	June 28 1813
Horace B. Owen	"	" 23. 1819
George Laub	"	Oct[ober]. 5 1814
Samuel Brown	"	Feb[ruar]y 1. 1801
Asahel A. Lathrop	"	Dec[embe]r 24. 1810

[T]hese were washed by [Jesse P.] Harmon and [Alexander] McRae, and anointed by Joseph Young and J[edediah]. M. Grant.

Finished at half past 3.

At 17 min[utes]. past 2. [we] commenced in the female department washing and anointing the following persons. viz;

Frances Wilson. born Feb[ruar]y 23. 1819 W[ashed]. by M[ercy]. R[achel]. Thompson an[ointed]. by Leonora Taylor[.]
Caroline Crosby born Jan[uar]y 5. 1807 W[ashed]. by Polly Zeruiah Johnson An[ointed]. by Patty Sessions[.]
Helenora Symons born Nov[embe]r. 26. 1794 or 5 W[ashed]. by M[ercy]. R[achel]. Thompson An[ointed]. by Leonora Taylor[.]
Philena Fulton born April 24 1797. W[ashed]. by P[olly]. Z. Johnson anointed by Patty Sessions[.]

Fanny Redfield born April 27. 1811 W[ashed]. by M[ercy]. R[achel]. Thompson an[ointed]. by Patty Sessions[.]
Ruth Robey born June 26. 1816 W[ashed]. by P[olly]. Z. Johnson, an[ointed]. by Leonora Taylor[.]
Charlotte Squires b[orn]. Nov[ember]. 19. 1825 W[ashed]. by M[ercy]. R[achel]. Thompson An[ointed]. by Leonora Taylor[.]
Adeline Hendrickson b[orn]. March 8. 1812 W[ashed]. by P[olly]. Z. Johnson An[ointed]. by Patty Sessions[.]
Julia Ann Allred born Feb[ruar]y 9. 1815 W[ashed]. by P[olly]. Z. Johnson, An[ointed]. by Leonora Taylor[.]
Abigail Woolsey born Sep[tember] 13. 1786 W[ashed]. by P[olly]. Z. Johnson an[ointed]. by Leonora Taylor[.]
Sally Ann Owens born Feb[ruar]y 21. 1829 W[ashed]. by M[ercy]. R[achel]. Thompson an[ointed]. by Patty Sessions[.]
Huldah Barnes born Oct[ober] 1, 1806 W[ashed]. by P[olly]. Z. Johnson. An[ointed]. [by] Leonora Taylor[.]
Lucretia Fulton born Oct[ober]. 26. 1818 W[ashed]. by P[olly]. Z. Johnson An[ointed]. by Patty Sessions[.]
Lydia Maria Brown born July 29. 1816 W[ashed]. by M[ercy]. R[achel]. Thompson An[ointed]. by Patty Sessions[.]
Jane Lathrop, born Nov[embe]r. 12. 1820 W[ashed]. by M[ercy]. R[achel]. Thompson An[ointed]. [by] Leonora Taylor[.]
Hannah Peacock born Sept[ember] 25. 1822 W[ashed]. by P[olly]. Z. Johnson, An[ointed]. by Patty Sessions[.]
Mary Ann Oakley, born March 20. 1821 W[ashed]. by M[ercy]. R[achel]. Thompson. An[ointed]. by Leonora Taylor[.]

Finished at 15 m[inutes]. past 4.

At half past 4 the bell rung, and those who are above mentioned were received in to the lower & middle departments, the following persons officiating, viz.

John Taylor	as	No.	1	}	
L[ucius]. N. Scovil	"	"	2	}	in upper dep[artmen]t
John Scott	"	"	3	}	
John Taylor	as	No.	1	}	
Alpheus Cutler	"	"	2	}	in middle dep[artmen]t
Jesse D. Hunter	"	"	3	}	
W[illiam]. W. Phelps	"	"	4	}	

F[ranklin]. D. Richards as Prompter—

At 15 minutes past 6, [we] commenced receiving into the upper department the company last washed and anointed—in the following order

William Symons by John Taylor[.]
Helenora Symons by W[illiam]. Symons & J[ohn]. Taylor[.]
Mary Ann Oakley by John Taylor[.]
Samuel Brown by L[ucius]. N. Scovil[.]
Lydia Maria Brown by S[amuel]. Brown & L[ucius]. N. S[covil].
Huldah Barnes by Jesse P. Harmon[.]
Adeline Hendrickson by Lorenzo Snow[.]
Charlotte Squires by Lorenzo Snow[.]
David H. Redfield by L[ucius]. N. Scovil[.]
Fanny M. Redfield by D[avid]. H. Redfield & [Lucius] Scovil[.]
Asahel A. Lathrop by L[ucius]. N. Scovil[.]
Jane Lathrop by A[sahel]. A. Lathrop & [Lucius] Scovil[.]
Hannah Peacock by A[sahel]. A. Lathrop & [Lucius] Scovil[.]
Jonathan Crosby by Aaron Johnson[.]
Caroline Crosby by Jonathan Crosby & A[aron]. J[ohnson].
Henry H. Wilson by John D. Lee[.]
Frances Wilson by H[enry]. H. W[ilson]. & J[ohn]. D. L[ee].
Abigail Woolsey by John D. Lee[.]
Horace B. Owens by John D. Lee[.]
Sally Ann Owen by H[orace]. B. Owen and J[ohn]. D. Lee[.]
George Laub by John D. Lee[.]
Lucretia Fulton by Stephen Winchester & [John D.] Lee[.]
Philena Fulton by " " " " [.]
Stephen Longstroth by J[ohn]. D. Lee[.]
Isaac Allred by J[ohn]. D. Lee[.]
Julia Ann Allred by Isaac Allred & [John D.] Lee[.]
Jeremiah Roby by John D. Lee[.]
Ruth Roby by Jeremiah Roby & [John D.] Lee[.]

Finished at ¼ before 9. Aaron Johnson officiating as prompter—

[A]t 6 o'clock [we] commenced washing & anointing in the Male department, the following persons belonging to the quorum of Seventies—viz

Jackson Smith	born	April 2. 1815
Salmon Warner	"	Oct[obe]r 27. 1798
Gad Yale	"	Aug[us]t. 21. 1790
Moses Martin	"	June 1. 1812

These were washed by John Lytle & Chauncy G. Webb, and anointed by

Joseph Young & J[ediah]. M. Grant. finished at 20 m[inutes]. past 6.

In the female department at 25 minutes before 7 [we] commenced washing & anointing the following persons viz;

Aphia W. Yale born Aug[us]t 28. 1795 W[ashed]. by M[ercy]. R[achel]. Thompson, anointed by Leonora Taylor[.]

Mary Smith, born September 13. 1818. W[ashed]. by Sophronia M. Harmon. an[ointed]. by Patty Sessions[.]

Julia P. Martin born March 5. 1815 W[ashed]. by Patty Sessions anointed by Patty Sessions[.]

Rebecca Warner born June 2 1807 W[ashed]. by S[ophronia]. M. Harmon anointed by Leonora Taylor[.]

Ruth Bosier born April 12, 1824 W[ashed]. by M[ercy]. R[achel]. Thompson anointed by Leonora Taylor[.]

Finished at 15 m[inutes]. after 7.

At 15 m[inutes]. past 7. [we] commenced receiving the above into the lower & middle departments.

Joseph Young	as	No.	1.	}
J[ediah]. M. Grant	"	"	2	} upper dep[artmen]t
L[evi]. W. Hancock	"	"	3	}
B[enjamin]. L. Clapp	as	No.	1	}
Henry Herriman	"	"	2	}
A[lbert]. P. Rockwood		"	3	} middle dep[artmen]t
W[illiam]. W. Phelps		"	4	}

F[ranklin]. D. Richards Prompter—

At half past 9 [we] commenced receiving into the upper department those whose washing & anointing commenced at 6 o'clock in the following order— viz;

Gad Yale by John D. Lee[.]

Aphia W. Yale by Gad Yale & L[ucius]. N. Scovil[.]

Jackson Smith by L[ucius]. N. Scovil[.]

Mary Smith by J[ackson]. Smith & L[ucius]. N. Scovil[.]

Salmon Warner by L[ucius]. N. Scovil[.]

Rebecca Warner by Salmon Warner & [Lucius N.] Scovil[.]

Moses Martin by J[ohn]. D. Lee[.]

Julia C. Martin by M[oses]. Martin & [John D.] Lee[.]

[F]inished at 10 O. clock. D[avid]. Candland officiating as prompter—

At 7 o'clock the following persons met in Elder [Heber C.] Kimball's room, clothed in priestly garments, and offered up thanks to our Heavenly

Father for the deliverance of Theodore Turley and others, that were in bondage by our enemies[.]

At 20 minutes before 8 the following persons met in council in Eld[er]. Kimballs room and made a selection of High Priests to be washed and anointed, [those in council being as follows,] viz. B[righam]. Young, H[eber]. C. Kimball Orson Hyde, Orson Pratt—Amasa Lyman, George A. Smith & George Miller. Pres[ident]. Young asked the question, Is it wisdom to send Hosea Stout and Jesse D. Hunter to England? Elder Hyde answered that the people in England expected that any one sent from America would be expected to be something more than ordinary— The subject was dropped at this point.

—William Clayton, Diary, kept for Heber C. Kimball.

....

This morning is quite ^cold^ indeed, it is now 9 o clock and the washing and anointing is about to commence, in both departments. — Pres[ident] Jos[eph] Young J[edediah] M Grant, [Henry] Herriman & B[enjamin] L Clapp & J[ohn] D L[ee] clerk here all the time as matter of course. The Names that were Selected to act in the different department were read and each man recived his appointment from Pres[ident] B[righam]. Young togeather with such instructions as he deemed necessary — for the benefit of the cause. the day before[,] said he[,] we have been thronged to that extent that it was almost impossible to move without running against some fifteen or 20 persons who were gawking round where they had no buissness & lauling [lolling?] & braking down Mahogany chairs worth $5.00 and tearing open the curtains & gazing in where they had no right. I dont ^know^ said he but what we will have to build plank P[ar]tition[s] before spring that men may learn manners[. If] one tenth Portion of the men that were here yesterday had been away[,] we would not be in one an others way — Now brethren let every man attend to that which is commited to his care and let other men [leave] matters alone and all will be well.

[See pages 95-97 for excerpted portion.]

The opperations of the day closed at ½ Past 11 at Night where as usual the persons who officiated principally retired to their separate [?] homes [illegible.] after all things were secure for the night, came Martin [with] his violin & his [illegible] Notes which riveborate [reverberate] back and forth within this sacred Edifice[,] following [with] ^heart^ gladness & dance before the Lord but as usual perfect ^order^ and decorum was observed in our little recreation. we truly felt grateful to our Eternal

[Washings and anointings for Friday, December 19, 1845]

The folling Person were washed and anointed 5 M. P 9. AM Namely

Isaac Haight	50	born	May 27, 1813
Wm A^n^derson	51	"	March 29 1803[?]
Vernon H. Bruce	52	"	Aug 18 1815
Hector C. Haight	53	"	June 17 1810[?]

The above were washed by J. P. Harmon & John Brown ^Anointed by^ J. Young J. M Grant —

	Sisters Names	Wash	Anoint }	born
At ½ past	Elizabeth Haight	{Patty Sessions	B. W. Smith }	Oct. 22 1815
8 in morn	Mary Ann Bruce	{ " "	Sarah D Rich }	April 27 1813
	Emolin T. Anderson	{ " "	B. W. Smith }	Sep 25 1812
	Julia Haight	{M. R. Thompson	S. D. Rich }	Jan 19 1801

I then coppeyed of a List of the Names of all the Seventies by request of Pres Brigham Young this ^he^ wished the better to refreshed his memory & there by aid him in the Selection of those who should pass through the ordinances of endowment first. Notwithstanding he is led by the spirit yet it is nessary that our own exertions skill and ability should be exercised or man would be entirely useless to his creatour.

6 m. 12

At 6 minets before 12 o.c. the following Persons were washed by Pres Harmon & John Kay — and anointed by Pres B. L Clapp & J M Grant Namely

J. W. Boynton born [illegible]

[illegible] Baxter Feb 10 1817 [illegible] May 13th [illegible] Wm Carmichel Augt 15 1804 [illegible]

Friday Dec 19th 1845

	No			
John S. Scofield	59	born Aug 2nd 1809	Wm Gray	Dec 30th 1811
Wm W. Phelps 61		Jan 23 1823 passed through at 21 m past 12		

In the Female Department

3 M p. 11 Mary J Brayton born Sep 13th 1818 W. Patey Sessions A L. Taylor
Mary Carmichael born Oct 29th 1808 w M R Thompson A " "
Julian Farnsworth May 18th 1819 W Patey Sessions A " "
Eunice Baxter Nov 25 1814 " M R Thompson A " "
Mary Winegar July 6th 1818 W " " A " "
Lydia C. Phelps Jan 12th 1824 W P Sessions A B Smith
Clarisa Scofield Nov 9th 1820 " M R Thompson P Sessions

At 25 minets past 2 P.M. comenced in Male department & Terminate as follows
Jonathan Crosby born July 20th 1801
Jeremiah Roby April 19. 1809 Wm Sessions April 25 1797
Isaac Allred 66 born June 28 1813 H. B. Owens June 23 1819
George Laub 67 Oct 5 1814 Samuel Brown Sept 1 1801
Asael ^a^ Lathrop 68 Dec 24 1810 were washed by Pres J P Harmon & A McRae and anointed by Pres Jos Young & J. M. Grant. finish at ½ P 3

in the Female Department

Caroline Crosby born Jan 5 1808 W [illegible] Johnson A. P. Session
Helena Lyman " Nov 26 1794 w. M R Thompson A L Taylor
Ruth Robey June 26. 1816. W [illegible] Johnson & A L Taylor
Julia M. Altez [?] Feb 9th 1815 W " A " "
Abigail Woolsy Sept 13 1786 " " A " "
Sarah Ann Owens Feb 21st 1829 W M R Thompson & P Session

At 6 oclock the last company commenced washing in the Male department —

Jackson Smith 69 April 2nd 1815 {Those Persons on the
Solomon Warner 70 Oct. 28. 1898 {left were washed by John
Gad Rule 71 Aug 21 1790 {Lytle & C. G. Webb & anointed
Moses Martin 72 June 1st 1812 {By Pres Jos. Young & J. M. Grant

In the Female department at 25 minuets before 8. commenced washing & anointing the following Persons to wit.

Aphia W. Rule born Augt 28 1795 W by M R Thompson & A L Taylor
Mary Smith " Sept 16 [?] 1818 W S Harmon & A Patty Sessions
Jane Lathrop " Nov 12 1820 " M R Thompson A L Taylor
Julia Martin " Mar 5 1805 " P Session & A P Session

—Seventies Record, Book B, oversized portion, December 19, 1845.

Benefactor — Pres[ident] B[righam] Young after his exercise felt much pained in his ^ancle^ which seemed [illegible] affiction, Pres[ident] Jos[eph] Young his Brother prepared a composition [of] liquors & [illegible] togeather with the Prayre of Faith which soon conquered and abated the Pain & he fell asleep in a few minets & was soon relieved —

—Seventies Record, Book B.

....

This morning Pres[ident] B[righam] Young after arranging and appointing each man his place in each department he drew the reigns rather closer than they were before[.] today I [John D. Lee] have been closely engaged in writing copying of the names of all the Seventies on the general records of the same[.] My occupation though was in different callings and capacities but [I] generally acted as prompter[.] The work of the anointing continued to near 10-11 at night[.] this evening at about 6 oclock 4 of my family had their washing and anointing namely Abigail Shaffer Lee[,] George L[aub] Lee[,] W B [Owens] Lee[,] & Sarah O[wens] Lee[.] we also after the buisy cares of the day closed we entered into the easy part of the Temple where we again took a little recreation to liven up our spirits while dancing before the Lord[.] The Twelve [apostles] participated in the mirth[.]

—John D. Lee, Diary.

....

About 4 p.m. bro[ther]. [Ezra T.] Benson notified me [Thomas Bullock] to appear at the Temple with my wife [Henrietta] on tomorrow morning at 8 oclock to attend to the ordinances of Washing and Anointing. Afterwards went to the Temple. Saw Pres[ident]. [Brigham] Young and received further instructions.

—Thomas Bullock, Diary.

....

... had prayer with the quorum at night.

—John Taylor, Diary (draft), LDS Archives.

....

I [Brigham Young] appointed the following elders to officiate and labor in the Temple today:

Heber C. Kimball,	George Miller,
George A. Smith,	Phineas H. Young,
Joseph Young,	Lucius N. Scovil,
Aaron Johnson,	John Smith,

W[illia]m. W. Phelps,	Jedediah M. Grant,
Hosea Stout,	John Scott,
W[illia]m. Crosby,	Charles C. Rich,
A[braham]. O. Smoot,	Daniel Garn,
Erastus Snow,	John L. Butler,
Jesse D. Harmon,	John Brown,
Orson Hyde,	Alexander McRae,
Amasa Lyman,	Benj[amin]. L. Clapp,
Orson Pratt,	Franklin D. Richards.

[At] 7 p.m., I met with the Twelve [apostles] in Elder [Heber C.] Kimball's room for prayer; after which we counseled on the propriety of sending certain brethren to England.

Ninety-eight persons received ordinances.

I remained in the Temple.

—"Manuscript History of Brigham Young," in *History of the Church,* 7:547-48.

....

Nauvoo temple endowments performed on this date:

First Company: Lorenzo Snow, Alice Hurst, Sarah M. Johnson, John Pea, Jane F. Pea, Elisabeth Pea, Harvey Green, Jane Ann Green, William Anderson, Emeline T. Anderson, Caleb Haight, Vernon H. Bruce, Mercy Ann Bruce, Hector C. Haight, Julia Haight, Isaac C. Haight, Eliza Ann Haight, Julia Ann Van Orden, and Lydia Moon.

Second Company: George W. Brayton, Mary P. Brayton, Stephen M. Farnsworth, Julia Ann Farnsworth, Margaret Ann Clapp, Joseph S. Scofield, Clarissa A. Scofield, Robert Stone, Julia Stone, Martha Knight, W. Waterman Phelps, Alvin Winegar, Lydia C. Phelps, Marcia Abbott, William Gray, Mary Winegar, Addison Everett, Orpha M. Everett, Zimri H. Baxter, Eunice Baxter, Margaret Riding, Sarah Jane Witte, Phebe Graves, Sarah M. Cleveland, William Carmichael, Mary Ann Carmichael, Edward Miller, Clarissa Miller, Wandel Mace, Margaret Mace, and Martha Bowker.

Third Company: William Symons, Helenora Symons, Mary Ann Oakley, Samuel Brown, Lydia Maria Brown, Huldah Barnes, Adeline Hendrickson, Charlotte Squires, David H. Redfield, Fanny M. Redfield, Asahel A. Lathrop, Jane Lathrop, Hannah Peacock, Jonathan Crosby, Caroline Crosby, Henry H. Wilson, Frances Wilson, Abigail Woolsey, Horace B. Owens, Sally Ann Owens, George Laub, Lucretia Fulton, Philena Fulton, Stephen Longstroth, Isaac Allred, Julia Ann Allred, Jeremiah Roby, and Ruth Roby.

Fourth Company: Gad Yale, Aphia W. Yale, Jackson Smith, Mary Smith, Salmon Warner, Rebecca Warner, Moses Martin, and Julia C. Martin.

—Summary of information compiled by the Temple Index Bureau, *Nauvoo Temple Endowment Register: 10 December 1845 to 8 February 1846*. Editors' note: According to the register, Ruth Bosier was washed and anointed on this date and therefore also probably endowed.

Saturday, December 20, 1845

Pres[ident]. [Brigham] Young having slept in the Temple last night was early at his post, and ~~after~~ dictating in relation to the business of the day, and arranging the workmen in order &c. &c. after which he listened to a reading from Capt[ain]. Fremonts Journal by Franklin D. Richards.[6] in the east room present at the same time [were] the following persons, viz; P[arley]. P. Pratt George A. Smith Orson Pratt, W[illiam]. W. Phelps, J[edediah]. M. Grant, George Miller, C[harles]. C. Rich, John Scott, Daniel Carn, Jesse P. Harmon Hosea Stout, Jesse D. Hunter, John Brown[,] W[illiam]. L. Cutler, H[enry]. G. Sherwood, Elijah Averett Bradford W. Elliott, David Candland and L[ucian]. R. Foster, the two latter acting as clerks. Pres[ident]. George Miller being engaged in revising and completing the list of High Priests to be admitted for washing and anointing, and several of the others mentioned above passing to and fro engaged in their several duties,— The morning was a very beautiful one, the sun shining clear and bright, through the east window of the room in which the party were assembled.

Pres[ident]. Young's son Joseph was present—also having slept with his father—Amasa Lyman came in during the reading also Elder H[eber]. C. Kimball, at a quarter to 10. the reading was finished at 10 o'clock. at which time Miss Eliza R. Snow handed in a list of the females washed this morning,—which lists she has taken for several days past.

At 17 minutes past 9 o'clock A.M. [we] commenced washing and

6. This latest published report of Frémont's travels was a gift from Stephen A. Douglas. Originally printed by 1843, the version available at this time was the *Report of the exploring expedition to the Rocky Mountains in the year 1842, and to Oregon and North California in the years 1843-44. By Brevet Captain J. C. Frémont. Printed by order of the Senate of the United States* (Washington, D.C.: Gales and Seaton, printers, 1845).

anointing in the male department, the following High Priests, viz.

Charles Allen,	born	Dec[ember]. 26. 1806
Joshua S. Holman	"	April 12. 1794
Samuel Gully	"	May 27. 1809
Samuel Ensign	"	May 24, 1805

These were washed by John Lytle and William Crosby and anointed by C[harles]. C. Rich and A[braham]. O. Smoot.

Also the following of the quorum of Seventies, viz

Benjamin Boyce,	born	Dec[embe]r. 28. 1812
Thomas Bullock	"	Dec[embe]r. 23. 1816
Lorenzo Clark	"	May 25 1806
Elijah J. Sabin	"	Jan[uar]y 12. 1806
James H. Glines	"	April 17. 1822
Roswell Stephens	"	Nov[embe]r. 17. 1808
Allen J. Stout	"	Dec[embe]r. 5 1815
Morgan Phelps	"	April 30. 1808
John Averett	"	Aug[us]t 15. 1821

These were washed by John Lytle & William Crosby, and anointed by Joseph Young and J[edediah]. M. Grant. They finished at 24 minutes past 9 o'clock.

In the female department the following persons were washed and anointed, commencing at 20 minutes past 8 o'clock viz;

Eliza Ann Graves born June 3. 1811 W[ashed]. by Sarah D. Rich, anointed by Sarah D. Rich[.]

Paulina Eliza Phelps born Mar[ch]. 20, 1827 W[ashed]. by S[arah]. D. Rich anointed by S[arah]. D. Rich[.]

Sarah Jane Peck born Sept[ember]. 15. 1825 W[ashed]. by S[arah]. D. Rich anointed by S[arah]. D. Rich[.]

Mary Ann Phelps born Aug[ust] 6 1829 W[ashed]. by S[arah]. D. Rich anointed by S[arah]. D. Rich[.]

Rebecca W. Holman born April 22. 1793 W[ashed]. by Patty Sessions. anointed by Agnes M. Smith[.]

Elisa Allen born August 28. 1808 W[ashed]. by Jane Bliven an[ointed]. by Agnes M. Smith[.]

Rebekah G. Holman b[orn]. Feb[ruar]y 20. 1824 W[ashed]. by Patty Sessions. An[ointed]. by Patty Sessions[.]

Polly Maria Stevens born June 29. 1811 W[ashed]. by Jane Bliven, an[ointed]. by Patty Sessions[.]

Henrietta Bullock born Feb[ruar]y 13. 1817 W[ashed]. by

M[ercy]. R. Thompson An[ointed]. by Agnes M. Smith[.]
Beulah A. Clark b[orn]. April 19. 1806 W[ashed]. by Jane Bliven, an[ointed]. by Patty Sessions[.]
Mary E. Ensign b[orn]. May 15, 1811 W[ashed]. by Jane Bliven an[ointed]. by Agnes M. Smith[.]
Polly Phelps born Dec[ember] 9. 1817 W[ashed]. By M[ercy]. R. Thompson An[ointed] by Patty Sessions[.]
Susannah C. Boyce b[orn]. Feb[ruar]y 25. 1815 W[ashed]. by Jane Bliven, an[ointed]. by Agnes M. Smith[.]
Pamela G. Holman b[orn]. March 31. 1827 W[ashed]. by Jane Bliven, an[ointed]. by Agnes M. Smith[.]
Rebecca Averett born April 18. 1822 W[ashed]. by M[ercy]. R. Thompson an[ointed] by Patty Sessions[.]
Ovanda Fuller born June 27. 1822 W[ashed]. by M[ercy]. R. Thompson anointed by Patty Sessions.
Elizabeth Ann Glines, born Feb[ruar]y 4. 1821 W[ashed]. by Jane Bliven anointed by Agnes M. Smith[.]
Ann Elizabeth Benson b[orn]. Feb[ruar]y 17. 1815 W[ashed]. by M[ercy]. R. Thompson A[nointed]. by Patty Sessions.
Finished at 22 minutes past 9.

[A]t 8 m[inutes]. past 10 [we] commenced receiving the foregoing into the lower & middle departments, as follows, viz; Joseph Young No. 1.— J[edediah]. M. Grant No. 2.— B[enjamin]. L. Clapp No. 3. in the upper department, and in the middle as follows, L[ucius]. N. Scovil No. 1.— Hosea Stout No. 2.— J[esse]. P. Harmon No. 3 W[illiam]. W. Phelps No. 4, John D. Lee as Prompter.

At 38 minutes past 11 o'clock [we] commenced receiving into the upper department those who have been washed and anointed this morning in the following order. viz,

Allen J. Stout. by L[ucius]. N. Scovil[.]
John Averett " " "
Rebecca Averett by John Averett & C[harles]. C. Rich[.]
Eliza Ann Graves by C[harles]. C. Rich[.]
Sarah Jane Peck by C[harles]. C. Rich[.]
Mary Ann Phelps by C[harles]. C. Rich[.]
Paulina ^Eliza^ Phelps by C[harles]. C. Rich[.]
James H. Glines by C[harles]. C. Rich[.]
Elizabeth Ann Glines by J[ames]. H. Glines & C[harles]. C. Rich[.]

Joshua S. Holman by C[harles]. C. Rich[.]
Rebecca W. Holman by J[oshua]. S. Holman & C[harles]. C. Rich[.]
Lorenzo Clark by Charles C. Rich[.]
Beulah A. Clark by Lorenzo Clark & C[harles]. C. Rich[.]
Elijah J. Sabin by C[harles]. C. Rich[.]
Morgan Phelps by C[harles]. C. Rich[.]
Polly Phelps by Morgan Phelps & C[harles]. C. Rich[.]
Thomas Bullock by C[harles]. C. Rich[.]
Henrietta Bullock by Thomas B[ullock]. & C[harles]. C. R[ich].
Charles Allen by C[harles]. C. Rich[.]
Eliza Allen by Charles Allen and C[harles]. C. Rich[.]
Roswell Stevens by C[harles]. C. Rich[.]
Polly Maria Stevens by R[oswell]. Stevens & C[harles]. C. R[ich].
Samuel Gully by John L. Butler & [Charles C.] R[ich].
Ovanda Fuller by S[amuel]. Gully & [John L.] Butler.
Benjamin Boyce by W[illiam]. L. Cutler[.]
Susannah C. Boyce by B[enjamin]. Boyce & [William] Cutler[.]
Ann Elizabeth Benson by Brigham Young[.]
Rebecca G. Holman by Brigham Young[.]
Pamela G. Holman by Brigham Young[.]
Samuel Ensign by Brigham Young[.]
Mary E. Ensign by S[amuel]. Ensign & B[righam]. Young.

Finished at half past 2. Prompters—Hosea Stout, John D. Lee.

At about 11 o clock [we] commenced washing and anointing in the Male department, the following High Priests, viz

William W. Major	born	January 27. 1804
Daniel S. Thomas	"	March 15 1803
Abraham Palmer	"	December 4 1807
Duncan McArthur	"	May 22. 1796

Quorum of Seventies.

William B. Benson	born	Feb[ruar]y 13. 1814
Simeon A. Dunn	"	Aug[ust] 7. 1804
Josiah Arnold	"	Oct[obe]r. 1 1800
Enoch Reese	"	May 25 1813
Stephen Luce	"	July 10. 1801
Benjamin Jones	"	Feb[ruar]y 24 1797.

William Pace	"	July 3. 1806
James Pace	"	June 15 1811
Madison D. Hambleton	"	Nov[embe]r. 2. 1811

These were washed by John Lytle & William Crosby. The High Priests were anointed by Charles C. Rich and Abraham O. Smoot, and the Seventies were anointed by Benj[amin]. L. Clapp John Pack, Joseph Young and J[edediah]. M. Grant. They finished at 10 minutes before 12.

In the Female department, the following persons were washed and anointed commencing at 15 minutes past 10. viz;

Elvira Randall. born February 26 1825 W[ashed]. by Mary Clapp anointed by Mary Clapp[.]

Sarah Major. born October 14 1812 W[ashed]. by Mercy R. Thompson A[nointed]. by Patty Sessions[.]

Anna Jones. born December 22. 1806 W[ashed]. by Jane Bliven. A[nointed]. by Agnes M. Smith[.]

Maria Crosby born May 7. 1808. W[ashed]. by Nancy Winchester. A[nointed]. by Agnes M. Smith[.]

Cynthia Shurtliff born June 19. 1806 W[ashed]. by Nancy Winchester. A[nointed]. by Patty Sessions[.]

Lucinda G. Pace born June 16 1805 W[ashed]. by M[ercy]. R. Thompson. anointed by Patty Sessions[.]

Margaret Pace born May 30 1808 W[ashed]. by Jane Bliven, anointed by Agnes Smith[.]

Martha P. Thomas born Feb[ruar]y 20. 1808 W[ashed]. by Mary Clapp anointed by Mary Clapp[.]

Betsey Arnold born October 21. 1799 W[ashed]. by Jane Bliven, anointed by Agnes M. Smith[.]

Mary Luce, born August 30, 1801 W[ashed]. by Jane Bliven, anointed by Patty Sessions[.]

Elizabeth Taylor born Dec[embe]r. 9, 1795 W[ashed]. by Nancy Winchester, A[nointed]. by Nancy Winchester[.]

Patience D. Palmer born Feb[ruar]y 15. 1809 W[ashed]. by Jane Bliven, anointed by Agnes M. Smith[.]

Susan McArthur born Oct[ober] 10. 1801 W[ashed]. by Jane Bliven An[ointed]. by Patty Sessions[.]

Hannah Reese born Feb[ruar]y 17. 1826 W[ashed]. by M[ercy]. R. Thompson an[ointed]. by Nancy Winchester[.]

Chelnetia Hambleton born March 5. 1818 W[ashed]. by Jane Bliven anointed by Agnes M. Smith[.]

Margaret Dunn born Mar[ch]. 12, 1812 W[ashed]. by Polly Y. Johnson A[nointed]. by Patty Sessions[.]

Finished at 10 Minutes to 1. o'clock.

At one o'clock the bell rung, and [we] commenced to receive into the lower and middle departments those whose washing & anointing commenced in the Male department at 11. o clock the following persons officiating—viz; in the upper department L[ucius]. N. Scovil as No. 1.—J[edediah]. M. Grant No. 2, B[enjamin]. L. Clapp No. 3

[A]nd in the middle department

Joseph Young	as	No. 1.	J[esse]. P. Harmonas	No. 2	
A[braham]. O. Smoot	"	" 3	W[illiam]. W. Phelps	"	4

John D. Lee as Prompter[.]

At 50 minutes past 2 [we] commenced receiving into the upper department the foregoing persons, in the following order, viz;

Enoch Reese by B[enjamin]. L. Clapp[.]
Hannah Reese " Enoch Reese & B[enjamin]. L. Clapp[.]
William W. Major by B[enjamin]. L. Clapp[.]
Sarah Major by W[illiam]. W. Major & B[enjamin]. L. C[lapp].

Elvira Randall	by B[enjamin]. L. Clapp[.]
Maria Crosby	" Samuel Bent.
Cynthia Shurtliff	" S[amuel]. Bent[.]
Willmer B. Benson	" John D. Lee[.]
Josiah Arnold	" John D. Lee[.]
Betsey Arnold	" Josiah Arnold & [John] Lee[.]
Duncan McArthur	" John D. Lee[.]
Susan McArthur	" D[uncan]. McArthur & [John] Lee[.]
Elizabeth Taylor	" Hosea Stout.
William Pace	" John D. Lee[.]
Margaret Pace	" W[illiam]. Pace & J[ohn]. D. Lee[.]
Abraham Palmer	" John Pack[.]
Patience Delila.	" A[braham]. Palmer & [John] Pack[.]
James Pace	" John Pack[.]
Lucinda G. Pace	" J[ames]. Pace & J[ohn]. Pack[.]
Simeon A. Dunn	" John Pack[.]
Margaret Dunn	" S[imeon]. A. Dunn & [John] Pack[.]
Benjamin Jones	" John Pack[.]

Anna Jones by B[enjamin]. Jones & J[ohn]. Pack[.]
Stephen Luce by John Pack[.]
Mary Luce by Stephen Luce & J[ohn]. Pack[.]

Daniel S. Thomas by John Pack[.]

Martha P. Thomas by D[aniel]. S. Thomas & J[ohn]. L. Butler[.]

Madison D. Hambleton by J[ohn]. L. Butler[.]

Chelnetia Hambleton. by her husband & J[ohn]. L. Butler[.]

Finished at half past 5 o'clock, Prompted by W[illiam]. L. Cutler, David Candland, Hosea Stout & John Pack—

At 27 m[inutes]. before 3 P.M. [we] commenced in the Male department washing & anointing the following High Priests viz;

Warren Smith born October 7. 1808

Gilbert D. Goldsmith[born] Nov[embe]r. 27 1811

Joseph L. Heywood [born] Aug[us]t. 1. 1815

Hiram Spencer [born] Nov[embe]r. 30. 179.

also the following Seventies—

Andrew Whitlock	born	Jan[uar]y 15 1805
William D. Huntington	"	Feb[ruar]y 28. 1818
Reuben W. Allred	"	Nov[embe]r 18 1815
Daniel M. Repsher	"	Dec[ember]. 23. 1804
Willard Smith	"	May 9. 1827
Claudius V. Spencer	"	April 2 1824

These were washed by William Crosby and John Lytle, and the High Priests were anointed by C[harles]. C. Rich & A[braham]. O. Smoot.—the Seventies by Joseph Young, J[edediah]. M. Grant and B[enjamin]. L. Clapp. Finished at half past 3 o'clock.

Willard Smith was ordained into the quorum of Seventies by H[eber]. C. Kimball, before being ~~ordained~~ washed & anointed[.]

At half past 2. [we] commenced in the female department washing & anointing the following persons. viz.

Catharine Clawson, January 27. 1804 Washed by Nancy Winchester. Anointed by Nancy Win[chester].

Ruth A. Reese born May 10. 1817 W[ashed]. by M[ercy]. R. Thompson. A[nointed]. by Patty Sessions[.]

Harriet A. Squires, born Sept[ember] 13. 1819 Wa[shed]. by Polly Z. Johnson A[nointed]. by Leonora Taylor[.]

Sarah Ann Prichard. b[orn]. Nov[embe]r. 29. 1826 W[ashed]. by P[olly]. Z. Johnson A[nointed]. by Patty Sessions[.]

Charity D. Pratt born Feb[ruar]y 24. 1776 W[ashed]. by Mercy R. Thompson A[nointed]. by Patty Sessions[.]

Caroline Huntington born Sept[ember] 15. 1819 W[ashed]. by Nancy Winchester. A[nointed]. by Leonora Taylor[.]

Amanda Smith. born Feb[ruar]y 22. 1808 W[ashed]. by M[ercy]. R. Thompson A[nointed]. [by] Leonora Taylor[.]
Lucy Ann Allred born Aug[us]t 6. 1814 W[ashed]. by Nancy Winchester A[nointed]. by Leonora Taylor[.]
Hannah Whitlock born Sept[ember] 20. 1808 W[ashed]. by P[olly]. Z. Johnson A[nointed]. by Patty Sessions[.]
Hannah Walton born July 1. 1826 W[ashed]. by Nancy Winchester A[nointed]. by Patty Sessions[.]
Sarepta M. Heywood born Nov[ember]. 21. 1821 W[ashed]. by M[ercy]. R. Thompson A[nointed]. by Leonora Taylor[.]
Abigail Goldsmith born May 22. 1814 W[ashed]. by P[olly]. Z. Johnson A[nointed]. by Catharine C. Spencer[.]
Cynthia Durfey b. February 6th 1800 W[ashed]. by Nancy Winchester. A[nointed]. by Nancy W[inchester].
Alzina Durfey born March 24. 1832 W[ashed]. by Polly Z. Johnson A[nointed]. by Patty Sessions[.]
Melissa Smith born Aug[us]t 12. 1830 W[ashed]. by P[olly]. Z. Johnson A[nointed]. by Patty Sessions[.]
Alvira Smith born Dec[ember]. 16. 1831 W[ashed]. by P[olly]. Z. Johnson A[nointed]. by Leonora Taylor[.]
Zeruah Goddard born Feb[ruar]y 20. 1832 W[ashed]. by Nancy Winchester A[nointed]. by Catharine C. Spencer[.]
Emily Spencer born Aug[us]t. 13. 1819 W[ashed]. by Nancy Winchester A[nointed]. by Patty Sessions[.]
Maria Antoinette Spencer b[orn]. Jan[uar]y 22. 1826 W[ashed]. by P[olly]. Z. Johnson A[nointed]. by Patty Sessions[.]

Finished at 24 minutes before 5.

At 15 m[inutes]. before 5, [we] commenced receiving the above into the lower & middle departments—

Joseph Young as No. 1. J[edediah]. M. Grant 2. [Lucius N.] Scovil 3.

and in the middle department

Orson Spencer No. 1. Geo[rge]. P. Dykes No. 2. Jesse P. Harmon No. 3 W[illiam]. W. Phelps No. 4 Prompter John D. Lee[.]

At half past 6 o'clock [we] commenced receiving into the upper department the company whose washings commenced at 27 m[inutes]. before 3 in the following order viz;—

Joseph L. Heywood by Orson Spencer[.]
Sarepta M. Heywood by J[oseph]. L. H[eywood]. and [Orson] Spencer[.]
Hiram Spencer by Orson Spencer[.]
Emily Spencer by H[iram]. Spencer & Orson [Spencer.]
Reuben W. Allred by Orson Spencer[.] ^John D. Lee Prompter^
Lucy Ann Allred by R[euben]. W. Allred & O[rson]. S[pencer].
Warren Smith by O[rson]. Spencer[.]
Amanda Smith by Warren Smith & O[rson]. S[pencer].
Charity D. Pratt by Parley P. Pratt[.]
Melissa Smith by Orson Spencer[.]
Elvira Smith by Orson Spencer[.]
Daniel M. Rep[s]her by Orson Spencer[.]
Hannah Walton by D[aniel]. M. Repsher & O[rson]. S[pencer].
William D. Huntington, by Geo[rge]. P. Dykes[.]
Caroline Huntington by W[illiam]. D. H[untington]. & G[eorge]. P. D[ykes].
Claudius V. Spencer by Orson Spencer[.]
Maria Antoinette Spencer by O[rson]. Spencer[.]
Ruth A. Reese by Orson Spencer[.]
Gilbert D. Goldsmith by Orson Spencer[.]
Abigail Goldsmith by G[ilbert]. D. Goldsmith & O[rson]. S[pencer].
Stephen H. Goddard by O[rson]. Spencer[.] he was washed and anointed on the 17th inst. but waited until to day for his wife Zeruah Goddarad. [She was received] by S[tephen]. H. Goddard & O[rson]. S[pencer].
Andrew Whitlock. by Orson Spencer[.]
Hannah Whitlock by A[ndrew]. W[hitlock]. and O[rson]. S[pencer].
Willard Smith by O[rson]. Spencer[.]
Alzina Durfey " O[rson]. Spencer[.]
Sarah Ann Prichard by O[rson]. Spencer[.]
Catharine Clawson by O[rson]. Spencer[.]
Harriet A. Squires by O[rson]. Spencer[.]
Cynthia Durfey by O[rson]. Spencer[.]

John Pack officiated as prompter. Also J[ohn]. D. Lee[.]

At 6 o'clock, Theodore Turley and his family having arrived at the Temple the ordinances were administered to them, as follows, viz;

Theodore Turley, ^H[igh]. Priest^ born April 10. 1801. was washed and anointed by William Crosby.

The females as follows, commencing at 15 minutes before 6 o'clock

Frances Turley, born June 22, 1800 w[ashed]. by Nancy Winchester A[nointed]. by Leonora Taylor[.]

Percila Turley born June 1. 1829 w[ashed]. by Polly Z. Johnson A[nointed]. by Patty Sessions[.]

Frances Amelia Turley born Jan[uar]y 1. 1825 w[ashed]. by Nancy Winchester. A[nointed]. by Patty Sessions[.]

Mary Ann Turley b[orn]. July 13. 1827 W[ashed]. by Nancy Winchester, A[nointed]. by Leonora Taylor[.]

Mary Henderson born Feb[ruar]y 18. 1823 w[ashed]. by P[olly]. Z. Johnson, A[nointed]. by Patty Sessions.

Finished at half past 6 o'clock. Eliza R. Snow, Clerk.

At 10 m[inutes]. past 7 [we] commenced receiving into the lower and middle department the above mentioned persons.

George A. Smith acting as No. 1
Amasa Lyman " " " 2
H[eber]. C. Kimball " " 3
Aaron Johnson as the Messenger
W[illiam]. W. Phelps as the tempter,
Orson Hyde as No. 1 }
John Taylor " " 2 } in middle dept.
P[arley]. P. Pratt " " 3 }

At half past 9 o'clock [we] commenced receiving Elder Turley & family into the upper department, in the following order

Theodore Turley by P[arley]. P. Pratt[.]
Frances Turley " T[heodore]. Turley & P[arley]. P. P[ratt].
Frances Amelia Turley by T[heodore]. Turley[.]
Mary Ann Turley by T[heodore]. Turley[.]
Mary Henderson by Isaac Allred[.]

Finished at 10 o'clock, John D. Lee officiated as prompter—

Pres[ident]. Young left the Temple about half past 4 o'clock, to be absent for the night.

At 5 o'clock a meeting was held in E[lde]r Kimballs room, present H[eber]. C. Kimball Orson Hyde, P[arley]. P. Pratt, Amasa Lyman George A. Smith, John Taylor, W[illiam]. W. Phelps and George Miller—Clothed in priestly apparel, they offered up thanks to God and asked for the health of Bishop Whitneys child, also Elder Kimballs, and that God would [sweep] away the wrath of this government from us and over rule all things for our good. Elder Kimball being mouth—

564 Persons have passed through—

95 this day—

—William Clayton, Diary, kept for Heber C. Kimball.

....

The weather is growing warmer, it was thought that we would stop giving endowments to day — in order to wash up the Garments & Clean up the rooms — But the call & anxiety of the Brethren Seemed to be so important & the anxiety so great that the Sisters, as well as the Brethren volunteered to wash ever[y] Night for the Next Day & continue on from day to day — giving the Endowment[.] near 100 have been Notified to attend to day to pass through the ordinance of the endowment.

9 o.clock[.] [A]t 9 o clock A.M. the following Persons passed th[r]u the ordinances (viz)

[See pages 111-12 for excerpted portion.]

The evening has come to a close & we are still at work in the diferent departments & some near 45 persons have passed through since Sun[day] Last, it has now got to be 10 o clock & we are just through with the last company making in all about 100 Persons that passed through the ordinances of the Endowment to day — Pres[ident] Jos[eph]. Young & Brigham [Young] have gone home & I [John D. Lee] think I will too as it is Saturday Night —

—Seventies Record, Book B.

....

[A]ccording to my [John D. Lee's] appointment[,] I acted as Prompter or the Guardian Angel of light in all three departments[.] Today 95 persons were taken through today[.] the services closed about 11 oclock at night & I went home[.]

—John D. Lee, Diary.

....

At sunrise I [Thomas Bullock] and Henrietta started to the Temple. We received the ordinances of Washing and Anointing &c &c. Pres[ident] Joseph Young anointed me to be K[ing] and P[riest] and he was in very good spirits and much pleased to see me as was also El[der]. H[eber]. C. Kimball. ^Prompter [was] Hosea Stout. Received by Charles C. Rich.^ After we had passed thro[ugh], we saw Pres[ident]. [Brigham] Young who took us into his private room and there we laid before him our Statement [regarding a plural marriage] and received his approval &c. I never was re-

[Washings and anointings for Saturday, December 20, 1845]

Benj Boice	b born Dec 28th 1812	Thomas Bullock Born Dec ~~11~~ ^23^ 1816	
Lorenzo Clark	May 25 1806	E J Sabin Jan 12 1806	Jos. H Glines April 17 1822.
Roswell Stepen	Nov 17 1808 was washed		
Allen G. Stout	Dec 5 1815	Morgan Phelps April 30 1808	
John Averitt [?]	Aug 18 1821 washed by John ^Lytle^ & Wm Crosby & anointed by Pres J. Young & J. M. Grant at 25M Past 9		

½ P. 2. PM Total No 81

Sisters department

20 M P. 8 Sarah M. Stephens	born June 29 1811 W Jane Blevins A. P Session
Heneretta ^Henrietta^ Bullock	" Feb 13 1817 W M R Thompson A A M Smith
Susanah C Dries	" 25th 1815 W Jane Blevin A by A M Smith
Rebeca Averett	" April 18-1827 " M R Thompson " "
½ P. 2 P.M. Elizabeth Ann Myers	" Feby 4th 1821 " Jane Blevin A "
Ann E. Benson	" 17th 1815 M R Thompson — P Session
Lucy Ann Allred	" Aug 6th 1814 Nancy Winchester — L Taylor
Hannah Pluttock [?]	" Sept 20th 1808 P Z Johnson A. P Session
Zeruah Goddard	" Feb 20. 1822 W Nancy Winchester [illegible]
Maria A Spencer	" Jan 22 1826 P Z Johnson A [illegible]

[illegible] 24 minets to 5 P.M. —

Saturday Evening 15 M. to 6 Dec 21st 1845

15 M to 6

Mary Henderson born Feby 18th 1823 W. by Polly Z Johnson A. by Patey Session

Wilbur Pace 83 July 3rd 1806 Benj Jones Feb 24 1797

James Pace 85 June 15th 1811 Madison D. Hamilton Nov 3d 1811

Claudius W. Spencer 86 April 3d 1815 washed by W. Crosby & J Lyttle & Anointed by Pres Jos. Young & Grant—

—Seventies Record, Book B, oversized portion, December 20, 1845.

ally happier than when I was in his room and hearkened to his council. My wife was really happy too. May the Eternal Father give us of his Spirit that we may ever bear in mind the truths that we this day learned, and ever keep them in sacred remembrance. We also feel glad and happy in the prospects that lie before us. We then went down to Dr. [Willard] Richards. Partook of bread and wine.

—Thomas Bullock, Diary.

... in the evening met with the quorum at Prayers.

—John Taylor, Diary (draft), LDS Archives.

I [Brigham Young] dictated the arrangements for the day. Afterwards, with a few of the Twelve [apostles] and others heard F[ranklin]. D. Richards read *Fremont's Journal,* giving an account of his travels to California.

We considered it prudent to devote today to cleaning and washing, and suspend operations in the Temple; but on account of the anxiety of the saints to receive their ordinances, the brethren and sisters volunteered to wash clothes every night. Ninety-five persons received their ordinances.

—"Manuscript History of Brigham Young,"
in *History of the Church,* 7:548.

Nauvoo temple endowments performed on this date:

First Company: Allen J. Stout, John Averett, Rebecca Averett, Eliza Ann Graves, Sarah Jane Peck, Mary Ann Phelps, Paulina Eliza Phelps, James H. Glines, Elizabeth Ann Glines, Joshua S. Holman, Rebecca W. Holman, Lorenzo Clark, Beulah A. Clark, Elijah J. Sabin, Morgan Phelps, Polly Phelps, Thomas Bullock, Henrietta Bullock, Charles Allen, Eliza Allen, Roswell Stevens, Polly Maria Stevens, Samuel Gully, Ovanda Fuller, Benjamin Boyce, Susannah C. Boyce, Ann Elizabeth Benson, Rebecca G. Holman, Pamela G. Holman, Samuel Ensign, and Mary E. Ensign.

Second Company: Enoch Reese, Hannah Reese, William W. Major, Sarah Major, Elvira Randall, Maria Crosby, Cynthia Shurtliff, Willmer B. Benson, Josiah Arnold, Betsey Arnold, Duncan McArthur, Susan McArthur, Elizabeth Taylor, William Pace, Margaret Pace, Abraham Palmer, Patience Delila Palmer, James Pace, Lucinda G. Pace, Simeon A. Dunn, Margaret Dunn, Benjamin Jones, Anna Jones, Stephen Luce, Mary Luce, Daniel S. Thomas, Martha P. Thomas, Madison D. Hambleton, and Chelnetia Hambleton.

Third Company: Joseph L. Heywood, Sarepta M. Heywood, Hiram Spencer, Emily Spencer, Reuben W. Allred, Lucy Ann Allred, Warren Smith, Amanda Smith, Charity D. Pratt, Melissa Smith, Elvira Smith, Daniel M. Repsher, Hannah Walton, William D. Huntington, Caroline Huntington, Claudius V. Spencer, Marie Antoinette Spencer, Ruth A. Reese, Gilbert D. Goldsmith, Abigail Goldsmith, Stephen H. Goddard, Zerah Goddard, Andrew Whitlock, Hannah Whitlock, Willard Smith, Alzina Durfey, Sarah Ann Prichard, Catharine Clawson, Harriet A. Squires, and Cynthia Durfey.

Fourth Company: Theodore Turley, Frances Turley, Frances Amelia Turley, Mary Ann Turley, and Mary Henderson.

—Summary of information compiled by the Temple Index Bureau, *Nauvoo Temple Endowment Register: 10 December 1845 to 8 February 1846*. Editors' note: According to the register, Percilla Turley was washed and anointed on this date and therefore also probably endowed.

Sunday, December 21, 1845

According to appointment on Sunday last, a meeting was held in the east room ^this day^ of all those who could clothe themselves in the garments of Priesthood[.] 75 persons were present, Elder H[eber]. C. Kimball presiding. The names of those present so far as the clerks could ascertain them, are as follows— H[eber]. C. Kimball, Vilate Kimball —John Taylor Leonora Taylor — P[arley]. P. Pratt. Mary Ann Pratt Orson Pratt, Sarah M. Pratt — Amasa Lyman Maria Louisa Lyman — George A. Smith, Bathsheba W. Smith, John Smith, Patriarch[,] Clarissa Smith — Alpheus Cutler, Lois Cutler — Reynolds Cahoon, Tirzah Cahoon George Miller, Clarissa Miller — C[harles]. C. Rich Sarah D. Rich — W[illiam]. W. Phelps — Sally Phelps Samuel Bent, Theodore Turley — F[ranklin]. D. Richards Jane S. Richards — David Fullmer, Rhoda Ann Fullmer — Reuben Miller — F[reeman]. Nickerson Simeon Carter — Lydia Carter — Thomas Grover — Caroline E. Grover G[eorge]. W. Harris Lucinda Harris — William Felshaw, Mary H. Felshaw, James Allred — Elizabeth Allred Elizabeth Taylor — Stephen Markham Levi Richards — W[illia]m. A. Sanger. Ma[r]y Sanger Louisa Sanger — William Crosby, Sally Crosby Joseph Fielding ^& wife^ Elijah Fordham. Anna B. Fordham — William Weeks — Caroline Weeks — David Candland — L[ucian]. R. Foster. Mary Smith — Mercy R. Thompson — John M. Bernhisel — Erastus

Snow — Ezra T. Benson & wife — John Pack & wife — Cynthia Durfee, Eliza R. Snow — James Taylor — Joseph L. Heywood & wife William Cahoon & wife — and 2 others whose names were not obtained[.]

At 5 min[utes] before 11, the song "Glorious things of thee are Spoken" was sung &—

Father John Smith then made a few remarks, blessed the bread and it [was] Handed round by Bishop Geo[rge]. Miller[.] the Wine was blessed by Geo[rge]. Miller and handed round by him[.] While the wine was passing round, Elder Geo[rge]. A. Smith arose and addressed the congregation[.] He thanked God for the privileges this day enjoyed and spoke of the difficulties under which the church had labored to attain to the blessings we now enjoy. Another thing he thanked God for [the fact that we] already had more than 500. persons passed through, and therefore if half of them should be like the foolish virgins, and turn away from the truth, ~~and~~ the principles of the Holy Priesthood, would be beyond the reach of mobs and all the assaults of the adversaries of the Church[.] Order was one of the laws of Heaven[.] there ought to be no whispering here[.] no difficulty ought to be mentioned, whatever transpires here ought not to be mentioned any where else[.]

When we pray to the Lord we ought to come together clad in proper garments and when we do so, and unite our hearts and hands together, and act as one mind, the Lord will hear us and will answer our prayers[.] Our garments should be properly marked and we should understand those marks and we should wear those garments continually, by night & by day, in prison or free and if the devils in hell cut us up, let them cut the garments to pieces also[.] if we have the garments upon us at all times we can at any time offer up the signs. ~~& tokens~~

He then related an instance of some children being healed & cured of the whooping cough in one night, through the prayers of himself and Elder [Wilford] Woodruff, in Michigan, while they were there on a mission. Said that whenever they could get an opportunity they retired to the wilderness or to an upper room [and] they did so and offered up the signs, and were always answered. It would be a good thing for us to put on our garments every day and pray to God, and in private circles, when we can do so with safety[.]

We are now different from what we were before we entered into this quorum. Speedy vengeance will now overtake the Transgressor[.] When a man and his wife are united in feeling, and act in union, I believe they can hold their children by prayer & faith and will not be obliged to give them up to death until they are fourscore years old[.]

Sometimes mere trifles, destroy the confidence which each ought to have in the other. this prevents a union of faith & feeling[.] The apostacy of Thomas B. Marsh was caused by so small a thing as a pint of strippings and his oaths brought the exterminating order which drove us all out of Missouri[.] The woman ought to be in subjection to the man[.] be careful to guard against loud laughter—against whispering—levity, talebearing[.] He expressed his unfeigned love for his brethren, and his confidence in their endeavors to keep these rules.

"The Spirit of God" was then sung[.]

Elder Kimball next addressed the meeting. He concurred in all that had been said[.] the observation of these things is most essential[.] about 4 years ago next May nine persons were admitted into the Holy order 5 are now living—B[righam]. Young—W[illard]. Richards George Miller—N[ewel]. K. Whitney & H[eber]. C. Kimball[.] two are dead, and two are worse than dead.[7] You have not got all you will have if you are faithful and keep your tongue in your mouth[.] You are pronounced clean, but were you pronounced clean from the blood of this generation? No! not all of you. only some few who have deserved it[.] Females were not received when we first received the Holy order[.] Men apostasized, being led by their wives[.] if any such cases occur again no more women will be admitted[.] He spoke of the Necessity of Women being in subjection to their husbands[.] I am subject to my God, my wife is in subjection to me and will reverence me in my place and I will make her happy I do not want her to step forward and dictate to me any more than I dictate to Pres[ident]. Young[.] In his absence I take his place according to his request[.] Shall we cease from loud laughter and mirth? will you never slander your brother or sister? I will refer your minds to the covenants you have made[;] by an observance of these things you will have dreams and visions. In the coming week we will take through 100 a day, we want no man to come in here unless he is invited, or on business. Let those having cloth to make up send it here and we will make it up, & put it to good use[.] Women should be appointed to attend to the washing and anointings of the High Priests wives. There is a large lot ahead, You are not yet ordained to any thing, but we

7. William Law and William Marks, both of whom had by this time left the church.

have the clay here[;] it is mellow & we shall soon put it on the wheel. If any brother divulges any thing we shall cut him off, We shall not be with you long. We cannot rest day nor night until we put you in possession of the Priesthood. We want you now to make up garments for yourselves[.] I want my own robe back again[.] If we have made you clean every whit, now go to work and make others clean[.] We will have a [screen?] put up before the vail, and will make an office of my room, and have a stairway leading down from it. No person will be allowed to take people through the vail but those appointed. Let women wait upon women & let men wait upon men, then no jealousies will arise. He closed at 5 m[inutes]. before one.

Elder P[arley]. P. Pratt approved of what had been said & said a few words about the fashion of our robes—his own robe, which was like those first used, was not sewed up at the sides, neither was it of more than one breadth.

Elder Kimball showed the right fashion for a leaf[.] Spoke of Elder Richards being protected at Carthage Jail—having on the robe, while Joseph & Hyrum [Smith]. and Elder Taylor were shot to pieces[.] said the Twelve [apostles] would have to leave shortly, for a charge of treason would be brought against them for swearing us to avenge the blood of the anointed ones, and some one would reveal it, and we shall have to part some day between sundown and dark[.]

George Miller said that when near the camp of Gen[eral]. Hardin, he was shot at, and the Sentinel who was near him was killed, but he escaped unhurt, having on his garment. He then spoke of the design and purpose for which all the ~~signs and tokens~~ Symbols in the garden were given &c. Paul said he bore in his body the marks of the Lord Jesus Christ—which was as plainly as he dare allude to these things in writing. But the marks Paul alluded to were just such as we now have on our garments. He spoke of the signs, tokens & penalties, and of the work in general, said it was the work of God, by which he designs to reinstate man into his presence &c.

Elder John Taylor confirmed the saying that Joseph and Hyrum & himself were without their robes in the jail at Carthage, While Doct[or] Richards had his on, but corrected the idea that some had, that they had taken them off through fear. W[illiam]. W. Phelps said Joseph told him one day about that time, that he had laid aside his garment on account of the hot weather[.]

Elder Kimball said word came to him & to all the Twelve [apostles] about that time to lay aside their garments, and take them to pieces, or cut them up so that they could not be found.

The Sisters ought not to gather together in schools to pray unless their husbands or some man be with them[.] every evening at 5 o clock the High Priests meet for prayer by themselves. Clothed in their robes of Priesthood—Also the High Council. and the Seventies.

There are from seven to twelve persons who have met together every day to pray ever since Joseph's death, and this people have been sustained upon this principle[.] Here is brother [Theodore] *Turley* [who] has been liberated by the power of God and not of man—and I have covenanted, and never will rest nor my posterity after me until those men who killed Joseph & Hyrum have been wiped out of the earth.

Elder Cahoon had permission to speak at 20 m[inutes]. past one. He bore testimony of the importance of those things which had been spoken. He rejoiced in the idea that the things he was taught in the beginning, were the same things now taught and remembered—and it is so because they are eternal things.

The whole assembly were then formed into 2 circles ^one within the other^ the signs & tokens were given, the proper attitude for prayer assumed, and Elder Taylor being mouth the whole congregation united with him in prayer to God[.] at 10 minutes past 2. the meeting was dismissed and all unclothed themselves of their robes and another congregation which had been waiting in the vestibul of the temple was admitted into the east room, not being clothed in the garments of Priesthood[.]

At 3 O'clock sung Hosanna. Prayer by E[lde]r Orson Hyde—after which by invitation of E[lde]r Kimball who presided, (Pres[ident]. Young not having been at the Temple today and the duty of presiding having devolved upon E[lde]r Kimball as the next in succession) Amasa Lyman, addressed the assembly. He said Doubtless with the most of the present assembly it is the beginning of a new era, in their lives—they have come to a ~~place the~~ time they never saw before[.] They have come to the commencement of a knowledge of things, and it is necessary they [tokens and covenants] should be riveted on their minds[.] one important thing to be understood is this, that those portions of the priesthood which you have received are all essential matters[.] it is not merely that you may see these things, but it is matter of fact, a matter that has to do directly with your salvation—for which you have talked and labored many years[.] It is not for amusement you are brought to receive these things but to put you in posession of the means of salvation and be brot into a proper relationship to God[.] Hence a man becomes responsible for his own conduct, and that of his wife, if he has one. It is not designed that the things that are presented to-day should be forgotten to-morrow but remembered and practiced through all coming life[.] Hence it is a step stone to approach to the favor of God. Having descended to the lowest state of degradation it is the beginning of a homeward journey. It is like a man lost in a wilderness and the means with which we are invested here are to direct us in our homeward journey. You then see the reason why you are required to put away your vain ties cease to talk of all those things which are not conducive to eternal life.

This is why you are required to be sober—to be honest, that you could ask and receive, knock and it should be opened, and that when you sought for things you would find them. It is putting you in possession of of those keys by which you can ask for things you need and obtain them[.] This is the Key by which to obtain all the glory and felicity of eternal life[.] It is the key by which you approach God. No impression which you receive here should be lost. It was to rivet the recollection of the tokens & covenants in your memory like a nail in a sure place, never to be forgotten[.]

The scenery through which you have passed is actually ~~putting you in~~ laying before you a picture or map by which you are to travel through life, and obtain an entrance into the celestial kingdom hereafter. If you are tempted in regard to these things here, you will be tempted when you approach the presence of God hereafter[.] You have, by being faithful[,] been brought to this point, by maintaining the things which have been entrusted to you. This is a representation of the Celestial Kingdom. It is not merely for the sake of talking over these things that they are given to you, but for your benefit, and for your triumph over the powers of darkness hereafter.

We want the man to remember that he has covenanted to keep the law of God, and the woman to obey her husband and if you keep your covenants you will not be guilty of transgressions. The line that is drawn is for you to maintain your covenant, and you will always be found in the path of obedience—after that which is virtuous and holy & good and will never be swallowed up by unhallowed feelings & passions.

If you are found worthy and maintain your integrity, and do not run away and think you have got all your endowment you will be found worthy after a while, which will make you honorable with God. You have not yet been ordained to any thing, but will be by and by. You have received these things, because of your compliance with all the requisitions of the law, and if faithful you will receive more.

You have now learned how to pray. You have been taught how to approach God, and be recognized. This is the principle by which the Church has been kept together, and not the power of arms. A few individuals have asked for your preservation, and their prayers have been heard, and it is this which has preserved you from being scattered to the four winds.

Those who have learned to approach God and receive these blessings, are they better than you? The difference is, they have been permitted to have these things revealed unto them.

The principles which have been opened to you are the things which ought to occupy your attention all your lives. They are not second to any thing You have the key by which if you are faithful, you will [have a] claim on you, and on your posterity, [and] all the blessings of the Priesthood.

Elder H[eber]. C. Kimball said, The ideas advanced by brother Lyman are good and true[.] We have been taken as it were from the earth, and have travelled until we have entered the Celestial Kingdom and what is it for, it is to personify Adam. And you discover that our God is like one of us, for he created us in his own image[.] Every man that ever came upon this earth, or any other earth will take the course we have taken[.] Another thing, it is to bring us to an organization and just as quick as we can get into that order and government, we have the Celestial Kingdom here. You have got to honor and reverence your brethren, for if you do not you never can honor God. The man was created, and God gave him dominion over the whole earth, but he saw that he never could multiply, and replenish the earth, without a woman. And he made one and gave her to him. He did not make the man for the woman; but the woman for the man, and it is just as unlawful for you to rise up and rebel against your husband, as it would be for man to rebel against God.

When the man came to the vail, God gave the key word to the man, and the man gave it to the woman. But if a man dont use a woman well and take good care of her, God will take her away from him, and give her to another.

Perfect order and consistency makes Heaven but we are now deranged, and the tail has become the head[.]

We have now come to this place, and all your former covenants are of no account, and here is the place where we have to enter into a new covenant, and be sealed, and have it recorded. One reason why we bring our wives with us, is, that they make a covenant with us to keep these things sacred. You have been anointed to be kings & priests, but you have not been ordained to it yet. and you have got to get it by being faithful[.] You can't sin so cheap now as you could before you came to this order. It is not for you to reproach the Lord's anointed nor to speak evil of him, You have covenanted not to do it.

One other thing. You all want to get garments, and you need not wait to get fine linen or bleached cotton for your garments. Shirting or sheeting will do for garments, The women can cut theirs from the cuts on their husbands[.] We dont want you to come here and take up the time to cut your garments. Go to a good faithful sister, & secrete yourselves, and make your garments. We have been crowded too much and we have got to stop it, and if you have cloth, and come here to get your cloth cut, we shall keep it here to make use of till we get through[.] We don't want one person that has come into the order the week past, to come into this room during the coming week except those who are to work. If you want any thing let it come in writing.

David Sessions, Gilbert D. Gouldsmith and Elam Ludington volunteered to draw water from the river in barrels for the use of the Temple.

Elder Kimball spoke of the confusion which had been in the house hitherto, None will be permitted to stand at the vail but the one that may be appointed by the President, You have been washed and pronounced clean, but not from the blood of this generation.

Elder George A. Smith, made a few remarks. He spoke principally in relation to the importance of keeping sacred those Signs & tokens & principles which we had received while passing along through the different degrees.

He was followed by Elder Orson Hyde who said a few words in approbation of what had been said by Elder Smith and followed up in the same matters[.]

The congregation was dismissed by prayer by Elder John Taylor and soon departed from the Temple to their respective homes[.]

At 5 o'clock P.M. the following High Priests met for prayer, clothed in their Priestly Garments, viz; Geo[rge]. Miller — Winslow Farr — Lucian Woodworth — William Crosby, Cornelius P. Lott.

—William Clayton, Diary, kept for Heber C. Kimball.

The brethren & sisters were instructed more fully into their duty by E[lde]rs A[masa]. Lyman, H[eber]. C. Kimball, George A. Smith and O[rson]. Hyde.

—William Clayton, Diary.

....

At a general meeting of the Seventies assembled in the Masonic Hall 10 0 clock A.M. Pres[ident] Jos[eph]. Young Said as the weather was extremely cold, and the Hall was not large enough to convened those who have assembled — I think it would not be a[d]missable to continue the meeting long — I want those that are ordained ^into the^ seventies, and are not recognized in the Quorim as an organized member to tarry after the meeting is dismissed — and we will put them into the 32nd Seventy & we will organize it to day — He also made [a] few verry appropriate remarks relative to the order of Endowment. He desired the Brethren to be patient & have no feelings[,] for everything will be conducted in wisdom acording to the revelation of God — he also observed that the Seventies for finishing off a room in the atic Story of the Temple might have the use of it, during the endowment — Where upon the following Brethren volunteered to fit up the room — Namely A. Baldwin Micah B. Welton E. M. Webb John Eldrige Elijah Newman A A Farnham John McDonald S. H. Earl — Hyrum Dayton — B R Bently M Masse L. Babbitt Seely Owens — He likewise said it was nessary to have a cook stove to put in the room when it should be finished[.] Br[other] W[illia]m Rowley observed that Bro[ther] [illegible] had a good cook [stove], that could be had on [illegible] prepare it immediately — After which a collection of $36 & 65 C[en]ts was taken up to finish garments &c nessessary for [illegible].

—Seventies Record, Book B.

....

I [John D. Lee] rode out [in] a carriage in company with Pres[ident] B[righam] Young and J[edediah] D Grant to visit Br[other] [A. P.] Freas['s] folks as 2 of his daughters to wit Emoline and Louisa were sick of a winter fever[.] after administering some nourishment and comfort to them we blessed them and returned. On our way home we stoped at Br[other]. Woodards, who was also sick. also at Br[other]. A[braham]. Washborns and [Freeman] Nickersons[.] at the latter I met my wife and her mother who was also on a visit and who was on their return home. They got into the carriage and rode home. I remained at home until midnight, when I arose dressed myself and went to the Temple[.] After passing the outer & lower door I rapt and soon obtained admission in through the inner courts to the East part of the temple where I found Pres[ident] B[righam] Young A[masa] Lyman Theodore Turley John L. Butler A L Robins E[lijah] averett & 2 Hansons all in silent repose[,] the watch excepted[,] who was the man that met me at the door & through whom I obtained admittance (J[ohn] L Butler)[.] [H]ere I took a turn of 2 hours as one of the watch after which I laid me down in one of the Sophias & took quite a knapp[.] at 6 oclock I was up making preparations for the day & at 8 the list was read & each person soon became acquainted with his station in the several departments for the day.

I will here observe that I was selected [to be] a prompter at the veil[.] I also acted [as] no 2 in the first department (that is Jehovah)[.] At 4 PM Nancy [Bean] and Rachel [Woolsey] Lee passed through the ordinances of endowment[.] 106 persons passed through the washing & anointing today[.] about midnight I returned home with Nancy & Rachel & tarried the balance of the night[.] at 8 in the morning I entered the temple[.] the order of the day was not changed from the arrangement of yesterday as the High Priests also had the liberty of the day generally[, but] their quorum being small[,] it was thought best for them to pass through in turns with the Seventies. I will here note a smawl item of Doctrine taken from a lecture delivered to the High Council & High Priests[:] in speaking of the Keys and callings of both H[igh] P[riests] & Seventies he observed that the calling of the Seventies was to carry the Gospel to all Nations & to build the Kingdom in all the world[.] if so then they will have authority to ordain and organize High Councils High Priests Seventies Elders Priests Bishops Teachers & Deacons[.] if this is not so then the Lord or his Prophet was mistaken in their calling[.] I must now stop writing as I am appointed to prompt at the veil & the first is to pass through[.] it is now 11 oclock[.]

Several officers are in the city with writs as I understand for the Twelve [apostles]—this being understood[,] Br[other]. W[illia]m. Miller was dressed in an atire representing Pres[ident] B[righam] Young and went down the stairs to a carriage that stood near the Temple door, for that purpose[,] in company with G[eorge] D Grant who[,] to carry out the design[,] said in the presence of the officers who stood around the carriage supposing it might be him (Pres[ident] Young) the atmosphere is rather cool to be comfortable[.] at this conjectures were confirmed and the one having the writ steped up with the writ in his hand said Mr

Young you are my Prisoner[.] the man on whom the writ was served submited & was carried to Carthage [Illinois] before they discovered the trick & had it not been for G[eorge] W Thatcher the clerk in the county commission Court—who was and is now an apostate from our church—they would in all probability have gone to Springfield [Illinois] before they would have found out their mistake but he being acquainted with both men Said this is not Pres[ident] Young it is W[illia]m Miller I know him like a book[.] as soon as they found out the joke they droped their countenances & dismissed the prisoner with this compliment[:] I think that you are a gentleman, sir for not making yourself known before[.] At 12 at night the prisoner returned bringing the word that a posse would likely be in on the morrow[.] we accordingly prepared for the worse[.]

The twelve [apostles] all being absent but one O[rson] P[ratt,] the arrangement of the endowment was placed under the direction or superintendance of Bishop G[eorge] Miller who gave me the keys of the different departments together with such instructions as was necessary to admit the officers in to search the temple for those for whom they have writs[.] We were prepared according to requirement[.] perfect order & decorum is observed here to day. I received at the veil a part of the day[.] in the evening I acted as J[ehovah] in the lower department No 2 and the same No in the upper department[.] it is now midnight and the last company is not yet through[.] I passed through the several departments set things in order for the night and at 2 oclock I layed me down to sleep on a splendid Sophais rapted up in a comforter belonging to Pres[ident] B[righam] Young[.]

—John D. Lee, Diary.

[T]here being a meeting in the Temple at 2 without garments[,] I [Thomas Bullock] returned there, heard some excellent instructions which causes my heart to rejoice much. At 5 went home.

—Thomas Bullock, Diary.

Jane [Richards] and myself [Franklin D. Richards,] both of us unitedly[,] enjoyed the Lords supper in the Lords House clothed in the "righteousness of the Saints" a blessing most precious to each of our souls for which will our Heavenly Father in the name of his son Jesus Christ be pleased to accept of our most devout & humble thanksgiving for this distinguished favor and may it have all that good effect upon each of our hearts which our Heavenly Father intended they should have upon all his faithful children when he instituted these things for their blessing and benefit[.] after meeting we went home[.] I spent until Thursday evening (christmas day) of this ^week^ assisting to give the Saints their endowments[.]

—Franklin D. Richards, Diary.

....

[T]hen went to a meeting in the Temple at two o'clock which was the first time which we ever met in a meeting of the Holy order.

—Hosea Stout, Diary, in *On the Mormon Frontier: The Diary of Hosea Stout, 1844-1861,* edited by Juanita Brooks (Salt Lake City: University of Utah Press/Utah State Historical Society, 1964).

....

According to appointment on Sunday last, a meeting was held in the Temple today of some of those who had received their ordinances. Seventy-five persons were present.

Elder Heber C. Kimball presiding.

The sacrament was administered by Father John Smith and Bishop George Miller.

Elders George A. Smith and Heber C. Kimball preached, others made a few remarks confirming what had been said.

Elder John Taylor was mouth in prayer.

Meeting dismissed at 2:10 p.m.

Three p.m., many others who had been invited met according to appointment.

Elders Amasa Lyman and Heber C. Kimball preached.

At ten a.m., the seventies met in the Music Hall. The thirty-second quorum of seventies was organized; and arrangements made to finish an upper room in the Temple for the benefit of the seventies.

—"Manuscript History of Brigham Young," in *History of the Church,* 7:548-49.

Monday, December 22, 1845

This week has been assigned principally to the High Priests for them to come in and receive their washings & anointing. Pres[ident]. George Miller was early at the Temple making preparations for the day's work. Pres[ident]. B[righam]. Young was at the temple having slept there the last night[.]

Each department and station having been filled by appointment of

Pres[ident]. Miller, at 17 minutes before 9, [we] commenced in the male department washing and anointing the following High Priests—viz;

Jonathan H. Hale,	born	Feb[ruar]y 1. 1800
Ira Price	"	Oct[ober]. 28 1792
Gardner Snow	"	Feb[ruar]y 15 1793
Dominicus Carter	"	June 21. 1806
William Garner	"	Jan[uar]y 22. 1816
Curtis E. Bolton	"	July 15. 1812
James C. Snow	"	Jan[uar]y 11. 1817
William D. Pratt	"	Sept[ember] 3. 1802
Dexter Stillman	"	March 23. 1804
John Patten	"	April 14. 1787
William G. Perkins	"	Jan[uar]y 11. 1801
Edward P. Duzette	"	Jan[uar]y. 24 1812
Levi Gifford	"	Aug[us]t 15, 1789
Jacob Foutz	"	Jan[uar]y 25 1800
Anson Call	"	May 13. 1810
George Burkett	"	Oct[ober] 18. 1788
John Coltrin	"	July 30, 1775
Edmund Fisher	"	July 7. 1803
James Sloan	born	Oct[ober] 28. 1792
Zebedee Coltrin	"	Sept[ember] 7 1804
Abel Lamb	"	March 9. 1801
Thomas Kington	"	May 1794
Evan M. Green	"	Dec[embe]r. 22. 1814
Edwin D. Woolley	"	June 28. 1807

Also of the quorum of Seventies,

William S. Covert	"	August 6. 1808.

These were washed by William Crosby and Jesse P. Harmon, and anointed by William Snow & A[braham]. O. Smoot.

Finished at 17 minutes before 12.

Also at 15 minutes past one o'clock

In the Male department [we] commenced washing and anointing the following persons, High Priests, viz;

Levi Stewart	born	April 28. 1812
Samuel Fowler	"	Dec[ember]. 14. 1790
Graham Coltrin	"	Dec[ember]. 11. 1796
James Newberry	"	May 29, 1791
George D. Watt	"	Jan[uar]y 16. 1816

Alvah L. Tippets	"	March 12. 1809
John Mackly	"	March 20 1796.
Isaac Beebee	"	July 31. 1806
Aaron Cheeney	"	July 14 1787
William Yocom	"	1805
John M. Burk	"	Feb[ruar]y 4 1793
Harvey Omstead	"	Feb[ruar]y 10. 1794
Henry Deam	"	March 5 1817
Cyrill Call	"	June 29 1785
Hugh McClelen	"	Feb[ruar]y 18. 1773

Washed by Jesse P. Harmon, & W[illiam]. Crosby an[ointed]. by W[illia]m. Snow, A[braham]. O. Smoot & Peter Haws. 26 m[inutes]. before 3.

Charles A. Burk, born Sept[ember]. 2. 1823 was ordained into the quorum of Seventies, by Joseph Young and Henry Harriman, washed by Jesse P. Harmon & W[illiam]. Crosby anointed by William Snow, A[braham]. O. Smoot & P[eter]. Haws[.]

[F]inished at 26 m[inutes]. before 3.

In the Female department [we] commenced washing and anointing at 17 m[inutes]. to 9. The following persons were washed & anointed.

Hannah Tupper born March 23. 1823 w[ashed]. by Caroline C. Grover. an[ointed]. by Caroline E. Grover[.]

Sarah A. Rice born Jan[uar]y 30. 1801 w[ashed]. by Sarah Crosby. An[ointed]. by Ma[r]y C. Miller[.]

Mary Pitt born Feb[ruar]y 17. 1806 W[ashed]. by Dorcas Dykes An[ointed] by C[atherine]. C. Spencer[.]

Olive B. Hale born July 30. 1805 W[ashed]. Dorcas Dykes An[ointed]. by C[atherine]. C. Spencer[.]

Rebecca Bolton born 1810 W[ashed]. by Amanda Rogers, An[ointed]. by Ma[r]y C. Miller[.]

Mary Carter born March 21. 1830 W[ashed]. [by] Sarah Crosby an[ointed] by Caroline E. Grover[.]

Sarah Garner [born] Jan[uar]y 27 1818 w[ashed] by Amanda Rogers an[ointed] by C[atherine]. C. Spencer[.]

Wealthy Pratt born March 24. 1810 W[ashed]. by Dorcas Dykes an[ointed] by C[aroline]. E. Grover[.]

Sarah S. Snow born Feb[ruar]y 2. [17]95 [washed] by Dorcas Dykes [anointed by] Ma[r]y C. Miller[.]

Barbara Stillman [born] Feb[ruary]. 5. 1808 [washed] by Dorcas Dykes [anointed by] C[atherine]. C. Spencer[.]

Eliza Ann Snow [born] Sep[tember]. 28. 1818 [washed] by Amanda Rogers [anointed by] Ma[r]y C. Miller[.]

Hannah Patten born May 10, 1788 W[ashed]. by Dorcas Dykes, anointed by Leonora Taylor[.]

Eliza Ann Duzette, b[orn]. May 29. 1817 [washed] by Sarah Crosby [anointed by] Caroline E. Grover[.]

Dicey Perkins b[orn]. Aug[us]t 12 1796 [washed] by Amanda Rogers [anointed by] Mary C. Miller[.]

Helen M. Averett b[orn]. Oct[ober]. 20. 1830 [washed] by Amanda Rogers [anointed by] Mary C. Miller[.]

[E]nded at 10 o'clock[.]

At eleven o'clock [we] commenced again and the following persons were washed and anointed, viz;

Deborah Gifford, born May 27. 1794 W[ashed]. by Sarah Crosby [anointed by] Ma[r]y C. Miller[.]

Cornelia Fisher b[orn]. May 11. 1812 [washed] by Ama[n]da Rogers [anointed by] Leonora Taylor[.]

Leah Coltrin, [born] Feb[ruar]y 8. 1775 W[ashed] by Margaret Smoot A[nointed] by Margaret Smoot[.]

Mary Coltrin, born Nov[ember]. 27. 1820 [washed] by Sarah Crosby [anointed by] Leonora Taylor[.]

Sarah Burkett born Jan[uar]y 5. 1788 or 9 [washed] by Amanda Rogers [anointed by] Mary C. Miller[.]

Catharine Lewis b[orn]. March 17. 1799 [washed] by Sarah Crosby [anointed by] Vilate Kimball[.]

Mary W. Woolley [born] Nov[ember]. 10. 1808 [washed] by Dorcas Dykes [anointed by] Leonora Taylor[.]

Louisa C. Rising. [born] Feb[ruar]y 28 1820 [washed] by Amanda Rogers [anointed by] Mary C. Miller[.]

Mary Sloan [born] Aug[us]t. 1. 1801. [washed] by Amanda Rogers [anointed by] Mary C. Miller[.]

Sarah McGill b[orn]. [blank] [washed] by Margaret Smoot [anointed by] Leonora Taylor[.]

Almira Lamb b[orn]. June 5. 1807 [washed] by Dorcas Dykes [anointed by] Leonora Taylor[.]

Margaret Kington born March 24. 1813 W[ashed]. by Dorcas Dykes anointed by M[argaret]. Smoot[.]

Margaret Foutz b[orn]. Dec[ember]. 14, 1802 [washed] by Amanda Rogers [anointed by] Mary C. Miller[.]

Mary Covert born Feb[ruar]y 7. 1809 [washed] by Margaret Smoot [anointed by] Vilate Kimball[.]

Nancy Kent b[orn]. Aug[us]t 6 1786 [washed] by Sarah Crosby [anointed by] Vilate Kimball[.]

Susan Green born April 3. 1816 [washed] by Dorcas Dykes [anointed by] Mary C. Miller[.]

[E]nded at 10 minutes past 12. at 20 m[inutes]. past one commenced again

Mary Watt	born Jan[uar]y 17 1807
by Dorcas Dykes	Mary C Miller
Mehitable Cheeney,	Jan[uar]y 31. 1787
by Sarah Crosby	Caroline Grover
Susanna Yocom	Nov[ember]. 5. 1807
by Amanda Rogers	Leonora Taylor
Elizabeth Deam	Sep[tember]. 11. 1815
by Sarah Crosby	Mary C. Miller
Melinda Stewart,	Nov[ember]. 7. 1816
by Margaret T. Smoot	Leonora Taylor
Nancy Bean	born Dec[ember]. 14. 1826
by Dorcas Dykes	Mary C. Miller
Rachel Woolsey	born Aug[us]t 18. 1818
by Dorcas Dykes	Caroline E. Grover
Polly McLellin	b[orn]. Dec[ember]. 20, 1776
by Amanda Rogers	Leonora Taylor
Aseneth Jones	born Aug[us]t 18. 1796
by Dorcas Dykes	Mary C. Miller
Phebe Beebe	born Aug[us]t 6, 1896
by Amanda Rogers	Leonora Taylor
Keziah Burk	born May 15. 1796
by Margaret T. Smoot	Leonora Taylor
Caroline Tippets	born Jan[uar]y 15. 1866
by Dorcas Dykes	Mary C. Miller
Eliza Ann Newberry	born Oct[ober] 24. 1824
by Margaret T. Smoot	Mary C. Miller
Elizabeth Newberry,	May 9. 1815
by Amanda Rogers	Leonora Taylor
Betsey Mackley	born, (unknown)
by Dorcas Dykes,	Margaret T. Smoot
Anna Omstead	born June 13. 1800
by Amanda Rogers	Leonora Taylor

Abi S. Burk	born April 8. 1825	
by Margaret T. Smoot		Mary C. Miller
Sally Call	born Nov[embe]r. 27. 1788	
by Dorcas Dykes		Leonora Taylor
Mary K. Miles	born April 29. 1809	
by Margaret T. Smoot		Mary C. Miller
Harriet Coltrin	July 8. 1813	
[not given]		[not given]

[E]nded at 3 o'clock. at 25 minutes to 5. [we] washed & anointed

Sarah Gibbons born Oct[ober]. 20. 1800 W[ashed]. by Margaret T. Smoot an[ointed]. by M[argaret]. T. Smoot[.]

Jemima Perkins. [born] June 27. 1808 W[ashed]. by Amanda Rogers an[ointed]. by Mary C. Miller[.]

Sarah Wood born March 31 1814 W[ashed]. by Sarah Crosby an[ointed]. by Mary C. Miller[.]

Esther Brown [born] Jan[uar]y 7th 1814 W[ashed]. by Sarah Crosby an[ointed]. [by] Leonora Taylor[.]

Constantine Hutchinson [born] Oct[ober] 14 1817 W[ashed]. by M[argaret]. T. Smoot anointed by M[argaret]. C. Miller[.]

Mary Downton born June 30, 1793 [washed] by ~~M. T. Smoot~~ Amanda Rogers [anointed by] Mary C. Miller[.]

Sarah Elizabeth Cook [born] Nov[ember]. 7. 1810 [washed] by Amanda Rogers [anointed by] M[ary]. C. Miller[.]

Alice Martin. born Mar[ch]. 28. 1816 [washed] by Amanda Rogers [anointed by] Leonora Taylor[.]

[E]nded at 20 min[utes] past 6.

At 16 m[inutes]. before 5. [we] commenced in the Male department washing & anointing the following persons. High Priests, viz;

Andrew H. Perkins,	born	Dec[ember]. 5, 1808,
James Brown	"	Sept[ember] 9 1801.

Also of the quorum of Seventies,

Jacob F. Hutchinson,	born	Aug[us]t 14, 1816
John M. Downton	"	Dec[ember]. 23 1794
Frederick Cook	"	April 17 1812
Edmund Martin	"	Nov[embe]r. 18. 1818

These were washed by Jesse P. Harmon and William Crosby[.] The High Priests were anointed by Abraham O. Smoot & William Crosby and the Seventies by Joseph Young and J[edediah]. M. Grant.

Finished at 10 m[inutes]. past 6.

At 3 m[inutes]. before 10 o'clock A.M. the Bell rung, and operations commenced to receive into the lower & middle departments, those that were washed & anointed this morning, the following persons officiating—viz.

in the upper department

Orson Spencer as No. 1. L[ucius]. N. Scovil No. 2
C[harles]. C. Rich as No 3.

In the Middle department

Erastus Snow	as	No.	1
Geo[rge]. P. Dykes	"	"	2
W[illiam]. A. Sanger	"	"	3
W[illiam]. W. Phelps	"	"	4

F[ranklin]. D. Richards Prompter—

At 10 minutes before 12 [we] commenced receiving into the upper department the company first washed this morning which we will [call?] Company No. 1[,] John D. Lee, Lorenzo Snow, and, Mrs. Catharine C. Spencer acting as prompters.

Jonathan H. Hale by Orson Spencer[.]
Olive B. Hale by J[onathan]. H. Hale & O[rson]. S[pencer].
Gardner Snow by Orson Spencer[.]
Sarah S. Snow by G[ardner]. Snow & O[rson]. Spencer[.]
Curtis E. Bolton by O[rson]. Spencer[.]
Rebecca Bolton " " " & C[urtis]. E. B[olton].
Ira Rice " George Miller[.]
Sarah Ann Rice by Ira Rice & G[eorge]. M[iller].
John Patten by Geo[rge]. Miller[.]
Hannah Patten by John Patten & G[eorge]. M[iller].
William Garner by H[eber]. C. Kimball[.]
Sarah Garner by W[illia]m. Garner & H[eber]. C. K[imball].
William D. Perkins by H[eber]. C. Kimball[.]
Wealthy Pratt by W[illiam]. D. Pratt and O[rson]. Spencer[.]
James C. Snow by Orson Spencer[.]
Eliza A. [?] Snow by J[ames]. C. Snow & O[rson]. S[pencer].
Mary Pitt by Orson Spencer[.]
Hannah Tupper by " " [.]
Helen M. Averett by " " [.]
Dominicus Carter " " " [.]
Mary Carter " " & D[ominicus]. C[arter].

[E]nded at half past 2.

At 20 minutes past 12, the bell rung for the second company to pass in the lower and middle departments—

Orson Spencer	officiated	as	No.	1	} in the
Lucius N. Scovil	"	"	"	2	} upper
Charles C. Rich	"	"	"	3	} dep[artmen]t
Erastus Snow	"	"	"	1	}
George P. Dykes	"	"	"	2	}
William A. Sanger	"	"	"	3	}
W[illiam]. W. Phelps	"	"	"	4	}
F[ranklin]. D. Richards	"	"	Prompter}		

At 3 o'clock [we] commenced receiving into the upper department company No. 2.— Lorenzo Snow and Mrs. Catharine C. Spencer being prompters. The persons were received in the following order viz;

George Burkett by H[eber]. C. Kimball[.]
Sarah Burkett by her husband G[eorge]. B[urkett].
Catharine Lewis by H[eber]. C. Kimball[.]
Nancy Kent by H[eber]. C. Kimball[.]
Dexter Stillman by H[eber]. C. Kimball[.]
Barbara Stillman by H[eber]. C. K[imball]. & D[exter]. S[tillman].
Abel Lamb by Amasa Lyman[.]
Almira Lamb by A[bel]. Lamb & A[masa]. Lyman[.]
John Coltrin by Orson Spencer[.]
Leah Coltrin by O[rson]. S[pencer]. & J[ohn]. Coltrin[.]
Thomas Kington by O[rson]. Spencer[.]
Margaret Kington by O[rson]. Spencer & T[homas]. K[ington].
Anson Call " O[rson]. Spencer[.]
Edwin D. Wolley by Orson Spencer[.]
Mary W. Woolley by E[dwin]. D. Woolley & O[rson]. S[pencer].
Louisa C. Rising by E[dwin]. D. Woolley & O[rson]. S[pencer].
Evan M. Green by H[eber]. C. Kimball[.]
Susa Green by E[van]. M. G[reen]. & H[eber]. C. K[imball].
William S. Covert by O[rson]. Spencer[.]
Mary Covert by W[illiam]. S. Covert & O[rson]. Spencer[.]
Levi Gifford by L[ucius]. N. Scovil[.]
Deborah Gifford by Levi Gifford & L[ucius]. N. S[covil].
Zebedee Coltrin by Lucius N. Scovil[.]
Mary Coltrin by Z[ebedee]. Coltrin & [Lucius] Scovil[.]
Jacob Foutz by L[ucius]. N. Scovil[.]
Margaret Foutz by J[acob]. Foutz & [Lucius] Scovil[.]

James Sloan by L[ucius]. N. Scovil[.]
Mary Sloan " James Sloan[.]
Sarah McGill " " " [.]
Edward Fisher by L[ucius]. N. Scovil[.]
Cornelia J. Fisher " " " [and] E[dward]. Fisher[.]
[E]nded at 15 minutes past 6.

At 3 o'clock the Bell rung for company No. 3. to enter the lower & middle dep[artments]. the following persons officiating, viz,

in the upper department
Orson Spencer as No. 1
John D. Lee " " 2
C[harles]. C. Rich " " 3.

In the middle department,
Erastus Snow No 1, G[eorge]. P. Dykes, No. 2
W[illiam]. A. Sanger " 3. W[illiam]. W. Phelps " 4.
Franklin D. Richards, prompter,

Almon W. Babbitt came into the Temple about this time—3 o'clock.

At 15 minutes past 6 [we] commenced receiving into the upper [illegible words crossed out] departments Company No. 3. Prompters J[ohn]. D. Lee. Lorenzo Snow and Catharine C. Spencer.

Alvah L. Tippetts, by P[arley]. P. Pratt.
Caroline Tippets " A[lvah]. L. Tippets[.]
Isaac Beebe " P[arley]. P. Pratt.
Phebe Beebe " Isaac Beebe[.]
Henry Deam " P[arley]. P. Pratt[.]
Elizabeth Deam " Henry Deam & P[arley Pratt.]
Harvey Omstead " J[ohn]. D. Lee.
Anna Omstead " " and H[arvey]. Omstead[.]
Hugh McLellin " P[arley]. P. Pratt.
Polly McLellin " " & H[ugh]. M[cLellin].
William Yocom " " [.]
Susan Yocom " " & W[illiam]. Yocom[.]
George D. Watt " P[arley]. P. Pratt.
Mary Watt " G[eorge]. D. Watt & P[arley]. P[ratt].
James Newberry " P[arley]. P. Pratt[.]
Elisabeth Newberry by J[ames]. Newberry & P[arley Pratt].
Elisa ^Ann^ Newberry by J[ames]. Newberry[.]

Aaron Cherry	by	P[arley]. P. Pratt.
Mehitabel Cherry	by	A[aron]. Cherry & P[arley Pratt].
Graham Coltrin	by	P[arley]. P. Pratt.
Hannah Coltrin	by	G[raham]. Coltrin.
Nancy Bean	by	John D. Lee[.]
Rachel Woolsy	by	J[ohn]. D. Lee[.]
~~Charles~~ ^John M.^ Burk	by	P[arley]. P. Pratt[.]
Keziah Burk	by	John M. Burk[.]
Samuel Fowler	by	John D. Lee[.]
Cyrill Call	"	Orson Spencer[.]
Sally Call	by	C[yrill]. Call & O[rson]. S[pencer].
John Mackley	by	O[rson]. Spencer[.]
Betsey Mackley	"	J[ohn]. Mackley[.]
Charles A. Burk	"	O[rson]. Spencer[.]
Abi Selina Burk	"	C[harles]. A. Burk[.]
Mary K. Miles	"	O[rson]. Spencer[.]
Aseneth Janes	"	O[rson]. Spencer[.]

[E]nded at 15 minutes before 10.

Levi Stewart.	by	[blank]
Melinda Stewart	"	Levi Stewart[.]

At 35 minutes past 6 the Bell rung for company No. 4 to enter the lower and middle departments—the following persons officiating, viz;

in the upper department

J[edediah]. M. Grant	as	No.	1.
L[ucius]. N. Scovil	"	"	2.
Aaron Johnson	"	"	3.

& in the middle department,

Orson Spencer	as	No.	1
George P. Dykes	"	"	2
William A. Sanger	"	"	3.
W[illiam]. W. Phelps	"	"	4

Prompter — F[ranklin]. D. Richards

At 5 o'clock the following High Priests met in room No. 8. viz; Pres[ident]. George Miller William Snow. John M. Bernhisel, Simeon Carter — Lucian Woodworth, Daniel Spencer — Erastus Snow — Winslow Farr William Felshaw — Stephen Markham, & F[ranklin]. D. Richards — Lucian Woodworth being mouth[.]

At 8 o'clock ^P.M.^ Pres[ident]. Brigham Young John Taylor, Amasa

Lyman, Geo[rge]. A. Smith, Orson Hyde, Lucian Woodworth and George Miller, met in Pres[ident]. Young's room, and consecrated thirty seven bottles of oil which had been prepared by Bishop Miller, for the purpose of anointing those who are prepared by washing[.]

[A]t Twelve o'clock P.M. all retired except Pres[ident]. B[righam]. Young, H[eber]. C. Kimball Amasa Lyman — John D. Lee — Lewis Rollins David Candland. Theodore Turl[e]y, H[ans]. C. Hanson — Peter Hanson — H[enry]. G. Sherwood these slept in the Temple[.]

At 10 o'clock [we] commenced receiving into the upper department company No. 4. Joseph Young being prompter, They were received in the following order—viz;

James Brown	by	Orson Spencer[.]
Esther Brown	"	J[ames]. Brown & O[rson]. S[pencer].
Sarah Wood	"	J[ames]. Brown & O[rson]. S[pencer].
Sarah Gibbons	"	A[braham]. O. Smoot.
Edward Martin	by	E[dward]. Martin & O[rson]. S[pencer].
Alice Martin	by	E[dward]. Martin & O[rson]. S[pencer].
Jacob F. Hutchinson	by	O[rson]. Spencer[.]
Constantia Hutchinson	by	O[rson]. S[pencer]. & J[acob]. F. H[utchinson].
Andrew H. Perkins	by	Orson Spencer[.]
Jemima Perkins	"	A[ndrew]. H P[erkins]. & O[rson]. S[pencer].
John M. Dunton	"	O[rson]. Spencer[.]
Mary Dunton	"	J[ohn]. M D[unton]. & O[rson]. Spencer[.]
Frederick Cook	"	O[rson]. Spencer[.]
Sarah Elizabeth Cook	by	F[rederick]. Cook & O[rson]. S[pencer].

[E]nded at 15 m. past 11.

—William Clayton, Diary, kept for Heber C. Kimball.

....

The day previous [i.e., December 21] some excellent instructions was offered in the Temple relative to order among the saints, and in the House of the Lord, more especially showing the wisdom & policy of the mind of the spirit in selecting or appointing Persons to officiate in the different departments in the House of the Lord that the innocent & just might not be exposed to the ignorance of inquisitive babler who ^know^ not how to keep from commiting [violations] themselves — [Only those should be present who are] responsible & confidential enough to [do so] & must be selected [on those terms] to officiate in giving the Endowment to the Saints — accordingly at 8 o clock A.M. the roll was called, and those persons who have been appointed to attend & officiate in the different departments received their several stations Namely O[rson] Spencer [as] E[lohim], No 1[;] L[ucius] N. Scovil [as] J[ehovah]. No. 2[;] C[harles]. C. Rich [as] M[ichael]. No. 3[;] & W[illia]m. W. Phelps [as the] S[erpent]. No. 4. F[ranklin]. D Richards[,] Promptors in the garden — Middle department Erastus Snow [as] P[eter,] No 1[;] G[eorge]. P. Dykes [as] No. 2 — John — W[illiam]. A. Sanger [as] John[,] No 3[;] & F[ranklin]. D. R[ichards,] P[rompter,] No. 4. [A]t the uper department O[rson] Spencer Screen at the v[eil]— J[ohn] D Lee Prompter A[t?]. V[eil?]. No 2 H[enry]. G. Sherwood Marshall — Daniel Carn ward Robe— A[ndrew] Lyttle John Scott & Elijah Averett attend to fire & water in the Female Department — Hosea Stout & J[esse]. D. Hunter in the male department — to wash W[illia]m Crosby Peter Haws. & J[ohn]. P. Harmon — to Anoint A[braham]. O. Smoot & W[illia]m Snow[;] Elisha Averett [and] Lewis Robbins Door Keepers[;] John L Butler Fireman[;] L[ucian] N Foster J[ohn] D Lee and David Candland — Clerks[.] This arrangment however was in[tended] not [to be] permanent[,] it being the order of the day only on acount of the member[s] or candidate[s] being chiefly High Priest[s] — which of course left Pres[ident] Jos[eph]. Young & council out until a company of the Seventies should be taken in —

12 O clock W[illia]m S. Covert born — Aug 6, 1808 washed by J[esse]. P Harmon & W[illia]m Crosby and anointed by A[braham]. O. Smoot Peter Haws & W[illia]m Snow —

$1.55 c[en]ts was Paid for the 30th Quorums by Pres[ident] W[illiam]. A. Sanger for the purpose of processing materials for garments. Preparatory for the Endowment.

Frederick Cook April 17. 1812. Edward Martin Nov 18 1818 — washed by J[esse]. P. Harmon & W[illia]m Crosby & anointed by A[braham]. O Smoot & W[illia]m Snow[. Number] 90[,] Jacob F. Hutchinson[,] d[itt]o by the same May 14, 1818[.]

Sisters

Constantine Hutchins June 14. 1811. Sarah E. Cook Nov 7 1810 Thea Martin Mar 28 ^1816^ washed by Amanda Rodgers & Anointed by M[ary]. C. Miller & L[eonora]. Taylor—

Cha[rle]s. A. Burk [was] ordained a Seventy under the hands of Pres[ident] Young — Pres[ident] Jos[eph]. Young and J[edediah]. M. Grant assisted in taking through the last company at ½ Past 11 at Night the services closed & Pres[ident] Young & Grant and myself [John D. Lee] returned home about midnight — to day 106 Persons passed through the ordinances of Endowment generally High priests [illegible.]

—Seventies Record, Book B.

I [Brigham Young] stayed in the Temple last night and early this morning gave direction for the arrangements of the day, assisted by George Miller, as the day was set apart more especially for the high priests.

One hundred and six persons received ordinances.

—"Manuscript History of Brigham Young,"
in *History of the Church,* 7:549.

Nauvoo temple endowments performed on this date for:

First Company: Jonathan H. Hale, Olive B. Hale, Gardner Snow, Sarah S. Snow, Curtis E. Bolton, Rebecca Bolton, Edward P. Duzette, Eliza Ann Duzette, Ira Rice, Sarah Ann Rice, John Patten, Hannah Patten, William Garner, Sarah Garner, William G. Perkins, Dicey Perkins, William D. Pratt, Wealthy Pratt, James C. Snow, Eliza A. Snow, Mary Pitt, Hannah Tupper, Helen M. Averett, Dominicus Carter, and Mary Carter.

Second Company: George Burkett, Sarah Burkett, Catharine Lewis,[8] Nancy Kent, Dexter Stillman, Barbara Stillman, Abel Lamb, Almira Lamb, John Coltrin, Leah Coltrin, Thomas Kington, Margaret Kington, Anson Call, Edwin D. Woolley, Mary W. Woolley, Louisa C. Rising, Evan M. Green, Susan Green, William S. Covert, Mary Covert, Levi Gifford, Deborah Gifford, Zebedee Coltrin, Mary Coltrin, Jacob Foutz, Margaret Foutz, James Sloan, Mary Sloan, Sarah McGill, Edmund Fisher, and Cornelia J. Fisher.

8. Three years later, Catherine Lewis would write an account of her experience in the temple; see her *Narrative of Some of the Proceedings of the Mormons; Giving an Account of Their Iniquities. With Particulars Concerning the Training of the Indians by Them, Description of the Mode of Endowment, Plurality of Wives, &c., &c.* (Lynn, MA: By the Author, 1848), 7-10.

Third Company: Alvah L. Tippets, Caroline Tippets, Isaac Beebe, Phebe Beebe, Henry Deam, Elizabeth Deam, Harvey Omstead, Anna Omstead, Hugh McLellin Polly McLellin, William Yocom, Susan Yocom, George D. Watt, Mary Watt, James Newberry, Elizabeth Newberry, Eliza Ann Newberry, Aaron Cheney, Mehitabel Cheney, Graham Coltrin, Hannah Coltrin, Nancy Bean, Rachel Woolsey, John M. Burk, Keziah Burk, Samuel Fowler, Cyrill Call, Sally Call, John Mackley, Betsey Mackley, Charles A. Burk, Abi Selina Burk, Mary K. Miles, Aseneth Jones, Levi Stewart, and Melinda Stewart.

Fourth Company: James Brown, Esther Brown, Sarah Wood, Sarah Gibbons, Edward Martin, Alice Martin, Jacob F. Hutchinson, Constantia Hutchinson, Andrew H. Perkins, Jemima Perkins, John M. Downton, Mary Downton, Frederick Cook, and Sarah Elizabeth Cook.

—Summary of information compiled by the Temple Index Bureau, *Nauvoo Temple Endowment Register: 10 December 1845 to 8 February 1846.*

Tuesday, December 23, 1845

The dry house of Gen[eral]. Charles C. Rich's emigrating company. No. 13. was burnt to the ground early this morning and about 300 dollars worth of spokes, felloes and other timber consumed. It was situated near the Seminary building, formerly the Arsenal. Gen[eral]. Rich came to the Temple and reported himself ready for the duties of the day, but on account of the accident above mentioned was excused for the day.

The High Council met this morning in room No. 4. for prayer, being clothed in the garments & Robes of Priesthood, They offered up prayer & thanksgiving to God, E[lde]r. [Alpheus] Cutler being mouth—present —Samuel Bent. G[eorge]. W. Harris Alpheus Cutler—James Allred,—Thomas Grover—Newell Knight—David Fullmer—Aaron Johnson—and Ezra T. Benson—closed at 8—30 m[inutes].

At 25 minutes before 9 o'clock A.M. [we] commenced in the Male department washing and anointing, the following High Priests, ~~viz~~[.] [B]efore being washed and anointed, Raymond Clark was ordained a High Priest under the hands of Pres[ident]. George Miller and William Crosby.

Benjamin Brown.	born	Sept[ember] 30. 1794
Raymond Clark	"	Feb[ruar]y 20. 1795
Daniel Carter	"	Aug[us]t 7. 1804
Gardner Clark	"	Jan[uar]y 15, 1791

Archibald Tanner " April 9. 1791
John Tanner " Aug[us]t 15. 1778
of the quorum of Seventies—
Thomas Woolsey, born Nov[embe]r. 3. 1806

[T]hese were washed by Jesse P. Harmon and William Crosby, and anointed by William Snow & Abraham O. Smoot.

[E]nded at 20 m[inutes]. past 9.

In the Female department [we] commenced washing, and anointing at 20 m[inutes]. to 9.

The following persons were washed & anointed,

Louisa Clark born Jan[uar]y 25. 1810. washed by Sarah Crosby anointed by Caroline C. Spencer[.]
Sarah Brown born April 20. 1795 W[ashed]. by Mary C. Miller. an[ointed]. by Mary C. Miller[.]
Delecta Clark b[orn]. Jan[uar]y. 30. 1796 W[ashed]. by Mary C. Miller an[ointed] by C[aroline]. C. Spencer[.]
Mary Ann Barker Feb[ruar]y 18. 1825 W[ashed]. by Sarah Crosby. A[nointed]. by C[aroline]. C. Spencer[.]
Huldah M. Clark. born Oct[ober] 22. 1823. w[ashed] by Sarah Crosby. anointed by Mary C. Miller[.]
Polly Thompson, born Jan[uar]y 29. 1822 W[ashed] by Sarah Crosby an[ointed]. by M[argaret]. T. Smoot.
Harriet A. Carter. born Nov[embe]r. 25. 1831 w[ashed] by Sarah Crosby An[ointed] by Pamela Lott.
Lucretia Marilla Johnson, Oct[ober] 12. 1830 w[ashed]. by Phebe Miller an[ointed]. by Mary C. Miller[.]
Mary Woolsey born May 11. 1813 w[ashed]. by Sarah Crosby. an[ointed]. by M[argaret]. T. Smoot[.]
Eliza Tanner born Nov[embe]r. 28. 1803 w[ashed]. by M[argaret]. T. Smoot an[ointe]d. by C[aroline]. C. Spencer[.]
Elizabeth Durfee born March 11. 1791 w[ashed]. by M[argaret]. T. Smoot ano[inted]. by Mary C. Miller[.]
Abigail Patten born Dec[embe]r. 13. 1791 W[ashed]. by Sarah Crosby an[ointed]. by Mary C. Miller[.]

[E]nded at 14 minutes to 10.

At 10 O'clock the bell rung and [we] commenced to receive in to the lower & middle departments those who had been washed and anointed this morning.

The following named persons officiated,

Orson Spencer as No. 1. }
Lucius N. Scovil " " 2. } upper dep[artmen]t.
George P. Dykes " " 3. }

In the middle department

Orson Pratt as No. 1
William Snow " " 2.
William Miller " " 3
W[illiam]. W. Phelps " " 4
F[ranklin]. D. Richards " Prompter—

At 15, m[inutes]. before 12, [we] commenced receiving into the upper department. company No. 1. Lorenzo Snow and Catherine C. Spencer officiating as prompters—also J[ohn]. D. Lee at first.

The persons washed and anointed were received in the following order, viz;

Benjamin Brown	by	Orson Spencer[.]
Sarah Brown	by	B[enjamin]. Brown & O[rson]. S[pencer].
John Tanner	by	Orson Spencer[.]
Elisa Tanner	"	John Tanner & O[rson]. S]pencer].
Daniel Carter	"	Orson Spencer [.]
Harriet Carter	"	Daniel Carter & O[rson]. S[pencer].
Elisabeth Durfee	"	Orson Spencer[.]
Thomas Woolsey	"	Orson Spencer[.]
Mary Woolsey	"	T[homas]. Woolsey & George Miller[.]
Lucretia Marilla Johnson	by	W[illia]m Miller[.]
Gardner Clark	"	George Miller[.]
Delecta Clark	"	G[ardner]. Clark & Geo[rge]. Miller[.]
Huldah M. Clark	"	Geo[rge]. Miller[.]
Raymond Clark	"	Geo[rge]. Miller.
Louisa Clark	"	R[aymond]. Clark & Geo[rge]. Miller[.]
Archibald Patten	"	George Miller.
Abigail Patten	"	A[rchibald]. Patten & G[eorge]. Miller[.]
Mary Ann Barker	"	George Miller[.]
Polly Thompson	"	George Miller[.]

[E]nded at 25 m[inutes]. past one.

At 5 minutes past one Almon W. Babbitt entered the Temple, was invited by Pres[ident]. [Brigham] Young into his room— he brings report that officers from Springfield [Illinois] are here and several of the State Troops—after some of the Twelve [apostles], particularly. Amasa Lyman[9]—

At 25 minutes to 11. [we] commenced in the male department, washing and anointing the following High Priests, viz;

Benjamin Covey.	born	March 9. 1792
William McCleary	"	Oct[ober] 9. 1793
Josiah W. Fleming	"	April 25. 1808
Henry W. Miller	"	May 1. 1807
Samuel Henderson	"	Feb[ruar]y 21. 1785
John Lamoreaux	"	July 19. 1779
Andrew L. Lamoreaux	"	Oct[ober]. 17. 1812

These were washed by Jesse P. Harmon and William Crosby, and the two first were anointed by Peter Haws & Th[eodore]. Turley the others by William Snow & A[braham]. O. Smoot.

[E]nded at 27 m[inutes]. past 12.

In the Female department, [we] commenced at 27 minutes before 11. to wash & anoint the following persons, viz;

Sophronia Mc.Clary born May 16. 1803 W[ashed]. by M[argaret]. T. Smoot, anointed by M[argaret]. T. Smoot[.]

Mary Wood. born June 18. 1819 w[ashed]. by Artemisia Snow, anointed by Pamela A. Benson[.]

Elisabeth Brotherton, born March 27. 1817 w[ashed]. by Polly Z. Johnson an[ointe]d. by Mary C. Miller[.]

Adeline B. Andrus b[orn]. March 18. 1813 W[ashed]. by Artemisia Snow an[ointed]. by Pamela A. Benson[.]

Diana Cole born May 27. 1819 w[ashed]. by Artemisia Snow. an[ointed]. by Mary C. Miller[.]

Nancy Fleming born Aug[us]t 6. 1810 W[ashed]. by A[rtemisia]. Snow anointed by Mary C. Miller[.]

Elmira Miller, born Feb[ruar]y 14. 1811 W[ashed]. by Pamela Lott, anointed by M[argaret]. T. Smoot.

9. Amasa Lyman, like Brigham Young, was wanted on counterfeiting charges. Warrants for their arrest had already been issued by a grand jury in Springfield, Illinois.

Minerva White born Mar[ch]. 22. 1822. W[ashed]. by Artemisia Snow. an[ointed] by Artemisia Sn[ow].

Axy White born March 15. 1789 w[ashed]. by Pamela Lott, an[ointed]. by Mary C. Miller[.]

Elizabeth Henderson [born] Dec[ember]. 3. 1800 w[ashed]. by Pamela Lott, anointed by Mary C. Miller[.]

~~Isabel Lamoreaux March 4 or 5 1808.~~— came into the washing room, but retired again without being washed or anointed.

Catherine Lamoreaux [born] Nov[embe]r. 30. 1779 [washed] by M[argaret]. T. Smoot an[ointed] by Mary C. Miller[.]

[E]nded at 20 min[utes] after 12.

At 25 minutes past 12. the bell rung, and operations commenced with company No. 2. in the lower & middle departments, the following persons officiating viz; in the upper department

Orson Spencer	as	No.	1
L[ucius]. N. Scovil	"	"	2
George P. Dykes	"	"	3

in the middle dep[artmen]t.

Erastus Snow	as	No.	1
William Snow	"	"	2
William Miller	"	"	3
W[illiam]. W. Phelps	"	"	4
F[ranklin]. D. Richards	"	Prompter—	

At 2 o'clock [we] commenced receiving into the upper department, company No. 2. whose washing and anointing commenced at 25 minutes before 11. in the following order—viz;

Henry W. Miller	by P[arley]. P. Pratt.
Elmira Miller	by H[enry]. W. Miller & P[arley]. P[ratt].
Adeline B. Andrew	" P[arley]. P. Pratt[.]
John Lamoreaux	" P[arley]. P. Pratt[.]
Catherine Lamoreaux	" J[ohn]. L[amoreaux]. & P[arley]. P. Pratt[.]
William McCleary	" P[arley]. P. Pratt.
Sophronia McCleary	by W[illiam]. M[c]C[leary]. & P[arley]. P. Pratt[.]
Mary Wood	" P[arley]. P. Pratt.
Elisabeth Brotherton	" P[arley]. P. Pratt[.]
Andrew L. Lamoreaux	" P[arley]. P. Pratt.

Axy White " P[arley]. P. Pratt[.]
Minerva White " Erastus Snow[.]
Samuel Henderson " P[arley]. P. Pratt[.]
Elisabeth Henderson " P[arley]. P. Pratt.
Benjamin Covey " P[arley]. P. Pratt.
Diana Cole by B[enjamin]. Covey & P[arley]. P. Pratt.
Josiah W. Fleming " P[arley]. P. Pratt.
Nancy Fleming " P[arley]. P. Pratt & J[osiah]. W. F[leming].
error ~~Isabel Lamoreaux " P. P. Pratt.~~

Finished at 25 minutes past 3.

At 5 m[inutes]. before 2. [we] commenced washing and anointing in the male department, the following High Priests, who were washed by Jesse P. Harmon and William Crosby, and anointed by William Snow and A[braham]. O. Smoot, viz;

John S. Higbee born March 7, 1804
Peter Joseph Fory " Dec[embe]r. 24 1777
John Zundell " April 15. 1792
William Marnham " Feb[ruar]y 13 1798
Ormus E. Bates " Mar[ch]. 25. 1815
Nelson Bates " Dec[embe]r. 23, 1813

Finished at 25 m[inutes]. to 3.

In the Female department [we] commenced Washing and anointing at 10 minutes before 2. & washed & anointed as follows

Sarah Ann Higbee. born April 16. 1805 W[ashed]. by Polly Z. Johnson an[ointed]. by M[argaret]. T. Smoot[.]
Anna Barbara Bowermaster. [born] Mar[ch]. 25. 1783 w[ashed]. by Sarah Crosby an[ointed]. by Mary C. Miller[.]
Cristina Zundall [born] July 31. 1811 [washed] by M[argaret]. T. Smoot an[ointed]. by M[argaret]. T. Smoot[.]
Jane Marnham born Feb[ruar]y 3. 1802 [washed] by P[olly]. Z. Johnson an[ointed]. by Mary C. Miller[.]
Elisabeth Fory born Aug[us]t 27. 1825 W[ashed]. by Sarah Crosby an[ointed] by Mary C. Miller[.]
Morilla Spink born Dec[ember]. 31. 1824 W[ashed]. by P[olly]. Z. Johnson an[ointed]. by M[argaret]. T. Smoot[.]
Amanda Bates born Aug[us]t 31. 1814 W[ashed]. by P[olly]. Z. Johnson an[ointed]. by M[ary]. C. Miller[.]

Phebe M. Bates born January 31. 1817 W[ashed]. by Heziah Hunter, an[ointed]. by M[argaret]. T. Smoot[.]
Finished at 8 m[inutes]. to 3.

At 3 o'clock [we] commenced receiving into lower and middle departments, company No. 3,

Orson Spencer as No. 1 L[ucius]. N. Scovil as No. 2
George P. Dykes as No. 3. in the up[p]er dep[artmen]t,
and in the middle department.

Erastus Snow as No. 1 W[illiam]. Snow. [as] No. 2
E[zra]. T. Benson " " 3. W[illiam]. W. Phelps " 4
F[ranklin]. D. Richards prompter

At 3 o'clock John Scott informed George D. Grant that an officer and assistants were watching for Pres[ident] Young and others at the front door of the Temple. Brother Grant carried the information to Pres[ident]. Young, who soon devised a scheme by which their intentions to carry him off might be frustrated.

He directed William Miller who was present at the time, to put on E[lde]r [Heber C.] Kimball's cloak, and go down with Geo[rge] D. Grant to his carriage, at the door. They accordingly went down, and as Miller was about to get into the carriage, with Elder Grant, the officer and 5 or 6 of his assistants arrested him, supposing it to be Pres[ident]. B[righam]. Young. They were about to drive away with him, having made their boasts that they would get as many of the Twelve as they could, take them down to Warsaw, and have a new Years frolic, killing them, but were persuaded to drive to the Nauvoo Mansion and tarry until tomorrow morning when the validity of the writ would be tested.

They were kept in profound ignorance of their mistake all the time, [also by] Esq[ui]r[e]. [Almon] Babbit[, who] takes the legal management of the case, and when they have stopped long enough to make a good tavern bill they will probably get their eyes open and put off—

At 12 minutes past 4 o'clock P.M. [we] commenced receiving through the vail company No. 3 (Lorenzo Snow and Catherine C. Spence acting as prompters—) in the following order, viz;

Peter Joseph Fory,	by	O[rson]. Spencer[.]
Elizabeth Fory	"	O[rson]. Spencer[.]
Anna Barbara Bowermaster	"	O[rson]. Spencer[.]
William Manham	"	O[rson]. Spencer[.]
Jane Manham	"	W[illiam]. Manham & O[rson]. S[pencer].

Nelson Bates	by George Miller[.]
Amanda Bates	by Nelson Bates & G[eorge]. M[iller].
John Zundall	by George Miller[.]
Christina Zundall	by J[ohn]. Zundall & G[eorge]. M[iller].
Ormus E. Bates	by Geo[rge]. Miller[.]
Phebe Bates	by Ormus E. Bates & G[eorge]. M[iller].
John S. Higbee	" George Miller[.]
Sarah Ann Higbee	" John S. Higbee & O[rson]. Spen[cer].
Morilla Spink	by O[rson]. Spencer[.]

Finished at half past 5.

Esq[ui]r[e]. Babbitt came in at 5 o'clock & reports that the officer who arrested W[illia]m Miller (supposing it to be Pres[ident]. Young) has left the city, and gone to Carthage [Illinois], with the prisoner, continuing ignorant of his mistake— Mr Edmonds, a partner of Mr. Babbitts, has gone with them to act as counsel for the prisoner[.] The officer has writs for ^B[righam]. Young^ P[arley]. P. Pratt, H[eber]. C. K[imball] John Taylor ^Geo[rge] A. Smith^ Amasa Lyman, & T[heodore]. Turly who are all charged with counterfeiting the coin of the United States, with Pres[ident]. Young[.]

At 15 minutes to 4 [we] commenced in the Male department washing & anointing the following persons. viz.

High Priests,

William Fausett, born Jan[uar]y 6. 1807.

Edward Rigby born June 17. 1789.

70's Bushrod W. Wilson. of the 70's [born] Aug[us]t 22. 1808[.]

These were washed by William Crosby and anointed by W[illia]m Snow & Peter Haws.

Finished at 30 minutes [after] 4.

In the female department [we] commenced washing and anointing at 10 m[inutes]. to 4 the following persons, viz;

Ann C. Z. Brimhall born. Feb[ruar]y 28. 1794 w[ashed]. by P[olly]. Z. Johnson anointed by M[argaret]. T. Smoot[.]

Mary Smith born Aug[us]t 13. 1797 w[ashed]. by M[argaret]. T. Smoot an[ointed]. by M[argaret]. T. Smoot[.]

Miranda Jones born Nov[embe]r. 16. 1804 w[ashed]. by Pamela Lott an[ointed]. by Mary C. Miller[.]

Matilda Fausett born August 13. 1809 w[ashed]. by Artemisia Snow. A[nointed]. by A[rtemisia]. Snow[.]

Rebecca Faussett, born March 12. 1829 W[ashed]. by P[olly]. Z. Johnson an[ointed] by Mary C. Miller[.]

Catherine Wilson born Jan[uar]y 18. 1815 W[ashed]. by Keziah Hunter, an[ointed]. by M[argaret]. T. Smoot[.]

Susanna Rigby born Dec[embe]r 23. 1791 w[ashed]. by Pamela Lott an[ointed]. by M[argaret]. T. Smoot[.]

Aseneth Sherman born Aug[us]t 2. 1780 W[ashed]. by P[olly]. Z. Johnson an[ointed]. by M[ary]. C. Miller[.]

Julia Hills born Sept[ember] 26. 1783. W[ashed]. by Artemisia Snow. An[ointed]. by Mary C. Miller[.]

Rebecca White, born April 29. 1788[.]

Finished at 16 min[utes]. to 5.

At 37 minutes past 4. the bell rung & [we] commenced receiving into the ~~upper~~ ^lower and middle^ department Company No. 4. the following persons officiating, viz; in the upper department,

Orson Spencer	as No. 1.
L[ucius]. N. Scovil	" " 2.
George P. Dykes	" " 3.

in the middle department,

Erastus Snow No. 1	Daniel Carter. No. 2
William Snow " 3	W[illiam]. W. Phelps " 4

Franklin D. Richards, Prompter

At 5 minutes past 6. [we] commenced receiving into the upper department company No. 4. in the following order,

Bushrod W. Wilson	by Orson Spencer[.]
Catharine Wilson	by O[rson]. S[pencer]. and B[ushrod]. W. W[ilson].
William Fausett	by O[rson]. Spencer[.]
Matilda Fausett	by W[illiam]. Fausett & O[rson]. S[pencer].
Edward Rigby	" O[rson]. Spencer[.]
Susanna Rigby	" O[rson]. Spencer[.]
Ann C. T. Kimball	" O[rson]. Spencer[.]
Miranda Jones, or Newton,	by John Smith[.]
Mary Smith	by John Smith[.]

Julia Hills, or Johnson	by John Smith[.]
Rebecca Fausett	by C[ornelius]. P. Lott and O[rson]. Spencer[.]
Aseneth Sherman	by John Smith[.]
Rebecca White	by John Smith[.]

Finished at 20 min[utes]. past. 7[,] Lorenzo Snow & Catharine C. Spencer officiating as prompters.

At 20 minutes before 6 o'clock [we] commenced in the male department, washing and anointing the following persons of the quorum of Seventies, viz;

Alfred Brown	born	Jan[uar]y. 17 1806
William Hyde	"	Sept[ember] 11. 1818
George Hales	"	Oct[ober] 30. 1822
Charles Smith	"	July 10. 1819
Jesse Haven	"	March 28. 1814
Charles H. Hales	"	June 17 1817
Ransom Shepard	"	May 5. 1812
Chandler Holbrook	"	Sept[ember] 16. 1807
Guy C. Barnum	"	April 5. 1825
Jonathan H. Holmes	"	March 11. 1806
also High Priest		
Job V. Barnum	"	March 14. 1788.

Guy C. Barnum was ordained into the quorum of Seventies, before washing & anointing, under the hands of Joseph Young and Henry Harriman.

These were all washed by Jesse P. Harmon and William Crosby, and anointed by Joseph Young, J[edediah]. M. Grant and Benj[amin]. L. Clapp.

Finished at 24 minutes past 6.

At a quarter past 5 o'clock, the following persons met for prayer in the High Priests room No. 8. Attic Story Temple viz; George Miller, Simeon Carter Winslow Farr, Daniel Spencer A[braham]. O. Smoot. W[illia]m Felshaw & F[ranklin]. D. Richards G[eorge]. Miller — mouth[.]

At 10 minutes before 6. [we] commenced in the female department, washing and anointing the following persons, viz;

Elizabeth Hyde born October 2. 1813 w[ashed]. by Sarah Crosby, anointed by M[ary]. C. Miller[.]

Hester Ann E. Brown [born] Nov[embe]r. 27. 1819 w[ashed]. by Artemisia Snow. a[nointed]. by A[rtemisia]. Snow[.]

Sarah Smith born July 1. 1821. W[ashed]. by M[argaret]. T.

Smoot an[ointed] by M[argaret]. T. Smoot[.]

Julia Ann Hales born Aug[us]t 10. 1824 [washed] by Mercy R. Thompson An[ointed]. by Mary C. Miller[.]

Sarah Ann Hales born Jan[uar]y 21. 1822 [washed] by Margaret T. Smoot, an[ointed]. by M[argaret]. T. Smoot[.]

Annis B. Thompson born July 24. 1788. [washed] by Sarah Crosby an[ointe]d [by] Mary C. Miller[.]

Marcia Barnum born Sept[ember] 8. 1798. [washed] by M[ercy]. R. Thompson an[ointed]. [by] M[argaret]. T. Smoot[.]

Eunia Holbrook born April 6. 1810 w[ashed]. by Artemisia Snow. A[nointed]. by Art[emisia]. Snow[.]

Martha S. Haven born Nov[ember]. 21. 1819 w[ashed]. [by] M[ercy]. R. Thompson An[ointed]. By Mary C. Miller[.]

Abigail H. Hale born Sept[ember] 26. 1790 w[ashed]. by Artemisia Snow. anointed by M[argaret]. T. Smoot[.]

Mary A. Shepard born May 26. 1818 w[ashed]. by M[ercy]. R. Thompson An[ointed] by M[argaret]. T Smoot[.]

Elvira A. Holmes born Nov[embe]r. 23. 1813 w[ashed]. by M[ercy]. R. Thompson An[ointed]. by M[ary]. C. Miller[.]

Miranda Barnham b[orn]. Sept[ember] 20. 1826 W[ashed]. by Artemisia Snow An[ointed]. by Mary C. Miller[.]

Ended at 5 min[utes] before 7 o'clock.

At 10 min[utes]. to 7 Bell rung & [we] commenced receiving into lower and middle departments, company No. 5, the following named persons officiating—viz; in the upper department

Jedediah M. Grant	as	No.	1.
Benjamin L. Clapp	"	"	2.
Lucius N. Scovil	"	"	3.

in the lower department

Joseph Young	as	No.	1
Daniel Carter	"	"	2
A[lbert]. P. Rockwood	"	"	3
W[illiam]. W. Phelps	"	"	4
F[ranklin]. D. Richards	"	"	5

[A]t half past 7. o'clock P.M. the following persons met in Pres[ident]. B[righam]. Youngs room clothed in sacerdotal garments and offered up thanks to God for his preserving care over them, in delivering them from all the snares of their enemies, and prayers that he would continue to do so. their names are. Brigham Young, Heber C. Kimball, John

Taylor, Orson Hyde George A. Smith, Amasa Lyman, & George Miller — Orson Hyde being mouth.

At 20 minutes past 8 o'clock, President Brigham Young, H[eber]. C. Kimball, P[arley]. P. Pratt, George A. Smith & Amasa Lyman, left the Temple, nearly at the same time disguised with other mens Hats & coats. The reason of this is that their enemies are seeking their lives, charging them with high crimes &c.

At 24 minutes before 9 [we] commenced receiving into the upper department company No. 5, in the following order

Jonathan H. Holmes.	by John Pack[.]
Elvira A. Holmes	by her husband & J[ohn]. P[ack].
George Hales	by John Pack[.]
Sarah Ann Hales	" G[eorge]. Hales &. J[ohn]. Pack[.]
George Hales	" John Pack[.]
Chandler Holbrook	" G[eorge]. H[ales]. & John Pack[.]
Alfred Brown	" John Pack[.]
Hester Ann Eliza Brown	" A[lfred]. Brown & J[ohn]. P[ack].
Charles H. Hales	by John Pack[.]
Julia Ann Hales	by C[harles]. H. Hale[s] & J[ohn]. Pack[.]
Annis B. Thompson	by John Pack[.]
Charles Smith	by John Pack[.]
Sarah Smith	by her husband & J[ohn]. Pack[.]
William Hyde	by John Pack[.]
Elizabeth Hyde	by W[illia]m. Hyde & J[ohn]. P[ack].
Jesse Haven	by David Candland[.]
Martha S. Haven	by Jos[eph]. Young & J[esse]. Haven[.]
Abigail Hale	by Jesse P. Haven & Jos[eph] Young[.]
Guy C. Barnum	by Joseph Young[.]
Miranda Barnum	by Guy C. B[arnum]. & J[oseph]. Y[oung].
Ransom Shepard	by Joseph Young[.]
Mary Ann Shepard	by R[anson]. S[hepard]. and J[oseph]. Y[oung].
Job V. Barnum	by [blank]
Marcia Barnum	by [blank]

Finished at ¼ before 11. Mercy Thompson & John D. Lee officiated as prompters.

Besides the persons whose names appear in the record of the proceedings of this day there are many others who have been very efficient in forwarding the work and have attended at the Temple not only today but several previous days, There is much labor to be done in keeping the utensils and garments in order.

Some of the names are as follows, viz; Cherizade Averett, Jane Sherwood Mary Ann Averett Jane Sherwood Mary Ann Turley Priscilla Turley Cynthia Durfee Aleinne Durfee Amanda Rogers[.] Henry Harriman takes the names and ages of the men who are washed and anointed, Miss Eliza R. Snow takes the names of the women[.] John D. Lee, David Candland & L[ucian]. R. Foster act as clerks[.] Brother Harmon has been sewing tent cloth to-day.

A stair case has this day been put up by which we can pass out through Elder Kimball's room, which has been converted into an office for the convenience of transacting business with persons from without[.]

—William Clayton, Diary, kept for Heber C. Kimball.

....

The atmosphere is still calm & serene though somewhat cloudy[,] presently a favorable omen [?] for a snow storm — about 8 oclock President Jos[eph]. Young — [Henry] Herriman & J[edediah]. M. Grant arrived in the Temple & after business[,] the order of the day[.] Pres[ident] Young returned home having nothing to do with the arrangement of the day — Employed officiating officers for the different departments until evening when a company of the Seventies are to go through
[Marginal notation: "12. oclock Ordinance Total 91 No 91"]

[A]fter the High Priest[s] that are notified receive[d] their washings & anointing ordinances[,] Thomas Woolsey & wife passed thorough born Nov 3d 1806 washed by J[esse] P Harmon & W[illia]m Crosby & anointed by A[braham]. O Smoot & W[illia]m [Snow?]

Mary Woolsey born May 11th 1812— Washed by [blank]
Bushrod Nelson [born] Aug 22nd 1808 washed by W[illia]m Crosby & anointed by Peter Haws & W[illia]m Snow.

At 20 minets past 6 at Night the following Persons received their washings & anointing washed by Jesse P. Harmon & W[illia]m Crosby and Anointed by Pres[ident] Jos[eph]. Young — & Benj[amin] L. Clapp — (Namely—)

[See pages 151-52 for excerpted portion.]

At 6. o.clock P.M. A company of the Seventies commenced going through under the direction of Pres[ident] Jos[eph]. Young — The

[Washings and anointings for Tuesday, December 23, 1845]

Alford Brown born Jan 17th 1806	Wm Hyde Sept 11th 1818
George Hales Oct 30th 1822	Job Bur Mar 18-1788
Chas Smith July 10th 1819	Jesse Haven Mar 28th 1814
Chas H. Hales June 17th 1817	Ransome Shepherd May 5th 1812
Chandler Holbrook Sept 16th 1807	Ivy C. Burnham April 5th 1825
	Jonathan H. Holmes March 11th 1806

Total ordained at the same time under the hands of Pres Jos. Young 103 and J. M. Grant

Female Department

At ½ Past 6. oclock in the evening the following Persons were washed and anointed (To Wit.)
Elizabeth Hyde born Oct 22d 1813 washed by Sarah Crosby & anointed by M. C. Miller
[Marginal notation: "30 p. 6 P.M."]

H. A. E. Brown Nov 14th 1819	washed & anointed	by Artemisia Snow		
Sarah Smith July 1st 1821	"			Margaret Smoot
Julia An Hales Augt. 10 1824	"	M R Thompson	"	M. C. Miller
Sarah An Hales Jan 26th 1822	"	M. S Smoot	"	[?] Lauck [?]
Marcia Bingham [?] Sept 8th 1788	"	S Crosby	"	M C Smith
Anesis B. Hampton July 25 1788	"	M R Thompson	"	M. S. Smoot
Eunice Holbrook April 6th 1810	"	A. Snow	"	A Snow
Martha S Haven Nov 21st 1819	"	M. R. Thompson	"	M. C. Miller
Abigail Hall Oct 20 1809	"	A Snow	"	M S Smoot
Mary S. Shepherd May 26th 1818	"	M. R. Thompson	"	"

E. A. Holmes Nov 23 1813	[washed by]	[M. R. Thompson]	[anointed by]	M C Miller
Marrinda Falkener [?] Sept 20 1826	"	A. Snow	"	" "

No of
Females
100

—Seventies Record, Book B, oversized portion, December 23, 1845.

Names, ages, togeather with those who officiated at the time[, of] Each Person [who] came through, are recorded on the Proceeding Page — Pres[ident] Young took an active part in the servises of the evening — this [after] about 3. o.clock Some 8 or 10 officers came in with writs from Springfield [Illinois] for the Twelve [apostles] & many others — they denied having any writs — but in order to attempt [to divulge] their corruption Pres[ident] [Brigham] Young sent down a man in disguise with a cloke on verry much like his own (P[resident]. Y[oung].) Pres[ident] J[edediah]. M. Grant — who acompanyed the man in disguise to the carriage [which] stood near the Temple [and] that was expected to convey Pres[ident] Young away[, said that] on reaching the carriage [he,] Pres[ident] Grant[,] said to Br[other] W[illia]m Miller who was the man in disguise, Pres[ident] Young the weather is growing colder —at this the officers surrounded the carriage & drew out a writ & read [it] & said Mr Young you are my prisoner[.] the Prisoner[,] apparently unconcerned[,] invited them to get into the carriage[,] or some of them, which some 2 or 3 did & Drove to the Mansion & finally started to Carthage [Illinois] being elated to the highest glory in immagination. Still they are gone & we hope all will be well — & that they will soon find out their mistake — we intended that they should have found out their blunder before they left the city but in this we have been mistaken[.] they may take him to Springfield before they discern the prank — at 11. o.clock opperations for the Night ceased —

—Seventies Record, Book B.

....

I worked in the Temple until evening and met the police and then came home and Br[other] James Pace came with me & brought some bleached cotton and let me have 23 yards to make me & my wife robes and other garments. It was bought for me by his [James Pace's] Br[other] W[illiam]. Pace for which may he be blessed.

—Hosea Stout, Diary, in *On the Mormon Frontier: The Diary of Hosea Stout, 1844-1861,* edited by Juanita Brooks (Salt Lake City: University of Utah Press/Utah State Historical Society, 1964).

....

The high council met in the Temple for prayer.

One-five p.m., Almon W. Babbitt came into the Temple and informed me [Brigham Young] that there were some federal officers from Springfield [Illinois] accompanied by several of the state troops in the city for the purpose of arresting some of the Twelve [apostles], especially Amasa Lyman and myself.

It was soon reported that they were at the door of the Temple and were intending to search it. George D. Grant, my coachman, went below and drove my carriage up to the door[,] as if he was waiting for me to come down.

William Miller put on my cap and Brother [Heber C.] Kimball's cloak and went downstairs meeting the marshal and his assistants at the door, as he was about getting into my carriage the marshal arrested him, on a writ from the United States court, charging him with counterfeiting the coin of the United States. Miller told him there must be some mistake about it, as he was not guilty of anything of the kind, but the marshal insisted it was right.

Miller desired the marshal to go down to the Mansion where he could get counsel and ascertain if the proceedings were legal. On reaching the Mansion they went into a private room where Esq[uire]. Edmonds examined the writ and pronounced it legal. Miller gave Edmonds the name of four [defense] witnesses for [Edmonds to] subpoena for him, and asked the marshal to remain until morning; he consented, but soon got uneasy and said he must go to Carthage [Illinois]. Miller then inquired if he would wait three quarters of an hour until he could get his witnesses, but in fifteen minutes he said he must go, and would wait no longer. Miller got into his carriage, Esq[uire]. Edmonds rode with the marshal's guard and they started for Carthage, Miller protesting there was some mistake about it, for he certainly was not guilty of any such things as were charged in the writ: on the way to Carthage the marshal was very social, and remarked that the people had got quite a joke upon him for letting [Theodore] Turley give him the dodge.[10] As they approached Carthage the troops began to whoop and holloa and went into town in high glee, performing the journey which was eighteen miles in two hours.

The marshal put up at Hamilton's Tavern, and the rumor soon spread through the town that Brigham Young was in the custody of the marshal at Hamilton's. Among others, George W. Thatcher,[11] county commissioner's

10. This is apparently in reference to Theodore Turley's release on bond earlier that month on counterfeiting charges.

11. George W. Thatcher, although once a member of the LDS church, is listed by Sheriff Jacob B. Backenstos (*History of the Church,* 7:144) as a member of the mob that killed Joseph and Hyrum Smith in Carthage Jail.

clerk, who was well acquainted with Miller came into the tavern to see me [Brigham Young]. The marshal at his [Thatcher's] request took Miller into a private room. After a little conversation one of the guards came in and the marshal went out. The marshal soon returned and said to Mr. Miller, "I am informed you are not Mr. Young;" "Ah!" exclaimed Miller, "then if I should prove not to be Mr. Young, it would be a worse joke on you than the Turley affair[.]" he replied, "I'll be damned if it won't."

The marshal asked Miller if his name was Young, he answered, "I never told you my name was Young, did I?" "No," replied the marshal, "but one of my men professed to be acquainted with Mr. Young, and pointed you out to me to be him." William Backenstos was called in and he told them William Miller was not Brigham Young. Another man came, and said he could swear Miller was not Brigham Young. The marshal said he was sorry, and asked Miller his name, he replied, "it is William Miller".

The marshal left the room and soon returned accompanied by [attorney] Edmonds who was laughing heartily at him. Edmonds inquired if he had anything more to do with "Mr. Young". The marshal replied that he did not know that he had anything further to do with Mr. Miller.

Eighty-seven persons received the ordinances.

Seven-thirty p.m., I met with the Twelve [apostles] in prayer, and thanked the Lord for deliverance from the snares of our enemies.

Eight-twenty, I left the Temple disguised and shortly after Brothers Heber C. Kimball, Parley P. Pratt, George A. Smith and Amasa Lyman left, to elude the vexatious writs of our persecutors.

—"Manuscript History of Brigham Young,"
in *History of the Church,* 7:549-51.

Nauvoo temple endowments performed on this date for:

First Company: Benjamin Brown, Sarah Brown, John Tanner, Eliza Tanner, Daniel Carter, Harriet Carter, Elizabeth Durfee, Thomas Woolsey, Mary Woolsey, Lucretia/Marilla Johnson, Gardner Clark, Delecta Clark, Huldah M. Clark, Raymond Clark, Louisa Clark, Archibald Patten, Abigail Patten, Mary Ann Barker, and Polly Thompson.

Second Company: Henry W. Miller, Elmira Miller, Adeline B. Andrus, John Lamoreaux, Catharine Lamoreaux, William McCleary, Sophronia McCleary, Mary Wood, Elisabeth Brotherton, Andrew L. Lamoreaux, Azy White, Minerva White, Samuel Henderson, Elisabeth Henderson, Benjamin Covey, Diana Cole, Josiah W. Fleming, and Nancy Fleming.

Third Company: Peter Joseph Fory, Elisabeth Fory, Anna/Barbara Bowermaster, William Manhard, Jane Manhard, Nelson Bates, Amanda Bates, John Zundall, Christina Zundall, Ormus E. Bates, Phebe M. Bates, John S. Higbee, Sarah Ann Higbee, and Morilla Spink.

Fourth Company: Bushrod W. Wilson, Catharine Wilson, William Faussett, Matilda Faussett, Edward Rigby, Susanna Rigby, Ann C. Y. Brimhall, Miranda Newton/Jones, Mary Smith, Julia Hills/Johnson, Rebecca Faussett, Aseneth Sherman, and Rebecca White.

Fifth Company: Jonathan H. Holmes, Elvira A. Holmes, George Hales, Sarah Ann Hales, Chandler Holbrook, Eunice Holbrook, Alfred Brown, Hester Ann/Eliza Brown, Charles H. Hales, Julia Ann Hales, Annis B. Thompson, Charles Smith, Sarah Smith, William Hyde, Elizabeth Hyde, Jesse Haven, Martha S. Haven, Abigail H. Hale, Guy C. Barnum, Miranda Barnum, Ransom Shepard, Mary Ann Shepard, Job V. Barnum, and Marcia Barnum.

—Summary of information compiled by the Temple Index Bureau, *Nauvoo Temple Endowment Register: 10 December 1845 to 8 February 1846.*

Wednesday, December 24, 1845

At half past 6 o'clock, the High Council met for prayer in the attic story of the Temple room No. 4. the following persons present, Samuel Bent — Alpheus Cutler — James Allred. G[eorge]. W. Harris. Newell Knight Thomas Grover — Charles C. Rich — David Fullmer — Aaron Johnson — and Ezra T. Benson — and being clothed in the Robes of Priesthood, offered up prayers to God for our prosperity, the preservation of the Twelve [apostles], for means to remove from this place — for the welfare of all the honest in heart — our wives & children &c. &c. Alpheus Cutler being mouth[.]

At 15 minutes before 9 [we] commenced in the male department washing & anointing the following persons, High Priests viz;

Isaac Decker	born	Nov[embe]r 29. 1799
Joseph A. Kelting	"	Oct[ober] 13. 1811
Joseph W. Johnson	"	Dec[ember]. 15. 1815
Herman Hyde	"	June 30. 1788
Benjamin Aber	"	April 25. 1790
Gustavus Hills	"	Janua[r]y 29. 1804

Luman H. Calkin " Jan[uar]y 15. 1816
Martin H. Peck " May 27 1806
Joseph Mount " Sept[ember] 10. 1806
William Davis " April 12 1795
Arza Judd " Nov[embe]r 4 1766
John Lowry " Aug[us]t 10 1799
Charles B. Thompson " Jan[uar]y 27 1814

also of the quorum of Seventies, the following persons. viz;

Randolph Alexander born Mar[ch]. 22 1802
Orlando Henry Carter " Jan[uar]y 27. 1820

These were washed by William Crosby & Ezra T. Benson, anointed by William Snow A[braham]. O. Smoot. Willard Snow and Peter Haws.

Finished at 10 m[inutes]. to 10.

In the female department [we] commenced washing and anointing the following persons at 27 minutes before 9 o'clock.

Minerva Wood. born Oct[ober] 18. 1827 Pamela Lott Mary C. Miller[.]
Myra Alexander. [born] Sept[ember] 20. 1815 M[argaret]. T. Smoot Mary C. Miller[.]
Elizabeth Johnson born July 22. 1817 Artemisia Snow M[argaret]. T. Smoot[.]
Elizabeth Kelting, born Ap[ri]l. 3. 1818 Lydia Carter Mary C. Miller[.]
Polly W. Hyde " Jan[uar]y 20. 1786. Artemisia Snow M[argaret]. T. Smoot.
Lois Judd " Sept[ember] 19. 1773 Artemisia Snow Caroline O. Spencer[.]
Phebe Angell " Mar[ch]. 17. 1786 M[ercy]. R. Thompson C[aroline]. C. Spencer[.]
Eunice Hyde " July 25. 1813 Artemisia Snow Mary C. Miller[.]
Mehitable Calkins " Oct[ober] 17. 1810 Artemisia Snow Mary C. Miller[.]
Sarah Davis " Sep[tember] 22 1799 M[ercy]. R. Thompson C[aroline]. C. Spencer[.]
Mary Lowry born Oct[ober] 6. 1802 ^washed & anointed by^ Artemisia Snow M[argaret]. T. Smoot[.]
Elisabeth Mount " July 5. 1813 Artemisia Snow Mary C. Miller[.]

Mary Peck " Feb[ruar]y 14. 1816 Elisabeth Durphee Elisabeth Durphee[.]

Elisabeth Ann Hills, [born] Jan[uary]. 23. 1803 E[lizabeth]. Durphee C[aroline]. C. Spencer[.]

Catharine A. Thompson [born] Aug[ust] 11. 1827 Pamela Lott M[argaret]. T. Smoot.

[E]nded at 20 minutes to 10.

[A]t 20 minutes before 10. [we] commenced receiving into the lower & middle departments company No. 1 for this day, the following persons officiating.

Orson Spencer	as No.	1. }	
L[ucius]. N. Scovil	"	2. }	upper department
George P. Dykes	" "	3. }	
Erastus Snow	" "	1 }	
William Snow	" "	2 }	middle
Theodore Turley	" "	3 }	
W[illiam]. W. Phelps	" "	4 }	department.
F[ranklin]. D. Richards	" "	5.}	

At 20 minutes past 11. [we] commenced receiving into the upper department company No. 1. in the following order

Joseph Mount	by Orson Spencer[.]
Elisabeth Mount	by J[oseph]. Mount & Geo[rge]. Miller[.]
Azra Judd	by Geo[rge]. Miller[.]
Lois Judd	by A[zra]. Judd & Geo[rge] Miller[.]
Herman Hyde	by Geo[rge]. Miller[.]
Polly W. Hyde	by H[erman]. Hyde & Geo[rge]. Miller[.]
Eunice Hyde received	by Geo[rge]. Miller[.]
Charles B. Thompson	" Geo[rge]. Miller[.]
Catharine A. Thompson	" C[harles]. Th[ompson]. & G[eorge]. Miller[.]
Randolph Alexander	" G[eorge]. Miller[.]
Myrza Alexander	by R[andolph]. Alexander & G[eorge]. Miller[.]
Lunian H. Calkins	by George Miller[.]
Mehitabel Calkins	" L[unian]. H. Calkins & G[eorge]. M[iller].
Joseph W. Johnson	" Erastus Snow[.]

Elisabeth Johnson	"	J[oseph]. W. Johnson & O[rson]. Spencer[.]
Orlando Henry Carter	"	Orson Spencer[.]
Sarah Carter	"	O[rlando]. H[enry]. Carter & O[rson] Spencer[.]
Joseph A. Kelting	"	Orson Spencer[.]
Elizabeth Kelting	"	J[oseph]. A. Kelting & O[rson]. S[pencer].
Minerva Wood	"	J[oseph]. A. Kelting & O[rson]. S[pencer].
Gustavus Hills	"	Orson Spencer[.]
Elisabeth Ann Hills	"	G[ustavus]. Hills & O[rson]. Spencer[.]
Phebe Angel	"	O[rson]. Spencer[.]
William Davis	"	O[rson]. Spencer[.]
Sarah Davis	"	W[illiam]. Davis & O[rson]. Spencer[.]
Martin H. Peck	"	Orson Spencer[.]
Mary Peck	"	M[artin]. H. Peck & J[ohn]. D. Lee[.]
John Lowry	"	John D. Lee[.]
Mary Lowry	"	J[ohn]. Lowry & J[ohn]. D Lee[.]
Benjamin Aber	"	J[ohn]. D. Lee[.]
Isaac Decker	"	J[ohn]. D. Lee.

Ended at 2 o'clock. Lorenzo Snow C[aroline]. C. Spencer } Prompters—

At 20 minutes past 12, William Miller who was arrested yesterday, came into the Temple, having been liberated from arrest at Carthage [Illinois] last evening, when they found that he was not Brigham Young. He was not ill treated.

At 25 minutes before 11. [we] commenced in the male department, washing & anointing the following persons, all High Priests, and forming company No. 2. for this day

Samuel Burton,	born	June 12 1783
Perry Durphy	"	Sept[ember] 21. 1797
Artimas Millet	"	Sept[ember] 11. 1790
Isaac Houston	"	Oct[ober] 5 1799
Joseph Fletcher	"	June 12 1787
Elisha H. Groves	"	Nov[embe]r. 5. 1797
John Telford	"	March 2 1802

William Munjar	"	Nov[embe]r. 25 1792
Henry B. Huffman	"	Aug[us]t 6. 1817
Sidney A. Knowlton	"	May 24. 1793
James Rawlins	"	Jan[uar]y 6. 1794
John A. Mikesell	"	Feb[ruar]y 8 1784
Roswell Stevens	"	Feb[ruar]y 17 1772
John Killion	"	April 25. 1796

[W]ashed by Peter Haws and William Crosby anointed by A[braham]. O. Smoot and Willard Snow

[E]nded at 26 minut[e]s before 12.

In the female department [we] commenced washing and anointing the following persons. viz,

Jane Telford, born Dec[ember]. 17. 1795 [washed by] M[argaret]. T. Smoot [anointed by M[ary]. C. Miller[.]

Silvina Huffman [born] Mar[ch]. 23. 1821 [washed by] Pamela Lott [anointed by] Mary C. Miller[.]

Almira Millet, born May 30. 1792 [washed by] Lydia Carter [anointed by] Mary C. Miller[.]

Katharine Mikesell " Oct[ober] 11, 1784 [washed by] Artemisia Snow [anointed by] Mary C. Miller[.]

Harriet Knowlton " Mar[ch]. 7. 1798 [washed by] Pamela Lott [anointed by] Elizabeth Durphee[.]

Lucy Groves, born Feb[ruar]y 1. 1807 [washed by] Artemisia Snow [anointed by] M[argaret]. T. Smoot[.]

Sybil Stevens " April 4. 1778 [washed by] Amanda Rogers [anointed by] Elisabeth Durphee[.]

Sally Killion " Oct[ober] 31. 1797 [washed by] Lydia Carter [anointed by] Elizabeth Durphee[.]

Hannah Burton " Oct[ober] 12, 1786. [washed by] Pamela Lott [anointed by] Mary C. Miller[.]

Melissa Burton " Mar[ch] 2. 1828 [washed by] Artemisia Snow [anointed by] Margaret T. Smoot[.]

Jane M. Houston " Mar[ch] 9. 1828 [washed by] Elisabeth Durphee [anointed by] Elisabeth Durphee[.]

Theodosia Houston " Sep[tember]. 27. 1804 [washed by] Artemisia Snow [anointed by] Elisabeth Durphee[.]

Mary Munjar " Sept[ember] 4. 1803 [washed by] M[argaret]. T. Smoot [anointed by] M[argaret]. T. Smoot[.]

Jane Rawlins " Mar[ch]. 22. 1793 [washed by] Arte-

misia Snow [anointed by] Mary C. Miller[.]
Armilla Fletcher " Oct[ober] 13. 1793 [washed by] Pamela Lott [anointed by] Mary C. Miller.
Jane Durphee " Apr[il]. 21. 1804 [washed by] Artemisia Snow [anointed by] Margaret T. Smoot[.]

[E]nded at 25 m[inutes]. past 11.

At half past 11. o'clock [we] commenced receiving into the lower & middle department the above company. No. 2, persons officiating viz;

Orson Spencer	as No.	1 }	
L[ucius]. N. Scovil	" "	2 }	upper dep[artmen]t
George P. Dykes	" "	3 }	
Erastus Snow	" "	1 }	
William Snow	" "	2 }	
Ezra T. Benson	" "	3 }	middle dep[artmen]t
W[illiam]. W. Phelps	" "	4 }	
F[ranklin]. D. Richards	" "	5 }	

At 30 minutes past 2. [we] commenced receiving into the upper department company No. 2. in the following order, viz;

Roswell Stevens,	rec[eive]d. by	John D. Lee[.]
Sybil Stevens	" "	R[oswell]. Stevens & J[ohn]. D. Lee[.]
James Rawlins	" "	John D. Lee[.]
Jane Rawlins	" "	J[ames]. Rawlins & J[ohn]. D. Lee[.]
William Munjar	"	by J[ohn]. D. Lee[.]
Mary Munjar	"	W[illia]m. Munjar & J[ohn]. D. Lee[.]
John Telford	"	John D. Lee[.]
Jane Telford	"	John Telford & J[ohn]. D. Lee[.]
Joseph Fletcher	"	John D. Lee[.]
Armilla Fletcher	"	J[oseph]. Fletcher & J[ohn]. D. Lee[.]
Perry Durphee	"	J[ohn]. D. Lee[.]
Jane Durphee	"	J[ohn]. D. Lee & P[erry]. Durphee[.]
John A. Mikesell	"	J[ohn]. D. Lee[.]
Katharine Mikesell	"	J[ohn]. A. Mikesell & J[ohn]. D. Lee[.]
x Samuel Burton	"	George Miller[.]

Hannah Burton	"	"	"	[.]
Melissa Burton	"	"	"	[.]
Isaac Houston	"	George Miller[.]		
Theodosia Houston	"	Isaac Houston & O[rson]. Spencer[.]		
Jane Maria Houston	"	I[saac]. H[ouston]. & O[rson]. Spencer[.]		
Henry B. Huffman	"	O[rson]. Spencer[.]		
Silvina Huffman	"	"	"	& H[enry]. B. H[uffman].
Sidney A. Knowlton	"	Orson Spencer[.]		
Harriet Knowlton	"	"	"	& S[ideny]. A. K[nowlton].
Artemas Millett	"	"	"	[.]
Almira Millett	"	"	"	& A[rtemas]. M[illett].
John Killion	"	"	"	[.]
Sally Killion	"	"	"	[and] J[ohn]. K[illion].

Finished at 5 minutes before 5 o'clock[.] Lorenzo Snow & Caroline C. Spencer officiated as prompters—

x Elisha H. Groves & Sally Groves, by Geo[rge]. Miller[.]

At 1 o'clock [we] commenced in the male department, washing and anointing the following persons, viz;

High Priests,

Howard Coray	born	May 6. 1817
Frederick M. Van Leuven	"	Feb[ruar]y 14. 1808
Stephen Litz	"	Feb[ruar]y 5 1798
Ebenezer Brown	"	Dec[ember]. 6. 1805
Joel Drury	"	April 6. 1794
Stephen Blackman	"	Dec[ember]. 2. 1784
John Sweat	"	Oct[ober] 18. 1796
George Coulson	"	Sept[ember] 22. 1801
Benjamin K. Hall	"	Dec[ember]. 10 1793
of the quorum of Seventies		
Alpheus P. Haws	"	Oct[ober]. 15. 1825

[W]ashed by William Crosby & Ezra T. Benson anointed by Abraham O. Smoot & Willard Snow.

[E]nded at 2 o'clock.

In the female department [we] commenced washing and anointing. at 2 m[inutes]. to one, the following persons. viz;

Martha Jane Corey, born June 3. 1822 washed by Artemisia Snow. Anointed by Pamela Lott.
Adeline Haws. born June 19. 1829 [washed] by Artemisia Snow an[ointed by] Mary C. Miller[.]
Abigail Haws born June 15. 1828 [washed] by Lydia Carter [anointed by] Elizabeth Durphee[.]
Lily Ann Haws born Jan[uar]y 11. 1833. [washed] by Lydia Carter [anointed by] Margaret T. Smoot[.]
Emily Whitmarsh, [born] July 22. 1823 [washed] by Elizabeth Durphee. [Anointed by] Mary C. Miller[.]
Lucy Ann Flanagan, [born] June 12, 1818 [washed] by Artemisia Snow [anointed by] Mary C. Miller[.]
Nancy Chapman, [born] April 10. 1808 [washed] by Artemisia Snow [anointed by] Elizabeth Durfee[.]
Eliza D. Burgess [born] Dec[embe]r. 8 1827 [washed] by Lydia Carter [anointed by] Margaret T. Smoot[.]
Tirzah Drury [born] Dec[embe]r. 1. 1791 [washed] by Sally Phelps [anointed by] Elizabeth Durfee[.]
Fanny Litz born Nov[embe]r. 22 1796 [washed] by Elizabeth Durfee. [anointed by] Elizabeth Durfee[.]
Phebe Brown born Oct[ober]. 9. 1797 [washed] by Lydia Carter [anointed by] Mary C. Miller[.]
Prudence Fairchild [born] Mar. 25 [blank] [washed] by Sally Phelps. [Anointed by] Elizabeth Durfee[.]
Betsy E. Fairchild [born] March 29. 1828 [washed] by Lydia Carter [anointed by] M[argaret]. T. Smoot[.]
Lydia Van Leuven [born] October 7. 1809 [washed] by Lydia Carter [anointed by] Elizabeth Durfee[.]
Polly Sweat born Feb[ruar]y 18. 1793. [Washed] by Artemisia Snow [anointed by] Margaret T. Smoot[.]
Catharine Wilkie [born] June 15. 1785 [washed] by Sally Phelps [anointed by] Mary C. Miller[.]
Deborah Blackman [born] July 1. 1791 [washed] by Sally Phelps [anointed by] Mary C. Miller[.]
Nancy Coulson [born] Dec[ember]. 27 1802 [washed] by Sally Phelps [anointed by] Margaret T. Smoot.
Fanny Hartshorn, [born] Oct[ober]. 1783. [Washed] by Lydia Carter, [anointed by] Elizabeth Durfee.

Finished at 8 min past 2.

At 20 minutes past 2 [we] commenced receiving into the lower and middle departments, Company No. 3, — persons officiating as follows, viz; Orson Spencer as No. 1. L[ucius]. N. Scovil as No. 2 Geo[rge]. P. Dykes " No. 3. in the upper department. and William Snow as No. 1 = E[zra]. T. Benson No. 2 Levi Stewart as No. 3. W[illiam]. W. Phelps as No. 4 F[ranklin]. D. Richards as No. 5 in the middle dep[artmen]t.

At 25 minutes past 5 o'clock [we] commenced receiving into the upper department Company No. 3 in the following order

Joel Drury	by Orson Spencer[.]
Tirzah Drury	" " "
Fanny Hartshorn	" "
John Sweat	" "
Polly Sweat	" "
Emily Whitmarsh	by Peter Haws [.]
Abigail Haws	" " "
Loly Ann Haws	" " "
George Coulson	" " Orson Spencer [.]
Nancy Coulson	" " "
Catharine Wilkie	" " "
F. M. Van Leuven	" " "
Lydia Van Leuven	" " " & F. M. V[an Leuven].
Alpheus P. Haws	" " "
Adeline Haws	" Alpheus Haws & O[rson]. S[pencer].
Stephen Blackman	" O[rson]. Spencer[.]
Deborah Blackman	" " " & S[tephen]. B[lackman].
Howard Coray	" " "
Martha Jane Coray	" " " & H[oward]. Coray[.]
Stephen Litz	" " "
Fanny Litz	" " " & S[tephen]. Litz[.]
Ebenezer Brown	" " "
Phebe Brown	" " " & E[benezer]. Brown[.]
Eliza D. Burgess	" " "
Lucy Ann Flanagan	" " "
Prudence Fairchild	" " "
Nancy Chapman	" " "
Betsey Fairchild	" " "
Benjamin H. Hall	" " "

Ended at 18 minutes past 8 o'clock[.] Lorenzo Snow, C[aroline]. C. Spencer & M[ercy]. R. Thompson officiating as prompters[.]

At 30 minutes past 5 o'clock, [we] commenced in the male department washing and anointing the following persons, of the quorum of Seventes viz;

Stephen Hales, Jun[io]r.		Oct[ober]. 17. 1820
John Hatfield	born	Nov[ember]. 29 1819
John M. Chidester	"	Jan[uar]y 22. 1809
Daniel S. Cahoon	"	April 7. 1822
Samuel Mulliner	"	Jan[uar]y 25 1808
Milo Andrus	"	March 6, 1814
Hiram Dayton	"	Nov[embe]r. 1. 1798
John Leeka	"	Feb[ruar]y 22. 1802
Lysander Dayton	"	Aug[ust]. 15 1820
Peter Hofheins	"	Nov[embe]r. 4 1809
Daniel McCall	"	Dec[ember]. 12. 1800
Joseph Cain	"	Nov[ember]. 5. 1822
William Taylor	"	Sept[ember] 2. 1823
Samuel Parker	"	April 7. 1790

also the following High Priests—

James Duncan	born	May 1. 1794
John Loveless	"	June 24. 1807

[W]ashed by Levi W. Hancock and Andrew Lytle—anointed by B[enjamin]. L. Clapp and Jedediah M. Grant—*10 m[inutes]. past 6.*

At 5 o'clock P.M. Pres[ident]. [Brigham] Young came in, and shortly after, George A. Smith — Amasa Lyman, and Orson Hyde came in — intending to meet for prayer, but not meeting with others whom they expected, several persons being at the same time in prayer in another room[,] they retired in a few minutes[.]

At 25 minutes past 4 [we] commenced washing and anointing in the female department the following persons

Abigail J. Andrus born Jan[uar]y 15 1805 W[ashed]. by Lydia Carter anointed by Mary C. Miller[.]

Lucinda Curtis born March 24, 1827 w[ashed].by Lydia Carter. anointed by M[argaret]. T. Smoot[.]

Lucy Hatfield " July 14. 1821. [washed] by Elizabeth Durfee[anointed by] Mary C. Miller[.]

Eveline Hales " Sept[ember] 24 1821 [washed] by M[argaret]. T. Smoot [anointed by] M[argaret]. T. Smoot[.]

Jane A. Cahoon " Oct[ober]. 11. 1822 [washed] by Pamela Lott [anointed by] Mary C. Miller[.]

Polly Chidester " April 2. 1809 [washed] by Elizabeth Durfee [anointed by] Pamela Lott[.]
Catharine Mulliner " June 4. 1804 [washed] by Elizabeth Durfee [anointed by] Pamela Lott[.]
Avis Brown " April 8. 1800 [washed] by Lydia Carter [anointed by] Pamela Lott[.]
Pamela Dayton " July 28. 1799 [washed by] Lydia Carter [anointed by] Pamela Lott[.]
Maria Dayton " July 15. 1829 [washed by] Lydia Carter [anointed by] Pamela Lott[.]
Sarah Leeka born Dec[ember]. 7. 1805 [washed by] Elizabeth Durfee [anointed by] M[argaret]. T. Smoot[.]
Huldah Duncan " May 4. 1813 [washed by] Lydia Carter [anointed by] Elizabeth Durfee[.]
Mahala Loveless " Aug[us]t 26. 1805 [washed by] Elizabeth Durfee [anointed by] Elizabeth Durfee[.]
Margaret McCall " Oct[ober] 12. 1805 [washed by] M[argaret]. T. Smoot [anointed by] M[argaret]. T. Smoot[.]
Sarah Ann Hofheins " July 4. 1811 [washed by] Lydia Carter [anointed by] Mary C. Miller[.]
Sarah Parker born March 28. 1799 [washed by] Elizabeth Durfee an[ointed by]. Mary C. Miller[.]

[E]nded at 6 min[utes]. after 6.

The Bell rung at 10 minutes past 6, and operations then commenced to receive into the lower and middle departments company No. 4. the following persons officiating viz; in the upper department

Benjamin L. Clapp	as	No.	1.
John D. Lee	"	"	2.
John Pack	"	"	3.

and in the middle department

J[edediah]. M. Grant	as	No.	1
John Scott	"	"	2
Levi W. Hancock	"	"	3
W[illiam]. W. Phelps	"	"	4
F[ranklin]. D. Richards	"	"	5

At 6 o'clock the following High Priests viz; George Miller — William Snow Lucian Woodworth — L[ucius]. N. Scovil Winslow Farr — Daniel Spencer William Crosby — Erastus Snow and Cornelius P. Lott, met together for prayer in Room No. 8, attic Story of the Temple Erastus Snow being mouth—

Pres[ident]. B[righam]. Young & H[eber]. C. Kimball came in at 20 minutes past 11 O'clock P.M.

At 10 minutes before 9 o'clock, [we] commenced receiving into the upper department, the persons composing company No. 4. John Pack & Mercy R. Thompson being prompters—

Joseph Cain, received by John D. Lee[.]
William Taylor " " " "
Hiram Dayton " " " "
Pamela Dayton by H[iram]. Dayton & " " "
Maria Dayton " H[iram]. Dayton & J[ohn]. D. Lee[.]
Stephen Hales Jun[io]r. by J[ohn]. D. Lee[.]
Eveline Hales by Stephen Hales & J[ohn]. D. Lee [.]
James Duncan by John D. Lee[.]
~~Huldah Duncan by John D. Lee & J. D.~~
John Hatfield by J[edediah]. M. Grant[.]
Lucy Hatfield by John Hatfield & J[edediah]. M. G[rant].
Lucinda Curtis by J[ohn]. Hatfield & [Jedediah M.] Grant[.]
Samuel Mulliner by J[edediah]. M. Grant[.]
Catharine Mulliner by S[amuel]. Mulliner & [Jedediah M.] Grant[.]
John Loveless by J[edediah]. M. Grant[.]
Mahala Loveless by John Loveless & J[edediah]. M. Grant[.]
Daniel S. Cahoon by J[edediah]. M. Grant[.]
Jane A. Cahoon by D[aniel]. S. Cahoon & [Jedediah M.] Grant.
John Leeka by J[ohn]. D. Lee[.]
Sarah Leeka by J[ohn]. Leeka & J[ohn]. D. Lee[.]
Avis Brown by Josiah Arnold & J[ohn]. D. Lee[.]
Milo Andrus by J[ohn]. D. Lee.
Abigail J. Andrus by Milo Andrus & J[ohn]. D. Lee[.]
Peter Hofheins by J[ohn]. D. Lee[.]
Sarah Ann Hofheins by P[eter]. H[ofheins]. & L[ucius]. N. Scovil[.]
Daniel McCall }
Margaret McCall } L[ucius]. N. Scovil[.]
John M. Chidester }
Polly Chidester } L[ucius]. N. Scovil[.]
Samuel Parker " " "

Sarah Parker	"	"	" & S[amuel]. Parker[.]
Lysander Dayton	"	"	"

[E]nded at eleven o'clock & 20 minutes—

The following persons have labored in the Temple this day—viz; President George Miller—presiding

Orson Pratt,	Mrs. Mary C. Miller
Orson Spencer	Catharine C. Spencer
Joseph Young	Pamela Lott
J[edediah]. M. Grant	Elizabeth Durfee
Lucius N. Scovil,	Alice ~~Warnock~~ ^Hurst^
George P. Dykes	Mercy R. Thompson
Erastus Snow	Artemisia Snow
William Snow	
Theodore Turley	
W[illiam]. W. Phelps	Sally Phelps
Franklin D. Richards	
Lorenzo Snow	Eliza R. Snow
Simeon Carter	Lydia Carter
Henry G. Sherwood	Jane Sherwood
John L. Butler	
Daniel Carn	Sopronia M. Harmon
Joshua S. Holman	
Willard Snow	[blank] Harmon
William Crosby	
Ezra T. Benson	Emmeline A. Benson
Abraham O. Smoot	Margaret T. Smoot
William Snow	
Peter Haws	
Elisha Averett	
Elijah Averett	
Lewis Robbins	
Hosea Stout	
Jesse D. Hunter	
John Pack.Julia Pack	
John D. Lee	
David Candland	
Lucian R. Foster	Henry Harriman

All the Twelve [apostles] have been absent from the Temple the greater part of this day except Orson Pratt, who has spent the greater part of the day here.

In the evening Pres[ident]. Brigham Young, Elder H[eber]. C. Kimball — Orson Hyde, Amasa Lyman & George A. Smith came in, but did not remain long. They soon retired, but at about 20 minutes past eleven, Pres[ident] Young & H[eber]. C. Kimball came in and remained the rest of the night— The labors of this day have been very arduous—122 persons having been washed and anointed and received into the upper department.

It was expected that troops would be in, with officers and writs, for the purpose of arresting the Twelve [apostles], who are mostly charged with counterfeiting the current coin of the United States. but no signs of troops, writs or officers have appeared to molest our peace. The day has been moderately cold, and in the evening a light flurry of snow.

Sister Huldah Duncan, whose name is among those who were washed & anointed did not go through the vail being obliged to turn back on account of the illness of her little child— See account of persons passed through January 20th—

—William Clayton, Diary, kept for Heber C. Kimball.

....

The weather is about the same Temporment — light flakes of Snow are frequently seen descending from the uper Hemisphere[.] the arrangements for the [officiators] — have not been altered from yesterday with the e[x]ception of one or 2 persons Namely E[zra]. T. Benson appointed Proterum to anoint in the room of P[eter]. Haws — absent Warren Snow in the Male department to wash — Simeon Carter in the room of Daniel Carn Absent — Previously 12 at Night a messenger came bringing the Joyful News of the liberty W[illia]m Miller the Suposed B[righam] Young that had been taken a Prisoner the night before — on entering Carthage [Illinois] J. W. Hacker the clerk of the county commissioners Court who was an apostate from our church, met the officers who had the Prisoner — & readily discovered the trick & said thats not B[righam]. Young it is W[illia]m Miller — I know him like a book — where upon the prisoner was Set at liberty — on his return the information came that they (the officers) wanted him [Brigham Young] in on the morrow with a Posse to to Search the Temple as well as the city — accordingly we listened as the Lord gave us wisdom[.] Prayers were offered up in the different departments by Each Q[uoru]m who [are] calling [upon God] — for in his hands we commit ourselves trusting in him to deliver his Saints from the voilence of the wicked men and preserve us to do his will on the Earth as it is done in Heaven[.] we are thankful for the [authority] & power that ^has^ already been confirmed on many of the Saints who [have been commissioned] unto confer[ring] the Keys of Endowment on the remaining faithful Saints — Should the Twelve be Forced to flee to some remote though congenial clime for safety[.] — Pres[ident] J[oseph]. Young [is] where [he can supervise] & Pres[ident] H[enry]. Herriman also who is & has been taking the names & ages of those who al[ready] are Passing through the ordinances of their Endowments — Pres[ident] J[edediah]. M. Grant came in at 25 Minets Past ten

1 o.Clock P.M.

No 104 Alpheus P. Haws born Oct 15th 1815 washed by William Crosby & E[zra]. T. Benson Anointed by A[braham]. O. Smoot and Willard Snow

Females

Adeline Haws — Females [—] born June 19-1819 washed by ^A[rtemisia] Snow & anointed [by] M[ary]. C. Miller^ No 104

Mary An[n] ^Mercy^ Alexander Sept 20th 1815 [by] M[argaret]. J. Smoot & M[ary]. C. Miller

Sarah Carter June 7th 1822 [by] L[ydi]a. [?] Carter & M[argaret]. C. Smoot 106

Males

10 AM
whole No

Randolph Alexander March 22nd 1802 washed [by Jedediah] G[rant and] W[illiam] C[rosby;] [anointed by] E[zra] T Benson

106

Henry Carter June 27 1820 Anointed by A[braham]. O. S[moot]. & W[illiam] Snow

Bushrod W. Wilson Augt. 22nd 1808 washed & anointed by the above

Stephen Hales Jr Oct 17th 1820

John Hatfield Nov 29. 1819

John M. Chitester Jan 22 1809

Samuel S. Cahoon Aug 7th 1822

Samuel Mulliner Jun 15th 1808

Milo Andrews Mar 6th 1814
Hyrum Dayton Nov 1st 1788
John Loecka Feb 22nd 1802
Lysander Dayton Aug 15th 1826
John Loveless June 24 1809 H[igh]. P[riest].
Peter Hoffines Nov 2nd 1809
David McCall Dec 12th 1800
John Cain Nov 5th 1822

Whole No.

W[illia]m Taylor Sept 2 1823

122

Samuel Parker April 7th 1790

The above named Persons were washed by Levi W. Hancock and Andrew Lyttle and anointed by Pres[ident]. B[enjamin] L Clapp J[edediah] M Grant John Pack & J[ohn]. D. Lee Henry Herriman clerk in the Preperatory Room. — Pres[ident] Jos[eph]. Young was called away about this time to accompany Pres[ident] B[righam] Y[oung] his Brother who was found [in need of assistance] to keep [him from] the group of wicked men who are seeking the distruction of the Lords anointed — & the overthrow of the Kingdom

[See page 172 for excerpted portion.]

[Marginal notation: "At 4 P.M. Co[mpany] No 43"]

Pres[ident] B[enjamin]. L. Clapp John D Lee & John Pack acted in the lower department as No 1 E[loheim] No 2 J[ehovah]. No 3. M[ichael]. W[illiam] W. Phelps No 4 S[erpent]. & F[ranklin] D Richards Prom[pter]. Pres[ident] J[edediah]. M. Grant [acted as] No. 1 P[eter]. in the middle department [with] Pres[ident] L[evi]. W. Hancock No 2. J[ames]. John Scott No 3 J[ohn]. W[illiam]. W. Phelps No 4 T[empter?]. F[ranklin]. D. Richards [illegible] Ricevers at the veil J[ohn] D Lee J[edediah] M Grant assisted by L[ucius]. N. Scovil — Prompters at the v[eil]— Pres[ident] L[evi]. W. Hancock John Pack & J[edediah]. M. Grant — it is now ½ past 12. oclock at Night & the last one of the co[mpany] N. 13, has Just passed through[.] 126 Persons have recived their washings and anointings to day — & out of that No[,] 20 Seventies & their wives have been washed — Pres[ident] L[evi] Hancock returned home about midnight Pres[ident] H[enry] Herriman also — Pres[ident] B[enjamin] L Clapp J[edediah]. M. Grant & J[ohn] D Lee Spent the Night in the Temple also Pres[ident] B[righam] Y[oung]. G[eorge]. Miller & H[eber]. C.

[Washings and anointings for Wednesday, December 24, 1845]

Femals	Washed by	Anointed by
Evelina Hales Sept 1821	M. T. Smoot	M. T. Smoot
Polly Chitister April 1809	E Durfee	P Lott
Jane A Cahoon Oct 11 1822	P Lott	M Collidge [?]
Cathorine Halliver June 4th 1814	E Durfee	P. Lott
Abigail Andrews June 2nd 1815	La. Carter	M. C. Miller
Permelia Dayton July 1791	" "	P Lott
Sarah Leeka Dec 7 1805	E Durfee	M. T. Smoot
Maria Dayton July 15 1829	La Carter	P Lott
Lucinda Curtis	E Durfee	M C Miller
Lucy Hatfield July 14th 1821	Lidia Carter	M. T. Smoot
Mahala Loveless Aug 26 1805	E Durfee	do do
Margaret McCall Oct 12th 1805	M. T. S.	M. T. Smoot
Sarah A. Hopkins July 4th 1811	La Carter	M. C. Miller
Sarah Parker Mar 28th 1799	Elizabeth Durfee	" "
Avis Brown April 8th 1800	L Carter	Females where No. 121

—Seventies Record, Book B, oversized portion, December 24, 1845

Kimball. No officers have been as was expected with writs for [subpoena] of the Saints. this Sentence closes the remarks for the day.

—Seventies Record, Book B.

....

At Eleven my wife [Louisa Stout] came to the Temple to cut out our robes and other garments.

—Hosea Stout, Diary, in *On the Mormon Frontier: The Diary of Hosea Stout, 1844-1861,* edited by Juanita Brooks (Salt Lake City: University of Utah Press/ Utah State Historical Society, 1964).

....

All the Twelve [apostles] have been absent from the Temple the greater part of this day except Orson Pratt. One hundred twenty-two persons received the ordinances.

At 11:20, Elder Heber C. Kimball and I [Brigham Young] returned to the Temple and remained all night.

William Miller remained last night at Carthage [Illinois] at Jacob B. Backenstos'. Miller said he could not sleep being interrupted by [attorney] Edmonds' continued roars of laughter at the marshal's discomfiture.

Miller saw two of the marshal's guards, one of whom threatened his life. Miller came in with the stage, the driver told him that the officers said it would be like searching for a needle in a hay mow now, to undertake to find Brigham Young in Nauvoo.

—"Manuscript History of Brigham Young," in *History of the Church,* 7:551.

....

Nauvoo temple endowments performed on this date for:

First Company: Joseph Mount, Elizabeth Mount, Arza Judd, Lois Judd, Herman Hyde, Polly W. Hyde, Eunice Hyde, Charles B. Thompson, Catharine A. Thompson, Randolph Alexander, Myrza Alexander, Luman H. Calkins, Mehitabel Calkins, Joseph W. Johnson, Elizabeth Johnson, Orlando Henry Carter, Sarah Carter, Joseph A. Kelting, Elizabeth Kelting, Minerva Wood, Gustavus Hills, Elizabeth Ann Hills, Phebe Angell, William Davis, Sarah Davis, Martin H. Peck, Mary Peck, John Lowry, Mary Lowry, Benjamin Aber, and Isaac Decker.

Second Company: Roswell Stevens, Sybil Stevens, James Rawlins, Jane Rawlins, William Munjar, Mary Munjar, John Telford, Jane Telford, Joseph Fletcher, Armilla Fletcher, Perry Durfee, Jane Durfee, John A.

Mikesell, Katharine Mikesell, Samuel Burton, Hannah Burton, Melissa Burton, Isaac Houston, Theodosia Houston, Jane Maria Houston, Henry B. Huffman, Silvina Huffman, Sidney A. Knowlton, Harriet Knowlton, Artemas Millet, Almira Millet, John Killion, Sally Killion, Elisha H. Groves, and Sally Groves.

Third Company: Joel Drury, Tirzah Drury, Fanny Hartshorn, John Sweat, Polly Sweat, Emily Whitmarsh, Abigail Haws, Loly Ann Haws, George Coulson, Nancy Coulson, Catharine Wilkie, F. M. Van Leuven, Lydia Van Leuven, Alpheus P. Haws, Adeline Haws, Stephen Blackman, Deborah Blackman, Howard Coray, Martha Jane Coray, Stephen Litz, Fanny Litz, Ebenezer Brown, Phebe Brown, Eliza D. Burgess, Lucy Ann Flanagan, Prudence Fairchild, Nancy Chapman, Betsey Fairchild, and Benjamin K. Hall.

Fourth Company: Joseph Cain, William Taylor, Hiram Dayton, Pamela Dayton, Maria Dayton, Stephen Hales Jr., Eveline Hales, James Duncan, John Hatfield, Lucy Hatfield, Lucinda Curtis, Samuel Mulliner, Catharine Mulliner, John Loveless, Mahala Loveless, Daniel S. Cahoon, Jane A. Cahoon, John Leeks, Sarah Leeks, Avis Brown, Milo Andrus, Abigail Andrus, Peter Hofheins, Sarah Ann Hofheins, Daniel McCall, Margaret McCall, John M. Chidester, Polly Chidester, Samuel Parker, Sarah Parker, and Lysander Dayton.

—Summary of information compiled by the Temple Index Bureau, *Nauvoo Temple Endowment Register: 10 December 1845 to 8 February 1846.*

III.

Late December

1845

"SIGNS & TOKENS"

Thursday, December 25, 1845

Present. Pres[ident]. Brigham Young, H[eber]. C. Kimball, George Miller and others who were here yesterday with some others, The morning is fine, the sun shining clear & bright upon the light covering of snow which fell last night—

At 9 o'clock [we] commenced in the male department, and the following persons were washed and anointed, all being High Priests— Joshua L. Miller being ordained to that office this morning in the Temple, under the hands of Pres[ident]. George Miller, his father and Theodore Turley— Their names are as follows, viz;

Joshua Mecham	born	April 12. 1773
Shadrach Roundy	"	Jan[uar]y. 1. 1789
Freeborn Demill	"	March 3. 1795
John Haven	"	March 9 1794
Nathaniel Taylor	"	March 15 1778
Barnet Cole	"	March 16 1796
Stephen Perry	"	August 12 1805
Frederick W. Cox	"	Jan[uar]y 20. 1812
Jacob G. Bigler	"	April 4. 1813
Israel Calkins Sen[io]r.	"	June 7, 1766

Joshua L. Miller " Jan[uar]y 4. 1827
Daniel Stanton " May 28. 1795

Washed by William Crosby and Joseph W. Johnson. Anointed by Abraham O. Smoot and Willard Snow.

[E]nded at 5 minutes to 10[.]

In the female department, commencing at 9 o'clock, the following persons were washed and anointed. viz;

Betsey Roundy born June 29. 1795. washed by Artemisia Snow, anointed by Mary C. Miller[.]

Sally S. Alvord born May 7. 1803 W[ashed]. by Amanda Rogers anointed by Elizabeth Durfee[.]

Anna Demill born March 5. 1804 W[ashed]. by M[argaret]. T. Smoot anointed by Elizabeth Durfee[.]

Amy L. Bigler born Nov[embe]r. 7. 1822 W[ashed]. by Artemisia Snow anointed by Mary C. Miller[.]

Laura Beck born September 26. 1821. W[ashed]. by Amanda Rogers an[ointe]d. by Artemesia Snow[.]

Surviah Taylor born Jan[uar]y 15. 1782 W[ashed]. by Amanda Rogers an[ointed]. by Elizabeth Durfee[.]

Samantha Roundy born June 2. 1824 W[ashed]. by Artemisia Snow an[ointed]. by Mary C. Miller[.]

Hannah Calkins born Sept[ember]. 4. 1773 W[ashed]. by Artemisia Snow an[ointed]. by Mary Ann Pratt[.]

Pamela Mecham born Jan[uar]y 25. 1787 W[ashed]. by Sally Phelps an[ointe]d. by Mary Ann Pratt[.]

Elizabeth Ann Miller born April 29. 1827 W[ashed]. by Amanda Rogers an[ointe]d. by Artemisia Snow[.]

Elizabeth Miller born April 7. 1817 W[ashed]. by Sally Phelps an[ointe]d. by Elizabeth Durfee[.]

Sophia Leyland born April 5. 1800 W[ashed]. by Amanda Rogers an[ointe]d. by Mary C. Miller[.]

Judith T. Haven born Dec[embe]r. 28. 1798 W[ashed]. by Amanda Rogers an[ointe]d. by M[argaret]. T. Smoot[.]

Roby Perry born July 23. 1794 W[ashed]. by Amanda Rogers an[ointe]d. by E[lizabeth]. Durfee[.]

Clarinda Stanton born March 8. 1797 W[ashed]. by Amanda Rogers an[ointe]d. by Mary Ann Pratt[.]

Maria S. Burton born April 10 1826 W[ashed]. by Amanda Rogers an[ointe]d. by Artemisia Snow[.]

Phebe Cole born January 8. 1809 W[ashed]. by Amanda Rogers an[ointe]d. by Mary C. Miller[.]

Harriet Parker born Jan[uar]y. 31. 1806 W[ashed]. by Mercy R. Thompson an[ointe]d. by Mary C. Miller[.]

Emeline Cox born Jan[uar]y 23 1817 [washed by] Amanda Rogers [anointed by] Mary C. Miller.

Ended at 14 m[inutes]. after 10.

21 [women washed and anointed.]

At 10 minutes past 10, the Bell rung for Company No. 1 to prepare for passing through. Persons officiating as follows, viz;

Orson Spencer	as	No.	1.}	
L[ucius]. N. Scovil	"	"	2 }	upper dep[artmen]t.
George P. Dykes	"	"	3 }	
Erastus Snow	"	"	1 }	
William Snow	"	"	2 }	middle
Ezra T. Benson	"	"	3 }	dep[artmen]t
W[illiam]. W. Phelps	"	"	4 }	
F[ranklin]. D. Richards	"	"	5 }	

Company No. 1.

At 15 minutes before 12 [we] commenced receiving into the upper department, company No. 1. Lorenzo Snow & Mercy R. Thompson and Julia Pack officiating as prompters

John Haven.	rec[eive]d.	by	Orson Spencer[.]
Judith T. Haven	"	"	J[ohn]. Haven & O[rson]. S[pencer].
Jacob G. Bigler	"	"	O[rson]. Spencer[.]
Amy L. Bigler	"	"	J[acob]. G. Bigler & O[rson]. S[pencer].
Shadrach Roundy		by	George Miller[.]
Betsey Roundy	"		S[hadrach]. Roundy & G[eorge]. Miller[.]
Maria S. Burton	"		Robert T. Burton & G[eorge]. M[iller].
Samantha Roundy	"		John D. Parker & G[eorge]. M[iller].
Laura Beck	"		Shad[rach]. Roundy & G[eorge]. M[iller].
Daniel Stanton	"		George Miller[.]

Clarinda Stanton	"	D[aniel]. Stanton & G[eorge]. M[iller].
Joshua Mecham	"	George Miller[.]
Pamela Mecham	"	J[oshua]. Mecham & G[eorge]. Miller[.]
Israel Calkins Sen[io]r.	"	George Miller[.]
Hannah Calkins	"	I[srael]. Calkins & G[eorge]. M[iller].
Frederick W. Cox	"	G[eorge]. Miller[.]
Emelina Cox	"	F[rederick]. W. Cox & G[eorge]. M[iller].
Barnet Cole	"	George Miller[.]
Phebe Cole	"	B[arnet]. Cole and Geo[rge]. Miller[.]
Stephen Perry	"	Geo[rge]. Miller[.]
Roby Perry	"	S[tephen]. Perry & G[eorge]. Miller[.]
Freeborn Demill	"	Geo[rge]. Miller[.]
Anna Demill	"	F[reeborn]. Demill & G[eorge]. Miller[.]
Nathaniel Taylor	"	George Miller.
Surviah Taylor	"	N[athaniel]. Taylor & G[eorge]. Miller[.]
Harriet Parker	"	H[enry]. G. Sherwood[.]
Joshua L. Miller	"	George Miller[.]
Elizabeth Ann Miller	"	J[oshua]. L. Miller & G[eorge]. Miller[.]
Sophia Leland	"	George Miller[.]
Elizabeth Miller	"	George Miller[.]
Jacob L. Bigler	"	George Miller
~~Amy L. Bigler~~	~~"~~	~~J L. Bigler G. M~~
~~John Haven~~	~~"~~	~~George Miller~~
Sally S. Alvord	"	George Miller[.]

[E]nded at 20 minutes before 3.

At 6 minutes past 11 o'clock [we] commenced in the male department, washing and anointing the following persons, viz

High Priests.

Thomas Carrico	born	Sept[ember]. 20. 1801
William Draper Sen[io]r	"	Sept[ember]. 6, 1774

Malatiah Luce	"	Jan[uar]y 30. 1772
Joseph L. Robinson	"	Feb[ruar]y 18. 1811
Elijah Williams	"	Aug[us]t 24. 1780
Joseph S. Allen	"	June 25. 1808
Joseph Mecham	"	Feb[ruar]y 1. 1806
William C. Gallaher	"	Jan[uar]y 16. 1807
Seventies		
Luman A. Shirtliff	"	March 13. 1807

These were washed by William Crosby Joseph W. Johnson & Andrew Lytle. Anointed, the High Priests by Willard Snow and Levi Stewart, and the Seventy by Benj[amin]. L. Clapp and Andrew Lytle[.]

Finished at 5 m[inutes]. before 12.

William C. Gallaher was taken from the quorum of Seventies, and ordained a High Priest, under the hands of Pres[ident]. George Miller and Daniel Carn, before being washed and anointed.

At a quarter past 12 o'clock George D. Grant brings word that the United States Marshall is in the city again,[1] Elder Kimball sent a message to him by Elder Grant, and at 15 minutes before one, Elders Young and Kimball left the Temple.

In the female department the following persons were washed and anointed, commencing at 5 minutes before 11 o'clock, viz;

Lydia Draper born Nov[embe]r. 5. 1775 W[ashed]. by Amanda Rogers anointed by Mary Ann Pratt[.]

Sarah Ellen Clift born May 3. 1817 W[ashed]. by Artemisia Snow, an[ointe]d. by Mary C. Miller[.]

Lucy D. Allen born Oct[ober] 4. 1815 W[ashed]. by Sally Phelps anointed by Mary Ann Pratt[.]

Aminta M. Williams born ~~Mar. 15. 1785~~ ^Sept[ember]. 20. 1815^ W[ashed]. by Amanda Rogers an[ointed] by Mary Ann Pratt[.]

Mary Williams born Mar[ch]. 15 1785 W[ashed]. by Amanda Rogers an[ointed] by Mary C. Miller[.]

Hannah Allen born Jan[uar]y 23. 1800 W[ashed]. by Artemisia Snow an[ointed]. by Mary C. Miller[.]

1. The marshal, a man named Roberts, possessed several writs for church leaders charged with "counterfeiting Mexican dollars and American half dollars, and dimes." Despite a circular from the Quorum of the Twelve Apostles denying the charges, the writs were issued in December 1845. See Glen M. Leonard, *Nauvoo: A Place of Peace, a People of Promise* (Salt Lake City: Deseret Book Co., 2002), 524.

Margaret Johnson born Dec[ember]. 16. 1819 W[ashed]. by Amanda Rogers an[ointe]d. by Elizabeth Durfee[.]
Maria Robinson born Jan[uar]y 5 1806 W[ashed]. by Sally Phelps an[ointed]. by Mary Ann Pratt[.]
Betsey Carrico born Dec[ember]. 4. 1811 W[ashed]. by Amanda A. Rogers an[ointed]. by Artemisia Snow[.]
Altamira Shirtliff born Aug[ust] 7. 1816 W[ashed]. by Sally Phelps an[ointed] by Artemisia Snow[.]
Charlotte Fox born Nov[embe]r. 6, 1801 w[ashed]. by Sally Phelps an[ointed] by Elizabeth Durfee[.]
Hannah Mecham, [born] Feb[ruar]y. 10. 1809 W[ashed]. by Sally Phelps an[ointed]. by Elizabeth Durfee[.]
Ruth Luce born Oct[ober]. 13. 1775 W[ashed]. by Sally Phelps an[ointed] by Elizabeth Durfee[.]
Elizabeth Gallaher born Oct[ober] 4. 1808 w[ashed]. by Amanda Rogers an[ointed]. by Mary C. Miller[.]

Finished at 10 m[inutes]. before 12.

At 12 o'clock the Bell rung for Company No. 2 to enter the lower & middle departments. Same persons officiating as for Co[mpany]. No. 1.

At 15 minutes after 3 o'clock [we] commenced receiving into the upper department, Company No. 2. in the following order. viz;

William C. Gallaher	by O[rson]. Spencer[.]
Sarah Ellen Clift	" Theodore Turley[.]
Elizabeth Gallaher	" W[illiam]. C. Gallaher & O[rson]. S[pencer].
William Draper Sen[io]r.	" Orson Spencer[.]
Lydia Draper	" W[illiam]. Draper & O[rson]. S[pencer].
Thomas Carrico	" O[rson]. Spencer[.]
Betsey Carrico	" T[homas]. Carrico & O[rson]. S[pencer].
Joseph Mecham Jr.	" Orson Spencer[.]
Hannah Mecham	" J[oseph]. Mecham Jr. & O[rson]. S[pencer].
Hannah Allen	" Simeon Carter[.]
Joseph S. Allen	" John D. Lee[.]
Charlotte Fox	" Lucian Woodworth[.]
Lucy D. Allen	" Joseph S. Allen & J[ohn]. D. Lee[.]

Margaret Johnson	"	Lucian Woodworth[.]
Araminta M. Williams	"	" "
Joseph L. Robinson	"	John D. Lee[.]
Maria Robinson	"	J[oseph]. L. Robinson & J[ohn]. D. Lee[.]
Elijah Williams	"	J[ohn]. D. Lee[.]
Mary Williams	"	E[lijah]. Williams & J[ohn]. D. Lee[.]
Malatiah Luce	"	John D. Lee[.]
Ruth Luce	"	M[alatiah]. Luce & J[ohn]. D. Lee[.]
Luman A. Shirtliff	"	John D. Lee[.]
Altamina Shirtleff	"	L[uman]. A. S[hirtliff]. & J[ohn]. D. Lee[.]

Finished at 20 m[inutes]. past 5. Lorenzo Snow, and Julia Pack. officiating as prompters[.]

At 5 o'clock, Pres[ident]. Young came into the Temple and remained about an hour overseeing, & directing in relation the business generally.

At 10 minutes before 3, [we] commenced in the male department washing and anointing the following persons, viz;

High Priests—

Isaac Behunin.	born	Oct[ober] 20 1803
Israel Calkins Jr.	"	Sept[ember]. 1. 1801
Parshall Terry	"	Sept[ember] 30 1778
Jeremiah Woodbury	"	March 9. 1791
Martin Bushman	"	April 1. 1802
John D. Chace	"	Aug[us]t 10, 1815

Seventy.

Francis Smith	"	October 15, 1816.

Washed by William Crosby & Joseph W. Johnson anointed by Willard Snow & Levi Stewart.

[E]nded at 10 minutes to 4.

At 5 minutes before 3 [we] commenced in the female department, washing and anointing the following persons, viz;

Elmira Behunin. born April 23. 1811. W[ashed]. by Artemisia Snow. anointed by Mary Ann Pratt.

Lavina Calkins born June 24. 1813 w[ashed]. by Amanda Rogers an[ointed]. by Mary C. Miller[.]

Sally Williams born Sept[ember]. 20. 1813 w[ashed]. by

Amanda Rogers an[ointed]. by Mary Ann Pratt[.]

Hannah Terry born Oct[ober] 8. 1786 w[ashed]. by Amanda Rogers an[ointed]. by Mary Ann Pratt[.]

Sarah E. Loveless [born] July 5. 1827 W[ashed]. by Artemisia Snow an[ointed]. by Mary Ann Pratt.

Elizabeth Bushman [born] Sep[tember] 12, 1802 W[ashed]. by Amanda Rogers an[ointed] by Mary Ann Pratt.

Elizabeth Woodbury born Ap[ri]l 24 1794 W[ashed]. by Amanda Rogers a[nointed]. by Mary C. Miller[.]

Isabella Smith born Oct[ober] 3 1821 W[ashed]. by Amanda Rogers a[nointed] by Mary Ann Pratt.

10 m[inutes]. to 4[.]

At 15 minutes past 4 the Bell rung for Company No. 3 to prepare to enter into the lower and middle departments, persons officiating as follows, viz, in the upper department, Orson Spencer as No. 1 L[ucius]. N. Scovil as No. 2. G[eorge]. P. Dykes as No. 3, and in the Middle department, William Snow as No. 1. E[zra]. T. Benson No. 2 Willard Snow [No.] 3. W[illiam]. W. Phelps [No.] 4. F[ranklin]. D. Richards [No.] 5, or prompter[.]

At 13 minutes before Six [we] commenced receiving Company No. 3 into the upper department, as follows, viz

Martin Bushman	by	Orson Spencer[.]
Elizabeth Bushman	"	M[artin]. Bushman & O[rson]. S[pencer].
Jeremiah Woodbury	"	O[rson]. Spencer[.]
Elizabeth Woodbury	"	J[eremiah]. Woodbury & O[rson]. S[pencer].
Isaac Behunin	"	Orson Spencer[.]
Elmira Behunin	"	~~I. Behunin & O. S.~~
John D. Chace	"	Orson Spencer[.]
Israel Calkins Jr.	"	" "
Lavina Calkins	"	Israel Calkins & O[rson]. S[pencer].
Francis Smith	"	Orson Spencer[.]
Isabella Smith	"	F[rancis]. Smith & O[rson]. S[pencer].
Sally Williams	"	John Loveless[.]
Sarah Ellen Loveless	"	" "
Parshall Terry	"	Orson Spencer[.]

Hannah Terry	"	P[arshall]. Terry & O[rson]. S[pencer].

Ended at 7 o'clock[.] Lorenzo Snow and Pamelia Benson officiated as prompters.

At 20 minutes before 6 came into the Temple Amasa Lyman & George A. Smith, Orson Hyde, [and] John Taylor[,] at 10 minutes past 6. P[arley]. P. Pratt and Orson Pratt, and at 18 min[utes]. past 6 Pres[ident]. Brigham Young & Heber C. Kimball came in.

At 20 minutes before 7 the Twelve [apostles] met in Pres[ident]. B[righam]. Young's room which is No. 1 for prayer. ^& council^ the following persons present, President Brigham Young — Heber C. Kimball — Orson Hyde, P[arley]. P. Pratt John Taylor — Orson Pratt — Amasa Lyman and George A. Smith— after considerable conversation about the western country they united in prayer & offered up the signs & tokens of the Holy Priesthood, Geo[rge]. A. Smith being mouth & afterwards laid hands on Pres[ident]. Geo[rge]. Miller who was in ill health. Closed at 8 o'clock.

The High Council met for prayer at 6 o'clock, in room No. 4. Present, C[harles]. C. Rich, Thomas Grover, Samuel Bent, Newel Knight, George W. Harris — David Fullmer, James Allred — Ezra T. Benson & H[enry]. G. Sherwood. Prayed for the prosperity & deliverance of the Twelve [apostles], and of the whole church &c.

The High Priests met in room No. 8 at 6 o'clock. for prayer, present — Freeman Nickerson — Stephen Markham W[illia]m. Felshaw — Winslow Farr Joseph B. Noble — L[ucius]. N. Scovil. Charles Allen. A[braham]. O. Smoot Willard Snow — William Snow. Erastus Snow — Joseph W. Johnson & F[ranklin]. D. Richards Stephen Markham was mouth—

At 20 minutes before 6 [we] commenced in the male department, washing & anointing the following persons, of the quorum of Seventies, viz;

William S. Muir	born	July 19 1822
Hiram Mace	"	May 5. 1811
John W. Farnham	"	Dec[ember] 15. 1794
Samuel Smith	"	June 11. 1807
Augustus A. Farnham	"	May 20. 1815
Jesse K. Nichols	"	Sept[ember] 15. 1812
Arieh C. Brewer	"	Jan[uar]y. 13. 1817

John E. Forsgren	"	Nov[embe]r. 7. 1816
Thomas J. Thurston	"	Feb[ruar]y 12. 1805
Waldo Littlefield	"	May 24. 1797
Jeter Clinton	"	Feb[ruar]y 17 1813
John Harvey	"	Dec[embe]r. 1816
George Cannon	"	Jan[uar]y 11. 1827
Truman Leonard Jr.	"	Sept[ember] 17. 1820
Jackson Redding	"	Sept[ember] 26. 1817
Hezekiah Peck	"	Mar[ch] 12. 1820
Also, High Priest,		
James Hoyt	"	Nov[embe]r 25. 1786

[E]nded at 25 minutes past 6.

In the Female department [we] commenced washing and anointing the following persons at 30 minutes past 5 o'clock—

Laura Owens born Jan[uar]y 11. 1806 washed by Amanda Rogers Anointed by Artemisia Snow[.]

Mary Ann Forsgreen " Sep[tember] 2. 1824 W[ashed]. by Sally Phelps an[ointed]. by Mary Ann Pratt[.]

Beulah Hoyt. born June 11. 1786 W[ashed]. by Amanda Rogers An[ointed]. by Julia ~~Peck~~ Pack[.]

Martitia Smith born Oct[ober] 28. 1812 W[ashed]. by Margaret T. Smoot an[ointed] by M[argaret]. T. Smoot[.]

Mary Jane Farnham " April 20. 1817 w[ashed] by Amanda Rogers an[ointed] by Julia Pack[.]

Margaret E. Brower [born] Sept[ember] 28 1818 w[ashed] by Sally Phelps an[ointed]. by Artemisia Snow[.]

Caroline Nichols " Jan[uar]y. 28. 1826 w[ashed]. by Julia Pack an[ointed]. by Julia Pack[.]

Jane Muir born Jan[uar]y 10. 1822 w[ashed]. by Sally Phelps an[ointed] by Mary Ann Pratt[.]

Ortensia White born Nov[embe]r. 30. 1825 W[ashed]. by Amanda Rogers an[ointed]. by M[argaret]. T. Smoot[.]

Jemima Peck born April 24. 1818 w[ashed]. by Amanda Rogers an[ointed]. by M[argaret]. T. Smoot[.]

Rozetta Thurston born Ap[ri]l. 25. 1809 w[ashed]. by Sally Phelps anointed by Arte[misia]. Snow[.]

Elizabeth Kahan [born] Sept[ember] 11. 1811 w[ashed]. by Mercy R. Thompson an[ointed]. by Leonora Taylor[.]

Elizabeth Mace born April 2. 1819 w[ashed]. by Mercy R.

Thompson an[ointed]. by M[ercy]. R. Thompson[.]
Eliza Harvey born July 12. 1814 w[ashed]. by Sally Phelps anointed by Julia Pack[.]
Mary Littlefield [born] July 8, 1815 w[ashed]. by Julia Pack An[ointed] by Mercy R. Thompson[.]
Melissa D. Clinton born Aug[us]t 20. 1836 w[ashed]. by Artemisia Snow an[ointed]. by Artemisia Snow[.]
Lydia Lewis born Dec[ember]. 7. 1823. w[ashed]. by Artemisia Snow an[ointed] by Mary Ann Pratt[.]
Louisa Redding [born] Feb[ruar]y 17. 1823 w[ashed]. by Sally Phelps anointed by Mary Ann Pratt[.]
Jane Bruce born Feb[ruar]y 29 1824 w[ashed]. by Sally Phelps an[ointed]. by Julia Pack[.]
Nancy Ann Redding, [born] Oct[ober] 6 1825 w[ashed]. by Sally Phelps anointed by Mary Ann Pratt[.]
Martha M. Redding [born] Aug[us]t 27 1814 w[ashed]. by Sally Phelps an[ointed]. by Julia Pack.

Ended at 5 m[inutes]. past 7 o'clock.

At 15 minutes past 7 the Bell rung and [we] commenced receiving into the lower and middle departments Company No. 4, the following named persons officiating viz;

Joseph Young	as	No.	1
B[enjamin]. L. Clapp	"	"	2
A[lbert]. P. Rockwood	"		3 in the upper department, and
Jedediah M. Grant,	as	No.	1
Levi W. Hancock	"	"	2
John Pack	"	"	3
W[illiam]. W. Phelps	"	"	4
F[ranklin]. D. Richards	"	"	5. in the middle department.

At 20 minutes before nine it was announced to the recorder [Lucian R. Foster?] ^by Elder Kimball^ that the Twelve [apostles] had decided in council, that George D. Watt should be sent to Scotland to preach the Gospel, and take his family with him.

At 10 minutes before 9 o'clock [we] commenced receiving into the upper department, the persons composing company No. 4 in the following order viz;

George Cannon,	Rec[eive]'d by	John Taylor[.]
Elizabeth Kahan	" "	John Taylor[.]
Arieh C. Brewer	" "	John Taylor[.]

Margaret E. Brewer	"	A]rieh]. C. Brewer & J[ohn]. T[aylor].
Augustus A. Farnham	"	John D. Lee[.]
Mary Jane Farnham		A[ugustus]. A. F[arnham]. & [John D.] Lee[.]
Lydia Lewis	Rec[eive]d. by	Jacob Gates[.]
James Hoyt	"	John D. Lee[.]
Beulah Hoyt	by	James Hoyt & J[ohn]. D. Lee[.]
Laura Owens	"	John D. Lee[.]
Jesse K. Nichols	"	John D. Lee[.]
Caroline Nichols	"	J[esse]. K. Nichols & J[ohn]. D. L[ee].
John Harvey	"	J[ohn]. D. Lee[.]
Eliza Harvey	"	J[ohn]. Harvey & J[ohn]. D. Lee[.]
Thomas J. Thurston	"	J[ohn]. D. Lee[.]
Rozetta Thurston	"	T[homas]. J. Thurston & J[ohn]. D. L[ee].
Waldo Littlefield	"	A[lbert]. P. Rockwood[.]
Mary Littlefield	"	W[aldo]. L[ittlefield]. & A[lbert]. P. R[ockwood]
William S. Muir	"	Albert P. Rockwood[.]
Jane Muir	by	W[illia]m S. Muir & A[lbert]. P. R[ockwood].
Jeter Clinton	"	A[lbert]. P. Rockwood[.]
Melissa D. Clinton	"	J[eter]. Clinton & A[lbert]. P. R[ockwood].
Hezekiah Peck	by	Albert P. Rockwood[.]
Jemima Peck	by	H[ezekiah]. Peck & A[lbert]. P. R[ockwood].
Truman Leonard Jr.	by	A[lbert]. P. Rockwood[.]
Ortensia White	by	T[ruman]. Leonard [Jr.] & A[lbert]. P. R[ockwood]
John W. Farnham	by	A[lbert]. P. Rockwood[.]
Samuel Smith	by	A[lbert]. P. Rockwood[.]
Martitia Smith	by	Samuel Smith & A[lbert]. P. R[ockwood].
John E. Forsgren	"	A[lbert]. P. Rockwood[.]

Mary Ann Forsgren	"	J[ohn]. E. Forsgren & A[lbert]. P. R[ockwood].
Hiram Mace	"	A[lbert]. P. Rockwood[.]
Elizabeth Mace	"	H[iram]. Mace & A[lbert]. P. R[ockwood].
Jackson Redding	"	A[lbert]. P. Rockwood[.]
Martha M. Redding	"	Jackson Redding & A[lbert]. P. R[ockwood].
Nancy Ann Redding	"	Jackson Redding & A[lbert]. P. R[ockwood].
Louisa Redding	by	J[ackson]. Redding & A[lbert]. P. R[ockwood].
Jane Bruce	"	Jackson Redding and A[lbert]. P. R[ockwood].

Finished at 15 minutes past 12 o'clock. John Pack, Julia Pack and Mercy R. Thompson officiating as prompters[.]

The following named persons have been present, and taken part in the business of the day, viz; President Brigham Young. —Elders Heber C. Kimball, Orson Hyde, Parley P. Pratt, John Taylor Orson Pratt, Amasa Lyman, George A. Smith of the Twelve [apostles]— Also, W[illiam]. W. Phelps, Orson Spencer, Lucius N. Scovil, Erastus Snow — William Snow Willard Snow. Joseph Young, Pres[ident]. of the Seventies, Jedediah M. Grant Benjamin L. Clapp. Albert P. Rockwood. William Crosby — Ezra T. Benson Abraham O. Smoot, Franklin D. Richards Henry Harriman — Hosea Stout, Jesse D. Hunter, John D. Lee. David Candland Henry G. Sherwood — George P. Dykes Joseph W. Johnson — Lewis Robbins — Elijah Averitt — Elisha Averitt — Joshua S. Holman — Daniel Carn — Simeon Carter — Andrew Lytle — Levi Stewart, Theodore Turley — Hans C. Hanson Peter Hanson — John L. Butler. John Pack. Levi W Hancock and President George Miller, who directed the business the principal part of the day, as to the initiation of those receiving their endowments & Lucian R. Foster. Recorder[.]

The Females present were as follows Mary C. Miller — wife of Pres[ident]. George Miller Eliza R. Snow, Mercy R. Thompson, Mary Ann Pratt — Artemisia Snow — Sally Phelps, Amanda Rogers — Elizabeth Durfee — Margaret T. Smoot — Pamela A. Benson Julia Pack, Alice ~~Walworth~~ ^Hurst.^, Abigail Hall. Martha H. Haven Ruth Mosher — Alvira Randall. Eliza J. Webb.

All the above mentioned persons have taken part in the business of the day, more or less— the females, many of them have been cutting out garments and sewing on them, for the use of those who are to receive their washing & anointing.

The business of the day closed at about 20 minutes past 10 o'clock.— notice was given that no ^more^ washings & anointings would be attended to at present.— Pres[ident]. Young & H[eber]. C. Kimball, with some few others, remained in the temple all night[.]

—William Clayton, Diary, kept for Heber C. Kimball.

....

The weather is Still cold, and Boreas[2] is still walking over the Plains causing his Power to be felt, by all living & moving creatures — it is clear over head & light under foot — that is there is Just snow enough to covering the dust & make the roads good as well the bridge over the great Mississippi [River] which [is] certainly favorable to the Poor Saints, in getting their wood [?] — Pres[ident] Jos[eph] Young & [Henry] Herriman came about [illegible] Pres[ident] J[edediah]. M. Grant left the Temple at 5 to [illegible]

	washed by	Anointed by
Lydia D. Clinton Aug 20th 1836	A. Snow	A[rtemisia]. Snow
Lydia Lewis Dec 7 1823	"	M[ary]. A[nn]. Pratt
Louisa Reddin Feb 17 1823	S. Phelps	M[ary]. A[nn]. P[ratt].
Jane Bruce " 29. 1827	" "	J[ulia]. Pack
Nancy An Redin Oct 6. 1825	" "	M[ary]. A[nn]. Pratt
Martha A. Reddin Aug 27 1814	" "	J[ulia]. Pack

Washing comenced in the Female department at ½ Past 5 PM the Station of Each [and all] officers that officiated in taking this co[mpany] through were as follows. In the Lower department Pres[ident] Young acted No. 1. Pres[ident] Clapp No 2 Pres[ident] Rockwood No 3 — W[illiam]. W Phelps No 4 D[avid]. Candland Prompter[.] [I]n the Midle department J[edediah]. M. Grant No 1 L[evi] Hancock No 2 J[ohn] Pack No. 3. F[ranklin]. D. Richards No 4. J[ohn]. D. Lee Receive[r] at the veil Pres[ident] H[enry]. Herriman clerk in the Preparation Room Pres[ident] J[oseph]. Young prompter at the veil J[ohn] Pack also Pres[ident] Rockwood receive[r] at the veil likewise, Pres[ident] B[righam]. Young & in fact all the 12 [apostles], that were at home have ^been^ & are still here this Evening — Pres[ident] B[righam]. Young informed the council that

2. The Greek god of the north wind.

we would Shut down the gate after to day for a short Season for the want of oil and to let the excitement cooll down a little — he further Said that it [occurred to him that he] would not suffer so Many Women to pass through as [he] has done ^in times past^ but to the contrary I will Stopp it — ~~Endow~~ it will be advisable, to give the Elders their endowments first & then should we have time, afterward we will then give the women their washings & anointing — after the operations of the day ceased which afterward Elder H[eber]. C. Kimble Set down & instructed us in the things that pertained to the Keys of the Priest Hood, which we have already reciveid[,] Pres[idents] Herriman [and] Grant — Rockwood & Hancock Returned home about one 1. o.clock at Night — Pres[ident]. Jos[eph]. B. Young ~~Returned~~ Spent the Night in the Temple.

—Seventies Record, Book B.

....

12:15 p.m., George D. Grant brought word that the United States marshal is in the city again. Elder [Heber C.] Kimball sent a message to him by Elder Grant, and at 1:15 Elder Kimball and I [Brigham Young] left the Temple.

Six p.m., the high council met for prayer in room No. 4; the high priests met in room No. 8.

At twenty minutes before six, Amasa Lyman, George A. Smith, Orson Hyde, and John Taylor went into the Temple, at 6:10 Parley P. Pratt and Orson Pratt, and at 6:18 Brother Heber C. Kimball and I went in.

The Twelve [apostles] met in my room for counsel and prayer. After considerable conversation about the western country we united in prayer: George A. Smith was mouth.

One hundred seven persons received their ordinances. The business of the day closed at twenty minutes past ten o'clock, and notice was given that no more washings and anointings would be attended to at present. Brother Kimball and I, with some few others, remained in the Temple all night.

—"Manuscript History of Brigham Young,"
in *History of the Church,* 7:551-52.

....

Nauvoo temple endowments performed on this date for:

First Company: John Haven, Judith T. Haven, Jacob G. Bigler, Amy L. Bigler, Shadrack Roundy, Betsey Roundy, Maria S. Burton, Samantha Roundy, Laura Beck, Daniel Stanton, Clarinda Stanton, Joshua Mecham,

Pamela Mecham, Israel Calkins Sr., Hannah Calkins, Frederick W. Cox, Emeline Cox, Barnet Cole, Phebe Cole, Stephen Perry, Roby Perry, Freeborn Demill, Anna Demill, Nathaniel Taylor, Surviah Taylor, Harriet Parker, Joshua L. Miller, Elisabeth Ann Miller, Sophia Leland, Elisabeth Miller, and Sally S. Alvord.

Second Company: William C. Gallaher, Sarah Ellen Clift, Elizabeth Gallaher, William Draper Sr., Lydia Draper, Thomas Carrico, Betsey Carrico, Joseph Mecham Jr., Hannah Mecham, Hannah Allen, Joseph S. Allen, Lucy D. Allen, Charlotte Fox, Margaret Johnson, Araminta Williams, Joseph L. Robinson, Maria Robinson, Elijah Williams, Mary Williams, Malatiah Luce, Ruth Luce, Luman A. Shirtliff, and Altamira Shirtliff.

Third Company: Martin Bushman, Elizabeth Bushman, Jeremiah Woodbury, Elizabeth Woodbury, Isaac Behunin, Elmira Behunin, John D. Chace, Israel Calkins Jr., Lavina Calkins, Francis Smith, Isabella Smith, Sally Williams, Sarah Ellen Loveless, Parshall Terry, and Hannah Terry.

Fourth Company: George Cannon, Elisabeth Kahan, Arieh C. Brewer, Margaret E. Brewer, Augustus A. Farnham, Mary Jane Farnham, Lydia Lewis, James Hoyt, Beulah Hoyt, Laura Owens, Jesse K. Nichols, Caroline Nichols, John Harvey, Eliza Harvey, Thomas J. Thurston, Rozetta Thurston, Waldo Littlefield, Mary Littlefield, William S. Muir, Jane Muir, Jeter Clinton, Melissa D. Clinton, Hezekiah Peck, Jemina Peck, Truman Leonard Jr., Ortensia White, John W. Farnham, Samuel Smith, Martitia Smith, John E. Forsgren, Mary Ann Forsgren, Hiram Mace, Elisabeth Mace, Jackson Redding, Martha M. Redding, Nancy Ann Redding, Louisa Redding, and Jane Bruce.

—Summary of information compiled by the Temple Index Bureau, *Nauvoo Temple Endowment Register: 10 December 1845 to 8 February 1846.*

Friday, December 26, 1845

The following Brethren & Sisters met in the Upper room of the Attic room of the Temple by my [Brigham Young's] request. H[eber] C Kimball ^O[rson] Pratt G[eorge] Miller^ Jo[seph] Young B[enjamin] L Clapp L[evi] Hancock H[enry] Herriman Peter Hawes [illegible] L[ucius] N Scovil H[enry] G. S[herwood] Lewis Robbins J[oshua] P Holman Elijah Averette Hans Hanson Theodore Turley John Butler & sisters.

I [Brigham Young] have concluded to dismiss or suspend work for the present. & take rest & when I begin to work again I shall select my men for work & shall stop the young women coming in because there [h]as been young babes taken through & I have and shall consider it an insult if a person come here to stay unless invited. I shall see these [selected] persons are place[d] on the vail to receive[.] I wish th[o]se persons not selected to retire [except] my doorkeepers and clerks[:] I shall keep [them] and sister [Mercy] Thompson & [Eliza] Snow to trim [?] an Altar. I shall have the cloth for robes removed to some more convenient place. & name the twelve the Seventies the High Council & H[igh] P[riests] to meet every day for prayer as we have done — there is too much confusion in these rooms[.] my office is now ready for the transaction of business with me[,] & the less some of us are here the better — how do you like it — I should like it [shouted] out as you like it to which they responded yes. I would caution you against attending the vail unless you are requested I have been Amused at the people making [use?] of their eyes to see who takes the sisters through the vail[.] it has nothing to do with the sealing power — they say they cannot receive their endowment without being sealed [and] this [is] to be known hereafter when persons come through the vail[.] those who have labor[ed] ^on^ the temple[,] they have all they can expect for a recompense[.] if we get more it is through the mercy of God. We shall[,] when we commence again[,] we shall have no respect to quorum but shall take them althogether. there is no difference between the Priesthood a man [has] to [be able to] preach [or] to [go into any part of the world and] open [up] the kingdom [if] he can [get the keys.][3] I say God bless you all [the] more. — we retain the two Brothers Hanson one of the Brothers Averett John Butler & our clerks are [illegible].

—William Clayton, "Copy of an address by B[righam] Young on Friday Morning in the Temple Dec[ember] 26 1845," photocopy in editors' possession, original in LDS Archives.

....

No persons having been notified to appear to day to receive their washings & anointings[,] very few persons were present in the morning[.] Pres[ident]. [Brigham] Young & H[eber]. C. Kimball were present[;] also Orson Pratt—no others of the Twelve [apostles.] a few of those who had officiated in the washing & anointing and as door keepers, fireman, Marshall, clerks, and so forth, and several of the women were present; Those

3. William Clayton subsequently incorporated and expanded these minutes in the diary he was keeping for Heber C. Kimball (following), from which the bracketed extrapolations (here) are drawn.

were all called to gether in the east room at about 11½ o'clock, and addressed by Pres[ident]. Young— He told them there would be no business done to day, and that they were all dismissed, except the two Brother Hansons [Hans Peter and Hans], Lewis Robbins & Bro[ther]. [Elisha] Averett, whom he wanted for door keepers & John L. Butler for fireman—also Sisters M[ercy]. R. Thompson & Eliza R Snow whom he wanted to do some sewing— We shall have no more washings & anointings at present, and if the brethren do not get any thing more than they have already got, they have got all they have worked for in building this house, and if there is any more to be received it is because the Lord is merciful and gracious. We shall not have any business done, except that the High Council and the High Priests will meet together once a day as usual for prayer. They will come in the back way, through the office door. Room No. 4 belongs to the High Council—No. 6 to the High Priests—No. 8 to the High Priests. No. 10 to the Elders[.] Pres[ident]. Young asked Pres[ident]. [George] Miller how many High Priests had been washed & anointed[.] Pres[ident]. Miller could not tell at the moment, but directed the clerk of the High Priests quorum to ascertain. The number was found to be 268.

Pres[ident]. Young said when he began again he should pay no respect to quorums—every man that comes in is washed & anointed by good men and it makes no difference. Every man that gets his endowment, whether he is High Priest or Seventy, may go into any part of the world and build up the kingdom if he has the keys—or on to any island. We have been ordained to the Melchisedeck Priesthood, which is the highest order of Priesthood, and it has many branches or offices— And those who have come in here and have received their washing & anointing will be ordained Kings & Priests, and will then have received the fullness of the Priesthood, all that can be given on earth, for Brother Joseph [Smith] said he had given us all that could be given to man on the earth.

I [Brigham Young] feel disposed to rest a few days, and let the Temple rest, and when I commence work again I am going to make a selection of my hands, and shall select those that will stay all the time. We will have no more cooking and eating going on in those rooms. No person will be allowed to come in unless they are invited, and I shall take it as an insult, if they come and stay— I feel it impressed upon me to rest a few days & make these regulations and as we have run out of oil we can't do much any way. I shall not have any more cutting & sewing of garments going on in the Temple. I shall have houses selected, where garments can be cut and made— It is my right to receive persons through the vail, and it does not belong to any one else, unless I put him there— When persons come into this house & receive the tokens, & signs and the key words, they have got all they have worked for in building this house. Pres[ident]. Young closed his remarks as the Temple Bell rung for noon.

All those who were not retained for door keepers, clerks &c. then departed and the rooms were cleared of those things with which they had been cumbered.

There was a necessity for a reformation of this sort, for some men were doing things which ought not to be done in the Temple of the Lord. Some three or four men & perhaps more, had introduced women into the Temple, not their wives, and were living in the side rooms, cooking, sleeping tending babies, and toying with their women The men who were guilty of these things were H[enry]. G. Sherwood, Benj[amin]. L. Clapp, L[ucius]. N. Scovil, & perhaps others[4]— There was also a great many men introduced & passed through the ordinances who were not so deserving as some that were passed by— There were also many women and children passed through who were not well entitled to the ordinances,[5] while none of the sons and daughters of the Twelve [apostles] had been permitted to enter—

There were also many persons lounging about, who had no particular duty to attend to, but who thought they had a right to be present, because they had once passed through the Vail. There was also a number of men taking their stations, at the vail without permission of the President, considering it their right to receive through the vail any female whom they might introduce into the washing & anointing room, while it is evidently the sole prerogative of the President, to officiate at that place or any one that he may authorize to do so, inasmuch as while there, the person stands in the place of the great Eloheim.

At a quarter past 3 P.M. Pres[ident]. Young & George Miller confirmed by the laying on of hands Robert ^B^ Barnes and Norman Barnes who had been baptized this day.

4. These men all continued to officiate in the temple after this date. The infractions mentioned here were apparently not sufficiently serious to prevent them from their temple duties.

5. Presumably this refers to passing through the door to the attic level of the temple, not to passing through the veil.

At about 6 o'clock in the evening, the Twelve [Apostles], The High Council, The High Priests, and the Presidents of Seventies met for prayer, each quorum in its own room—

At about half past 6 sheriff [Jacob] Backenstos came to the Temple. was admitted to the office. Room No. 3, by the back Stairs,[6] had a conference with Pres[ident]. Young, H[eber]. C. Kimball, Orson Hyde, P[arley]. P. Pratt, John Taylor, Amasa Lyman, & George A. Smith. He gave an account of the occurrences at Carthage [Illinois], when William Miller arrived there— Said the United States Deputy Marshall was in town with writs for the Twelve [apostles] & Pres[ident]. G[eorge]. Miller. He remained about half an hour & retired.

Pres[ident]. Young and H[eber]. C. Kimball left the Temple at 8 o'clock, and did not return again during the night. Sisters Snow & Thompson have been sewing and Sisters [Huldah] Barns, Margaret Moon and Sophronia M. Harmon have been washing garments in the evening—

—William Clayton, Diary, kept for Heber C. Kimball.

....

Pres[ident] Jos[eph]. Young went home about 8 o.clock in the morning. I [John D. Lee] also left the Temple about the Same time — to arrange ^some^ matters at home — It being an idle moment with me in the Temple as the work of Washing & anointing had ceased for the want of Oil & for other purposes —

Friday Dec 26th 1845 The Twelve [apostles] are taking a little resting Spell — while their enemies were prowling around like so many deamons — seeking to arest them & take them from our midst — in order to Stop the progress of the work of the Lord — through the Day Pres[ident] Jos[eph]. Young — Grant Pack L[evi] Hancock were here frequently.

At 6. P.M. Pres[ident] Jos[eph]. Young Levi Hancock J[edediah]. M. Grant John D Lee & John Pack Dresed in [marginal notation: "Dresed Priesthood"] the [robes of the] Priesthood & went in to Pres[ident] J[oseph] Youngs room [and] offered our devotion to the great Elohim in the Holy Temple of the Lord — after which Pr[e]s[ident]. Hancock & Br[other]. Hans C. Hanson, & B[rother]. E[lisha?]. Averitt made melody on their Sweet instruments of Music while Pres[ident]. J[oseph]. Young J[ohn]. Pack & J[ohn] Butler L[evi] Hancock D[avid]. Candland & myself

---

6. Office Number 3 was the only office in the attic that had a staircase to access a lower floor of the temple.

danced before the Lord[.] Before Pres[ident] B[righam]. Young left the Temple to Night he informed us that we might have a few days rest —

The Pres[idents] of all the Seventis that convened here this evening went to their respective homes about 10. at Night — which closes the records for the day.

—Seventies Record, Book B.

....

[T]he evening before [i.e., December 26, 1845] at 6 oclock Pres[ident] Jos[eph]. Young [Levi] Hancock [Jedediah M.] Grant Myself [John D. Lee] & John Pack of the eighth quorum convened in Pres[ident] Youngs room[7] & [prayed as a] council in the House of the Lord[.] Presided (or I presided) in the Priesthood & prayed after offering up the signs—it being the first time that we the Quorum of Seventy [had met] in this capacity—after which I went home by permission from Pres[ident] B[righam] Y[oung] who told (me) that I could have leisure for a few days to keep my records in order[.]

—John D. Lee, Diary, entry dated December 27, 1845.

....

When I [Hosea Stout] came to the Temple I found all the hands engaged in the endowment in a meeting. President [Brigham] Young called a meeting and concluded not to work for a few days and also made new arraingements about the order of business.

—Hosea Stout, Diary, in *On the Mormon Frontier: The Diary of Hosea Stout, 1844-1861,* edited by Juanita Brooks (Salt Lake City: University of Utah Press/ Utah State Historical Society, 1964).

....

Elders Heber C. Kimball, Orson Pratt and I [Brigham Young] were present in the Temple this morning and a few of those who had been officiating: I called them together in the east room about 11:30 a.m., and told them there would be no business done today and that they were all dismissed except the two Brothers Hanson, and three brethren for officers.

I said we shall have no more anointing at present, and if the brethren do not get anything more than they have already received, they have got

7. Room Number 1. This room also had an altar that was used for administering second anointings beginning in January 1846. See David John Buerger, "'The Fulness of the Priesthood': The Second Anointing in Latter-day Saint Theology and Practice," *Dialogue: A Journal of Mormon Thought* 16 (Spring 1983): 25.

all they have worked for in building this house; and if there is any more to be received it is because the Lord is merciful and gracious.

The high council and high priests will meet together once a day as usual for prayer.

Two hundred sixty-eight high priests were reported to have received their endowments.

I further remarked, that when we began again we should pay no respect to quorums. Every man that comes in, is washed and anointed by good men and it makes no difference. Every man that gets his endowments, whether he is a high priest or seventy may go into any part of the world and build up the kingdom if he has the keys. We have been ordained to the Melchizedek priesthood which is the highest order of the priesthood, and it has many branches or appendages.

I said, my feelings were to rest a few days and let the Temple rest, and when we commenced work again I would make a selection of hands who will remain and officiate daily. No persons will be allowed to come in unless they are invited, and I shall feel insulted if they remain here. I felt it impressed upon me to rest a few days and make these regulations, and as our oil is done we cannot do much anyway.

Six p.m., the Twelve [apostles], the high council, the high priests and the Presidents of Seventies met for prayer, each quorum in their own apartment. Sheriff [Jacob] Backenstos informed me that the United States deputy marshal was in town with writs for the Twelve [apostles] and Brother George Miller.

Eight p.m., Elder Kimball and I left the Temple.

—"Manuscript History of Brigham Young,"
in *History of the Church,* 7:552-53.

Saturday, December 27, 1845

This morning was a very pleasant one, being moderately cold, and the Sun Shining clear & bright in the heavens.

None of the Twelve [apostles] present at the Temple except Orson Pratt.

At 15 minutes past 10 o'clock the United States Deputy Marshall, from Springfield [Illinois], by the name of Roberts, came to the Temple in company with [church attorney] Almon W. Babbitt. He was freely admitted to every part of the Temple; to which he desired access. He went into the tower, on the roof, and into the Attic Story, passed through the various departments into the east room, where he very intently examined the portraits, and made enquiries as to whose they were, severally[,] but obtained no correct information on the subject. He was requested to take off his boots in the preparation room, which request he complied with.

After remaining about half an hour he departed— At about 2 o'clock he returned in company with Sheriff [Jacob] Backenstos, and a gentleman whom the Marshall introduced as from New Orleans — They visited the Middle room and the tower, and departed after about half an hour.

Doct[or]. [John] Bernhisel came in at about One o'clock, and borrowed the "New York Sun" of Dec[ember]. 9th, 1845, which contains a letter said to have been written by Emma Smith, to the Editor[8]—

Brother [David] Candland has been so fortunate as to find at Lathrops store this morning, some crimson Damask cloth, and some fringe for covering the new Altar that is to be used in the further ordinances of the Temple.

Sisters Mercy R. Thompson & Eliza R. Snow are engaged in preparing the covering. Sister [Huldah] Barns is engaged in ironing the garments that were washed last night. Lewis Robbins is cleansing & putting in order the washing Rooms & apparatus, Hans C. Hanson is sewing tent cloth together. Peter Hanson is translating the Book of Mormon into the Danish language, E[lisha]. Averett is door keeper, J[ohn]. L. Butler, Fireman. David Candland & L[ucian]. R. Foster, as Clerks— Orson Pratt has been engaged in making Astronomical calculations. From several observations, he makes the latitude of Nauvoo to be 40°35'48"—

In the evening several of the Twelve [apostles] came in, viz; Pres[ident]. Brigham Young, H[eber]. C. Kimball, P[arley]. P. Pratt, Orson

8. This letter, dated November 20, appeared in the *New York Sun* on December 9, 1845. The editor of the paper prefaced the letter by asserting that James Arlington Bennett "pronounces it genuine." In the letter, the author criticized church members as "infatuated, simple-minded people," and leaders as "petty tyrants." Most disturbing was the revelation that "I must now say, that I have never for a moment believed in what my husband called his apparitions and revelations, as I thought him laboring under a diseased mind." Emma Smith denied writing the letter and wrote to chastize Bennet for believing it was authentic. She wrote the *Sun* on December 30: "Sir: I wish to inform you, and the public through your paper, that the letter published Tuesday morning, December 9th, is a forgery, the whole of it, and I hope that this notice will put a stop to all such communications. Emma Smith." For the text of the forged letter, and the aftermath, see Linda King Newell and Valeen Tippetts Avery, *Mormon Enigma: Emma Hale Smith* (New York: Doubleday, 1984), 222-26.

Pratt, Amasa Lyman, & George A. Smith— these met for prayer in Pres[ident]. Young's room at 15 minutes befor 7 o'clock. Bishop [Newel] Whitney was with them also. all were clothed in priestly garments. Elder John Taylor came in just as they were commencing their exercises, and ~~without~~ having clothes himself united with them in prayer—Elder Kimball being mouth— Elder Orson Hyde came in after they had finished, and was asked by Pres[ident]. Young what made him always so late— He replied that the officers had been watching his house.[9] The High Council met in room No. 4 at 6 o'clock. Present, Isaac Morley, James Allred — Samuel Bent, Newel K. Knight — Alpheus Cutler, David Fullmer, Geo[rge]. W. Harris — Thomas Grover, Ezra T. Benson, William Huntington, Henry G. Sherwood, Lewis D. Wilson & Aaron Johnson — prayed for Pres[ident]. Brigham Young and all the Twelve [Apostles] that they might be preserv[e]d. from their enemies — that all the faithful Saints may be permitted to receive all the ordinances of the Lord's house, that the Lord will bless all the different quorums — for Father [John] Smith & wife — for sister Isabella Smith & child — and Eliphalet Rogers — for the High Council, their wives & children — for means to enable us to remove from this place — also for the restoration to health of Sister Slade and brother Lish—

The High Priests met in room No. 6, for prayer at half past 6 o'clock — present as follows. Daniel Spencer — Hiram Spencer. W[illia]m Felshaw Charles Allen — Winslow Farr — Joseph S. Heywood, Daniel Carter — Isaac Higbee — Abraham Palmer — Stephen Markham Albert Petty, Freeman Nickerson Elizur G. Terrill, Cornelius P. Lott — Reynolds Cahoon Franklin D. Richards Isaac Chase — & Joshua Holman — Stephen Markham and Winslow Farr being Mouth—

The following named High Priests met for prayer in room No. 8.— viz; President George Miller, L[ucien]. Woodworth Joshua S. Holman, William Crosby Peter Haws — Joseph B. Noble & Simeon Carter — Lucian Woodworth being mouth. Prayed that those persons and those who are seeking our hurt may find themselves hedged up — prayed for deliverance from bondage, — means to remove — that Pres[ident] Young may be sustained, in conjunction with all the quorums, [and] for the sick — for Elder [Wilford] Woodruff, Elder [Benjamin] Grouard and all the Missionaries on the Globe. —&c.&c.&c.

9. Orson Hyde was among those wanted for "bogus-making" (counterfeiting).

The Quorum of Seventies met in their room for prayer, present President Joseph Young, B[enjamin]. L. Clapp, J[edediah]. M. Grant, Levi W. Hancock — John D. Lee & John Pack. Joseph Young being mouth.

After the meeting was over in the room of Pres[ident]. Young, Bishop N[ewel]. K. Whitney counted out Two hundred dollars, which came in as tithing from Bro[ther]. [blank] through the hands of Elder Orson Pratt.

A general conversation ensued, in which Pres[ident]. B[righam]. Young, and all the Twelve [apostles] above mentioned, & Bishops Whitney & Miller, L[ucien]. Woodworth, J[edediah]. M. Grant & one or two others took part. The visit of the Marshall—and California were the prominent topics— Elder P[arley]. P. Pratt read from Hastings' Book.[10]

At 35 minutes past 9 P.M. there was a council of the Twelve [apostles] which continued until about 11 o'clock. at which a selection was made of men and women to labor in the Temple the ensuing week. The list is as follows—viz;

Joseph Young,	Abraham O. Smoot
William Crosby,	Henry Harriman,
Jedediah M. Grant	Benjamin L. Clapp
Erastus Snow	Charles C. Rich
Orson Spencer	William Snow
Willard Snow	Ezra T. Benson
Lorenzo Snow	F[ranklin]. D. Richards
Lewis Robbins	Elisha Averett
John L. Butler	
Catharine C. Spencer	Lois Cutler
Thirzah Cahoon	Mercy R. Thompson
Eliza R. Snow	Artemisia Snow
Diantha Billings	Sarah D. Rich
Huldah Barnes	Margaret Moon &
Sophronia M. Harmon	

The above in addition to those of the Twelve [apostles] who will be present, are considered sufficient to perform the work—

Pres[ident]. Brigham Young. H[eber]. C. Kimball Amasa Lyman George A. Smith, N[ewel]. K. Whitney and a few others remained in the Temple all night[.]

—William Clayton, Diary, kept for Heber C. Kimball.

10. This is Lansford W. Hastings's *Emigrants' Guide to Oregon and California* (Cincinnati: G. Conclin, 1845).

10 minutes past ten A.M. the united States Deputy Marshall (Roberts) from Springfield [Illinois], came with [church trustee] A[lmon]. W. Babit accompanied by [church] Lawyer Edmonds & searched the Temple for [the] Twelve & others for whom they had writs — though illegal[.] [A]fter a diligent and careful search of about ½ an hour — they left the House of the Lord put on their Boots & Hats & went their way — for they were not permited to enter without first taking the Shoes from off their feet as well as uncovering their Heads — for we gave them to understand that the Spot on which they stood was conscered [consecrated] and Holy — After ro[a]ming arround the city to Satisfy their curiosity — they [the marshal and "a gentleman from New Orleans"] came back in company with Br[other]. Babbit, and went up into the Tower of the Temple and walked out on the Deck [?] where they had a majestic view of all the surrounding country — [which] filled [the marshal] with admiration and wonder — Seeing the splendor magnificinse and Grandures that Saluted his eyes as he caught sight of the Mormon population — so called — & Knowing the inconvenience under which we had to Labor[,] while searching this the House of the Lord as well as our beautiful city — it was enough to astound [him regarding the] thing — for in fact no other people as they acknowledge Could have accomplished such [illegible] work under the same circumstances but the Saints — Say they[,] we [law enforcement] are completely whipped and acknowledge ourselves fairly out done or rather to use to use their own words fairly tuckered [?] by [the church leadership] Palming W[illia]m Miller on them for Pres[ident] B[righam]. Y[oung]. which they carried to Carthage [Illinois] before they discovered the Prank — which[,] said they[,] g[a]ve the Twelve [apostles] & other[s] for whom they had writs — oppertunity to Step out of the way — This was what we intended to do Precicily —

At 6 o.clock P.M. the following Persons — met Namely Pres[ident] Jos[eph]. Young — B[enjamin]. L. Clapp L[evi]. Hancock. J[edediah] M. Grant J[ohn] D Lee & Pres[ident] J[ohn] Pack of the 8th Seventy — Pres[ident] Jos[eph]. Young was mouth[;] the Subject of our Prayer was that the great Elohim would turn Rule and overturn the Schemes and designs of our Enemies that those who have writs may be buffeted in all their attempts & that the Twelve [Apostles] & all Faithful and good men might be delivered from their hands — and that the Lord would put it into the Hearts of the rich to come and buy our possession that we may have wherewith to remove West in the Spring — The twelve [apostles] also met & dressed in the Priesthood [robes] & offered up the signs & tokens and prayed for the Same things and so did the High Priests in their appartment and the High council likewise Making in all 4 Quorums —

—Seventies Record, Book B.

....

Mr Roberts the Deputy Marshall of the United States from Springfield Co[unty] Ill[inois] came into the Temple by permission & searched the different departments for the apprehension of the Twelve [apostles] and others for whom they had writs[.] on entering the sacred departments they were required to take off their shoes & Hats—for the ground on which they stood was holy—which they did[.] they searched about ½ an hour [and] went away without making any discoveries[. They roamed the city, and when they were] through [with] this[,] they returned and went up into the Tower of the Temple & walked out on the [blank] which presented to the eye a splendid cenery as one could overlook the surrounding country for many miles—the grandeur and sublimity with which this sacred edifice is embellished[.] they went down filled with wonder and admiration [and] acknowledged that they were completely whipped & said that it was entirely useless for them to try to get the uper hand of the Mormons for they could not[.] At 6 in the evening Pres[ident] J[oseph] Young L[evi] Hancock B[enjamin] L Clapp J[edediah] M Grant J[ohn] D Lee & John Pack of the 8th Quorum met in the Temple, [in one of the rooms] of the temple[,] dressed[,] offered up the signs [and] prayed for our deliveries from our enemies[,] for wisdom to contrive[,] & power to control our actions that we may rear our families in the fear of the Lord and the rich would come and buy our possessions & let us have gold silver horses waggons oxen cows mules sheep & clothing &c for our journey West in the spring[.] after [this,] a[nother] quorum met & prayed in the same manner[.] The twelve [apostles] sat read[ing] a california book and gave some excellent instructions[.] at 10 I returned home with Br[other] Grant who was quite unwell.

—John D. Lee, Diary.

....

Orson Pratt was the only one of the Twelve [apostles] present in the Temple [this morning].

Ten-fifteen a.m., the United States Deputy Marshal Roberts, went to the Temple in company with Almon W. Babbitt and searched for the Twelve [apostles] and others. He was freely admitted to every part of the

Temple, to which he desired access; he went into the tower, on to the roof, into the attic story and while viewing the city from the tower he expressed his astonishment at its magnificence and extent and said considering the unfavorable circumstances with which the people had been surrounded it seemed almost impossible that so much should have been accomplished. He passed through the various departments into the east room where he very intently examined the portraits, and made inquiries as to whose they were.

On entering the attic hall he was requested to take off his boots and uncover his head, to which he complied; after remaining about half an hour he departed.

About two p.m., the marshal returned accompanied by a gentleman whom he introduced as from New Orleans, and Sheriff [Jacob] Backenstos. They visited the middle room and the tower and departed after about half an hour.

Dr. [John M.] Bernhisel went to the Temple about one p.m. and borrowed the *New York Sun* of December 9, 1845, which contains a letter said to have been written by Emma Smith, to the editor.

Lewis Robbins is cleaning and putting in order the washing rooms and furniture, Peter Hanson is translating the *Book of Mormon* into the Danish language, Elisha Averett is doorkeeper, John L. Butler, fireman, David Candland and L[ucian]. R. Foster, clerks. Orson Pratt has been engaged in making astronomical calculations. From several observations he makes the latitude of Nauvoo 40° 35' 48" north.

In the evening I went to the Temple and met with Brothers Heber C. Kimball, Parley P. Pratt, Orson Pratt, Amasa Lyman and George A. Smith.

We retired to my room for prayer at six-forty-five. Elder John Taylor came in and joined us. Elder Heber C. Kimball was mouth. Elder Hyde arrived after prayers, and informed us he could not come at the hour as the officers were watching his house.

The high council met and prayed for me and all the Twelve [apostles], that we might be preserved from our enemies that the faithful saints may be permitted to receive all the ordinances of the Lord's House that the Lord would bless the quorums, and for several sick persons.

The high priests met in rooms Nos. 6 and 8 and prayed that those persons who are seeking our hurt may find themselves hedged up—for deliverance from bondage—[and the] means to remove [ourselves from here], that I [Brigham Young] and all the quorums in the church may be sustained—for the sick Elders [Wilford] Woodruff, [Benjamin] Grouard [in the Pacific Islands] and all the missionaries on the globe, etc.

The First Presidency of the Seventies met for prayer.

After prayers a general conversation ensued, in which the Twelve [apostles] and bishops, J[edediah]. M. Grant, and several others took part. The visit of the marshal and the emigration to California were the prominent topics. Elder Parley P. Pratt read from Hastings' account of California.

Nine-thirty-five the Twelve [apostles] met in council and selected the names of persons who would be called upon to labor in the Temple the ensuing week.

The list is as follows, *viz.:*

Joseph Young,	Lorenzo Snow,
Abraham O. Smoot,	Lewis Robbins,
W[illia]m. Crosby,	Benj[amin]. L. Clapp,
Henry Harriman,	Charles C. Rich,
J[edediah]. M. Grant,	William Snow,
Erastus Snow,	Ezra T. Benson,
Orson Spencer,	Franklin D. Richards,
Willard Snow,	Elisha Averett,

John L. Butler.

The above in addition to those of the Twelve [apostles] who will be present are considered sufficient to perform the work.

Elders Heber C. Kimball, Amasa Lyman, George A. Smith, Newel K. Whitney, and a few others remained in the Temple all night.

—"Manuscript History of Brigham Young,"
in *History of the Church,* 7:553-55.

Sunday, December 28, 1845

The [sic] A large concourse of people assembled in the attic story of the Lords House. the song of Zion was sung. (The Morning breaks. the shadows flee) Present of the Twelve B[righam] Young. H[eber] C Kimball P[arley] P Pratt O[rson] Pratt G[eorge] A Smith A[masa] Lyman Father & Uncle John Smith all robed and dressed. P[arley] Pratt opened by prayer after which they sung ("Come to me") [At] ¼ [past] 12[,] I [Brigham Young] came into the Room [and said], I suppose here is a part [?] of those who have received ~~unto~~ their endowments. Those who desire to be sure [of the meaning of the endowment] and do have [commitment] to the cause they espouse and bring no reproach upon the character of him who has given of his kingdom liberally[;] for the benefit of the [illegible,] I will commence with the beginning — The keys or sign of the priesthood is for the purpose of impressing on the mind [the order] of the creation. Penal Signs. In the first place, the name of the man is given. A New name Adam signifies the first man or Eve the woman. Adam['s] name was more Ancient than he was[;] it was a name [of a man] long before him who enjoyed the priesthood[. The] New name should be after some Ancient Man whereby you are enabled to ask for present future & past[.] [A]fter his [Adam's] fall another name was given — he being full of integrity & [having learned] not to listen to the woman[,] he was permitted to receive the tokens of the priesthood I wish you to learn one lesson[, and] you will find [that] one lesson [is] that you [should] hold your tongues [and then] you will never be extricated [from your kingdom] unless you go to hell[;] unless you learn[,] you will be damned — ~~we~~ let no person assemble except in an Upper room according to the priesthood. I have been saluted by [people with] the grips & tokens [and] I have felt to slap their faces. — look at the result of persons rushing to the vail — one of the most sacred places on the earth. The two key words were received in the garden. the first was his [the first man's] new name. the other is our [new] name — all such should be Ancient — the Aaronic is for helps and to assist the Melchisedec priesthood or [in] Temporal things[, and those who hold it] are entitled to those two signs[.] the man having the Mel[chizedek]. priesthood [receives more]. I will [say] there are 4 token[s,] 4 Signs[, and] 4 Penal signs[, but] the ancient name will enable [all] to ask for blessings or [for] views of ancient things. I will use the very first token — sign & penal[ty.] David [said,] Let my arm forget not the order done of the Lord & thee O Jehovah[.] [I]f [I have a question] about Modern [events,] my own name [is sufficient] — there is the thing of present [concern,] now what about future events [?] My last name.[11] In prayer you use the fir[st] tokens in your own name[.] This quorum is the more important [because] you are washed — it is [not] trifling. no[.] ...[12] I believe God & the son are

11. From the other sources for this day's events, including the content of Brigham Young's sermon, Young seems to have referred to the last names revealed to an initiate in the temple, not to Young's personal last name.

12. This portion of William Clayton's minutes is undecipherable, even though readers will notice occasional words and wording in common with Clayton's more polished account in the succeeding diary entry. What follows below is replaced by the ellipses above: "— The acting of Br Phelps — it is a well [?] privilege even

personages of tabernacle [and] the Holy Ghost is a personage of a spirit[.] God dwells in eternal fire [and] it would consume all matter that will [be] consume[d.] I do not believe any man [can] see his glory & live[,] as we but [see the writing] as ^on^ [the wall or through] the vail [as] the hand is pass[ed] through. so the finger [of God] or the knuckle [?] so the Lord will sometimes pass through his hand & the wicked may see so much & no more because He is behind the vail. if you do not sanctifie [yourselves before] the Lord and [purify] your heart[,] you will go quick to Hell & be dammed four fold. I am rough but I mean what I say. [I] do not like the Dumb Ass that ~~Pr~~ brays in the St[r]eets. — I have shut down the gates for the present — When I begin again[,] I shall bring in such as are worthy & good Men & women. Many children were brought here[;] it does not belong [to] them[,] no more than the Throne of God belongs to us[.] we will give an endowment to the good & faithful — I care not who so much [as whether they are worthy] — he [Brigham Young] also stated the impractability of there being [large gatherings in the attic, that there should be] no more meeting[s] here. The [illegible] of Workm[e]n were called over. I shall forbid you taking away your own garments — they have taken away many robes & garments [and] this I call stealing — we could dress a company of thirty when we commenced[, but today] we ~~could~~ ^cannot^ take a company of eighteen through. (I would not say every body is honest[;] I would not for my right arm) I would wish some person to take [inventory] & see every one [illegible] of all they wore while passing through. — On vote of how many will [volunteer to] fur[n]ish robes & garments[:] you are coming to a close connection with God[;] beware of your covenants how you break ~~it~~ them. If a man who works ^here^ if he mouths [complaints, this] is evil [and I] can ride him

---

when this world is [illegible] is prove the principle taught in the Bible they should have their love [illegible] so see all over use it [illegible] supremely. by all things past rather than [illegible] my [illegible] although foreordain Man should follow his wife out of the Garden it follows the woman should be led back — he related an anecdote of Uncle John & the [illegible] kitchen [?] so with us I want this to be understood all things sacred not Eternity will never become upon the world until they learn the principle No No never you lives [?] must be in subjection yes in by [illegible] do you understand the love of David & Jonathan it was above the law; Women it was the love of the Priesthood I could say Good by to the Mountain as freely could to the woman yet I love the priesthood & the principles of righteousness they may go. God told eve your desires shall be to your husband & not ~~her~~ ^his^ desire to her & he shall rule over him for if God rules over a Man he ought to rule over his household. & you ought to submit to it. I have heard upon the principle of men & Joseph Smith being God I will explain — in your prayer you ask for food."

[too,] at least with my tongue[.] We want Oil. you shall furnish it. some has been furnished[.] let the H[igh] P[riests]. [and] Seventies [contribute] & some [should be furnished] by the Bishops. I am now going to lay a plan for 1000 cords of wood[.] I will propose that the seventies shall[,] when they come here[,] they shall provide their own lights & oil. when they will[,] they [can] say to us we have furnished oil [for] above 800 persons. all vote for the different quorums furnishing their own oil & lights. I am determined to stick to this point & do away with the technicalities. & [with] the different quorums assuming a portion[,] they ought not but let us have oneness in the Lord[.] unless we would use [an opportunity for offense, we] shall have [no] trouble. the different men of different [rank] we have passed through & esteemed themselves better than another it is a paltry affair. let the Brethren start from this room & raise Men able to throw an [axe]. & let us have trains ready for wagons [for] the quorums [to gather wood.] will you do it. On motion of H[eber] C Kimball[, resolved] that we go and get it. I [will] commence to Morrow. I [propose to] continue till Wednesday as far as we can. dispatch a note to Br[other] J[oseph] Young urging his co-operation at his meetings of the seventies. previous to the sacrament being administered[,] they sung (Glorious things —) [At] 1-20 [the] Bread [was] blessed by E[lde]r. A[masa] Lyman, P[arley] P Pratt the wine. O[rson] Hyde came in at 20—2.

Elder H[eber] C Kimball cautioned the Brethren against making public w[h]ere we are. you need tell no lies about it — the Marshall survey[s] through here [and] they may come here again. we do not want to kill [?] them[,] for if we should[,] we might have to leave in the bad time of year. for if the boys get hold of them[,] we shall [not] stay [their hand] & [will say,] go you your length. if any one of you betray us you are traitors of course [and] you must expect the penalties [to be] put in force. I should not cut your throats but pray God to intervene to cut your own throat & thusly atone for his own blood. P[arley] P Pratt suggested the propriety of keeping it from ^[illegible] we do [not] tell your wives & husbands^ their own friends. on motion of B[righam] Young[, moved] that all in favor of the Motion manifest it by holding their tongues — those of a contrary mind & the same sign. H[eber] C Kimball spoke upon the flying reports about our nakedness [and] the breath of many having [been] stopped [by strangulation,] all calculation[s] to [distort] events [and elicit] the wrath of our enemies — I have not given the grips to any man but have received it from many. the giving of endowments bring[s] us in peril — The great lesson to learn [is] to hold your tongue. & mind your own business. [It] Is [from Joseph Smith;] to us[,] the key of salvation is in this — and I know it [because] I have ever preached it all my days[.] O[rson] Hyde spoke — [He] gave a figure of [a] bottle of unbottled beer which has been unstopped [and] it loses its spirits & ~~h~~ is [leaking, and] so with us when we open our mouths.

H[eber] C Kimball, by request of B[righam] Young[, said] we will form a ring around the stove of the old [initial] Member[s]. [A]fter offering up the signs. they prayed ^ except [?] one[,] Ashael Smith^ John Taylor mouth. ~~10~~ 2 o clock. The meeting was dismissed by singing the Hymn (the Praise of God that await for thee).

Dismissed by O[rson] Hyde.

W[illiam] Major. John Lytel. J[ames] Harmon. D[aniel] Carter. J[ohn] D Lee. L[ucian] R Foster M[adison] D. Hambleton. C[harles] C Rich V[ernon] H Bruce S[idney] A Knowlton J[oseph] L Heywood N[orton] Jacob. Elijah Fordham J[oshua] S Holman D[aniel] Spencer. W[ilmer] Benson. H[iram] Spencer. L[yman] O Littlefield J[ohn] R Bernhisel. [Zimri] H Baxter A[ndrew] Whitlock W[illiam] A Sanger J[oseph] G Hovey. S[tephen] Winchester Jun[ior]. John Garfield W[illiam] S Covert. J[oseph] P Cain P[errigrine] Session E[zra] T Benson. W[illiam] Matthews A[braham] Palmer & wife.

—William Clayton, "Minutes of Sunday Dec[ember] 28 1845," photocopy in editors' possession, original in LDS Archives.[13]

....

Meeting at half past 10 o'clock this day in the attic story of the Temple, for those who could clothe themselves in the garments of Priesthood. A very large congregation was present, the side rooms were some of them filled, the curtain was withdrawn, and the other rooms besides the east room were filled. About 200 persons were present, clothed in priestly garments— Pres[ident]. [Brigham] Young addressed the meeting, it having been opened by prayer by P[arley]. P. Pratt, & singing the songs of Zion, "The morning breaks the shadows flee" & "Come to me" &c. Pres[ident]. Young came into the room at ¼ before 12 M. He said he supposed those present were a part of those who had received their endowment, that they were those who desired to be wise and do honor to the cause they have

13. William Clayton subsequently incorporated and expanded these minutes in the diary he was keeping for Heber C. Kimball.

espoused, and bring no reproach upon the character of him who has given us of the things of his Kingdom liberally. The keys or signs of the Priesthood are for the purpose of impressing on the mind the order of the Creation— In the first place the name of the man is given, a new name, Adam, signifying the first man—or Eve, the first Woman— Adam's name was more ancient than he was— It was the name of a man long before him, who enjoyed the Priesthood The new name should be after some ancient man. Thus with your ancient name, your modern name, and the name that was last given you [in the temple], you enquire concerning things past present & future—

After his fall, another name was given to Adam, and being full of integrity, and not disposed to follow the woman nor listen to her[,] was permitted to receive the tokens of the priesthood.

I [Brigham Young] wish you to cease talking about what you see and hear in this place. No man or woman has a right to mention a work or the appearance of this building in the least, nor to give the signs & tokens except when assembled together, according to the order of the Priesthood, which is in an upper room. There are not a dozen persons that can give the signs & token correct & the reason [for discretion] is that person would run to that vail, one of the most sacred places on the face of the earth, that had not understood the right manner of giving the signs & tokens[.]

The order and ordinances passed through here prove the principles taught in the Bible— First men should love their God supremly[.] Woman will never get back, unless she follows the man back— if the man had followed the woman he would have follow[e]d her down until this time— Light, liberty and happiness will never shine upon men until they learn these principles— The man must love his God & the woman must love her husband— The love which David & Jonathan had for each other was the love of the priesthood[.] God is a personage of tabernacle— the Son is a personage of tabernacle— the Spirit or Holy Ghost is also a personage, but not a personage of tabernacle, but is a personage of Spirit— God dwells in eternal burnings [and] puts his hand through the vail & writes on the wall— Any persons that goes through these ordinances, unless ^they cleanse^ their hearts & sanctify themselves, & sanctify the Lord, it will damn them— When we begin again I shall select those that are worthy— We shall not be able to have another public meeting here on account of the weight on the floor, it has already caused the walls to crack—prevents the doors from shutting, and will injure the roof. I see here 200 persons, all clothed in their garments, and tomorrow I suppose we cannot find half enough [priesthood vestments] to work with, unless we lay an embargo on your garments, and forbid any of you carrying away your garments. When we began we could dress a company of 30. now we cannot dress 18. For my right arm I would not ^say^ that every body is honest, for I do not believe they are.

The names of those who would volunteer to furnish a suit of garments, to be used by those who were yet to go through the ordinances[,] was then taken, [and] they are as follows, viz — W[illiam]. W. Major — John Lytle James Harmon — Daniel Carter — John D. Lee, L[ucian]. R. Foster, M[adison]. D. Hambleton, Vernon H. Bruce — Sidney A. Knowlton — Charles C. Rich, J[ohn]. L. Haywood, Elijah Fordham — Norton Jacob — Daniel Spencer Joshua S. Holman, Willmer B. Benson, Hiram Spencer, L[yman]. O. Littlefield, J[ohn]. M. Bernhisel, Zimri H. Baxter, Andrew Whitlock, William A. Sanger, J[oseph]. G. Hovey — Stephen Winchester Jr. W[illia]m. S. Covert, John Hatfield — Joseph Kain, P[errigrine]. G. Sessions — Ezra T. Benson W[illia]m Matthews, Abraham Palmer & wife, 32 in all, each of these agreed to furnish one suit of garments for Temple use—

It was decided that when the High Priests were washed & anointed they should find the oil, and the lights, and the Seventies do the same when they occupied the rooms— and the wood is to [be] supplied as follows—1,000 men, or as many as can be obtained, to go to the [nearby Mississippi River] islands and cut wood, and teams to go and draw it to the Temple until 1,000 cords have been obtained.

Sung the hymn "Glorious things of thee are spoken". Prayer by Amasa Lyman asking a blessing on the bread— Bread passed round by Charles C. Rich and George Miller, Blessing on the wine asked by P[arley]. P. Pratt— While the wine was passing, sung the hymn Adam Ondi Ahman—

Elder H[eber]. C. Kimball cautioned the brethren and sisters against telling that the Twelve [apostles] were in the Temple— P[arley]. P. Pratt said a few words to the same point.

Elder ^Kimball^ moved that no man tell his wife what he has seen— Pres[ident] Young said "all that are in favor of this signify it by holding your tongues when you go away from here. P[arley]. P. Pratt.—"Contrary mind by the same sign".

Elder Kimball continued his remarks, [and] alluded to the stories in circulation that several persons, had been killed on their way through the ordinances, and that men and women were stripped naked here. Joseph [Smith] said that for men and women to hold their Tongues, was their Salvation.

A circle was formed, composed of about 20 persons, most of whom had received the ordinances, and [had] been admitted to the first quorum at a previous time— They united in prayer—Elder John Taylor being mouth— A hymn was sung, being led by Goddard, [John] Kay & Cahoon— notice was given that no more meetings would be held in the Attic story, for the present, and the congregation [was] dismissed after prayer by Elder Orson Hyde—

The people soon retired from the Temple and no other meeting was held—

At 5 o'clock Pres[ident]. Young & H[eber]. C. Kimball, assisted by their wives and sister Whitney, washed and anointed for their health their three children, whose names are.

John Willard Young.	born	Oct[ober]. 1, 1844
Brigham Willard C. Kimball	"	Jan[uar]y 29. 1845
Mary Jane Whitney	born	[blank]

The following High Priests met at 6 o'clock. for prayer in their room, ^No.8^ viz; George Miller — Robert Pierce — Gardner Clark — L[ucien]. Woodworth — Winslow Farr, Addison Everett W[illia]m. Felshaw, Erastus Snow. Daniel Carn, Elizur G. Terrill. — John M. Bernhisel and Albert Petty — Erastus Snow mouth.

They adjourned at 8 o'clock—

Also the following High Priests met in room No. 6. for prayer, viz; Joseph C. Kingsbury, George P. Dykes — Ormus E. Bates, Benj[amin]. Brown — Daniel Carter, Joshua S. Holman David H. Redfield — William Crosby—

Joseph C. Kingsbury mouth, closed at 8.

Three of the Dragoons stationed at Carthage [Illinois] came in with a man named Noah Miles, whom they wished to deliver up to the proper officers[.] He was charged with swindling several persons out of their property—such as horses & a waggon, pistol &c. &c.— They brought a letter from Major Warren, the commanding officer, the tenor of which was as above—the letter is on file among Pres[ident]. Young's papers— This occurred just at dark. Pres[ident]. Brigham Young and his wife &

child, Eld[er]. H[eber]. C. Kimball and his wife & child—and several other persons remained in the temple over night—

The High Council met for Prayer at the usual time, about 6 o'clock—Present Isaac Morley — David Fullmer, William Huntington — James Allred — Alpheus Cutler George W. Harris — Aaron Johnson. Thomas Grover — Ezra T. Benson & Newel Knight Prayed for the health of H[enry]. G. Sherwood — W[illia]m. Huntington — James Allred's wife — and a boy in his family & for all the sick among the saints — For Pres[ident]. B[righam]. Young, that he might have wisdom, & bodily & mental Strength, & be able to lead his people.

—William Clayton, Diary, kept for Heber C. Kimball.

At 10. o.clock A.M. in the House of the Lord Such of the Saints as were provid[ed] with Priestly Robes convened for worship all being arrayed in Priestly attire[,] Linen clean and white which is the Token of the righteousness of the Saints[.] the congregation were Seated in perfect order — then called to order by Elder P[arley]. P. Pratt. A Hymn was sung by the concourse[.] The Theme of Grace was then addressed by Elder P[arley]. P. Pratt[.] while supplicating the Throne of God[,] the Supplement was fully overcome while remembering the condition of the Scattered remnant of the House of Iseral — who are still under the hand of oppresion[.] after Prayer the Hymn titled ["]come to me["] was sung. led by Elder [John] Kay— 3d Pres[ident]. B[righam]. Young then arrived and said that in as much as this congregation that are present are those that have recived their Endowments & only administered part of them — therefore I will give some general instructions while the Bread & wine are preparing — the ordinances that you have recived in the garden togeather with the performances of those things that has been presented are to represent the creation of the world. the Name that was given to Adam was more Ancient than he was[:] the Name Adam was given him because he was the first man[;] but his New Name pertained to the Holy Priesthood & as I before stated is more Ancient than he was — there are 4 Penal signs & 4 Penal Tokens and [if I] should want to address the thorne (the throne) to enquire after Ancient things which transpired on to plannets that rol[l]ed away befofore [sic] this Plannet came into existence — I should use my New Name which is Ancient & refered to Ancient things — should I wish to Enquire for ~~modern~~ ^present^ things I should use my own name which refers to present things[. If] I Should want to enquire for

~~modern~~ ^future^ things — I would use the 3rd Name which refers to the first token of the Mel~~keze~~chizadich Priesthood. or is this token that is given[, which] refers to the son — [T]he 2nd Token of the M[elchizedek]. Priesthood is to be given only in one place & not where [the other side of the veil is in] clear [sight.] — but these signs & tokens that pertain to the Priesthood should never be given any where only in such places as belong to the P[riest]. H[ood]. & that too by none but such as belong to the order of the Priesthood — but there are not 6 Persons that have gone through those ordinances that can offer them correctly — & some has had the presumption to approach this veil which is [for] the most Sacred ordinances that is performed in this House — and have Marked the garments wrong & levity has been used here which was not pleasing in the sight of the Lord. therefore I have shut down the gate & came to the conclusion that when we can come again — we need [to] make a selection of such Persons as are worthy & will give them their endowments first & when they get their Endowments then the remainder may get their Endowment — I dont know but what I shall displease some of you but I dont care if I do — here are about 900 Persons that are dressed here to day and unless I lay an embargo on the Brethren we will not find garments enough to take 1 company through tommorow without changing them from one to another[.] the Seventies have had about 18 garments made — & this morning there were not more th[a]n 5 or 6 to be found — some have taken garments & carried them off — I call such conduct stealing & it must be stoped — Brethren cease from lightmindedness & be careful & not take the Name of the Lord in vain [and] cease from all evil speaking & backbiting[.] unless your Endowment form a cure to them [whose conduct has not been right, and] which will certainly [need reform, it] will bring in condemnation upon all who do not observe the nature of their obligations — lay aside all party strife — such as the Seventies & the H[igh]. P[riests]. striving to excell each other in Power[.] this ought [not] to be — I intend to put a stop to all such feelings[.] the H[igh]. P[riests]. commenced it in Kirtland [Ohio] — The Seventies commenced in it Quincy [Illinois] & to let it go we shall soon be split up & divided into parties — let the Saints be united that the voice of all be as the voice of one man —

Again the Tithing of the Brethren are not so promptly attended to Since the Endowment commenced as it should be — we are now about out of wood & oil — I want about 1,000 cords of wood cut & hauled this week — let every man that can lift up an axe go to morrow & continue until that amount is procured — I again Motion[ed] that Each [of the] Q[uorum]s furnish the light & oils for them selve[s] — to all the above motioned propositions entire assent was manifested by the Multitude — The blessing was then asked on the Bread by Elder Amasa Lyman — carried around by Bishop G[eorge]. Miller & Elder C[harles]. C. Rich — The Blessing was then asked by P[arley]. P. Pratt on the wine & passed around by P[arley]. P. Pratt Bishop Miller C[harles]. C. Rich & A[masa] Lyman — while Partaking of the wine — Hymn ["]Adam on Di ahman["] was sung by the Multitude — Elder H[eber]. C. Kimble then observed, that in as much you (the multitude) have seen the Twelve here to day — for the Marshal has been here & Searched the Temple yesterday & we were not here & perhaps they will come again — they have already said that [they] would have [the intent] of killing the Twelve — we dont want to kill them but if they attempt this we will not say to the Boys hold still — but go your length — I motion[,] said he[,] that no person be permitted to tell their wives what took place here to day[.] Pres[ident]. B[righam]. Young motioned that all that was in favor of this Motion should manifest it by holding their Tongues & keeping close[d] mouths[.] By permission Elder O[rson]. Hyde said with regard to telling things reminded him of an old story or [illegible] — A Botle of wine that is kept stoped close[d] has much better flavor th[a]n one that is leaking & suffering [air] to enter it — & so it is with those [who] hold their tounges until at a proper time & place — About 20 Persons, all of whom but one rec[ei]v[e]d the Priesthood before the Dedication of the Temple — formed a circle [and] offered up the Signs & Tokens & then Prayed in the Priesthood after which Elder Orson Hyde dismissed the Meeting Sine die, the Quorums excepted who were to meet every evening for Prayre Namely the Quorum of the Twelve [apostles] First Presidency of the Seventies the High Priesthood & Bishop.[14] at ½ past 2 P.M the Servises closed —

Dec. 28, 1845 Minutes of a General Conference of Seventies. The meeting assembled at the Council Hall pursuant to adjournment. The meeting was called to order by Pres[iden]t Herriman. After Singing, the Pres[iden]t. called on Pres[iden]t. B[enjamin]. L. Clapp to open the meeting by prayer. Pres[iden]t. J[oseph]. Young having arrived, rose and remarked that he knew the anxiety of the brethren to receive their endow-

14. These quorum leaders had been assigned specific offices in the attic story. The apostles had rooms 3, 5, and 7; the presidency of the Seventy, room 9; the high priests, rooms 6 and 8; and the Presiding Bishop, room 2.

ments, and [advised] them to be patient, and every worthy man should recive his blessing; [and] if we could not get them in the House of the Lord, we should have them in the wilderness; for we had built a house to the name of the Lord, and he had accepted it at our hands[.] He then answered a question which was often asked him, viz. Would the Quorums go in the Temple according to order beginning with the first, and so on to the last. He said he would answer it once for all, and in order to make it plain he would [draw] a figure. If (said he) a man have twenty-five sons, and half of them had worked all day in his vineyard, and had ate nothing; and the other half had been visiting and had not worked any, then at eve he should send his servant to call his children to supper; he would ask which should come first; the answer would be, — those who had worked all day, and so it will be with the Endowments[.] Pres[ident] Pulsipher gave the brethren much good instruction on the same subject, and exhorted all to be prayerful &c.

Pres[iden]t Clapp also gave the brethren much good instruction concerning the great work which was now resting upon them, even of carrying out the work which the prophet Joseph had commenced, and the Twelve Apostles ~~on~~ were the pillars on which the work rested, and we under them to bear it to the nations of the earth.

The meeting then adjourned to meet on Sunday Evening next. At 4 o'clock P.M. by request of Pres[iden]t B[righam]. Young I [John D. Lee] went to Benjamin McGennis to solemnize the rite of matrimony between Mary Ann his daughter and George L. Lee, it being distant about 4 miles & tarried over night, and returned to the temple about 10 o'clock this day Jan 7 [1846].

—Seventies Record, Book B.

[A]t 10 in the morning I [John D. Lee] entered the Temple of the Lord[,] arrayed my self in Priestly attire[,] and took my station near the head of the company by the speaker in order to take minutes of the discourse[.] Elder P[arley] P Pratt addressed the Throne of Grace[.] Pres[ident] Brigham Young then arose draped in linen clean & white in the midst of about 300 that were arrayed in white robes which is an emblem of the righteousness of the saints[.] He spoke in reference to the order of the Priesthood[,] the signs and tokens connected therewith[.] He observed that there were 4 penal signs & 4 penal tokens and each one of them aludes to certain names[.] the first aludes to your New or 1st name the 2nd to the 2nd & so on & should I or any of you want to enquire of the Lord for anything ancient that transpired on Plannetts that roled into existence long after this world or theater of action was organized[,] I would use my New Name because it is more ancient [than] that [of] my self & refers to ancient times[.] and should I want to enquire for things that are modern I would use my own name & to enquire for things that are future I would use the name which refers to things in future using the signs that are connected with the 3 names[.] The spirit of Elijah's God was in our midst and surely we had a time of rejoicing while we partook of the Bread & Wine & that of our own make[,] pure and good[.] Such a scene mine eye never beheld before[.] it certainly reminded me of that company that John saw while caught away in the spirit & I dont know but what [it] alluded to those that were here today[,] as a portion of them at least[.] but [as many] of [those in attendance who had] this happy prevelege[, many others of] the saints were deprived for the present, as the floor in the atic story—or more properly speaking—the trams and joists that support the floor[,] was not sufficiently strong to bear up such an immence weight as would nesarily be upon it when filled with people[.] the ceiling has already cracked [and] in many places the door frames were also cracked by the weight in so much that it actually became nessary—for the preservation of the building—to stop holding any more public meetings.

I returned home when [the meeting was over,] where I remained transacting business till near 9 at Night for the Seventies when I went up to the House of God and commenced setting things aright for the day[.] this morning produced new rules & regulations prohibiting loafers from lounging & ga[w]king around medling with [an]other mans matters & indulging in levity nonsense and folly and making light of things that are sacred and holy[.] several persons that officiated in the beginning were drop[p]ed[.] this new arrangement rather placed [me?] in an awkward position[.] I became the actor in No 4 but few persons received their endowments on Mon[day]. Tuesday the washing & anointing rooms were filled to overflowing.

—John D. Lee, Diary.

....

About two hundred of the brethren and sisters met at ten-thirty a.m. in the attic story of the Temple, some of the side rooms were filled, and the curtains withdrawn.

After singing and prayer, I [Brigham Young] addressed the meeting. The sacrament was administered. Elder [Heber C.] Kimball made a few remarks. After prayer the meeting was dismissed by benediction from Elder Orson Hyde.

Six p.m., the high council and the high priests met for prayer.

Elder Kimball and I remained in the Temple.

—"Manuscript History of Brigham Young," in *History of the Church,* 7:555-56.

Monday, December 29, 1845

Pres[ident]. B[righam]. Young. H[eber]. C. Kimball and their wives, Orson Pratt, Amasa Lyman, George A. Smith Joseph Young, Parley P. Pratt. J[edediah]. M. Grant, A[braham]. O. Smoot, W[illia]m. Crosby. Henry Harriman Erastus Snow, C[harles]. C. Rich, Orson Spencer Willard Snow — William Snow — E[zra]. T. Benson Lewis Robbins — Elisha Averett John L. Butler Lorenzo Snow. & George P. Dykes, John D. Lee, David Candland & L[ucian]. R. Foster [were present].

The carpets were taken up to some extent and shook, and the floors swept, stoves blacked, trees and shrubbery arranged in the garden, and a general arrangement of matters attended to in the morning— Sisters [Mercy] Thompson & [Artemisia] Snow engaged on the drapery & cushions for the new Altar, Sisters [Margaret] Moon & [Sophronia] Harmon sewing garments, Sisters [Vilate] Kimball, [Mary Ann] Young, [Lois] Cutler & [Tirza] Cahoon, engaged in arranging the Furniture &c. in the east room.

Several men presented themselves at the dwelling of Pres[ident]. George Miller this morning, some came in the house & enquired for him while others remained outside— It was suspected they were after him with a writ, and although Pres[ident]. Miller was present and before them all the time[,] no one knew him, neither did any of the brethren, several of whom were present [and] seem[ed] to know where he was, and the suspicious individuals soon left.

At 2 o'clock word was brought that a company of Soldiers were in, from Carthage [Illinois]. Brother Willmer B. Benson, clerk in the office of Doct[or]. Willard Richards, the General Church Recorder & Historian brought in a book for revision, it being part of the Church History: Elders George A. Smith & Amasa Lyman attended to the revision. Half past 2 o'clock P.M. Pres[ident]. Young, H[eber]. C. Kimball & Pres[i-dent] George Miller have been listening to Elder P[arley]. P. Pratt, who has been reading from Capt[ain] Fremont's narrative of a journey to California—

At 15 minutes past 3 O'clock P.M. Noah Rogers, just arrived from his mission to the Society Islands, in the South Pacific ocean[,] came in to the office—room No. 3 of the Attic Story of the Temple— He brought with him a Mr. [Franklin] Tower, a fellow passenger on board ship— whom he baptized. He brings a favorable report of the progress of the gospel on those islands. He came on foot from Paducah, [Kentucky,] on the Ohio River.

The soldiers above mentioned proved to be 4 Dragoons, they came up the hill, went around by the east end and north side of the Temple, out of the yard by the north gate, and drew up in front of the house of Pres[ident]. Geo[rge]. Miller— They made some enquiries of the women at the door and after a few moments passed on—

At 20 minutes before 4 [we] commenced washing and anointing the following persons.

Louisa Beman born Feb[ruar]y 7. 1815 washed by Artemisia Snow. A[nointed]. by Artemisia Snow.

Emily D. Partridge, born Feb[ruar]y 28, 1824 w[ashed]. by Lois Cutler anointed by Lois Cutler[.]

Harriet E. Cook born Nov[embe]r. 7. 1824. washed and anointed by Artemisia Snow[.]

Belinda B. Martin born Dec[embe]r. 24. 1820 washed and anointed by Bathsheba W. Smith[.]

Diantha Farr. born Oct[obe]r. 12, 1828 washed & anointed by Artemisia Snow[.]

Emily T. Cutler, born Feb[ruar]y 23. 1828 washed and anointed by Lois Cutler[.]

Lucy Walker born A[p]ril 30. 1826 washed & anointed by Bathsheba W. Smith[.]

Clarissa C. Cutler. [born] Dec[embe]r. 23, 1824 ^Louisa Cutler [born] March 16. 1816^ washed and anointed by Lois Cutler[.]

Lucy Smith, born Feb[ruar]y 9, 1817. washed & anointed by Bathsheba W. Smith[.]

Nancy Clement, born Oct[ober] 31. 1815 washed by Artemisia Snow, an[ointed] by B[athsheba]. W. Smith[.]

Zilpha Starks born July 3. 1818. washed and anointed by
Bathsheba W. Smith[.]

[E]nded at 20 minutes to 5—

At 11 minutes past 5 the Bell rung, and operations commenced to introduce those who had been washed & anointed into the lower and middle departments — The following persons officiating—viz; Orson Pratt—as No. 1. Amasa Lyman as No. 2. Orson Spencer as No. 3.—in the first department. and Orson Spencer Orson Pratt, and Amasa Lyman, in the middle department, J[ohn]. D. Lee as No. 4. B[righam]. Young as Prompter—

At 10 minutes before 6. Pres[ident]. Young ordered the lights taken out of the stair case as the troops were endeavoring to get into the Temple— It was soon after ascertained to be a false alarm— They were searching for hogs said to have been stolen from Mr. Hibbard—

At 20 minutes past 6. [we] commenced receiving into the upper department, those who were washed and anointed this evening—in the following order, viz;[15]

Louisa Beman	by	Brigham	Young[.]	
Emily D. Partridge	"	"	"	
Harriet E. Cook	"	"	"	
Louisa Cutler	"	"	"	
Lucy Walker	"	H[eber]. C.	Kimball[.]	
Clarissa C. Cutler	"	"	"	
Emily T. Cutler	"	"	"	
Belinda B. Martin	"	P[arley]. P.	Pratt[.]	
Lucy Smith	"	Geo[rge]. A.	Smith[.]	
Nancy Clement	"	"	"	"
Zilpha Starks	"	"	"	"
Diantha Farr	"	W[illia]m	Clayton[.]	

Finished at 8 minutes past 7.

The following High Priests met in Room No. 8 for prayer at about 6 o'clock—Pres[ident]. Geo[rge]. Miller—who was mouth —Daniel Spencer Harvey Green — Howard Coray W[illia]m C. Gallaher — E[lizur]. G. Terrill — Th[omas]. Burdick William Crosby — W[illia]m. Felshaw. L[uman]. H. Calkins Joshua S. Holman — Jon[atha]n. Becklehymn and Edward Hunter—

The High Council met in their Room, No. 4 for prayer, at the usual

15. The women here are all plural wives of the men receiving them through the veil.

time, about 6 o'clock P.M.— several High Priests not members of the High Council met with them. The names of those present are as follows. viz; C[harles]. C. Rich, Thomas Grover Geo[rge]. W. Harris — David Fullmer, Aaron Johnson Newel Knight, Ezra T. Benson & James Allred ~~of~~ the High Council — also Abraham Palmer, Daniel Carn, Stephen Markham — Cha[rle]s. W. Patten, Addison Everett Geo[rge]. P. Dykes, Cornelius P. Lott, Peter Haws Robert Pierce, & David Sessions, H[igh]. P[riests].

Prayed for the prosperity of the Church, and for several individuals out of health, and for many matters, which cannot well be written here—

The Seventies also met for prayer in their Room which is No. 9— present Pres[ident]. Joseph Young, Benj[amin] L. Clapp, Henry Harriman, John Pack, John D. Lee[.]

The Twelve [apostles] met for prayer in Pres[ident]. Young's Room. No. 1, at about half past. 10 P.M. Present—Pres[ident]. B[righam]. Young, H[eber]. C. Kimball Orson Hyde, P[arley]. P. Pratt, Amasa Lyman, John Taylor & George A. Smith— they were dressed in their garments of Priesthood, as were all the others who have met this evening— They prayed for deliverance from their enemies & that they might be spared to give all the faithful Saints their endowment, that they might be clothed with the power & have the keys of Priesthood.

Orson Hyde was mouth.

After prayer was over, P[arley]. P. Pratt, G[eorge]. A. Smith John Taylor & Orson Hyde went home, Amasa Lyman laid down on a sofa. Pres[ident]. Young & Elder Kimball went into the Tower & on to the roof of the Temple[,] spent half an hour, and returned. & Pres[ident]. Young spent near an hour reading Capt[ain] Fremonts Narrative—after which he retired for the night—

—William Clayton, Diary, kept for Heber C. Kimball.

At 8. O.clock in the morning Pres[ident] Jos[eph] Young H[enry]. Herriman J[edediah]. M. Grant B[enjamin]. L. Clapp — L[evi] Hancock & myself reported our selves on hands ready for servises Br[other] Jeddediah went home before night on acount of his health being much impaired — the other Presidents remained until after the hour of our evening appointment for prayer which was in a measure frustrated — from these causes[:] the first — that interfered was that a No of Sister[s] passed through the ordinances of Endowment — 2nd an alarm though false reached the Sacred apartments that the govenors People were below at the outer Door, & had expresed a determination to enter in Search of the hogs that were said to have been Stolen, the evening previous from Mr. Hibbard one of his Apostate citizens — this However was only a pretext the better to carry out their Murderous designs — I [John D. Lee] at that moment was acting No. 4 the S[erpent]. Pres[ident] Brigham Young said Bro[ther]. Lee come go down quickly & see that they do not enter[, also] furnishing me with a six shooter well loaded at the Same time — I ran down stairs to the outer door where I met the Porter Tho[ma]s Woolsey a Brother in law [?] of mine[.]

Whole Nos of both Male & Female [were] Rec[e]i[v]ed up to [illegible] who informed me & those that were with me — that the alarm was false in part — I then gave the tyler instructions to let no officer pass that Night — at the peril of his Life[.] I then returned and corrected the rumor — and after assisting in the present servises I recorded the acts of the previous evening as well as the minets of this evening — the weather was much warmer th[a]n it was some few days ago — it is now about ten at Night — at ½ Past 10 the following were of the Quorum of the Twelve [apostles] who Dressed in the Priesthood [robes] & Prayed that the Saints might be delivered out of the hands of their enemies that the Twelve might be permit[te]d to continue giving the Saints their Endowments until all the faithful should be clothed with the Keys and Power of the Priesthood Namely Pres[ident] B[righam]. Young ~~who mouth~~ [who] ^was^ [presiding,] 2nd H[eber]. C. Kimble [3rd] Orson Hyde 4th P[arley]. P. Pratt 5th A[masa]. Lyman 6th John Taylor 7 G[eorge]. A. Smith — Orson Hyde was mouth — after Prayre P[arley]. P. Pratt G[eorge]. A. Smith John Taylor and Orson Hyde disguised themselves to avoid suspicion of their [departure] and went home — Elder A[masa] Lyman layed down in a sofa to repose for the Night while Pres[ident] B[righam]. Young and Elder H[eber]. C. Kimble went into the Tower which led out on the deck and Promenade of the Temple where they spent about ½ an hour in Serenading the city in immagination — while they walked arround the Decks to take the Sweet & [illegible] Air — The bright luminaires that Shone from the habitations of the Saints presented a pleasing Aspect — for at 1 glanc[e] almost a thousand [illegible] appeared bright through dark Curtains of the Night At 11. o.clock they returned again — threw off their overcoat[s] & Set down Pr[esident] B[righam] Young read something near an hour from a [illegible] work Entitled The Narative of the exploring expedition to the Rocky Mountains & to Oregon & North California in the year 42-3 & 44 By Brevet Capt. J. C. Fremont which gave an interesting acount the locality of the country — togeather with a discription of the Animal Race [as] well as the feathered Fowls. it is now about midnight — I [John D. Lee] will here mention that Twelve persons that were taken through the ordinance to day — which were all women — Just filled up the No to 1,000 Persons — Pres[ident] B[righam] Young says that it is time for me to go Bed so I must stop writing for the Night.

—Seventies Record, Book B.

....

Elder [Heber C.] Kimball and I [Brigham Young] assisted by our wives, and the laborers in the Temple, cleaned up and arranged the furniture in the rooms. ...

Three-forty, a company numbering twelve commenced receiving their ordinances; this makes 1000 who have received the ordinances.

Six p.m., the high council, the high priests and the seventies met for prayer.

The Twelve [apostles] met for prayer. We prayed for deliverance from our enemies, and that we might be spared to give the faithful saints their endowments, Orson Hyde being mouth.

I spent an hour reading, and with Brothers Kimball and [Amasa] Lyman remained in the Temple all night.

—"Manuscript History of Brigham Young,"
in *History of the Church,* 7:556.

....

Nauvoo temple endowments performed on this date for:

Louisa Beman, Emily D. Partridge, Harriet E. Cook, Louisa Cutler, Lucy Walker, Clarissa C. Cutler, Emily T. Cutler, Belinda B. Martin, Lucy Smith, Nancy Clement, Zilpha Starks, and Diantha Farr.

—Summary of information compiled by the Temple
Index Bureau, *Nauvoo Temple Endowment Register:*
10 December 1845 to 8 February 1846.

Tuesday, December 30, 1845

The morning was pleasant, and at an early hour a very large number were at the Temple waiting for their washing & anointing—they having been notified the day before to attend at an early hour— Geo[rge]. P. Dykes—Messenger—

At 10 minutes past 8 o'clock [we] commenced in the male department, washing & anointing the following persons, viz, ^washed by William Snow & Geo[rge]. P. Dykes anointed by A[braham]. O. Smoot & W[illia]m. Crosby^

High Priests;

James Henricks,	born	June 23. 1808
Eliphalet Bristol	"	Aug[us]t 30. 1811.

Seventies.

Welcome Chapman	"	July 24. 1805
James H. Rollins	"	May 27. 1816
John Gaylord	"	July 12 1797
David Wilding	"	Nov[embe]r. 29 1804
James Downing	"	Feb[ruar]y 12 1816
Alfred Alexander Smith	"	Dec[ember]. 6. 1816
Solon Foster	"	Jan[uar]y 8. 1811
Lewis Mecham	born	Sept[ember] 4. 1814
Moses Mecham	"	Feb[ruar]y 19. 1804

Elders

Andrew Woods	"	May 23. 1780
William E. Murray	"	Oct[ober] 4. 1802

[F]inished at 22 minutes to 10.

In the female department the following persons were washed and anointed, commencing at 20 minutes after 8, viz;

Ann Smith, born Aug[us]t 20. 1813 washed by Catharine C. Spencer, Anointed by Thirza Cahoon[.]

Jane Wood, born March 21. 1787 w[ashed] by Lois Cutler, anointed by Lois Cutler[.]

Elizabeth M. Hendricks. [born] May 10. 1828 w[ashed] by Mercy R. Thompson. An[ointed]. by Thirza Cahoon[.]

Sarah Foster born Oct[ober] 11. 1819 w[ashed] by C[atherine]. C. Spencer an[ointed]. by Lois Cutler[.]

Margaret P. Downing. [born] Nov[ember]. 1. 1823. w[ashed] by Sarah D. Rich an[ointed] by Lois Cutler[.]

Nancy Walker born Jan[uar]y 20. 1780 w[ashed]. by C[atherine]. C. Spencer anointed by Lois Cutler[.]

Mary Murray born Sept[ember] 29. 1811 washed & anointed by Sarah D. Rich[.]

Diomitia Walker [born] March 10. 1816 w[ashed]. by Sarah D. Rich, an[ointed]. by Lois Cutler.

Eveline Rollins[16] born May 26. 1823 w[ashed] by C[atherine]. C. Spencer. anointed by Thirza Cahoon[.]

Rena Bristol born Aug[us]t 25 1810 washed & anointed by Sarah D. Rich[.]

Elvira Gaylord b[orn]. July 23. 1807 w[ashed]. by C[atherine]. C. Spencer an[ointed]. by Thirza Cahoon[.]

Alice Wilding born April 8. 1810 w[ashed]. by Catharine C. Spencer An[ointed]. by Sarah D. Rich.

Elvira Mecham born Nov[ember]. 6. 1811. w[ashed]. by Catharine C. Spencer. an[ointed]. by Thirza Cahoon[.]

Lydia Mecham b[orn]. Aug[us]t 6. 1817 w[ashed]. by Catharine C. Spencer an[ointed] by Thirza Cahoon[.]

Susan A. Chapman. b[orn]. Aug[us]t 24. 1807 w[ashed]. by C[atherine]. C. Spencer anointed by Lois Cutler.

Finished at 25 minutes to 10.

At half past 9 o'clock 18 bottles of oil which had been prepared with perfume, were consecrated for the anointing in Pres[ident]. Young's room, the following persons of the quorum of the Twelve [apostles] being present, and clothed according to the Holy Order, viz; Pres[ident]. Brigham Young, Elders H[eber]. C. Kimball Parley P. Pratt, Amasa Lyman & George A. Smith, also Pres[ident] Joseph Young of the Seventies—Pres[ident]. B[righam]. Young was mouth, for the first 12. and George A. Smith for the other Six.

At 10 O'clock the Bell rung, and [we] commenced to receive into the upper department, those whose names are above written, who have been washed and anointed this morning—

Persons officiating as follows, viz; P[arley]. P. Pratt, as No. 1. Orson

16. Eveline Rollins is one of several possible candidates for authorship of a letter published four months later headlined "Mormon Endowments" to the editor of the *Warsaw Signal,* April 13, 1846. Whereas the author signed her name "Emeline," this was probably a pseudonym. One potentially telling detail is her mention of fourteen other women who comprised her endowment company. Although there were fifteen women, including Eveline Rollins, in her company; this was not true for any of the Emelines who were endowed, according to the available records (see Emeline Waterman, Dec. 18; Emeline Anderson, Dec. 19; Emeline Cox, Dec. 25, 1845; Emeline Harris, Jan. 3; Emeline Grover, Jan. 5; Emeline Free, Emeline Kessler, and Emeline Houghton, Jan. 9; Emeline Tinker, Jan. 21; Harriet Emeline Barney and Emeline Curtis, Jan. 22; Emeline Hess, Jan. 29; Maria Emeline Mott, Jan. 30; and Emeline Potter, Feb. 6, 1846). Still, the identification of "Emeline" as Eveline Rollins remains conjectural.

Spencer as No. 2. Erastus Snow as No. 3. in the upper department. and in the middle department, as follows George A. Smith. No. 1. C[harles]. C. Rich No. 2 — Lorenzo Snow [No.] 3. John D. Lee [No.] 4 F[ranklin]. D. Richards [No.] 5.

At 10 m[inutes]. before 11. John M. Bernhisel brought in a suit of garments for the use of the persons receiving their endowments. Robe, Garment, Apron. Cap, Moccasins & Socks.

[A]t 10 minutes past 11. [we] commenced receiving the first company into the upper department, in the following order

William E. Murray	by	P[arley]. P. Pratt.
Mary Murray	"	W[illiam]. E. Murray & P[arley]. P. P[ratt].
Moses Mecham	"	P[arley]. P. Pratt[.]
Elvira Mecham	"	M[oses]. Mecham & P[arley]. P. P[ratt].
Eliphalet Bristol	"	Brigham Young[.]
Brother Bristol was brought through in his bed[.]		
Rena Bristol	"	Parley P. Pratt.
James Hendricks	"	" " "
Elizabeth M. Hendricks	"	" " "
Welcome Chapman	by	Parley " "
Susan Amelia Chapman	"	" " " & W[elcome]. C[hapman].
David Wilding	"	Amasa Lyman[.]
Alice Wilding	by	D[avid]. Wilding &. " "
James Downing	"	Amasa Lyman[.]
Margaret P. Downing	"	" " & J[ames]. Downing[.]
Lewis Mecham	"	Amasa Lyman[.]
Lydia Mecham	"	" " & L[ewis]. Mecham[.]
Nancy Walker	"	" "
Diomitia Walker	"	" "
James H. Rollins	"	" "
Eveline Rollins	"	" " & J[ames]. H. Rollins[.]
Solon Foster	"	" "
Sarah Foster	"	" " & Solon Foster[.]
John Gaylord	"	" "

Elvira Gaylord	"	"	"	& John Gaylord[.]
Andrew Woods	"	"	"	
Jane Woods	"	"	"	& Andrew Woods[.]
Alfred A. Smith	"	"	"	
Ann Smith	"	"	"	& A[lfred]. A. Smith[.]

Finished at 20 minutes past One. Lorenzo Snow and Catharine C. Spencer officiated as prompters, also Artemisia Snow.

At 30 minutes past 11, [we] commenced in the male department, washing & anointing the following persons, viz;

High Priest		
Aaron F. Farr	born	Oct[ober] 31. 1818
Seventy.		
William Walker,	born	Aug[ust] 29 1820
Lorin Walker	"	July 25 1822
William Cottier	"	March 3. 1820
Samuel Russell	"	Sept[ember] 25. 1812
David Brinton	"	Dec[embe]r. 29 1814
Joseph Horne	"	Jan[uar]y 17 1811
Daniel C. Davis	"	Feb[ruar]y 23 1804
Edmund Ellsworth	"	July 1. 1819
Nathaniel Ashby	"	April 15. 1805
John S. Gleason	"	Jan[uar]y 13. 1819
Isaac Outercark	"	April 1. 1809
Elder		
Jonathan Taylor	"	June 6. 1793

Finished at 10 minutes before one o'clock. These were washed by George P. Dykes and Phineas H. Young, and anointed by Abraham O. Smoot & William Crosby.

At half past 11. Almon W. Babbitt came in, & reported that the Marshall had left Carthage [Illinois] for Springfield [Illinois], and there would be *no more danger from Writs.*[17]

At half past 12. William E. Murray was ordained an High Priest, in Room No. 2. by William Snow, and Orson Spencer—

In the female department [we] commenced washing and anointing the following persons at 20 minutes to 11. viz;

17. This refers to the writs issued for church leaders on counterfeiting charges.

Sarah Smith born May 15, 1794 w[ashed] by Lois Cutler, an[ointed]. by Elizabeth Ann Whitney[.]

Lydia Granger born April 5, 1790 w[ashed] by Lois Cutler, an[ointed]. by Elizabeth Ann Whitney[.]

Cynthia Weston born Feb[ruar]y 2. 1783 w[ashed] by Thirza Cahoon an[ointed by]. Vilate Kimball[.]

Sarah P. Noon, born May 3. 1811 w[ashed]. by Lois Cutler, an[ointed]. by Vilate Kimball[.]

Lovina Walker born Sept[ember] 16. 1827 w[ashed]. by Mercy R. Thompson An[ointed] by E[lizabeth]. A[nn]. Whitney[.]

Olive H. Walker [born] March 8. 1824 washed and anointed by Lois Cutler.

Persis Farr born May 27. 1820 w[ashed] by Thirzah Cahoon an[ointed]. by Vilate Kimball[.]

Elizabeth Ellsworth born Sept[ember] 26. 1825 w[ashed]. by Lois Cutler an[ointed] by Vilate Kimball[.]

Martha Taylor born Mar[ch]. 10. 1822. w[ashed]. by Lois Cutler an[ointed]. by Vilate Kimball[.]

Esther Russell born March 21. 1816 w[ashed]. by M[ercy]. R. Thompson an[ointed]. by Sarah D. Rich[.]

Elizabeth H. Brinton [born] Sept[ember] 8. 1817 w[ashed]. by Lois Cutler an[ointed] by Sarah D. Rich[.]

Eliza Outercark. born Jan[uar]y 25. 1813 w[ashed]. by Lois Cutler an[ointed]. by Sarah D. Rich.

Mary Isabella Horne. [born] Nov[ember]. 20. 1818 w[ashed] by M[ercy]. R. Thompson an[ointed] by Vilate Kimball[.]

Julia E. Stone, born Nov[ember]. 16. 1827 w[ashed]. by Julia Stone an[ointed]. by Lois Cutler.

Desdemona Gleason born April 3. 1821 w[ashed]. by Lois Cutler an[ointed] by Lois Cutler[.]

Susan Ashby [born] Aug[us]t 28. 1808 w[ashed]. by L[ois]. Cutler. an[ointed]. by V[ilate]. Kimball[.]

Susan Davis. [born] Feb[ruary]. 16 1824 w[ashed] by M[ercy]. R. Thompson. an[ointed] by Vilate Kimball.

Finished at 10 o'cl[oc]k 30 m[inutes].

At One o'clock the Bell rung for the introduction of Company No. 2, into the lower and middle departments the following persons officiating, viz; in the upper department, Orson Pratt, Orson Spencer, & B[enjamin]. L. Clapp. and in the middle department,

Orson Spencer	as No. 1	J[edediah]. M. Grant No. 2
Lorenzo Snow	" " 3.	John D. Lee " 4
F[ranklin]. D. Richards	" " 5,	or prompter—

At a quarter past 2 [we] commenced receiving into the upper department, company No. 2 in the following order. viz.

Edmund Ellsworth,	by Orson Pratt[.]
Elizabeth Ellsworth.	" O[rson]. Pratt & E[dmund]. Ellsworth[.]
David Brinton	by Orson Pratt.
Elizabeth H. Brinton	" " " & D[avid]. Brinton[.]
Sarah P. Noon	" H[eber]. C. Kimball[.]
Julia E. Stone	" " " "
Aaron F. Farr	" " " "
Persis Farr	" " " " & A[aron]. F. Farr[.]
Isaac Outercark	" Orson Pratt[.]
Eliza Outercark	" " " & I[saac]. Outercark[.]
Jonathan Taylor	" " "
Martha Taylor	" J[ohn]. Taylor & Orson Pratt[.]
Lydia Granger	" Orson Pratt.
Lorin Walker	" " "
Lovina Walker	" " " & Lorin Walker[.]
Daniel Davis	" O[rson]. Pratt.
Susan Davis	" O[rson]. Pratt & D[aniel]. C. Davis[.]
Samuel Russell	" O[rson]. Pratt.
Esther Russell	" " " & S[amuel]. Russell[.]
John S. Gleason	" " "
Desdemona Gleason	by J[ohn]. S. G[leason]. & O[rson]. P[ratt].
Joseph Horne.	by Orson Pratt.
Mary Isabella Horne	by J[oseph]. Horne & O[rson]. Pratt.
William Walker	" Orson Pratt[.]
Olive H. Walker	" O[rson]. Pratt & W[illia]m. Walker[.]
Nathaniel Ashby	" O[rson]. Pratt[.]
Susan Ashby	" O[rson]. P[ratt]. & N[athaniel]. Ashby[.]

William Cottier " O[rson]. Pratt[.]
Cynthia Weston " O[rson]. Pratt[.]
Sarah Smith " O[rson]. Pratt[.]

Finished at 25 m[inutes]. past 4. Prompters Lorenzo Snow. & Artemisia Snow ~~and~~

At 23 minutes to 2 [we] commenced in the Male department, washing & anointing the following persons, viz;

High Priests.

Alexander Williams	born	Oct[ober] 10. 1803
Thomas Richardson	"	1804
Martin Littlewood	"	Jan[uar]y 28. 1817

Seventies

Stillman Pond	"	Oct[obe]r. 26. 1803
Nathaniel H. Felt	"	Feb[ruar]y 6. 1816
William Pool	"	Nov[embe]r. 22 1812
Benjamin T. Mitchell	"	Jan[uar]y 12 1816
William Blackhurst	"	June 22 1807
William Kelly	"	April 6 1828
Charles White	"	March 30. 1812
Elder George Whiting (Elder)	"	April 6. 1816
John G. Tanner	"	Dec[embe]r. 19 1811
Sidney Tanner	"	April 1. 1809
Nathan Tanner	"	May 14. 1815

Washed by Geo[rge]. P. Dykes, & Phineas H. Young Anointed by A[braham]. O. Smoot & William Crosby[.]

Ended at 15 m[inutes]. to 3.

In the Female department, the following persons were washed and anointed, commencing at 5 m[inutes]. to 2.

Maria L. Pond, born May 2. 1813 W[ashed]. by Sarah D. Rich, an[ointed]. by E[lizabeth]. A[nn]. Whitney[.]

Abigail A. Pond, born July 14. 1828 W[ashed]. by Lois Cutler, anointed by E[lizabeth]. A[nn]. Whitney[.]

Loenza A. Pond, born Feb[ruar]y 15, 1830 w[ashed]. by Thirza Cahoon an[ointed]. by E[lizabeth]. A[nn]. Whitney[.]

Dolly Mecham born Aug[us]t 26. 1801 washed & anointed by Lois Cutler[.]

Elizabeth Pool born May 8. 1814 W[ashed]. by Thirza Cahoon an[ointed]. by Lois Cutler[.]

Louisa Tanner born Feb[ruar]y 5. 1811 w[ashed]. by Thirza

Cahoon an[ointed] by Lois Cutler[.]

Nancy Whiting born Sept[ember] 11. 1828 w[ashed]. by Lois Cutler an[ointed] by Lois Cutler[.]

Mary Richardson [birth date] unknown 41. or 42 y[ea]rs old W[ashed]. & an[ointed]. by Thirza Cahoon[.]

Lovina Mitchell [born] Jan[uar]y 28. 1822. washed & anointed by Sarah D. Rich[.]

Eliza Ann Felt. born Nov[embe]r. 10. 1824 w[ashed]. by Julia Stone an[ointed]. by Sarah D. Rich[.]

Margaret Blackhurst. [born] May 5. 1804 W[ashed by]. Julia Stone an[ointed]. by Thirza Cahoon[.]

Catharine Stephenson. [born] March 1771 [washed by] Julia Stone [anointed by] Lois Cutler[.]

Isabella Williams [born] Sept[ember] 11. 1806 [washed by] Julia Stone. [anointed by] Lois Cutler[.]

Rachel W. Tanner [born] May 1. 1818 [washed by] Julia Stone [anointed by] Sarah D. Rich[.]

Rebecca Tanner [born] April 17. 1818. [washed by] Julia Stone [anointed by] Lois Cutler[.]

Sarah Littlewood, [born] July 10. 1818. [washed] by Sarah D. Rich [anointed] by Lois Cutler[.]

[Finished at] 4, o'cl[oc]k[.]

At 10 m[inutes]. past 4, the bell rung for Company No. 3 to commence operations for entering the lower & middle departments. the following persons officiating viz; in the upper department,

Orson Spencer	as	No.	1.
Amasa Lyman	"	"	2
Parley P. Pratt	"	"	3

and in the middle department,

Erastus Snow	as	No.	1.
Charles C. Rich	"	"	2
Willard Snow	"	"	3.
John D. Lee	"	"	4
F[ranklin]. D. Richards	"	"	5.

At 4 o'clock, Pres[ident]. Brigham Young left the Temple and was gone until 25 minutes past 5. o'clock.

Bishop [Newel K.] Whitney has been engaged in arranging some business matters with Almon W. Babbitt Esq[ui]r[e] as counsel for the Lawrence Estate—

Bishop George Miller, has been in the Temple all day, considering it unsafe for him to be out much on account of the writ said to be out for him.[18]

P[arley]. P. Pratt has been engaged part of the time in forming a schedule for a pioneer company of 1,000 men, to preceed the body of emigrants, find a proper location, & put in seed early in the summer.

At 35 minutes past 5 o'clock [we] commenced receiving into the upper department, company No. 3. in the following order, viz;

Alexander Williams	by Amasa Lyman[.]
Isabella Williams	" A[lexander]. Williams & A[masa]. Lyman[.]
Abigail A. Pond	" Amasa Lyman[.]
Martin Littlewood	" Orson Hyde[.]
Sarah Littlewood	" O[rson]. Hyde & M[artin]. Littlewood[.]
William Blackhurst	" O. Hyde[.]
Margaret Blackhurst	" W[illiam]. Blackhurst & O[rson]. H[yde].
Catherine Stephenson	" O[rson]. Hyde & W[illia]m. Blackhurst[.]
John J. Tanner	" O[rson]. Hyde[.]
Rebecca Tanner	" O[rson]. Hyde & J[ohn]. J. Tanner[.]
Thomas Richardson	" O[rson]. Hyde[.]
Mary Richardson	" O[rson]. Hyde & Th[omas]. Richardson[.]
Nathaniel H. Felt	" O. Hyde[.]
Eliza Ann Felt	" O[rson]. Hyde & N[athaniel]. H. F[elt].
William Pool	" O[rson]. Hyde[.]
Elizabeth Pool	" O[rson]. Hyde & W[illiam]. Pool[.]
Benjamin T. Mitchell	" O[rson]. Hyde[.]
Lovina Mitchell	" O[rson]. Hyde & B[enjamin]. F. M[itchel].
Nathan Tanner	" O[rson]. Hyde[.]

18. The writ issued on charges of counterfeiting.

Rachel Tanner	"	O[rson]. Hyde & N[athan]. Tanner[.]
Stillman Pond	"	O[rson]. Hyde[.]
Maria L. Pond	"	O[rson]. Hyde & S[tillman]. Pond[.]
Loenza A. Pond		O[rson]. Hyde & S[tillman]. Pond[.]
George Whiting	"	O[rson]. Hyde[.]
Nancy Whiting	"	O[rson]. Hyde & G[eorge]. W[hiting].
Dolly Mecham	"	O[rson]. Hyde[.]
Charles White	"	O[rson]. Hyde[.]
Sidney Tanner	"	O[rson]. Hyde[.]
Louisa Tanner	"	O[rson]. Hyde & S[idney]. Tanner[.]
William Kelly	"	O[rson]. Hyde[.]

Finished at 15 m[inutes]. past 8. Lorenzo Snow & [blank] Prompters.

The labors of the day having been brought to a close at so early an hour viz; half past 8. it was thought proper to have a little season of recreation.[19] accordingly, Brother [Hans] Hanson was invited to produce his violin— He did so, and played several lively airs, among the rest some very good lively dancing tunes. This was too much for the gravity of Bro[ther]. Joseph Young, who indulged in a hornpipe, and was soon joined by several others, and before the dance was over several French fours were indulged in. The first was opened by Pres[ident] B[righam]. Young with Sister [Elizabeth Ann] Whitney and Elder H[eber]. C. Kimball with Sister ~~Whitney~~ ^[Catherine] Lewis^[.] The spirit of dancing increased until the whole floor was covered with dancers[.] After this had continued about an hour, several excellent songs were sung, in which several of the brethren and sisters joined— The Upper California was sung by Erastus Snow. After which Sister Whitney being invited by Pres[ident]. Young, stood up and invoking the gift of tongues, sung one of the most beautiful songs in tongues, that ever was heard. The interpretation was given by her husband, Bishop Whitney, it related to our efforts to build this House, and to

19. This is the second mention of dancing in the temple. For more on these events, and LDS attitudes toward dancing generally, see Davis Bitton, "'These Licentious Days': Dancing among the Mormons," *Sunstone* 2 (Spring 1977): 16-27, rpt. in Bitton's *The Ritualization of Mormon History and Other Essays* (Urbana: University of Illinois Press, 1994), 98-114.

the privilege we now have of meeting together in it, — of our departure shortly to the country of the Lamanites, and their rejoicing when they hear the gospel. and of the ingathering of Israel. Altogether, it was one of the most touching and beautiful exhibitions of the power of the Spirit in the gift of tongues which was ever seen—(So it appeared to the writer of this)[.] After a little conversation of a general nature, the exercises of the evening were closed by prayer by Pres[ident]. B[righam]. Young—and soon after most of the persons present left the Temple for their homes. The persons present at this interesting meeting were. Pres[ident]. B[righam]. Young, Elder H[eber]. C. Kimball, Orson Hyde, Joseph Young, Erastus Snow — John D. Lee Bishop N[ewel]. K. Whitney, Elisha Averett, David Candland — L[ucian]. R. Foster — John L. Butler — Lewis Robbins — [Welcome] Chapman Hans C. Hansen — Horace Whitney W[illia]m. H. Kimball — little Joseph Young Bishop Whitneys son ^John^ — and Sisters Kimball Whitney, Artemisia Snow. Eliza R. Snow. Mercy R. Thompson [and] sisters: [Huldah] Barns — S[ophronia]. M. Harmon & Margaret Moon and Catharine Lewis.

At 12 o'clock most of the brethren who staid had prepared their beds, some on the floor, and some on sofas, and were ready for sleep.

Amasa Lyman came in at 12.—and with Pres[ident]. Young, ~~Elder~~ and 5 or 6 others remained in the Temple over night.

At 6 o'clock the following High Priests met for prayer in Room No. 8 clothed in the robes of Priesthood. viz; Pres[ident]. George Miller, Abraham O. Smoot who was mouth, Hiram Spencer, Peter Haws, James Brown, Simeon Carter — Samuel Gully Isaac Chase, William Felshaw — Hezekiah Peck, Albert Petty Benjamin Brown William Crosby — Philo Dibble & Joseph B. Noble—

Another company met in room No. 10.

The High Council met for prayer in room No. 6 clothed in the robes of Priesthood, Present Isaac Morley, Tho[ma]s. Grover, — C[harles]. C. Rich James Allred, Alpheus Cutler Lewis D. Wilson — George W. Harris — Newel Knight — Aaron Johnson — W[illia]m. Huntington & David Fullmer— Also the following H[igh]. P[riests]. not members of the Council, met with them, viz; Joshua S. Holman, Isaac Higbee Winslow Farr, & Freeman Nickerson—

They united in prayer, for the preservation of Pres[iden]t. Brigham Young & his Council from all their enemies—for the protection of the Church of God from all our enemies & that our enemies might be frustrated in all their plans—for all the sick in the Church, especially Brigham Willard Kimball—Sisters Hyrum Smith & Huldah Nickerson—Bro[ther]. Scotts two children, and Brother Daniels & Andrew Smith, for means for our removal—for the blessing of God upon all our possessions &c.

—William Clayton, Diary, kept for Heber C. Kimball.

....

The weather this morning is in a moderate temperment pleasant & warm[.] at about 8 oclock A.M. Pres[ident] B[righam]. Young H[eber]. C. Kimble P[arley]. P. Pratt A[masa]. Lyman & G[eorge]. A. Smith of the Twelve [apostles] — and Pres[ident] Jos[eph] Young of the Seventies Arayed themselves in Priestly attire — offered up the signs & Prayed for the deliverance of the People[.] then We ^consecrated 18 bottles of oil —^ again commenced giving the Saints that were and are faithful in Christ their Endowments[.] those of the 12 [apostles] that were present (or rather are) were as follows~~ing~~ B[righam]. Young H[eber]. C. Kimble P[arley]. P. Pratt O[rson]. Pratt A[masa]. Lyman G[eorge]. A Smith — Presant of the 1st Presidency of the Sev[enties] — Jos[eph] Young Henry Herriman B[enjamin]. L. Clapp J[edediah]. M. Grant & J[ohn]. D. Lee[,] here all the time or nearly so — The Name[s] of those that officiated in the Several departments were Orson Spencer No 1 in the garden or tower department — P[arley]. P. Pratt No 2 — Erastus Snow No 3 —John D Lee No 4 & F[ranklin]. D. Richards No 5 — The Same Persons above refered too also officiated in the Middle department or more properly speaking the uper or 4th apartment — G[eorge]. A. Smith Acted the part of No 1 Lorenzo Snow No 2 — & C[harles]. C. Rich No 3 — in the 2 middle apartment — Lorenzo Snow Prompter at the veil — P[arley]. P. Pratt reciever at the veil in the Morning.

The washing commenced in the Male department

1. At 10 minutes Past 8th A.M		
2. Welcome Chapman	born	July 4th 1805
3. John H. Rollins		May 27th 1816
4. John Gaylord		July 12th 1798
5. David Wilding		Nov 29th 1804
6. James Downing		Feb 12th 1816
7. Alvah Alexander		Dec ^4^ 6. 1816
8. Solon Foster		Jan 8th 1814
9. Lewis Mecham		Feb 19th 1804
10. Moses Mecham		Feb 19th 1804

The above named Persons were washed by George P. Dykes & W[illia]m Snow Anointed by Abraham O. Smoot & W[illia]m Crosby.

At 30 minutes past 11. the following Persons were washed & anointed under the hands of Phineas Young & G[eorge]. P. Dykes [and] they were washed & under the hands of A[braham]. O. Smoot & W[illia]m Crosby —

11.	W[illia]m Walker	Aug 29th 1820 [?]
12.	Loren Walker	July 25th 1822
13.	W[illia]m Cotton	March 3d 1820
14.	Samuel P. Russell	Sep 25th 1812
15.	David Brinton	Dec 28th 1814
		Males Sev[enties?]
16	John Horne	Jan 17th 1811.
17	Daniel C. Davis	Feb. 23d 1804
18	Edmund Ellsworth	July 14 1819
19	Nathaniel Ashby	April 15th 1805
20	John Gleason	June 13th 1819
21	Isaac Ondercark	April 14 1809

Commenced washing & anointing in the Female Department 20 minutes after 8. A.M.

[See pages 235-37 for excerpted portion.]

At 6 or near that hour Pres[ident] Jos Young L[evi]. Hancock Henry Herriman A[lbert]. P. Rockwood and Br[other]. Mathews Dressed in Priestly attire, offered the signs & tokens [of] the great Elohim & prayred in Pres[ident] J[oseph]. Youngs Room or Rather the room ^that^ is prepared for the council of the Seventies — About 10 at Night the last company got through — I [John D. Lee] will here mention that Br[other] Alexander P. Chealy was ordained into the 32nd [Quorum of the] Seventy — under the hands of Pres[ident] J[oseph]. Young[,] J[ohn]. D Lee[,] J[edediah?]. D. Grant[,] & P[hineas]. Young — to return [to the present time:] after the Servises of the day closed, Br[other]. Herriman & Bro[ther]. Elisha Averett by request struck up several lively and animating tunes upon the violin & Flute — the spirit of the Lord Rested down in power upon us & while our hearts were filled full we danced [before] the Great I [A]m & Shook the dust off our feet as a Testimony As a testimony against the Nation — After pleasing the Lord on the dance we set down & celebrated his Name in songs divine — in fine we were led by the influence of the comforter — Sister Elizabeth An[n]. Whitney Sung one of the songs of Zions in an un-

[Washings and anointings for Tuesday, December 30, 1845]

1.	Sarah Foster born Oct 11th 1819	W.	by C C Spencer	A.	Lo Cutler
2	Margarett Downing " Nov 1st 1823	"	Sarah D Rich	"	" "
3	Nancy Walker " Jan 20th 1780	"	C C Spencer	"	" "
4	Diontha Walker " No 10th 1816		S. D. Rich	"	" "
5	Emoline Rollins " May 26th 1823		"		
6	Elvira Gaylord " July 23 1807		C C Spencer		Thirza Cahoon
7	Alice Wilding Ap 8 1810	"	" "		S D Rich
8	Elvira Meecham Nov 6 1811	"	" "		Thirza Cahoon
9	Lydia Meecham Aug 6 1814	"	" "		" "
10	Susan A Chapman " 24 1807	"	" "		Lois Cutler
	Commenced washing in the Female Department at 20 Minutes to 11.				
11	Lovina Walker born Sept 16th 1825	W.	M R. Thompson	A.	E. A. Whitney
12	Olive H. Walker " Mar 8th 1824	"	Los Cutler	"	Louisa Cutler
13	Elizabeth Ellsworth " Sept 26th 1825	"	" "	"	" "
14	Esther Russell " Mar 21st 1816	"	M R Thompson		S. D. Rich
15	Elizabeth H Brinton Sept 8th 1811		Lois Cutler	"	" "
16	Eliza Ondercark Jan 25th 1813	"	"		" "
17	Mary Isabella Horn " Nov 20th 1818	"	M R Thompson	"	V. Kimble
18	Desdemona Gleason " April 8th 1821	"	L Cutler	"	L. Cutler
19	Susan Ashby " Feby 26th 1808	"	" "		V. Kimble
20	Susan Davis Feb 16. 1827		M R Thompson	"	" "

Washing commenced at 5 minits past 2. P.M.

21	Dolly Meecham Aug 26th 1801			W.	Lois Cutler	[A.]	L. Cutler
	Washing commenced in the Male department at						
22	32 minits to 2. P.M						
23	Stillman Pond		Oct 26th 1813				
24	Nathaniel H Felt		Feb 6th 1816				
25	Wm Pool	born	Nov. 22nd 1812				
26	Benjamin F Milchel	"	Jan 12th 1816				
27	Wm Blackhurst	"	Jan 12th 1816				
28	Wm Kelly	"	April 6th 1828				
29	Charles While	"	March 4th 1812				
30	John J Tanner	"	Dec 17th 1811				
31	Sidney Tanner	"	April 1st 1809				
32	Nathan Tanner	"	May 1st 1815				

Washed by G. P. Dykes & Phinehas Young — and Anointed by A. O. Smoot & Wm Crosby.

1.	Maria Pond				Females		
2	Maria Pond	born	May 2nd 1813	W.	S D. Rich	A.	E. A. Whitney
3	Abigail L Pond	"	July 4th 1828	"	L Cutler	"	" "
4	Louisa Pond	"	Feb 15th 1830	"	Thirza Cahoon	"	" "
5	Elizabeth Pool	"	May 8th 1814	"	" "		L Cutler
6	Louisa Tanner	"	Feb 6th 1811	"	" "	"	" "
7	" Mitchell	"	Jan 28th 1822		S D Rich	"	S. D. Rich
8	Elizabeth Fott	"	Nov 10th 1820	"	Julia Stone	"	" "

9	Margaret Blackhurst		May 5th 1804	"	"		"	"	"
10	Rachel W Tanner	"	" 1st 1818	"	"			"	"
11	Rebecca Tanner	"	April 17th 1816		" "			L Cutler	
12	Sarah Littlewood	"	July 10th 1818		S. D. Rich		"	"	"

Commenced washing at 5 Minets to 2 P.M —

—Seventies Record, Book B, oversized portion, December 30, 1845.

known tongge — to those Save to such as the Lord shall give the interpretation & understanding thereof — Pres[ident] B[righam]. Young & Bishop Whitney gave the interpretation which was that the Lord ~~that~~ looked down upon our devotion & was well pleased & that he would soon gather in the Lamanites & remnant of the House of Iseral & bring them to the knowledge of the Truth & then they will join in the dance before the Lord of Hosts when our Enemies shall be crumble[d] to death & fall to rise no more — Pres[ident] B[righam] Young & Heber C. Kimball also spoke in foreign tongue[s] — The house was filled to overflowing so that we breathed the soft soothing breezes that descends from the Throne of Peace — Pres[ident] B[righam] Young then concluded in prayer & thanksgiving to the author of all good for our deliverance & protection from the hands of our enemies — Pres[ident] Jos[eph]. Young & Bishop Whitney & Lady W[illia]m Kimble & Mother Horace Whitney & O[rson] Hyde went [illegible.] Elder A[masa] Lyman came about midnight when we all prepared to repose by Spreading down Pallets upon the carpets over the room as well as filling the sofas[.] those that spent [the night] in the Temple were B[righam]. Young H[eber]. C. Kimble A[masa] Lyman Erastus Snow J[ohn]. D. Lee D[avid] Candland John L Butler H[ans] Hansen Lewis Robbins Elisha Averett & little Jos[eph Young and] John [Whitney]— the 2 sons of Pres[ident] B[righam]. Young & B[ishop] Whitntney [sic] — it is now 1. o.clock & I [John D. Lee] will stop writing for the presant — [although] courtesy & respect brings me back to my duty — while I take conizence [cognizance] of the Females that were preasant [at] the scene of rejoicing & merriment before the Lord[.] Margaret Miller Artimisia Snow Eliza Snow Mercy R. Thompson Sophronia M Harmon Huldah Armstrong — Vilalate [sic] Kimble & Elizabeth A. Whitney were the happy Participants of our much favored & varried scene of Enjoyment.

—Seventies Record, Book B.

....

At eight-ten a.m., [we] commenced to administer the ordinances. Elders Heber C. Kimball, Parley P. Pratt, George A. Smith, Amasa Lyman, Joseph Young and myself [Brigham Young] consecrated oil.

Eleven-thirty, Almon W. Babbitt reported that the marshal had left for Springfield [Illinois], and there would probably be no more danger of writs for the present.

Eighty-eight persons received ordinances.

Elder Parley P. Pratt has been engaged part of the time in forming a schedule for a Pioneer Company of 1000 men to precede the body of emigrants, to find a proper location and put in seed early in the summer.

The labors of the day having been brought to a close at so early an hour, *viz.:* eight-thirty, it was thought proper to have a little season of recreation, accordingly Brother Hanson was invited to produce his violin, which he did, and played several lively airs accompanied by Elisha Averett on his flute, among others some very good lively dancing tunes. This was too much for the gravity of Brother Joseph Young who indulged in dancing a hornpipe, and was soon joined by several others, and before the dance was over several French fours were indulged in. The first was opened by myself with Sister [Elizabeth Ann] Whitney and Elder Heber C. Kimball and partner. The spirit of dancing increased until the whole floor was covered with dancers, and while we danced before the Lord, we shook the dust from off our feet as a testimony against this nation.

After the dancing had continued about an hour, several excellent songs were sung, in which several of the brethren and sisters joined. The "Upper California" was sung by Erastus Snow, after which I called upon Sister Whitney who stood up and invoking the gift of tongues, sang a beautiful song of Zion in tongues. The interpretation was given by her husband, Bishop [Newel K.] Whitney, and me, it related to our efforts to build this house to the privilege we now have of meeting in it, our departure shortly to the country of the Lamanites, their rejoicing when they hear the gospel and of the ingathering of Israel.

I spoke in a foreign tongue; likewise, Brother Kimball.

After a little conversation of a general nature I closed the exercises of the evening by prayer.

Six p.m., the high council, and two companies of high priests met for prayer.

—"Manuscript History of Brigham Young,"
in *History of the Church,* 7:556-58.

....

Nauvoo temple endowments performed on this date for:

First Company: William E. Murray, Mary Murray, Moses Mecham, Elvira Mecham, Eliphalet Bristol, Rena Bristol, James Hendricks, Elisabeth M. Hendricks, Welcome Chapman, Susan Amelia Chapman, David Wilding, Alice Wilding, James Downing, Margaret P. Downing, Lewis Mecham, Lydia Mecham, Nancy Walker, Dionitia Walker, James H. Rollins, Eveline Rollins, Solon Foster, Sarah Foster, John Gaylord, Elvira

Gaylord, Andrew Woods, Jane Woods, Alfred A. Smith, and Ann Smith.

Second Company: Edmund Ellsworth, Elizabeth Ellsworth, David Brinton, Elizabeth H. Brinton, Sarah P. Noon, Julia E. Stone, Aaron F. Farr, Persis Farr, Isaac Outercark, Eliza Outercark, Jonathan Taylor, Martha Taylor, Lydia Granger, Lorin Walker, Lovina Walker, Daniel C. Davis, Susan Davis, Samuel Russell, Esther Russell, John S. Gleason, Desdemona Gleason, Joseph Horne, Mary Isabella Horn, William Walker, Olive H. Walker, Nathaniel Ashby, Susan Ashby, William Cottier, Cynthia Weston, and Sarah Smith.

Third Company: Alexander Williams, Isabella Williams, Abigail A. Pond, Martin Littlewood, Sarah Littlewood, William Blackhurst, Margaret Blackhurst, Catharine Stephenson, John J. Tanner, Rebecca Tanner, Thomas Richardson, Mary Richardson, Nathaniel H. Felt, Eliza Ann Felt, William Pool, Elisabeth Pool, Benjamin T. Mitchell, Lovina Mitchell, Nathan Tanner, Rachel Tanner, Stillman Pond, Maria L. Pond, Loenza A. Pond, George Whiting, Nancy Whiting, Dolly Mecham, Charles White, Sidney Tanner, Louisa Tanner, and William Kelly.

—Summary of information compiled by the Temple Index Bureau, *Nauvoo Temple Endowment Register: 10 December 1845 to 8 February 1846.*

Wednesday, December 31, 1845

The morning cloudy and the ground Soft and muddy— At an early hour a company had assembled at the Temple for the purpose of receiving their washing and anointing—

At 30 minutes past 7 [we] commenced in the male department, washing and anointing the following persons, viz;

Noah Rogers	born	March 17. 1799
Ira Clothier		April 29. 1792
Richard H. Kinnaman		May 11. 1818
Jesse B. Martin		April 11. 1825
W[illia]m. E. Higginbotham		Feb[ruar]y 26. 1811
Philip B. Lewis		Jan[uar]y 16. 1804
Albert Merrill	"	July 17. 1815
Henry Bigler	"	Aug[us]t 28. 1815
~~Priddy~~ ^Allen^ Weeks	"	Jan[uar]y 24, 1813
Charles A. Harper	"	Jan[uar]y 27 1817
Philander Colton	"	Oct[ober] 19 1811

Isaac Fuller " Oct[ober] 25 1811

The above mentioned are of the quorum of Seventies— The following persons are High Priests—viz;

Lyman Leonard, born June 3. 1793
Priddy Meeks " Aug[ust] 29, 1795

These were washed by William Snow Ezra T. Benson & Benj[amin] L. Clapp. Anointed by Abraham O. Smoot William Crosby & B[enjamin]. L. Clapp— Finished at 20 minutes to 9—

In the Female department [we] commenced at 10 minutes to 8, washing & anointing the following persons, viz;

Lucinda Johnson, born March 5. 1806 w[ashed]. by Thirza Cahoon anointed by Thirza Cahoon[.]
Amy Clothier, born Aug[us]t 3. 1794 w[ashed]. by Lois Cutler anointed by Lois Cutler[.]
Lovina W. Harper born Nov[embe]r. 5. 1818 w[ashed] by Thirza Cahoon an[ointed] by Thirza Cahoon[.]
Sarah Jane Weeks born Nov[embe]r. 26. 1814 w[ashed] by S[ophronia]. M. Harmon an[ointed]. by Lois Cutler[.]
Maris T. Lewis b[orn]. March 26. 1817 w[ashed] by Sophronia M. Harmon An[ointed]. by Lois Cutler.
Louisa Higgenbotham b[orn]. March 12 1811 w[ashed]. by Thirza Cahoon an[ointed]. [by] Thirza Cahoon[.]
Margaret Kinnaman [born] July 17. 1827 w[ashed]. by S[ophronia]. M. Harmon an[ointed]. by Lois Cutler.
Polly M. Colton born Oct[ober] 15. 1816 w[ashed]. by S[ophronia]. M. Harmon an[ointed]. by Lois Cutler[.]
Abigail Leonard b[orn]. April 11. 1795 w[ashed]. by S[ophronia]. M. Harmon an[ointed]. by Lois Cutler[.]
Adelia Ann Bishop b[orn]. Nov[ember]. 5. 1825 w[ashed]. by S[ophronia]. M. Harmon an[ointed]. by Sarah D. Rich[.]
Mary Ann Merrill. b[orn]. June 2. 1819 w[ashed]. by Thirza Cahoon An[ointed] by Thirza Cahoon.
Margaret Ann Merrill [born] Nov[ember]. 15. 1816 w[ashed]. by S[ophronia]. M. Harmon an[ointed]. by Lois Cutler[.]
Elizabeth Meeks b[orn]. July 2. 1823. w[ashed]. by S[ophronia]. M. Harmon an[ointed] by Sarah D. Rich[.]
Eda Rogers, born Aug[us]t 19. 1801. w[ashed]. by S[ophronia]. M. Harmon an[ointed]. by Lois Cutler[.]
Sarah Meeks b[orn]. Dec[ember] 12 1801 w[ashed]. by Thirzah

Cahoon an[ointed]. by S[arah]. D. Rich.

Laurinda M. Fuller. [born] May 2. 1821 [washed by] S[ophronia]. M. Harmon [anointed by] Lois Cutler[.]

Adeline Hamblin [born] Sept[ember] 18. 1823 [washed by] S[ophronia]. M. Harmon [anointed by] Thirza Cahoon[.]

17 [women. Finished at] 25 m[inutes]. to 10.

At 5 m[inutes]. before 10. at the ringing of the bell [we] commenced receiving into the lower & middle departments Company No. 1 for this day, the following persons officiating—viz: in the upper department,

Orson Pratt as No. 1
Erastus Snow as No. 2.
and Charles C. Rich as No. 3.

in the middle department,

Orson Spencer	as No.	1.	J[edediah]. M. Grant	No.	2
Lorenzo Snow	"	3	J[ohn]. D. Lee as	"	4
F[ranklin]. D. Richards	"	5.			

At 10 minutes past 11. [we] commenced receiving company No. 1 into the upper department, as follows, viz;

Philip B. Lewis,	by	Orson Pratt[.]		
Maria T. Lewis	"	"	"	& P[hilip]. B. Lewis[.]
Lucina Johnson	"	"	"	
Allen Weeks	"	"	"	
Sarah Jane Weeks	"	"	"	& Allen Weeks[.]
Priddy Meeks	"	O[rson]. Pratt[.]		
Elizabeth Meeks	"	"	"	& P[riddy]. Meeks[.]
Rich[ar]d. H. Kinnamon	"	"	"	
Margaret Kinnamon	"	"	"	& R[ichard]. H. K[innamon].
Ira Clothier	"	"	"	
Amy Clothier	"	"	"	& Ira Clothier[.]
Noah Rogers	"	"	"	
Eda Rogers	"	"	"	& Noah Rogers[.]
Philander Colton	"	"	"	
Polly M. Colton	"	"	"	& Philander Colton[.]
W[illia]m E. Higginbotham	"	"	"	

Louisa Higginbotham	"	"	" & W[illia]m. E. H[igginbotham].
Jesse B. Martin	"	"	"
Isaac Fuller	"	"	"
Laurinda Fuller	by Orson Pratt & I[saac]. Fuller[.]		
Lyman Leonard	by O[rson]. Pratt.		
Abigail Leonard	"	"	" & L[yman]. Leonard[.]
Charles A. Harper	"	"	"
Lovina W. Harper	"	"	" & C[harles]. A. Harper[.]
Henry W. Bigler	"	"	"
Albert Merrill	"	"	"
Margaret Ann Merrill	"	"	"
Mary Ann Merrill	"	"	"
Adelia Ann Bishop	"	"	"
Adeline Hamblin	"	"	"
Sarah Meeks	"	"	"

Finished at 20 m[inutes]. past. 1, Lorenzo Snow and Catharine C. Spencer as prompters—

No. 2

Commencing at 25 minutes past 10, the following persons were washed and anointed— viz—

High Priests		
William Stringham,	born	May 2. 1787
Lebbeus T. Coons	"	May 13. 1811.
Jonathan C. Wright	"	Nov[embe]r. 29. 1808.
Edson Whipple	"	Feb[ruar]y 5. 1805
Stephen Hales Sen[io]r.	"	Sept[ember] 10. 1791
Isaac Perry	"	May 4. 1807
Seventies.		
George Myers	"	March 2. 1805
James Davenport	"	May 1. 1802
Richard Harrison	"	March 8. 1808
Rufus Beach	"	May 8. 1795
Melvin Wilber	"	Aug[us]t 10. 1801
Henry W. Hales	"	Aug[us]t 7, 1829
Elders.		
Richard Ballantyne	"	Aug[us]t 15. 1817

James Lake " Oct[obe]r. 7. 1790

W[ashed]. by G[eorge]. P. Dykes & Phineas H. Young. anointed by A[braham]. O. Smoot. W[illia]m. Crosby — B[enjamin]. L. Clapp. J[ohn]. D. Lee & L[evi]. W. Hancock.

[Finished at] 15 m[inutes]. p[ast] 11.

In the female department, commencing at 20 minutes to 11, the following persons were washed and anointed, viz;

Lavinia Whipple, born June 7. 1811. washed by Sarah Smith, anointed, by Sarah Smith[.]

Busmath Whipple born Sept[ember] 7 1769 w[ashed]. by Artemisia Snow an[ointed]. by Sarah D. Rich[.]

Mary Ann Harrison. [born] Aug[ust] 10. 1811. w[ashed]. by Artemisia Snow an[ointed]. by M[ercy]. R. Thompson[.]

Mary E. Lincoln b[orn]. June 18. 1820 w[ashed]. and anointed by Sarah D. Rich[.]

Mary Ann Hales born Oct[ober] 11. 1799 w[ashed]. by Lois Cutler. an[ointed] by Sarah Smith[.]

Mary Ann Coons born Aug[us]t 11. 1812 W[ashed]. by Artemisia Snow an[ointed] by M[ercy]. R. Thompson[.]

Philomela Lake born April 13. 1793 W[ashed]. by Artemisia Snow an[ointed]. by Sarah D. Rich[.]

Frances G. Swan born June 20. 1822. Washed and anointed by Lois Cutler[.]

Ann Myers born Dec[ember]. 1809 w[ashed]. by Artemisia Snow. an[ointed] by Sarah D. Rich[.]

Eunice Wilber. born Jan[uar]y 20. 1808 w[ashed] by Artemisia Snow an[ointed] by M[ercy]. R. Thompson[.]

Margaret McCall born Oct[ober] 16. 1771 Washed & anointed by Lois Cutler[.]

Abigail Andrews [born] Oct[ober] 4 1780 w[ashed] by S[ophronia]. M. Harmon An[ointed]. by Lois Cutler[.]

Dicey C. Allen born Oct[ober] 26. 1802 W[ashed]. by S[ophronia]. M. Harmon An[ointed] by Lois Cutler[.]

Annie Ballantyne born Sep[tember] 2. 1819 washed and anointed by Mercy R. Thompson[.]

Jane Ballantyne born Apr[il] 11 1813 w[ashed] by S[ophronia]. M. Harmon an[ointed]. [by] Leonora Taylor[.]

Anne Ballantyne born Oct[ober] 1791 w[ashed]. by S[ophronia]. M. Harmon an[ointed] by Lois Cutler[.]

Rebecca Wright, born Sept[ember] 22 1813 w[ashed]. by Sarah Smith, an[ointed] by Sarah Smith[.]

Henrietta C. Cutler born Nov[ember]. 16. 1821 w[ashed]. by S[ophronia]. M. Harmon an[ointed]. by Lois Cutler[.]

Almira Davenport b[orn] Jan[uar]y 23. 1805 w[ashed]. and anointed by Sarah Smith.

Finished at 25 minutes to 1. o'clock

At 15 minutes before 1 P.M. at the ringing of the bell, [we] commenced receiving into the lower and middle departments, those whose washing & anointing commenced at 25 m[inutes]. past 10. constituting Co[mpany]. No. 2, the following persons officiating in the upper department, viz; Orson Spencer, Orson Hyde & P[arley]. P. Pratt, and in the middle department, the following viz.

John Taylor as No. 1		
Erastus Snow as No. 2.	Willard Snow	No. 3.
John D. Lee as No. 4, &	F[ranklin]. D. Richards	" 5.

Pres[ident]. [Brigham] Young ~~& Elder~~ [and] ^myself^ [Heber C.] Kimball are superintending the operations of the day, examining maps with reference to selecting a location for the Saints west of the Rocky Mountains and reading the various works which have been written & published by travellers in those regions. also making selections of names of persons to come in and receive their endowment.

At 10 minutes past 2 [we] commenced receiving into the upper department company No. 2 in the following order—viz;

Richard Ballantyne,	by John Taylor[.]
Ann Ballantyne	" " "
James Davenport	" " "
Almira Davenport	" " " & J[ames]. D[avenport].
Edson Whipple	"
Lavinia Whipple	" E[dson]. Whipple & J[ohn]. Taylor[.]
Basmath Whipple	" " " " " "
Stephen Hales Sen[io]r.	" John Taylor[.]
Mary Ann Hales	" St[ephen]. Hales & John Taylor[.]
Jonathan C. Wright	" John Taylor[.]
Rebecca Wright	" J[ohn]. C. Wright & J[ohn]. T[aylor].
Frances G. Swan	" H[eber]. C. Kimball[.]
Melvin Wilber	" John Taylor[.]

Eunice Wilber	" M[elvin]. Wilber & J[ohn]. Taylor[.]		
Jane Ballantyne	" John Taylor[.]		
Annie Ballantyne	" John Taylor[.]		
Richard Harrison	" John Taylor[.]		
Mary Ann Harrison	" "	"	& R[ichard]. H[arrison].
Margaret McCall	" "	"	
Rufus Beach	" "	"	
Libbeus T. Coons	" "	"	
Mary Ann Coons	" "	"	& L[ibbeus]. T. C[oons].
Mary E. Lincoln	" Phineas Young[.]		
Dicey C. Allen	" John Taylor[.]		
Abigail Andrews	" "	"	
Henrietta C. Cutler	" "	"	
James Lake	" "	"	
Philomela Lake	" "	"	& J[ames]. Lake[.]
Henry W. Hales	" "	"	
George Myers	" "	"	
Ann Myers	" "	"	& Geo[rge]. Myers[.]
Isaac Perry	" "	"	John Taylor[.]
William Stringham	" John Taylor[.]		

[Finished at] half p[ast] 4. Lorenzo Snow, Artemisia Snow & C[atherine]. C. Spencer prompters[.]

At 5 minutes past 2. P.M. [we] commenced in the male department, washing & anointing the following persons. viz;

High Priests.

Joel H. Johnson.	born	March 23. 1802
Albert Brown	"	Nov[embe]r. 13 1807

[W]ashed by Geo[rge]. P. Dykes & Phineas Young anointed by William Crosby.

Seventies

Jeremiah Willey	born	Nov[ember]. 6. 1804
Zadoc Parker	"	Oct[ober]. 27. 1804
Henry Royle	"	April 1. 1813
Chauncey Gaylord	"	Oct[ober] 29. 1821
James Rigby	"	March 23 1809
Arza Adams	"	Jan[uar]y 22 1804

[W]ashed by G[eorge]. P. Dykes & Phineas Young—anointed by B[enjamin]. L. Clapp & Levi W. Hancock[.]

Finished at 15 minutes to 3.

In the female department, commencing at half after One, the following persons were washed and anointed. viz;

Sarah Brown, born Oct[ober] 24. 1816 washed by S[ophronia]. M. Harmon, An[ointed]. by Lois Cutler[.]

Susan Johnson born Aug[ust]. 28. 1812 w[ashed]. by Sarah D. Rich, an[ointed]. by Sarah D. Rich[.]

Mary E. Gaylord b[orn]. Sept[ember] 5. 1821 w[ashed]. by S[ophronia]. M. Harmon An[ointed]. by Thirza Cahoon[.]

Mariam Parker, b[orn]. Oct[ober] 14. 1799 w[ashed]. by Sarah D. Rich, an[ointed]. by Lois Cutler.

Samantha Willey b[orn]. Nov[ember]. 15. 1814 W[ashed]. by S[ophronia]. M. Harmon An[ointed]. by Thirza Cahoon[.]

Sabina Adams. born Sept[ember] 1. 1812 w[ashed]. by Sarah D. Rich an[ointed] by Sarah Smith[.]

Matilda A. Royle [born] Aug[us]t 22. 1828 w[ashed]. by Sarah D. Rich an[ointed]. by Lois Cutler[.]

Martha Royle born Jan[uar]y 1823 w[ashed]. by Sarah D. Rich an[ointed] by Thirza Cahoon[.]

Sarah M. Gee born Jan[uar]y 24. 1795 w[ashed] by Sarah D. Rich an[ointed] by Lois Cutler[.]

Sarah C. Botsford b[orn]. Aug[us]t 30. 1820 w[ashed]. by M[ercy]. R. Thompson an[ointed] by Sarah Smith[.]

Jane Rigby born Oct[ober] 1. 1813 Washed & anointed by Sarah D. Rich[.]

Hannah Grinnell [born] Nov[ember]. 3. 1783 W[ashed]. by M[ercy]. R. Thompson an[ointed] by Mary Smith[.]

Ended at 20 m[inutes]. to 3.

At 10 minutes ^past 3^ at the ringing of the bell, [we] commenced receiving into the upper department, company No. 3, the following persons officiating in the upper department.

Orson Hyde	as No.	1
Orson Spencer	" "	2
Charles C. Rich	" "	3

and in the middle department,

Erastus Snow	as No.	1
R[ichard]. Ballantyne	" "	2
Willard Snow	" "	3

John D. Lee	"	"	4
F[ranklin]. D. Richards	"	"	5.

Elder Kimball's Son Heber P. Kimball came in at 15 minutes to 4.

At 5 minutes to 5. [we] commenced receiving company No. 3 into the upper department, in the following order. viz;

Joel H. Johnson	by P[arley]. P. Pratt[.]
Susan Johnson	" " " " & Joel Johnson[.]
Albert Brown	" " " "
Susan Brown	" " " " & A[lbert]. Brown[.]
Jeremiah Willy	" " " "
Samantha Willy	" " " " & J[eremiah]. Willey[.]
Henry Royle	" " " "
Matilda Royle	" " " " & H[enry]. Royle[.]
Martha Royle	" " " " " "
Zadoc Parker	" " " "
Mariam Parker	" " " " & Zadoc Parker[.]
Sarah W. Gee	" " " "
Sarah C. Botsford	" " " "
Hannah Grinnel	" John Taylor[.]
Arza Adams	" " "
Sabina Adams	" A[rza]. Adams & J[ohn]. Taylor[.]
Chauncey Gaylord	" Amasa Lyman[.]
Mary C. Gaylord	" C[hauncey]. Gaylord & A[masa]. Lyman[.]
James Rigby	" A[masa]. Lyman[.]
Jane Rigby	" James Rigby &. A[masa]. Lyman[.]

Finished at 20 m[inutes]. past 6. Lorenzo Snow & Artemisia Snow. prompters.

At 6 o'clock the High Council, the High Priests and the Seventies met together for prayer, each quorum by itself, and all dressed in the garments & Robes of the Holy Order of the Priesthood.

—William Clayton, Diary, kept for Heber C. Kimball.

....

At Sun rise the weather is still warm and pleasant — the washing commenced in the Male department at 9 A.M.

[1]	Noah Rodger	born	Mar 19th 1777
2	Richard H Kinnamin	"	May 17th 1818

3	Jesse B Martin	"	April 11th 1825
4	W[illia]m E. Higginbotham	"	Feb 26th 1811
5	Philip B. Lewis	"	[~~illegible~~] January 16th 1804
6	Albert Merril	"	Aug 28th
7	Henry W. Bigler	born	Aug 28th 1815
8	Priddy Meeks	"	Aug 29th 1787
9	Allen Weeks		Jan 24th 1813
10	Charles ^A^ Harper	"	Jan 28 1817
11	Philander Colton	"	" 25 1811
12	Isaac Fuller	"	" 25 1811

The above Name[d] Persons were washed by John D Lee and Anointed by Pres[ident] B[enjamin]. L. Clapp —

Washing commenced in Female Department at the Hour of 9 A.M. & the following persons are the wives or family of the foregoing Persons already registered

[See pages 250-52 opposite for excerpted portion.]

The No. of Men and Women that Passed through the ordinances of Endowment to day are 84 — 56 of that No were Seventies & their familys — the others were High Priests & some few Elders. the greater portion of the Brethren are included in the quorums of the Seventies or High Priest[.] After the opperations closed I [John D. Lee] went home with the intention of returning back within a few hours — but in this I was disapointed ~~for~~ by a tremendous Rain Storm — which continued the the [sic] whole night incessantly — and is still poaring down like a torrent from the Heavens — almost covering the face of the earth in watter[.] it is now 9 oclock AM & the Prospect for the continuation of the Storm is as good as it was in the beginning — Pres[ident] Jos[eph] Young — L[evi] Hancock — B[enjamin] L Clapp J[edediah]- M- Grant A[lbert]. P Rockwood H[enry] Herriman Clothed themselves in Robes Clean & white (it being an emblem of righteousness) in the order of the Priest-hood — then offered the signs and prayed Ater [sic] or rather at the same time the Twelve [apostles] Dressed & [illegible] in their in their depart-ment in the same [illegible,] After which they and all that were presant [gathered together and] we danced in an [illegible] and ~~cold~~ civil recre-ation — The violin & Flute also performed their part genteely — after dancing before the King of Kings — they all united in Singing Praises to his Name —

—Seventies Record, Book B.

[Washings and anointings for Wednesday, December 31, 1845]

Namely ~~Mary~~ ^Rodgers^ born Aug 3rd 1793		C M Herriman		Ls Cutler
2 Margaret Kinnamin " July 19th 1827		M Harmon	A.	Ls Cutler
3 Louisa Higginbotham " Mar 20th 1809	Washed	Thurza Cahoon	A.	Ls Cutler
4 Maria C. Lewis " " 26 1817	Washed	S. M. Harmon	A.	Ls Cutler
5 Sarah Jane Weeks " Nov 26th 1814	"	" "	"	" "
6 Polly M Cutler " Oct 15th 1816	"	" "	"	" "
7 Louisa D Harper " Nov 5th 1818	"	Thurza Cahoon	A	[illegible]
8 Mary A. Merril " June 2nd	"	" "	"	"
9 Margarett A. Merril " Nov 15th 1816	"	S. M. Harmon	"	L Cutler
10 Elizabeth Meeks " July 2d 1823	"	" "	"	S D Rich
11 Sarah Meeks " Dec 12th 1801	"	T Cahoon	"	" "
12 Lovinda M Fuller " Mar 2nd 1821	"	S M Harmon	"	L Cutler

Washing commenced in the Male department at, 25 minets Past 10 A.M —

13 George Meyres	born	2nd 1805
14 Malvin Wilber	"	Aug 10th 1801
15 James Devenport	"	May 1st [?] 1802
16 Richard Harris	"	Mar 8th 1808
17 Rufus Beach	"	May 8th 1795
18 Henry W Hales	"	Aug 7th 1827
19 Jas Lake	"	Oct 9 1790

washed by G. P. Dykes & Phinihas Young Anointed by B. L Clapp & John D. Lee — Washing commenced at 20 minets to 11 in the morning.

			Washed by & Anointed by	
13 Mary Harrison	"	Aug 10th 1811	Artemisia Snow	M B Thorpe
14 Mary E Lyncoln	"	June 18 1821	S D Rich	S D Rich
15 Philomila Lake	"	April 15th 1793	A Snow	" " "
16 Ann Meyres	"	Dec 1817	" "	" " "
Whole No of Sev 201 —				Total Femals 213
17 Eunice Walber	"	Jan 20th 1808	A — Snow	M. R. Thompson
18 Margaret McCall	"	Oct 16th 1781	L Cutler	L Cutler
19 Disey C. Allen	"	" 26th 1802	S — M— Harmon	L Cutler
20 Rebea Wright	"	Sept 22 1813 —	Sarah Smith	Sarrah Smith
21 Almyra Devenport	"	Oct. 1805	" "	" "

3rd Co.— Male Department

washing commenced at 5 minets Past 2 P-M-

24 Jeremiah Willey	born	Nov 6th 1804
25 Zadeck Parker	"	Oct 22d " "
26 Henry Royal	"	April 15th 1813
27 Chaney Gaylord	"	Oct 29th 1821
28 James Rigsby	"	Mar 23 1809
29 Arza Adams	"	Jan 22 1804

washed by G. P. Dykes & J Young Anointed by B. L C & L Hancock.

3rd Co of Females c. at ½ Past 1—

22 Mary E. Gaylord	[born]	Sept 5th 1821	S. M. Harmon &	A	T Cahoon
23 Marryann Parker		Oct 4th 1799	S D Rich	A	L Cutler
24 Samantha Willy		Nov 15th 1844	S. M. H.	"	S Smith
25 Sabina Adams	"	Sept 1st 1813	S. D. Rich	"	" "
26 Matilda Royale	"	Aug 22d 1828	" " "	"	" "
27 Jane Rigsley	"	Oct 1st 1813	" " "	"	S— D— R—

—Seventies Record, Book B, oversized portion, December 31, 1845.

[L]ike wise[.]

—John D. Lee, Diary.

Elder Heber C. Kimball and I [Brigham Young] superintended the operations in the Temple, examined maps with reference to selecting a location for the saints west of the Rocky Mountains, and reading various works written by travelers in those regions; also made selections of names of persons to be invited to receive their endowments.

Eighty-four persons were received into the Temple.

Six p.m., the high council, high priests, and seventies met in their respective rooms and prayed.

—"Manuscript History of Brigham Young,"
in *History of the Church,* 7:558.

Nauvoo temple endowments performed on this date for:

First Company: Philip B. Lewis, Maria T. Lewis, Lucina Johnson, Allen Weeks, Sarah Jane Weeks, Priddy Meeks, Elizabeth Meeks, Richard H. Kinnamon, Margaret Kinnamon, Ira Clothier, Amy Clothier, Noah Rogers, Eda Rogers, Philander Colton, Polly M. Colton, William. E. Higginbotham, Louisa Higgenbotham, Jesse B. Martin, Isaac Fuller, Laurinda Fuller, Lyman Leonard, Abigail Leonard, Charles A. Harper, Lovina W. Harper, Henry W. Bigler, Albert Merrill, Margaret Ann Merrill, Mary Ann Merrill, Adelia Ann Bishop, Adeline Hamblin, and Sarah Meeks.

Second Company: Richard Ballantyne, Anne Balantyne, James Davenport, Almira Davenport, Edson Whipple, Lavina Whipple, Basmath Whipple, Stephen Hales Sr., Mary Ann Hales, Jonathan C. Wright, Rebecca Wright, Frances G. Swan, Melvin Wilber, Eunice Wilber, Jane Balantyne, Annie Ballantyne, Richard Harrison, Mary Ann Harrison, Margaret McCall, Rufus Beach, Libbeus T. Coons, Mary Ann Coons, Mary E. Lincoln, Dicey C. Allen, Abigail Andrews, Henrietta C. Cutler, James Lake, Philomena Lake, Henry W. Hales, George Myers, Ann Myers, Isaac Perry, and William Stringham.

Third Company: Joel H. Johnson, Susan Johnson, Albert Brown, Susan Brown, Jeremiah Willey, Samantha Willey, Henry Royle, Matilda Royle, Martha Royle, Zadoc Parker, Mariam Parker, Sarah W. Gee, Sarah C. Botsford, Hannah Grinnel, Arza Adams, Sabina Adams, Chauncey Gaylord, Mary E. Gaylord, James Rigby, and Jane Rigby.

—Summary of information compiled by the Temple
Index Bureau, *Nauvoo Temple Endowment Register:
10 December 1845 to 8 February 1846.*

IV.

Early January

1846

"INSTRUCTIONS MOST BEAUTIFUL TO THE MIND"

Thursday, January 1, 1846

This day is the first of another year— the morning is rainy. The ground very soft, and the mud very deep. A heavy mist rests upon the low ground under the bluff— the sun light is very dim being nearly shut out by the dark heavy clouds which overspread the whole face of the sky and every thing around wears a gloomy and dismal aspect— But notwithstanding the unfavorable appearance of things, the brethren and sisters are assembling together to the house of the Lord, to receive their washings & anointings

Pres[ident]. Brigham Young came in at an early hour, having left the Temple about 6 o'clock last evening in company with Elder H[eber]. C. Kimball[.]

The plasterers have commenced this morning to plaster the arched ceiling of the lower hall of the Temple, the floor is laid, the frame work of the pulpets and surrounding seats for the Choir and band, is put up and the work of fitting the room for dedication & holding meetings therein progresses very fast—

At 10 minutes past 8 [we] commenced in the male department, washing & anointing the following persons, viz;

High Priests.

Joseph Rich.	born	April 16. 1786
Jacob Anderson	"	June 15 1807
Dwight Webster	"	April 13. 1814
Enos Curtis	"	Oct[ober] 9 1783
Erastus Bingham	"	March 12 1778
Isaac Hill	"	Sept[ember] 26 1806
Hazen Kimball	"	March 31. 1812
James S. Kimball	"	Nov[embe]r 17. 1785

Seventies

Thomas Spiers	"	July 14 1804
James W. Huntsman	"	Oct[ober]. 8. 1806
Oliver H. Dudley	"	Feb[ruar]y 22 1809
David DeVol	"	Nov[embe]r. 27 1805
John W. Bell	"	May 28. 1805
Burr Frost	"	March 4. 1816
William Dorland	"	July 14 1787

15 [men] These were all washed by George P. Dykes and Phineas H. Young, & anointed, the High Priests by A[braham]. O. Smoot & William Crosby and the Seventies by Joseph Young, B[enjamin]. L. Clapp and William Crosby.

Finished at 5 minutes past 10.

In the female department, commencing at 10 m[inutes]. past 8, the following persons were washed & anointed, viz;

Nancy Rich, born April 24, 1782 washed and anointed by Lois Cutler[.]

Serene Anderson born Jan[uar]y 1. 1814 washed & anointed by Sarah D. Rich[.]

Lucinda Bingham born Sep[tember]. 19 1797 washed by Thirzah Cahoon anointed by Thirza Cahoon[.]

Mary Atherton born Oct[ober] 21. 1784 or 5[,] washed & anointed by Thirza Cahoon[.]

Lydia Judah born Feb[ruary] 17. 1813 W[ashed]. by Sarah D. Rich, an[ointed] by Diantha Billings[.]

Mary Dryer born June 27. 1803 w[ashed] by Thirza Cahoon an[ointed] by Lois Cutler[.]

Ruth B. Kimball born Dec[ember]. 3 1791 w[ashed] by Sarah Smith an[ointed]. by Diantha Billings[.]

Eunice Webster born June 19. 1820 w[ashed] by Sarah Smith

an[ointed]. by Diantha Billings[.]

Mary E. Frost born Sept[ember]. 4. 1815 w[ashed]. by Catharine C. Spencer an[ointed]. by C[atherine]. C. Spencer[.]

Derinda C. Kimball born May 4. 1819 W[ashed]. by Thirza Cahoon an[ointed]. by Lois Cutler[.]

Louisa C. Smith born July 30. 1815 W[ashed]. by Sarah Smith an[ointed]. by Mary Smith[.]

Elizabeth Dorland born Mar[ch]. 10/96 W[ashed] by Thirza Cahoon An[ointed]. by Lois Cutler[.]

Delia Devol, born Jan[uar]y 9. 1812. W[ashed]. by Sarah D. Rich an[ointed]. by Diantha Billings[.]

Hannah Huntsman [born] Feb[ruary]. 8. 1816 W[ashed]. by Thirza Cahoon an[ointed]. by Lois Cutler.

Elisa Hill born Dec[ember]. 16. 1805 w[ashed]. by Sarah Smith, an[ointed]. by Lois Cutler.

Mary Ann Dudley born Mar[ch]. 19 1811 w[ashed]. by Sarah Smith, an[ointed]. by Lois Cutler[.]

Ann Bell born Jan[uar]y. 21. 1812 w[ashed]. by C[atherine]. C. Spencer an[ointed]. by Diantha Billings[.]

Ruth Curtis born Nov[ember]. 14. 1790 W[ashed]. by C[atherine]. C. Spencer an[ointed] by Lois Cutler[.]

Mary Spiers born Sep[tember]. 30. 1804 W[ashed]. by Thirza Cahoon an[ointed] by Sarah Smith[.]

Mary Spiers born Oct[ober] 16 1830 w[ashed] by C[atherine]. C. Spencer an[ointed] by Lois Cutler[.]

20 [women washed and anointed.] [Finished at] 10 m[inutes]. past 10.

At 15 minutes before 10, the following persons assembled in Pres[ident]. B[righam]. Young's Room, clothed themselves, and consecrated 14 bottles of oil, which had previously been perfumed, viz; Pres[ident]. Brigham Young Amasa Lyman & George A. Smith, of the quorum of Twelve, and Joseph Young, Orson Spencer, C[harles]. C. Rich, Erastus Snow and Benjamin L. Clapp, after which they united together in prayer to God that he would preserve us from all the snares and traps that were laid by our enemies, that he would paralyze their power, and turn away their wrath, that we might have means & power to remove from this place, and for the continued prosperity of the Church &c. &c. &c.

After this was over Pres[ident]. Young had a short conference with Father Isaac Morley, who had been waiting to see him, for half an hour in the Office—

Elder Kimball came in about 10 o'cl[oc]k.

At 25 minutes past 10, at the ringing of the bell[, we] commenced receiving into the upper department, those who have been washed and anointed this morning.

Orson Spencer; officiating as No. 1.
Orson Pratt " " " 2
Willard Snow " " " 3.

and in the middle department,

Erastus Snow officiating as No. 1
C[harles]. C. Rich as No. 2. Morris Phelps " 3
John D. Lee " 4 F[ranklin]. D. Richards " 5

At 10 minutes before 12 [we] commenced receiving into the upper department company No. 1. in the following order—viz;

Joseph Rich	by H[eber]. C. Kimball[.]
Nancy Rich	" " " " & J[oseph]. Rich[.]
David Devol	" Parley P. Pratt[.]
Delia DeVol	" David DeVol & P[arley]. P. Pratt[.]
Dwight Webster	" P[arley]. P. Pratt.
Eunice Webster	" " " " & D[wight]. Webster[.]
Mary Dryer	" Truman Leonard Jr.
Isaac Hill	" Orson Spencer[.]
Eliza Hill	" " " & I[saac]. Hill[.]
John W. Bell	" " "
Ann Bell	" " " & J[ohn]. W. Bell[.]
Lydia Judah	" Amasa Lyman[.]
Jacob Anderson	" " "
Serena Anderson	" " " & J[acob]. Anderson[.]
Burr Frost	" " "
Mary E. Frost	" " " & B[urr]. Frost[.]
Oliver H. Dudly	" " "
Mary Ann Dudley	" " & O[liver]. H. Dudley[.]
William Dorland	" " "
Elizabeth Dorland	" " " & W[illia]m. Dorland[.]
Erastus Bingham	" Orson Pratt[.]
Lucinda Bingham	" " & E[rastus]. Bingham[.]
James S. Kimball	" "
Ruth B. Kimball	" " & James S. K[imball].
James W. Huntsman	" "

Hannah Huntsman	"	"	& J[ames]. W. H[untsman].
Thomas Spiers	"	"	
Mary Spiers	"	"	& Th[omas]. Spiers[.]
Mary Spiers	"	"	" " "
Enos Curtis	"	"	
Ruth Curtis	"	"	& E[nos]. Curtis[.]
Hazen Kimball	"	"	
Derinda C. Kimball	"	"	& Hazen Kimball[.]
Mary Atherton	"	"	
Lovina C. Smith	"	"	

Finished at 20 m[inutes]. to 3. Lorenzo Snow & Artemisia Snow. Prompters[.]

At 10 o'clock [we] commenced washing and anointing in the male department the following persons, viz;

High Priests

Sanford Porter,	born	March 7. 1790
Timothy B. Clark	"	March 15 1778
Harrison W. H. Sagers	"	May 3. 1814
James S. Holman	"	Sept[ember] 17. 1805
Chauncey W. Porter	"	Oct[ober] 20. 1812
Ezekiel Kellogg	"	Jan[uar]y 20, 1801

These were washed by Geo[rge]. P. Dykes & Phineas Young, & anointed by A[braham]. O. Smoot and William Crosby.

Seventies.

Benj[amin] Sweat		May 22, 1793
John W. Clark		Feb[ruary] 4. 1819
Alonzo LeBaron		
Loren Babbitt	born	Sept[ember] 19. 1806
George Woodward	"	Sept[ember] 9 1817
David B. Dille	"	April 5. 1812
Thomas Whittle	"	May 21. 1812
William O. Clark	"	June 25 1817
John H. Tippets	"	Sept[ember] 5 1810
Ezra T. Clark	"	Nov[ember]. 23. 1823
John Bowen	"	Sept[ember] 23 1803
Alborn Allen	"	May 22 1802
Chapman Duncan		July 1 1812
Lindsay A. Brady		June 11. 1811

14 [men] These washed by Levi W. Hancock and Alexander McRae, and anointed by B[enjamin]. L. Clapp Levi W. Hancock, and Phineas H. Young.

John Bowen, was ordained a High Priest under the hands of A. O. Smoot and Phinehas H. Young

~~Hazen Kimball, was ordained a High Priest at the time of anointing under the hands of ^Wm Snow^ Phinehas H. Young William Crosby & Geo. P. Dykes. see next page~~

Timothy B. Clark was ordained a High Priest, before being washed & anointed, under the hands of Phineas H. Young — A[braham]. O. Smoot William Crosby & Geo[rge]. P. Dykes.

Hazen Kimball was ordained a High Priest, before being washed & anointed, under the hands of William Snow, Phineas H. Young and George P. Dykes[.]

John Bowen was ordained a High Priest, before being washed & anointed under the hands of George P. Dykes Phinehas H. Young & W[illia]m. Crosby[.]

In the female department, commencing at 15 minutes after 11. the following persons were Washed & anointed. viz

Caroline Tibbetts born July 24. 1808 washed & anointed by Sarah D. Rich[.]

Persis Tippets born Mar[ch]. 15. 1821. Washed & anointed by Diantha Billings[.]

Mary Whittle born June 18. 1817 W[ashed]. by Thirza Cahoon An[ointed]. by Diantha Billings[.]

Polly Conklin born Oct[ober] 18. 1791 W[ashed]. and anointed by Ma[r]y Smith[.]

Thomazin D. Woodward, [born] Dec[ember]. 10 1814 w[ashed] by Thirza Cahoon an[ointed]. by Mary Smith[.]

Ann Bowen born Ap[ril]. 11 1813 w[ashed]. by Lois Cutler an[ointed]. by Sarah Smith[.]

Nancy Porter born July 23, 1790 w[ashed]. by Lois Cutler, an[ointed] by Diantha Billings[.]

Harriet L. Dille b[orn]. Oct[ober] 23. 1820 w[ashed]. by Thirza Cahoon an[ointed]. by Diantha Billings[.]

Mary Brown b[orn]. Jan[uar]y 4. 1806 w[ashed]. by Lois Cutler. an[ointed] by Sarah Smith[.]

Laurena Clark b[orn]. Nov[embe]r. 19. 1815 Washed and anointed by Mary Smith[.]

Julia R. Clark born June 25. 1817 washed & anointed by Sarah D. Rich[.]

Mary Clark born Sept[ember] 29, 1816 washed & anointed by Sarah D. Rich.

Olive Amanda Sagen. [born] Jan[uar]y 26. 1813 w[ashed]. by Lois Cutler an[ointed]. by Diantha Billings[.]

Marcia Allen b[orn]. Oct[ober]. 6. 1804 w[ashed]. by Lois Cutler an[ointed] by Sarah Smith[.]

Amy Porter, born Feb[ruar]y 22. 1815 w[ashed]. by Thirza Cahoon an[ointed]. by Mary Smith[.]

Naomi Kellogg b[orn]. May 5. 1800 w[ashed]. by Thirza Cahoon an[ointed]. by Mary Smith[.]

Clarissa LeBarron b[orn]. Dec[ember]. 16. 1824 Washed and anointed by Lois Cutler.

Eda Sweat born Aug[us]t 12, 1806 W[ashed]. and an[ointed]. by Diantha Billings[.]

Elizabeth Brady b[orn]. Oct[ober] 23, 1813, w[ashed]. and anointed by Thirza Cahoon.

19 [women washed and anointed.] Finished at 3 minutes to 1.

At half past one, at the ringing of the bell, [we] commenced receiving into the Lower and middle department, company No. 2.—

persons officiating in the upper department

Orson Spencer,	as	No. 1	George Miller No. 2.
Charles C. Rich	"	"	3 & in the middle department
Erastus Snow,	as	No.	1. P[arley]. P. Pratt as No. 2
[blank]	"	"	3. David Candland 4
F[ranklin]. D. Richards	as	No.	5.

At 4 o'clock [we] commenced receiving into the upper department company No. 2.

John W. Clark	by Amasa Lyman[.]
Lurena Clark	" & J[ohn]. W. Clark[.]
Harrison W. H. Sagers	by A[masa]. Lyman[.]
Olive Amanda Sagers	by " " & H[arrison]. Sagers[.]
Benjamin Sweat	by A[masa]. Lyman[.]
Eda Sweat	by B[enjamin]. Sweat & Geo[rge] Miller[.]
Ezra T. Clark	by Geo[rge] Miller[.]
Mary Clark	by E[zra]. T. Clark & G[eorge]. Miller[.]

John Bowen	by Geo[rge]. Miller[.]
Ann Bowen	" J[ohn]. Bowen & Geo[rge]. Miller[.]
William O. Clark	by Geo[rge]. Miller[.]
Julia R. Clark	" " " & W[illiam]. O. C[lark].
Chapman Duncan	by John D Lee[.]
Alonzo LeBaron	by J[ohn]. D. Lee[.]
Clarissa LeBaron	by J[ohn]. D. Lee[.]
George Woodward	" J[ohn]. D. Lee[.]
Thomazin ^D.^ Woodward	" G[eorge]. W[oodward]. & J[ohn]. D. Lee[.]
Timothy B. Clark	" J[ohn]. D. Lee[.]
Loren Babbitt	" Orson Hyde[.]
Mary Brown	by Loren Babbitt & O[rson]. Hyde[.]
David B. Dille	" Orson Hyde[.]
Harriet L. Dille	" " "
Polly Conklin	" " "
Alborn Allen	" " "
Marcia Allen	" " " & A[lborn]. Allen[.]
John H. Tibbets	" " "
Caroline Tibbets	" " "
Persis Tibbets	" " "
Lindsay A. Brady	" " "
Elizabeth Brady	" " "
Sanford Porter	" " "
Nancy Porter	" " "
Ezekiel Kellogg	" " "
Naomi Kellogg	" " "
Chauncey W. Porter	" " "
Amy Porter	" " "
James S. Holman	" " "
Thomas Whittle }	
Mary Whittle }	by Orson Hyde[.]

Finished at half past 4. Lorenzo Snow [and] M[ercy]. R. Thompson and [blank] Prompters[.]

At 10 minutes past 3 o'clock P. M. in President Brigham's Young's room No. 1. in the Attic Story of the Lord's House, Truman Leonard Jun[io]r. and Ortensia White, were united in the bonds of matrimony, by Pres[ident]. Brigham Young, and were sealed for time and for eternity, in the presence of George A. Smith, and Parley P. Pratt, as Witnesses.[1]

At 6½ O'clock, the High Priests met in room No. 8 attic Story of the Temple[.] The following persons were present, all clothed in the robes of the Priesthood. viz; Pres[ident]. George Miller, Edwa[rd]. Hunter Isaac Higbee — Isaac Chase, Winslow Farr, Charles W. Patten, Elijah Fordham Anson Call, Elizur G. Terrill, Joshua S. Holman, Stephen Markham, Luman H. Calkins — William C. Gallaher and Franklin D. Richards. Meeting opened by singing "Come all ye Sons of Zion". then prayer by Winslow Farr. President Miller gave instruction most beautiful to the mind, explaining the signs, tokens and names of the Priesthood after which they all offered up the Signs and united in prayer with President Miller who was mouth.

Several members of the High Council came to the place of meeting but the number not being large, and No President being. there[,] no meeting was held.

At 10 minutes past 6 o'clock [we] commenced in the male department, washing and anointing the following persons.

High Priest.		
John Young	born	May 22. 1791
Seventies.		
William H. Kimball	born	Ap[ri]l. 10. 1827
William G. Young	"	Feb[ruar]y 22. 1827
Orson K. Whitney	"	Jan[uar]y 20. 1830
Elders.		
Brigham H. Young	born	Jan[uar]y 3. 1824
Horace K. Whitney	"	July 25. 1823

[W]ashed by Phineas H. Young, William Crosby and N[ewel]. K. Whitney. Anointed by Brigham Young & H[eber]. C. Kimball[.]

Orson K. Whitney was ordained into the quorum of Seventies before being washed and anointed, under the hands of Pres[ident]. Brigham Young, Heber C. Kimball & N[ewel]. K. Whitney.

At 10 minutes past 6 [we] commenced in the Female department, washing & anointing the following persons, viz;

1. This may mark the first eternal marriage sealing performed in the Nauvoo temple.

Mary M. Kimball, born Feb[ruar]y 27. 1824 washed and anointed by Vilate Kimball[.]

Sarah Ann Kingsbury, born Mar[ch]. 22, 1826 washed and anointed by Elizabeth A. Whitney[.]

Helen Kimball. born Aug[ust] 25. 1828 Washed & anointed by Vilate Kimball and Elizabeth Ann Whitney[.]

Helen Genet Murray born Feb[ruary] 18. 1826 washed and anointed by E[lizabeth]. A[nn]. Whitney[.]

Mary Huston, born Sept[ember] 11. 1818 washed and anointed by E[lizabeth]. A[nn]. Whitney[.]

Eliza M. Partridge b[orn]. Ap[ri]l. 20. 1820 w[ashed] by Maria L. Lyman anointed by E[lizabeth]. A[nn]. Whitney[.]

Caroline E. Partridge born Jan[uary] 8. 1827 washed and anointed by Maria Louisa Lyman[.]

Cedenia O. Clark born July 15. 1828 washed by Mercy R. Thompson an[ointed]. by Mary Smith[.]

Adelia C. Clark born Jan[uar]y 28. 1826 washed by Lovina C. Smith an[ointed] by Mary Smith[.]

Lucy Ann Seely [born] May 17. 1822 washed and anointed by E[lizabeth]. A[nn]. Whitney[.]

Clarissa C. Decker born July 22. 1820 w[ashed]. by M[ercy]. R. Thompson an[ointed]. by E[lizabeth]. A[nn]. Whitney[.]

Persis Young born March 15. 1806 w[ashed]. by M[ercy]. R. Thompson An[ointed]. by Mary Smith[.]

Finished at 15 minutes after 7.

At 20 minutes to 8, at the ringing of the bell [we] commenced receiving into the lower and middle departments, the before mentioned company whose washings & anointings commenced at 10 minutes past 6.—the following persons officiating in the upper department, viz;

Orson Hyde	as	No.	1.	Orson Pratt " No. 2.
Amasa Lyman	"	"	3.	

in the middle department.

Orson Pratt	as	No.	1. }
Erastus Snow	"	"	2 }
Lorenzo Snow	"	"	3. }
John D. Lee	"	"	4 }
F[ranklin]. D. Richards	"	"	5. }

At 10 minutes to 9, [we] commenced receiving into the upper department company No. 3, in the following order

John Young	received by	Brigham Young[.]
Lucy Ann Seeley	"	" "
Clarissa C. Decker	"	" "
William H. Kimball	"	H[eber]. C. Kimball[.]
Mary M. Kimball	"	W[illia]m. H. [Kimball] & H[eber]. C. Kimball[.]
Sarah Ann Kingsbury	"	H[eber]. C. Kimball[.]
Persis Young	"	H[eber]. C. Kimball[.]
Helen Mar Kimball	"	H[eber]. C. Kimball[.]
Helen Genet Murray	"	H[eber]. C. Kimball[.]
Mary Huston	"	H[eber]. C. Kimball[.]
Horace K. Whitney	"	N[ewel]. K. Whitney[.]
Orson K. Whitney	"	N[ewel]. K. Whitney[.]
Eliza Maria Partridge	"	Amasa Lyman[.]
Caroline E. Partridge	"	Amasa Lyman[.]
Brigham H. Young	"	Phineas H. Young[.]
Cedenia O. Clark	"	B[righam]. H. Young & P[hineas]. H. Young[.]
William G. Young	"	Phineas H. Young[.]
Adelia C. Clark	"	W[illia]m G. Young & P[hineas]. H. Y[oung].

Finished at 20 minutes past 10. Franklin D. Richards, Elizabeth Ann Whitney, and Artemisia Snow officiated as prompters.

After a little time had elapsed; the whole company were assembled together in the east room, in number about fifty and all kneeled down upon the carpet and united with Elder H[eber]. C. Kimball in thanksgiving to God for his great mercy, and goodness to us in granting us this opportunity of meeting together in the House of the Lord, and in prayer to him that he would continue to bless us—that he would bless Pres[ident]. Brigham Young with health and wisdom, that he might be able to lead and direct this people, and that the same blessings might be extended to all his brethren of The Twelve [apostles], and on all the Saints, and that God would bless our wives and give unto them strength of body, that they might live and administer to the servants of God that they might see three score years and ten, and behold the kingdom of God established in the earth.— And that we might be enabled to continue in Nauvoo in peace, until all the faithful Saints had received their endowment, and that when the time to leave here should arrive, that we might have those things that we need to enable us to go away in comfort,—that to this end our possessions might look good to those who are round about us that they may buy them and pay us gold and silver, and such things as we need.

[A]lso that God would bless our children, and all that pertains to us, and dedicating the whole company to God, [we] gave him the glory through our Lord Jesus Christ. Amen.

William G. Young, and Adelia C. Clark were then married by Pres[ident]. Brigham Young, in the following order, viz; chairs were placed for them near the west side of the room by Phineas H. Young, in which they were seated, and Brigham H. Young and Cedenia O. Clark officiated as Groomsman & Bridesmaid. Pres[ident]. Young then asked the Groom if it was the understanding that they were to be married for time and for eternity and receiving an answer in the affirmative, asked the Bride the same question, and received the same answer. He then asked Hazen Kimball & his wife if the Bride's parents understood their intentions and and approved of them and received the same answer— He also asked the Bride how old she was, and was answered that she would be 20 years old the 28th of this month— These questions having all been satisfactorily answered, he requested them to stand up, & they did so. and by his direction joined their right hands together, He then said nearly as follows, William G. Young, you take Adelia C. Clark by the right hand to be your lawful wedded wife, and promise, in the presence of God and Angels, and these witnesses to observe all the laws and obligations and duties pertaining or belonging to this order of the Priesthood, do You? to which the Groom answered Yes Sir— He then asked the same question or nearly so of the Bride, and received a like answer. He then pronounced them husband & wife and sealed them together as such for time and for all eternity, and also sealed them up to eternal life, against all sins, except the sin against the Holy Ghost, which is the shedding of innocent blood, & pronounced various blessings upon them, and when he had done. told William to kiss his wife.

Two or three songs were then sung, and Pres[ident]. Young invited the company to supper, which had been prepared in another part of the hall, viz; the garden. Bishop N[ewel]. K. Whitney & his wife led the way, and were followed by about half the company, the table not being extensive enough to accommodate more than that number. Supper was soon ended and the sound of [Hans] Hanson's violin ^and Brother [Elisha] Averett's flute^ in the east room gave notice that business of a different nature would soon be attended to. The floor was cleared of chairs & tables, and filled up with two sets of dancers, one on each side of the stove[2]— After dancing a few figures, Pres[ident]. Young called the attention of the whole company, and then gave them a message, of this import, ~~that~~ viz; that this Temple was a Holy place, and that when we danced we danced unto the Lord, and that no person would be allowed to come on to this floor, and afterwards mingle with the wicked, He said the wicked had no right to dance, that dancing and music belonged to the Saints— and he strongly impressed upon the mind of those present the impropriety of mingling again with the wicked after having come in here, and taken upon them the covenants which they had— He spoke pointedly to his daughter Vilate and told her that if she should do so after this, she might expect to meet the frowns of a father who held the keys of the Priesthood— He was followed by L[ucian]. R. Foster, who concurred in the remarks of Pres[ident]. Young, and said he would like to have the question put, that it might be known how many of those present were willing to make a covenant to this effect, that they would not mingle with the wicked any more in their amusement, Elder H[eber]. C. Kimball said before the question was put he wished to say a few words. He felt thankful that Pres[ident] Young had touched this subject, & also that we had this opportunity of meeting together in this manner— said that those who were parents had become responsible for the conduct of their children, and for his part he should not be willing that his children should meet with the wicked, or have any thing to do with their amusements— He said to his own children, that they had covenanted here this evening, that they would receive the instruction, and listen to the counsel of their father & mother—and he hoped they would remember it.

Erastus Snow, expressed his feelings in a few words, [and] said he had never attempted to dance in his life, until he came on to this floor, and he must say that since he had commenced he had enjoyed himself very well in the exercise, and felt grateful to God that he had the privilege—

The question was then put— the Pres[ident]. invited all those who were willing to covenant that they would keep themselves from mingling with the wicked to rise upon their feet— whereupon all rose up.—

2. This was the room representing the Garden of Eden. Evidently the rooms of the endowment departments were also used at times for meetings or in this case a wedding meal and dance. The Garden Room was the only room of the temporary departments other than the Celestial Room that could accommodate a large gathering.

L[ucian]. R. Foster said again, that he was willing to serve the Lord, and look to him for the things that were necessary, and do the work he had for him to do, if the Lord would permit him to enjoy himself in the dance once in a while. Hans C. Hanson enquired if it would be permitted for him to speak a few words on this occasion & receiving an approving nod from the President, said he had been in the habit of playing the fiddle for mixed companies among the wicked, and that in such companies he had always seen very ungodly conduct, that on a certain occasion he played for some who were called saints, but they went down to a steam Boat & got about 25 passengers to join them, and said he[,] they wanted to get away all our gals, and there was very bad talk there,—and that when he saw the saints enjoying themselves in the dance as they did the last night here, he made a covenant with himself that he would no more play the fiddle for the wicked—but that the saints should have the use of his fiddle, and that when he went on a mission he would leave the fiddle with the Saints, and asked them if they would take care of it. They answered Yes.—

The Spirit of the Lord was present, and the spirit of meekness & humility & gratitude to God, for the great privileges we enjoy, that tears came into the eyes of many of those present.— Love and union, peace & harmony prevailed, the utmost decorum was observed, not a loud laugh, nor a rude jest saluted the ear.— All were in the most perfect subjection to the word of the President, and when he told them at about half past 2 o'clock, that it was time to quit and seek repose the whole company assented without a murmur, although many would have been glad to have continued the exercises longer—

The sisters retired to the side rooms, & the brethren stretched themselves on the floor, or on the sofas and all were soon in the embraces of "tired nature's sweet restorer, balmy sleep."[3] with the exception of the Bridegroom & Bride, and a few of their friends, who, being unable to close their eyes in sleep, from the abundance of their joy, passed the short hours of the morning, in agreeable conversation, in the office.

The persons present on this occasion were as follows, viz; Pres[ident]. Brigham Young & his wife, his daughter, Vilate, & sons Joseph, & Brigham, & two little girls & infant.—Elder H[eber]. C. Kimball & wife, his son William H. Kimball with his wife,—his daughter Helen M. Kim-

3. Those sleeping in the temple gathered in the Celestial Room.

ball,—John Young,—Lorenzo Young—. & his wife, his son William G. the bridegroom,—Phineas H. Young, & his Son Brigham H. Young—N[ewel]. K. Whitney & wife, Horace K. Whitney, Orson K. Whitney, John Whitney—Amasa Lyman, & his wife, Eliza Maria Partridge[;] Caroline E. Partridge. Lucy Ann Seeley—Clarissa C. Decker Joseph C. Kingsbury. Sarah Ann Kingsbury Helen Genet Murray Mary Huston Cedenia O. Clark—Adelia C. Clark ~~Joseph C. Kingsbury~~—Hazen Kimball & wife Erastus Snow & wife—Catharine Lewis. Lorenzo Snow—Eliza R. Snow. Mary Smith—

—William Clayton, Diary, kept for Heber C. Kimball.

....

This morning is the beggining of A New year — warm though not verry pleasant for its raining like a torrent upon the veil or vally — Making it quite disagreeable indeed to both Man & Beast it continued to rain all the day. Pres[ident]. B[righam] Young quite unwell & much fatigued this Morning[.] the Twelve [apostles] met in the room No 1 and consecrated fourteen bottles of oil for the endowment at 8. ^Minets to.^ 10 The following brethren were washed and anointed[:] washed by George P. Dykes and Phinehas Young[,] Anointed by Pres[idents] J[oseph] Young [Benjamin] Clapp & W[illiam] Crosby

[See pages 270-71 for excerpted portion.]

Orson Whitney was ordained a Seventy under the hands of Pres[ident] B[righam]. Young H[eber]. C. Kimble [and] Newell K. Whitney the Father of the Said O[rson]. Whitney —

The following persons were washed ~~& anointed~~ by N[ewel] K. Whitney G[eorge] Miller Phineas Young & W[illia]m Crosby — And anointed by Pres[ident] Brigham Young H[eber]. C. Kimble & Newell K. Whitney. Namely —

John Young H[igh]. P[riest]. born May 22nd 1791—
223 W[illiam] H. Kimble " April 10th 1827— Seventy
224 W[illia]m G. Young " Feb 22nd 1827
225 Orson H. Whitney " Jun 20th 1830
Brigham H. Young " Jan 3d 1824 Elder
Horace K Whitney " July 25th 1823 "

10 Minets after 6 in the evening the washing commenced in both departments — & the following Ladies were washed and anointed by Vilate Kimble Elizabeth An Whitney Mercy R. Thompson Louisa M. Lyman & Mary Smith[,] Namely

[Washings and anointings for Thursday, January 1, 1846]

1 Thos Spears July 14. 1804	Mary Spiers Sept 30 1804
2 Jas W Huntman Oct 8. 1806	Hannah Huntsman Feb 8. 1816
3 Oliver W Dudley Feb 28 1809	Mary Ann Dudley 1811
4 David De Vol Nov 27. 1805	Delia De Vol. Jan 9. 1812
5 John W Bell May 28 1805	Ann Bell 1812
6 Benj Frost Mar 9. 1816	Mary Frost Sep 19 1815
7 William Dorland July 14. 1789	Elizabeth Dorland 1796

finished 10. 5

At 11. o.clock A.M. Co. No 2 commenced ~~their~~ going through the ordinances — under the direction of Pres B. Young — Namely

8 Lorrin Babbitt " Sept 19th 1806	~~T D~~ Mary Brown 1805	
9 George Woodard " " 9th 1817	T. D. Woodard 1803	
10 David B. Dille " April 5th 1812	Harriet Dille born Oct 23d 1820	
11 Thos Whittle " May 21st 1812	Mary Whittle " Jun 18 1817	
12 Wm O. Clark " June 25th 1818	Julia R- Clark June 25th 1825	
13 John H. Tibbets " Sept 5th 1810.	Caroline Tibitts 1808	Percy Tibbitts
14 Ezra T. Clark " Nov 23rd 1823	Mary Clark— 1827	
15 John Bowen " Sept 23rd 1813	An Bowen 1816 ord H P	
16 Abern Allen " May 22nd 1802	Maria Allen 1804	

the Persons above refered too were washed by Pres L Hancock & B. L Clapp, Phineas Young — Pres Henry Herriman [illegible] Pres Jos Young where to day & in fact has been here every day Since the Endowment commenced preparing garments oil essence

&c- and has occasionally [acted] officially when ever circumstances would permit Brother Jedediah M Grant is with us Generally, but unable to labour much on account of his Health being much impairied — The weather grows colder this evening — the wind has Shifted arround to the N. W. —

The following Names belong to co[mpany]. No. 2

17 Chapman Duncan " July 4th 1812	
18 John W. Clark " Feb 4th. 1819	Luremnda Clark — 1816
19 Benj Sweat " May 22nd 1793	Elda Sweat
20 Alonzo LeBarron " Nov 18- 1818	Clarisa Lebarron Dec 16th 1825
222 Linzey A Brady " June 11th 1811	Elizabeth Avon[?] Oct 23rd 1813

Seventies Record, Book B, oversized portion, January 1, 1846.

Mary M Kimble	born	Feb 27th 1824
Sarah A Kimball	"	May 22 1825
Helen "	"	Aug 25th 1828
Helen G. Murray		Feb 18 1826
Mary Huston		Sept 10 1818
Eliza M Partridge		Apr. 20. 1820
Caroline A "	"	Jan 8 1827
Cedina O Clark		July 15 1828
Adelia C Clark		Jan 28 1826
Lucy Ann Seely		May 17 1822
Clarissa C Decker		July 22 1820
Persis Young		Mar 15 1802

Finished 15 Min[utes] [illegible]

After the business of the [day] was laid [to rest] — The congregation assembled to the End room of the the Temple where they were seated in order under the direction of Pres[ident] Brigham Young — who staid in the midst of the concourse — and Solemnized the right of Matrimony between Elder W[illia]m G Young & sister Adelia Clark — The eloquence meekness and sobriety with which he address[ed] ^the company^ himself — Truly beholden [to] the character of a Man clothed with authority from the great Elohim[,] & that he was Sensible of the important Station & keys of his calling; under which he was ad[d]ing [to] such authority humility [?] & reverence [that] I [John D. Lee] [had] never before witnessed [on] any occasion at [illegible] any circumstances whatever — the congregation consisted chiefly of the children & kinfolks of Pres[ident] B[righam]. Young Heber C. Kimble Bishop Whitney & the relations of the Bride — after the ceremony was over the concourse walked unto the garden [room] to Sup[p]er — the probable No were about 150 presant[.] the Festival — the Supper was prepared by Pres[ident] B[righam] Young — with the exception of the Turkeys that was furnished by Br[other]. David Yearsley[.] after partaking of the said banquet the assembly ~~its~~ was again conducted to the east part of the Temple where they found the room filled with the melodious sounds of violin & Flute — here the young man & the Maden, as also the old man & the Maden went forth in the dance — fulfilling the Predictions of the [illegible] but before we had, indulged to any great extent — The President called the House to order & said that he had a message to this [group] which mostly were young, in the bloom of youth & when I have declared my message then I shall have done what the

Lord has commanded me to do — verrily thus saith saith [sic] the voice of the spirit to you!! This is mine holy House which I have caused to be built to my Holy Name[;] therefore let no Person go fourth in the Dance unless they will covenant to Sepperate themselves from the world & never again mingle in their Society nor Participate in their mirth or amusements from this time forth & for ever — I have said ^this to the^ children here & should they transend these bounds they may expect to merit the frowns of an offended Father!! that holds the keys of the Priesthood — mirth & recreation belongs to the people of God[;] it does[, just] as it [does not] belong to the unbelieved! & they participate in them & they usurp that privelege right or [illegible] [of] what belongs to the Saints alone — Now Dance [illegible] yourselves — but first learn to reverence & adorn that House of the most high in all your devotion & recreation —

Pres[ident] H[eber] C Kimble [began] Friday Jan 2nd 1845 by saying that he had sepperated himself from the world more than 10 years ago & will never mingle with ^them^ again Br[other] L[ucian] R. Foster E[rastus]. Snow & Br[other] C[hristian] Hanson all spoke their feelings freely on the subject — A vote was then taken of those ~~who~~ who would observe to do those things[.] the vote was unanimous — we then recommenced our recreation & continued until ½ past 2. o.clock when Pres[ident]-Young Said that we had better close our amusements & lay down & take a little sleep & thereby afresh ourselves for the work of the Morrow — there are bedding & matrasses sufficient in the small rooms to accommodate the sister[s] — let them occupy them — & let the Brethren lye down in the large rooms on the Carpets by the Stoves & rest 2 or 3 hours — all order[s] were strictly obeyed. because we were of one heart & mind and with propriety it might be said that this Jubilee of the Saints are only the preludes of the enjoyment of those who inhabit celestial Homes —

—Seventies Record, Book B.

....

[I]t rained like a torrent all the long [day] and the day before[. Nevertheless,] I [John D. Lee] had the pleasure [of] realizing the answer to Prayer[.] In meeting the stuborn feeling of Br[other] Benj[amin] M[e]-Ginnis who had sworn vengance against Br[other] George Lee; because of his being under promise to his (Magginis) daughter though against the consent & wish of her father—and had they or she not [been] past the Flour [flower] of her age—I dont know whether he ever would have consented[;] but seeing that he could not get his endowment while such feelings existed[,] he at length offered to do as I said. [T]hat was[,] Pres[ident] Young & myself showed him by the Power of the Spirit so that he wept like a child while I taught him the law of the Priesthood[.] Pres[ident] Young confirmed what I said to him which seemed to reconcile his mind and soon I expect a wedding to take place instead of a trial before the Mormons as was contemplated but a few days before[.] But to return[,] I got permission to leave the Temple a few hours on business for my family who was unwell[.] returned again about 3 oclock PM & officiated some at the veil[.] This being New years day Pres[ident] B[righam] Young H[eber] C Kimble [and Newel K.] Whitney prepared quite a genteel supper so after the opperations of the day ceased the house was called to order and the congregation seated in regular form Elder Heber C Kimble offered up a tribute of praise to the Ruler of all Good for the pleasure of having our friends & Kinfolk together in the Holy sanctuary of the Lord[.] After prayer Pres[ident] B[righam] Young arrose and [performed] the right of matrimony between Bro[ther] W[illia]m Young & Miss [A]delia Clark[.] The soft serene Spirit that was manifested on the occasion was more like a celestial or Heavenly being than a Finite one[.] The grace modesty and sobriety with which the minister addressed him self truly bespeak[s] the character of a Prophet[.] after the ceremony was over the company sat down to a table well furnished with the rich dainties of the earth[.] after supper we retired to the east part of the Temple where we were all again seated[.][4] Pres[ident] B[righam] Young then arose and in an affectionate air said that he had a message to deliver to his people— You are young the most of you & have been in the habit of mingling with the world[.] harken[,] thus saith the voice of the Spirit that in [me,] as much as you [have] gone through the sacred ordinance of the Priesthood remember your covenants and never again mingle with the world, that is unbelievers[.] I have children here and want them to understand that if they ever participate in Mirth or recreation with the world that they may expect to meet a Fathers fro[w]n[.] furthermore I [want] no person [to] go on this floor that holds the keys of the Priesthood that ever intends to mingle with the unbelievers again[.] this is a sacred place & must not be defiled[.] The Lord is pleased to have his people enjoy themselves in righteousness[.] pleasure belongs to the saints but it does not belong to the wicked and when they enjoy pleasure, they usurp that that does not be-

4. This was the Celestial Room.

long to them[.] I want my children & all others that are under my Jurisdiction to learn to serve the Lord in the dance and in all things whatsoever we do[.] Pres[ident] H[eber] C Kimble offered the same instructions to his children & said that he had sepperated himself from the world 10-15 years ago and would never again participate with them[.] L[ucian] R Foster & E[rastus] Snow & Hans Osborne all freed their minds in turn and [the entire assemblage] was then called to know whither they (the congregation) would agree to the above proposition & terminated [the discussion with a] unamious [consent.] They no doubt felt the weight & importance of the instruction that was given by both Pres[ident] B[righam] Young and H[eber] C Kimble[.] Now said Pres[ident] B[righam] Y[oung] and H[eber] C K[imball] then in as much as you have been willing to harken to council Now enjoy your selves & we will participate with you[.] So they joined in the dance & truly we had a scene of rejoicing & merriment accompanied by the spirit of the Lord that gladen[ed] the hearts of the Saints[.] our amusement continued till near 3 in the morning[.] Pres[ident] Young then said that it was enough let all merriment cease & let us now repose in sleep in the small rooms[.] there are beds and bedding sufficient to make the wimen comfortable & the men can lie down upon the carpet around the stoves & should You go home to refresh yourselves in sleep it would be near the day light before you could get to sleep & you can just rest a few hours here as not[.] In a few moments the large room [was] almost covered with men strewed around over the room upon palletts & in the Sophias while the wimen were in the side rooms[.] Pres[ident] B[righam] Young stretched himself down upon the carpet before the stove having given up his bed to accomodate some others[.] and soon we were all wraped in the arms of sleep & seemed as in Heaven while we dreamed[.] After a pleasant nap of 3 hours all was up & s[e]tting [the] house in order[,] replacing the furniture which had been taken out & used in the garden for the sup[p]er the evening previous[.] However on account of this little New Year recreation we declined working much to day but the anxiety was apparantly so great that we were obliged to commence as the vestry was already full of candidates waiting for admission[.] at 12 oclock the first company came through[.] I officiated as prompter at the veil & received some at the veil[.]

—John D. Lee, Diary.

....

I [Franklin D. Richards] went to the Temple [and] assisted to give the blessings of the endowment to 92 persons among whom were a company in the evening of Young relatives[,] at the close of which W[illia]m Young and Delia Clark were united for time and eternity and I was blessed with a seat near the head of the table next [to] the Bridesgroom at 11 oclock P.M.

[A]t 6 P.M. I met with the following H[igh]. P[ries]ts President George Miller, Bishops Edward Hunter, & Isaac Higbee, Isaac Chase, Winslow Farr, Charles W. Patten, Elijah Fordham, Anson Call, Elishur G. Terrell, Joshua S. Holman, Stephen Markham, Luman H. Calkins, [and] W[illia]m G. Gallaher. Pres[iden]t Miller explained most beautifully the nature of the tokens, signs, names & Covenants of the Priesthood which we had received saying in the course of his observations that he had the utmost confidence that we should all of us continue faithful & not one of us turn from the faith & Covenants which we had made[.] May God grant it in the name of Jesus Christ, Amen. Pres[iden]t Miller after we had offered up the signs was mouth for us in prayer and enjoyed that measure of the Spirit by which he was led to ask for that which I had long desired to ask for in that circle[.] we also prayed that Jane [Richards] might be healed of all her infirmities and be made strong and her heart be made to leap for joy and be lifted up above all her troubles which is the devout and fervent supplication of my heart in the name of the Holy one "Jesus Christ[.]"

At the close of the prayer I told the brethren that I felt that we had received at the hand of the Lord in our endowments a New Years blessing of a superlative degree for which may the good Spirit enable us to feel that proper Gratitude and be able even to exercise it too, which is due to the giver for this benevolent act[.] After supper which was at 11 the east room was arranged, br[other]s Hanson a Dane and a brother Averett an American[,] the former with a violin the latter with a flute, made melody and the sons and daughters of the Lord went forth and praised him in the dance[.][5] some 10 or 12 couples [were] on the floor at once and so arousing was the scene that although I had never danced a figure of any kind in my life[,] after being introduced to sister Eliza Partridge, by Elder [Heber C.] Kimball[,] I ventured on to the floor with her and danced an Opera reel twice in succession and enjoyed it much[,] after which Sister Livona Smith was my partner in a "double French four[.]"

5. This dance was held in the Celestial Room.

In the course of our recreation Pres[ident] [Brigham] Young called the company to order and addressed them saying that it was the mind of the spirit that there should no one of the company occupy the floor any more for dancing in that holy temple of the Lord who was not willing to abstain from & not meet with the wicked in any of their recreations but those who were willing to do so might continue to praise the Lord in the dance in his *holy House* and according to the blessings and addressing himself to his daughter who was in the room and had been in the dance he said —you cannot mingle again with the wicked in their vain amusements without incurring the frowns of a Father who holds the Keys of the Priesthood and you will have to feel his indignation if you do[.] after a short interchange of sentiment by Elder Kimball, Erastus Snow, L[ucian]. R. Foster, the company all arose as testimony that they would not unite with the wicked in future in recreation.

—Franklin D. Richards, Diary.

....

At an early hour, Elder Heber C. Kimball and I [Brigham Young] went to the Temple. The plasterers have commenced to plaster the arched ceiling of the lower hall, the floor is laid, the framework of the pulpits and seats for the choir and band are put up; and the work of finishing the room for dedication progresses rapidly.

6:30 p.m., the high priests met and prayed, eighty-nine persons received ordinances.

10:20 p.m., after finishing the labors of the day, the company assembled in the large room in the attic story and united in prayer with Elder Heber C. Kimball, thanking God for his great mercy and goodness to us in granting this opportunity of meeting together in the House of the Lord, asking him that he would continue to bless us, that he would bless President Brigham Young with health and wisdom, that he might be able to lead and direct this people; and that the same blessings might be extended to all his brethren of the Twelve [apostles] and all the saints; and that God would bless our wives and give unto them strength of body that they might live and administer to the servants of God, that they might see three score years and ten, and behold the kingdom of God established in the earth; and that we might be enabled to continue in Nauvoo in peace, until all the faithful saints had received their endowments; and that when the time to leave here should arrive that we might be able to sell our possessions and obtain those things that we need to enable us to go away in comfort. Also, that God would bless our children, and all that pertains to us.

—"Manuscript History of Brigham Young," in *History of the Church,* 7:560-61.

....

Nauvoo temple endowments performed on this date for:

First Company: Joseph Rich, Nancy Rich, David DeVol, Delia DeVol, Dwight Webster, Eunice Webster, Mary Dryer, Isaac Hill, Eliza Hill, John W. Bell, Ann Bell, Lydia Judah, Jacob Anderson, Serena Anderson, Frost Burr, Mary E. Frost, Oliver H. Dudley, Mary Ann Dudley, William Dorland, Elizabeth Dorland, Erastus Bingham, Lucinda Bingham, James S. Kimball, Ruth B. Kimball, James W. Huntsman, Hannah Huntsman, Thomas Spiers, Mary Spiers, Enos Curtis, Ruth Curtis, Hazen Kimball, Derinda C. Kimball, Mary Atherton, and Lovisa C. Smith.

Second Company: John W. Clark, Lurena Clark, Harrison W. H. Sagers, Olive Amanda Sagers, Benjamin Sweat, Eda Sweat, Ezra T. Clark, Mary Clark, John Bowen, Ann Bowen, William O. Clark, Julia R. Clark, Chapman Duncan, Alonzo LeBaron, Clarissa LeBaron, George Woodward, Thomazin D. Woodward, Timothy B. Clark, Loren Babbitt, Mary Brown, David B. Dille, Harriett L. Dille, Polly Conklin, Alborn Allen, Marcia Allen, John H. Tibbets, Caroline Tibbets, Persis Tibbets, Lindsey A. Brady, Elizabeth Brady, Sanford Porter, Nancy Porter, Ezekiel Kellog, Naomi Kellog, Chauncey W. Porter, Amy Porter, James S. Holman, Thomas Whittle, and Mary Whittle.

Third Company: John Young, Lucy Ann Seeley, Clarissa C. Decker, William H. Kimball, Mary M. Kimball, Sarah Ann Kingsbury, Persis Young, Helen Mar Kimball, Helen Genet Murray, Mary Hustin, Horace K. Whitney, Orson K. Whitney, Eliza Maria Partridge, Caroline E. Partridge, Brigham H. Young, Cedenia O. Clark, William G. Young, Adelia C. Clark, and John Price Wriston.

—Summary of information compiled by the Temple Index Bureau, *Nauvoo Temple Endowment Register: 10 December 1845 to 8 February 1846.*

Friday, January 2, 1846

The weather was clear & cold this morning, and the mud which was very abundant yesterday, was dried up this morning, At an early hour those who slept in the Temple were stirring, and [a] large company had assembled in the vestry, waiting for their washing and anointing, although it had been supposed the work must cease for a short time for want of oil, ~~which has been~~ but several bottles had been brought in for Temple use by various individuals so that by the time it was wanted, there were 17 bottles, These were perfumed, and consecrated for washing & anointing those who were invited to the Temple. The oil was consecrated, by the following persons who assembled together in room No. 4, clothed in their robes & garments, viz; Amasa Lyman, Geo[rge]. A. Smith Joseph Young — William Crosby, A[braham]. O. Smoot, C[harles]. C. Rich and F[ranklin]. D. Richards— they commenced at 20 minutes before One and continued 10 minutes— after which they united in prayer to God for the welfare of the Church in general &c. and for the restoration to health of a few sick persons.

At 22 minutes to 11. [we] commenced in the Male department, washing & anointing the following persons. viz;

High Priests		
Jefferson Hunt	born	January 22. 1804
Thomas Guyman	"	March 10. 1787
Samuel Miles	"	Sept[ember] 3. 1779
Anson Matthews	"	Dec[embe]r. 1. 1787
John Kempton	"	Sept[ember] 8 1777
Amos C. Deuel	"	March 4 1797
Seventies		
Stephen M. St. John	"	April 10. 1810
John Eldridge	"	April 21. 1804
Samuel Moore	"	Jan[uar]y 19. 1804
Elders		
Osmyn M. Deuel	"	Jan[uar]y 1. 1802
William Sears	"	Aug[us]t 4, 1798
Alfred Sears	"	Aug[us]t 26. 1821

The above were washed by William Snow Geo[rge]. P. Dykes & Levi W. Hancock—anointed by A[braham]. O. Smoot & William Crosby.

Amos C. Deuel was ordained a High Priest, under the hands of A[braham]. O. Smoot, George P. Dykes and Jefferson Hunt.— before being washed and anointed—

In the female department[,] commencing at half past 10. the following persons were washed & anointed—viz;

Elizabeth Matthews, born Aug[ust]. 4. 1787 w[ashed]. by Sarah D. Rich, an[ointed]. by Thirza Cahoon[.]

Roxana Freeman born Sept[ember] 18. 1791. w[ashed]. by Olive Farr, anointed by Olive Farr[.]

Mary Deuel born Nov[ember]. 23. 1807 w[ashed]. by Thirza Cahoon an[ointed]. by Thirza Cahoon[.]

Celia Hunt born [blank] 1805 washed and anointed by Lois Cutler.

Mary Little, born Feb[ruar]y 6. 1813 washed & anointed by Sarah D. Rich[.]

Hannah Kempton. born May 22. 1791 w[ashed]. by Olive Farr an[ointed] by Lois Cutler[.]

Sally St. John. born Sept[ember] 7. 1809 w[ashed]. by M[ercy]. R. Thompson an[ointed]. by Lydia Granger[.]

Margaret Sears born Dec[ember]. 25. 1801 w[ashed]. by Sarah D. Rich an[ointed] by Lois Cutler[.]

Eunice S. Moore, born Mar[ch]. 2. 1807 w[ashed]. by Sarah D. Rich an[ointed] by Thirza Cahoon[.]

Cynthia Ann Eldridge. born Oct[ober] 3. 1820 w[ashed]. by Sarah D. Rich an[ointed]. by Lois Cutler[.]

Sarah Guyman b[orn]. Nov[ember]. 20. 1789 w[ashed] by Sarah D. Rich an[ointed]. by Thirza Cahoon[.]

Prudence Miles b[orn]. May 1. 1795 w[ashed]. by Olive Farr an[ointed]. by Thirza Cahoon[.]

Polly Ann Guyman b[orn]. July 11. 1829 w[ashed] by Sarah D. Rich an[ointed]. by Thirza Cahoon[.]

Olive Littlefield [born] Sept[ember] 24. 1818 washed & anointed by Sarah D. Rich.

Luana H. Beebee, [born] Oct[ober] 3. 1814 Washed & anointed by Lois Cutler.

Finished at 5 m[inutes]. past 12.

At 20 m[inutes]. to One, at the ringing of the Bell [we] commenced receiving into the lower & middle departments the company washed & anointed this morning.

P[arley]. P. Pratt as No. 1. John Taylor as No. 2.
H[eber]. C. Kimball " " 3. in the upper dep[artmen]t
Orson Spencer as No. 1. Erastus Snow as No. 2
Lorenzo Snow " 3 J[ohn]. D. Lee " 4.
F[ranklin]. D. Richards as No. 5.

At 20 minutes past 2. [we] commenced receiving into the upper department company No. 1, in the following order. viz;

Amos C. Deuel	by Orson Hyde[.]
John Eldridge	" " "
Cynthia Ann Eldridge	By J[ohn]. Eldridge & O[rson]. H[yde].
William Sears	" O[rson]. Hyde[.]
Margaret Sears	" " "
Stephen M. St. John	by O[rson]. Hyde[.]
Sally St. John	by Stephen [St. John] & O[rson]. Hyde[.]
Anson Matthews	by O[rson]. Hyde[.]
Elizabeth Matthews	by O[rson]. Hyde & A[nson]. Matthews[.]
John Kempton	" O[rson]. Hyde[.]
Hannah Kempton	" " " & J[ohn]. Kempton[.]
Alfred Sears	" " "
Jefferson Hunt.	" O[rson]. Hyde[.]
Celia Hunt	" O[rson]. Hyde & J[efferson]. Hunt[.]
Mary Little	" O[rson]. Hyde[.]
Roxana Freeman	" O[rson]. Hyde[.]
Thomas Guyman	" O[rson]. Hyde[.]
Sarah Guyman	" O[rson]. Hyde & Th[omas]. Guyman[.]
Osmyn M. Deuel	" O[rson]. Hyde.
Polly Ann Guyman	" O[rson]. Hyde[.]
Mary Deuel	" O[rson]. Hyde & O[smyn]. M. Deuel[.]
Samuel Moore	" O[rson]. Hyde[.]
Olive Littlefield	" O[rson]. Hyde[.]
Eunice S. Moore	" O[rson]. Hyde & Sam[ue]l Moore[.]
Luana H. Beebee	" O[rson]. Hyde[.]
Samuel Miles	" O[rson]. Hyde[.]
Prudence Miles	" O[rson]. Hyde & S[amuel]. Miles.

Finished at 25 minutes past 3—Lorenzo Snow and Catherine C. Spencer officiating as prompters[.]

At 15 minutes to 11, [we] commenced in the Male department, washing and anointing the following persons. viz;

High Priests.		
Lyman L. Corey,	born	Jan[uar]y 18. 1809
William Scearce	"	Aug[us]t 15. 1779
Ebenezer Page	"	Oct[ober] 7. 1807
~~William Scearce~~	"	
Philip H. Buzzard	"	Feb[ruar]y 10. 1814
Seventies		
David P. Rainey	born	Feb[ruar]y 1. 1817
John Rowberry	"	Aug[us]t 16, 1823
Amos Davis Jr.	"	May 28. 1811
William McBride	"	March 22 1807
Daniel Davis	"	Dec[embe]r. 18 1808
Amos Babcock	"	Aug[us]t 15. 1808
Benj[ami]n. Maginniss	"	May 3. 1803
James Smithies ~~Kimball~~	"	Oct[ober] 29. 1807
Robert W. Bidwell	"	Aug[us]t 29 1794
Elder[s]		
James Lemon	"	March 12. 1815
Isaiah Whitesides	"	March 28 1816
William H. Woodbury	"	Aug[us]t 28 1816

Washed by Levi Hancock & William Huntington Anointed by B[enjamin]. L. Clapp. Joseph Young & J[edediah]. M. Grant.

At ~~10 minutes to one.~~ ^half after 11^ in the Female department [we] commenced washing & anointing the following persons

Margaret M. Rainey, born Oct[ober] 21. 1816 washed by Sarah D. Rich, An[ointed]. by Olive Farr[.]

Mary Jane Davis, b[orn]. Mar[ch]. 10. 1822. w[ashed]. by Sarah D. Rich an[ointed]. by Thirza Cahoon[.]

At 10 minutes before 1. [we] commenced in the female department washing & anointing the following persons—viz;

Sarah Gibbs born June 11, 1827 washed and anointed by Lois Cutler[.]

Eliza Gibbs born May 8. 1831 w[ashed]. by M[ercy]. R. Thompson and an[ointed]. by Lois Cutler[.]

Elizabeth Corey b[orn]. March 6. 1816 w[ashed]. by M[ercy]. R. Thompson an[ointed] by Lydia R. Granger[.]

Eliza Rowberry born Aug[us]t 22. 1813 W[ashed]. by Sarah D. Rich an[ointed]. by Thirza Cahoon[.]

Louiza Lemmon b[orn]. Oct[ober] 4. 1816 Washed & anointed by Thirza Cahoon[.]

Elizabeth Blood b[orn]. Jan[uar]y 7. 1790 W[ashed] by M[ercy]. R. Thompson an[ointed]. by Lois Cutler[.]

Nancy Smithies born Aug[us]t 2. 1809 W[ashed]. by Mercy R. Thompson & an[ointed]. by Lois Cutler[.]

Maria Gribble born Oct[ober] 14. 1820 washed and anointed by Olive Farr[.]

Elizabeth S. Blood [born] April 3. 1829 w[ashed]. by Rebecca W. Holman an[ointed]. by Lois Cutler[.]

Sarah Meginniss born Sept[ember] 4. 1802 w[ashed]. by Rebecca W. Holman an[ointed]. by T[irza]. Cahoon[.]

Hannah Maginn b[orn]. June 20. 1824 Washed and anointed by Mercy R. Thompson[.]

Harriet Clark born Aug[us]t 2. 1825 W[ashed]. by Mercy R. Thompson An[ointed]. by Thirza Cahoon[.]

Hannah Page born Ap[ri]l. 28, 1798 W[ashed]. by Rebecca W. Holman An[ointed]. by Lois Cutler[.]

Elizabeth Bidwell b[orn]. Oct[ober] 6. 1803 washed & anointed by Rebecca W Holman[.]

Elizabeth H. McBride b[orn]. Jan[uar]y 7. 1813 washed by Sarah D. Rich An[ointed]. by Lois Cutler[.]

Mary Ann Babcock born Jan[uar]y 8. 1813 w[ashed]. by R[e-becca]. W. Holman An[ointed]. by R[ebecca]. W. Holman[.]

Eliza Buzzard b[orn]. May 17. 1820 washed & anointed by Sarah D. Rich[.]

Clarissa Woodbury [born] May 16. 1818 washed & anointed by Sarah D. Rich[.]

Margaret Whitesides, b[orn]. Mar[ch]. 22. 1816. w[ashed]. by Olive Farr. An[ointed]. by Lois Cutler[.]

[E]nded at 15 minutes past 2.

At half past 2. Pres[ident]. [Brigham] Young in Company with his wife & children went on to the roof of the Temple— He returned at 15 minutes past 3.

At 35 minutes past 2, at the ringing of the bell [we] commenced receiving into the lower & middle departments, company No. 2. the following persons officiating, viz; Orson Spencer as No. 1. B[enjamin]. L. Clapp as No. 2. Henry Harriman as No. 3. in the upper dep[artment]. and in the middle department,

Orson Pratt	as No. 1.	P[arley]. P. Pratt	as No. 2.
John Taylor	" " 3.	J[ohn]. D. Lee	" " 4

F[ranklin]. D. Richards as No. 5.

William Scearce was ordained a High Priest, under the hands of H[eber]. C. Kimball, Geo[rge]. P. Dykes & Ezra T. Benson, at about 12 o'clock this day.

At 5 minutes to 4, [we] commenced receiving into the upper department company No. 2. in the following order

David Rainey	by John Taylor[.]
Margaret M. Rainey	" " " & D[avid]. P. R[ainey].
Harriet Clark	" " "
Hannah Maginn	" " "
Lyman L. Corey	" " "
Elizabeth Corey	" " " & L[yman]. L. C[orey].
William Scearce	" " "
John Rowberry	" " "
Eliza Rowberry	" " " & John R[owberry].
Benjamin Meginnis	" " "
Sarah Meginnis	" " " & B[enjamin]. M[eginnis].
Elizabeth Blood	" " "
Ebenezer Page	" " "
Hannah Page	" " " & E[benezer]. Page[.]
Elizabeth Blood	" " "
Amos Babcock	" " "
Mary Ann Babcock	" " " & A[mos]. Babcock[.]
James Lemmon	" " "
Maria Gribble	" " "
W[illia]m. McBride	" " "
Maria Louisa Lemmon	" " " & James Lemmon[.]
Daniel Davis	" " "
Eliza J. Gibbs	" " "
Robert W. Bidwell	" " "
Elizabeth H. McBride	" " " & W[illia]m. McBride[.]
James Smithies ~~Kimball~~	" " "
Elizabeth Bidwell	" " " & R[obert]. W. Bidwell[.]
Nancy Smithies	" " " & James Smithies[.]
Isaiah Whitesides	" " " & [blank]

W[illia]m. St. Woodbury	" " "
Margaret Whitesides	" " " & Isa[iah] Whitesides[.]
Clarissa Woodbury	" " " & W[illia]m. H. W[hitesides].
Amos Davis Sr.	by John Taylor[.]
Philip Hammon Buzzard	by John Taylor[.]
Mary Jane Davis	by Amos Davis & J[ohn]. T[aylor].
Eliza Buzzard	by P[hilip]. H[armon]. Buzzard & J[ohn]. T[aylor].
Sarah Gibbs	" John Taylor[.]

Finished at 5 minutes past 6.—Lorenzo Snow and Artemisia Snow officiating as prompters—also Mercy R. Thompson—

The High Council met at 6 o'clock P.M. Present—Isaac Morley, David Fullmer — Charles C. Rich, Ezra T. Benson Geo[rge]. W. Harris W[illia]m. Huntington Sr. Aaron Johnson, Newel Knight — James Allred— Also present the following High Priests, viz Joseph Rich, Jacob Anderson & Harvey Green— Prayed as usual for the deliverance & prosperity of Zion; and the healing of the sick.

The High Priests met for prayer. in room No. 6[,] present, Peter Haws, who was mouth — W[illia]m. Snow. W[illia]m Crosby — Geo[rge]. P. Dykes — Stephen Markham, Charles W. Patten — Nelson Bates, Ormus E. Bates — Benj[ami]n. Brown — Anson Call — David H. Redfield — Joseph B. Noble, Jonathan C. Wright, Addison Everett, & Cyrill Call—

Also in Room No. 10. the following persons[:] Geo[rge]. Miller — Albert Carrington — Abel Lamb Joshua S. Holman—who was mouth— William Felshaw Elam Ludington — Daniel Carter — Stephen Winchester, Job V. Barnum — Joseph Kelting — Elijah Fordham — Samuel Gully, Hiram Spencer — S[imeon]. Carter — L[ucien]. Woodworth — Isaac Chase L[uman]. H. Calkins — E[lizur]. G. Terrill.

The persons who have officiated in the ordinances of the Lord's House, this week so far, are as follows, viz; Pres[ident]. Brigham Young, Elder H[eber]. C. Kimball. Orson Hyde, P[arley]. P. Pratt, John Taylor, Orson Pratt, Amasa Lyman, George A. Smith, Joseph Young Orson Spencer — Abraham O. Smoot. William Crosby — Henry Harriman — Jedediah M. Grant, Benjamin L. Clapp — Erastus Snow Charles C. Rich — Willard Snow — William Snow — Ezra T. Benson Lewis Robbins — Elisha Averett — John L. Butler — Lorenzo Snow — Franklin D. Richards — George P. Dykes — Phineas H. Young John D. Lee, David Candland, L[ucian]. R. Foster George Miller — William Stringham — Daniel [blank].

The names of the Females are as follows, viz; Catharine C. Spencer, Lois Cutler — Thirza Cahoon. Mercy R. Thompson. Mary Smith. Eliza R. Snow Artemisia Snow — Diantha Billings — Sarah D. Rich — Huldah Barns Margaret Moon — Sophronia M. Harmon Sarah Smith — Lydia Granger, Olive Farr, Rebecca W. Holman — Maria Louisa Lyman, Elizabeth Ann Whitney — Vilate Kimball — Mary Ann Young—

After the regular exercises and business of the day was over, and the meetings of the High Council, & the High Priests, were closed, we had some excellent instrumental and vocal music.—Several members of the Band having been invited in by Elder Kimball viz; W[illia]m. Pitt — W[illia]m. Clayton — J[acob]. F. Hutchinson, and James Smithies— They performed several very beautiful pieces of music—and at the request of Joseph Young, played Fishers Hornpipe, upon which brother Joseph broke the gravity of the scene by dancing a hornpipe by himself, he was soon joined by John L. Butler, Ezra T. Benson. & A[lbert]. P. Rockwood— These danced until they were weary & sat down.

Pres[ident] ^B.[righam]^ Young then invited some one to join him in the dance, and found a partner in Bro[ther]. [Isaac] Chase— A french four was indulged in by these & others— After a short time, spent in dancing Elder Hyde made a short address, and requested those present to unite with him in thanksgiving & prayer to God, which they did— A new song, composed by W[illia]m. Clayton called "Come go with me" was ~~then~~ ^first^ sung by Clayton, & Hutchinson, accompanied on the violin by [William] Pitt, and on the Bass viol by [James] Smithies. When this was over—the address was made by Elder Hyde, and after the address & prayer, the President gave permission to any one to speak or pray, or shout, or speak in tongues— No one seemed disposed to use the opportunity, where upon the Pres[ident]. arose and made a short address to those present, himself— Some of the topics which he spoke upon are as follows. He alluded to the privilige which we now have of meeting in this house— and said that we could worship God in the dance, as well as in other ways.— He alluded to the ordinances of the endowment, and said they must always be attended to in an upper room. When we see a temple built right, there will be places for the Priests to enter and put on their robes, and offer up sacrifices, first for themselves, and then for the people—

The way for us to grow & thrive is for us to serve the Lord in all we do.—and as we have called upon the different quorums to meet together once a day, so it will eventually be with the whole church. There will be houses for them to meet in.— Remember the covenants that we have entered into. No man is to be filled with lightness— No brother or sister will be allowed to speak evil of his brother or sister—or speak against them— It is the duty of the quorums to meet together, we cannot enjoy it but a short time—

No person is at liberty to reveal any thing that takes place here to any mortal upon the face of the earth, ~~anythin~~ unless they know that person to be a good one, and one that the Lord is well pleased with. We have not the privilege of telling what we have seen here to night, but we will praise the Lord as we please.

Now as to dancing in this house— There are thousands of brethren and Sisters that have labored hard to build these walls and put on this roof, and they are shut out from any opportunity of enjoying any amusement among the wicked—or in the world—and shall they have any recreation? Yes! Where? Why in the Temple of the Lord. that is the very place where they can have liberty—and we will enjoy it this winter and then leave it.— And we will go to a land where there are at last no old settlers to quarrel with us—where we can say that we have killed the snakes & made the roads. and we will leave this wicked nation, to themselves, for they have rejected the gospel, and I hope and pray that the wicked will kill one another & savc us the trouble of doing it.

We cannot have another public meeting in this room, for if we do our roof is ruined.

But this church have obtained already all they have labored for in building this temple, but before we leave here, (I feel it in my bones)[6] there will be thousands and thousands of men that can go into any part of the world and build up the kingdom. and build temples. If any want to faint let them faint— If there are any that don't want to go with us don't urge them.

The U.S. Government says if we let the Mormons go out from this nation they will give us trouble— Well perhaps their fears will come upon them— Where is there a city of refuge, on the face of the earth but this, They have tried to break us up. But with all their officers, all their troops, & all their power we are here yet. They have got writs out for me [Brig-

6. It is not clear if William Clayton is representing Brigham Young's or William Clayton's own voice in this parenthetical admission.

ham Young], but they have not got me yet, and when they do get me they will get some thing else, I assure you.

From [James K.] Polk,[7] down to the nastiest Bogus maker or whiskey seller—it was resolved to break up the Mormons this fall. And if I had hearkened to Col[onel]. Backenstos we should have broken up, and all put out of the way— But when he received correct instruction he acted right, and the plan & trap which our enemies laid for us, worked to [our benefit in] that it gave us the advantage over them, and when he went according to counsel he came off victorious every time,

And we are hunted, and persecuted, & our enemies try to trouble us every way.— And now brethren will it hurt your feelings any if we dance a little. We need a little recreation— My mind is continually upon the stretch, because I know that this church must be saved, The Gospel must be preached to all the world. Temples must be built. and then add to this all minor matters— I tell you no man knows nor can know, the burden & responsibility that rests upon my mind, unless he experiences it.— One thing I will do, I will do my utmost to break down every thing that divides— I will not have divisions & contentions[.]

I mean that there shall not be a fiddle in this church but what has holiness to the Lord upon it—nor a flute; nor a trumpet, nor any other instrument of music—and if they will not make music exclusively for the Lord's house, they shall not play at all.

If Joseph Smith had lived we should not have been here at this time, we should have been in some other country. We can't stay in this house but a little while. We have got to build another house, it will be a larger house than this, and a more glorious one. and we shall build a great many houses, we shall come back here and we shall go to Kirtland [Ohio], and build houses all over the continent of N[orth]. America[.] Last night we had some of our young folks here—some of our children, and they all covenanted that they would no more mingle with the wicked.

After closing his remarks he gave permission for all that wished to retire to do so. Many of the High Council, and High Priests were present, in all as many as forty, some of whom were perhaps at first a little doubtful as

---

7. James K. Polk (1795-1849) was eleventh president of the United States and served from 1845 to 1849. He died of cholera just months after leaving office. Prior to the presidency, he had been a member of the Tennessee House of Representatives (1823-25), U.S. Representative (1825-39), and Speaker of the House (1835-39). He also served as governor of Tennessee from 1839 to 1841.

to the propriety of praising the Lord in this way, but probably their prejudices were dissipated, or removed, when they heard the remarks of Pres[ident]. Young.

—William Clayton, Diary, kept for Heber C. Kimball.

....

At 6- in the morning the men that were appointed to officiate in the several departments were up & seting thing[s] to right for the opperations of the Day — but on acount of the Furniture being taken from the different rooms (such for instance, as Tables and chairs) and [because others had] placed ^them^ in the garden [room] for the purpose of spreading the rich comforts of [a wedding feast] upon [tables arranged for that purpose,] the better to accommodate [the wedding party] — the hapy Participants at the Banquets of refreshments [having since left the temple] — The Bell toll[ed] for mid Day — before the the [sic] first company were washed — However Pres[ident] B[righam]. Young Heber C. Kimble Or[son]. Hyde P[arley]. P. Pratt John Taylor Orson Pratt G[eorge]. A. Smith & A[masa] Lyman are here & officiated in turns all the Day — Bishop G[eorge]. Miller & O[rson] Spencer is here daily almost & has taken an active part in the great work of Endowment, Bishop Whitney & Elder W[illia]m Clayton are engaged at the [illegible] the Store — transacting business for the Temple — Pres[ident] Jos[eph] Young B[enjamin] L Clapp H[enry]. Heriman & J[edediah]. M. Grant are here & have been pretty much all the while[.] Pres[ident] L[evi] Hancock is also here occasionally — Pres[ident]. A[lbert]. P. Rockwood is engaged in Superintending the Milling and wood departments for the advancements of the great cause — at 20 minets to 1. P.M. Elder A[masa]. Lyman Jos[eph]. Young — C[harles]. C Rich A[braham]. O. Smoot F[ranklin]. D. Richards & W[illia]m Crosby — Dressed themselves & consecrated 17 Bottles of oil, it being procured promiscuously from the Seventies — the following Persons were washed by Pres[ident] L[evi]. Hancock G[eorge]. P. Dykes & W[illia]m Snow — & anointed by A[braham]. O. Smoot & W[illia]m Crosby[.]

1 Jefferson Hunt born Jan 22d 1814 H[igh]. P[riest].
2 Tho[ma]s Guyman " Mar 10th 1784
3 Samuel Miles " Sept 30 1788
4 Anson Matthews " Dec 1 1787
5. John Kempton born Sept 1st 1787 H[igh]. P[riest].
6. Amos C. Duell " March 4th 1797

No [of] Elders

1. Osmyn M. Duel " Jan 1st 1809
2. James Lemans " Mar 11th 1815
3. W[illia]m Sears " Aug 4th 1798
4. Alford Sears " " 26th 1821

No [of] Sev[enties].

1. Stephen M. St. John " April 10th 1810 Seventies
2. David P. Rainy " Feb 11 1817
3. John Rowberry " Aug 16th 1823
4 Amos Davis Jr. " May 18 1811
5 W[illia]m McBride " Mar 22 1807
6 John Eldri[d]ge " April 22 1814
7 Samuel Moore " Jun 14 1814

Co[mpany]. No. 2

8. Daniel C Davis " Dec 28th 1808
9. Amos Babcock " Aug 15th "
10. Benj[amin] Magginis " May 3rd 1803
11 Jos[eph] [illegible] Kimble " Oct 23rd 1807
12 Robert W Bidwell " Aug 29 1724

H[igh]. P[riest].

7. Lyman L. Coray " Jan 18th 1809

H[igh]. P[riest].

8. Ebenezer Page " Oct 7 1807
9. W[illia]m Scearce " Aug 15 1779 o[r]d[ained] H[igh]. P[riest]. by H[eber]. C. Kimble & G[eorge]. P. Dykes & E[zra]. T Benson[. The members of Company] No 2 were washed by L[evi] Hancock & W[illia]m Huntington & anointed by Pres[ident] Jos[eph] Young B[enjamin]. L. Clapp & J[edediah]. M. Grant[.]

[See pages 291-92 for excerpted portion.]

At 6 o c[l]ock evening Pres[ident] Jos[eph]. Young B[enjamin]. L. Clapp J[edediah]. M. Grant & A[lbert]. P. Rockwood of the [illegible] & Br[other] J[ohn] Pack of the 8th Sev[enties]. Met in Room No 8. arrayed themselves [in] Priestly attire [and] offered the Signs & then prayed for the deliverance of this People[,] at least until the [illegible] be given — This morning Elder Heber C. Kimble related a dream that he had the Night Previous[:] as he lay down to repose in sleep[,] he asked the Great Elohim to enlighten his mind, with regard to the work of the endowment[.] And [as] he was enwraped in the arms of sleep[,] Behold[,] a large field of corn

[Washings and anointings for Friday, January 2, 1846]

at ½ Past 12 — The washing was carried on in the Female department by Lois Cutler Thurza Cahoon, Olive Farr, Sarah D. Rich Mercy R. Thompson & Lydia Granger commencing at Past 10 in the morning — finished at 5 m. after 11— Namely

Elizabeth Martins born Aug 4th 1787	w.	S. D. R	Anointed	by T. C.
Rosana Freeman " Sep 18 1796		O. F.	"	" O. F.
Mary Duell " Nov 28 1807		T. C.	"	T. C.
Celia Hunt " " 1805		L. C.	"	L. C.
Mary Lyttle " Feb 6th 1813		S. D. R.	"	S. D. R.
Hannah Kempton May 28th 1791		O. F.	"	L. C.
Sally St. John Sept 7 1809		M. R. T.	"	L. C.
Margaret An Rainey Oct 21 1816		S. D. R.	"	O. F.
Margaret Sears Dec 15 1801		" " "	"	L. C.
Eunice S. Morro Mar 2 1807		" " "	"	L. C.
Cynthia A. Eldridge Oct 3 1820		" " "	"	L. C.
Sarah Lyman Nov 20 1789		" " "	"	L. C.
Prudence Miles May 1 1795		O. F.	"	L. C.
Mary Jane Davis Mar 10 1822		S. D. R.	"	" "
Born				
Polly Ann Guyman July 11 1829		S D R		L. C.
Laura H Beebe Oct 3 1814		L. C.		L. C.

finished 5 min past 12.

Sarah Gibbs	June 21 1827
Eliza Gibbs	May 8 1831

Making in all 43. Persons taken through to day.

—Seventies Record, Book B, oversized portion, January 2, 1846.

^that^ was fully ripe was placed before him & he and a number of others were commanded to take Baskets & Pick off the corn with all possible speed! for soon there wood be a storm that would hinder the gathering of the Harvest. The hands [who were] engaged in gathering the Harvest were heedless and unconcerned & did not haste as they were commanded[.] But he and the man that he [was] at first [assigned to work with] had a much larger basket than the rest & [yet they] picked with all their might, of the largest ears of the Field. they once in a while would Pick an ear that had a long tail on each end & but a few grains scatter[ed] in the center of the cobb, and were very light. The interpretation of the Dream was, that the work [was meant to be that] of the endowment[,] the field was the church[,] the corn that was good is the good Saints — the light corn are the light or indiferent Saints — the laborers are those that are apointed to officiate & labor in the Several departments[.] the storm is [the] trouble that is near upon us & requeres an imediat united exertion of all engaged in giving the Endowment to the Saints — or else we will not get through before we will be compeled to flee for our lives — after the Fatigues [?] of the day was past, the Persons that were employed in the work of the Endowment related their feeling[s] by taking a litle recreation — which served to refresh the mind as well as to invigorate the body — in dancing before the Great Eloheim — we have an eye single to his glory & designate[d it] as a tribute of Praise —

—Seventies Record, Book B.

....

This morning Elder [Heber C. Kimball] related a dream that he had the night before[.] as he lay down to repose himself he asked the Lord to enlighten his mind or more properly speaking to give him information relative to the endowment[.] & as he fell asleep lo & behold a large field of corn partly ripe, with labourers [who] were placed into [the field to] gather the corn[.] there was also a large basket given to him & to the one that was appointed to labor with him[.] they commenced to gather the Harvest with all possible speed for there will be a tremendous storm & it is near to hand[.] there fore hasten that the corn may not be lost[.] He [did] as he was commanded and so did the man that was with him but the other men were indifferent & careless & did not seem to care much about hastening as they were commanded[.] The interpretation is as follows the field is the church the grain is the saints & the good corn is the good Saints, in ears that had [been] scattering grain[,] & light cobs are those that are not true & have but little faith or works[.] The storm signifies Trouble that awaits This Place[.] the idlers means thos that are around through the temple laughtering [loitering?] about where they have no business just as you see them here.

—John D. Lee, Diary.

Night went to the Temple and F[ranklin]. D. Richards lent me [his] robes in order to cut the patterns for my holy robes. ... Went home [and] cut my robes.

—Thomas Bullock, Diary.

Sixty-four persons received ordinances.

At 6 p.m., the high council, high priests, and seventies met in their several apartments for prayer.

This morning Elder Heber C. Kimball related the following dream: Last evening, before retiring to bed he asked God to enlighten his mind with regard to the work of endowment; while sleeping he beheld a large field of corn that was fully ripe, he and a number of others were commanded to take baskets and pick off the corn with all possible speed, for there would soon be a storm that would hinder the gathering of the harvest. The hands engaged in gathering the harvest, [but] were heedless and unconcerned and did not haste, as they were commanded; but he and the man he assisted had a much larger basket than the rest, and picked with all their might of the largest ears of the field[.] they once in a while would pick an ear that had a long tail on each end and but a few grains scattering over the center of the cob, which were very light.

The interpretation of the dream is, that the field represented the church, the good corn represented good saints, the light corn represented the light and indifferent saints, the laborers are those appointed to officiate in the Temple, the storm is [the] trouble that is near upon us, and requires an immediate united exertion of all engaged in giving the endowments to the saints, or else we will not get through before we will be obliged to flee for our lives.

Elder Kimball having invited Brothers William Pitt, William Clayton, J[acob]. F. Hutchinson and James Smithies [musicians], they performed several very beautiful pieces of music.

After a short time spent in dancing, Elder Orson Hyde delivered a short address and requested the company present to unite with him in prayer.

I [Brigham Young] addressed the brethren at length, alluding to the privileges we enjoy of the order of administering endowments: that the way to grow and thrive was to serve the Lord in all we did, [and I] exhorted the brethren to remember their covenants and not to speak evil of each other, and related some of the efforts made to arrest me and persecute the saints. If Joseph Smith had been living, we should have already been in some other country, and [instead,] we would go where we would be "the old settlers", and build larger Temples than this.

—"Manuscript History of Brigham Young,"
in *History of the Church,* 7:561-62.

....

Nauvoo temple endowments performed on this date for:

First Company: Amos C. Deuel, John Eldridge, Cynthia Ann Eldridge, William Sears, Margaret Sears, Stephen M. St. John, Sally St. John, Anson Matthews, Elizabeth Matthews, John Kempton, Hannah Kempton, Alfred Sears, Jefferson Hunt, Celia Hunt, Mary Little, Roxana Freeman, Thomas Guyman, Sarah Guyman, Osmyn M. Deuel, Polly Ann Guyman, Mary Deuel, Samuel Moore, Olive Littlefield, Eunice S. Moore, Luana G. Beebee, Samuel Miles Sr., and Prudence Miles.

Second Company: David P. Rainey, Margaret M. Rainey, Harriet Clark, Hannah Maginn, Lyman L. Corey, Elizabeth Corey, William Scearse, John Rowberry, Eliza Rowberry, Benjamin Meginnis, Sarah Meginnis, Elizabeth Blood, Ebenezer Page, Hannah Page, Elizabeth S. Blood, Amos Babcock, Mary Ann Babcock, James Lemmon, Maria Gribble, William McBride, Maria Louisa Lemmon, Daniel Davis, Eliza J. Gibbs, Robert W. Bidwell, Elizabeth H. McBride, James Smithies, Elizabeth Bidwell, Nancy Smithies, Isaiah Whitesides, William. H. Woodbury, Margaret Whitesides, Clarissa Woodbury, Amos Davis Jr., Philip Harmon Buzzard, Mary Jane Davis, Eliza Buzzard, and Sarah Gibbs.

—Summary of information compiled by the Temple
Index Bureau, *Nauvoo Temple Endowment Register:*
10 December 1845 to 8 February 1846.

Saturday, January 3, 1846

This was a clear & beautiful morning, the air comfortably warm. Pres[ident][Brigham] Young having been up late last night did not rise very early— Elder [Heber C.] Kimball was up somewhat earlier.

Uncle John Smith & his wife Clarissa Smith, came in early in the morning—Also Isaac Morley, Barnet Cole, Joseph Rich Jacob Anderson, Benjamin Aber, Joseph A. Keltin[g], & others, they having friends who were passing through the ordinances—whom they were waiting to receive.

At 25 minutes past 8 [we] commenced in the Male department, washing & anointing the following persons, viz;

High Priests.

John M. King	born	Sept[ember] 23. 1809
Ephraim Badger	"	Sept[ember] 17. 1802
John Cooper	"	Sept[ember] 15. 1803
James Cummings	"	Jan[uar]y 26. 1780

Seventies

Edward Tuttle	"	July 1. 1792
Daniel Bailey	"	Sept[ember] 27. 1804
George Alley	"	Dec[ember] 30. 1792
Joseph Stallings	"	Aug[us]t 26. 1783
Thomas Callister	"	July 17. 1821
John L. Smith	"	Nov[embe]r. 17. 1828
John Tidwell	"	Jan[uar]y 14 1807
Eli Chase	"	Nov[embe]r. 9, 1808
Nathan B. Baldwin	"	Jan[uar]y 27. 1812
Hiram W. Mikesell	"	June 13. 1812
Henry B. Jacobs	"	May 5, 1817

15 [men] These were washed by John Lytle and William Crosby—and were anointed by Levi Hancock, John Pack & W[illia]m. Pitt, except James Cummings & Henry B. Jacobs, who were anointed by Levi Hancock, John Lytle & W[illia]m. Pitt.

In the Female department, commencing at 9 o'clock, the following persons were washed and anointed, viz;

Caroline Callister, born June 6. 1820 w[ashed] by M[ercy]. R. Thompson an[ointed] by Lois Cutler[.]

Augusta B. Smith born Dec[embe]r. 7. 1828 w[ashed]. by M[ercy]. R. Thompson an[ointed] by Lois Cutler[.]

Sarah A. Baldwin born July 4. 1819 w[ashed]. by Julia Pack. anointed by Thirza Cahoon[.]

Rhoda Cooper born Oct[ober] 25 1809 washed & anointed by Sarah D. Rich.

Sarah Bailey born Aug[us]t 15. 1806 washed & anointed by Julia Pack[.]

Olive Chase born Aug[us]t 12. 1815 W[ashed]. by Mary Clapp an[ointed] by Diantha Billings[.]

Hannah Aber born Oct[ober] 10. 1827 washed and anointed by Julia Pack.

Mary Ann Scheffalin b[orn]. Oct[ober] 31. 1815 w[ashed]. by Diantha Billings anointed by the same[.]

Margaret Stallings born May 1. 1817 w[ashed]. by Mary Clapp an[ointed]. by Thirza Cahoon.

Abigail Abbott born Sept[ember] 11. 1806 W[ashed]. by M[ercy]. R. Thompson an[ointed] by Lois Cutler.

Harriet Badger born Feb[ruar]y 28. 1804 W[ashed]. by Julia Pack an[ointed]. by Diantha Billings[.]

Almena Randall, born Nov[ember]. 28. 1814 w[ashed]. by Julia Pack an[ointed]. by Sarah D. Rich[.]

Jane Tidwell born June 5 1812 washed by Sarah D. Rich an[ointed]. by Thirza Cahoon[.]

Caroline Conrad born Sept[ember] 10. 1828 W[ashed]. by Julia Pack an[ointed]. by Thirza Cahoon[.]

Susanna Cummings born Mar[ch]. 3. 1792 w[ashed] by Sarah D. Rich an[ointed] by Lois Cutler[.]

Lucinda Allen born June 2. 1824 W[ashed]. by Julia Pack an[ointed] by Lois Cutler[.]

Sally Ann King born March 5. 1814 W[ashed]. by Julia Pack an[ointed]. by Sarah D. Rich[.]

Ann A. Mikesell born March 3. 1819 w[ashed]. by Julia Pack an[ointed] by Lois Cutler[.]

Zina D. Jacobs born Jan[uar]y 31. 1821 w[ashed] by Julia Pack an[ointed]. by Lois Cutler[.]

Mary Alley born Aug[us]t 7 1795 w[ashed]. by Julia Pack an[ointed] by Julia Pack[.]

Catharine B. Tuttle born Aug[us]t 3. 1797 w[ashed]. by Julia Pack an[ointed]. by Sarah D. Rich[.]

Mehitabel Barr born July 8. 1797 washed & anointed by Thirza Cahoon.

22 [women washed and anointed.] Finished at 11. O'clock—

At 10 minutes past 11 o'clock at the ringing of the Bell [we] commenced receiving into the lower and middle departments, company No.

1.— the following persons officiating in the ~~upper~~ ^middle^ department[:] Orson Spencer as No. 1. C[harles]. C. Rich as No. 2. George P. Dykes as No. 3. J[ohn]. D. Lee No. 4 / F[ranklin]. D. Richards as No. 5. ~~and in the middle department.~~ and in the upper department Joseph Young, as No. 1. J[edediah]. M. Grant No. 2 and Benjamin L. Clapp as No. 3.

At 8 minutes to 12 [we] commenced receiving into the upper department, those who have been washed & anointed this morning, constituting Company No. 1. in the following order viz;

John Cooper	by Orson Hyde[.]
Rhoda Cooper	by John Cooper & O[rson]. H[yde].
John M. King	by O[rson]. Hyde[.]
Sally Ann King	" " " & J[ohn]. M. King[.]
Joseph Stallings	" " " & [blank]
Margaret Stallings	" " " & J[oseph]. Stallings[.]
Mary Ann Schaffelin	" "
Hiram W. Mikesell	" "
Ann A. Mikesell	" " & H[iram]. W. M[ikesell].
Henry B. Jacobs	" " "
Zinah D. Jacobs	" " " & H[enry]. B. Jacobs[.]
Mehitabel Barr	" " "
James Cummings	" " "
Susanna Cummings	" " " & J[ames]. Cummings[.]
Abigail Abbott	" " "
Ephraim Badger	" " "
Harriet Badger	" " " & E[phraim]. Badger[.]
Daniel Bailey	" " "
Caroline Conrad	" " "
Sarah Bailey	" " " & John Taylor[.]
Nathan P. Baldwin	" " "
Lucinda Allen	" Joseph Young[.]
Sarah Ann Baldwin	" J[ohn]. Taylor & N[athan]. P. B[aldwin].
Eli Chase	" " "
Olive Chase	" Eli Chase & J[ohn]. Taylor[.]
Almena Randall	" John Taylor[.]
George Alley	" " "
Mary Alley	" George Alley & J[ohn]. Taylor[.]
Edward Tuttle	" John Taylor[.]

Caroline B. Tuttle	"	E[dward]. Tuttle &. [blank]
John Tidwell	by	John Taylor[.]
Jane Tidwell	"	John Tidwell & J[ohn]. Taylor[.]
Thomas Callister	"	John Taylor[.]
Caroline Callister	"	Th[omas]. Callister —
John L. Smith	"	John Taylor[.]
Augusta B. Smith	by	John L. Smith & J[ohn]. T[aylor].
Hannah Aber	by	Benjamin Aber & J[ohn]. Taylor[.]

Finished at 10 m[inutes]. past 2. Prompters, Lorenzo Snow, Catharine C. Spencer[.]

At 15 minutes to 12 [we] commenced in the male department, washing & anointing the following persons, viz;

High Priest.

Gideon Brownell	born	May 5, 1790
Albert G. Fellows	"	Sept[ember] 5 1799
John A. Bouck	"	Jan[uar]y 6. 1797.

Seventies.

Charles W. Wandell	born	Ap[ri]l. 12. 1819
Benj[amin]. F. Cutler	"	April 13. 1823
Moses Thurston	"	Sept[ember]. 13. 1819
Buckley B. Anderson	"	Jan[uar]y 14. 1819
Alvin Horr	"	Sept[ember] 5. 1799
Charles Bird	"	Sept[ember] 19. 1803
Chester Loveland	"	Dec[ember]. 30. 1817
William ^A^. Empy	"	July 4 1808
Andrew Moore	"	Dec[ember] 25 1792
Readin A. Allred	"	Feb[ruar]y 21. 1822
William M. Allred	"	Dec[ember]. 24, 1819
Johnson F. Lane	"	Feb[ruar]y 22 1803
John Faussett	"	Dec[embe]r. 22 1804

[W]ashed by William Crosby, John Lytle, and Ezra T. Benson, anointed by Levi W. Hancock. John Pack & W[illia]m. Pitt.

16 [men.] Finished at 25 m[inutes]. to 1.

Albert G. Fellows was ordained a High Priest, under the hands of President George Miller, before being washed & anointed[.]

In the Female department, commencing at half after 12, the following persons were washed and anointed—viz;

Euphemia Bouck born Oct[ober] 20. 1799 w[ashed]. by Lydia Granger an[ointed]. by Elizabeth A[nn]. Whitney[.]

Mary Ann Empy born Dec[ember]. 3. 1808 w[ashed]. by Lydia Granger an[ointed]. by Vilate Kimball[.]

Olive M. Bishop born Mar[ch]. 17. 1807 w[ashed]. by E[lizabeth]. A[nn]. Whitney an[ointed]. by E[lizabeth]. A[nn]. Whitney[.]

Elizabeth A. Pond born May 2. 1827 w[ashed] by E[lizabeth]. A[nn]. Whitney an[ointed]. by E[lizabeth]. A[nn]. Whitney[.]

Emeline B. Harris born Feb[ruar]y 29. 1828 w[ashed]. by Vilate Kimball an[ointed]. by Elizabeth Ann Whitney[.]

Eunice Billings born Jan[uar]y 3. 1830 w[ashed]. by Diantha Billings an[ointed] by E[lizabeth]. A[nn]. Whitney[.]

Ellen Sanders, born March 3. 1825 Washed and anointed by Vilate Kimball[.]

Harriet Sanders born Jan[uar]y 25. 1824 washed and anointed by Vilate Kimball[.]

Sabra Gribble born Febr[uar]y 17. 1794 w[ashed]. by Lydia Granger an[ointed] by E[lizabeth]. A[nn]. Whitney[.]

Eliza A. Gibbs born May 30. 1825 W[ashed]. by Lydia Granger anointed by Vilate Kimball[.]

Margaret Cutler, born Sept[ember] 26 1827 W[ashed]. by E[lizabeth]. A[nn]. Whitney an[ointed] by Lois Cutler[.]

Sarah Horr, born Oct[ober] 16. 1809 W[ashed]. by Julia Pack an[ointed] by Lois Cutler[.]

Mary Ann Greenalgh born Oct[ober] 1. 1807 Washed and anointed by Mercy R. Thompson[.]

Mary Ann Bird, born Dec[embe]r. 7. 1806 w[ashed]. by Julia Pack anointed by Julia Granger[.]

Fanny Loveland born May 11. 1815 W[ashed]. by Julia Pack an[ointed]. by Lois Cutler[.]

Mary B. Wandell born July 21. 1811 W[ashed]. by M[ercy]. R. Thompson an[ointed]. by Vilate Kimball[.]

Sally S. Carter born Sept[ember] 1. 1826 W[ashed]. by Lydia Granger an[ointed] by Lois Cutler[.]

Orissa A. Allred born Aug[ust] 17. 1823 W[ashed]. by Julia Pack an[ointed] by Julia Pack[.]

Julia ^A.^ Allred born Feb[ruar]y 7. 1828 W[ashed]. by Julia Pack an[ointed] by Julia Pack[.]

Margaret Fossett born May 18. 1796 W[ashed]. by Julia Pack

an[ointed] by Lois Cutler[.]

Mary Leech born Sept[ember] 1787 W[ashed]. by Mercy R. Thompson an[ointed]. by Vilate Kimball[.]

Almira Covey born April 28. 1826 Washed and anointed by Mercy R. Thompson[.]

Temperance Mack born Sept[ember] 8. 1771 washed and anointed by Vilate Kimball[.]

Phebe Leavitt born July 6. 1794 washed by Julia Pack an[ointed]. by Lois Cutler[.]

Rebecca Moore born June 7, 1797 W[ashed]. by Lydia Granger an[ointed]. by Lois Cutler[.]

Sally M. Anderson born Sept[ember] 3. 1818 W[ashed]. by Lydia Granger an[ointed] by Lois Cutler[.]

Hannah B. Merriam [born] Mar[ch]. 19 1811 W[ashed]. by Julia Pack an[ointed] by Lois Cutler[.]

Matilda Lane born April 8. 1811 w[ashed] by M[ercy]. R. Thompson an[ointed]. by Lois Cutler[.]

Mary Sturdevant born Jan[uar]y 2. 1781 W[ashed]. by Julia Pack an[ointed] by Julia Pack[.]

Henrietta Rich born Aug[us]t 2. 1823 W[ashed]. and anointed by Sarah D. Rich[.]

Elizabeth Brownell born Oct[ober] 16. 1789 w[ashed]. by M[ercy]. R. Thompson an[ointed] by Lois Cutler[.]

[Finished at] 20 m[inutes]. to 3.

[A]t 5 minutes past 2, at the ringing of the bell, [we] commenced receiving into the lower and middle departments Company No. 2. the following persons officiating in the upper department, viz; Orson Spencer as No. 1. J[edediah]. M. Grant as No. 2 — B[enjamin]. L. Clapp as No. 3.

in the middle department

Orson Pratt	as	No.	1
George P. Dyke	"	"	2
P[arley]. P. Pratt	"	"	3
John D. Lee	"	"	4
F[ranklin]. D. Richards		"	5.

At 15 minutes past 3, [we] commenced receiving into the upper department, Company No. 2. in the following order

John A. Bouck	by N[ewel]. K. Whitney[.]				
Euphemia Bouck	"	"	"	" & John A. Bouck[.]	

William A. Empy	"	"	"	"
Mary Ann Empy	"	"	"	" & W[illiam]. A. Empy[.]
Olive M. Bishop	"	"	"	"
Elizabeth A. Pond	"	"	"	"
Emeline B. Harris	"	"	"	"
Albert G. Fellows	"	"	"	"
Eunice Billings	"	"	"	"
Moses Thurston		"	"	"
Helen Sanders	"	H[eber]. C. Kimball[.]		
Charles W. Wandell	"	"	"	"
Mary B. Wandell	"	C[harles]. W. W[addell]. & H[eber]. C. K[imball].		
Harriet Sanders	"	H[eber]. C. Kimball[.]		
Sabra Gribble	"	"	"	"
Mary Leech	"	"	"	"
Temperance Mack	"	"	"	"
Buckley B. Anderson	by	H[eber]. C. Kimball[.]		
Sally Maria Anderson	by	B[uckley]. B. Anderson & H[eber]. C. K[imball.		
Hannah B. Merriam	"	Isaac Morley[.]		
Eliza A. Gibbs	"	H[eber]. C. Kimball[.]		
Andrew Moore	"	"	"	"
Rebecca Moore	"	"	"	"
William M. Allred	"	Orson Hyde[.]		
Orissa A. Allred	"	W[illiam]. M. Allred & O[rson]. H[yde].		
R[eddin]. A. Allred	"	O[rson]. Hyde[.]		
Julia A. Allred	"	R[eddin]. A. Allred & O[rson]. H[yde].		
Benj[amin]. F. Cutler	"	O[rson]. Hyde[.]		
Margaret Cutler	"	B[enjamin]. F. Cutler & O[rson]. H[yde].		

Finished at 5 m[inutes]. to 5. Lorenzo Snow and Catharine C. Spencer officiating as prompters also. Sisters [Vilate] Kimball, [Elizabeth Ann] Whitney, A[rtemisia]. Snow.

At 25 minutes to 3 [we] commence[d] in the male department washing and anointing the following persons—

High Priests.

Stephen Sturdevant	b[orn].	May 25. 1771
John C. Annis	b[orn].	Nov[ember]. 17. 1784
Ezra Bickford	b[orn].	May 19. 1806
Samuel Snyder	b[orn].	Feb[ruary]. 14 1808
Elijah Cheeney	b[orn].	[blank]
Seventies		
Urban V. Stewart	b[orn].	Nov[ember]. 9. 1817
Ara W. Sabin	b[orn].	Aug[us]t 4. 1822
Moses M. Sanders	b[orn].	Aug[ust]. 17. 1803
Joseph Hutchinson	b[orn].	Jan[uar]y 21, 1813
Thomas Rich	b[orn].	Nov[ember]. 29. 1817
Seeley Owen	b[orn].	March 20. 1805
Lemuel Lewis	born	March 19. 1801
John Miller	"	Aug[us]t 15 1801
Chauncey W. West	"	Feb[ruar]y 6. 1826
Cyrus H. Wheelock	"	Feb[ruar]y 28. 1813
Joseph H. Swimely	born	[blank]
Fred H. Moeser	"	[blank]

Washed by John Lytle & W[illia]m. Crosby anointed by Levi W. Hancock, John Pack, & William Pitt—except Samuel Snyder who was anointed by Franklin D. Richards and William Crosby.

In the Female department, the following persons were washed and anointed—commencing at 25 minutes past 4, viz

Abigail Bickford. born Aug[us]t 29. 1802 washed and anointed by Lydia Granger[.]

Lydia G. Stewart b[orn]. Dec[ember]. 25. 1822 w[ashed]. by Sarah D. Rich, an[ointed] by Lois Cutler.

Olive M. Lewis b[orn]. April 29. 1809 W[ashed]. by Julia Pack an[ointed]. by Julia Pack[.]

Cordelia C. Morley [born] Nov[ember]. 28. 1823 w[ashed]. by Sarah D. Rich an[ointed]. by Lydia Granger[.]

Amanda A. Sanders b[orn]. May 6. 1810 w[ashed]. by Sarah D. Rich an[ointed]. by Lois Cutler[.]

Mary Hutchinson b[orn]. Aug[us]t 3. 1813 w[ashed]. by Sarah D. Rich an[ointed]. by Julia Pack[.]

Lydia A. Owen born July 1. 1811 w[ashed]. by Sarah D. Rich an[ointed]. by Lois Cutler[.]

Magdalene Moeser b[orn]. Nov[ember]. 11. 1807 w[ashed]. by Sarah D. Rich an[ointed]. by Julia Pack[.]

Hannah Annis b[orn]. Sept[ember] 19 1786 w[ashed]. by Lydia Granger an[ointed]. by Lois Cutler[.]

Hannah Annis born Dec[ember]. 7. 1824 w[ashed]. by Lydia Granger an[ointed]. by Lois Cutler[.]

Lovisa Snider born May 22, 1789 w[ashed]. by Jane Richards, an[ointed]. by Sarah D. Rich[.]

Henrietta M. Snider b[orn]. Sept[ember] 4, 1809 w[ashed]. by Jane Richards an[ointed]. by Sarah D. Rich[.]

Lucinda Miller [born] Feb[ruar]y 18. 1807 w[ashed]. by Lydia Granger an[ointed]. by Lois Cutler[.]

Sarah D. Cheney born July 20. 1829 washed & anointed by Julia Pack[.]

Ended at 15 minutes past 5.

At 15 minutes to 4, at the ringing of the Bell[, we] commenced receiving into the lower and middle department Company No. 3. the following persons officiating, in the upper department, viz;

Joseph Young	as	No.	1. }
J[edediah]. M. Grant	"	"	2. }
Levi W. Hancock	"	"	3. }

and in the middle department

Orson Spenceras		No.	1
Charles C. Rich	"	"	2
Ezra T. Benson	"	"	3
John D. Lee as	"	"	4
Franklin D. Richards	"		5.

At 5 o'clock, Pres[ident]. [Brigham] Young came out of his room into the Large Hall. He has been quite out of health today suffering from chills & fever & and pain in his bones &c.

At 15 minutes past 5, [we] commenced receiving into the upper department, company No. 3—in the following order, viz

Almina Covey,	by	Benj[amin]. Covey & O[rson]. Hyde[.]		
Thomas Rich	"	O[rson]. Hyde[.]		
Henrietta Rich	"	Th[omas]. Rich & O[rson]. Hyde[.]		
Sally Carter	by		"	"
Elijah Cheney	"		"	"
~~Sarah D. Cheney~~	~~"~~	~~E. Cheney &~~	~~"~~	~~"~~
Phebe Leavitt	"	B[enjamin]. Covey &	"	"
Mary Ann Greenalgh	"		"	"

Charles Bird " " "
Mary Ann Bird by C[harles]. Bird" " "
Chester Loveland by O[rson]. Hyde[.]
Fanny Loveland " Ch[ester]. Loveland & O[rson]. H[yde].
Gideon Brownell by O[rson]. Hyde[.]
Elizabeth Brownell by G[ideon]. Brownell & O[rson]. H[yde].
John Faussett " " "
Margaret Faussett " J[ohn]. Faussett & O[rson]. Hyde[.]
Alvin Horr by O[rson]. Hyde[.]
Sarah D. Horr by A[lvin]. Horr & O[rson]. Hyde[.]
Johnson F. Lane " O[rson]. Hyde[.]
Matilda Lane by J[ohnson]. F. Lane & O[rson]. H[yde].
Chauncey W. West by O[rson]. Hyde[.]
Cyrus H. Wheelock " " "
Ara W. Sabin " " "
Joseph H. Swimely " " "

[E]nded at half past 6, o'clock[.] Lorenzo Snow, & C[atherine]. C. Spencer officiated as prompters[.]

At 6 o'clock, [we] commenced receiving into the lower & middle departments, Company No. 4.[,] the following persons officiating in the upper department, viz;

P[arley]. P. Pratt as No. 1
Joseph Young " 2
Erastus Snow " 3.

in the middle department as follows,

Orson Pratt as No. 1
J[edediah]. M. Grant " " 2
A[lbert]. P. Rockwood " " 3
John D. Lee as " 4
F[ranklin]. D. Richards " " 5

At 20 minutes past 7 [we] commenced receiving into the upper department, company No. 4, in the following order

Cordelia C. Morley by P[arley]. P. Pratt[.]
Ezra Bickford by P[arley]. P. Pratt[.]
Abigail Bickford " E[zra]. Bickford & P[arley]. P. P[ratt].

Seeley Owen	"	P[arley]. P. Pratt[.]
Lydia Owen	"	S[eeley]. Owen & P[arley]. P. P[ratt].
Urban V. Stewart	by	P[arley]. P. Pratt[.]
Lydia G. Stewart		[blank]
Samuel Snyder	by	P[arley]. P. P[ratt].
Lovisa Snyder	by	S[amuel]. Snyder & P[arley]. P. P[ratt].
Henrietta M. Snyder	by	S[amuel]. Snyder & P[arley]. P. P[ratt].
Moses M. Sanders	by	P[arley]. P. P[ratt].
Amanda Sanders	by	M[oses]. M. S[anders]. & P[arley]. P. P[ratt].
Joseph Hutchinson	by	P[arley]. P. P[ratt].
Mary Hutchinson	by	J[oseph]. Hutchinson & P[arley]. P. P[ratt].
Fred[eric]k. H. Moeser	"	P[arley]. P. Pratt[.]
Magdalena Moeser	"	P[arley]. P. P[ratt]. & F[rederick]. H. M[oeser].
John Miller	by	P[arley]. P. Pratt[.]
Lucinda Miller	"	J[ohn]. Miller & P[arley]. P. P[ratt].
John C. Annis	by	P[arley]. P. Pratt[.]
Hannah Annis	"	" " " & J[ohn]. C. Annis[.]
Stephen Sturdevant	by	P[arley]. P. Pratt[.]
Mary Sturdevant	"	S[tephen]. S[turdevant]. & P[arley]. P. P[ratt].
Lemuel Lewis	"	P[arley]. P. Pratt[.]
Olive M. Lewis	"	L[emuel]. Lewis & P[arley]. P. Pratt[.]
Hannah Annis	"	P[arley]. P. Pratt.
S[arah]. Delina Cheeney	"	P[arley]. P. Pratt.

Finished at 9 o'clock[.]

The following High Priests met for prayer about 5 o'clock— viz; Daniel Spencer L[ucius]. N. Scovil, Simeon Carter, W[illia]m. Felshaw — Samuel Rolfe — Stephen Winchester Abel Lamb — Elizur G. Terrill — Joshua S. Holman — Job V. Barnum Albert Carrington, Elijah Fordham and Isaac Higbee, who was mouth[.]

After the above had finished their business they retired, and another meeting was held in the same room, No. 8. by the following persons—viz; Abraham O. Smoot, Elam Ludington, Samuel Gully — Hiram Spencer — Luman H. Calkins, Phineas Richards — Charles Allen — and Joseph L. Heywood — A[braham]. O. Smoot was mouth—

In Room No. 10 the following persons met for prayer—viz; William Snow — Benj[amin] Brown — D[avid]. H. Redfield — Addison Everett Edw[ar]d. Hunter — Hezekiah Peck — Ormus E. Bates—

—William Clayton, Diary, kept for Heber C. Kimball.

....

This morning the weather is mild & pleasant — the weather [illegible] day — it has been for several days past. The 1st co[mpany] commenced reciving their endowments at 25 M[inutes]. Past 8, morning[,] washed by John Lytle & W[illia]m Crosby and anointed by Pres[ident] Levi Hancock John Pack & W[illia]m Pitt

[Marginal notation: "No. of the day"]

1st Edward Tuttle born July 1st 1892 [1792] Seventy
2 David Bailey " Sept[ember] 29th 1804 "
3 George Alley " Dec[ember] 30 1792 "
4 Jos[eph] Stalling " Aug[ust] 26 1813 "
5. Tho[ma]s Callister " July 17 1821 "
6 John C. L. Smith " Nov[ember] 17 1828 "
7 John Tidwell " Jan[uary] 14 1807 "
8 Eli Chase " Nov[ember] 9 1808 "
9. Nathan B. Baldwin " Jan[uary] 27- 1812 "
10 Hyrum McMikeseler " " 13 " "

[Marginal notation: "H. P."]

1 John Cooper " Sep[tember] 15 1803 H[igh]. P[riest].
2 Ephraim Badger " " 17th 1802 "
3 John Mc King " Sept[ember] 23 1809 "
4 James Cumming " July 26th 1780 "

[Marginal notation: "Sev[enty]"]

11 Henry B. Jacobs " May 6th 1819 Seventy

(Co[mpany]. No. 2)

Cha[rle]s W. Wandall " April 12 1819 Sev[enty]. Pres[ident]
Benj[amin] F. Cutler " " 13 1823 "
Moses Thurston " Sep[tember] 13 1817 "
Buckly B. Anderson " Jun[e] 12 1819 "
Alvin Horr " Sept[ember] 5th 1799 " Pres[ident]

Cha[rle]s Bird " " 19. 1803 " Pres[ident]
Chester Loveland " Dec[ember] 30 1817 "
W[illia]m. Empy " July 4 1808 " Pres[ident]
Andrew Moore " Dec[ember] 25 1792 " Pres[ident]
Redding A Allred " Feb[ruary] 21 1822 "
W[illia]m M Allred " Dec[ember] 24 1819 "
Johnson F Lane " Feb[ruary] 22nd 1803 "

[Marginal notation: "H. P."]

5. Gideon Brewnell " May 5 1790 H[igh]. P[riest].
6 Albert G Fellows " Sep[tember] 5 1799 "
7 John A Burk " Jun[e] 6 1797 "
John Fawcitt " Dec[ember] 22 1844 Sev[enty]

The above persons were washed by John Lyttle E[zra]. T. Benson & W[illia]m Crosby. & anointed by Pres[ident] L[evi] Hancock John Pack & W[illia]m Pitt —

Co[mpany] No. 1. in the Female department 9. O.clock — [illegible]

[See pages 309-12 for excerpted portion.]

1	Urban V. Stewart born	Nov[ember] 9 1817	Seventy
2	Aron W Sabin	Aug[ust] 4 1822	"
3	Moses M Sanders	Aug[us]t 17 1803	Pres[ident]
4	Joseph Hutchinson	Jan[uary[26, 1813	"
5	Thomas Rich	Nov[embe]r 29 1817	"
6	Luby Owen	Mar[ch] 20 1805	"
7	Lemuel Lewis	Mar[ch] 19 1801	"
8	John Miller	Aug[ust] 15 1801	"
9	Chauncy W West	Feb[ruar]y 6 1814	"
10	Cyrus H Wheelock	Feb[ruar]y 28 1813	"
1	Stephen Sturdevant	May 25 1771	H[igh]. Priest
2	John C. Annis	Nov[embe]r 17 1784	"
3	Esra Bickford	May 19 1806	"
4	Samuel Snider	Feb[ruar]y 14 1808	"

Saturday January 3rd 1846 Co[mpany] No 3 — 25 M[inutes] to 3 P.M.

The above named persons were washed by John Lytle, William Crosby, and Anointed by Levi Hancock, John Pack & William Pitt, and Samuel Snider was washed by John Lytle & William Crosby Anointed by Franklin D. Richards and William Crosby.

The above statement that John Lytle assisted to wash Samuel Snyder was a mistake as Franklin D. Richards assisted W[illia]m Crosby to wash him & anoint him.

[Washings and anointings for Saturday, January 3, 1846]

	by whom washed	by whom anointed
Caroline Callister born June 6 1820	M. R. T	
Augusta B. Smith " Decr 7 1828	M. R. T.	L. C.
Sarah A. Baldwin " July 4 1819	J. P.	T. C.
Rhoda Cooper " Decr 25th 1809	S. D. R	S. D. R.
Olive Chase " Aug 12 1813	M. C.	D. B.
Hanah Haber " Oct 10 1827	J. P.	J. P.
Mary Ann Chaffin " Oct 31 1815	D. B.	D. B.
Margaret Stallings " May 1 1817	M. C.	T. C.
Abigail Abbot " Sept 11 1806	M. R. T.	L. C.
Harriet Badger " Feb 28 1804	J. P	D. B.
Almira Randall " Nov 28 1814	J. P.	S. D. R.
Jane Tidwell " Jun 5 1812	S. D. R.	T. C.
Caroline Conrad " Sep 10 1828	J. P.	T. C.
Susannah Cummings " Mar 3 1792	S. D. R.	L. C.
Lucinda Allen " Jun 2 1824	J. P.	L. C.
Sally Ann King " Mar 5 1814	J. P.	S. D. R.
Ann A Mikesell " Mar 3 1819	J. P.	L. C.
Mary Alley " Augt 7 1795	J. P.	J. P.

Co No 2. in the Female Department commenced washing at ½ Past 12 & were washed by & anointed by Vilate Kimble Elizabeth A Whitney Diantha Billings Lydia Granger Julia Pack Mercy R Thompson- & Louis Cutler —

	washed	Anointed
1st Ellen Sanders born May 3d 1825	Vilate Kimball	Vilate Kimball
Harriett Sanders " Jan 25 1824	" "	" "
Eunice Billings " " 3d 1830	D. B.	E. A. W.
Olive M. Bishop " Mar 17 1807	E. A. W.	" " "
Elizabeth A. Pond " May 2nd 1827	" " "	" " "
Emoline S Harris " Feb 29 1828	V. K.	" " "
Sabra Grible " " 17 1794	L. C.	" " "
Eliza A. Gibbs " May 20th 1825	" "	V. K.
Margaret Cutler " Sept 26th 1829	E. A. W.	L. C.
Sarah Horr " Oct. 16 1809	J. P.	" "
Margaret Greendal " " 1st 1807	M. R. T.	M. R. T.
Eupheurna Bouck " Oct 20 1799	L. G.	E. A. W.
Mary A. Bird " Dec 7 1806	J. P.	J. P.
Fanny Loveland " May 11 1815	" "	" "
Mary B. Wandall " July 21 1811	M. R. T.	V. K.
Sally S. Carter " Sept 15 1826	L. G.	L. C.
Orisa C. Allred born Aug 17 1823	J. P.	J. P.
Julia A. Allred " Feb 1 1828	"	"
Margaret Fawcett " May 18 1796	"	L. C.

Mary Leech " Sep - 1787	"	V. K.
Almira Corray " April 18 1806	"	M. R. T.
Temperence Mack " Sep 5 1771	V. K.	V. K.
Phebe Leavitt " July 6 1824	J. P.	J. P.
Rebecca Moon " June 7 1797	L. G.	L. C.
Mary Ann Empy " Decr 3 1808	L. G.	V. K.
Sally M Anderson " Sept 3 1808	L. G.	L. C.
Hannah B Muriem " May 19 1811	J. P.	L. C.
Matilda Luni " Aprl 8 1811	M. R. T.	L. C.
Mary Sturdavant " Jun 21 1781	J. P.	J. P.
Henrietta Rich " Augt 2 1823	S. D. R.	S. D. R.
Elizabeth Brownell " Oct 11, 1789	M. R. T.	L. C.
Company No 2 in the Temple department at 25 past O clock A.M		
Catharine B Tuttle " Augt 3 1797	J. P.	S. D. R.
Mahitable Barr " July 8 1797	T. C.	T. C.
Abigail Bickford " Augt 29 1802	L. G.	L. G.
Lydia G Steward " Dec 25 1822	S. D. R.	L. C.
Olive M Lewis " April 29 1809	J. P.	J. P.
Cordelia C Morley " Novr 28 1823	S. D. R.	L. C.
Amanda A Sanders " May 1, 1810	S. D. R.	L. C.
Mary Hutchason " Aug 3 1813	S. D. R.	J. P.
Lydia A Oven " July 1 1811	S. D. R.	L. C.
Magdelina Moeser " Nov 11 1807	S. D. R.	J. P.

	[washed]	[anointed]
Hannah Annis " Dec 7 1824	L. G.	L. C.
Louisa Snider " May 22 1789	J. P.	S. D. R.
Hinnitta M Snider " Sept 4 1809	J. P.	S. D. R.
Lucinda Miller " Feby 18 1807	L. G.	L. C.
Sarah D Chenny " Feby 20 1827	J. P.	J. P.

—Seventies Record, Book B, oversized portion, January 3, 1846.

A[t] 7 o'clock the following of the first presidency of the Seventies met in room No 9 clothed [in priesthood robes] and offered up the signs and prayers viz: Jos[ep]h Young, Henry Herriman, Benj[amin]. L. Clapp, A[lbert]. P. Rockwood, J[edediah]. M. Grant, [and] Pres[iden]t. Young mouth after making out a list of names for Monday they retired to their respective homes at 9 o clock. Pres[iden]t. Brigham Young has had a chill & fever today and is quite ill [and] unable to attend to business much.

There has been 114 persons washed anointed and received through the vail this day.

The council of 12 [apostles] returned to their homes at 9½ o clock except Pres[iden]t B[righam]. Young being unwell[.] J[ohn]. D. Lee s[t]aid for his assistance. Several others s[p]ent the Night in the Temple Namely F. D. Richards John Lytle John L. Butler, Lewis Robbins W[illia]m Stringham Hans C Hanson & E[rastus]. Snow. Sisters that Staid to wash the garments for Monday were E[liza]. R. Snow Mercy R. Thompson Sop[h]ronia Harmon Huldah Barns & Lydia Granger —

—Seventies Record, Book B.

....

I [John D. Lee] passed the day of [Saturday, January 3,] in my former service in the Temple[.] Saturday evening Pres[ident] B[righam] Young was taken quite unwell had a chill & Fever[.] he requested we tarry with him the night Peradventure I might afford him some assistance which I cordially did & slept but little [through] the night[.]

—John D. Lee, Diary.

....

One hundred and fourteen persons received their ordinances.

At 5 p.m., several companies of high priests met for prayer.

At 7, the seventies met for prayer.

I [Brigham Young] had a chill today, accompanied by fever, and felt unable to attend to business. I remained in the Temple all night.

—"Manuscript History of Brigham Young,"
in *History of the Church,* 7:562.

....

Nauvoo temple endowments performed on this date for:

First Company: John Cooper, Rhoda Cooper, John M. King, Sally Ann King, Joseph Stallings, Margaret Stallings, Mary Schuffalin, Hiram W. Mikesell, Ann A. Mikesell, Henry B. Jacobs, Zinah D. Jacobs, Mehitabel Barr, James Cummings, Susanna Cummings, Abigail Abbott, Ephraim

Badger, Harriet Badger, Daniel Bailey, Caroline Conrad, Sarah Bailey, Nathan P. Baldwin, Lucinda Allen, Sarah Ann Baldwin, Eli Chase, Olive Chase, Almena Randall, George Alley, Mary Alley, Edward Tuttle, Catharine B. Tuttle, John Tidwell, Jane Tidwell, Thomas Callister, Caroline Callister, John L. Smith, Augusta B. Smith, and Hannah Aber.

Second Company: John A. Bouck, Euphemia Bouck, William A. Empy, Mary Ann Empy, Olive M. Bishop, Elisabeth A. Pond, Emeline B. Harris, Albert G. Fellows, Eunice Billings, Moses Thurston, Helen Sanders, Charles W. Wandell, Mary B. Wandell, Harriet Sanders, Sabra Gribble, Mary Leech, Temperance Mack, Buckley B. Anderson, Sally Maria Anderson, Hannah B. Merriam, Eliza A. Gibbs, Andrew Moore, Rebecca Moore, William M. Allred, Orissa A. Allred, R. A. Allred, Julia A. Allred, Benj[amin] F. Cutler, and Margaret Cutler.

Third Company: Almira Covey, Thomas Rich, Henrietta Rich, Sally Carter, Elijah Cheney, Phebe Leavitt, Mary Ann Greenalgh, Charles Bird, Mary Ann Bird, Chester Loveland, Fanny Loveland, Gideon Brownell, Elisabeth Brownell, John Faussett, Margaret Faussett, Alvin Horr, Sarah D. Horr, Johnson F. Lane, Matilda Lane, Chauncey W. West, Cyrus H. Wheelock, Ara W. Sabin, and Joseph H. Swimely.

Fourth Company: Cordelia C. Morley, Ezra Bickford, Abigail Bickford, Seeley Owen, Lydia Owen, Urban V. Stewart, Lydia G. Stewart, Samuel Snyder, Lovisa Snyder, Henrietta M. Snyder, Moses M. Sanders, Amanda Sanders, Joseph Hutchinson, Mary Hutchinson, Frederick H. Moeser, Magdalena Moeser, John Miller, Lucinda Miller, John C. Annis, Hannah Annis, Stephen Sturdevant, Mary Sturdevant, Lemuel Lewis, Olive M. Lewis, Hannah Annis, and Delina S. Cheney.

—Summary of information compiled by the Temple Index Bureau, *Nauvoo Temple Endowment Register: 10 December 1845 to 8 February 1846.*

Sunday, January 4, 1846

No public meeting was held in the Temple this day, on account of the floor being not stiff enough to support so large a company as would have come in, without swaying too much—

There was a council in Pres[ident]. [Brigham] Young's room No. 1 at which the following persons were present, in the morning, viz. Pres[ident]. Brigham Young — Elders H[eber]. C. Kimball, Orson Hyde, P[arley]. P. Pratt, & Bishops N[ewel]. K. Whitney, & George Miller.

Sisters Mary Ann Young, Vilate Kimball, Elizabeth Ann Whitney — Eliza R. Snow — Mary Smith, Mercy R. Thompson & Sarah Ann Kingsbury—were employed most of the day in working at the cushions for the new altar.

In the afternoon, at 20 minutes past two, at a council held in Pres[ident]. B[righam]. Young's room[,] at which the following persons were present, viz; Pres[ident]. B[righam]. Young, H[eber]. C. Kimball — Orson Hyde — P[arley]. P. Pratt, and Joseph Young, it was decided that David Candland be sent to England to preach the gospel,— Bro[ther]. Candland was present at the council, and of course was officially notified.

A letter was received this day, from Samuel Brannan in New York— also one from Pittsburg, signed W[illia]m. W. Salt, both of which were answered—the one to Brannan under the signature of Brigham Young— the other was signed Willard W. Pepper—. by David Mustard Clerk— both written by Elder Hyde—

A copy of the New York Sun of Dec[embe]r. 19. 1845, containing a letter from James Arlington Bennett to the Editor, in which he refers to a letter bearing the signature of Emma Smith, published in that paper on the 9th of Dec[ember]. was also received by Pres[ident]. Young.

Bennett's letter to the Editor contained some things which were considered as evidence that he was also the author of the letter signed Emma Smith— at least that idea was advanced by L[ucian]. R. Foster, and was generally concurred in by those present. and was referred to in Pres[ident]. Young's letter to Brannon.

The different quorums met in their respective rooms for prayer, at the usual time, viz; The High Council & the High Priests—

In the High Council, were present, Charles C. Rich, Newel Knight, Ezra T. Benson — Samuel Bent — Thomas Grover Alpheus Cutler — George W. Harris — W[illia]m. Huntington — James Allred — David Fullmer Henry G. Sherwood — Aaron Johnson & Lewis D. Wilson— Also the following High Priests, — Freeman Nickerson, Erastus Snow. & Jacob Anderson. Prayer for President Young—and his council, that all necessary blessings might rest upon them—for the sick—for means for our removal—for scattered Israel—for our reception by them—and for the general prosperity and welfare of Zion.

The following named High Priests met in No. 8. Isaac Chase — Zebedee Coultrin — Hezekiah Peck — Samuel Williams, Jesse Baker — Gustavus Hills — James S. Holman — Ormus E. Bates — Caleb Haight

— Simeon Carter — John D. Packer Albert Petty — Winslow Farr — Joseph W. Johnson — Lucius N. Scovil — and George Miller who was mouth.

The following named H[igh]. P[riests]. met in No. 4. at 5 o'clock P.M.—viz; Daniel Spencer, who was mouth — Reynolds Cahoon, Cornelius P. Lott — Samuel Rolfe — William Manhard — Sol[omo]n. Chamberlain Hiram Spencer — Elijah Fordham — William Felshaw — Daniel Carn — Henry H. Wilson D[avid]. H. Redfield — Stephen Winchester, Wandel Mace — Jonathan Becklehymn, & A[braham]. O. Smoot[.]

The following named met in No. 10. at 6 o'cl[oc]k, George P. Dykes, who was mouth, William Crosby — Luman H. Calkins — W[illia]m. C. Gallaher Joseph C. Kingsbury — Job V. Barnum, Elam Ludington — Philo Dibble, Elizur G. Terrill — Nelson Bates — Benjamin Brown — George Coulson — Noah Hubbard — Raymond Clark & Addison Everett—

—William Clayton, Diary, kept for Heber C. Kimball.

....

A convention of the sixth Quorum of Seventies was was held in the upper room of their Hall at half past ten. The house was called to order by J[edediah]. M. Grant — opened by singing and prayer — after which the President [Jedediah Grant] made some general remarks touching the necessity of having oil &c. He spoke upon the various requirements necessary for the Temple [illegible]. He spoke also upon the necessity of upholding the hands of the Twelve to heaven, and not seek to injure the cause by withholding their help.

An inquiry was then made as to who had oil, upon which the following persons replied as follows: —

[See page 317 for excerpted portion.]

The President then spoke of the Gentile merchants who shave the saints; they in return shall be shaved with the razor of hell; this may be spiritualizing but it means a remarkable truth with regard to the man who is called [out] by me, [whether] or [not it is a] Gentile [or] Mormon Merchant[.] The members of the sixth Quorum are requested to meet here to night.

Bro[ther] Noah Rogers, by invitation, spoke upon the feelings he had while in the distant Islands of the sea — The anxious feelings of himself and his brethren — their thirst for news; and the pleasure he had in be-

[Replies to inquiry regarding oil, Sunday, January 4, 1846]

Miles Anderson	1	Bottle	William Sykes	1	Bottle
John McGotha	1	"	David W. Rogers	1	"
M[atthew]. McEwan	1	"	Henry Standage	1	"
Hiram B. Byington	1	"	George C. Riser	1	"
N[elson]. Higgins	1	"	J[ohn] J. Riser	1	"
David Jones	1	"	Darwin Chase	1	"
J[oseph]. B. Peck	½	"	Hiram W. Mikesell	1	"
Sixth Quorum	14	"	W[illiam]. K. Rice	1	"
Thirtieth Quorum has			B[enjamin]. R. Bentley	1	"
enough for their Quorum			G[eorge]. W. Oman	1	"
Twelfth Quorum	37		Owen Batson	1	"
Twenty-third Quorum			Robert Covington	1	"
has six dollars on ha[n]d			Norman Williams	1	"
for Oil			Sixth Quorum has		
Seventh Quorum has			five dollars		
money enough for their Quorum					
Nineteenth Quorum					
has sixteen dollars					
[F]ifth Quorum has					
sixteen dollars					
Thirty-first Quorum					
has five dollars					

—Seventies Record, Book B., oversized portion, January 4, 1846 holding the faces of his old friends. I fully appreciate (said he) the blessings and knowledge you have here, (This day, Pres[iden]t. B[righam]. Young, H[eber]. C. Kimball, O[rson]. Hyde, P[arley]. P. Pratt, and Joseph Young met in room No 1 about 2 oclock P.M. in council and appointed David Candland on a mission to England. He was present, and officially notified.) and I desire to become more intimately acquainted with the same. You are now in the way to obtain power by which to overcome Satan. Let us use our utmost endeavors to obtain the blessings of the endowment before we leave this place in the ensuing Spring. I think I shall write a Synopsis of my travels for the Times and Seasons where all can read it. I rejoice to see and know that no more have fallen away.

President Grant then gave a very long address, much to the purpose and edifying.

A messenger now arrived from the Concert Hall bringing word of the arrangement there made for obtaining oil.

Moved, Seconded, and carried that this meeting adjourn, to meet at this place on Sunday next at Ten O'clock A.M.

Dismissed by prayer by President Grant.

—Seventies Record, Book B.

....

I [John D. Lee] remained with him [Brigham Young] until 2 oclock PM when [he] sent me in his own carriage to Br[other] A[bsalom] P Free's where I spent night with Louisa next morning early[.] I returned to the Temple leaving my girl in good spirits[.] I entered the Temple & Pres[ident] B[righam] Young sitting up by the stove, feeling much better than when I left him the evening previous[,] I here remained in service writing and acting in the several departments until Tuesday evening [January 6] when by permission of Pres[ident] B[righam] Young I rode in a carriage to Br[other] [Benjamin] Meginnis[.] I after reasoning upon the Scripture with them till near midnight (as they [are] not to[o] firm) I solomized the right of matrimony between Br[other] George L Lee & Mary Jane Megines ————[.] Here I formed a slight acquaintance with Sister Cathrine Mchering who felt much desirous to know and understand certain points of doctrine which had caused her considerable trouble[.] my statements she believed and expressed her gratitude to me for the information that she received from me. About 10 oclock I reached the Temple & commenced my daily opperations[.] for 2 weeks past I have been acting in the garden and middle department No 4[.] Thursday [January 8] I threw a part of this burden of[f] my shoulders upon the shoulders of [Wilber J.] Earl who has since that time acted in that capacity[.] Wednesday night [January 7] I went home about 11 oclock [and took] Some little particulars home such [as] for instance some fowls [to] roust [roast] [and offals] out [of which to make] Pork [sweet]bread &c[.] Thursday [January 8] I acted the part of Eloheim which is No 1 in the 1st & last department[.]

—John D. Lee, Diary.

....

Morning at home. Cutting out green silk leaves [for temple aprons].

—Thomas Bullock, Diary.

....

No public meeting was held in the Temple this day, on account of, the floor being insufficient to support a large congregation.

I [Brigham Young] attended a council of the Twelve [apostles] in the Temple. David Candland was appointed a mission to England.

A letter was received from Samuel Brannan, New York, also one from Pittsburg, signed W[illia]m. W. Salt: both of which were answered.

The different quorums met in their respective rooms for prayer, at the usual hour.

—"Manuscript History of Brigham Young,"
in *History of the Church,* 7:562.

Monday, January 5, 1846

This was a pleasant morning, and many persons were early at the Temple to receive their washings & anointings. Pres[ident]. [Brigham] Young's health is almost restored. He was ready for duty at an early hour, spent the morning in hearing letters, and newspapers, and giving directions as to the business of the day.

At 15 minutes to 9 [we] commenced in the Male department washing & anointing the following persons, viz;

High Priests.

Thomas Domville	born	March 27 1792
Alvah Keller	"	April 17 1809

Seventies.

Orson B. Adams	"	March 9. 1815
Truman Gillet	"	May 21. 1811
William Austin	"	March 10. 1800
Reuben M. Jolly	"	Oct[ober] 1. 1808

Gustavus Williams	"	April 11. 1807
Henry B. M. Jolly	"	Oct[ober]. 11. 1813
Jacob Hamblin	"	April 2 1819
Gilbert H. Rolfe	"	Aug[us]t 25. 1820
Orvil M. Allen	"	June 9. 1805
Daniel Browitt	"	Dec[embe]r. 18 1810
Simeon J. Comfort	"	Dec[embe]r. 10. 1816
Lucius A. Bingham	"	Sept[ember] 1. 1804
Augustus Stafford	"	June 24. 1805

Washed by Harrison Burgess & W[illia]m. Hyde anointed by J[edediah]. M. Grant. Jacob Gates, & Ezra T. Benson & William Pitt—

Finished at 25 m[inutes]. to 10.

In the female department, the following persons were washed and anointed, commencing at 25 minutes after 9, viz;

Susanna Adams, born May 30. 1819 washed by Nancy H. Rockwood anointed by Nancy Winchester[.]

Martha Stafford born March 5. 1805 w[ashed]. by Clarissa Harriman an[ointed]. by Nancy Winchester[.]

Fidelia Gillet born May 1. 1814 w[ashed]. by Nancy H. Rockwood an[ointed] by Lois Cutler[.]

Agnes Austin born May 22. 1803 w[ashed]. by Clarissa Harriman an[ointed]. by Lois Cutler[.]

Maria Williams born Aug[us]t 12. 1811 washed & anointed by Catharine C. Spencer[.]

Jane Allen born March 2. 1810 W[ashed]. by Nancy H. Rockwood an[ointed] by Nancy Winchester[.]

Elizabeth Browett born June 11. 1814 W[ashed]. by Clarissa Harriman an[ointed] by Nancy Winchester[.]

Martha Browett born June 4. 1779 W[ashed]. by Clarissa Harriman an[ointed] by C[atherine]. C. Spencer[.]

Louisa Chandler born Mar[ch]. 12. 1822 W[ashed]. by Nancy H. Rockwood an[ointed] by Lois Cutler[.]

Harriett Browett born Oct[ober]. 10. 1810 W[ashed]. by Nancy H. Rockwood an[ointed] by Lois Cutler[.]

Lodoska Tupper born May 22. 1828 w[ashed]. by Clarissa Harriman an[ointed] by Lois Cutler[.]

Emeline Grover born July 30. 1830 W[ashed]. by Nancy H. Rockwood an[ointed]. by Nancy Winchester[.]

Charity Butler born Jan[uar]y 13. 1782 w[ashed]. by Julia Pack an[ointed] by C[atherine]. C. Spencer[.]

Sarah Bingham born Ap[ri]l 21. 1806 W[ashed]. by Clarissa Harriman An[ointed] by Nancy Winchester[.]

Sarah Jolley born May 28. 1812 W[ashed]. by Nancy H. Rockwood An[ointed] by Lois Cutler[.]

Maria Domville born July 10. 1797 W[ashed]. by Julia Pack an[ointed]. by C[atherine]. C. Spencer[.]

Lucinda Hamblin born Aug[us]t 24. 1823 W[ashed]. by Nancy H. Rockwood an[ointed]. by Lois Cutler[.]

Eliza Jane Rolfe born Dec[ember]. 20. 1823 washed & anointed by Clarissa Harriman.

Susan Comfort born Oct[ober] 11. 1817 w[ashed]. by Julia Pack an[ointed]. by C[atherine]. C. Spencer[.]

Brittania Jolly supposed [birth] 1813 w[ashed]. by Nancy H. Rockwood an[ointed] by N[ancy]. Winchester[.]

Finished at 25 min[utes]. to 11.

At 11 o'clock [we] commenced receiving into the lower & middle departments, those who were washed & anointed this morning, being company No. 1. the following persons officiating in the upper department, viz;

Orson Pratt	as	No.	1
C[harles]. C. Rich	"	"	2
Erastus Snow	"	"	3

and in the middle department.

Orson Spencer	as	No.	1.
Lucius N. Scovil	"	"	2.
Abraham O. Smoot	"	"	3.
W[illiam]. W. Phelps	"	"	4
Geo[rge]. P. Dykes	"	"	5

At 10 o'clock. the following named persons met in room No. 9, which is the one used by the President of the Seventies, viz; Joseph Young, — Charles C. Rich — Abraham O. Smoot, Geo[rge]. P. Dykes and Lucius N. Scovil — and consecrated Seventeen Bottles of Oil, for the anointing[.]

At 12 o'clock [we] commenced receiving into the upper department company Number One, in the following order, viz;

Alvah Keller	by Orson Pratt[.]
Charity Butler	" " "

Martha Browett	"	"	"	
Emeline Grover	"	"	"	
Thomas Domville	"	"	"	
Mary Domville	"	"	"	& Thomas D[omville].
Lucius A. Bingham	"	"	"	
Lodoska Tupper	"	"	"	
Sally Bingham	"	"	"	& L[ucius]. A. Bingham[.]
Gustavus Williams	"	"	"	
Louisa Chandler	"	"	"	
Maria Williams	"	"	"	& Gustavus Williams[.]
Simeon J. Comfort	"	"	"	
Susan Comfort	"	"	"	& S[imeon]. J. Comfort[.]
Gilbert H. Rolfe	"	"	"	
Eliza Jane Rolfe	"	"	"	& G[ilbert]. H. Rolfe[.]
Henry B. M. Jolly	"	"	"	
Brittania Jolly	"	"	"	& H[enry]. B. M. Jolly[.]
Orvil M. Allen	"	"	"	
Jane Allen	"	"	"	& O[rvil]. M. Allen[.]
Daniel Browett	"	"	"	
Elizabeth Browett	"	"	"	& Daniel Browett[.]
Harriet Browett	"	"	"	& " "
Reuben M. Jolly	"	"	"	
Sarah Jolly	"	"	"	& R[euben]. M. Jolly[.]
Orson B. Adams	"	"	"	
Susanna Adams	"	"	"	& O[rson]. B. Adams[.]
Jacob Hamblin	"	"	"	
Lucinda Hamblin	"	"	"	& J[acob]. Hamblin[.]
Truman Gillet	"	"	"	
Fidelia Gillet	"	"	"	& Truman Gillet[.]
William Austin	"	"	"	
Agnes Austin	"	"	"	& W[illia]m. Austin[.]
Augustus Stafford	"	"	"	
Martha Stafford	"	"	"	& A[ugustus]. Stafford[.]

[Finished at] 5 m[inutes]. p[ast]. 2[.] Erastus Snow & Artemisia Snow prompters.

At 25 minutes before 12 [we] commenced in the Male department, washing and anointing the following persons. viz;

High Priests

Bechias Dustin born Oct[ober]. 5, 1793

McCaslin Frost	"	Dec[embe]r. 16. 1785
Seventies		
Jacob Stoker	"	April 7 1812
Edward M. Webb	"	Aug[us]t 17 1815
Michael Stoker	"	Feb[ruar]y 10. 1805
John W. Cooley	"	Nov[embe]r. 29. 1811
George C. Riser	"	July 16 1816
Jacob Hofheins	"	Dec[ember] 4 1812
John Dolton	"	July 10 1801
Peter W. Counover	"	Sept[ember]. 19. 1807
Alvah Alexander	"	March 12. 1799
Eli Tibbets	"	January 11. 1812
Henry P. Hoyt	"	Aug[us]t 2. 1815
Lewis Eager	"	Sept[ember] 5. 1791
David W. Rogers	"	Oct[ober] 4 1787
John Bourne	"	Nov[embe]r. 13. 1821
Easton Kelsey	"	March 9. 1813
Josiah Boyce	"	March 10. 1802
Nelson Higgins	"	Sept[ember] 1. 1806
Jehiel Savage	"	Oct[ober] 3. 1800

Washed by William Hyde & Harrison Burgess—anointed by Levi W. Hancock Jacob Gates, and William Pitt.— Finished at 30 minutes past 12[.]

A letter from William Smith to George D. Grant, was read to Pres[ident]. [Brigham] Young and 10 or 12 others, this morning, by Bro[ther]. Grant's permission— The letter was dated at Cincinnati, and was very scurrillous & slanderous—

In the Female department, the following persons were washed and anointed, commencing at 10 minutes to 12. viz;

Panina Frost born 1788 washed by Julia Pack anointed by Clarissa Herriman[.]

Mary Eager born Nov[embe]r. 30. 1803 w[ashed]. by Nancy H. Rockwood an[ointed]. by Nancy Winchester[.]

Rebecca Dolten born Apr[il] 24. 1796 W[ashed]. by Julia Pack. an[ointed]. by Nancy Winchester[.]

Rozina Northrup. born June 14. 1793 W[ashed]. by Julia Pack an[ointed]. by Catharine C. Spencer[.]

Catharine Stoker born Aug[us]t 14 1818 W[ashed]. and anointed by Clarissa Harriman[.]

Clarissa Ross born June 16. 1814 w[ashed]. by Phebee Chase an[ointed]. by Phebe Chase[.]
Elizabeth Bourne born Oct[obe]r. 1. 1822 W[ashed]. by Julia Pack an[ointed]. by C[atherine]. C. Spencer[.]
Martha Rogers born Aug[us]t 22 1793 W[ashed]. by Julia Pack an[ointed]. by Nancy Winchester[.]
Sarah Higgins born Ap[ri]l 5. 1806 W[ashed]. by Julia Pack an[ointed]. by Nancy Winchester[.]
Mary Cooley born May 16 1794 W[ashed]. by Julia Pack an[ointed]. by Nancy Winchester[.]
Ruth Tibbets born Ap[ri]l. 16. 1815 W[ashed]. by Clarissa Harmon An[ointed]. by Phebe Chase[.]
Martha Stoker born Feb[ruar]y 24. 1808 W[ashed]. by Julia Pack, an[ointed] by Nancy Winchester[.]
Phebe Alexander born June 4. 1804 W[ashed]. and anointed by Clarissa Harriman[.]
Elizabeth Hofheins born Dec[ember]. 25. 1819 W[ashed]. by Julia Pack an[ointed]. by Phebe Chase[.]

Finished at 5 m[inutes]. past one— 14 [women washed and anointed.]

At 15 minutes past 1. [we] commenced receiving into the Lower & middle department Company No. 2.[,] the following persons officiating in the upper department, viz; John Taylor as No. 1 P[arley]. P. Pratt as No. 2 — J[ediah]. M. Grant No. 3. and in the middle department, Orson Spencer as No. 1. L[ucius]. N. Scovil as No. 2. A[braham]. O. Smoot as No. 3. John D. Lee No. 4 and Geo[rge]. P. Dykes as No. 5.—

~~At 2~~ A[t] 20 minutes past 2 [we] commenced receiving Co. No. 2. into the upper department. as follows.

David W. Rogers	by	John	Taylor[.]	
Rozina Northrup	"	"	"	
John W. Cooley	"	"	"	
Martha Rogers	"	"	"	& D[avid]. W. Rogers[.]
Mary Cooley	"	"	"	& J[ohn]. W. Cooley[.]
Lewis Eager	"	"	"	
Mary Eager	"	"	"	& Lewis Eager[.]
Clarissa Ross	"	"	"	
Eli Tibbets	"	"	"	
Ruth Ribbets	"	"	"	& Eli Tibbets[.]
Jacob Hofheins	"	Orson Hyde[.]		
Elizabeth Hofheins	"	"	"	& Jacob H[ofheins].

Jacob Stoker	"	"	"	
Catharine Stoker	"	"	"	& J[acob]. Stoker[.]
John Bourne	"	"	"	
Elizabeth Bourne	"	"	"	& John Bourne[.]
John Dolten	"	"	"	
Rebecca Dolten	"	"	"	& John Dolten[.]
Alvah Alexander	"	"	"	
Phebe Alexander	"	"	"	& A[lvah]. Alexander[.]
McCaslin Frost	"	"	"	
Panina Frost	"	"	"	& M[cCaslin]. Frost.
Nelson Heigins	"	"	"	
Sarah Heigins	by Orson Hyde & N[elson]. H[eigins].			
Michael Stoker	"	"	"	
Martha Stoker	"	"	"	& Michael [Stoker].
Josiah Boyce	"	"	"	
Bechias Dustin	"	"	"	
Edward M. Webb	"	"	"	
~~Schiel Savage~~	~~"~~	~~"~~	~~"~~	

Finished at 15 m[inutes]. to 4.—Geo[rge]. P. Dykes John Pack — Catharine C. Spencer Prompters[.]

President Young left the Temple in his carriage, at 3 o'clock in company with his brother Lorenzo Young and [blank.]

At 10 minutes before 2 o'clock, [we] commenced washing & anointing in the male department the following persons. viz;

High Priests		
Robert Clift	born	Sept[ember]. 20. 1791
Henry Hoagland	"	Jan[uar]y. 17. 1796
Orrin Porter Rockwell	"	Jan[uar]y 8. 1814
Seventies		
Thoret Parsons	"	Sept[ember] 5. 1802
Alexander Neibaur	"	Jan[uar]y 8. 1808
John I. Riser	"	June 4. 1824
Homer C. Hoyt	"	July 31. 1820
Gilbert Belknap	"	Dec[ember]. 22 1821
Andrew S. Gibbons		
William Wordsworth	born	March 5. 1810
Henry Wilcox	"	Jan[uar]y 13. 1812
George F. Hanson	"	April 19. 1820
Thomas Heap	"	April 1. 1809

12 [men] Washed by William Hyde & Harrison Burgess, anointed by Levi W. Hancock. Jacob Gates and James Brown.

Finished at 15 minutes to 3.

In the Female department, commencing at 10 minutes to 2[,] the following persons were Washed and anointed. viz;

Eveline Counover born May 25. 1808 w[ashed]. by Julia Pack an[ointed]. by Phebe Chase[.]

Christiana Riser, born Dec[ember]. 3. 1821 W[ashed]. by Clarissa Harriman An[ointed]. by Phebe Chase[.]

Ruth L. Crosier born Feb[ruar]y 11. 1818. W[ashed]. by Julia Pack an[ointed] by Nancy Winchester[.]

Eliza E. Jones born Jan[uar]y 5. 1790 washed and anointed by Julia Pack[.]

Abigail Kelsey born Nov[embe]r. 14. 1805 w[ashed]. by Clarissa Harriman an[ointed]. by Phebe Chase.

Martha Langley born Oct[ober] 7. 1825 w[ashed]. by Clarissa Harriman An[ointed] by Nancy Winchester[.]

Nancy Ann Haines b[orn]. Nov[ember]. 12. 1828 w[ashed]. by Julia Pack An[ointed]. by Julia Pack[.]

Mary Ann Burnham, [born] Mar[ch]. 14. 1816 w[ashed]. by Julia Pack An[ointed] by Phebe Chase[.]

Irena C. Hoyt. born Sept[ember]. 5. 1819 W[ashed]. by Nancy H. Rockwood An[ointed] by N[ancy]. Winchester[.]

Sarah Ann Hampson born July 22. 1828 W[ashed]. by Clarissa Harriman An[ointed] by Phebe Chase[.]

Alice Heaps. born 1815. W[ashed]. by Julia Pack An[ointed] by Nancy Winchester.

Adeline Belknap born, May 4. 1832 w[ashed]. by Nancy H. Rockwood An[ointed] by Nancy Winchester[.]

Ellen Neibaur born Feb[ruar]y 28. 1811 W[ashed]. by Julia Pack A[nointed]. by Julia Pack[.]

Catharine Savage [born] Aug[us]t 8. 1822 W[ashed]. [by] Nancy H. Rockwood An[ointed]. by Julia Pack[.]

Rizpah Gibbons born May 13. 1829 W[ashed]. by Nancy H. Rockwood An[ointed] by N[ancy]. Winchester[.]

Ann Wordsworth born July 31. 1812 W[ashed]. by Nancy H. Rockwood An[ointed] by Julia Pack[.]

Sarah Rockwell born Sept[ember] 9. 1785. W[ashed]. and anointed by Nancy Winchester.

[Finished at] 18 min[utes]. past 3.

[A]nd at 28 minutes past 3. the following persons were washed & anointed,

Naomi Holman born Oct[ober] 7. 1811. Washed & anointed by Clarissa Harman[.]

Julia Ann Hoyt. born Feb[ruary] 27. 1821 w[ashed]. by Julia Pack anointed by Nancy Winchester[.]

Alvira M. Rockwell born Oct[ober] 7. 1820 w[ashed]. by Phebe Chase An[ointed]. by Nancy Winchester[.]

Priscilla Clift born Aug[us]t 1815 W[ashed]. & anointed by Julia Pack[.]

Angeline Horn born Feb[ruar]y 19 1820 washed & anointed by Nancy H. Rockwood.

Finished at 7 minutes to 4.

At 27 m[inutes]. past 3. at the ringing of the Bell [we] commenced receiving into the lower and middle departments, company No. 3.[,] the following persons officiating in the upper department. viz; Orson Spencer as No. 1. J[edediah]. M. Grant as No. 2. and Erastus Snow as No. 3 — and in the middle department, Lucius N. Scovil as No. 1 A[braham]. O. Smoot as No. 2 Israel Barlow as No. 3. W[illiam]. W. Phelps as No. 4 Geo[rge]. P. Dykes as No. 5.

At 5 o'clock[,] commencing receiving into the upper department, company No. 3 in the following order viz,

Ruth L. Crosier	by John Taylor[.]
Gilbert Belknap	" " "
Adeline Belknap	" G[ilbert]. Belknap & J[ohn]. Taylor[.]
William Wordsworth	" John Taylor[.]
Ann Wordsworth	" W[illiam]. Wordsworth[.]
Mary Ann Burnham	" John Taylor[.]
Peter W. Counover	" John Taylor[.]
Eveline Counover	" P[eter]. W. Counover[.]
Thoret Parsons	" John Taylor[.]
Eliza E. Jones	" John Taylor[.]
Jehiel Savage	" Orson Pratt[.]
Nancy Ann Haines	" " "
Catharine Savage	" Jehiel Savage[.]
George C. Riser	" Orson Pratt[.]
Christiana Riser	" Geo[rge]. C. Riser[.]
Sarah Rockwell	" Orson Pratt[.]

Easton Kelsey	"	" "
Abigail Kelsey	"	Easton Kelsey[.]
George F. Hampson	"	Orson Pratt[.]
Alexander Neibaur	"	Orson Pratt[.]
Ellen Neibaur	"	Alex[ander] Neibaur[.]
Sarah Ann Hampson	"	Geo[rge]. F. Hampson[.]
Andrew S. Gibbons	"	Orson Pratt[.]
Rizpah Gibbons	"	A[ndrew]. S. Gibbons[.]
Henry Hoagland	"	Orson Pratt[.]
Thomas Heap	"	" "
John I. Riser	"	" "
Alice Heap	"	" "
Martha Langley	"	Orson Pratt[.]
Henry Wilcox	by	Orson Pratt[.]
Henry P. Hoyt	"	" "
Irene E. Hoyt	"	Henry P. Hoyt.

Ended at 35 m[inutes]. past 6—103 this day.

President Young returned at 30 m[inutes]. past 6.

At 15 m[inutes]. past 4. [we] commenced receiving into the lower & middle departments company No. 4.[,] the following persons officiating in the upper department, viz; Joseph Young as No. 1. A[lbert]. P. Rockwood as No. 2. & L[evi]. W. Hancock No. 3. and in the middle department, Erastus Snow as No. 1. John Pack as No. 2 B[enjamin]. L. Clapp as No. 3. W[illiam]. W. Phelps as No. 4. George P. Dykes as No. 5.

At 5 m[inutes]. before 7. [we] commenced receiving company No. 4 into the upper department, in the following order—viz;

Orrin Porter Rockwell by P[arley]. P. Pratt.
Alvira M. Rockwell by O[rrin]. P[orter]. Rockwell[.]
Homer C. Hoyt by P[arley]. P. Pratt[.]
Julia Ann Hoyt by H[omer]. C. Hoyt[.]
Naomi R. Holman by James S. Holman[.]
Robert Clift by P[arley]. P. Pratt[.]
Priscilla Clift by Robert Clift[.]
Angeline Horn by A[lbert]. P. Rockwood.
Prompters. A[lbert]. P. Rockwood—and Artemisia Snow—.

Finished at 25 m[inutes]. past 7.

At 6 o'clock the following named High Priests, met for prayer in room No. 6, viz; William Crosby, chosen to preside, George P. Dykes.

mouth, Jefferson Hunt W[illia]m. C. Gallaher, Edward Hunter, Peter Haws, Anson Call, Cornelius P. Lott, Benj[ami]n Brown, Jonathan Becklehymn, Joseph W. Johnson, James Brown, Joseph A. Kelting, Albert Petty, Dan[ie]l. Spencer Ormond Butler — Isaac Higbee — Hezekiah Peck Stephen Winchester — and Samuel Williams, President of the Elders quorum.

In room No. 8 the following named High Priests met also, viz; George Miller, who was mouth, Daniel Carter, Simeon Carter, Andrew L. Lamoreaux Joseph Mount — Jesse Baker Elijah Fordham — Joshua S. Holman — Samuel Cully — Ormus E. Bates — Nelson Bates, Caleb Haight — Abel Lamb, E[lizur]. G. Terrill — Edward Rigby — W[illia]m. Felshaw Jacob Foutz — Job V. Barnum — Harvey Green & Gustavus Hills—

The High Council met a[t] 6 O'clock[.] Present, Isaac Morley Samuel Bent James Allred — David Fullmer H[enry]. G. Sherwood — C[harles]. C. Rich — Thomas Grover Lewis D. Wilson — Newel Knight, George W. Harris & Ezra T. Benson— prayed for the preservation of Pres[iden]t B[righam]. Young, & his Council—and all the quorums, & for blessings upon all the Saints, the overthrow of our enemies, the healing of the sick that are among us, for blessings upon the house of Israel, & for our reception among them, and for all the saints abroad.

After the labors of the day were over, which was soon after nine o'clock P.M.[,] the violin and flute, played by brothers [Hans C.] Hanson & [Elisha] Averett, in the east room, enlivened the spirits of the saints that were present,— and they soon joined in the dance, during which the High Council adjourned, and the members thereof came into the room, and some of them, viz, Isaac Morley, Samuel Bent, James Allred, C[harles]. C. Rich, E[zra]. T. Benson C[alvin]. C. Pendleton Thomas Grover & L[ewis]. D. Wilson ^joined in^— Efforts were made to induce Brother George W. Harris to join in it also, but his great gravity & superior wisdom forbade ^him^ to do so, & he thought that as he had not yet danced in his life, he would not begin at the present time. after continuing the dance until about 12 o'clock, all retired except the few who generally remain over night. President Young left the Temple shortly after 12—and went home in his carriage. Elder [Heber C.] Kimball also with his wife and William [Clayton?] took their departure about the same time—for home. Also Bishop [Newel K.] Whitney & his family.

—William Clayton, Diary, kept for Heber C. Kimball.

Monday morning at 8 in [the] morning the list of the Names of those that were selected to labour in several departments were read, & each mans station was appointed him — which were as follows — E[zra]. T. Benson & Hyrum Dayton, water & fireman in both Departments[,] W[illia]m Hyde & Harrison Burgess were appointed to wash in the Male department — and Pres[ident] Levi Hancock & Jacob Gates to anoint[;] Pres[ident] H[enry]. Herriman Clerk in the Preparation Room — Lewis Robbins & Elisha Averett Door Keepers — William Snow — Wardrobe — John L. Butler Fireman & candle Snuffer — W[illia]m Stringham Chief Cook — Sister Huldah Barns[,] assistant[;] the Twelve[;] the 1st Presidency of the [Seventies;] & clerk were instructed to act — [illegible] in the other departments in Turns — Br[other] Orson Spencer Erastus Snow & L[ucius]. N. Scovil were with us through the week —

Company No. 1[. We] commenced washing in the male department at 9 o'clock a. m. [T]he following persons were washed and anointed[.] William Hyde and Harrison Burgess administered the ordinance of washing, and Levi Hancock, Jacob Gates, and William Pitt administered the ordinance of anointing.

Seventy		Orson B. Adams	born	Mar[ch] 9 1815
	1	Truman Gillett	"	May 21 1811
	2	William Austin	"	Mar[ch] 10 1800
	3	Reuben M. Jolly	"	Oct[ober]. 1, 1808
	4	Gustave [illegible]	"	Apr[il] 11, 1807
Seventies		Henry B. Jolley	born	Oct[ober]. 11, 1813
	7	Jacob Hamblin	"	Apr[i]l. 2, 1819
	8	Gilbert H. Rolfe	"	Aug[ust]. 25 1820
	9	Orvil M. Allen	"	June 9, 1809
	10	David Browett	"	[illegible]
Seventies	11	Simeon J. Comfort	Born	Dec. 10, 1816
	12	Lucius A. Bingham	"	Sep[tember] 1 1804
	13	Augustus Stafford	"	June 24, 1805
High Priests		Thomas Doniville	born	Mar[ch] 27 1792
	2	Alva Vielleu	"	Ap[ri]l. 17, 1809
		Co[mpany]. No. 2 [Seventies]		
	14	Thomas Parsons	"	Sep[tember]. 5, 1802
	15	Alexander Neibaur	"	Jan[uary] 8, 1808
	16	John J. Riser	"	June 4, 1824
	17	Honcer [?] C. Hoyt	"	July 31, 1820
	18	Gilbert Belknap	"	Dec[ember]. 22, 1821

19 William Wadsworth	"	Mar[ch] 5, 1810
20 Henry Wilcox	"	Jan[uary]. 13, 1812
21 George F Hanson	"	Ap[ri]l 19, 1820
2 Thomas Heap	"	Ap[ri]l. 1, 1809
Co[mpany]. No. 2 [High Priests]		
3 Robert Clift	"	Sep[tember] 20, 1791
4 Henry Hoagland	"	Jan[uary] 17, 1796
5 Oren Porter Rockwell	"	June 3, 1814

The above named persons were washed by William Hyde and Harrison Burgess, Anointed by Levi Hancock, Jacob Gates, and James Brown.

[See pages 332-33 for excerpted portion.]

This days operations closed at 9 o'clock A. M. at which time the High Priests and Seventies arrayed themselves in priestly attire, and retired to their respective apartments for prayers, the High council also prayed; after which Brother Anson & Elisha Effort [Averett] brought in their violin and flute and commenced discoursing music, when some of the Twelve, High Priests, ^&^ Seventies danced before the Lord, after which, all, except those who labored in the Temple, retired to their respective homes.

—Seventies Record, Book B.

....

Morning at home cutting out green leaves. ... Borrowed Joseph [L. Heywood]'s garment. Went home, cut out mine, returned his at 5 ...

—Thomas Bullock, Diary.

....

My [Brigham Young's] health being better I was ready for duty at an early hour. Spent the morning in hearing letters and newspapers, and giving directions as to the business of the day.

8:45 a.m., commenced washing and anointing.

Seventeen bottles of oil were consecrated.

One hundred four persons received their endowments.

The high council, two companies of high priests, and the seventies met in their respective rooms for prayer.

9 p.m., the labors of the day being over, Brothers Hanson and E[lisha]. Averett played on the violin and flute and enlivened the spirits of the saints present: some embraced the opportunity and danced to the lively strains of music.

Elder Heber C. Kimball and I returned home about midnight.

—"Manuscript History of Brigham Young," in *History of the Church,* 7:564.

[Washings and anointings for Monday, January 5, 1846]

No 1 Susanna Adams born May 30, 1819	Washed by	Nancy H. Rockwood,	Anointed by	Nancy Winchester
Martha Stafford " Mar 5, 1805	"	Clarissa Herriman	"	"
Fidelia Gilbert " May 1, 1814	"	Clarissa Spencer	"	Lois Butler
Agnes Austin " May 22, 1803	"	Clarissa Herriman	"	"
Maria Williams " Aug 12, 1811	"	Catharine C. Spencer	"	Catharine C. Spencer
Jane Allen " Mar 2, 1810	"	Nancy H. Rockwood	"	Nancy Winchester
Elizabeth Browett " June 1, 1814		Clarissa Herriman	"	"
Martha Browett " June 4, 1779	"	"	"	Catharine C. Spencer
Louisa Chandler " Mar 12, 1822	"	Nancy H. Rockwood	"	Lois Butler
Harriet Browett " Oct 10, 1810	"	"	"	"
Lodeska Tupper " May 22, 1828	"	Clarissa Herriman	"	Nancy Winchester
Emeline Grover " July 30, 1830	"	Nancy H. Rockwood	"	"
Charity Butler " Jan. 13, 1782	"	Julia Pack	"	Catharine C. Spencer
Sarah Bingham " Apl 21, 1806	"	Clarissa Herriman	"	Nancy Winchester
Sarah Jolly " May 28, 1812	"	Nancy H. Rockwood	"	Lois Butler
Mary Dunbilla " July 10, 1797	"	Julia Pack	"	Catharine C. Spencer
Lucinda Hamblin " Aug 24 1823	"	Nancy H. Rockwood	"	Lois Butler
Eliza Jane Rolfe " Dec 20, 1823	"	Clarissa Herriman	"	Clarissa Herriman
Susan Comfort " Oct 11, 1817	"	Julia Pack	"	Catharine C. Spencer
Christianna Jolly " About 1813	"	Nancy H. Rockwood	"	Nancy Winchester
No. 2 Pamina Frost born 1788	Washed by	Julia Pack	Anointed by	Clarissa Herriman
Mary Eager " Nov 30 1803	"	Nancy H. Rockwood	"	Nancy Winchester

Rebecca Dalton " Apl. 24, 1796	"	Julia Pack	"	"
Rosina Northrop " June 14, 1793	"	"	"	Catharine C. Spencer
Catharine Stoker " Aug 14, 1818	"	Clarissa Herriman	"	Clarissa Herriman
Clarissa Ross " June 16, 1812	"	Phebe Chase	"	Phebe Chase
Elizabeth Birn " Oct. 1, 1822	"	Julia Pack	"	Catharine C. Spencer
Martha Rogers " Aug. 22, 1793	"	"	"	Nancy Winchester
Sarah Higgins " Apl 18, 1794	"	"	"	"
Mary Cooley " May 18, 1794	"	"	"	"
Ruth Tibbets " Apl. 16, 1815	"	Clarissa Herriman	"	Phebe Chase
Martha Stoker " Feb. 24, 1808	"	Julia Pack	"	Nancy Winchester
Phebe Alexander " June 4, 1804	"	Clarissa Herriman	"	Clarissa Herriman
Elizabeth Hofines " Dec. 25, 1819	"	Julia Pack	"	Phebe Chase
Naomi Holman ^born^ Oct. 7, 1816	washed by	Clarissa Herriman	Anointed by	Clarissa Herriman
Julia Ann Hoyt Feb. 27, 1821	"	Julia Pack	"	Nancy Winchester
Alvira M. Rockwell Oct. 7, 1820	"	Phebe Chase	"	"
Priscilla Clift Aug 1815	"	Julia Pack	"	Julia Pack
Angeline Horn Feb 19, 1820	"	Nancy H. Rockwood	"	Nancy H. Rockwood

—Seventies Record, Book B, oversized portion, January 5, 1846.

Nauvoo temple endowments performed on this date for:

First Company: Alvah Keller, Charity Butler, Martha Browett, Emeline Grover, Thomas Domville, Mary Domville, Lucius A. Bingham, Lodoska Tupper, Sally Bingham, Gustavas Williams, Louisa Chandler, Maria Williams, Simeon J. Comfort, Susan Comfort, Gilbert H. Rolfe, Eliza Jane Rolfe, Henry B. M. Jolly, Brittania Jolly, Orvil M. Allen, Jane Allen, Daniel Browett, Elizabeth Browett, Harriet Browett, Reuben M. Jolly, Sarah Jolly, Orson B. Adams, Susanna Adams, Jacob Hamblin, Lucinda Hamblin, Truman Gillet, Fidelia Gillet, William Austin, Agnes Austin, Augustus Stafford, and Martha Stafford.

Second Company: David W. Rogers, Rozina Northrup, John W. Cooley, Martha Rogers, Mary Cooley, Lewis Eager, Mary Eager, Clarissa Ross, Eli Tibbets, Ruth Tibbets, Jacob Hofheins, Elisabeth Hofheins, Jacob Stoker, Catharine Stoker, John Bourne, Elisabeth Bourne, John Dolten, Rebecca Dolten, Alvah Alexander, Phebe Alexander, McCaslin Frost, Panina Frost, Nelson Heigins, Sarah Heigins, Michael Stoker, Martha Stoker, Josiah Boyce, Bechias Dustin, and Edward M. Webb.

Third Company: Ruth L. Crosier, Gilbert Belknap, Adeline Belknap, William Wordsworth, Ann Wordsworth, Mary Ann Burnham, Peter W. Cownover, Eveline Cownover, Thoret Parsons, Eliza E. Jones, Jehiel Savage, Nancy Ann Haines, Catharine Savage, George C. Riser, Christiana Riser, Sarah Rockwell, Easton Kelsey, Abigail Kelsey, George F. Hampson, Alexander Neiba[u]m, Ellen Neiba[u]m, Sarah Ann Hampson, Andrew S. Gibbons, Rizpah Gibbons, Henry Hoagland, Thomas Heap, John J. Riser, Alice Heap, Martha Langley, Henry Wilcox, Henry P. Hoyt, Irene E. Hoyt, Orrin Porter Rockwell, Alvira M. Rockwell, Homer C. Hoyt, Julia Ann Hoyt, Naomi R. Holman, Robert Clift, Priscilla Clift, and Angeline Horn.

—Summary of information compiled by the Temple Index Bureau, *Nauvoo Temple Endowment Register: 10 December 1845 to 8 February 1846.*

Tuesday, January 6, 1846

This morning I [Brigham Young] came to the Temple with my wife [and] spent the day in assisting her about preparing the alt[a]r. In the evening met the council.

—Brigham Young, Diary.

In the male department. commencing at 25 minutes to 9. the following persons were washed and anointed, viz;

High Priests		
William Black	born	Aug[us]t. 20. 1784
Moses Clawson	"	Oct[ober] 8. 1801
Seventies		
Edward Mecham	"	Feb[ruar]y 22. 1802
James Bean	"	March 3. 1804
Joseph Busby	"	Nov[ember]. 5. 1810
Nathaniel Leavitt	"	Nov[ember]. 17. 1823
Darwin Chase	"	Feb[ruar]y 25. 1816
Ephraim Mecham	"	March 7 1808
Alphonso Green	"	July 8 1810
George Black	"	May 6 1823
David Jones	"	Aug[us]t 20 1799
Charles Lambert	"	Aug[us]t 30 1816

12 [men.] Washed by William Hyde & Harrison Burgess[,] anointed by Levi Hancock, Jacob Gates and Ezra T. Benson— ended 20 m[inutes]. to 10.

In the Female department, commencing at 25 minutes to 9, the following persons were washed and anointed, viz;

Eliza Ann Raven born May 15. 1829 Washed by Nancy H. Rockwood. An[ointed]. by Nancy Winchester[.]

Sally Maria Wade born May 13. 1798 W[ashed]. by N[ancy]. H. Rockwood An[ointed]. by Clarissa Herriman[.]

Sally Murdock, born April 22. 1788 w[ashed] by Artemisia Snow. An[ointed]. by Nancy Winchester[.]

Cornelia Clawson born Oct[ober]. 22. 1803 w[ashed]. by Nancy H. Rockwood An[ointed]. by Nancy Winchester[.]

Betsey Green born May 6. 1810 w[ashed]. by N[ancy]. H. Rockwood An[ointed] by Clarissa Hancock[.]

Ann C. Busby b[orn]. March. 9. 1813. w[ashed]. by Nancy H. Rockwood An[ointed]. by Clarissa Herriman[.]

Jane Black, born. June 11. 1801 w[ashed]. by Artemisia Snow An[ointed] by Clarissa Hancock[.]

Polly Mecham born Aug[us]t 13. 1814 w[ashed]. by Nancy H. Rockwood An[ointed] by Nancy Winchester[.]

Irene Mecham born Nov[ember]. 18, 1807 W[ashed]. by Artemisia Snow An[ointed]. by Clarissa Hancock[.]

Elizabeth Bean born Sept[ember]. 22. 1803 W[ashed]. by Artemisia Snow An[ointed]. by Clarissa Hancock[.]

Mercy Jones born July 19. 1806 w[ashed] by Nancy H. Rockwood An[ointed] by Clarissa Herriman[.]

Elizabeth Stout, born Oct[ober] 13, 1823 W[ashed]. by Nancy H. Rockwood An[ointed]. by N[ancy]. Winchester[.]

Sarah Alley born Oct[ober] 19 1819 w[ashed]. by Artemisia Snow An[ointed] by Mary A. Noble[.]

Mary Alice Lambert born Dec[ember]. 9. 1828 w[ashed]. by N[ancy]. H. Rockwood An[ointed] by Clarissa Hancock[.]

Charlotte Baker born Dec[ember]. 5. 1820. W[ashed]. by N[ancy]. H. Rockwood An[ointed]. by Clarissa Hancock[.]

S[arah]. Susanna Divine, born Jan[uar]y 16, 1823 w[ashed]. by N[ancy]. H. Rockwood An[ointed]. by Clarissa Herriman.

[E]nded at 5 min[utes]. past 10.

At 15 min[utes]. past 10, [we] commenced receiving into the lower and middle departments the company [that was] washed & anointed this morning[,] the following persons officiating in the upper department, viz; John Taylor as No. 1. J[edediah]. M. Grant as No. 2. L[evi]. W. Hancock No. 3. and in the middle department, B[enjamin]. L. Clapp as No. 1 L[ucius]. N. Scovil as No. 2. John Pack No. 3, J[ohn] D. Lee No. 4. Geo[rge]. P. Dykes No. 5

Elder H[eber]. C. Kimball came into the temple at 5 minutes before 11 o'clock. and in a few moments called upon all the others of the Twelve [apostles] to unite with him in consecrating some oil for the anointing[.] The following persons therefore retired [to] room No. 9, clothed themselves in their Priestly Robes and garments, and consecrated 17 Bottles of oil, viz ~~H. C. Kimball, John Taylor~~ P[arley]. P. Pratt, Amasa Lyman J[edediah]. M. Grant, A[braham]. O. Smoot, John D. Lee. George Miller, W[illiam]. W. Phelps & Joseph B[ates]. Noble, after consecrating the oil, they united in prayer.

At 20 minutes past 11. Pres[ident]. Young came in with Mrs Young—his health not very good, but being quite comfortable. He slept at home and dreamed the same dream three times in the course of the night—

Elder [Almon W.] Babbitt came in at 15 minutes before 12, bringing a letter, written by Gov[ernor]. Thomas Ford,[8] to J[acob]. B. Backenstos,

8. Thomas Ford (1800-50) served as governor of Illinois from 1842 to 1846. He had earlier been a judge of the circuit court in northern Illinois (1835-37) and

dated Springfield [Illinois], Dec[ember]. 19, in which he refers among other matters to the probability that the U.S. Government would send a military force to Nauvoo to assist in arresting the Twelve [apostles], who are charged with counterfeiting.

At 30 minutes past 11, [we] commenced receiving into the upper department, company No. 1. in the following order, viz;

Sarah Susannah Divine,	by	John Taylor[.]
Charles Lambert	"	" "
Mary Alice Lambert	"	Cha[rle]s. Lambert[.]
Sally Murdock	"	John Taylor[.]
David Jones	"	John Taylor[.]
Mercy Jones	by	David Jones[.]
Elizabeth Stout	"	Allen J. Stout.
Sarah Alley	by	Joseph B. Noble[.]
Joseph Busby	"	John Taylor[.]
Ann Busby	"	Joseph Busby[.]
James Bean	"	Jed[ediah]. M. Grant.
Elizabeth Bean	"	James Bean[.]
James Black	"	J[edediah]. M. Grant[.]
Jane Black	"	James Black.
Eliza Ann Haven	"	J[edediah]. M. Grant[.]
Moses Clawson	"	J[edediah]. M. Grant[.]
Cornelia Clawson	"	Moses Clawson[.]
Alphonso Green	"	J[edediah]. M. Grant[.]
Betsey Green	"	Alphonso Green[.]
Ephraim Mecham	"	J[edediah]. M. Grant.
Polly Mecham	"	Ephraim Mecham[.]
Edward Mecham	"	J[edediah]. M. Grant[.]
Irene Mecham	"	Edward Mecham[.]
Sally Maria Wade	"	J[edediah]. M. Grant[.] deaf lady
Darwin Chase	"	J[edediah]. M. Grant[.]
Nathaniel Leavitt	"	J[edediah]. M. Grant[.]
George Black	"	J[edediah]. M. Grant[.]
~~Charlotte Baker~~	~~"~~	~~J. M. Grant~~

27 [men and women received through the veil.]

---

for the Galena district (1839). He was appointed to the state supreme court in 1841, but resigned to accept the Democratic nomination for governor. After serving his term as governor, he authored *A History of Illinois: From Its Commencement as a State in 1818 to 1847* (Chicago: S. C. Griggs, 1854).

Finished at one o'clock— George P. Dykes, John D. Lee, and Artemisia Snow officiating as prompters.

At 20 minutes past 10 [we] commenced in the Male department, washing & anointing the following persons, viz;

High Priests.		
Nahum Bigelow	born	Feb[ruar]y 9. 1785
William Burgess Sen[ior].	"	May 20. 1794
James Tomlinson	"	April 17. 1800
Lemuel Mallory	"	April 2. 1801
James Davis	"	Aug[us]t 12. 1793
Selah VanSickle	"	June 8. 1812
Seventies		
Elisha Edwards	"	Dec[ember]. 13 1806
John Groesbeck	"	July 3 1801
David Elliott	"	Nov[embe]r 18 1799
George Gates	"	Dec[embe]r 24. 1811
Simon Baker	"	Oct[obe]r. 18 1811
Nathan Wixom	"	Nov[embe]r. 22. 1805
James Moses	"	Feb[ruar]y 28 1806
William Mendenhall	"	April 8. 1815
Lysander Gee	"	Sept[ember] 1. 1818
Preston Thomas	"	Feb[ruar]y 15. 1814
James Bulloch	"	Nov[embe]r. 16. 1806

Washed by William Hyde & Harrison Burgess Anointed by Levi Hancock Ezra T. Benson and Jacob Gates— ended at 25 m[inutes]. p[ast]. 11.

Nahum Bigelow was ordained a High Priest, under the hands of Abraham O. Smoot, and Joseph B. Noble, before being washed and anointed—

In the female department, the following persons were washed and anointed, commencing at 3 minutes past 11.

Elizabeth Gates. born Feb[ruar]y 4. 1811. Washed and anointed by Clarissa Hancock[.]

Betsey Eliza Wixom born April 16. 1813 W[ashed]. by Artemisia Snow. An[ointed] by Clarissa Herriman[.]

Mary Bigelow born June 26 1809 W[ashed]. by Nancy H. Rockwood An[ointed]. by N[ancy]. Winchester[.]

Maria E. Edwards born July 25. 1814 W[ashed]. by Nancy H. Rockwood An[ointed]. by Clarissa Herriman[.]

Margaret Groesbeck born Oct[ober] 7. 1797 W[ashed]. by Nancy H. Rockwood An[ointed]. by Nancy Winchester[.]

Vilate Burgess b[orn]. Oct[ober] 10 1794 Washed & anointed by Nancy H. Rockwood[.]

Laura Lovina Shimer born, Mar[ch]. 23. 1827 Washed & anointed by Nancy Winchester[.]

Nancy Booth born April 11. 1826 Washed & anointed by Julia Pack[.]

Elizabeth Davis b[orn]. April 1797 w[ashed] by Clarissa Hancock An[ointed]. by Clarissa Herriman[.]

Amanda M. Gee born May 5, 1821 W[ashed]. by Clarissa Hancock An[ointed]. by Nancy Winchester[.]

Sarah Ann Jane Thomas b[orn]. Feb[ruar]y 23. 1817 washed & anointed by Clarissa Hancock[.]

Eliza Graham born Nov[embe]r. 6. 1825 washed and anointed by Julia Pack[.]

Elizabeth Mallory born March 9. 1801 washed by Clarissa Hancock An[ointed] by Nancy Winchester[.]

Mary VanSickle born May 20 1816 W[ashed]. by Clarissa Hancock An[ointed]. by Clarissa Harriman[.]

Margaret Curtis born April 20. 1816 W[ashed]. by Mary Noble An[ointed], by Nancy Winchester[.]

Sarah Tomlinson born Mar[ch]. 10, 1802 W[ashed]. by Julia Pack An[ointed] by Clarissa Harriman[.]

Mary Bulloch born Aug[us]t 2. 1812 w[ashed]. by Clarissa Hancock, An[ointed]. by Clarissa Herriman[.]

Eliza Moses born June 15. 1813. w[ashed]. by Julia Pack. An[ointed]. by Nancy H. Rockwood[.]

Caroline Murdock born Oct[ober] 2. 1804 W[ashed]. by Mary Noble. An[ointed] by Nancy Winchester[.]

Sarah Mendenhall born March 12 1818 w[ashed]. by Mary Noble An[ointed] by Nancy Winchester[.]

20 [women washed and anointed.] Ended at 10 m[inutes]. past 12.

At 25 m[inutes]. past 12, [we] commenced receiving into the lower & middle departments company No. 2, the following persons officiating, viz, in the upper department,

Joseph Young	as	No.	1.
Levi W. Hancock	"	"	2.
John Pack	"	"	3.

in the middle department.

Lucius N. Scovil	as	No.	1

A[braham]. O. Smoot	"	"	2
Joseph B. Noble	"	"	3
W[illiam]. W. Phelps	"	"	4
Geo[rge]. P. Dykes	"	"	5.

The following named persons are engaged in finishing the upholstery work on the new Altar, which is to be used in the second washings & anointing, viz; Sister Mary Ann Young, and Agnes Smith—

At 25 minutes to 2, [we] commenced receiving into the upper department company No. 2 in the following order, viz;

Theodore Curtis,	by P[arley]. P. Pratt[.]
Margaret Curtis	by Theodore Curtis[.]
Laura Lovina Shimer	by Edward Hunter[.]
Preston Thomas	by P[arley]. P. Pratt[.]
Sarah Ann Jane Thomas	by Preston Thomas[.]
Simon Baker	by P[arley]. P. Pratt[.]
Charlotte Baker	" S[imon]. Baker[.]
Caroline Murdock	by P[arley]. P. Pratt[.]
Nathan Wixom	by P[arley]. P. Pratt[.]
Betsey Eliza Wixom	by Nathan Wixom[.]
Lemuel Mallory	by P[arley]. P. Pratt[.]
Elizabeth Mallory	by Lemuel Mallory[.]
James Davis	by P[arley]. P. Pratt[.]
Elizabeth Davis	by James Davis[.]
George Gates	by P[arley]. P. Pratt[.]
Elizabeth Gates	by George Gates[.]
William Mendenhall	by Orson Hyde[.]
Sarah Mendenhall	by W[illia]m. Mendenhall[.]
Elisha Edwards	by Orson Hyde[.]
Maria E. Edwards	by Elisha Edwards[.]
William Burgess Sen[io]r.	by Orson Hyde[.]
Vierlaty Burgess	by William Burgess[.]
Nahum Bigelow	by Orson Hyde[.]
Mary Bigelow	by Nahum Bigelow[.]
John Groesbeck	by Orson Hyde[.]
Margaret Groesbeck	by John Groesbeck[.]
Lysander Gee	by Orson Hyde[.]
Amanda M. Gee	by Lysander Gee[.]
David Elliott	by O[rson]. Hyde[.]
Nancy Booth	by O[rson]. Hyde[.]

Eliza Graham	by	O[rson]. Hyde[.]
James Bullock	by	Orson Hyde[.]
Mary Bullock	"	James Bullock[.]
James Moses	"	Orson Hyde[.]
Eliza Moses	"	James Moses[.]
James Tomlinson	"	Orson Hyde[.]
Sarah Tomlinson	"	James Tomlinson[.]

37. [men and women received through the veil.]

Ended at 10 minutes to 4. Prompters, Joseph A. Kelting, Jacob Gates, and Artemisia Snow.

At 25 minutes to 1, [we] commenced in the Male department, washing & anointing the following persons, viz;

High Priests.

John Bair	born	Nov[ember]. 26. 1810
Charles Crisman	"	Dec[ember[. 25 1807.

Seventies.

Thomas Tanner	born	March 18 1804
Warren S. Snow	"	June 15 1818
Levi S. Nickerson	"	April 2. 1814
Zenos H. Gurley	"	April 29 1801
Abraham Washburn	"	March 17 1805
Wilkinson Hewitt	"	March 20. 1812
Erastus H. Derby	"	Sept[ember] 14 1801

9 [men] Washed by William Hyde & Harrison Burgess, anointed by Jacob Gates, Ezra T. Benson and James Brown[.]

Finished at 30 m[inutes]. past 1.

In the Female department, commencing at 25 minutes after One, the following persons were washed & anointed, viz;

Tamar Washburn b[orn]. July 4, 1805 washed and anointed by Mary A. Noble[.]

Mary Ann Washburn born Nov[ember]. 18. 1827 Washed and anointed by Mary A. Noble[.]

Margaret Gurley born Jan[uar]y 1. 1808 w[ashed]. by Clarissa Hancock An[ointed] by Nancy Winchester[.]

Mary Ann Snow born Dec[ember]. 2. 1822 washed and anointed by Nancy H. Rockwood[.]

Mary Ann Nickerson born Sept[ember]. 5. 1823. w[ashed]. by Clarissa Hancock An[ointed]. by Nancy Winchester[.]

Ruth Tanner born Feb[ruar]y 17. 1814. w[ashed]. by Clarissa Hancock An[ointed] by Nancy Winchester[.]

Mary Catharine Aber born Dec[ember]. 24. 1825 washed and anointed by Nancy H. Rockwood[.]

Eliza Jane Fosdick born April 16. 1823. w[ashed]. by Clarissa Hancock An[ointed] by Nancy Winchester[.]

Mary Crisman born Oct[ober] 1. 1815 W[ashed]. by Clarissa Hancock An[ointed] by Nancy H. Rockwood[.]

Lucinda Bair born Jan[uar]y 10. 1819 W[ashed]. by Clarissa Hancock An[ointed]. by N[ancy]. H. Rockwood[.]

Molly Slade born June 22 1783 w[ashed]. by Mary A. Noble An[ointed] by Nancy Winchester[.]

Mary Beach born Sept[ember] 12 1826 w[ashed] by Mary A. Noble An[ointed]. by Nancy Winchester[.]

Sarah Lawrence born May 13. 1826 w[ashed] by Clarissa Hancock An[ointed] by Nancy H. Rock[woo]d.

Rumanah B. Derby b[orn]. Sept[ember] 6 1817 w[ashed]. by Clarissa Hancock An[ointed]. by Clarissa Harriman[.]

Sarah Ann Hewitt b[orn]. Ap[ri]l. 9. 1816 w[ashed]. by Mary A. Noble An[ointed] by Nancy Winchester[.]

15 [women washed and anointed.] Ended at 25 m[inutes]. to 3[.]

At 10 m[inutes]. to 3 [we] commenced receiving into the lower and middle departments Company No. 3 J[edediah]. M. Grant, B[enjamin]. L. Clapp, & John Pack officiating in the upper department, and Lucius N. Scovil, Joseph B[ates]. Noble, Israel Barlow, Eratus Snow and Levi W. Hancock in the Middle department.

At 20 m[inutes]. past 4 [we] commenced at the vail.

Molly Slade	received by	H[eber]. C. Kimball[.]
Sarah Lawrence	" "	" " "
Erastus H. Derby	" "	" " "
Rumanah B. Derby	"	E[rastus]. H. Derby[.]
Mary Ann Washburn	"	J[oseph]. B. Noble[.]
Zenos H. Gurley	"	H[eber]. C. Kimball[.]
Margaret Gurley	"	Z[enos]. H. Gurley[.]
Abraham Washburn	"	H[eber]. C. Kimball[.]
Tamar Washburn	"	A[braham]. Washburn[.]
Charles Crismon	"	H[eber]. C. Kimball[.]
Mary Crismon	"	Ch[arles]. Crismon[.]
Thomas Tanner	"	H[eber]. C. Kimball[.]

Ruth Tanner	"	Thomas Tanner[.]
Levi S. Nickerson	"	H[eber]. C. Kimball[.]
Mary Ann Nickerson	"	Levi S. Nickerson[.]
Wilkinson Hewitt	"	A[lbert]. P. Rockwood[.]
Sarah Ann Hewitt	"	W[ilkinson]. Hewitt[.]
John Bair	"	A[lbert]. P. Rockwood[.]
Lucinda Bair	"	John Bair[.]
Warren S. Snow	"	A[lbert]. P. Rockwood[.]
Mary Ann Snow	"	Warren S. Snow[.]
Selah Vansickle	"	A[lbert]. P. Rockwood[.]
Mary Vansickle	"	Selah Vansickle[.]
Eliza Jane Fosdick	"	A[lbert]. P. Rockwood[.]
Mary Beach	"	" " "
May Catharine Aber	"	" "

Ended at 5 m[inutes]. to 6.— Prompters were [blank]

24. [men and women received through the veil.]

At 6 o'clock P.M. Pres[ident]. B[righam]. Young and Heber C. Kimball with their wives Mary Ann Young & Vilate Kimball left the temple, to go to Elder John Taylor's to attend a party, to which they were invited.

The following named High Priests met in room No. 8 for prayer, clothed in the Robes of the Holy Priesthood, viz; Simeon Carter who was mouth — Joseph B. Noble, William Felshaw — Benj[ami]n. Brown, Amos C. Deuel — Hiram Spencer Elijah Fordham — Elan Ludington — Joshua S. Holman, [David] H. Redfield — Abel Lamb — Jacob Foutz John S. Higbee Samuel Gully — Isaac Chase — Caleb Haight[.]

In room No. 10 the following High Priests met — viz; Stephen Markham, Pres[ident]. — Winslow Farr — Aaron F. Farr — Daniel Carn — W[illia]m. Manhard[,] Freeman Nickerson and Elders Jesse Baker — Sam[ue]l. Williams William Sears — [and] O[smyn]. M. Deuel—

In room No. 6 the following named High Priests met.— viz; George Miller President, Samuel Rolfe — Geo[rge]. P. Dykes William Crosby — Harvey Green — W[illia]m. C. Gallaher — Jonathan Becklehymer — Job V. Barnum — Samuel Miles, — James Brown John Murdock — Zebedee Coltrin — Albert Petty — Charles W. Patten — Raymond Clark[,] Alphonso Young — Hezekiah Peck — F[ranklin]. D. Richards — John Brown[,] Seventy.

The High Council met at 15 m[inutes]. past 6 in room No. 4, the following persons being present viz; — Charles C. Rich, Samuel Bent,

George W. Harris — James Allred — Henry G. Sherwood — David Fullmer — Aaron Johnson, Thomas Grover Newel Knight — Lewis D. Wilson & Calvin C. Pendleton[,] clerk—

The Quorum of Seventies, met in room No. 9, clothed, and offered up prayers—for the preservation of the Twelve [apostles] and all the different quorums and for the continuation of the blessings of the endowment—

After the business of the day was over the brethren & Sisters, indulged in a dance— The musicians were Hans C. Hanson, Jacob F. Hutchinson and Levi W. Hancock on the Violin, James Smithies on the Bass Viol, Elizha Averett on the Flute. After dancing two figures, Joseph Young addressed the party at considerable length, and made a prayer in which all joined after which the music & dancing was continued to a late hour, say 12. o'clock.

Pres[ident]. B[righam]. Young returned to the Temple a few minutes after 10, and took part in the exercises— By his directions, Lucian R. Foster and Ann Maria, his wife, and Stephen Markham and his wife, danced a French four— This was the first time that L[ucian]. R. Foster & his wife danced together.

—William Clayton, Diary, kept for Heber C. Kimball.

....

Services commenced at 9 20/60 [9:20] o'clock A M ~~by~~ in the male department by washing & anointing the following persons, viz,

Seventies			
1	Edward Mecham	born	^Feb[ruary]^ 22, 1802
2	James Bean	"	Mar[ch] 3, 1804
3	Joseph Busby	"	Nov[ember]. 5, 1810
High Priest			
	Moses Clawson	"	Oct[ober] 8, 1801
2	William Black	"	Aug[ust] 20, 1784
Seventy			
4	Nathaniel Leavitt		
Seventies			
	Darwin Chase	born	Feb[ruary]. 25, 1816
6	Ephraim Mecham	"	Mar[ch]. 7, 1808
7	Alphonso Green	"	July 8, 1810
8	George Black	"	May 6, 1823
9	David Jones	"	Aug[ust] 20, 1799
10	Charles Lambert	"	Aug[ust] 30, 1816

The above persons were washed by William Hyde & Harrison Burgess, and anointed by Levi Hancock Jacob Gates & Ezra T. Benson, who finished at 10 20/60 [10:20] o'clock A.M.

[A]t 11 0'clock Pres[iden]t B[righam]. Young and H[eber]. C. Kimball came in the room, the rest of the Twelve [apostles] (except W[illard]. Richards and G[eorge]. A. Smith, who were absent on account of sickness) were present; after which they with P[arley]. P. Pratt, A[masa]. Lyman, J[edediah]. M. Grant, G[eorge]. Miller, W[illiam]. W. Phelps, Joseph B. Nobles and J[ohn]. D. Lee dressed in priestly robes, offered up the signs and prayed & consecrated 19 bottles of oil.

No. 2 Sev[enties]

11	Elisha Edwards	born	Dec[ember] 13, 1806
12	John Groesbeck	"	July 3, 1801
13	David Elliott	"	Nov[ember]. 18, 1799
14	George Gates	"	Dec[ember]. 27, 1811
15	Simeon Baker	"	Oct[ober] 15 1811
16	Nathan Wixom	"	Nov[ember] 22, 1805
17	James Moses	"	Feb[ruary] 28, 1806
18	William Mendenhall	"	Ap[ri]l 8, 1815
Seventies			
19	Lysander Gee	born	Sep[tember] 1, 1818
20	Preston Thomas		Feb[ruary] 15, 1814
21	James Bullock		Nov[ember]. 16, 1805
High Priests			
	Nahum Bigelow		Feb[ruary] 9, 1785
2	William Burgess		May 20, 1794
3	James Tomlinson		Apr[i]l 17, 1800
4	Lemuel Mallony		April 2, 1801
5	James Davis		Aug[ust] 12, 1793
6	Selah Van Liskle		Jun[e] 8, 1818

Washed by William Hyde and Harrison Burgess Anointed [illegible]

Co[mpany]. No. 3

Seventies			
23	Thomas Tanner	born	March 18, 180[0?]
24	Warren Snow	"	June 15, 1818
25	Levi P. Nickerson	"	Ap[ri]l. 2, 1814
26	Zenos ~~W~~ ^H.^ Gurley	"	Ap[ri]l 9, 1801
27	Abraham Washburn	"	Mar[ch]. 17, 1805

Seventy			
	Wilkinson Hewit	born	Mar[ch]. 20, 1812
29	Erastus W. Derby	"	Sep[tember] 11, 1801
High Priest			
	Charles Crismon	"	Dec[ember] 25, 1807
2	John Bair	"	Nov[ember 25, 1810

Washed by William Hyde and Harrison Burgess; Anointed by Jacob Gates, Ezra T. Benson, and James Brown.

Female Department

[See pages 347-49 for excerpted portion.]

At about 8 o'clock P.M. Several of the Twelve [apostles], part of the High Council, several Seventies & [the] High Prsts retired to their respective rooms for prayers, offering up the signs &c. After which several musicians came into the room, when Pres[iden]t ^B[righam]^ Young, J[oseph]. Young, with several Seventies and High Priests joined in the holy dance, after which Br[other]s. [Levi] Hancock and E[rastus]. Snow each sang a California hymn, when at 4 40/60 [4:40] o'clock all retired to their respective houses except those who labored in the Temple.

—Seventies Record, Book B.

....

Evening went into the Temple [and] sat about two hours. I [Thomas Bullock] esteemed my great privilege. Shook hands with B[righam]. Young, H[eber]. C. Kimball, O[rson]. Hyde, P[arley]. P. Pratt, O[rson]. Pratt, and many others. Felt very happy ...

—Thomas Bullock, Diary.

....

Seventeen bottles of oil were consecrated.

Ninety persons received ordinances.

6 p.m., Elder H[eber]. C. Kimball and I [Brigham Young] with our wives attended a party at Elder John Taylor's.

Three companies of high priests, the high council, and the seventies met for prayer in their respective rooms in the Temple.

Several musicians were present in the evening, some of the brethren danced.

I returned to the Temple about 10 p.m. and took part in the exercises. Brothers Erastus Snow and Levi W. Hancock sang hymns.

—"Manuscript History of Brigham Young,"
in *History of the Church,* 7:565.

[Washings and anointings for Tuesday, January 6, 1846]

	washed by		anointed by	
Eliza Ann Haven born May 1, 1798		Nancy H. Rockwood		Nancy Winchester
Sally M. Wade May 13, 1788	"	"	"	Clarissa Herriman
Sally Murdock Apl 22, 1788	"	Artimisia Snow	"	Nancy Winchester
Cornelia Clawson Oct 22, 1803	"	Nancy H. Rockwood	"	"
Betsey Green May 6, 1810	"	"	"	Clarissa Hancock
Ann C. Buzby Mar 9, 1813	"	"	"	Clarissa Herriman
Jane Black June 11, 1801	"	Artimisia Snow	"	Clarissa Hancock
Polly Mecham Aug 13, 1814	"	Nancy H. Rockwood	"	Nancy Winchester
Irena Meckham Nov. 18, 1807	"	Artimisia Snow	"	Clarissa Hancock
Elizabeth Bean Sep 22, 1803	"	"		"
Mercy Jones July 19, 1806	"	Nancy H. Rockwood	"	Clarissa Herriman
Elizabeth Stout Oct 13, 1823	"	"	"	Nancy Winchester
Sarah Ally Oct 19, 1819	"	Artimisia Snow	"	Mary A. Noble
Mary Alice Lambert Dec 9, 1828	"	Nancy H. Rockwood	"	Clarissa Hancock
Charlotte Baker Dec 5, 1820	"	"	"	
S. Susannah Divine Jan 16, 1833	"	"	"	Clarissa Herriman
Elizabeth Gates ~~b~~ Feb 4. 1811	"	Clarissa Hancock	"	Clarissa Hancock
Bestey Eliza Wixom Apl 16, 1813	"	Artimisia Snow	"	Clarissa Herriman
Mary Bigelow June 26, 1809	"	Nancy H. Rockwood	"	Nancy Winchester
Mariah E. Edwards July 25, 1814	"	"	"	Clarissa Herriman
Margaret Groesbeck Oct. 7, 1797	"	"	"	Nancy Winchester

	[washed by]		[anointed by]	
Vierlaty Burgess Oct 10, 1774	"	"		Nancy H. Rockwood
Laura Lovina Shiver May 23, 1827	"	Nancy Winchester	"	Nancy Winchester
Nancy Booth Apl. 11, 1826	"	Julia Pack	"	Julia Pack
Elizabeth Davis Apl. 1797	"	Clarissa Hancock	"	Clarissa Herriman
Amanda M. Gee May 5, 1821	"	"	"	Nancy Winchester
Sarah A Jane Thomas Feb 23, 1817	"	"		Clarissa Herriman
Eliza Graham Nov. 6, 1825	"	Julia Pack	"	Julia Pack
Elizabeth Mallory Mar 9, 1801	"	Clarissa Hancock	"	Clarissa Herriman
Mary Ann Sickle May 20, 1816	"	"	"	
Margaret Curtis Apl 20, 1816	"	Mary Noble	"	Nancy Winchester
Sarah Tomlinson Mar. 10, 1802	"	Julia Pack	"	Clarissa Herriman
	washed by		anointed by	
Mary Bullock b. Aug. 2, 1812	"	Clarissa Hancock	"	Clarissa Herriman
Eliza Moses June 19, 1813	"	Julia Pack	"	Nancy H. Rockwood
Caroline Murdock Oct 2, 1804	"	Mary ^A^ Noble	"	Nancy Winchester
Sarah Mendenhall Mar 12, 1818	"	"	"	"
No 3				
Tamar Washburn July 4, 1805	"	"	"	Mary A Noble
Mary Ann Washburn Nov. 18, 1827	"	"	"	
Margaret Greeley Jan 1, 1808	"	Clarissa Hancock	"	Nancy Winchester
Mary Ann Snow Dec. 2, 1822	"	Nancy H. Rockwood	"	Nancy H. Rockwood
Mary Ann Nickerson Sep 5, 1823	"	Clarissa Hancock	"	Nancy Winchester

Ruth Tanner Feb 17, 1814	"	"	"	
Mary C. Aber Dec. 24, 1825	"	Nancy H. Rockwood	"	Nancy H. Rockwood
Eliza Jane Fosdick Apl. 16, 1823	"	Clarissa Hancock	"	Nancy Winchester
Mary Crisman Oct 1, 1815	"	"	"	Nancy H. Rockwood
Lucinda Bear Jan. 10, 1819	"	"	"	
Molly Slade June 22, 1783	"	Mary A. Noble	"	Nancy Winchester
Mary Beach Sep. 12, 1826	"	"	"	
Sarah Lawrence May 13, 1826	"	Clarissa Hancock	"	Nancy H. Rockwood
Rumamah B. Derby Sep 6, 1817	"	"	"	Clarissa Herriman
Sara Ann Hewitt Apl. 9, 1816	"	Mary A Noble	"	Nancy Winchester

—Seventies Record, Book B, oversized portion, January 6, 1846.

Nauvoo temple endowments performed on this date for:

First Company: Sarah Susannah Divine, Charles Lambert, Mary Alice Lambert, Sally Murdock, David Jones, Mercy Jones, Elizabeth Stout, Sarah Alley, Joseph Busby, Ann Busby, James Bean, Elisabeth Bean, William Black, Jane Black, Eliza Ann Haven, Moses Clawson, Cornelia Clawson, Alphonso Green, Betsey Green, Ephraim Mecham, Polly Mecham, Edward Mecham, Irene Mecham, Sally Maria Wade, Darwin Chase, Nathaniel Leavitt, and George Black.

Second Company: Theodore Curtis, Margaret Curtis, Laura Lovina Shimer, Preston Thomas, Sarah Ann Jane Thomas, Simon Baker, Charlotte Baker, Caroline Murdock, Nathan Wixon, Betsey Eliza Wixom, Lemuel Mallory, Elizabeth Mallory, James Davis, Elizabeth Davis, George Gates, Elizabeth Gates, William Mendenhall, Sarah Mendenhall, Elisha Edwards, Maria E. Edwards, William Burgess Sr., Vierlaty Burgess, Nahum Bigelow, Mary Bigelow, John Groesbeck, Margaret Groesbeck, Lysander Gee, Amanda M. Gee, David Elliott, Nancy Booth, Eliza Graham, James Bullock, Mary Bullock, James Moses, Eliza Moses, James Tomlinson, and Sarah Tomlinson.

Third Company: Molly Slade, Sarah Lawrence, Erastus H. Derby, Rumanah B. Derby, Mary Ann Washburn, Zenos H. Gurley, Margaret Gurley, Abraham Washburn, Tamar Washburn, Charles Crismon, Mary Crismon, Thomas Tanner, Ruth Tanner, Levi S. Nickerson, Mary Ann Nickerson, Wilkinson Hewitt, Sarah Ann Hewitt, John Bair, Lucinda Bair, Warren S. Snow, Mary Ann Snow, Selah Vansickle, Mary Vansickle, Eliza Jane Fosdick, Mary Beach, and Mary Catharine Aber.

—Summary of information compiled by the Temple Index Bureau, *Nauvoo Temple Endowment Register: 10 December 1845 to 8 February 1846.*

Wednesday, January 7, 1846

[S]pent this day also in assisting about the alt[a]r which [was] completted & arranged [in] my room. In the evening the council met[.] after sing[ing] & prayers we put on our [temple] robes & proceeded to dedicate the alter and I pronounced the ~~following~~ dedication prayer[.]

—Brigham Young, Diary.

....

Dedication of the Altar.

On January 7th 1846 at 6 P.M.: President Brigham Young, H[eber].

C. Kimball, O[rson]. Hyde, P[arley]. P. Pratt, O[rson]. Pratt, W[illard]. Richards, John Taylor, A[masa]. Lyman, George Miller, N[ewel]. K. Whitney, Mary A. Young, Vilate Kimball, Leonora Taylor, & Elizabeth Ann Whitney met in room No 1[.] after singing, and prayer by Bishop N[ewel]. K. Whitney and singing again the brethren proceeded to put on their robes and surrounding the Alter Pres[iden]t Brigham Young pronounced the following prayer[:]

Our father in heaven in the name of the Lord Jesus Christ we ask thee to forgive us of our sins and cleanse our hearts from ever[y] impure spirit that we may offer unto thee an acceptable offering. We present ourselves before thee and bow down upon this alter which we have been enabled to prepare for thy servants and handmaids to receive their sealing blessings. We present it unto thee with ourselves and dedicate and consecrate it in the name of the Lord Jesus Christ unto thy most holy name; and we ask thee to receive this our dedication & sanctify this Alter to thy servants and handmaids and that all those who come unto it may feel the power of the Holy Ghost resting upon them and realize the covenants they enter into upon this alter; unto this end we ask thee to dedicate, consecrate, and sanctify this holy alter that our covenants and contracts that we enter into with each other may be dictated by thy Holy Spirit and sacredly kept by us and accepted of thee, and all these blessings be realized by all thy saints who come unto this alter in the morning of the resurrection of the just, and all the Glory honor praise and power be unto God & the Lamb forever and ever Amen. & Amen. The alter being now ready for use.

—Book of Living Sealings.[9]

....

This morning there was an immense crowd at the reception room,

9. The "Book of Sealings (Living)" is one of four ledger books recording the various sealing ordinances performed in the Nauvoo temple. The three others are: "Book of Adoptions," "Book of Anointings," and "Book of Proxey [Sealings]." The information—names, birth dates, etc.—was first written on loose pieces of paper and then transferred to these books. In 1869-70, Joseph F. Smith used information from these books, as well as from other early records, to compile "Sealings and Adoptions." Smith's compilation contains: (1) sealings of couples in Salt Lake City, 1849-57; (2) sealings of couples, as well as adoptions and other sealings, in the Nauvoo temple, 1846; (3) sealings and marriages in Nauvoo and Winter Quarters, 1846-48; (4) a list of people to be adopted to Brigham Young, 1846-54; and (5) cancellations of one marriage and two adoptions. Lyndon W. Cook summarized all known early proxy marriage sealings in his *Nauvoo Marriages Proxy Sealings 1843-1846* (Provo, UT: Grandin Book, 2004); see especially his biographical annotations.

waiting for admission into the washing & anointing rooms[,] The brethren as they came along bearing Baskets, Pails & other vessels filled with all kinds of provisions, for the use of those who are attending on the ordinances of the Lord's House.— The supply is much greater than the consumption.

At 7 minutes to 8 o'clock [we] commenced in the Male department, washing and anointing the following persons, viz;

High Priests.		
Henry Mower,	born	Dec[embe]r. 18. 1798.
David Manhard	"	Aug[us]t 16 1802.
Wheeler Baldwin	"	March 7. 1793.
Seventies.		
Robert Campbell	"	March 31. 1810
Eli B. Kelsey	"	Oct[ober] 27. 1819
Jared Porter	"	March 23. 1812
Roswell Hyde	"	May 20. 1816
Aaron Hart	"	April 1. 1803
Charles S. Peterson	"	July 28 1818
Henry A. Cleaveland	"	Jan[uar]y 4. 1809
William A. Beebe	"	June 9. 1813
Levi North	"	July 17. 1817
George W. Rosencrantz	"	Feb[ruar]y. 6 1812
Nathan Cheney	"	Feb[ruar]y 11. 1811
John B. Walker	"	March 24 1814

[W]ashed by Jacob Gates, & W[illia]m. Hyde Anointed by J[edediah]. M. Grant Ezra T. Benson Harrison Burgess James Brown—

[F]inished at 9 o'clock.

In the Female department, commencing at 25 minutes after 8. the following persons were washed and anointed, viz;

Mary Jane Manhard.	born	Feb[ruar]y 9. 1815
Mary Mower	"	Oct[ober]. 1803
Agnes Flake	"	Nov[embe]r. 6 1819
Rhoda Matthews	"	April 6. 1817
Eliza Rosencrans	"	Dec[embe]r. 15, 1811
Mary Ann Hyde	"	Dec[ember]. 31 1820
Araminta North	"	Feb[ruar]y 25, 1819
Abiah Porter	"	Feb[ruar]y 1. 1813
Mary Kelsey	"	June 28. 1791

Letitia Kelsey	"	Oct[ober]. 24. 1816
Louisa Beebe	"	Aug[us]t. 10. 1817
Mary Baldwin	"	July 20. 1793
Isabel Hart	"	April 7. 1808
Elizabeth Walker	"	Oct[ober]. 24. 1816
Samantha Baldwin	"	May 13. 1820
Delilah Campbell	"	July 27. 1813
Susannah Warm	"	Feb[ruar]y 18. 1825
Eliza Ann Cheney	"	Jan[uar]y 11. 1815
Ann Cleaveland	"	March 10. 1803
Mary Ann Peterson	"	July 23. 1822

Finished at 12 m[inutes]. to 10.

[W]ashed by Eliza Jane Webb — Elizabeth Barlow, Mary Clapp, Nancy H. Rockwood and Nancy Winchester— Anointed by Nancy Winchester, Clarissa Harriman and Nancy H. Rockwood.

At 10 o'clock [we] commenced receiving into the lower & middle departments, those who were washed & anointed this morning— The following persons officiating, viz; Joseph Young, J[edediah]. M. Grant, John Pack. L[ucius]. N. Scovil, A[braham]. O. Smoot — L[evi]. W. Hancock, E[rastus]. Snow. & G[eorge]. P. Dykes.

At 15 m[inutes]. past 11. [we] commenced receiving into the upper department, company No. 1 in the following order—viz;

Agnes Flake	by	P[arley]. P. Pratt[.]
Levi North	"	P[arley]. P. Pratt[.]
Araminta North	"	Levi North.
Mary Kelsey	"	P[arley]. P. Pratt[.]
Henry Mower	"	P[arley]. P. Pratt[.]
Mary Mower	"	Henry Mower[.]
David Manhard	"	P[arley]. P. Pratt.
Mary Jane Manhard	by	D[avid]. Manhard[.]
John B. Walker	by	P[arley]. P. Pratt[.]
Elizabeth Walker	"	J[ohn]. B. Walker[.]
Samantha Baldwin	"	P[arley]. P. Pratt[.]
Jared Porter	"	P[arley]. P. Pratt[.]
Abiah Porter	"	Jared Porter[.]
Aaron Hart	"	Orson Spencer[.]
Isabella Hart	"	Aaron Hart[.]
Rhoda Matthews	"	Orson Spencer[.]

Henry A. Cleaveland	"	Orson Spencer[.]
Ann Cleaveland	"	H[enry]. A. Cleaveland[.]
Robert Campbell	"	Orson Spencer[.]
Delilah Campbell	"	R[obert]. Campbell[.]
Roswell Hyde	by	Orson Spencer[.]
Mary Ann Hyde	"	R[oswell]. Hyde[.]
George W. Rosecrans	"	Orson Spencer[.]
Eliza Rosecrans	"	G[eorge]. W. Rosecrans[.]
Susannah Warm	"	Edward Hunter.
Eli B. Kelsey	"	O[rson]. Spencer[.]
Letitia Kelsey	"	E[li]. B. Kelsey[.]
William A. Beebee	"	John Taylor[.]
Louisa Beebe	"	W[illiam]. A. Beebe[.]
Nathan Cheney	"	John Taylor[.]
Eliza Ann Cheney	"	N[athan]. Cheney[.]
Wheeler Baldwin	"	John Taylor[.]
Mary Baldwin	by	Wh[eeler]. Baldwin.
Charles S. Peterson	"	John Taylor[.]
Mary Ann Peterson		Ch[arles]. S. Peterson[.]

Finished at 10 minutes past one, Prompters—Geo[rge]. P. Dykes, L[evi]. W. Hancock, & C[atherine]. C. Spencer.

A letter was received this morning from Mr. Tucker, the Catholic Priest, informing us that the Bishop could not raise money enough to purchase our property, but would either purchase or rent one of our public building but would not insure it against fire or mobs. A council was held in Pres[ident]. [Brigham] Young's room, and the letter was taken into consideration,— The result of the deliberations was that they would not answer the letter, and that the Catholics might go to hell their own way.

President B[righam]. Young, H[eber]. C. Kimball — P[arley]. P. Pratt, Orson Pratt William Clayton & Peter Haws were present at the council.

At 10 minutes past 10 [we] commenced in the male department, Washing & Anointing the following persons, viz;

High Priests.

Pliny Fisher	born	Aug[us]t 5. 1775
Rufus Fisher	"	Dec[embe]r. 11. 1804
Almon W. Babbitt	"	Oct[ober] 29 1813

Seventies

Dana Jacobs	"	July 16. 1808

Walter E. Wilcox	"	April 11. 1821
Ira N. Spaulding	"	April 16 1809
Samuel W. Richards	born	Aug[us]t 9 1824
William Rowley	"	June 21. 1798
Ethan Griffith	"	April 15 1803
Silas W. Condit	"	June 27. 1819
Enoch P. Rollins	"	Jan[uar]y 14 1805
Lauren H. Roundy	"	May 21. 1814
John Woodman	"	Oct[ober] 8. 1789
Gilbert Hunt	"	April 11. 1825
Simpson D. Huffaker	"	July 23. 1812
George P. Stiles	"	July 18. 1816

Washed by Jacob Gates & W[illia]m. Hyde[;] Anointed by John Pack — Harrison Burgess James Brown & Ezra T. Benson.

Finished at 10 m[inutes]. past. 11.

In the Female department, commencing at 18 minutes to 11, the following persons were washed and anointed—viz;

Fanny Murr[a]y	born	Nov[embe]r. 8. 1787
Nancy Ingersoll	"	Oct[ober] 18. 1785
Olive Fisher	"	April 18. 1821
Isabel Hollister	"	Aug[us]t 20. 1825
Maria W. Wilcox	"	June 17, 1827
Sophia Janette Stiles	"	Dec[ember]. 17. 1814
Jemima Stringham	"	Oct[ober] 5. 1804
Mary Ann Rowley	"	Jan[uar]y 21. 1810.
Cynthia Nichols	"	Jan[uar]y 11. 1816
Ruth A. Griffith	"	Feb[ruary] 16. 1800 Sup[posed?].
Johanna Roundy	"	Nov[ember]. 26 1824
Zilpha Jacobs	"	Sept[ember] 28. 1811
Mehitabel Hall	"	Oct[ober] 1. 1806
Sarah Condit	"	Dec[ember] 18. 1824
Lucy Bishop	"	Jan[uary]. 20. 1783
Ann Eliza Spaulding	"	Sept[ember] 2 1817
Sally Parker	born	Dec[ember]. 8. 1778
Betsey Pinkham	"	Dec[ember]. 12 1789
Sophia W. Rollins	"	Dec[ember]. 12. 1805
Priscilla Huffaker	"	April 16. 1784
Lucretia Hupper	"	Sept[ember] 15. 1818
Julia Ann Babbitt	"	Nov[ember]. 9. 1809

Washed by Nancy Winchester, Mary Ann Young, Nancy H. Rockwood, Elizabeth Barlow & Eliza Jane Webb— Anointed by Nancy Winchester, Nancy H. Rockwood, Clarissa Harriman, and Vilate Kimball— ended at 20 minutes to 1.

Almon W. Babbitt was washed by Jos[eph]. Young and Ezra T. Benson— anointed by H[eber]. C. Kimball and Joseph Young.

At 5 minutes before 1. [we] commenced receiving into the lower & middle departments, company No. 2. the following persons officiating in the upper department, viz; J[edediah]. M. Grant as No. 1. John Pack 2. Abraham O. Smoot No. 3, and in the middle department[,] Orson Pratt as No. 1. Levi W. Hancock as No. 2. Erastus Snow as No. 3. John D. Lee as No. 4, G[eorge]. P. Dykes No. 5.

At 10 minutes past 2 [we] commenced receiving into the upper department Company No. 2 in the following order—

Ethan Griffith	by	P[arley]. P. Pratt[.]
Ruth A. Griffith	"	P[arley]. P. Pratt[.]
Almon W. Babbitt	"	P[arley]. P. Pratt[.]
Julia Ann Babbitt	"	A[lmon]. W. Babbitt[.]
Nancy Ingersol	"	P[arley]. P. Pratt[.]
George P. Stiles	by	P[arley]. P. Pratt[.]
Sophia Janette Stiles	"	Geo[rge]. P. Stiles[.]
Isabel Hollister	"	G[eorge]. P. Stiles[.]
Lauren H. Roundy	"	P[arley]. P. Pratt[.]
Fanny Murray	"	Joseph Young[.]
Joanna Roundy	"	L[auren]. H. Roundy[.]
Rufus Fisher	"	P[arley]. P. Pratt.
Olive Fisher	"	Rufus Fisher[.]
Cynthia Nichols	"	Rufus Fisher[.]
Silas W. Condit	"	P[arley]. P. Pratt[.]
Sarah Condit	"	S[ilas]. W. Condit[.]
Pliny Fisher	"	P[arley]. P. Pratt.
Sally Parker	"	P[arley]. P. Pratt.
Simpson D. Huffaker	"	P[arley]. P. Pratt[.]
Priscilla Huffaker	"	S[impson]. D. H[uffaker]. & Amasa Lyman[.]
Enoch P. Rollins	"	Amasa Lyman[.]
Sophia W. Rollins	"	E[noch]. P. Rollins[.]
John Workman	"	Amasa Lyman[.]
Betsey Pinkham	"	" "

Jemima Stringham	"	" "
Walter E. Wilcox	"	" "
Maria W. Wilcox	"	Walter E. Wilcox[.]
Mehitabel Hall	"	Amasa Lyman[.]
Samuel W. Richards	"	Amasa Lyman[.]
Lucretia Hupper	"	Amasa Lyman[.]
William Rowley	"	A[masa]. Lyman[.]
Mary Ann Rowley	"	William Rowley[.]
Lucy Bishop	"	A[masa]. Lyman[.]
Ira N. Spaulding	"	Amasa Lyman[.]
Eliza Spaulding	"	I[ra]. N. Spaulding[.]
~~Julia Ann Babbitt~~	~~"~~	~~Almon W. Babbitt~~
Dana Jacobs	"	Amasa [Lyman.]
Zilpha Jacobs		[blank]

Prompters, A[braham]. O. Smoot, & Artemisia Snow.

At 10 min[utes]. past 1, [we] commenced in the Male department, washing & anointing the following persons. viz;

High Priests

Amos Cox.	born	March 26. 1821
Orville S. Cox	"	Nov[ember]. 25. 1814
Edwin Whiting	"	Sept[ember] 9. 1809
Thomas Pearson	"	March 1. 1802

Seventies.

William Burgess Jr.	born	Mar[ch]. 1. 1822
Isaac Morley Jr.	"	May 2. 1829
John Alger	"	Nov[ember]. 5. 1820
Joseph B. Peck	"	Jan[uar]y 7. 1819
Rowland Shannon	"	Oct[ober] 11. 1820
Chauncey Whitney	"	Aug[us]t 19. 1819
Horace Burgess	"	Jan[uar]y 23. 1816
James McClelan	"	Aug[us]t 8. 1804
John Bills	"	Sept[ember] 17. 1819
David LeBaron	"	Nov[embe]r 24. 1822.

Elders.

James M. Works	"	Oct[ober] 5. 1822.

Ended 2 o'clock— washed by Jacob Gates & William Hyde anointed by Benj[ami]n. L. Clapp, Harrison Burgess and James Brown.

Isaac Morley Jun[io]r. was ordained into the quorum of Seventies, under the hands of Joseph Young & Isaac Morley. before being washed & anointed[.]

At 23 <m[inutes].> before 2 [we] commenced in the Female department, washing & anointing the following persons viz;

Lucia L. Leavitt	born	Aug[us]t 9. 1826
Mary E. Cox	"	Dec[embe]r. 15. 1826
Theresa A. Morley	"	July 18 1826
Elizabeth P. Whitney	"	April 15. 1814
Nancy Ann Hunt	"	Aug[us]t. 10. 1827
Matilda Neas	"	Jan[uar]y 1. 1828
Almira Palmer	"	May 13. 1824
Catharine Pearson	"	April 3. 1809
Maria Burgess	"	June 17. 1823
Susanna Peck	"	Mar[ch]. 12 1821
Phebe Danfield	"	Sept[ember] 20. 1807
Harriet L. Cox	"	Jan[uar]y 20. 1823
Editha A. Whiting	"	Jan[uar]y 25. 1820
Mary G. Pearson	"	Oct[ober] 2. 1828
Elizabeth Bills	"	Jan[uar]y 1. 1817
Sarah Alger	"	Nov[ember]. 2, 1824
Philena Cox	"	Oct[ober] 2. 1813
Pamela Elvira Cox	"	Mar[ch]. 2. 1820
Esther M. LeBaron	"	Jan[uary] 12. 1827
Lucretia Shannon	"	June 7. 1823
Cynthia McClelan	"	April 28. 1810
Almira Burgess	born	"

Washed by Eliza Jane Webb. and Clarissa Hancock— anointed by Nancy Winchester, Clarissa Herriman & Nancy H. Rockwood. Elizabeth Barlow held the horn.

Ended at. 10 minutes past 3.

~~At 15 M. past commenced receiving co. No. 3 into lower & middle department. J. D. Lee acting in the upper department as No. 1. A. P. Rockwood as No. 2. and Harrison Burgess as No 3.~~

error—

At 15 minutes past 3. [we] commenced receiving into the lower & middle departments, company No. 3.[,] the following persons officiating in the upper department. viz;

Joseph Young	as	No.	1.
Levi W. Hancock	"	"	2.

Jacob Gates	"	"	3.

and in the middle department,

L[ucius]. N. Scovil	as No.	1
Israel Barlow	"	2
Jacob Gates	"	3
W[illiam]. W. Phelps	"	4
Geo[rge]. P. Dykes	"	5

At 15 minutes before 5 o'clock [we] commenced receiving into the upper department Company No. 3. in the following order—viz;

William Burgess Jr.	by	B[enjamin]. L. Clapp[.]
Maria Burgess	"	William Burgess[.]
Lucia L. Leavitt	"	B[enjamin]. L. Clapp[.]
Joseph B. Peck	"	B[enjamin]. L. Clapp[.]
Susanna Peck	"	J[oseph]. B. Peck[.]
Matilda Neas	"	[Benjamin] Clapp[.]
James McClellan	"	[Benjamin] Clapp[.]
Cynthia McClellan	"	James McClelan[.]
Nancy Ann Hunt	"	[Benjamin] Clapp[.]
Chauncey Whiting	"	[Benjamin] Clapp[.]
Editha Ann Whiting	"	C[hauncey]. Whiting[.]
Theresa A. Morley	"	[Benjamin] Clapp[.]
Almira Palmer	"	[Benjamin] Clapp[.]
John Alger	"	[Benjamin] Clapp[.]
Sarah Alger	"	J[ohn]. Alger[.]
Thomas Pearson	"	B[enjamin]. L. Clapp[.]
Catharine Pearson	"	Th[omas]. Pearson[.]
Mary G. Pearson	"	" "
John Bills	"	B[enjamin]. L. Clapp[.]
Elizabeth Bills	"	John Bills[.]
Harriet L. Cox	"	B[enjamin]. L. Clapp[.]
Horace Burgess	"	[Benjamin] Clapp[.]
Almira Burgess	"	H[arrison]. Burgess[.]
Edwin Whiting	"	[Benjamin] Clapp[.]
Mary Elizabeth Cox	"	[Benjamin] Clapp[.]
Elizabeth P. Whiting	"	E[dwin]. Whiting[.]
Phebe Danfield	"	[Benjamin] Clapp[.]
Amos Cox	"	[Benjamin] Clapp[.]
Philena Cox	"	A[mos]. Cox[.]
Orville S. Cox	"	[Benjamin] Clapp[.]

Pamela Elvira Cox	"	O[rville]. S. Cox[.]
David LeBaron	"	[Benjamin] Clapp[.]
Esther M. LeBaron	"	D[avid]. LeBaron[.]
Isaac Morley Jr.	"	[Benjamin] Clapp[.]
Rowland Shannon	"	[Benjamin] Clapp[.]
Lucretia Shannon	"	R[owland]. Shannon[.]
James M. Works	"	[Benjamin] Clapp[.]

Finished at 33 [minutes] p[ast]. 6. Jacob Gates, Joseph A. Kelting and Artemisia Snow—officiating as prompters[.]

The supply of provisions brought in to day has been very abundant—and much of it has been sent away to those families that are destitute.

At 15 min[utes]. to 4 [we] commenced in the female department, washing, and anointing, the following persons. viz;

Harriet P. Decker	born	Sept[ember] 7. 1803
Susan Ann Ashby	"	Feb[ruar]y 1. 1830
Elizabeth Brunelle	"	April 28. 1824
Mary Ellen Harris	"	Oct[ober] 5 1818
Betsey Herrington or Landers	"	July 15. 1790
Nabby Works	"	Nov[ember]. 6. 1781
Maria Lawrence	"	Dec[ember]. 18. 1823
Nancy Richardson	"	Sept[ember] 27. 1784
Adaline Melimical	"	Mar[ch]. 24. 1824
Mary A. Sherman	"	Feb[ruar]y 17 1830
Dulcinea D. Sherman	"	Nov[embe]r. 19. 1806

These were washed by Elizabeth A. Whitney Vilate Kimball — Nancy Winchester — Nancy H. Rockwood & Eliza Jane Webb. Anointed by Elizabeth Ann Whitney, Vilate Kimball Nancy Winchester & Mercy R. Thompson[.]

Ended at 5 minutes to 5.

At 15 minutes past 5 the Bell rung, & [we] commenced receiving into departments lower & middle the above company, also Almon W. Babbitt who had been washed & anointed in the previous company, the following persons officiating in the upper department, viz; John D. Lee as No. 1[,] A[lbert]. P. Rockwood No. 2[,] Harrison Burgess as No. 3.[,] and in the middle department, Erastus Snow as No. 1.[,] W[illia]m. Snow as No. 2[,] W[illia]m. Miller as No. 3.[,] Wilber J. Earl 4, [and] J[acob]. Gates 5.

At 10 minutes to 7 [we] commence[d] receiving into the upper department, company No. 4, being 11 women and 1 man.

Almon W. Babbitt	by John D. Lee[.]
Dulcinea D. Sherman	by A[lmon]. W. Babbitt[.]
Maria Lawrence	" " " "
Mary Ann Sherman	" " " "
Elizabeth Brunelle	" J[ohn]. D. Lee[.]
Harriet P. Decker	" " " "
Susan Ann Ashby	" " " "
Mary Ellen Harris	" " " "
Nabby Works	" " " "
Adaline Melimical	" Lyman Whitney[.]
Nancy Richardson	" " "
Betsey Herrington (Sanders)	by J[ohn]. D. Lee.

Finished at 36 m[inutes]. past 7. Prompters, Artemisia Snow & M[ercy]. R. Thompson[.]

The High Council met at 6 o'clock in room No. 10. — Present as follows. C[harles]. C. Rich, Samuel Bent, G[eorge]. W. Harris, Aaron Johnson David Fulmer Henry G. Sherwood, Lewis D. Wilson — Ezra T. Benson, Thomas Grover Newell Knight, James Allred — and the following names [of] High Priests, viz, Joseph B. Noble — Aaron F. Farr[,] Lorin Farr Elam Ludington — Stephen Winchester—

Prayed as usual for Pres[ident]. B[righam]. Young & his council, for the defeat of our enemies, the continuation of the endowment, and for the general welfare of all the Saints.

The High Priests held three different meetings, in Rooms No. 8 and 10. — Those who were present are as follows, Lucian Woodworth. — Abel Lamb[,] Cornelius P. Lott — William Crosby — Freeman Nickerson, — Simeon Carter[,] William Felshaw — Luman H. Calkins[,] Gustavus Hills — Samuel Rolfe, Samuel Gully — Jacob Foutz — Daniel Davis[,] Dexter Stillman — Isaac Houston — Jacob Wieler[,] A. L. Lamoreaux. Joseph Mount — Lyman Leonard — William Snow — William Crosby. Edward Hunter — Daniel Spencer. Anson Call — Zebedee Coltrin[,] W[illia]m. C. Gallaher[,] Jonathan Becklehymer — John S. Higbee — John Bowen—

The three meetings were conducted by persons chosen in each one to preside and all the individuals in them were clothed in priestly apparel—and the greatest unanimity of feeling prevailed. The most prominent things prayed for were, the preservation of President B[righam]. Young and all the Twelve [apostles], and that the ordinances of the endowment might continue, until all the elders had received their washings & anointings and that the Saints might all be able to procure means by which they could remove from Nauvoo to the West in comfortable manner—and for the sick, that they may be healed—and that God would disappoint our enemies in all their places.

Mrs. Ann Maria Foster, wife of L[ucian]. R. Foster, left the Temple about 6 o'clock, and went home with her little boy, Lucian R. Foster Jun[io]r.—having been in the Temple all the time since yesterday noon— Her little boy was quite sick when he came, but went away quite well— On Sunday last she brought him to the Temple also, and at the request of his Father, Elders H[eber]. C. Kimball Brigham Young and P[arley]. P. Pratt laid their hands upon him and asked the Lord to restore him to health—and pronounced upon him the blessings of life & health.

About 9 o'clock this evening, Elders H[eber]. C. Kimball, and his wife, Bishop [Newel] Whitney & his wife, left the Temple and went to Joseph Kingsbury's—to remain until William Kimball should carry a load of persons, viz; L[ucian]. R. Foster, Horace Whitney and Mary Ellen Harris, to their respective homes— after which he returned and carried home his Father & mother in the carriage, with the grey horses— Bishop Whitney & his wife went home also in the same carriage—

President Brigham Young left the Temple about 10 o'clock—and went home for the night.

This afternoon and evening the new altar was used, for the first time—and four individuals and their wives were sealed— The altar is about 2½ feet high, and 2½ feet long, and about one foot wide—rising from a platform about 8 or 9 inches, high and extending out on all sides about a foot, forming a convenient place to kneel upon— The top of the altar and the kneeling place are covered with cusions of scarlet damask cloth— The sides of the upright part, or body of the altar are covered with white linen—

The Twelve [apostles] and the Bishops with their wives, were present at the dedication this afternoon—

William Pack revealed what he was while coming through[10]—

—William Clayton, Diary, kept for Heber C. Kimball.

10. This sentence fragment is curious since there has been no previous reference to a "William Pack." Clayton's frequent mention of "William Pitt and John Pack," the two names often associated together, may point to his intention here. In any case, whether he or they revealed what was said to them while coming through the

Services commenced in the Males Department at 8 o'clock A.M. when the following persons were washed and anointed, viz.

Seventies

1	Robert Campbell	born	Mar[ch]. 31, 1810
2	Eli B. Whitney	"	Oct[ober]. 27, 1819
3	Jared Porter	"	Mar[ch] 23, 1812
4	Roswell Hyde	"	May 20, 1816
5	Aaron Hart	"	Ap[ri]l. 1, 1803
6	Charles S. Peterson	"	July 28, 1818
7	Henry A. Cleaveland	"	Jan[uary]. 4, 1809
8	William A. Beebe	"	June 9, 1813
9	Levi North	"	July 17, 1817
10	George W Rosecrans	"	Feb[ruary]. 6, 1812
11	Nathan Cheney	"	Feb[ruary] 11, 1811
12	John B. Walker	"	Mar[ch]. 29, 1819

High Priests

	Henry Mower	born	Dec[ember]. 18, 1798
2	David Manhard	"	Aug[ust] 16, 1802
3	Wheeler Baldwin	"	Mar[ch]. 7, 1793

Washed by Jacob Gates and William Hyde. Anointed by J[edediah]. M. Grant, E[zra]. T. Benson, Harrison Burgess, and James Brown. Finished at 9.

Female Department.

Services commenced at 8 20/60 o'clock A.M. the following persons were washed and anointed, viz.

[See pages 364-66 for excerpted portion.]

Present this Morning Pres[iden]t. B[righam]. Young, H[eber]. C. Kimball, W[illard]. Richards, P[arley]. P. Pratt, O[rson]. Pratt, John Taylor, and Amasa Lyman, Bishops [Newel] Whit[n]ey & G[eorge]. Miller, and others. News has been recived from Washington [D.C.] that Congress has passed a [blank]

---

veil is left to conjecture. It is also significant that this is the last entry Clayton made in the diary he was keeping for Heber C. Kimball. Why it stops here in unknown. However, it seems likely that the number of people coming through the temple increased at such a rapid rate between this date and when the temple closed on February 8 that continuing such a comprehensive record would have been impractical. Or perhaps Clayton meant to return to the diary and was simply overwhelmed by other duties.

[Washings and anointings for Wednesday, January 7, 1846]

Margaret Manhart b.	Feb. 9, 1815	Mary Mower	born	Oct 1803
Rhoda Matthews	Apl 6, 1817	Agness Kater	"	Nov. 6 1819
Mary Ann Hyde	Dec. 31, 1820	Eliza Rosecrans	"	Dec. 15 1811
Abiah Porter	Feb 1, 1813	Artiminta North	"	Feb 25 1819
Louisa Beebe	Aug 10, 1817	Mary Kilsey	"	June 28, 1791
Mary Baldwin	July 20, 1793	Letitia Kelsey	"	Oct 24, 1816
Elizabeth Walker	Oct. 24, 1816	Isabel Hart	"	Apl 7, 1808
Delilah Campbell	July 27, 1813	Samantha Baldwin	"	May 13, 1820
Elizabeth Cheney	Jan 11, 1815	Susannah Warm	"	Feb 28, 1825
Mary Ann Peterson	July 23, 1822	Ann Cleaveland	"	Mar. 10, 1805

Washed by Eliza Jane Webb, Elizabeth Barlow, Mary Clapp, Nancy H. Rockwood, and Nancy Winchester. Anointed by Nancy Winchester, Clarrisa Herriman, and Nancy H. Rockwood. Finished at 10 A.M.

Male Department No. 2.

Seventies

13	Dana Jacobs	born	July 16, 1808
14	Walter E. Wilcox		Apl. 11, 1821
15	Ira Spaulding		Apl 16, 1809
16	Samuel W. Richardson		Aug 9, 1824
17	William Rowley		June 21, 1798
18	Ethan Griffith		Apl 15, 1803
19	Silus W. Condit		June 27, 1819
20	Enoch P. Rollins		Jan. 14, 1805

21 Lauren W. Roundy May 21, 1814
22 John Woodman Oct. 8, 1789

High Priests

Pliny Fisher born Aug 5, 1775
5 Rufus Fisher Dec 11, 1804
6 Almon W. Babbit Oct 29, 1813

Brother Babbit was washed by Joseph Young and E. T. Benson, and anointed by H. C. Kimball and Joseph Young.

Seventies

23 Gilbert Hunt born Apl. 11, 1825
24 Simpson D. Huffaker July 23, 1812
25 George P. Styles July 18, 1816

Washed by Jacob Gates and William Hyde. Anointed by John Pack, Harrison Burgess, James Brown, and Ezra T. Benson. Finished at 10 11/60 A.M.

Female Department No. 2, com. 18 minutes to 11 A.M.

Fanny Murray born Nov 8 1787
Olive Fisher " Apl. 18, 1821
Mariah W. Wilson " June 17, 1827
Jemima Stringham " Oct. 5, 1804
Cynthia Nichols " Jan 11, 1816
Johanna Roundy " Nov. 26, 1824
Mehitable Hall " Oct 1, 1806
Lucy Bishop " Jan 20, 1783
Nancy Ingersol born Oct 18, 1785
Isabel Holister " Aug 20, 1825
Sophia Janet Stiles " Dec 17, 1814
Mary Ann Rowley " Jan 21, 1810
Ruth A Griffith " Feb. 16, 1800
Zilpha Jacobs " Sep 28, 1810
Sarah Condit " Dec 18, 1822
Ann Eliza Smalling " Sep 2, 1817

Sally Parker [born] Dec 8, 1778	Betsey Parkham [born] Dec 12, 1780
Sophia W. Rollins " Dec 12, 1802	Priscilla Huffaker " Apl. 16, 1781
Lucretia Tupper " Sep 15, 1818	Julia [illegible] " Nov 9, 18[?]

The foregoing named persons were washed by Mary Ann Young, Nancy H. Rockwood, Nancy Winchester, Elizabeth Barlow and Eliza Jane Webb. Anointed by Vilate Kimball, Clarissa Herriman, Nancy H. Rockwood and Nancy Winchester. Finished at 20, min to 1 P.M.

—Seventies Record, Book B, oversized portion, January 7, 1846.

The number of applicants for endowments this morning is immense, the greatest number that has passed through at a time, has passed through to day, and beside them, Pres[iden]t. J[oseph]. Young is obliged to turn many away, not being able to give them their endowments to day.

Male Department Co[mpany]. No. 3 commenced 10 min[utes] past 1.

High Priests			
	Amos Cox	born	Mar[ch]. 26, 1821
8	Orville Whiting	"	Nov[ember]. 25, 1814
9	Edwin Whiting	"	Sep[tember]. 9, 1809
10	Thomas Pearson	"	Mar[ch]. 1, 1802
Seventies			
26	William Burgess Jr	"	Mar[ch]. 1, 1822
27	Isaac Morley	"	May 2, 1829
28	John Bills	"	Sept[ember]. 19, 1819
29	David LeBaron	"	
30	John Algerborn		Nov[ember]. 5, 1820
31	Joseph B. Peck	"	Jan[uary]. 7, 1819
32	Rowland Shannon		Oct[ober] 11, 1820
33	Chauncy Whiting		Aug[ust] 19, 1819
34	Horace Burgess		Jan[uary]. 23 1816
35	James McLellan		Aug[ust]. 8, 1804.
Elder			
	James M. Works		Oct[ober]. 5, 1822

Washed by Jacob Gates and William Hyde. Anointed by B[enjamin]. L. Clapp, Harrison Burgess and James Brown.

Female Department Co[mpany]. no. 3 commenced 23 Min[utes] [past?] 2

[See page 368 for excerpted portion.]

After the 4th Co[mpany]. came through the council of the seventies convened in Room No 9 & took into consideration the nature & calling of the 1st Quorum of Presidents or Presidency — relative to giving of the Endowments to the different Quorums of the seventies Also the officers to officiate in the different departments — the subject was laid before the House for deliberation — & after each one of the council had spoken their feelings upon the subject finally resolved that in as much as the Twelve [apostles], had Rol[l]ed the responsibility of giving the endowment upon the shoulders of the Council — and consiquently & consi-

[Washings and anointings for Wednesday, January 7, 1846—second excerpt]

Lucia L. Leavitt born Aug 9, 1826	Mary E. Cox born Dec 15, 1826
Theresa A Morley " July 18, 1826	Elizabeth P Whiting " Apl. 15, 1814
Nancy Ann Hunt " Aug 10, 1827	Matilda Neas " Jan 1, 1828
Almira Palmer " May 13, 1824	Catharine Pearson " Apl. 3, 1809
Maria Burgess " June 17, 1823	Susanna Peck " Mar. 12, 1821
Phebe Danfield " Sep 20, 1807	Harriet Le Cox " Jan 20, 1823
Editha A Whiting " Jan 25, 1820	Elizabeth Bills " Jan 1, 1817
Mary G. Pearson " Oct. 2, 1828	Sarah Alger " Nov. 2, 1824
Philena Cox " Mar. 2, 1820	Esther M. Le Baron " Jan 12, 1827
Lucretia Shannon " June 7, 1823	Synthia McLellin " Apl. 28, 1810

Washed by Eliza Jane Webb and Clarissa Hancock, Anointed by Nancy Winchester, Clarrissa Herriman, Nancy H. Rockwood, Elizabeth Barlow held the oil Finished 10 min after 3.

Harriet P. Decker born Sep. 7, 1803	Elizabeth Brunelle born Apl 28, 1824
Susan Ann Ashby " Feb. 4, 1830	Mary Ellen Harris " Oct 5, 1818
[illegible]	
Betsey Herrington born July 15, 1790	Nabby Woods born Nov. 6 1781
Maria Lawrence " Dec 18, 1823	Nancy Richardson " Sep 27 1784
Adaline Melimical [?] " Mar 24, 1825	Mary A. Sherman " Feb 17 1830
	Delcena D. Sherman " Nov 19 1806

Washed by Vilate Kimball, Nancy H. Rockwood, Elizabeth Ann Whitney, Nancy Winchester, and Eliza Jane Webb. Anointed by Vilate Kimball, Elizabeth Ann Whitney, Nancy Winchester, and Mercy R. Thompson. Finished at 5 minutes to 5 P.M.

—Seventies Record, Book B, oversized portion, January 7, 1846.

quently they hold us responsible for the strict performance of every ordinance, that is & will be performed in this House ac[c]ording to the patron [pattern?] that they have set. Furthermore in as much as the seventies are the men, that are to revolutionize the world by carrying the gospel of his Kingdom to all Nations & errecting the standard in every land — They certainly are the Men that should have the prevelge [privilege] of officiating in giving the Endowments to their several Quorums For they will no doubt[,] ma[n]y of them, be called to administer these ordinances to Nations & People remote f[rom] here — consiquently they should have the advantage of practice — through which Knowledge is obtained, which is Power: the High Priests have pretty much all gone through & when they were receiving their Endowments they[,] the High Priests[,] officiated well [and] it was all right — For it was their perogative Now it is ours to do after this week — we will select out of the Presidents of the Seventies to act in every department under our direction in this Temple. There is Tallent wisdom & ability among the seventies sufficient for any thing that we are called to do & as bright Tallent as there is in the world & we will use it where it belongs and take the privilege[s] of the seventies & give them to others[.] we will appoint a Martial [marshal] to Keep the house in order. He will require of the Twelve to invite such as they wish to come here through us — & we will enter there Names on a list & will commit it to the door Keeper, with such instructions as will prohibit any further imposition from being practiced upon us. The Twelve has already said that the seventies have that[,] the right [illegible] — since the work has begun [to be] committed to them — the provisions that are brought daily is [sufficient] to sustain the hands that labor here[,] & also the Families of this council[.] ...[11] [As we spoke, we felt] the spirit & presence of Elijah [illegible][12] in our midst, which filled our hearts to overflowing — before we left the room we all raised to our feet & rendered thanks to the Great Elohimie for his preserving kindness over his Saints — Those of the council that were presant were Pres[ident] Jos[eph]. Young H[enry]. Herriman B[enjamin]. L. Clapp A[lbert]. P. Rockwood

11. Although unintelligible, the missing line reads: "... also the Families of this council [illegible] get it — but it is [illegible] by roofer that never brought any thing [illegible] when do they care for their work but this must be at [illegible] ..."

12. This seems to read "God abode," which might be integrated into the sentence as: "... [we felt] the spirit and presence of Elijah [in] God['s] abode[, with God's Spirit] in our midst" or as "[T]he spirit and presence of Elijah['s] God ab[i]de[d] in our midst."

J[edediah] M Grant & J[ohn]. D. Lee[,] clerk[.] Br[other]. Jack Gates of the 4th [Quorum of] Sev[enties] was also here[.] Pres[idents] Jos[eph]. Young & [Jedediah] Grant spent the Night in the Temple — it is now 10 at Night.

—Seventies Record, Book B.

....

Continued work as usual on the Temple of the Lord until morning of the 7th of January when[,] being called upon[,] I [Samuel Richards] went to receive my endowment. Went in about 10 in the morning with the second company, [and] was the first of the company that was washed[,] at the same time with Walter N. Wilcox[,] done by Jacob Gates, and anointed by Harrison Burgess, also received a new name by him. B[enjamin]. L. Clapp, Eloheim & Orson Pratt, Peter. Received through the v[eil]. by Amasa Lyman: Got through about 4 in the afternoon and left the house[.] while passing out *Pres[ident]* Joseph Young informed me that, he should depend upon me to come and assist in giving the endowment. On the morn[ing] of the 8th [I] commenced my work as usual on [the construction of] the Temple, and continued thereat untill the morn[ing] of the 20th when I was sent for by Bro[ther]. [Joseph] Young, to come and labour in the Endowments and [I] immediately went for that purpose. [At] First [I] commenced writing for *Pres[ident].* Joseph [Young] and the next day commenced labour at the veil, and continued administrating and officiating in all the departments of the first endowment with the exception of the [role of the] serpent, [all of] which I esteemed as a great blessing and privilege, affording me a knowledge of those things which had been concealed before.

—Samuel W. Richards, Diary, typescript, L. Tom Perry Special Collections, Harold B. Lee Library, Brigham Young University, Provo, Utah.

....

This morning there was an immense crowd at the reception room waiting for admission. The brethren brought all kinds of provisions for the use of those who are attending on the ordinances of the Lord's House.

A letter was received this morning from Father Tucker, informing us that the Catholic bishop could not raise money enough to purchase our property, but would either purchase or rent one of our public buildings, but would not insure it against fire or mobs.

One hundred twenty-one persons received ordinances.

The supply of provisions brought in today has been very abundant, and much has been sent away to those families that are destitute.

The high council and three companies of high priests met for prayer.

The Presidents of Seventies met in council, in relation to keeping order in the Temple.

The Twelve [apostles] delegated to them the government of the Temple, while the ordinances were being administered to their quorums. This afternoon, the new altar was used for the first time, and four individuals and their wives were sealed. The altar is about two and one-half feet high and two and one-half feet long and about one foot wide, rising from a platform about 8 or 9 inches high and extending out on all sides about a foot, forming a convenient place to kneel upon. The top of the altar and the platform for kneeling upon are covered with cushions of scarlet damask cloth; the sides of the upright part or body of the altar are covered with white linen.

The Twelve [apostles] and presiding bishops with their wives were present at the dedication of the altar this afternoon.

—"Manuscript History of Brigham Young,"
in *History of the Church,* 7:565-66.

....

Nauvoo temple endowments performed on this date for:

First Company: Agnes Flake, Levi North, Araminta North, Mary Kelsey, Henry Mower Sr., Mary Mower, David Manhard, Mary Jane Manhard, John B. Walker, Elizabeth Walker, Samantha Baldwin, Jared Porter, Abiah Porter, Aaron Hart, Isabella Hart, Rhoda Matthews, Henry A. Cleaveland, Ann Cleaveland, Robert Campbell, Delilah Campbell, Roswell Hyde, Mary Ann Hyde, George W. Rosecrans, Elisa Rosecrans, Susannah Wann, Eli B. Kelsey, Letitia Kelsey, William A. Beebe, Louisa Beebe, Nathan Cheney, Elisa Ann Cheney, Wheeler Baldwin, Mary Baldwin, Charles S. Peterson, and Mary Ann Peterson.

Second Company: Ethan Griffith, Ruth A. Griffith, Almon W. Babbitt, Julia Ann Babbitt, Nancy Ingersol, George P. Stiles, Sophia Janett Stiles, Isabel Hollister, Lauren H. Roundy, Fanny Murray, Joanna Roundy, Rufus Fisher, Olive Fisher, Cynthia Nichols, Silas W. Condit, Sarah Condit, Pliny Fisher, Sally Parker, Simpson D. Huffaker, Priscilla Huffaker, Enoch P. Rollins, Sophia W. Rollins, John Workman, Betsey Pinkham, Jemima Stringham, Walter E. Wilcox, Maria W. Wilcox, Mehitabel Hall, Samuel W. Richards, Lucretia Hupper, William Rowley, Mary Ann

Rowley, Lucy Bishop, Ira N. Spaulding, Eliza Spaulding, Dana Jacobs, and Zilpha Jacobs.

Third Company: William Burgess Jr., Maria Burgess, Lucia L. Leavitt, Joseph B. Peck, Susanna Peck, Matilda Ness, James McClellan, Synthia McClellan, Nancy Ann Hunt, Chauncey Whiting, Editha Ann Whiting, Theresa A. Morley, Almira Palmer, John Alger, Sarah Alger, Thomas Pearson, Catharine Pearson, Mary G. Pearson, John Bills, Elizabeth Bills, Harriet L. Cox, Horace Burgess, Almira Burgess, Edwin Whiting, Mary Elizabeth Cox, Elisabeth P. Whiting, Phebe Danfield, Amos Cox, Philena Cox, Orville S. Cox, Pamela Elvira Cox, David LeBaron, Esther M. LeBaron, Isaac Morley Jr., Rowland Shannon, Lucretia Shannon, and James M. Works.

Fourth Company: Almon W. Babbitt, Dulcinea D. Sherman, Maria Lawrence, Mary Ann Sherman, Elisabeth Brunelle, Harriet P. Decker, Susan Ann Ashby, Mary Ellen Harris, Nabby Works, Adaline Melimical, Nancy Richardson, and Betsey Herrinton/Sanders.

—Summary of information compiled by the Temple Index Bureau, *Nauvoo Temple Endowment Register: 10 December 1845 to 8 February 1846.* Editors' note: According to the register, Gilbert Hunt was washed and anointed on this date and therefore probably received through the veil.

....

No. 1[.] Jan[uary] 7 '46. Brother Heber Chase Kimball born June 14 1801 in Shelden Franklin Co[unty]. Vermont. Vilate ~~Kimball~~ Murray born June 1, 1806 [in] Teorida Montgomery Co[unty] N[ew]. Y[ork]. were sealed husband & wife for time and for all eternity according to the holy order of God. upon the Alter by Pres[iden]t B[righam]. Young in presence of P[arley]. P. Pratt, O[rson] Pratt, O[rson] Hyde, and others. E[van]. M. Greene clerk.

No. 2[.] Jan[uary] 7 '46. Pres[iden]t Brigham Young [born] June 1, 1801 [in] Whitingham, Windham Co[unty]. Vermont. Mary Ann Angel, [born] June 8 1803 [in] Seneca Ontario Co[unty] N[ew]. Y[ork]. were sealed husband & wife for time and all eternity according to the holy order of God on the Alter by Heber Chase Kimball in presence of P[arley]. P. Pratt, O[rson]. Pratt, O[rson]. Hyde & others. E[van] M. Greene clerk.[13]

—Book of Living Sealings.

---

13. Also sealed on this date were Leonora Cannon to John Taylor and Elizabeth Ann Smith to Newel K. Whitney.

Sealing for the dead performed on this date

Miriam Works (Mary Ann Angel, proxy) to Brigham Young (Heber C. Kimball officiating).

—Summarized from the Book of Proxy Sealings.

V.

January and Early February 1846

"THE PATTERN OF HEAVENLY THINGS"

Thursday, January 8, 1846

Bro[ther]. H[eber]. C. K[imball] and others received the ordin[an]ces according to the law of the Lord upon the alt[a]r followed by John Taylor and N[ewel]. K. Whitney, ... little Brigham [i.e., Brigham H. Young] came to the vestry with his company where I married him to Miss Cedenia Cyphrona Clark— In the evening the council met at my [office] Where after prayers we consecrated fourteen bottles of oil, anointed bro[ther]. H[eber]. C. K[imball]. & wife and bro[ther]. O[rson]. Pratt attended to the ordinancies on the alter.

—Brigham Young, Diary (includes some text from the entry dated January 7, 1846).

....

President Brigham Young as president of the whole church anointed brother Heber C. Kimball first, this being according to the order[,] in which the ordinances of the Lord's House are at all times first communicated to the children of men[,] that he who holds the Keys of the Kingdom of Heaven to minister to men on earth as President Brigham Young now does, should confer the ordinances upon some faithful man who should in turn minister to him according to the pattern of heavenly beings.

This is the order observed by the Prophet Joseph [Smith], he first baptized Oliver [Cowdery], then Oliver baptised him.

6. o. clock eve[ning]. Pres[ident]. Brigham Young, Heber Chase Kimble, Parley Parker Pratt, Orson Pratt, John Taylor, Amasa Lyman, Newell Kimble Whitney, Vilate Kimble, Elizabeth Ann Whitney, Sarah Marinda Pratt, & Leonora Taylor — Assembled in Pres[ident]. B[righam]. Young's Room No. 1. Dressed themselves [in] Holy Robes. The hymn now let us rejoice in the Day of Salvation, was sung and Elder Heber C. Kimble offered Prayer at the Alter after offering up the Signs of the Priesthood. Pres[ident]. Brigham Young proceeded to anoint Br[other]. Heber C. Kimble and Vilate his wife[1]—and pronounced the following blessing namely[:]

Bro[ther] Heber C. Kimble in the name of Jesus Christ we pour upon thy head this Holy oil & we anoint thee a King and Priest unto the most High God & in & over the Church of Jesus Christ of Latter Days Saints and also Iseral in this the Holy Temple of the Lord, at Nauvoo the City of Joseph State of Ill[inoi]s. & I seal upon you power to bind on Earth & it Shall be bound in Heaven & whomsoever thou Shalt loose on Earth shall be loosed in Heaven, & whomsoever thou shalt curse Shalt be cursed, & whomsoever thou shalt bless, shall be blessed & I anoint thy head that it may be sound & thy brains shall be quick to think & to regulate thy whole body. & thine ears to hear the cries of the Poor & needy of thy Brethren, who shall come to thee for council & thine eyes that thou mayest see and understand the things of God—& that thou mayest behold Angels & thy mouth that thou mayest speak forth the great things of God[,] & [I] Seal upon you all the blessings of thy Progenitors Even Abraham Isaac & Jacob & even as Far back as the Priesthood: & I say that thou shalt live to a good old age Even to three score & ten & longer if thou desire it—& thou shalt have Power to redeem thy progenitors & thou shalt have power over thy Posterity & shall Save all of them & bring them into thy Kingdom we also seal upon thee all the power & blessing of the Holy Reserection Even to the Eternal God head & no blessing that thy heart can conceive will be withheld from you & in the name of the Father & of the Son & of the Holy Spirit Amen.

---

1. This was the first time the second anointing was administered in the Nauvoo temple.

He then anointed Sister Vilate Kimble a queen and Priestess unto her Husband [Heber C. Kimball] in the Church of Jesus Christ of Latter Days Saints & in Iseral. & pronounced all the blessings upon her head in common with her husband.

—"Book of Anointings."

....

An account of the resolutions of the Seventies[:] Resolutions, passed last evening[.] there is much order and quietness in the Temple this morning. At about 9 a.m. H[eber]. C. Kimball came into the room, and missing a six shooter pistol, and not getting any information of its whereabouts, after some remarks on the subject of stealing, said that the person who had taken the pistol (if done purposely) should be cursed. He then said, that there had been too much confusion, talking, and running about the rooms: those that washed (said he) will scarcely get through before you may see them around the stove in the Holy of Holies, this should not be, Were Parley and Orson Pratt officiating in the ordinance of washing, you would not see them until they were through their day's work, except to go down to their meals. The order is, that no person come into this room unless he be invited ~~and~~ ^by^ the Twelve [apostles] ~~invite nobody.~~ The government of the Temple is committed to the Seventies, and they are afraid to do their duty. This must not be.

Pres[iden]t. B[righam]. Young came in at 20 minutes past 11, A.M. Present this morning Pres[iden]t B[righam]. Young, H[eber]. C. Kimball. P[arley]. P. Pratt O[rson]. Pratt, and Amasa Lyman of the Twelve[.] [Others who] were present[:] George Miller, Pres[iden]t. J[oseph]. Young, [Henry] Herriman, B[enjamin]. L. Clapp, J[edediah]. M. Grant, of the Seventies.

~~Ever~~ Labor commenced in the No. 1 Male Department at 20 min[utes]. to 11 A.M. when the following persons were washed and anointed viz.

Seventies

1.	Alvin M. Harriding	born	July 12, 1816
2	Nicholas H. Silcock	"	Sep[tember] 29, 1819
3	Joseph T. Palmer	"	Oct[ober]. 7, 1802
4	Henry Grow	"	Oct[ober]. 1, 1817
5	Hyrum Gates	"	Aug[ust] 11, 1802
6	Lorenzo A Quick	"	July 2, 1813
7	William H. Folsom	"	Mar[ch] 25, 1815
8	John H. Atwood	"	Ap[ri]l 21 1822

High Priests		
David H. Parsons	born	Oct[ober] 22, 1801
2 Silas Maynard	"	Ap[ri]l. 1, 1787
Elder		
Cha[rle]s. W. Hyde	"	July 16, 1814
Seventies		
George J. Fordham	"	Ap[ri]l. 21, 1825
10 George Crooks	"	June 28, 1825
11 Vincent M. Conrad	"	Sep[tember]. 15, 1812
12 Charles Maxham	"	Ap[ri]l. 26, 1813
13 Hezekiah H. Brannan	"	June 30, 1812
14 Ph^a^res Wells	"	June 7, 1814

[W]ashed by William Hyde and James Brown. Anointed by J[edediah]. M. Grant, Harrison Burgess and Jacob Gates, [illegible]

No. 1; Female Department commenced at 25 min[utes]. p[ast]. 8[.]

Delight Maynard	b[orn].	Mar[ch], 6, 1804
Violette O Harding	"	Dec[ember] 6, 1821
Mary Grow	"	Ap[ri]l 28, 1817
Lydia Taylor Parsons	"	July 5, 1798
Jane Silcock	"	Nov[ember]. 6, 1826
Barbara Heath	"	Mar[ch]. 20, 1796
Indiana Brannan	"	Nov[ember]. 17, 1813
Electa Conrad	born	Aug[ust] 10, 1808
Mary A. Palmer	"	June 26, 1803
Zerviah Eliza Johnson	"	Feb[ruary] 5, 1816
Sarah M. Gates	"	May 10, 1808
Sarah Atwood	"	May 8, 1822
Matilda Maxham	"	Jan[uary]. 17, 1819
Elizabeth L. Quick	"	Aug[ust] 7, 1818
Maria Wells	"	Dec[ember] 22, 1813

Washed by Mary Winchester, Mercy R. Thompson, Eliza Jane Webb, Clarissa Herriman, Nancy H. Rockwood, and Sophia M. Burgess. Anointed by Nancy Winchester, Artimisia Snow, Clarissa Herriman, and Nancy P. Rockwood. Finished at half p[ast] 9.

Male Department No. 2 commenced at 4 min[utes]. to 10[.]

Seventies		
15 Albert Gregory	born	Sep[tember] 15, 1802
16 John Wardrobe	"	Dec[ember]. 26, 1810
17 Horace L. Eldridge	"	Feb[ruary] 6, 1816

18	Phineas K. Wright	"	Jan[uary] 15, 1826
19	James Olive	"	June 4, 1817
20	Elias Gardner	"	Ap[ri]l 2, 1807
21	Willis R. Johnson	"	Sep[tember] 13, 1828

Seventies

	Oren Jefferds	born	Ap[ri]l 19, 1801
23	Michael Viats [?]	"	Dec[ember]. 5, 1814
24	William Price	"	Dec[ember]. 4, 1818
25	John Oakley	"	Nov[ember] 12, 1819
26	Leonard W. Randall	"	Nov[ember] 16, 1814

High Priest

Thomas Green	"	Jan[uary]. 27, 1802

Elder

Ezra Oakley	"	Ap[ri]l 10, 1788

Washed by Harrison Burgess and James Brown. Anointed by J[edediah] Grant, William Hyde, and John Pack. Finished at 11 o'cl[oc]k.

Female Department No. 2 commenced at 10 15/60[.]

Elizabeth Oakley	born	Jan[uary]. 26, 1795
Jane Scott	"	July 10, 1822
Betsey Ann Eldridge	"	Sep[tember] 23, 1818
Lucy McIntosh	"	May 18, 1814
Alta Wright	"	Ap[ri]l 10, 1823
Zerena Jefferds	"	Sep[tember] 28, 1806
Sena Olive	"	Nov[ember] 7, 1818
Mary M. Oakley	b[orn].	Feb[ruary]. 11, 1826
Betsey Markham	"	Oct[ober] 18, 1815
Mary Green	"	Feb[ruary]. 25, 1825
Charlotte Ann Stilwell	"	Nov[ember]. 1828
Catharine Katz	"	Aug[ust] 22, 1819
Maria L. Randall	"	Dec[ember]. 18, 1815
Margaret Bryson	"	Aug[ust] 12, 1789

Washed by Sophia M. Burgess and Ruth Bovier. Anointed by Nancy Winchester, Clarissa Herriman and Nancy H. Rockwood. Eliza Jane Webb held the horn [of consecrated oil]. Finished at 20 min[utes] after 11.

Male Department List 3 commenced 35 to 12 [o'clock.]

Seventies

27	William Brown	born	Jan 3, 1816
28	Nathan A. Wood	"	Ap[ri]l 10, 1808
29	James Goff	"	Ap[ri]l. 27, 1808

30	David J. Mayberry		Oct[ober] 6, 1825
31	Joseph Mayberry	"	Sep[tember] 1, 1823

Seventies

	Gabriel Mayberry	born	Sep[tember] 14, 1821
33	Samuel Pitchforth	"	Nov[ember] 23, 1825
34	Rufus Pack	"	July 24 1803
35	James B. Woodward	"	July 1, 18 [illegible]

Elder

Cyrus Daniels	"	Sep[tember] 12 [illegible]

Washed by [Hyrum?] Dayton. Anointed by John Pack, Harrison Burgess.

Jan. 8, 1846. This day H[eber]. C. Kimball, P[arley]. P. Pratt, A[masa]. Lyman, George Miller, J[edediah]. M. Grant, E[rastus]. Snow, B[enjamin]. L. Clapp, clothed themselves in priestly apparel and offering up the signs consecrated 11 bottles of oil for the Anointing; then prayed for the sick, and for three men who had just fallen from a scaffold in the Temple; and for the safety of Israel and the heads of the church &c. This was done in the Seventies room at 11 A.M. N[ewel]. K. Whitney came in about 1 o'clock P.M.

Female Department List 3 commenced at 15 min[utes] p[ast]. 12

Catharine Wilson	born	Ap[ri]l 15, 1782
Mary Goff	"	Oct[ober] 16, 1811
Rebecca Hall	"	May 23, 1788
Clara K. F. Mayberry	"	May 28, 1827
Maria L. Woodworth	"	Nov[ember]. 12, 1782
Mary A. De La Woodward	"	May 7, 1803
Adaline West	born	Dec[ember]. 21, 1816
Phebe M. Brown	"	July 4, 1822
Mary Maybeary	"	Mar[ch] 11, 1792
Mary Pitchforth	"	Aug[ust] 26, 1825
Ann Pitchforth	"	Jan[uary] 30, 1801
Jane Fields	"	Aug[ust] 4, 1811

Washed by Nancy Winchester, Nancy H. Rockwood, Eliza Jane Webb, Sophia M. Burgess, Ruth Bosier. Anointed by Leonora Taylor, Nancy H. Rockwood, Clarissa Herriman, and Nancy Winchester.

Finished at 25 minutes past 2 P.M. C[harles]. W. Wandell Scribe for J[ohn]. D. L[ee].

After the services of the day closed the Quorum of the Twelve [apostles] Seventies the High Council & High Priests retired to their respective

Rooms, where they arrayed themselves in Priestly Robes[,] offered the Signs[,] & Prayed — Pres[ident] Jos[eph]. Young went home on acount of his helth & ^was^ not with us at the hour of Prayer which was 6 o clock. The following were the Names of those that were presant (Q[uorum] S[eventies]) Pres[ident] Levi Hancock H[enry] Herriman B[enjamin]. L. Clapp, A[lbert]. P. Rockwood J[edediah]. M. Grant & J[ohn]. D. Lee of the council & Pres[ident] Jacob Gates of the 4th [Quorum of] Sev[enties] Also Pres[ident]. W[illia]m Hyde of the 8th [Quorum of] Sev[enties]. After Prayre a list of candidates were Selected by order of the council for Saturday & Monday next & were placed in the care of Bishop Edward Hunter — who was appointed to notifie them — about 8 o.clock in the evening Pres[ident] W[illia]m. A. Sanger came in to let us [k]now that that [sic] he could not obtain the oil, at the Town of Burlington as was anticipated[.] he consiquently would be under the necessity of going to the city of Chigcago [sic] as it was the nearest point ^where^ oil could be obtained (for the endowment)[.] [A]t 8 o. clock the Twelve all returned Elder Taylor came back again at 9 & spent the Night after which we celebrated the praise of Zions King on the violin & Flute, joining in the Dance at the Same with motive pure before the Lord — after our merryment ceased the [hymn] calld the Seer was sung & Prayre offered by Elder Erastus Snow [illegible] all returned to rest[,] leaving [illegible] sufficient to keep up Fire & [illegible] of the light &c.

—Seventies Record, Book B.

....

[W]ent to the Temple at 10 a.m. In Council in relation to our intended movements westward.

Eighty-one persons received ordinances.

After the services of the day closed, the Twelve [apostles], Seventies, High Council and High Priestho[od] retired to their respective rooms and prayed.

The Twelve [apostles] consecrated 14 bottles of oil.

I [Brigham Young] attended to ordinances at the altar.

—"Manuscript History of Brigham Young," in *History of the Church,* 7:566, and *Manuscript History of Brigham Young,* p. 9.

....

Nauvoo temple endowments performed on this date for:

First Company: Charles W. Hyde, Alvin M. Harding, Violette O. Harding, Phares Wells, Maria Wells, Henry Grow, Mary Grow, David H. Parsons, Lydia Parsons, Hiram Gates, Sarah Ann Gates, John F. Atwood, Sarah Atwood, Vincent M. Conrad, Electa C. Conrad, Nicholas T. Silcock, Jane Silcock, Silas Maynard, Barbara Heath, Delight Maynard, William H. Folsom, Zerviah Eliza Folsom, Lorenzo A. Quick, Elizabeth S. Quick, Joseph F. Palmer, Mary Palmer, Hezekiah H. Brannan, Indiana Brannan, Charles Maxham, Matilda Maxham, George Crooks, and George F. Fordham.

Second Company: John Wardrobe, Lucy Wardrobe, John Oakley, Mary M. Oakley, James Olive, Zina Olive, Horace S. Eldridge, Betsey Ann Eldridge, Albert Gregory, Charlotte/Ann Stillwell, Phineas R. Wright, Alta Wright, Thomas Green, Mary Green, Michael Katz, Catharine Katz, Elias Gardner, Betsey E. Markham, Leonard L. Randall, Maria L. Randall, Oren Jefferds, Zerena Jefferds, William Price, Willis K. Johnson, Margaret Bryson, Jane Scot, Ezra Oakley, and Elizabeth Oakley.

Third Company: James B. Woodward, Mary A. Woodward, Jane Fields, James Goff, Mary Goff, Catharine Wilson, Cyrus Daniels, Mary Mayberry, William Brown Jr., Phebe N. Brown, Rebecca Hall, Nathan A. West, Adaline Louisa West, Gabriel Mayberry, Maria L. Mayberry, Joseph Mayberry, Ann Pitchforth, Samuel Pitchforth, Mary Pitchforth, David F. Mayberry, Rebecca Frances Hall, and Rufus Pack.

—Summary of information compiled by the Temple Index Bureau, *Nauvoo Temple Endowment Register: 10 December 1845 to 8 February 1846.*

....

Sealings performed for the living on this date:

Samuel Pitchforth to Mary Mitchell; Orson Pratt to Sarah Marinda Bates.

—Summarized from the Book of Living Sealings.

Friday, January 9, 1846

[S]pent the former part of the day in and about the Temple with the brethren: about 11. oc[lock] bro[ther]. Jno [John] Wooley came to my room and was married to Sister Lucy Dewey. In the evening. bro[ther]'s. W[illia]m Crosby, W[illia]m Mathews. Jno. [John] Brown A[braham]. O. Smoots & G[eorge]. P. Dykes attended to the ordinances upon the alt[a]r—I then went home[.]

—Brigham Young, Diary.

[A]t 4 O clock P.M. Pres[ident]. B[righam]. Young, H[eber]. C. Kimball, P[arley]. P. Pratt, O[rson] Pratt, O[rson]. Hyde, W[illard]. Richards, John Taylor, A[masa]. Lyman, Geo[rge]. Miller, N[ewel]. K. Whitney, Mary A[nn]. Young, [and] Elizabeth Ann Whitney, met in room No 1[.] Pres[iden]t. B[righam]. Young proposed the matter of proceeding to the second anointing & drop the first for one week, and talk over matters relative to the dress of our children. &c then proceeded to appoint 30 men to officiate as a committee to proceed with the second anointing and sealing ...[2]

—Book of Living Sealings.

....

The atmospher[e] is heavy yet warm[.] At 8 A.M. the Twelve [apostles] & all of the Seventies [met,] Pres[ident] Z[erah] Pulsipher excepted who has not been with [us], only to recive the Endowment — The Twelve are now almost entirely engaged in preparing & administering higher ordinances in a more retired and private appartment — consiquently the burden of the Endowment, now rests on the 1st Presidency of the Seventies.

Male Department Co[mpany]. No. 1 comenced washing at 15 to 8

[See pages 384-87 for excerpted portion.]

At the usual appointed hour [illegible] Several of the Quo[rum]s ^met &^ prayed in their Several appartments — after which the services of the day closed 9 at Night. Pres[ident] B[righam]. Young observed that all merriment & dancing should cease least the Brethren & Sisters be carried away in Levity — the Name of the Great Elohime, should be held in reverence, with all due deference — that belongeth to an infinanate Being of his character.

—Seventies Record, Book B.

....

I took a little rest having Br[other] C[harles] W Wandal to assist me in writing through the day[.] I acted the part of No 2 in the 1st [and] last department[s] also No 4 in the Garden & middle department [as] Prompter and Tempter[.] 125 Persons passed the ordinances to day about [blank] I

2. Within a month, just over 600 second anointings would be performed in the temple. See David John Buerger, "'The Fulness of the Priesthood': The Second Anointing in Latter-day Saint Theology and Practice," *Dialogue: A Journal of Mormon Thought* 16 (Spring 1983): 26.

[Washings and anointings for Friday, January 9, 1846]

[Male Department]		Female Department
Seventy		
Jesse Terpin born June 22d 1816	Sev	
Frederick Kesler " Jan 20 "	"	Jan Butterfield Jan 21 1817
John M. Wooley " Nov 20 1822	"	Matilus Thompson Feb 16 1822
Daniel Hunt " Feb 1st 1798	"	Susan Hunt Feby 14 1824
Samuel L. Sprague " May 3d 1805	Elder	Sarah Edwards Apl 1, 1824
		Mary McMallin Aug 16 1820
Thos. Butterfield " June 17 1811	Sev	Ruth Davis " 13 1821
		Permelia M Bassett Feb 11 1823
Abraham D. Boynton " March 12	"	Ann Phippins Jan 5, 1826
Geo. W. Potter " Oct 11 1816	"	Sarah Ann Church May 2 1824
		Emeline Young Ap 28, 1824
Chals A. Davis " 13 1810	"	Margaret M. Allen Dec 19 1825
Elias Edwards " April 10 1812	"	Sarah Coleman June 11 1804
		Lucretia Gay May 21 1809
Moses Gay " Mar 21 1804	"	Maria Boynton July 22 1817
Hayden W Church " Aug 29 1819	"	Charlotte B Potter Oct 8, 1817
Williard G. McMullin " Feb 21 1823	"	Julia Bayles Jan 12, 1810
		Catherine Jolly Feb 15, 1810
Jos. L. Thompson " Jan 22 1818	"	Mary W. Sprague Mar 1, 1804
Allen Talley " Jan 27 1810	"	Emeline Meslen Mar 26 1816

		Maria L Dewey Aug 3 1823
Joseph F Phippin " Sep 20 1823	"	washed by Eliza Webb Sophia M Burgess
Chas H Bassett " Mar 4 1828		Nancy H Rockwood
		Anointed by Leonora Taylor Nancy Winchester
Harmon A Bayles " July 28 1812		Clarissa Herriman N. H. Rockwood
		13 min to 10.

Washed by Ezra T Benson & W Hyde Anointed by Jacob Gates Harrison Burgess & James Brown.

Male Department No 2.

Daniel Rent " Dec 31 1787	Elder Ordained H P.	
William Coray May 14 1823	Seventy	Elizabeth Ackley Jan 26. 1795
		Mary M Ackley Feb 11 1824
Francis A Brown Nov 14 1822		Jane Scott July 10 1828
Osias Milbourne Mar 20 1810	H P	Betsy Markham Oct 18 1815
Jas Worthington Jan 9 1803		Betsy A Hanago Sep 23, 1819
		Mary Greyin Sep. 25 1805
Wm Vanausdall Feb. 23 1788		Lucy McIntyre May 18 1814
Jas Brinkeroff May 22 1816		Charlotte A Stewill Nov. 18 1828
		Alta Wright Ap 10 1823
Isaac Phippin Feb 15 1793		Catharine Bates Aug 22 1819
		Yereno Giffords Sep 28 1806
Stephen Niscon Mar 7 1807		Maria Randall Dr 18 1815
Benj R Lamb Aug 23 1821		Sina Olive Nov 7 1818
Jos Clement Sep 27 1817		Margaret Bryson Aug 12 17[?]

Washed & Anointed by Brigham Young and George Miller.

Stephen Richardson Feb 11 1799	H. P. —
John M Ewell Aug 5. 1828	Seventy

Washed by Jacob Gates & William Hyde Anointed by Levi Hancock Harrison Burgess & James Brown finished 20 p. 11.

Male Department Co. No 3 10 Mi 1.				[Female Department]
Alvah Phelps	Born	Nov 15. 1813	Sev	Amanda M McEwan May 20 1816
David Dixon		Jan 28 1817	"	Mary Corey Feb 27 1792
Christopher Merkly		Dec 18 1808	"	Rosella Carter " 22, 1825
John P McEwan		Feb 24 1824	"	Nancy Ackley Sep 27 1816
Wiley B Alrea		Mar 31, 1818	"	Hulda Deeples Jan 4, 1812
George N Corey		May 4 1819	"	Julia A Phippins Aug 31 1826
J G S Alread		Ma. 28 1825	"	Sally Alread Aug 8 1814
George W Price		Oct 24 1815	"	Eliza B Alread Nov 23, 1821
John C. Ackly		July 6, 1815	"	Lucy S McOlney Nov 22, 1804
Jas W Phippins		Oct 12 1819	"	Harriett Johnson Sep 4, 1823
Henry Stead		May 24 1800	"	Nancy Tracey May 14 1816
Samuel H Rogers		Mar 1 1819	"	Lydia R Steaou May 15 1827
David Seelye		Oct 12 1819	"	~~Elin~~ ^Emeline A^ Houghton Sep 3 1807
Jos E Johnson		Ap 28 1817	Elr.	Margaret Phelps May 13, 1819
Saml Eggleston		Mar 30 1804	Sev	Hannah Howe Feb 5 1802
Davis McOlney		Feb 24 1796	Pres	Susanah Eggleston Aug 15 1808
Richard P Keel		Nov 7, 1786	~~Sev~~ Elr	Sarah Makley May 19, 1810
Alanson Colly		May 9 1813	Sev	Ellen Keele Ap 14, 1790

Moses Gracey   Ap 11, 1810   Total 64   Alice Charlesworth Nov 5, 1827

Washed by James Brown & Hiram Dayton Anointed by Jacob Gates & Harrison Burgess. Finished 30 Min past 1. o clock.

Joseph Smith   May 5 1822   Sev

Thos Charlesworth   Feb 6, 1823

Washed by W. Hyde & ~~Ezra~~ Jas. B~~enson~~^rown^ & Harrison Burgess.

—Seventies Record, Book B, oversized portion, January 9, 1846.

went to Br[other] A[bsalom] P Frees where [I] staid over night & enjoyed my self well[;] better should [it] never be desired[,] so note it [to] be[.]

—John D. Lee, Diary.

....

[D]ictated history till ½ past 4 when I went to the Temple [and] spent an hour and a half with my quorum & returned home[.]

—Willard Richards, Diary.

....

On the 9th, returned to the Temple, in the afternoon I was called to the Sacred altar in the House of the Lord to receive the seal of the covenant between myself & wife [Margaret Smoot], & also Sariah Gibbon was there [and] given me in the Seal of the covenant, President Brigham Young, administering the ordinance.

—Abraham Owen Smoot, Diary, LDS Archives.

....

One hundred and five persons received ordinances in the Temple. I [Brigham Young] attended to ordinances at the altar. The several quorums met for prayer.

I observed to the brethren that it was my wish that all dancing and merriment should cease, lest the brethren and sisters be carried away by vanity; and that the name of the Deity should be held in reverence, with all the due deference that belongeth to an infinite being of his character.

—"Manuscript History of Brigham Young,"
in *History of the Church,* 7:566.

....

Nauvoo temple endowments performed on this date for:

First Company: Samuel L. Sprague, Mary W. Sprague, Emeline Free, Willard G. McMullen, Mary McMullen, Jesse Turpin, Sarah Coleman, Margaret M. Allen, Hayden W. Church, Sarah Ann Church, Abram D. Boynton, Hannah M. Boynton, Hanah M. Boynton, James L. Thompson, Matilda Thompson, Frederick Kessler, Emeline Kessler, Charles A. Davis, Ruth Davis, Daniel D. Hunt, Susan Hunt, Moses Gay, Lucretia Gay, George W. Potter, Charlotte B. Potter, Thomas Butterfield, Mary Jane Butterfield, Allen Tally, Catharine Tally, Harmon D. Bayles, Juliette Bayles, Essias Edwards, Sarah Edwards, Joseph F. Phippen, Ann Phippen, John M. Woolley, Maria L. Dewey, Charles H. Bassett, and Permelia M. Bassett.

Second Company: Elizabeth Canfield, Eliza Ann Dibble, Joseph Clements, Deborah Ann Clements, James Brinkerhoff, Sally Ann Brinkerhoff, Sarah Canfield, Daniel Kent, Ozias Kilbourn, Electa Kilbourn, John M. Ewell, Charlotte L. Lorenzen, Elizabeth Ewell, Stephen Nixon, James Worthington, Rachel Worthington, Francis A. Brown, Harriet Nixon, Benjamin R. Lamb, Elizabeth Lamb, William Van Ausdall, Polly Van Ausdall, William Coray, Isaac Phippen, Adah Phippen, Stephen Richardson, Erepta Richardson, and Christeen Golden.

Third Company: John P. McEwan, Amanda M. McEwan, Christopher Merkley, Sarah Merkley, Moses Tracy, Nancy Ann Tracy, Richard J. Keele, Ellen Keele, Rozilla Carter, Alvah Phelps, Margaret Phelps, Wily P. Allred, Sally Allred, David Dickson, Nancy Dickson, Fanny Howe, Joseph E. Johnson, Harriet Johnson, John C. Ackley, Percy Ackley, James W. Price, Emeline A. Houghton, Alanson Colby, Huldah Teeples, James T. S. Allred, Eliza B. Allred, J. W. Phippen, Julia A. Phippen, David Seelye, Samuel H. Rogers, Samuel Eggleston, Lurenna Eggleston, Davis McOlney, Lucy S. McOlney, George W. Coray, Mary Coray, Henry Steed, and Lydia Rebecca Steed.

Fourth Company: Thomas Charlesworth, Alice Charlesworth, and Joseph Smith II.

—Summary of information compiled by the Temple Index Bureau, *Nauvoo Temple Endowment Register: 10 December 1845 to 8 February 1846.*

....

Sealings performed for the living on this date:

John Brown to Elizabeth Crosby; William Crosby to Sarah [Sally] Harmon; George Parker Dykes to Dorcus Keeling, Alzina [Alciva] Durfey [Durfee], and Cynthia Sloes [Soles]; William Matthews to Elizabeth Adaline Henderson; Freeman Nickerson to Hulda [Huldah] Chapman; Isaac Phippen to Ada Stewart; Abraham Owen Smoot to Margaret Thompson McMeans, Sarah Gibbons, and Emily Hill Harris; William Weeks to Caroline Matilda Allen; and John Mills Woolley to Maria Lucy Dewey.

—Summarized from the Book of Living Sealings.

Saturday, January 10, 1846

[S]pent the afternoon and evening in attend[ing] the business of the alt[a]r[.] staid at the Temple this night[.]

—Brigham Young, Diary.

Washing commenced in the Male Department 15 to 8.

[See pages 391-94 for excerpted portion.]

At 7 o clock the council of the 1st Seventy retired to their apartments in Room No. 9 in council & took into consideration the circumstances & condition of the poor — who are suffering in our Midst[.] Pres[ident] Jos[eph] Young said that there were both Men and Women among the Quorums of the Seventies that[, he] has no doubt[,] brought the last Fowl, that they [own] & some men that are in rags & Scarcely Sustain Life have borrowed 15 c[en]ts &c to buy oil for this Endowment — while there are others in our midst who want to be in advance that had thousands & [more,] Both of Gold & Silver[,] gold chain necklaces, Silks & Sattans & clothing of every kind that grind the Face of the Poor — all the day long — This was the case in Kirtland [Ohio] & when the Kirtland[,] or rather the Zion[,] Camp was called to go west to defend the cause of bleeding [and suffering Saints.] There were 500 or about[,] but [illegible] we were all poor[.] not withstanding we had to Sustain ourselves[,] we [combined our] expenses and raised about $5.00 in cash — we afterward called the Brethren to geather in order to know what assistance could be raised, should we [be] under the [necessity] of all removing west[,] & to our astonishment $9.00 were raised in Jewels & gold rings [and] that from the Sisters — which of course were things that could be spared as well as not — what amount could be raised from the Seventies Wives[,] such a large body as we now have — why it would be nearly [a] thousand dollars. this is a subject that ought to be laid before the Quorums that the frequent calls of suffering [and appeals to] humanity may be [answered.]

—Seventies Record, Book B.

....

[A]t 9 AM I acted No 1 in the 1st & last apartment[s and] also kept up the minets of the day[.] in the evening I went home and spent the Night[.] My wife however was not at home[.] She was on a visit to Br[other] A[bsalom] P Frees[.]

—John D. Lee Diary.

....

Sisters Rhoda [Richards] and Amelia [Pierson] went to the Temple with the Dr. [Willard Richards] and attended to the first ordinances.

—Thomas Bullock, Diary.

....

Went to the Temple at ½ past 8—with Sister Rhoda [Richards] & my

[Washings and anointings for Saturday, January 10, 1846]

[Male Department]		
Stephen Richardson born Feb 11 1797	H. P.	
John McEwell " Aug 5 1823	Sev	
Miles Anderson " Oct 30 1795		
		Female Department commenced washing & anointing at 2 m. to 8 A.M.
Wm A Lutz born Oct 6 1818	Sev	Mary Hamilton born Sep 26 1807
John D Martin " Aug 28 1816	"	Louisa C. Earl " Jan 4 1818
Sylvester H Earl " " 15, 1815	"	Mariah Kempton " April 15 1826
Jerome B. Kempton " Oct 13 1820	"	Charity Riley " Dec 11 1816
Wm W. Riley " Feb 8 1813	"	Lucy Watterman " Feb 25 1829
John Hamilton " July 12, 1807	"	Sophrona Babcock " July 24 1822
Joseph Wilder " Oct. 22 1798	"	Eliza Babcock " Oct. 1828
Adelphia Young " Feb 27, 1816	"	Louisa Pratt " Nov 10 1802
		Sarah Nickerson " Oct 2, 1820
Geo. W. Nickerson " Dec 13 1813	"	Rhoda Young " " 24 1820
		Lydia Gates July 11 1810
Samuel Gate " Mar 14 1804	"	Sarah Martin " April 14 1823
		Enda Cordon " May 26 1819
Benj West " Sept 13 1801	"	Rhoda Richards " Aug 11 1783
Alford Cordon " Feb 20 1817	"	Amelia Pearson " April 16 1815

Washed by Jacob Gates & Wm Hyde & anointed by Hyrum Dayton & Dominicus Carter finished 15 m. to 9.
washed by E. J. Webb Sophronia M. Burgess Lydia Granger Phebe Bl[?] Nancy Winchester & Mercy R Thompson Anointed by

N Winchester C. Herriman Nancy H. Rockwood & Phebe Chase Eliza Ann Whitney also —

½ past 7. A.M. the following Persons met in Room No 9 Dresed in Robes after the order of the Priesthood, offered up the Signs then consecrated 16 Bottles of oil Namely A. Lyman Geo. Miller Henry Herriman Erastus Snow L. N. Scovil Wm. Hyde and Harrison Burgess & Amasa Lyman mouth in consecrating Geo Miller in offering up the Signs took the lead —

Male department No. 2
30 Minets past 10 A.M.

James Houston born June 4 1818	Sev
1 Abram C. Hodge " July 10 1806	Elder
2 Alber Smith " Nov 18. 1804	Sev
3 Cyrus C. Canfield " Dec 20 1817	"
4 Jas. Cummings " Mar 10 1819	"
5 David M Gammet " Dec 4 1802	"
1 Chas. Dolton " Aug 22 1810	H. P.
Simon C. Dolton " Jan 14, 1806	Sev
John A. Wooley " July 31 1805	"
Stepen Shelton " Mar 1809	"
Edward Johnson " Aug 18 1785	H. P.
Wm G Steritt " June 4 1813	Sev

washed by Wm Hyde & Jacob Gates
& anointed by H. Dayton John Brown
& Wilber G. Earl 20 M. past 10

Female Department 20 m. to 11

Christeen Golden born
Lydia Canfield " Oct. 17 1812
Esther Smith " Feb 25. 1811
Percy Johnson " Sept 12th 1802
Hannah P. Grant " Mar 6 1815
Abigail L Leavitt " Aug 23 1801
Hannah Carter " Oct 9th 1786
Sarah Ann Wolf " April 10 1814
Cathrine Rhodes " Jan 19 1824
Rebeca Hodge " Nov 13 1816
Cathrine Miller " Feb 16 1798
Louisa Miller " Jan 8. 1822
Anna Dolton " May 5 1828
Elizabeth Miles " July 17 1788

Margarett Knowlton " Jar 1st 1825
Ana S. Cummings " Feb 17 1809
Anna Atwood " April 9 17[?]

Female Department

Hannah Wright born April 20 1823
Eliza An Turpin " Aug 28 1824
Almira Teeples " Nov 11 1819
Emily S Hoyt " Sept. 1806
Esther Fuller [?] " " 20 1810
Lydia Brown " Mar 4 1814

Rachel Colmer " " 21 1823

Sarah Winters " " 31 1803

Betsey L. Henderson " " 8 1813
Sarah [illegible] " July 1 1804
Margarett Standing " Aug 23 1823
Maryan Grant " Sep 18 1810
[illegible] " Mar 11 1823
Anna Partridge " Sep 27 1794
Elizabeth Green " Nov 24 1811
Nancy Green " Sept. 17 1828
Male Department
10 M. to 4 P.M.

Abigail Shelton " [illegible]
Mary E. Dolton " July 19 [illegible]

Cordia E. Leavitt born Jan 5 1825
Lydia Partridge " May 8 1830
Dolly Bullock " Aprl 6 1799
Louis Lords " May 5 1813

The above named persons were washed by Lydia Granger E. J. Webb Surphrona M Burges, N. M. Lyman & Nancy Winchester & anointed by N. M. Lyman Nancy Winchester [illegible] & Nancy H. Rockwood

Cy. No. 4 —
52 M. to 3. P.M.

Eliza Staford born Jun 16 1821
Elizabeth Lee " Aug 25 1805
Hanah E. Crosby " Mar 4 1820
Jane Patten " Jan 31, 1820
Mary Wilson " Sep 8, 1788
Lorena Barrows " Aug 4 1820

Geo M Grant born July 14 1820	Sev
Ethan Burrows " Jan 12 1817	"
David Grant " July 21 1816	"
Amos B Fuller " Mar 24 1810	"
Ichabod W Beach " May 13 1817	"
Leslie Symes " Sep 30 1816	"
Isaac S. Brown " Dec 15th 1806	"
Wm Standing " Oct 13 1821	"
Alexander Wright " Jan 27 1815	"
James Jones " " 1st 1818	"
George Colmeure " Nov 6 1814	"
Jesse W Crosby " " 15 1820	"
Hosea Cusher " April 2 1826	"
John Henderson " Nov 20 1810	
Samuel P. Hoyt " " 21 1807	"
Wm A. King " July 3 1821	"
Louis Robinson	"
Samuel M Rice " July 25 1823	
Andrew Cahoon Aug 4 1829	
Jacob D. Allen " 1804	
Jacob Gates "	
Alford [illegible] Dec 12 1805	

Betsey Foot [born] Oct. 18 [1820]
Mary D. Grant " Jan 28 1823
Lydia Allen " Aprl 8, 1829
Emma Beach " Oct 7, 1820
Naomah K. J. Twist " Mar 20 1821
Meary An Powers " Dec 28 1816
washed & anointed by L. Granger
S. M. Burgess, N. H. Rockwood
N. Winchester & M. R. Thompson
Anointed by N Winchester N. H. R
C. Herriman Eliza Webb
& Mercy R. Thompson finished 10 to 4

Male Department
Wm Allred born July 21 1819
Total washed by Wm Hyde
1,25
James Brown Jacob Gates & Hyrum Dayton
Anointed by the Same

—Seventies Record, Book B, oversized portion, January 10, 1846.

Niece E. [Amelia] Pierson—attended to the first ordinances, and returned a little after 12[.]

—Willard Richards, Diary.

....

Afternoon and evening in the Temple administering at the Altar. One hundred and eighteen received ordinances.

—"Manuscript History of Brigham Young," in *History of the Church,* 7:566-67, and *Manuscript History of Brigham Young,* p. 10.

....

Nauvoo temple endowments performed on this date for:

First Company: Willard Richards, Rhoda Richards, Amelia E. Pearson, Vilate Young, Alfred Cordon, Emma Cordon, Lucy Waterman, Presenda Buel, Jerome B. Kempton, Maria Kempton, Louisa Pratt, John Hamilton, Mary Hamilton, Sophronia Babcock, William W. Riley, Charity Riley, Eliza Babcock, George W. Hickerson, Sarah Hickerson, Samuel Gates, Lydia Gates, William A. Litz, Rebecca Litz, Adolphia Young, Rhoda Young, Sylvester H. Earl, Lois C. Earl, John D. Martin, Sarah Martin, Benjamin West, Miles Anderson, and Joseph Wilder.

Second Company: Lois Low, John A. Woolf, Sarah Ann Woolf, Dolly Bullock, Abram C. Hodge, Rebecca Hodge, Catharine Rhodes, Stephen C. Shelton, Abigail Shelton, James Houston, Margaret Houston, Cyrus C. Canfield, Cornelia E. Leavitt, Louisa Canfield, Lydia Partridge, Elizabeth Miles, Abigail L. Leavitt, Hannah Carter, Louisa Minnerly, David M. Gamet, Hannah P. Gamet, Catharine Minnerly, James W. Cummings, Aura Anette Cummings, Anna Atwood, Charles Dalton, Mary E. Dalton, Simon C. Dalton, Anna Dalton, William G. Sterredd, Edward Johnson, Percy Johnson, Albert Smith, and Esther Smith.

Third Company: Alexander Wright, Hannah Wright, Samuel P. Hoyt, Emily S. Hoyt, David Grant, Mary Ann Grant, James D. Allen, Sarah Allen, Amos B. Fuller, Esther Fuller, John Henderson, Betsey Jane Henderson, Alvira Teeples, George Colemere, Rachel Colemere, Leslie Syme, Eliza Ann Turpin, James Jones, Mary Ann Jones, Elisa M. Green, Anna Partridge, Nancy Z. Green, Sarah Winter, William Standing, Margaret Standing, James Hawkins, Isaac S. Brown, Lydia Brown, William A. King, Samuel M. Price, Andrew Cahoon, and Hosea Cushing.

Fourth company: George R. Grant, Mary D. Grant, Ichabod W. Beach, Emma Beach, Alfred Lee, Elizabeth Lee, Mary Wilson, Jesse W. Crosby,

Hannah E. Crosby, William C. Patten, Jane Patten, William Alford, Eliza Alford, Naamah K. J. Twiss, Ethan Barrows, Lorena Barrows, Mary Ann Powers, Lydia Allen, and Betsey Foote.

—Summary of information compiled by the Temple Index Bureau, *Nauvoo Temple Endowment Register: 10 December 1845 to 8 February 1846.*

....

Sealings performed for the living on this date:

James Brown to Esther Jones, Martha Stephens, and Sarah Steadwell Wood; David Candland to Mary Ann Barton; Amos Botsford Fuller to Esther Victoria Smith; William Culbertson Gallaher to Elizabeth Orton; Peter Haws to Charlotte Harrington, and Betsey Harrington; Parley Parker Pratt to Elizabeth Brotherton, Mary Ann Frost, and Mary Wood; and John Smith to Ann Carr.

—Summarized from the Book of Living Sealings.

....

Sealings for the dead performed on this date:

Thankful Halsey (Elizabeth Brotherton, proxy) to Parley P. Pratt, Brigham Young officiating; and Martha Hopkins and Susan Foutz (Ester Jones, proxy) to James Brown, Brigham Young, officiating.

—Summarized from the Book of Proxy Sealings.

Sunday, January 11, 1846

I spent the day in the Temple[.] about 3. o[clock] my family came up into The Temple, also Bro[ther]. [Heber C.] Kimballs [family and] Bro[ther]. O[rson] Hyde's & N[ewel]. K. Whitney's [families.] we had a good visit [where]in they met in my room together with others & I received my last anointing under the hand of brother H[eber]. C Kimball[.]

—Brigham Young, Diary.

....

31 minutes to 7 P.M. Assembled in Pres[ident]. Brigham Young's Room No. 1. in the atic Story of the Lords House[:] Pres[ident]. B[righam]. Young Heber C. Kimble, Orson Hyde, P[arley]. P. Pratt, Orson Pratt, Willard Richards, John Taylor, Amasa Lyman, N[ewel]. K. Whitney, Geo[rge]. Miller Edmund Ellsworth, Mary Young[,] Vilate Kimble[,] Leonora Taylor, Elizabeth An[n] Whitney & Elizabeth Ellsworth. Bro[th-

er]. J[ohn]. Taylor started the hymn This Earth was once a garden place[,] all being clothed in Priestly garments—Pres[ident]. B[righam]. Young Prayed. all having nelted [knelt] a round the Alter—previous to prare [prayer] they all arose sang a Hymn & offered up the signs of the Holy Priesthood then Br[other] Heber C. Kimball proceeded to anoint and consecrate Pres[ident]. Brigham Young a King & a Priest unto the most High God over the Church of Jesus Christ of Latter Day Saints & over the whole House of Iseral—

Brother Brigham Young, I pour this holy, consecrated oil, upon your head, and anoint thee a King and a Priest of the Most High God over the Church of Jesus Christ of Latter Day Saints, and unto all Israel: and I anoint thy head, that thy brain may be healthy and active and quick to think and to understand and to direct thy whole body and I anoint thy eyes that they may see and perceive, and that thou mayest not be deceived in what thou beholdest, and that thy sight may never fail thee: and I anoint thy ears that they may be quick to hear and communicate to thy understanding; and that thou mayest hear the secret deliberations of thy enemies, and thereby thou shalt be enabled to overreach their designs: and I anoint thy nose that thou may scent, and relish the fragrance of the good things of the earth: and I anoint thy mouth that thou mayest be enabled to speak the great things of God, and confound all the wisdom of man, and put to nought all who shall raise up to oppose thee, in all countries where thou goest for thou shalt build up the Kingdom of God among many people, and in the midst of mighty nations; so thy glory shall be established, and whatsoever thou shalt bind on earth, shall be bound in heaven, and whomsoever thou shalt loose on earth, shall be loosed in heaven; for there shall be given unto thee crowns, and kingdoms, and dominions; and thou shalt receive all thy heart shall desire; and thy soul shall be satisfied with a multitude of blessings which thou shalt receive; for princes shall bow at thy feet and deliver unto thee their treasures; and thou shalt teach them the principles of salvation. And I seal thee up unto Eternal Life, that thou shalt come forth in the morn of the first resurrection, and receive all these blessings, in their fulness. And thou shalt attain unto [the] Eternal Godhead, and receive a fulness of joy, and glory, and power; and that thou mayest do all things whatsoever is wisdom that thou shouldest do, even if it be to create worlds and redeem them: so shall thy joy be full to the praise and glory of God: Amen.

Elder Heber Chase Kimbal then anointed Mary Ann Young a Queen

& Priestess unto her husband [Brigham Young] in the Church of Jesus Christ of Latter Day Saints & in the house of Iseral—

Sister Mary Ann Young, I pour upon thy head this holy, consecrated oil, and seal upon thee all the blessings of the everlasting priesthood, in conjunction with thy husband: and I anoint thee to be a Queen and Priestess unto thy husband, over the Church of Jesus Christ of Latter Day Saints; and thou shalt be heir to all the blessings which are sealed upon him, inasmuch as thou dost obey his counsel; and thou shalt receive glory, honor, power and exaltation in his exaltation: and thou shalt be a strength in thy mind for thou shalt have visions, and manifestations of the Holy Spirit, and the time shall come that Angels shall visit thee, and minister unto thee, and teach thee: and in absence of thy husband shall comfort thee, and make known his situation.

Thou shalt be a wise counsellor to many of thy sex, and they shall look unto thee for precept and for example.

Thou shalt be noted and honored for thy generosity, and the freedom and good feelings with which thou shalt relieve the wants of the distressed; and the disgression [discretion] with which thou shalt act in thy sphere in all things. And I seal thee up unto Eternal Life, thou shalt come forth in the morning of the first resurrection and inherit with him all the honors, glories, and power of Eternal Lives, and that thou shalt attain unto the eternal Godhead, so thy exaltation shall be perfect, and thy glory be full, in a fulness of power and exaltation.

And the glory, honor and power shall be ascribed unto the Father, Son, and Holy Ghost, Amen.

—"Book of Anointings."

....

A.M. in the Temple with the Council of Fifty, arranging to make an early start West.

—William Clayton, Diary.

....

[A]t 10 in the morning I [John D. Lee] met in council in [the] atic story of the Lords House[.] it being 60 feet above the surface of the Earth[, it] enabled us to breathe pure air and also placed us out of the reach of [blank] and eve[s]droppers[.] at this council the subject of leaving this place was taken into consideration[,] the time when [we should leave,] &c[.] Trouble was near at hand was the decided oppinion of the c[o]uncil[.] about 3 PM the council adjourned to Tuesday 10 PM[.] I then took dinner after which I went to Pres[ident] B[righam] Yo[u]ng &

took his carriage & conveyed about 15 of the apostles families to the Temple[.] & when I had done this I drove to Br[other] A[bsalom] P Free's & took my wife & sister Louisa Lee home[.] about dark I reached home[.] leaving a part of my load I went to the Pres[ident] & left the carriage & horses[.] & when I had reached home again I found several of the High [Priests] were collected in my house & had in the South part in the 2nd story about 30 in No. [including] Bro[ther] Jefferson Hunt & daughter Br[other] Bean & family in connection with many other good friends who help[ed] pass off the evening[.] We had a variety of music [and] we enjoyed (ourselves well)[.] after our merriment ceased we bowed in Prayer before the great Eloheme & rendered thanks for his presance this evening[.] our Co[mpany] having retired to their respective places of abode I found myself seated in a small company who spent the night[.] here I had application made to me; to receive a man and his wife into my Family[.] after speaking freely upon the law of adoption, I accepted James Woolsey & Lovina his wife into my family by the Law of adoption[,] he choosing to retain his Sir name for the presant & to have mine named upon[.] this however was a perogative that I gave him[.]

—John D. Lee, Diary.

....

The General Council [of Fifty] met and arranged to make an early start west.

—"Manuscript History of Brigham Young,"
in *History of the Church,* 7:567.

....

Sealings performed for the living on this date:

Edmund Lovell Ellsworth to Elizabeth Young; Emer Harris to Polly Chamberlain; Orson Hyde to Nancy Marinda Johnson, Martha Rebecca Browett, and Mary Ann Price; William Henry Kimball to Mary Marie Davenport William Seely Lish to Veronica Cornwall [Cornwell].

—Summarized from the Book of Living Sealings.

....

Adoptions performed on this date:

To William H. and Martha D. Kimball: Ellen Vilate Kimball, sealed by Brigham Young: "Done in the order before written, the covenants by the parents"; and to Brigham Young and Miriam Young (Mary Ann Young as proxy): Joseph Angel Young, Brigham Young Jr., John Willard Young, Elizabeth Young, Vilate Young, Roxy Erma Alice Young, Eunice Caroline

Young, and Edmund Ellsworth, sealed by Heber C. Kimball: "These persons were adopted unto their parent in the usual form, and by the Sealing ordinance at the alter, &c."

—Summarized from "Sealings and Adoptions."

Monday, January 12, 1846

The remiand[er] of the day I [Brigham Young] spent at the alt[a]r officiating in the ordinances of Sealing— In the evening Evan M. Greene: my clerk[,] through sickness[,] was compelled to retire from his labour— Br[other]. John D. Lee I appointd to take his place. ~~there~~ being a few records to be kept sepperately & apart contanning the first Sealings of the living & of Proxy [and] of adoption & also that of the 2d anonitings which I found to be quite a task for one man to perform therefore I employed Bro[ther]. Franklin D. Richard to assist in keeping those Records above aluded too— Such was the anxiety manifested by the Saints to receive the ordinances of Endowment & no less on our part to have them get the keys of the Priesthood—that I gave myself up entirely to the work of the Lord in the Temple[.] almost night & Day I have spent[,] not taking more than 4 hours upon an average out of 24 to Sleep—& but seldom ever allowing myself the the [sic] time & opportunity of going home once in a week.

—Brigham Young, Diary.

....

[A]t 12. o. clock[,] Assembled in Room No. 1[:] Pres[ident] Brigham Young, Heber C Kimble, P[arley]. P. Pratt, Amasa Lyman, John Taylor, Geo[rge] Miller, Isaac Morl[e]y, Orson Spencer, Ezra T Benson, Newell K Whitney—after the usual ceremony pre-requisite to the ordinance of anointing—Pres[ident] Brigham Young anointed Newell Kimble Whitney a King & a Priest unto the Most [High] God—in the church of Jesus Christ of Latter Days Saints & in the House of Iseral & among thy Brethren in this the House of the Lord[.] Elizabeth An[n] Whitney was then anointed a Queen & Priestess unto her Husband N[ewel]. K. Whitney, in the Church of Jesus Christ of Latter Day Saints & to all Iseral.

—"Book of Anointings."

....

Ellen Sanders [born] Mar[ch] 3 1825 [in] Presteel [Telemark] Norway was sealed to Heber Chase Kimball for time & all eternity by B[righam]. Young in presence of John Taylor, A[masa]. Lyman [and] Joseph Young[,] Vilate Kimball presenting her to him at the alter.

Sarah Ann Whitney was also sealed to President Joseph Smith (deceased) for time & all eternity as his wife[,] Heber Chase Kimball acting as proxy for & in behalf of Joseph Smith (deceased) by B[righam]. Young in presence of ~~the~~ J[ohn]. Taylor, A[masa]. Lyman, Joseph Young, & others[.] She was then sealed to Heber Chase Kimball as his wife for time[,] his wife Vilate presenting her to him at the Alter[,] her father & mother having presented her to him [f]or the above named purpose[.]

—Book of Living Sealings.

....

[T]his day George Miller Henry Herriman Jedediah Grant, and William Hyde clothed themselves in Priestly apparel at 8 oclock in Room No 9 [and] offered up the Signs & consecrated 18 Bottles of oil after which the order of the day [was given] & each appointed his Station[. Those who] were present of the council the 1st Seventy this morning[:] 6 Persons Namely Pres[ident] Young B[enjamin] L Clapp H[enry] Herriman J[edediah]. M. Grant Zerah Pulsipher & [illegible] that this is the Lords House [and] that Pres[ident] Pulsipher has [illegible]

Male Department Company No 1 commenced washing 8 of A.M.

[See pages 402-406 for excerpted portion.]

The giving of endowments is now for a time ^suspended^; it being considered wisdom by the council. At the usual hour the High Priests and Seventies met at their respective apartments, and offered up the signs and prayed for such blessings as we need.

—Seventies Record, Book B.

....

At 9 oclock the services commenced & through the day I [John D. Lee] acted from the [role of the] Tempter in the G[arden of] E[den][.] Also kept up the records[.] 145 persons passed through the ordinances today[.] it is now 10 at night & we would like to retire to rest but the Twelve [apostles] are in council[.] I had an invitation to spen[d] the evening in the Temple[, but] peradventure my services or person would be wanted[,] I tarried but without embracing the promise but saw it not a far off[.] at 11 oclock I returned home & spent the night[.] Tuesday noon [January 13] I walked to the Temple[,] but on my way I stoped to procure Materials to paint my house[.] some 8 or 10 of the Painters proposed to bestow 1 or 2 days labor on my house[.] Br[other] [blank] Sterriot profered to paint my huse & risk my selling to get his pay[.] at 10 I set in council in the atic

[Washings and anointings for Monday, January 12, 1846]

[Male Department]		Female Dept Co No 1
Samuel White born March 9th 1818	Sev	commenced
Caleb Ayers " Novbr 13th 1816	S H. P. 8	
James Nixon " March 2nd 1823	"	Fanny Spillsberry born Jan 1825
George Spilbury " " 25th "	"	Eliza Jenkins " Aug 24 1811
John Rollins " Nov 20th 1805	"	Malvina G. Owman " " 12 1812
Joseph S Hutchins " March 17th 1825	"	Ann McIntire " Dec 19 1811
George N Omand " Jany 30th 1802	"	Margarett Dayna " April 1st 1807
Shepard P Hutchins " Nov 29th 1818	Sev	Elizabeth Clark " May 1788
Thomas Kay " Sept 1st 1815	"	Abigail Ashton " Feb 15 1821
William Jenkins " Oct 3rd 1814	"	Mary Ann Roslana " June 22 1811
William P McIntyre " May 29th 1813	"	Mary H. White " Aug 31 1818
Isaac Ashton " July 4th 1811	"	Sarrah Wixom " Dec 12 1817
Amos P. Rodgers " Sept 27th 1820	Pres	Margarett Avery " Aug 20 1809
Myron Higly " Dec 29th 1807	Sev	Charlotte Allen " Oct 10 1817
Nathan Allen " Nov 10, 1812	H P	Cornelia M Waterman " April 19 1829
Solomon Wixom " Mar 26 1809	"	Lucinda Hutchings " Jan 15 1822
Chas R. Dana " Nov 8 1802	"	" Eyers " " 29 1816
James Pettit " Oct. 13, 1793	Elder	Sally Hutchins " Feb 20 1794
The above Named Persons were		Lovina W. Lee " Jan 9 1824
washed by Isaac Allred & Jos		Ann Hall " Dec 30 1818
G Hovey And anointed by Edson	"	M. Doolittle " " 24 1820

Barney Randolph Allexander &
Ransome Shepherd —

Finished 8 Minits to 10.
Male Department
Co No 2.

John Adams born Mar 23 1799	Sev
Ephraim Green " " 5th 1807	H P
Elbridge Tufts " Oct. 5, 1812	
Thomas Atkinson " Sept 1st 1810	
Francello Surfee " May 17, 1812	
Isaac Clark " " 7 1806	H P
Wm A Perkins " Dec 17th 1815	Elder
Jerome M Benson " Nov 5 1800	H P
Guy M Keyser " Oct. 16 1805	Sev
John G Luce " Sept 30 1817	"
Wm C Stain^e^s " " 26 1818	"

20. Phebe Pettit " Jan 2 1796
Females washed by Lydia Granger
Sophia M. Burgess
Malvina Snow
Mary Gates
Anointed by
Nancy H. Rockwood
Sophiah M. Burgess
Mary Gates &
Mercy R Thompson
Female Department
No 2 commenced 20 m to 11
Elmira Tufts born Sept 24 1812
Sarah Winston " Aug 3 1822
Elizabeth Gregory " Jun 16 1806
Loisia Elliot " Aug 1793
Martha ^R^ Perkins " Jan 19 1819
Lydia C. Flemming " Oct 31 1816
Eliza Cravath " April 27 1808
Matilda Bassett " July 14 1800
Mary Benson " " 1820
Margarett Atkinson " " 13 1818
Mary Clark " Mar 1804

Wm Hutchins [born] April 1823	[Seventy]
Cornelius Cox " Sept 13 1813	"
Isaac Lossee " Oct 5 1816	"
Jas Adams " Mar 23 1799	"
Franklin Bovier " Dec 15 1805	"
Samuel A P. Kelsy " April 27 1815	"
Co. No. 3.	
Andrew G. Stewart " Sep 12 1819	"
John M Stewart " " 15 1808	"
Daniel Corbitt " May 16 1809	"
Jesse Spirgin " June 30 1780	H P.
John Houston " May 13 1816	Sev
Jas Garrett " " 1 1807	Elder
Levi Empy " Nov 15 1813	Eld
James Waters " Mar 9, 1814	Sev
Uriah Curtis " " 5 1805	"
Hiram B. Bassett " Mar 11 1820	"
Richard Brush " " 13 1820	"
Alonzo H Raliegh " Nov 7 1818	"
Ira. E. West " " 20 1824	Eder
Royal Barney Jr " Dec 8 1880	Pres
Geo. W. Taggart " Nov 6, 1810	Sev
Daniel Hendrix " Jan 6 1806	Elder

Pricilla Eberson [born] Aug 1st 1799
Elizabeth Cox " May 15 1814
Fidelia Thompson " Jan 12 1818
Betsey Adams " Nov 12 1804
Susan Hovy " Mar 12 1808
Harriet N Luce " Oct 11 1822
Susan Thomas " Jun 7 1808
Jennet Kelsy " Feb 20 1809
Ruth C Hutching " Jan 28 1827
Sarah Lossee " May 7 1822
Agness Rich " Oct. 2 1819
Frances Brown " " 31 1818

Co. No. 3.

Elizabeth A Benedict " Nov 1 1825
Mary Houston " " 2 1785
Nancy Stewart " Dec 6 1813
Mary An Robinson " " 2 1818
Phebe Curtis " May 7 1806
Christana Houston " " 6 1823
Fanny Taggart " Oct 25 1821
Susana P. Houston " Feb 11 1826
Lucinda M Bassett " Aug 24 1829
Charlotte A West " Jan. 13 1828

Lorenzo Owen " Feb 2 1820 Sev
Matthew L Peck " Nov 21. 1822 Elder
Geo Snider " June 12 1819 Sev
washed by Iseral Barlow & Rudolph
Alexander & anointed J G Hovy &
Edson Barney [illegible] George [illegible]
Male Department
Co. No. 4
Erastus O. Beach born Mar 5 1829 Sev
John Spires " Feb 19 1822 "
Chas H Dewey " Aug 14 1825 "
Wm F Babbett " " 10 1820 "
Edwin B. Harris " July 3 1823 "
Lorenzo B Harris " Nov 13 1818 "
Elijah Thomas " Jan 22 1815 "
Joel Terry " May 23 1812 "
Jos Smith " Dec 2d 1828 "
Jos H Thomas " June 11 1815 "
John Brush " May 22 1815 "
Russell Rodgers " 17 1824 "
George S Clark " Nov 7 1816 "
Robert Clift " Jan 4 1824 70
Jacob Shewmaker " Oct 17 1798 Elder

Lidia Spirgin " May 9 1781
Mary Pulsipher " Mar 2 1799
Elmira B Corbett " Jun 13 1811
Elouisa Hendrix " [illegible]

Sarah Snider born Nov 21 1821
Unice Stewart " July 12 1825
Eliza Tabor " Feb 17 1814
Elizabeth Saveill[?] " " 25 1807
Mary Jared " May 15 1806
Caroline F Raliegh " Nov 12 1820
Margarett J Empy " Dec 5 1822
Ann Boice " April 5 1788
Co. No. 4. 15 M. Past 3
Nancy Shewmaker " Nov 18 1799
Martha Brush " Jan 17 1815
Susan Thomas " Oct. 15 1828
Maria Terry " Mar 23 1818
Matilda King " " 11 1812
Sarah S. O. Banks " Sept 22 1822
washed by Sophia Burgess Mary Gates

Chas. D. Barnham [born] May 9 1800	Sev	Nancy H Rockwood & Lydia Granger
Thos. R. King " Mar 9 1813	"	Anointed Nancy Rockwood L Granger
Samuel C Hall " Aug 25 1813	"	

Total 45

Washed by Edson Barney & Randsome Shepherd & S- Mo- Burgess Anointed by Isaac Allred Iseral Barlow & J. G. Hovey at 10 minets to 9. the last company came through the veil, making in all one hundred & 45 that passed through to day.

—Seventies Record, Book B, oversized portion, January 12, 1846.

story of the Lords House[.] The capt[ain]'s of the several companies reported the amount of waggons & teams provisions & cash that was on hand & ready to start whenever called on[.] The Spirit of the Lord guided our council to leave[, and in this there was] entire & full satisfaction Pres[ident] B[righam] Young said that the saying of the Prophets would never be verified unless the House of the Lord be reared in the Tops of the Mountains & the Proud Banner of Liberty wave over the valley's that are within the Mountains & I know where the spot is & I know how to make the Flag[.] Jos[eph] [Smith] sent out the coulours and Said where ever the coulours settled there would be the spot[.] There is another thing that I [Brigham Young] wish to say to this council[.] let an influence go out[.] we intend that every worthy man will receive his endowment[;] if not here[,] he will have it in the wilderness & to[morrow if not today.] I [John D. Lee] will here observe Pres[ident] Brigham Young called & set me apart for the purpose of keeping the records of sealings and anointings which were sacred & precious & will of course be handled to future generations[.] quite a number of cases having already occured without ever having been recorded & what was recorded was not in a correct form consiquently had to be rectified—which of course produced much labor which has been our ocupation through the week[.] finding the task more arduous than what we expected Br[other] Franklin D Richards was appointed to assist in getting the records properly arranged up with the opperations of the [day] or rather each day.

—John D. Lee, Diary.

....

On the 12th of January 1846 I received the first degree of my endowment under the hand of the Presidency of the Seventies, was washed anointed with oil ordained to be a King and Priest unto God, in his own due time[,] and introduced through the signs and orders of the Priesthood.

—John Spiers, Autobiography, LDS Archives.

....

One hundred and forty-three persons received their endowments in the Temple. I [Brigham Young] officiated at the altar. Such has been the anxiety manifested by the saints to receive the ordinances, and such the anxiety on our part to administer to them, that I have given myself up entirely to the work of the Lord in the Temple night and day, not taking more than four hours sleep, upon an average, per day, and going home but once a week.

Elder Heber C. Kimball and the others of the Twelve Apostles were in constant attendance but in consequence of close application some of them had to leave the Temple to rest and recruit their health.

—"Manuscript History of Brigham Young," in *History of the Church,* 7:567.

....

Nauvoo temple endowments performed on this date for:

First Company: James Pettitt, Phebe Pettitt, Elizabeth Clark, Caleb Ayers, Lucinda Ayers, Amos P. Rogers, Ann Matilda Doolittle, Shepherd P. Hutchings, Samuel White, Mary H. White, Cornelia M. Waterman, William Avery, Margaret Avery, Solomon Wixom, Sarah Wixom, John Roylance, Mary Ann Roylance, Jonathan Allen, Charlotte Allen, James W. Lee, Lovina W. Lee, William P. McIntire, Ann McIntire, Thomas Hall, Ann Hall, George W. Oman, Malvina G. Oman, William Jenkins, Eliza Jenkins, Joseph S. Hutchings, Sally Hutchings, George Spilsbury, Fanny Spilsbury, Isaac Ashton, Abigail Ashton, Charles R. Dana, and Margaret Dana.

Second Company: William J. Perkins, Martha R. Perkins, Lydia C. Fleming, Susan Harvey, Jerome M. Benson, Mary Benson, Myron Higley, Priscilla Higley, Elbridge Tufts, Elmira Tufts, Louisa Follet, John G. Luce, Harriet N. Luce, Elizabeth Gregory, Cornelius Cox, Elizabeth Cox, Elias Bassett, Matilda Bassett, Francillo Durfey, Thomas Atkinson, Margaret Atkinson, Agnes Rich, James Adams, Betsey Adams, Susan Thomas, Isaac Clark, Mary Clark, William W. Hutchings, Ruth C. Hutchings, Samuel A. P. Kelsey, Jennet Kelsy, Isaac H. Losee, Sarah Losee, Ephraim Green, Fidelia Thompson, Eliza Cravath, Franklin Bevier, William C. Staines, Guy M. Keyser, and Sarah Huston.

Third Company: Mary Pulsipher, Elizabeth A. Burkitt, Royal Barney Jr., Levi Empy, Margaret Empy, George Snider, Sarah Snider, George Boyes, Ann Boyes, Elizabeth Swan, Uriah Curtis, Phebe Curtis, Lorenzo Brown, Frances Brown, Daniel Corbett, Elmira B. Corbett, Daniel Hendrix, Louisa Hendrix, John Huston, Christiana Huston, John M. Stewart, Nancy Stewart, Jesse Spurgin, Lydia Spurgin, Alonzo H. Raleigh, Caroline L. Raleigh, Mathew L. Peck, Mary Ann Robinson, George W. Taggart, Fanny Taggart, Mary Huston, Susanna Huston, Eliza Tabor, Andrew J. Stewart, Eunice B. Stewart, Hiram D. Bassett, Lucinda Bassett, James Jarret, Mary Jarret, Ira E. West, Charlotte Amelia West, James Walters, and Richard Bush.

Fourth Company: Jacob Shoemaker, Nancy Shoemaker, Thomas King,

Matilda King, Joseph M. Thomas, Susan Jane Thomas, John Brush, Matilda Brush, Sarah S. Obanks, Charles D. Barnum, Lorenzo B. Harris, Robert Clift, Edwin B. Harris, Charles H. Drury, Samuel E. Hull, Russell Rogers, Elijah Thomas, Erastus O. Beach, John Spiers, Job Smith, George S. Clark, and Milton F. Bartlett.

—Summary of information compiled by the Temple Index Bureau, *Nauvoo Temple Endowment Register: 10 December 1845 to 8 February 1846*. Editors' note: According to the register, Joel and Maria Terry were washed and anointed on this date and therefore probably received through the veil.

....

Second anointings performed on this date:

Parley P. Pratt, Elizabeth (Brotherton) Pratt, and Mary (Wood) Pratt, anointed by Orson Hyde; Heber C. Kimball and Ellen (Sanders) Kimball, anointed by [not given]; Sarah Ann Kimball to Heber C. Kimball for time and Joseph Smith (deceased) for eternity, anointed by Brigham Young; and Orson Hyde and Marinda Nancy (Johnson) Hyde, anointed by Heber C. Kimball.

—Summarized from "Book of Anointings."

....

Sealings performed for the living on this date:

Thomas Atkinson to Margaret Ann Olden Fields; Hiram [Hyram] David Bassett to Lucinda Mathena Stout; Thomas Hall to Ann Hughes; Isaac Higbee to Eliza Darling; Myron Spencer Higley to Priscilla Ebberson [Eberson]; Joshua Holman to Rebecca Whitcomb Greenleaf; Parley Parker Pratt to Belinda Marden; Amos Philemon Rogers to Ann Matilda Doolittle; Willard Trowbridge Snow to Melvina [Malvina] Harvey and Susan Harvey; Joseph Morehead Thomas to Mary Ann Thomas; and Judson Tolman to Sarah Lucretia Holbrook.

—Summarized from the Book of Living Sealings.

....

Sealing for the dead performed on this date:

Joseph Smith (Heber C. Kimball, proxy) to Sarah Ann Whitney, Brigham Young officiating.[3]

—Summarized from the Book of Proxy Sealings.

3. Sarah Ann Whitney was also sealed to Heber C. Kimball for time.

Adoptions performed on this date:

To Orson and Nancy Marinda Hyde: Laura Marinda Hyde and Emily Matilda Hyde ("Conducted in the same order as President [Brigham] Young, [Heber C.] Kimball &c."); to Heber C. and Vilate Kimball: William Henry Kimball, Heber Parley Kimball, David Patten Kimball, Charles Spaulding Kimball, Brigham Willard Kimball, Helen Mar Kimball, and Martha Mariah Davenport; and to Newel K. and Elizabeth Ann Whitney: Horace Kimball Whitney, Orson Kimball Whitney, John Kimball Whitney, Joshua Kimball Whitney, Don Carlos Whitney, Sarah Ann Whitney, Ann Maria Whitney, and Mary Jane Whitney: "Horace K. and Sarah Ann holding the birthright of their sexes. The children[,] having been washed and anointed by their parents[,] were (at the Alter, in Holy Order, clad in white) Sealed up unto their Parents for time and all eternity (with the usual reserve in case of mutual agreement) and also unto eternal life against all sins and blasphemies, except the Sin against the Holy Ghost which is the shedding of innocent blood, or the consenting thereunto with all the blessings ~~thereunto~~ which appertain to the fulfillment of the covenant which they mutually entered into at the Alter. Done in the same Holy order and covenant as President Brigham Young and Heber C. Kimball which are before written in full as a pattern of the ceremony, in presence of the witnesses named above."

—Summarized from "Sealings and Adoptions."

Tuesday, January 13, 1846

[A]t 7. o. clock. P.M. the Quorum assembled in Room No. 2. Being arrayed in Priestly Robes according to the Holy Order—Prayer was offered by Bro[ther]. Orson Pratt who afterward was anointed a King & a Priest unto the Most High God in the Church, of Jesus Christ of Latter Day Saints & to all Iseral ... Sarah Marinda [Bates], Mary Ann [Merrill, and] Adelia Ann [Bishop] [were anointed] by Heber C. Kimball.

—"Book of Anointings."

....

This day a council was held in the House of the Lord, for the purpose of inquiring as to who had the means, and where prepared to go West immediately, if worst comes to worst. The Captains of Fifties, and tens were questioned on this matter and made their report. They reported Seventy span of horses and seventy waggons ready for immediate service. In the evening at 6 P.M. the High Council, High Priests, Seventies, and Elders met at their respective appartments and[,] offering up the signs[,] prayed for blessings. the following persons met in room No. 10, viz. A[lbert]. P. Rockwood Pres[iden]t. of Seventy[,] Samuel Williams Pres[iden]t. Elders, Jesse Baker Pres[iden]t Elders, O[smyn]. M. Dewel Elder, W[illia]m Sears Elder, Ransom Shepherd Pres[iden]t Seventies, W[illia]m J. Cahoon Pres[iden]t Seventi[e]s, W[illia]m D Huntington Seventy, Joseph Stallings, Seventy; M[adison]. D. Hamilton Pres[iden]t. Seventy, W[illiam]. S. Covert Seventy[,] Norton Jacob Pres[iden]t. Seventy; Joseph B. Peck Seventy. Randolph Alexander Pres[iden]t Seventy; John Butler Seventy; Charles Wesley Wandell Pres[iden]t. Seventy. We then offered up the signs and prayed[,] A[lbert]. P. Rockwood leading[, and] Prayed for Lucius N. Scovil's wife, Sister Hamilton. W[illiam]. S. Hovey and wife, Alford Sears and Jacob B. Gates after which two brethren came in, when we again offered up the signs and prayed, Samuel Williams leading[, and] prayed for Lyman White and Brother Emmet and those that were with them; also for the Lamanites, that they might be favorably disposed towards the saints, also for the First Presidency and those who are associated with them in council; also for the saints that they might be favored in makings waggons and this [m]ay [be the] means to migrate west.

—Seventies Record, Book B.

....

This evening at 6 oclock I attended prayers among the anointed ones in the Temple.

—"Life of Norton Jacob," typescript, L. Tom Perry Special Collections, Harold B. Lee Library, Brigham Young University, Provo, Utah.

....

[O]n Tuesday evening I [Franklin D. Richards] went to the Temple [and was] called in to the Presidents room ^(No 1 attic story)^[.] found that that [sic] Evan M. Greene, who had been his clerk[,] was ill and unable to serve[.] brother John D. Lee was serving in stead[,] and while sitting by[, I] was requested to assist in recording which I did & the President (Brigham Young) wished me to come the next day which I did & continued to write the labors of sealing so long as the ordinances were administered ^in^ the Temple in Nauvoo[,] much of the time writing from morning till midnight & sometimes until 2 & even 3 o clock in the morning[,] seldom getting an opportunity to go home to see my family[.] of the things of which I wrote ^there^ I will only write here that they were the sealing ordinances of the Lords House and belong to him or those who hold the Keys of the Kingdom & is one of the books out of which men will be judged[.]

For the privilege of assisting in this part of the endowment I know not how to be so thankful[,] as I desire & I pray that the knowledge which I have here obtained of the laws of the kingdom of God ^may^ prove an eternal blessing unto me and redound to my salvation Redemption, & Exaltation to a far more exceeding Crown of glory[.] Give me wisdom I pray thee to use the knowledge which I have obtained for good & not for evil for the glory & not the reproach of thy holy name[.]

—Franklin D. Richards, Diary.

....

I went to the house of the Lord with my wife, Bathsheba W., and were sealed by President Brigham Young, in the presence of witnesses, which was duly recorded. We then received a second anointment under the hands of Elder Orson Hyde.

—George A. Smith, "History of George Albert Smith."

....

Spent the afternoon of the 13th, in the Temple, and received a promise from Heber C. Kimball to receive my second ordinances during the week upon a condition of being prayerful and faithful which was complied with to the best of my ability.

—Abraham Owen Smoot, Diary, LDS Archives.

....

A council was held in the Temple.

The captains of fifties and tens made reports of the number in their respective companies, who were prepared to start west immediately, should the persecutions of our enemies compel us to do so: one hundred and forty horses and seventy wagons were reported ready for immediate service.

At 6 p.m., the High Council, High Priests, Seventies and Elders met for prayer.

—"Manuscript History of Brigham Young," in *History of the Church,* 7:567, and *Manuscript History of Brigham Young,* p. 11.

Second anointings performed on this date:

George A. Smith and Bathsheba W. (Bigler) Smith, anointed by Orson Hyde; Orson Pratt, Sarah (Bates) Pratt, Mary Ann (Merrill) Pratt, and Adelia Ann (Bishop) Pratt, anointed by Heber C. Kimball; Amasa M. Lyman, Mary (Tanner) Lyman, Caroline (Partridge) Lyman, and Eliza Maria (Partridge) Smith to Amasa M. Lyman for time and Joseph Smith (deceased) for eternity, all anointed by Heber C. Kimball; and George Miller and Mary (Fry) Miller, anointed by Heber C. Kimball.

—Summarized from "Book of Anointings."

....

Sealings for the living performed on this date:

Dominicus Carter to Mary Durfee, Sylvia Amaret Mecham, and Sophronia Babcock; Benjamin Lynn Clapp to Mary Rachael Shulz and Elvira Randall; Hiram Dayton to Pamela Bundy; Hiram Gates to Sarah Maria Sayles and Maryetta Rowe; Lemuel Lewis to Weighty Stanton and Olive Matilda Stow; Amasa Mason Lyman to Maria Louisa Tanner, Caroline Ely Partridge, Cornelia Eliza Leavitt, and Laura Read; George Miller to Mary Catherine Fry; Noah Packard to Sophia Bundy; Martin Horton Peck to Susan Caroline Clough and Mary Thorn; Orson Pratt to Mary Ann Merrill and Adelia Ann Bishop; Joseph Lee Robinson to Maria Wood; George Albert Smith to Bathsheba Wilson Bigler; Levi Stewart to Charity Holdaway; and Richard Thorn to Harriet Anna [Ann] Glines.

—Summarized from the Book of Living Sealings.

....

Sealings for the dead performed on this date:

Joseph Smith (Amasa M. Lyman, proxy) to Eliza M. Partridge, Brigham Young officiating;[4] Lydia Smith (Mary Durfee, proxy) to Dominicus Carter, Brigham Young officiating; and Susan Caroline Clough (Mary Thorn, proxy) to Marton Horton Peck, Brigham Young officiating.

—Summarized from the Book of Proxy Sealings.

Wednesday, January 14, 1846

This day occupied in various duties pertaining as the further ordinances of the Lord's House. at 6 o clock the following Seventies Met in

4. Eliza Partridge was also sealed to Amasa Lyman for time.

No 10 for prayer having offered up the signs[;] the prayers circle was formed as follows[:] A[lbert] P Rockwood who was mouth[,] David Candland[,] H[arrison] Burgess[,] R[andolph] Alexander[,] C[handler]. Holbrook[,] R[anson] Shephard[,] Cha[rle]s Shumway[,] S[amuel] W Richards[,] Jos[eph] B Peck[,] Jos[eph] Stallings[,] Norton Jacob[,] V[ernon] H Bruce[,] C[hester] Loveland[,] S Moon[, and] A[lbert] Merrill[.] closed at 20 Min[utes] to 7.

Note January [1]4, 1846. An adjourned meeting was held in the Music hall[,] called to order by Pres[ident] Herriman[.] Prayer was offered by Pres[ident] A[lbert] P. Rockwood when Pres[ident] Jos[eph] Young arrived and wished to ascertain what number of bottles of Oil were now on hands [and it was] reported (18 bottles) further. I [Joseph Young] wish some measure taken to raise $200 dollars for oil[.] it was then suggested that all the quorums act in unison on this and to this end let all the quorums meet this Afternoon so as to be able to report to morrow evening at this place. the business being done[,] Much valuable instructions was given on several points of doctrine. On Motion the Meeting adjourned to meet to morrow[,] Monday evening at this place[,] but let those Members now unorganized Meet at the seventies Hall.

—Seventies Record, Book B.

....

2 of my [John D. Lee's] family came through the washings and anointings[.] after which Louisa Free[,] Abigail Sheffer[,] Rachel Woolsey[,] & Caroline Williams went into room No 1 where we[,] being clothed in Priestly apparel[,] kneeled over the alter[,] rather before the Holy Alter[,] & over it the sacred [and] the solemn covenant & sealing was entered into & ratified in [the] presance of 3 witnesses[,] Pres[ident] Brigham Young officiating at the alter[.] From thus we were conducted to Room No 2 where we received our anointings yea, Holy anointings in the Temple of the Lord under the hands of Elder Orson Hyde[.] this certainly produced more joy comfort and pleasure & reconciliation of feeling than could possibly have been imagined[.] About midnight Bro[ther] Milo Andrews with his carriage took us home[.] it was snowing rapidly[.] Bro[ther] Heber C Kimball left the Temple at the same time [and] took his 15 shooter under his cloke the better to keep it dry[.] it is now Saturday Night [January 17] & I have not [had] time to Journalize any through the week until this eve[.] about an hour is left me to improve in private writing having brought up the book to the present dates[.]

Every exertion is made to forward the work of the Endowment also every preperation is making [way] for a move West[,] not knowing when necissity will force us away to seek refuge in the wilds [and the protection] of the Church[.] on the morrow I expect to take another step[.] at 2 oclock [in the] morning I returned home & slept till 7 [in the] morn[ing] when I arose dressed my self & went to the temple[.] my services were confined to record keeping through the week[.]

—John D. Lee, Diary.

....

On the 14th [I] attended [a meeting] in the Temple and was favored with the privilege of helping to form a Quorum of Priesthood to the receiving of the Second ordinances &c.

—Abraham Owen Smoot, Diary, LDS Archives.

....

This day I [Brigham Young] was occupied in various duties pertaining to the further ordinances of the Lords House.

—"Manuscript History of Brigham Young," in *Manuscript History of Brigham Young,* p. 11.

....

Second anointings performed on this date:

Samuel Bent, Lettis (Palmer) Bent, Phebe (Palmer) Bent, Cynthia (Noble) Bent, and Maria (Thompson) Bent, anointed by Parley P. Pratt; Isaac Morley, Lucy (Gunn) Morley, Abigail (Snow) Morley, and Hannah (Finch) Morley, anointed by Parley P. Pratt; John D. Lee, Agatha Ann (Woolsey) Lee, and Nancy (Bean) Lee, anointed by Orson Hyde; Alpheus Cutler, Lois (Lathrop) Cutler, and Luana (Rockwell) Cutler, anointed by Parley P. Pratt; James Allred and Lydia ([Elizabeth] Warren) Allred, anointed by Orson Hyde; Lucy Ann (Decker) Young, Harriet (Cook) Young, Emmeline (Free) Young, and Margaret (Alley) Young to Brigham Young for eternity and Emily D. (Partridge) Smith and Louisa (Beaman) Smith to Brigham Young for time and Joseph Smith (deceased) for eternity, anointed by Heber C. Kimball.

—Summarized from "Book of Anointings."

....

Sealings for the living performed on this date:

James Allred Sr. to Elizabeth Warren; Samuel Bent to Phebe Palmer, Cynthia Noble, and Maria [Mariah] Thompson; Daniel Carter to Sally

Sylvia Perry; John Alpheus Cutler to Luana Hart Beebe Rockwell; John Doyle Lee to Agatha Ann Woolsey and Nancy Bean; Isaac Morley to Lucy Gunn, Hannah Blakeslee Finch, and Abigail Leonora Snow; Levi M. Stewart to Melinda Stewart Howard; John Taylor to Elizabeth Kaighin [Kahan], Jane Ballantyne, and Mary Ann DeGroot Oakley; Thomas Williams to Nancy Bean; Brigham Young to Lucy Ann Decker, Harriet E. Cook [Campbell], Emeline Free, and Margaret Mariah Alley.

—Summarized from the Book of Living Sealings.

Sealings for the dead performed on this date:

Edward Partridge (William D. Huntington Sr., proxy) to Lydia Clisbee, Brigham Young officiating;[5] Zina Barker (Lydia Clisbee Partridge, proxy) to William D. Huntington Sr., Brigham Young officiating; Clarrisa Amelia Foster (Sally Lydia Perry, proxy) to Daniel Carter, Brigham Young officiating; Keziah String (Elizabeth Darling, proxy) to Isaac Higbee, Brigham Young officiating; Ambroze Palmer (Samuel Bent, proxy) to Lettis Hawk, Heber C. Kimball officiating; Mary Kilborn (Lettis Palmer, proxy) to Samuel Bent, Heber C. Kimball officiating; and Joseph Smith (Brigham Young, proxy) to Louisa Beaman and Emily Dow Partridge, Heber C. Kimball officiating.[6]

—Summarized from the Book of Proxy Sealings.

Thursday, January 15, 1846

Room No. 2[:] B[righam]. Young Orson Hyde, Orson Pratt, Orson Spencer, Daniel Spencer, Amasa Lyman, Jedediah M. Grant, George A. Smith, Isaac Morley, Benjamin L. Clapp, George Miller, William Snow, Willard Snow, [and] John Taylor[, who] was mouth in prayer[.] B[righam]. Young[,] assisted by Aaron Johnson[,] anointed John Taylor, King [and] Priest[;] Leonora Taylor, Elizabeth Taylor, Jane Taylor, [and] Mary Ann Taylor queens [and] priestesses &c & to their husband[;] & [the session was] closed by prayer by O[rson] Hyde [at] 18 minutes to 1 p.m.

—"Book of Anointings."

5. Lydia Clisbee was also sealed to William Huntington for time.

6. Louisa Beaman and Emily Partridge were also sealed to Brigham Young for time.

Second anointings performed on this date:

Charles C. Rich, Sarah (Pea) Rich, Emeline (Grover) Rich, Eliza Ann (Graves) Rich, Sarah Jane (Peck) Rich, and Mary Ann (Phelps) Rich, anointed by Parley P. Pratt; John Taylor, Leonora (Cannon) Taylor, Elizabeth (Kaighan) Taylor, Jane (Ballantyne) Taylor, and Mary Ann (Oakley) Taylor, anointed by Brigham Young; William W. Phelps and Sally (Waterman) Phelps, anointed by Amasa M. Lyman; John Smith, Clarissa (Lyman) Smith, Ann (Carr) Smith, and to John Smith for time and Joseph Smith (deceased) for eternity, Marinda Jones and Sarah M. (Kingsley) Smith, anointed by Parley P. Pratt; Aaron Johnson, Polly (Kelsey) Johnson, and Sarah (Johnson) Johnson, anointed by Parley P. Pratt; Orson Spencer, Catherine (Curtis) Spencer, and Eliza (Dibble) Spencer, anointed by Orson Hyde; Lucy (Walker) Smith to Heber C. Kimball for time and Joseph Smith (deceased) for eternity, anointed by Brigham Young; Sarah (Peake) Kimball to Heber C. Kimball, anointed by [officiator unknown]; Mary Elizabeth (Rollins) Lightner to Brigham Young for time and Joseph Smith (deceased) for eternity, anointed by Heber C. Kimball

—Summarized from "Book of Anointings."

....

Sealings for the living performed on this date:

Isaac Allred to Julia Ann Taylor and Mary Polly Henderson; Solomon Chamberlain to Emiline Shepherd; Philo Dibble to Hannah Ann Dubois; Stephen M. Farnsworth to Julia Ann Clark; John Solomon Fullmer to Mary Ann Price; John Hatfield to Lucy Clark and Lucinda Curtis; Henry Wells Jackson to Eliza Ann Dibble; James Davis to Miranda Jones; Aaron Johnson to Polly Zuriah Kelsey and Sarah Maria Johnson; Joseph Watkins Johnson to Elizabeth Knight; Heber Chase Kimball to Sarah Perry Peak, Hezekiah Peck, and Jemima Smoot; William Wines Phelps to Sally Waterman; George White Pitkin to Amanda Egglestone; Charles Coulson Rich to Sarah DeArman Pea, Eliza Ann Graves, Mary Ann Phelps, and Sarah Jane Peck; Samuel Jones Rolfe to Elizabeth Hathaway; William Sears to Margaret Stanley; John Smith to Clarissa Lyman, Ann Carr [Cain], and Marinda Jones; Orson Spencer to Catherine Curtis and Eliza Ann Dibble; Alvah Lewis Tippets to Caroline Beard; John Harvey Tippets to Abigail Harvey Smith; Nathaniel Prentiss Warden to Ann Cowley; Nathan Ayers West to Adaline Lousia Follett and Louisa Turner; Solomon Wixom to Sarah Avery; Brigham Young to Emily Haws Smith.

—Summarized from the Book of Living Sealings.

Sealings for the dead performed on this date:

Joseph Smith (Brigham Young, proxy) to Olive Andrews, Heber C. Kimball officiating;[7] Mary Smith Hulet (Adaline Louisa Smith, proxy) to Nathan Ayres, Heber C. Kimball officiating; Silas Smith (John Smith, proxy) to Ruther Steavors (Mary Aikin, proxy), Heber C. Kimball officiating; Silas Smith (John Smith, proxy) to Mary Aikin [officiator not given];[8] Joseph Smith (John Smith, proxy) to Sarah M. Kingsley [officiator not given][9]; Abigail Tippets (Caroline Beard, proxy) to Alvah Tippets, Brigham Young officiating; Joseph Smith (Heber C. Kimball, proxy) to Lucy Walker, Brigham Young officiating;[10] Hyrum Smith (Heber C. Kimball, proxy) to Jerusha Bardon (Mary Fielding Smith, proxy), Brigham Young officiating;[11] Celia Kent (Keziah Ann Amboy, proxy) to Philo Dibble, Brigham Young officiating; and Matilda Johnson (Sarah Avery, proxy) to Solomon Wixom [officiator not given].

—Summarized from the Book of Proxy Sealings.

Friday, January 16, 1846

Second anointings performed on this date:

Jedediah M. Grant and Caroline (Van Dyke) Grant, by Brigham Young; Daniel Spencer and Mary Spencer, anointed by Parley P. Pratt; Ezra T. Benson, Permelia (Andrus) Benson, and Adelia (Andrus) Benson, anointed by Orson Hyde; Joseph Young, Jane (Bicknell) Young, Lucinda (Allen) Young, and Lydia (Hagar) Young, anointed by Heber C. Kimball; Peter Haws, Charolette (Harrington) Haws, and Betsy (Cook) Haws, anointed by Parley P. Pratt; Cornelia (Leavitt) Lyman, Dionetia Paulina (Walker) Lyman, Eliza (Gray) Lyman, and Prescilla (Turley) Lyman to Amasa M. Lyman, anointed by Orson Hyde; William Snow and Lydia (Adams) Snow, anointed by Orson Pratt; Truman O. Angell and Polly (Johnson) Angell, anointed by Heber C. Kimball; and Reynolds Cahoon, Thirza (Stiles) Cahoon, Lucinda (Roberts) Cahoon, and Mary (Hildrath) Cahoon, anointed by Parley P. Pratt.

—Summarized from "Book of Anointings."

7. Olive Andrews was also sealed to Brigham Young for time.
8. Mary Aikin was also sealed to John Smith for time.
9. Sarah Kingsley was also sealed to John Smith for time.
10. Lucy Walker was also sealed to Heber C. Kimball for time.
11. Mary Fielding Smith was also sealed to Heber C. Kimball for time.

Sealings for the living performed on this date:

Reuben Warren Allred to Lucy Ann Butler; Truman Osborne Angell [Angel] to Polly Ann Johnson; Elijah Averett to Cherizade [Cherrizade] Grimes; Ezra Taft Benson to Pamelia Andrus and Adeline Brooks Andrus; John Bills to Elizabeth Scott; Joseph Busby to Ann Cady Eldridge; Reynolds Cahoon to Theresa Stiles, Lucina Roberts Johnson, and Mary Hildrath; Aaron Cheney to Mehitable Wells; Wilber Joseph Earl to Harriet Beard; William Felshaw to Mary Harriet Gilbert; Elijah Fordham to Anna Bibbins Chaffee; Jedediah Morgan Grant to Caroline Van Dyke; Levi Ward Hancock to Clarrisa Reed; Henry Harriman to Clarissa Boynton and Eliza Elizabeth Jones; Samuel Henderson to Elizabeth Harris; William Dresser Huntington to Caroline Clark and Harriet Clark; Alonzo Harrington LaBaron to Clarisa Bostwich [Bostwick]; Amasa Mason Lyman to Dionitia Walker and Pauline Eliza Phelps; Elijah Funk Sheets to Susanna Musser; Willard Trowbridge Snow to Mary Bingham Freeman; William Snow to Lydia Adams; Daniel Spencer Jr. to Mary Woolerton; Hiram Spencer to Emily Shafter Thompson; Allen Joseph Stout to Elizabeth Anderson; Andrew Hiram Whitlock to Caroline Hannah Allred; Melvin Wilber to Eunice Dennis and Melinda Eddy; Samuel Williams to Ruth Bishop; Joseph Young to Jane Adeline Bicknell and Lucinda Allen.

—Summarized from the Book of Living Sealings.

....

Sealings for the dead performed on this date:

Sophronia Eliza Pomeroy and Sariah Lester (Mary Spencer, proxy) to Daniel Spencer, Heber C. Kimball officiating; Mary Spencer (Emily Thompson, proxy) to Hiram Spencer, Amasa M. Lyman officiating; Mary Goforth (Elizabeth Harris, proxy) to Samuel Henderson, John Taylor officiating; Isaac Fleming (Joseph Young, proxy) to Lydia Caroline Hagar [officiator not given];[12] Jane Ann Fisher and Bothian Fisher (Ann Bibbins Chaffee, proxy) to Elijah Fordham, Heber C. Kimball officiating; and Hannah Miles (Lydia Adams, proxy) to William Snow, Brigham Young officiating.

—Summarized from the Book of Proxy Sealings.

Saturday, January 17, 1846

The following persons were washed and anointed, viz.

---

12. Lydia Hagar was also sealed to Joseph Young for time.

[See page 421 for excerpted portion.]

Mary C. Miller washed two, and anointed ten.
Catharine C. Spencer washed three and anointed eight[.]
Sophronia M. H[armon]. washed twelve[.]
Pheebe Woodworth anointed one[.]
Pamelia Benson held the Horn[.]
Mercy R. Thompson washed two, and took ^account^ of the names &c.

—Seventies Record, Book B.

....

Sealed to Sally Coburn [deceased] and Lydia Goldthwait as wives for time and eternity and we the same Day was anointed King and Priest, and Queen and Priestess by the hand of Heber C. Kimball, for which we feel to thank the Lord for his mercy towards us, by the power of the Priesthood with the Lord confered upon his church in these last days.

—Newel Knight, Diary, LDS Archives.

....

The 17th, was a day of great enjoyment for me [Abraham O. Smoot], it gave birth to the greatest blessings and an higher exaltation in the Priesthood than ever had been anticipated by me. I received my Second ordinances in the Priesthood with my wife Margaret and Sister Sariah Gibbon, under the hands of George Miller, President of the High Priest Quorum, in room No. 4 attick story of the Temple of the Lord. I was called upon by the President [Brigham Young] to open the Meeting by prayer which I complied with, with feelin[g]s of much gratitude to my Heavenly Father and my brethren that surrounded us. The Services of this holy anointing commenced at the hour of 6 o'clock in the afternoon and closed at 7. We then resumed our seat in the celestial department of the Temple and heard a number of lectures from the brethren on the principles of Priesthood pertaining to exaltation. We also listened with pleasure to the verses of Solomon Hancock, composed on the removal of the Saints to California, with a number of others of the songs of Zion.

—Abraham Owen Smoot, Diary, LDS Archives.

....

Thirty-six persons received ordinances in the Temple.

—"Manuscript History of Brigham Young,"
in *History of the Church,* 7:568.

[Washings and anointings for Saturday, January 17, 1846]

High Priests	Seventy
" Hiram Kimball born May 31, 1806	1 David H. Keeler born July 25, 1811
" 2 John Vance " Nov 8, 1794	" 2 Neilson Harison " Mar. 26, 1800
" 3 Isaac Allred " Jan. 27, 1788	" 3 William Leyland " May 16, 1828
" 4 Samuel Shepherd " Nov, 10, 1792	" 4 Henry G. Boyle " Mar 7, 1823
" 5 Daniel A. Miller " Aug. 11, 1809	" 5 William Greenwood " Aug 7, 1821
" 6 Joseph Knight Jr. " June 21, 1808	" 6 David Boss sometime in 1800
" 7 David Avery " July 1, 1797	H. Priests John G. White " Oct 21, 1775
" 8 Solomon Hancock " Aug 15, 1794	10 Luman Heath " Sept 12, 1803
	11 Nahum Ward " Aug 7, 1780

Washed by Ezra T. Benson and Willard Snow. Anointed by Isaac Morley and Charles C. Rich. Finished at ½ past 10 a.m.

Female Department commenced at ½ past 9.

Mary Allred born Mar 19, 1793	Elizabeth Vance " born Jan. 25, 1801
Lydia Ann Edwards " Jan. 22, 1824	Lucy White " Feb 6
Margaret O. Banks " May 26, 1800	Margaret Avery " Aug 26, 1802
Merrilla Harrison " July 2, 1823	Mary Elizabeth Lightner " Apl. 9, 1818
Philinda E. Heeler " Aug 2, 1809	Lucina Snow " Oct. 16, 1785
Betsey Knight " July 24, 1813	Charity Shepherd " May 4, 1794
Hannah Miller " June 24, 1820	Louisa Heath " May 1, 1822
Flora Ann Gove " June 14, 1826	Alice Greenwood " May 8, 1823
Silence M. Ward " Apl 17, 1785	Sarah A Saunders " May 6, 1810
Mary Carter " Nov. 25, 1810	

—Seventies Record, Book B, oversized portion, January 17, 1846.

Nauvoo temple endowments performed on this date for:

Mary Carter, Solomon Hancock, Nahum Ward, Silence W. Ward, Luman Heath, Louisa Heath, William Greenwood, Alice Greenwood, Joseph Knight Jr., Betsey Knight, Isaac Allred, Mary Allred, Margaret Obanks, Flora Ann Woodworth, Lucina Snow, Sarah Ann Saunders, Samuel Shepherd, Charity Shepherd, Lydia Ann Edmonds, Daniel Avery, Margaret Avery, John G. White, Lucy White, Daniel A. Miller, Hannah Miller, Philinda Keeler, Daniel H. Keeler, John Vance, Elizabeth Vance, Neilson Hanson, Marilla Hanson, David Boss, Hiram Kimball, Henry G. Boyle, William Leyland, and Mary Elizabeth Lightner.

—Summary of information compiled by the Temple Index Bureau, *Nauvoo Temple Endowment Register: 10 December 1845 to 8 February 1846.*

....

Second anointings performed on this date:

Henry Harriman, Clarissa (Boynton) Harriman, and Eliza (Jones) Harriman, anointed by Orson Hyde; Sarah (Chandler) Pratt to Orson Pratt, anointed by Orson Hyde; Benjamin L. Clapp, Mary (Shultz) Clapp, and Elivra (Randall) Clapp, anointed by Orson Hyde; Albert P. Rockwood and Nancy (Haven) Rockwood, anointed by Parley P. Pratt; Phebe (Watrous) Smith to Lucien Woodworth for time and Joseph Smith (deceased) for eternity, anointed by Parley P. Pratt; Abraham O. Smoot, Margaret (McKeans) Smoot, and Sarah (Gibbens) Smoot, anointed by George Miller; and Levi Hancock and Clarissa (Reed) Hancock, anointed by Parley P. Pratt.

—Summarized from "Book of Anointings."

....

Sealings for the living performed on this date:

Isaac Allred to Mary Culvert; Israel Barlow to Elizabeth Haven, Zimri Hafford Baxter, and Eunice Abigail Seaby; David Marks Burbank to Abigail Blodget; Israel Calkins Sr. to Hannah Calkins and Mary Grigg; Gardner Clark to Delecta Farrer; Theodore Curtis to Margaret Morgan; Sylvester Henry Earl to Lois Caroline Owen; James Goff to Mary Elizabeth Kimbrough, and Lydia Smith; Samuel Gully to Ovanda [Ovenda] Fuller; Zenos Hovey Gurley to Margaret Hickey; Luman Heath to Louisa Young; Gustavus Hills to Elizabeth Ann Mansfield; Elam Luddington to Mary Eliza Clark; Amasa Mason Lyman to Priscilla Rebecca Turley; Wandle Mace to Margaret Merkle; Duncan McArthur to Susan McKeen;

Daniel Arnold Miller to Hannah Bigler; Benjamin Thomas Mitchell to Lovina Buckwalter, and Caroline Conrad; William Smith Muir to Jane Stewart Robb; Jesse Kenney Nicholas to Caroline Pinkham; Horace Burr Owens to Sally Ann Layne; Abraham Palmer to Patience Delilah Pierce; Orson Pratt to Sarah Louisa Chandler; Albert Perry Rockwood to Nancy Haven; Miles Romney to Elizabeth Gaskell; Lorenzo Snow to Mary Adaline Goddard [Goodard], Sarah Ann Prichard, Charlotte Merrill Squires, and Harriet Amelia Squires; Samuel Lindsey Sprague to Mary W. Woodard; James Taylor to Agnes Taylor; John Taylor to Mary Amanda Utley; John Vance to Elizabeth Campbell; James Whitehead to Jane Marshall; and Alphonzo Young to Nancy Robinson.

—Summarized from the Book of Living Sealings.

....

Sealings for the dead performed on this date:

Sarah Traceback (Lovina Buckwater, proxy) to Benjamin Thomas Mitchell [officiator not given]; Joseph Smith (Elam Luddington, proxy) to Jane Tibbets, Heber C. Kimball officiating;[13] Eliza Caroline Averill (Mary Woodward, proxy) to Samuel Lindsay Sprague, Brigham Young officiating; Sarah Perkins (Elizabeth Campbell, proxy) to John Vance [officiator not given]; Joseph Smith (Lucien Woodworth, proxy) to Phoebe Watrous, Heber C. Kimball officiating;[14] Joseph Smith (Brigham Young, proxy) to Mary Elizabeth Rollins Lightner, Heber C. Kimball officiating;[15] and Clerisa Kingston (Louisa Young, proxy) to Luman Heath, Brigham Young officiating.

—Summarized from the Book of Proxy Sealings.

....

Adoptions performed on this date:

To Orson Pratt and Sarah Marinda Pratt: Orson Pratt Jr. and Celestia Larissa Pratt, sealed by Heber C. Kimball: "Same as Pres[iden]t. [Brigham] Young & [Heber] Kimball"; and to John and Leonora Taylor: George John Taylor, Joseph Taylor, and Mary Ann Taylor, sealed by Heber C. Kimball: "Same order as Pres[iden]ts. [Brigham] Young & [Heber] Kimball."

—Summarized from "Sealings and Adoptions."

13. Jane Tibbets was also sealed to Elam Luddington for time.

14. Phoebe Watrous was also sealed to Lucian Woodworth for time.

15. Mary Elizabeth Lightner was also sealed to Brigham Young for time.

Sunday, January 18, 1846

E[dward]. P. Dusett, H[ezekiah] P[eck,] Martin H. Peck.[,] N[oah]. P[ackard,] Allen Weeks, James Pace, Isaac Ashton, G[eorge]. W. Brayton, Jessee Baker, C[harles]. W. Hubbard, Joseph Burley, Royal Barney, [and] S[amuel]. L. Sprague met in room No. 10, and being arrayed in Priestly attire, offered up the signs and prayed for J[oseph]. H. Tippets, Laura P[itkin], Abigail [illegible] S[amuel]. L. Sprague, Mary A. Hubbard, [Allen] Weeks, Joseph Busby, and wife, [and] Edward Busett, all of whom were sick. Brother [John] Hayward and others spoke in favor of the work of the last days.

—Seventies Record, Book B.

....

In the Temple with the Council of Fifty and also Captains of Companies.

—William Clayton, Diary.

....

A meeting of the captains of Emigrating Companies was held in the attic story of the Temple, to ascertain the number ready and willing to start should necessity compel our removal, being aware that evil is intended towards us, and that our safety alone will depend upon our departure from this place, before our enemies shall intercept and prevent our going.

A general interest in the movement was manifested by the whole council, every man felt willing to yield to the circumstances that surround us, and let their property be used for the purpose of accomplishing the removal and salvation of this people.

We selected Almon W. Babbitt, Joseph L. Heywood, John S. Fullmer, Henry W. Miller and John M. Bernhisel, a committee to dispose of our property and effects and aid such in emigrating as may have to go, it was agreed that they should have letters of attorney to authorize them to act for us legally.

They were instructed to enclose the Nauvoo House and complete the first story of the Temple.

Meetings for prayer in the several rooms.

—"Manuscript History of Brigham Young,"
in *History of the Church,* 7:569-70.

....

Second anointings performed on this date:

Joshua S. Holman and Rebecca (Greenleaf) Holman, anointed by

George Miller; and John Tanner and Eliza (Boswick) Tanner, anointed by George Miller.

—Summarized from "Book of Anointings."

....

Sealings for the living performed on this date:

Simpson David Huffaker to Elizabeth Melvina Richardson; and John Tanner to Eliza Boswick.

—Summarized from the Book of Living Sealings.

....

Sealings for the dead performed on this date:

Tabitha Bently and Lydia Steward (Eliza Boswick, proxy) to John Tanner, Brigham Young officiating; Clarrisa Hamilton (Mary Elvira Beecher, proxy) to Phineas Howe Young "with the understanding that P[hineas]. H. Young will deliver up Mary Elvira [Beecher] Lincoln to her husband I[ra]. E. Lincoln in the Resurrection," Brigham Young officiating; and Ira Elisha Lincoln (Phineas Howe Young, proxy) to Mary Elvira Beecher, Brigham Young officiating.

—Summarized from the Book of Proxy Sealings.

Monday, January 19, 1846

I stood at the Alt[a]r all day—with the exception of time alone to take refreshment[.] about 30 minutes to 9 at Night I left the Temple & attended a concert held in the concert Hall ... Through the week [i.e., January 19 to January 23] my labours were entirely confined to the Sealings & anointings of the Saints[.]

—Brigham Young, Diary.

....

[O]n the 19th of January, 1846, in the Temple of the Lord at Nauvoo we [David and Rhoda Ann Fullmer] received our second anointings and ordination and the next day, the 20th of January we attended to the last anointings, that of the feet.

—Rhoda Ann Fullmer, "Experiences in the Life of Rhoda Ann Fullmer," typescript, L. Tom Perry Special Collections, Harold B. Lee Library, Brigham Young University, Provo, Utah.

....

[W]ent with my wife [Emily Jacob] to the Temple in the morning to attend to our sealing, but there was a council to be held, which put other business [first].

In the evening I went into the Holy of Holies with Emily, my wife, where, by President Brigham Young[,] we were, according to the holy order of the Priesthood, sealed together for time and all eternity and sealed up unto eternal life and against all sin except the sin against the Holy Ghost. May God keep us faithful in his ordinances. Amen!

—"Life of Norton Jacob," typescript, L. Tom Perry Special Collections, Harold B. Lee Library, Brigham Young University, Provo, Utah.

....

I went to the Temple a few minutes after 10. attended Council and returned home at 5[.]

—Willard Richards, Diary.

....

I [Brigham Young] administered at the altar all day with the exception of thirty minutes in which I took some refreshments.

Evening, I attended a concert in the Music Hall.

—"Manuscript History of Brigham Young," in *History of the Church,* 7:570.

....

Second anointings performed on this date:

Newell Knight and Lydia (Goldthwaite) Knight, anointed by Heber C. Kimball; Lucinda (Pendleton) Harris to George W. Harris for time and Joseph Smith (deceased) for eternity, anointed by Amasa M. Lyman; David Fullmer, Rhoda Ann (Marvin) Fullmer, Margaret (Philips) Fullmer, and Sarah Sophronia (Oysterbanks) Fullmer, anointed by Parley P. Pratt; and Charolette (Fox) Woodworth, Araminta (Williams) Woodworth, Margaret (Johnston) Woodworth, and Rachel (Kingsley) Woodworth to Lucien Woodworth, anointed by George Miller.

—Summarized from "Book of Anointings."

....

Sealings for the living performed on this date:

Simeon Carter Allen to Hannah Dunham; Elijha Averett to Sarah Jane Witt [Witte]; Benjamin Brown to Sarah Mumford and Mary Ann Barker; William Black to Jane Johnston; David Fullmer to Rhoda Ann Marvin, Margaret Phillips, and Sarah Sophronia Banks [Oysterbanks]; Stephen Hezekiah Goddard to Zeruah Norwood Roby; John Henderson to Betsey Jane Ohaver; Daniel Durham Hunt to Susan Davis; Heman [Herman] Hyde to Polly Wyman Tilton; William Hyde to Elizabeth Howe Bullard; Norton Jacobs to Maria [Mariah] Van Valkenburg and Emily Horton Heaton; Newel Knight to Lydia Goldthwaite; William Miller to Phoebe Scott and Lucrettia Marilla Johnson; Lemuel Mallory to Elizabeth Kennedy; Hezekiah Peck to Martha Long; Morris Charles Phelps to Sarah Thompson; George Philander Stiles to Isabella K. Hollister and Sophia Janett Williamson [Williaman]; John Stiles to Persis Cole; Theodore Turley to Frances Amelia Kimberley and Sarah Ellen Clift; Fredrick Matthew Van Leuven to Lydia Draper; Lucien Woodworth to Charlotte Fox, Aminta Maria Williams, Margaret Johnston, Rachel Kingsley, and (for time only) Phebe Watrous.

—Summarized from the Book of Living Sealings.

....

Sealings for the dead performed on this date:

Dorcas Willis (Sarah Jane Willis, proxy) to Elisha Averett, Brigham Young officiating; Sally Colburn (Lydia Goldthwaite, proxy) to Newel Knight, Brigham Young officiating;[16] Nancy Davis (Susan Davis, proxy) to Daniel Durham Hunt, Brigham Young officiating;[17] Belinda Barker and Sally Tufts (Elizabeth Kennedy, proxy) to Lemuel Mallory, Brigham Young officiating; Elizabeth Scott (Phoebe Scott, proxy) to William Miller, Brigham Young officiating; Laura Clark (Sarah Thompson, proxy) to Morris Phelps, Brigham Young officiating; and Isabell Bisbee (Zeriah N. Roby, proxy) to Stephen H. Goddard, Brigham Young officiating.

—Summarized from the Book of Proxy Sealings.

Tuesday, January 20, 1846

Council convened in room No 2, Prayer having been offered by William Davis it being a prerequisite to the anointing in all cases wherever a candidate, is presented for anointing. This is required[,] to offer up a prayer[,] before the ordinance of anointing can be administered[.] The council all being arrayed in priestly robes (previous to prayer) a circle was formed the signs were offered after which Elder Orson Spencer anointed

16. Lydia Goldthwaite was also sealed to Newel Knight for time.

17. Susan Davis was also sealed to Daniel Hunt for time.

William Davis a Priest unto the Most High God in the Church and among his brethren in Israel after which his wife Sarah was anointed a Queen and Priestess unto her husband etc done in the presence of William Snow, J[oshua] S Holman, L[ucian]. Woodworth, Willard A Johnson, Daniel Spencer[,] William Miller[,] and J[oseph] A Kelting at 13 minutes to 12[.]

—"Book of Anointings."

....

Altho a violent storm is raging, a multitude of people are at the door awaiting to receive their endowment; Pres[iden]t J[oseph]. Young was obliged to send many of them away. In the

Female Department, list one,

The following persons were washed and anointed, viz.

[See pages 429-31 for excerpted portion.]

Public prejudice is so great against us, and the excitement is so alarming that we may not be able to continue giving the endowment more than three weeks longer; therefore it is determined that we continue night and day in the administration of the ordinances of endowment.

Present of the Twelve [apostles] this day Pres[ident] ^B[righam].^ Young, H[eber]. C. Kimball, P[arley]. P. Pratt, Orson Pratt. Orson Hyde, and Amasa Lyman. Of the Trustees in trust, G[eorge]. Miller. Several of the High Council also, who were officiating in the higher ordinances.

[See pages 432-35 for excerpted portion.]

—Seventies Record, Book B.

....

[A]t 2 went to the Temple—sat in Council and returned at 5.

—Willard Richards, Diary.

....

One hundred and ninety-five persons received ordinances in the Temple.

Public prejudice being so strong against us, and the excitement becoming alarming we determined to continue the administration of the ordinances of endowment night and day.

—"Manuscript History of Brigham Young,"
in *History of the Church,* 7:570.

....

Nauvoo temple endowments performed on this date for:

First Company: Thomas B. Parker, Martha Ann Parker, James Duncan,

[Washings and anointings for Tuesday, January 20, 1846]

No. 1

Phebe Ann Hanks born, July 4, 1803
Mary Eliza Jackson " Aug 31, 1820
Phebe Hallet " Apl 25, 1806
Sophia Aldridge " July 16, 1819
Sarah Head " Dec 31, 1804
Hannah Loveland " Mar. 23, 1814
Sarah Coltron " Apl 25, 1821
Fanny M. Huntington " Oct. 26, 1810
Emily Harris " Nov. 25, 1815
Hellen M. Marr " July 14, 1829
Ann Condit " Apl 9, 1808

Abigail Robinson born July 13, 1792
Mary Jane Warner " Feb. 13, 1819
Betsey A Snow " Apl. 12, 1822
Jane Conner " Aug 23, 1819
Martha Ann Parker " Oct 16, 1800
Sarah H Bracken " Feb. 27, 1817
Lucinda E. Perry " Nov. 7, 1820
Elizabeth Bobbitt " Nov. 14, 1818
Sarah Ann Liby " May 7, 1818
Hannah Maria Libby " June 29, 1828
Kiziah Henrixson " Mar. 15, 1785

Bathsheba anointed 3 persons.
Patty Sessions washed and anointed 3 persons.
Sophia M. Burgess washed 1 anointed 3.
Elizabeth Barlow washed 2 anointed 3.
Nancy Rockwood washed 2 anointed 3.
Nancy Winchester washed washed 3.
Clarissa Herriman anointed 3.
Lydia Granger washed 6.
Margaret T. Smoot washed 6 anointed 2;
Sisters Barlow, Burgess, Rockwood, Herriman, held the horn.

Male Department
No. 1

Seventies		H. Priests	
"	1 Levi Loveland born Feb 20, 1816	"	Dimick B. Huntington born May 26, 1808
"	2 John Robinson " Dec 27, 1792	"	William Aldridge " June 27, 1787
"	3 Josiah H Perry " Apl 5, 1818	"	Clark Hallet " May 5, 1810
"	4 William J. Conner " Nov 2, 1819	"	Amos W. Condit " Nov 23, 1815
"	5 James B. Bracken " Jan 16, 1816	Elders	Joseph Hawks " May 24, 1799
"	6 Norval M. Head " Feb, 18, 1815	"	2. Simeon Henderson " Mar 7 1783
"	7 James J. Jackson " Feb 2, 1819		Washed by Iseral Barlow,
"	8 Thomas B. Parker " Oct. 1, 1797		and Edson Barney.

Anointed by Isaac Allred, Joseph G. Hovey, Samuel Moore held the horn.

Male Department Co. No. 2.

Seventies		Seventies	
"	Dwight Harding born Apl. 27, 1807		Cyrus A. Mead born July 13, 1804
"	10 Stephen C. Perry " Dec 22, 1818	"	21 William H. Covington " July 13, 1818
"	11 Joseph Egbert " Mar. 10, 1818	"	22 William K. Parker " Aug 11, 1803
"	12 Allen Taylor " Jan. 17, 1844	"	23 Robert Snyder " Mar. 5, 1810
"	13 Elles Stoker " July 28, 1816	"	24 Daniel M. Burbank " Dec. 3, 1813
"	14 Thomas L. Johnson " June 1, 1818	H. Priests	5 Marcellus McKown " Sep 9, 1807
"	15 William L. Davis " May 4, 1822	"	6 Aaron M. York " Aug 27, 1807
"	16 William Meeks " Jan. 9, 1815	"	7 Benjamin Slade " June 4, 1800
"	17 Archibald Herr " Feb. 2, 1813		8 Joseph W. Pierce " June 5, 1805
"	18 Robert D. Covington " Aug. 22, 1820	"	9 Daniel Russell " Jan. 28, 1717

" 19 Bradley D. Wilson " Oct. 11, 1806

Washed by Israel Barlow, and Edson Barney.
Anointed by Isaac Allred, Joseph G. Hovey, and Israel Barlow. Finished at 10 minutes past 12.

Female Department.

Jemima C. Mead born Jan 24, 1815
Sarah L. Taylor " Nov. 14, 1814
Nancy Covington " Nov 3, 1820
Amelia M. Snyder " Sep 20, 1815
Susan Ann McKown " Nov 20, 1806
Ann B. Thomas " Apl 1, 1813
Margaret Stoker " May 29, 1822
Jane Davis " Feb. 11, 1824
Abigail Burbank " Mar 26, 1811
Patience Johnson " Oct. 30, 1821
Harriet E. Russel " Apl. 22, 1806
Arlytia L. Carter " May 18, 1829
Francis M. Stilman " May 29, 1830

Mary C. Egbert born Dec 9, 1824
Margaret Parker " Feb 18, 1820
Roxy Slade " Mar 20, 1800
Amanda Mary Pierce " Jan 17, 1811
Elizabeth Covington " Apl. 20, 1820
Mary Anna Thorn " Sep. 22, 1784
Nancy J. Kerr " Aug 11, 1812
Elizabeth Meeks " Jan 23, 1818
Agnes Wilson " Dec. 24, 1811
Ann Mariah Perry " Dec. 11, 1814
Phebe Hardin " Mar. 16, 1810
Abigail Thorn " Apl. 2, 1821

Washed by Margaret T Smoot, Clarissa

Washed by Margaret T. Smoot, Clarissa Herriman, Patty Sessions, Elizabeth Barlow, Nancy Winchester, and Sophia M. Burgess. Anointed by the same persons except Margaret T. Smoot, Nancy Winchester, Elizabeth Barlow and Sophia M. Burgess held the oil. Finished at 30 p. 12.

—Seventies Record, Book B, oversized portion, January 20, 1846.

[Washings and anointings for Tuesday, January 20, 1846—second excerpt]

Male Department Co. No. 3 ½ M.

Seventies		Seventies	
"	James Morehead born Feb. 28, 1809		Ute Perkins born Mar 5, 1816
"	26 William A. Duncan born Mar. 6, 1803	"	35 Isaac Y. Vance " Dec. 18, 1818
"	27 Smith Humphrey " Nov. 1, 1805	"	36 Alfred B. Benson " Apl. 7, 1817
"	28 Samuel Henderson Jr " Oct. 19, 1820	"	37 John Evarts " July 10, 1811
"	29 Chevey G. Van Beuren " Jan. 26, 1811	H. Priests	James Randall " May 22, 1793
"	30 Aaron Roger " July 9, 1809	"	11 John Walker " June 20, 1794
"	31 Hiram F Dayton " June 12, 1824	"	12 Henry Thomas " Dec 27, 1781
"	32 William H. Perry " Aug. 2, 1823	"	13 Josiah Butterfield " Mar 13, 1795
"	33 William Richey " Feb. 1, 1796		

Washed by Israel Barlow, and Edson Barney. Anointed by Isaac Allred, Joseph G. Hovey and Hiram Dayton. Finished anointing at ½ past one; Allred B. Benson was ordained to the office of Seventy by Henry Herriman and Hiram Dayton. John Evarts was ordained to the same office at the same time, by the same persons.

Female Department co. no. 3. 10 min. to one

Mary Casson born Dec. 1, 1814	Dolly Duncan born Feb 24, 1811
Charity Holdaway " May 26, 1824	Eliza A Dayton " Nov. 2, 1826
Esther S. Tyler " Apl. 24, 1804	Lucy Van Buren " June 11, 1813
Sarah Ann Evart " June 3, 1811	Rosilla Cowan " Nov. 8, 1814
Louisa Free " Aug 9, 1824	Sarah C. Williams " Nov. 19, 1830
Eliza Humphrey " Feb. 6, 1799	Martha A. Vance " Mar, 30, 1822
Ann Perkins " Jan. 5, 1814	Hetty Benson " Apl. 14, 1821

Sally Randall " May 22, 1815	Margaret Butterfield " Apl. 29, 1801
Elizabeth Morehead " July 31, 1812	Rosannah Virgin " Apl. 1, 1820
Mary Call " Feb 21, 1824	Rebecca Rager " May 29, 1814
Jane Glen " July 20, 1805	Mary Ann Greenwell " Mar. 21, 1816
Emily Richards " Mar. 12, 1831	Nancy J. Putman " Feb. 20, 1825
Anabella McMurray " Nov. 4, 1827	Margaret Ritchey " 1818
Elizabeth Shimer " Jan. 1, 1805	Marietta Henderson " Jan. 31, 1827

Washed and anointed by Nancy Winchester, Clarissa Herriman, Patty Sessions, Sophia M. Burgess, Elizabeth Barlow, and Mary Henderson. Finished at 10 minutes past 2 P.M.

Female Department co no. 4 6 min p. 3

Harriet Lamareaux born Aug 20, 1826	Elizabeth Sabin born May 31, 1811
Catharine Etleman " May 25, 1796	Alice Weinel " Jan. 16, 1821
Sarah Carter " Aug 25, 1812	Rebecca Bass " Sep. 30, 1782
Ann Steele " Aug 28, 1787	Margaret Thomas " Feb. 1823
Sally Ann Sellew " Feb. 9, 1812	Lucinda Bass " May 22, 1824
Matilda Cochran " Jan. 26, 1828	Mary Cook " Feb. 8, 1800

Washed and Anointed by Lydia Granger, Sophia Harmon, Nancy Winchester, Patty Sessions, Elizabeth Barlow [illegible]

Male Department co no. 4 3 o'clock

1846

Jan. 20

Seventies		Seventies	
"	Henry E. Lamoreaux born Mar 5, 1817		William F. Carter born May 1, 1811
"	Ekells Truly " Mar 1, 1813	45	Elijah H Fuller " June 13, 1811

[Seventies]	40 Washington R. Cook [born] Oct. 4, 1804	[Seventies]	46 Robert J. Thomas [born] Jan 8, 1820
"	41 Daniel Thomas " Dec. 6, 1809		47 Philip Ethelman " Mar. 2, 1791
"	42 William Thomas " Apl. 21, 1811	H. Priest	14 David Sabin " Mar. 31, 1807
"	43 Nathan J. Thomas " May 22, 1811		3 John Weinel " Nov. 26

William Thomas was ordained to the office of Seventy by President B. L. Clapp and H. Herriman. The foregoing persons were washed by Israel Barlow and Edson Barney. Anointed by Isaac Allred and Joseph G. Hovey. 4 P.M.

Co. No. 5 commenced at 8 P.M.

Seventies			
"	48 Horace Roberts born Sept. 1, 1807	"	Joseph Jackson born Sep. 1807
"	49 Timothy B. Foot " Dec. 29, 1799	"	60 Galen Cole " Feb. 6, 1819
"	50 Michael Jacobs " Dec. 12, 1794	"	61 Albert Miles " Jan. 22, 1812
"	51 Joseph Warthan " Dec. 1, 1811	"	62 M J. Daley " Nov. 22, 1822
"	52 Theodore Rogers " Feb. 3, 1824	"	63 Leonard Hill " May 2, 1800
"	53 Washington B Rogers " Sep. 16, 1826	"	64 Charles F. Hill " Jan. 6, 1824
"	54 David Rogers " May 24, 1828	H. Priests	David Lewis " Apl. 10, 1814
"	55 Mark Rogers " Feb. 21, 1830	"	16 William Hickenlooper Sep. 22, 1804
"	56 Andrew J. Clothier " Jan. 15, 1823	"	17 Edward M. Fuller Jan 26, 1792
"	57 Thomas E. Fuller " Apl. 23, 1818	"	18 William Leffingwell " Oct. 31, 1805
"	58 Daniel R. Williams " Aug 7, 1802	Elder	4 Milton Rogers " Mar. 23, 1786

David and Mark Rogers were ordained Seventies by A. P. Rockwood, Noah Rogers and Hiram Dayton. They received their washings and anointings but went no farther. The above named company was washed by Andrew L. Lamoreaux, and John Lytle. Anointed by Hiram Dayton, Noah Rogers and Joseph G. Hovey. Finished at 9 ¼ o'clk. P.M.

Female Department. Co. No. 5. commenced at 7- 45/60

Clara Rogers born Sep. 20, 1791	Emily Hoagland born Feb 25, 1804
Sibble Jacobs " Jan 7, 1791	Sarah Hickenlooper " June 1, 1803
Lucy Ann McOlney " Dec 22, 1831	Lutitia Warthen " Feb. 9, 1822
Sophronia Moor " May 14, 1832	Duritha Lewis " Jan 5, 1813
Sarah Rogers " Mar 19, 1831	Henretta Rogers " May 30, 1831
Harriet Roberts " Sep 3, 1808	Sarah Fuller " Feb 22, 1824
Electa C. Williams " Jan. 26, 1806	Hannah Fuller " Jan 24, 1797
Ann Jackson " Dec. 22, 1807	Sally Ann Fuller " Oct. 24, 1815
Lucinda Cole " Feb. 28, 1822	Sally Hill " Mar. 15, 1808
Lucy Ann Cole " Mar. 22, 1826	Harriet F Daley " Dec 26, 1822
Mariah Miles " Jan. 31, 1812	Unice Leffingwell " Mar 1, 1805

Washed and anointed by Nancy Winchester, Mary Ann Pratt, Lois [illegible]

—Seventies Record, Book B, oversized portion, January 20, 1846.

Huldah Duncan, Dimick B. Huntington, Fanny Maria Huntington, Mary Jane Warner, Betsey Arseno Davis, Sarah M. Kimball, Josiah H. Perry, Lucinda Perry, James J. Jackson, Mary Eliza Jackson, Sarah Coltrin, Amos W. Condit, Ann Condit, Sarah Ann Libby, Hannah Maria Libby, Helen Marr Clark, Elizabeth Bobbitt, Levi Loveland, Hannah Loveland, Joseph B. Hawks, Phebe Ann Hawks, William Aldridge, Sophia Aldridge, William James Connor, Jane Connor, Simeon Hendrickson, Keziah Hendrickson, John Robinson, Abigail Robinson, Morvil M. Head, Sarah Head, Clark Hallet, Phebe Hallet, James B. Bracken, Sarah H. Bracken, and Emily Harris.

Second Company: Thomas Smith Johnson, Patience Johnson, Robert Snyder, Almeda M. Snyder, David M. Burbank, Abigail Burbank, Joseph W. Pierce, Amanda M. Pierce, Abigail Thorn, Frances M. Stillman, Benjamin Slade, Roxy Slade, Allen Taylor, Sarah Louisa Taylor, Robert D. Covington, Elizabeth Covington, William H. Covington, Nancy Covington, Ann Thompson, Bradley B. Wilson, Agnes Wilson, Arlytia L. Carter, William K. Parker, Margaret Parker, Mary Anna Thorn, Eller Stoker, Margaret Stoker, Stephen C. Perry, Anna Maria Perry, Cyrus A. Mead, Jemima C. Mead, Archibald Kerr, Nancy Kerr, Daniel Russell, Harriet E. Russell, Dwight Harding, Phebe Harding, Aaron M. York, Hannah York, William L. Davis, America Jane Davis, Marcellus McKown, Susan McKown, William Meeks, Elizabeth Meeks, Joseph Egbert, and Mary C. Egbert.

Third Company: Eliza Lee, William H. Perry, Caroline Lee, Rosilla Cowan, John Evarts, Sarah Ann Evarts, Rosanna Virgin, Aaron Rager, Rebecca Rager, Mary Call, Jane Glen, Isaac Y. Vance, Martha E. Vance, Charity Holdaway, Hiram F. Dayton, Eliza A. Dayton, Esther S. Tyler, Elizabeth Shimer, James Randal, Sally Randall, Smith Humphrey, Elisa Humphrey, Cheney G. Van Buren, Lucy Van Buren, John Walker, Arabelle Walker, William A. Duncan, Dolly H. Duncan, Mary Ann Greenwell, Josiah Butterfield, Margaret Butterfield, Nancy J. Putman, Henry Thomas, Ute Perkins, Anna Perkins, James M. Morehead, Elizabeth T. Morehead, Mary Casson, Alfred B. Benson, Hetty Benson, Samuel Henderson Jr., Mariette Henderson,[18] William Richey, Margaret Richey, and Emily Richey.

---

18. For the published account of her endowment on this date, see Marietta (Coray) Henderson Jones Smith in Nelson Winch Green, *Fifteen Years Among the Mormons: Being the Narrative of Mrs. Mary Ettie [sic] V. Smith ...* (New York: Charles Scribner, 1858), 42-49. It is interesting that, throughout her memoir, Smith identi-

Fourth Company: Rebecca Burss, Sally Ann Sellew, Ekells Truly, Ann Steed, Elijah K. Fuller, Matilda Cochran, Laura L. Burss, Henry E. Lamoreaux, Harriet Lamoreaux, Robert T. Thomas, Nathan T. Thomas, John Weinel, Alice Weinel, David Sabin, Elizabeth Sabin, Daniel Thomas, Margaret Thomas, William F. Carter, Sarah Carter, Philip Ettleman, Catharine Ettleman, Washington M. Cook, and Mary Cook.

Fifth Company: Daniel R. Williams, Sophrinia Moore, Electa C. Williams, Joseph Jackson, Ann Jackson, Horace Roberts, Harriet Roberts, Edward M. Fuller, Hannah Fuller, Theodore Rogers, Leonard Hill, Sarah Hill, David Lewis, Duritha Lewis, M. J. Daley, Harriet Daley, Albert Miles[,] Maria Miles, Michael Jacobs, Emily S. Hoagland, Sybil Jacob, William Leffingwell, Eunice Leffingwell, William Hickenlooper, Sarah Hickenlooper, Thomas E. Fuller, Sarah Fuller, Sally Ann Fuller, Milton Rogers, Clara Rogers, Joseph Warthan, Lutitia Warthan, Timothy Foot, A. J. Clothier, and W. B. Rogers.

—Summary of information compiled by the Temple Index Bureau, *Nauvoo Temple Endowment Register: 10 December 1845 to 8 February 1846.* Editors' note: According to the register, Louisa Free, Charles F. Hill, Arabella McMurray, Lucy Ann McOlney, David Rogers, Henrietta Rogers, Mark Rogers, Sarah Rogers, and William Thomas were washed and anointed on this date and therefore probably received through the veil.

....

Second anointings performed on this date:

Zebedee Coltrin and Mary (Mott) Coltrin, anointed by Parley P. Pratt; Simeon Carter and Hannah (Dunham) Carter, anointed by Parley P. Pratt; John M. Bernhisel, Julia Ann (Haight) Bernhisel, Catherine (Paine) Bernhisel, Dolly (Ransome) Bernhisel, and Fanny (Spafford) Bernhisel, anointed by Heber C. Kimball; John D. Lee, Louisa (Free) Lee, Abigail (Woolsey) Lee, Rachel (Woolsey) Lee, and Sarah Caroline (Williams) Lee,

---

fies her first husband as Wallace Henderson, whom she wed civilly in Nauvoo on January 30, 1843, Elias Higbee performing the ceremony. However, her own genealogical records as well as the registry of Nauvoo marriages report that she married Wallace's brother, Samuel Goforth Henderson Jr., a year later in Nauvoo, William Earl performing the civil ceremony (see Lyndon W. Cook, comp., *Nauvoo Deaths and Marriages, 1839-1845* [Orem, UT: Grandin Book, 1994], 109). Her narrative of her first marriage combines details from the lives of both Wallace and Samuel. She subsequently separated from Samuel and married Nathaniel V. Jones, then Reuben P. Smith in 1852.

anointed by Heber C. Kimball; and William Davis and Sarah (McKee) Davis, anointed by [not given].

—Summarized from "Book of Anointings."

....

Sealings for the living performed on this date:

Lewis Abbott to Ann Marsh [March]; William Aldridge to Elizabeth [Betsey] Van Blarcum; Wiley Payne Allred to Sarah [Sally] Zabriskie; Caleb Baldwin to Nancy Kingsbury; Caleb Clark [Clarke] Baldwin to Ann Eliza Robinson; Job Vassal Barnum to Marcia [Martha] Collins; John Milton Bernhisel to Julia Haight [Van Orden], Dolly Ranson, Catherine Paine, and Fanny Spafford [Howe]; Thomas Butterfield to Mary Jane Parker; Cyrill Call to Sally Tiffany; Simeon Carter to Matilda Phebe Cochran; Lorenzo Clark to Beulah Ann Rodgers; Henry Alanson Cleveland to Ann Slade; Zebedee Coltrin to Mary Mott; Charles Crismon to Elizab[e]th Hill and Mary Hill; William Davis to Sarah McKee; Thomas Grover to Caroline Eliza Nickerson, Hannah Tupper, and Laduska [Lodoska] Solome Tupper; Samuel Henderson Jr. to Marietta Coray; John Somers [Summers] Higbee to Sarah Ann Voorhees; Isaac Houston to Theodocia Keys [Keyes]; Eli Brazee Kelsey to Letitia Sheets; Joseph Andrew Kelting to Elizabeth Ann Martin and Minerva Orvilla Woods; Joseph Corrodon Kingsbury to Caroline Whitney; George Washington Langley to Mary Turner and Martha McKinney Frost; John D. Lee to Rachel Woolsey, Louisa Free, Abigail Shaeffer Woolsey, and Sarah Caroline Williams; Albert Miles to Margaret Mariah Veets [Veits]; James Pace to Lucinda Gibson Strickland; William Franklin Pace to Margaret Nichols; Samuel Parker to Sarah Bidell; Martin H. Peck to Arlytia Long Carter; James Rigby to Jane Lovenia [Lavinia] Littlewood; John Robinson to Abigail Parson; Samuel Russell Jr. to Frances Maria Stillman, Ester Hill, and Mary Abigail Thorn; Lorenzo A. Quick to Elizabeth Smith Allen; Moses Martin Sanders to Amanda Armstrong Fausett [Faucett]; George Albert Smith to Bathsheba Wilson Bigler; Levi Stewart to Charity Holdaway; Bushrod W. Wilson to Catharine Iona Anderson; Lewis Dunbar Wilson to Nancy Ann Wagoner; and Henry Hardy Wilson to Frances Kelly.

—Summarized from the Book of Living Sealings.

....

Sealings for the dead performed on this date:

Hannah Edgecomb and Mary Bracey Trueworthy (Sarah Bedell,

proxy) to Samuel Parker, Brigham Young officiating; and Julia Ann Jennings (Mary Mott, proxy) to Zebedee Coltrain, Brigham Young officiating.

—Summarized from the Book of Proxy Sealings.

Wednesday, January 21, 1846

Male Department. co[mpany]. 1. comm[enced] 9 A.M.

Seventy

This day a great crowd in the vestry, At 9 o'clock A.M. operations commenced in the washing rooms when the following persons were washed and anointed viz.

[See pages 440-41 for excerpted portion.]

Present of the Twelve [Apostles] this morning Pres[iden]t. B[righam]. Young, H[eber]. C. Kimball, P[arley]. P. Pratt, Orson Hyde, and Amasa Lyman. Yesterday evening the High Council of the church prepared an article to be printed and circulated through the country, stating our design in going West and settling land, and censuring severely the base, lying spirit in our enemies who accuse us of treasonable designs, bogus making &c. and stating th[at] we are true to the institutions of our Country: and offered to build those block houses and stockade forts spoken of by President [James K.] Polk in his message to Congress, if the General Government thought fit to employ us for that purpose.[19] That a company of pioneers go out in March next for the purpose of selecting a fertile valley in order to put in a Spring crop; erect houses &c. Cha[rle]s W. Wandell [illegible]

---

19. James K. Polk (1795-1849), U.S. president from 1845 to 1849, had pledged himself to further expand the boundaries of the country, as begun during the previous administration under John Tyler in annexing Texas (Texas became a state on December 29, 1845). Polk's goals as president were to settle the Oregon boundary and acquire California, and he publicly recommended the following: "For the protection of emigrants whilst on their way to Oregon against the attacks of the Indian tribes occupying the country through which they pass, I recommend that a suitable number of stockades and blockhouse forts be erected along the usual route between our frontier settlements on the Missouri and the Rocky Mountains, and that an adequate force of mounted riflemen be raised to guard and protect them on their journey. The immediate adoption of these recommendations by Congress will not violate the provisions of the existing treaty. It will be doing nothing more for American citizens than British laws have long since done for British subjects in the same territory." (James K. Polk, 1st Annual Message, December 2, 1845.)

[Washings and anointings for Wednesday, January 21, 1846]

Seventies		Seventies	
	1 Ira P. Hatch born Feb 9, 1802		Berrill Covington born Nov 27, 1817
"	2 Almond L. Tulman " Sep. 7, 1816	"	10 Robert E Byard " May 15 1817
"	3 Benjamin R. Bently " July 10, 1816	H. Priests	1 Thomas Taylor " Oct 6, 1771
"	4 Huntington Johnson " Feb. 15, 1796	"	2 Jeremiah Hatch " Sep. 25, 1766
"	5 H. W. Tinker " Sep. 4, 1818	"	3 Benjamin Johnson " Apl. 20, 1794
"	6 Edward Dolten " Mar. 23, 1827	"	4 Thomas Kidd " July 17, 1790
"	7 Josiah Mounton Jr. " Mar. 15, 1805	Elder	1 Alexander Hill " Aug. 1, 1789
"	8 George W. Boyd " Oct. 30, 1825	"	2 Joel Ricks " Feb 18, 1804

Washed by Noah Rogers and Samuel Moore. Anointed by Israel Barlow, Edson Barney and L. A. Shirtliff. Finished 15 min to 9.

Female Department. List 1 com 9 A.M.

Catharine Stoker born Mar. 6, 1773	Abigail Bradford born Aug 14, 1812
Lovina Johnson " Apl. 17, 1792	Elizabeth Walker " Feb 22, 1800
Elizabeth Hatch " Apl. 24. 1772	Eleanor Ricks " Dec 25, 1807
Abigail Hatch " Dec. 19, 1798	Emiline Tinker " Aug 12, 1814
Jemima Johnson " Nov. 4, 1796	Susannah Kidd " June 9, 1789
Elizabeth Hill " Dec. 1, 1777	Sarah B. Barney " June 12, 1811
Hannah Mounton " Oct. 16, 1805	Rhoda Ann Bently " Sep. 12, 1807
Desdimona C Fulmer " Oct. 6, 1809	Caroline A. Webb " July 9, 1821
Lancy Durfee " June 3, 1788	Amelia Wilsey " Feb. 19, 1790
Mary Brower " Apl. 8, 1792	Jane Wilsey " Jan. 14, 1827

Mary Ann Buchanan " Aug. 1, 1822	Elizabeth Tuttle " Sep 6, 1823
Sarah Ann Fulmer " Oct 26, 1823	Hannah E. Biard " Dec. 10, 1817

Washed and anointed by Lydia Granger, Sophia M. Burgess, Nancy Winchester. Elizabeth Barlow, Mary Gates, Sophronia Harmon, Elizabeth Cooledge. Finished 20 minutes past 10 A.M.

—Seventies Record, Book B, oversized portion, January 21, 1846.

1846 House of the Lord.
Jan[uary]. 21

In consequence of so many persons eating in the Temple yesterday, the offerings this morning have failed to supply the workmen with food; so that Pres[iden]t. J[oseph]. Young was obliged to send a man with a note to some wealthy brethren, in order to obtain a supply for the day.

[See pages 443-46 for excerpted portion.]

January 21, 1846 House of the Lord

The following persons met in room No. 9 at the usual hour for prayer viz. B[enjamin]. L. Clapp, P[resident]. S[eventies]. — A[lbert]. P. Rockwood P[resident]. S[eventies]. — Addison Pratt — H[igh]. P[riest]. — Jos[eph] Pace, Job V. Barnum, Joseph Bushby, H. A. Cleveland, Elijah Fordham H[igh]. P[riest]. — Elisha N. Graves H[igh]. P[riest]. — W[illia]m Felshaw H[igh]. P[riest]. — George W. Brayton. After arraying themselves in priestly attire, and offering up the signs, the circle was formed and prayer was made as follows Pres[iden]t. Clapp leading. For the general welfare of the church — for the confusion of our enemies — for special blessings on the Twelve [apostles] and all Pres[iden]ts of the different quorums. Also for Jedediah Grant who is sick, also for Miles Romney and sister Barnes three children.

[See pages 446-48 for excerpted portion.]

—Seventies Record, Book B.

....

At the temple at Nauvoo she [Nancy Wilson] received her washings and anointings even to become a queen and a priestess, after which time she attended to one other ordinance which was to wash the feet of her husband [Lewis Dunbar] and anoint him to be her king and priest and Savior, that she might have claim on him at the resurrection[.]

—"Record of Lewis Dunbar Sr. and
Nancy Ann Wilson," LDS Archives.

....

Two hundred and eight persons received ordinances

—"Manuscript History of Brigham Young,"
in *History of the Church,* 7:572.

....

Nauvoo temple endowments performed on this date for:

First Company: Jeremiah Hatch, Elizabeth Hatch, Alexander Hill Sr.,

[Washings and anointings for Wednesday, January 21, 1846—second excerpt]

Male Department Co. No. 2 11 oclock A.M.

Seventies		High Priest	
"	John P. Parker born July 28 1811		Samuel Parker born Jan. 26 1796
"	12 John Perry " June 22 1799	Seventies	Jacob Peart " June 3 1801
"	13 John H. Mikesell " Mar. 29 1815		19 Ransom A Beecher " Dec. 2 1813
"	14 Joseph I. Murdoch " June 26 1822		20 Benj F. Cummings " Mar. 3 1821
"	15 Richard Bentley " Oct 1 1820		21 George P. Billings " July 25 1828
"	16 Peter Shirts " 1808	High Priest	Lyman Stephens " Feb. 7 1812
"	17 James W. Walker " Jan. 17 1825		7 Silas S. Davis " Jan. 12 1793

John Perry was ordained to the office of Seventy by Pres Joseph Young and Ezra T. Benson. Silas S. Davis was ordained to the office of High Priest by Isaac Morley and Ezra T. Benson. George J. Billings was ordained a Seventy by Joseph Young.

	22 Myron Tanner born June 7 1826	High Priest	Abraham Hoagland born Mar. 24 1797
	23 Orlando D. Hovey " Sept. 12 1809	"	9 Benj. Wilcox " Aug 23 1796

Abraham Hoagland was ordained a High Priest by Ezra T. Benson & Isaac Morley. Benj Wilcox was ordained a High Priest by Isaac Morley & Ezra T. Benson.

The above named company was washed by Noah Rogers & Samuel Moore and anointed by Israel Barlow, Edson Barney and L. A. Shirtliff.

Finished 12 oclock & 10 Minutes P.M

Co. No. 3 Male Department com. 15 min 2 P.M.

Seventies		Seventies	
	Daniel Wood born Oct. 11, 1790		Joseph West born June 23, 1822
"	25 Andrew B. Williams " Nov 7, 1818	"	33 Julius J. Guiand " Apl. 28, 1818

[Seventies]		[Seventies]	
"	26 Jeremiah Hatch [born] July 7, 1823	"	34 Carlos Stevens [born] Feb 3, 1825
"	27 William B. Lindsey " Dec. 25, 1821	"	35 James Townsend " Feb. 20, 1808
"	28 John B. Fairbanks " Apl. 28, 1817	"	36 Jas. Green " May 1, 1812
"	29 Andrew Lamoraux " Mar. 17, 1817	"	37 Jacob Morris " Aug. 1797
"	30 William H. Jordan " Aug. 31, 1802	H. Priests	David Nelson " Jan 6, 1801
"	31 James Lighthead " July 1, 1816	"	11 Elisha Cragon " Feb. 22, 1786

Washed by Noah Rogers and Samuel Moore. Anointed by Israel Barlow, Edson Barney, L. A. Shirtliff and Hiram Daton. Fin[ished]. at 3 P.M.

Female Department List 2 11-½ o'clk ~~P.~~^A^M.

Anna Allen born Feb 12, 1796	Lurena Luce born Apl. 12, 1812
Margaret Sutherland " Oct. 21, 1729	Agnes Sutherland " Apl. 8, 1792
Lucretia Davis " Sep. 13, 1796	Elizabeth Bentley " June 29, 1821
Ann Parry " Feb. 21, 1801	Ruth Maxon " Aug. 13, 1786
Eliza Ann Parry " Mar 30, 1828	Sylvia H. Mecham " July 22, 1820
Martha Stevens " Nov. 17, 1811	Elizabeth Hutchins " July 7, 1826
Nancy Porter " Dec. 3, 1821	Margaret Hoagland " Apl. 18, 1802
Sylvia D. Beecher " Apl. 17, 1821	Anna Welker " Jan 31, 1820
Susannah Lipthorp " May 27, 1809	Ann Braddock " Mar. 5, 1794
Phebe Peart " Aug 30, 1805	Margaret Mikesell " May 7, 1827
Deiany Parker " Aug 15, 1798	Mary Wilcox " Mar. 3, 1801
Margaret Shirts " Dec. 26, 1802	Mary Jane Sanderson " Nov. 16, 1809
Mary Cummings " Apl. 8, 1830	Abigail D. Hovey " Aug 31, 1817

Rosanna Winter " Dec. 6, 1825	Eliza Dollinger " Dec. 22, 1813
Jannette Snively " Oct 23, 1812	Susannah Snively " Oct. 30, 1805

Washed and Anointed by Lydia Granger, Sophia M. Burgess, Lucinda Harris, Mary Winchester, Mary Gates, Elizabeth Barlow, S. Harmon, Jane Green. 1, 12 P.M.

Female Department List 5 com. 2 P.M.

Electa Lamoreaux born Oct. 7, 1825	Lucretia Fisher born Mar 13, 1831
Mary T. Nelson " Dec. 31, 1817	Elizabeth Barton " Sep. 10, 1803
Lucinda West " [blank]	Elizabeth Guinand " June 7, 1829
Abigail Williams " July 26, 1823	Julia Lindsay " Feb. 2, 1822
Floretta Green " Mar. 1, 1816	Rebecca Ann Marshall " May 13, 1825
Mary Gordon " Nov. 10, 1816	Louisa Hatch " Jan. 2, 1825
Elizabeth L. Taft " Dec. 6, 1827	Deborah Leithead " Feb. 4, 1808
Sarah Fairbanks " July 11, 1822	Mary Ann Knowlton " Sep. 11, 1829
Mary Wood " Nov. 25, 1803	Jane Stevens " June 8, 1827
Perina Wood " Mar. 12, 1827	Amelia A. Stevens " May 7, 1828
Catharine Gray " Oct. 13, 1817	Elizabeth Graygun " May 1, 1799
Susan Townsend " Apl. 10, 1795	Nancy Anderson " Mar. 20, 1801
Jane Molton " Apl. 14, 1820	

Washed and Anointed by Lydia Granger, Mary Gates, Sophia M. Burgess, Lucinda Harris, Nancy Winchester, Sophronia Harmon, Martha J. Codey, Elizabeth Barlow.

Male Department List 4. com. 15 to 6.

Seventy		Seventies	
"	John W. Stoker born Mar. 16, 1802		Lorenzo D. Butler born July 13, 1826

[Seventy]		[Seventies]	
"	39 John Stoker [born] Mar 8, 1817		43 James M. Butler [born] Apl. 20, 1821
"	40 Moses Whitaker " Apl. 22, 1818		44 Caleb G. Edwards " June 18, 1819
"	41 John Cole " Jan. 16, 1807		

Washed by Noah Rogers and Samuel Moore. Anointed by Edson Barney and L. A. Shirtliff.

. . . .

[Washings and anointings for Wednesday, January 21, 1846—third excerpt]

List 4 Female Department Commencing 35 minutes after 3.

Susan Miller born Jan 25, 1812	Alice Whitaker born Jan 25 1824
Sarah J. Goff " Mar. 22, 1831	Elizabeth Foutz " Sep 25 1827
Catharine McAll " May 18 1828	Olive A. Smith " Sep 15, 1825
Anna Cole " Mar. 18, 1812	Jane Stoker " Feb 24, 1810
Cynthia Shephard " Feb. 9, 1819	Sarah Stoker " May 26 1806

Washed and anointed by Caroline Crosby Jane Ann Green, Lucinda Harris, Lydia Granger, Nancy Winchester, Phebe Miller, Elizabeth Barlow, Merillu Johnson. Finished 4 oclock P.M.

List 5. Male Department

Seventies		Seventies	
"	Alfred Randall born June 13, 1844		Dorr P. Curtiss born Jan. 21 1809
"	William D. Morton " June 22 1816	"	Charles C. Robbins " July 24 1819
"	Jonathan S. Wells " Jan 3 1808	"	James Kibby " July 17 1824
"	Samuel B. Merrill " Jan 4 1812	"	Gideon D. Wood " June 30 1808

"	Worthy Clark " Sept 12 1811	"	Gad Sprague " Nov 2 1810
"	William W Patten " Oct 4 1816	"	Philip Klingensmith " Apr. 3 1810
"	William Somerville " Apr 4 1817	"	Horace Fish " Jan 6, 1799
"	Ebenezer Hanks " Feb. 11 1808	"	Thomas Dunn " Jan 2 1822
"	William W. Rust " Aug 14 1808	"	John Lawrence " June 21 1803
"	Alfred B. Lamson " Aug 27 1819	High Priest	Justin Morse " Mar. 27 1809
"	John Edger " Apr. 22 1811	"	Thomas Matthews " Apr. 24 1799
"	Philemon C. Merrill " Oct. 12 1820	"	James Eastman " Oct. 20 1786
"	Shadrach Driggs " Aug. 28 1813	Elders	Elias Langdon " Jan 2 1798
"	James Burgess " Feb. 25 1818	"	Henry Doremus " June 4 1801
"	Thomas Weir " July 26 1808		
"	Charles Barnum " Aug 11 1809		

5th Company was washed by Stephen H Goddard Welcome Chapman, and Jesse P. Harmon. Anointed by Andrew Lytle Andrew L Lamaraux, William Cahoon and Joseph G. Hovey — Shadrach Driggs, James Eastman ^and^ Horace Fish were ordained Seventies by [illegible]

Female Department list 5 com. ½ p. 6

Anna Mariah Morton born Jan. 22, 1819	Mercy Cady Matthews born Nov. 13, 1801
Milissa Jane Lambson " Mar. 24, 1825	Mary Jane Robbins " Oct. 23, 1820
Elizabeth Barnum " May 24, 1801	Eliza Driggs " July 11, 1808
Emoret L. Randall " May 18, 1818	Syrena Merrill " Jan. 6, 1814
Sally Sprague " June 7, 1820	Jane Hanks " Oct. 4, 1817
Emily P. Merrill " Feb 2, 1806	Sarah Langdon " Mar 10, 1792
Lydia Clark " Mar. 15, 1820	Rhoda Lawrence " June 15, 1812

Mary Darrow [born] Apl. 30, 1791	Hannah Fish [born] Dec. 26, 1806
Hannah Wood " Aug. 21, 1804	Elizabeth Daley " June 14, 1791
Mary Thompson " Oct. 21, 1827	Catharine Adelia Curtis " Nov. 28, 1820
Mary Rust " Jan. 8, 1815	Clarissa Eastman " Mar. 8, 1792
Margaret Wells " Sep. 15, 1811	Elizabeth Wier " Mar. 3, 1814
Harriet Doremus " Mar. 28, 1819	Hannah Clingingsmith " Apl. 11, 1826
Nancy Moss " June 7, 1824	Harriet Dunn " Feb 4, 1815

Washed and Anointed by Jane F. Rea, Phebe Miller, Anna Harmon, Lucinda Harris, L. C. Butler, S. Harmon, M. Johnson, M. Henderson.

—Seventies Record, Book B, oversized portions, January 21, 1846.

Caroline A. Webb, Almond L. Fullmer, Sarah Ann Fullmer, Elizabeth Hill, Thomas Kidd, Susannah Kidd, Benjamin R. Bentley, Rhoda Ann Bentley, Huntington Johnson, Jemima Johnson, Elizabeth Tuttle, Mary Ann Buchanan, Amelia Wilsey, Jane Wilsey, Catharine Stoker, Elizabeth Welker, Lancy Durfee, Josiah Mounton Jr., Hannah Moulton, Mary Brower, Desdemona C. Fullmer, Benjamin Johnson, Lovina Johnson, Abigail Bradford, Joel Ricks, Eleanor Ricks, Sarah B. Barney, Ira S. Hatch, Abigail Hatch, Robert E. Baird, Hannah E. Baird, Thomas Taylor, Edward Dolton, Hosea W. Tinker, Emeline Tinker, Berrill Covington, and George W. Boyd.

Second Company: Eliza Dollinger, Silas S. Davis, Lucretia Davis, Elizabeth Hutchins, Susanna Snively, John P. Porter, Nancy Porter, Mary Jane Sanderson, Lyman Stevens, Martha Stevens, Ruth Maxson, Richard Bentley, Elizabeth Bentley, Orlando D. Hovey, Abigail D. Hovey, Abraham Hoagland, Margaret Hoagland, John Parry, Ann Parry, Eliza Parry, Rose Ann Winter, Lurena Luce, Benjamin Wilcox, Mary Wilcox, Peter Shirts, Delaney Parker, Ann Read Braddock, Margaret Shirts, Samuel C. Parker, Susanna Liptrot [Lipthrop], Joseph S. Murdock, Eunice Murdock, Sylvia A. Mecham, James W. Welker, Anna Welker, Jacob Peart, Phebe Peart, Margaret Sutherland, Agnes Sutherland, R. A. Beecher, Sylvia D. Beecher, George P. Billings, B[enjamin]. F. Cummings, Mary Cummings, Anna Allen, John H. Mikesell, Margaret Mikesell, and Myron Tanner.

Third Company: Catharine Gray, William H. Jordan, Mary Jordan, Elizabeth L. Taft, Job E. Green, Floretta Green, Jeremiah Hatch, Louisa Hatch, David Nelson, Mary T. Nelson, Lucretia Fisher, Joseph West, Lucinda West, Nancy Anderson, Jane Holten, Elisha Cragun, Elizabeth Cragun, Elizabeth Barton, John B. Fairbanks, Sarah H. Fairbanks, Julius J. Guinard, Elizabeth Guinard, James Leithead, Deborah Leithead, Jacob Morris, Mary Ann Knowlton, William Lindsay Jr., Julia Lindsay, Electa Lamoreaux, Andrew Lamoreaux, Daniel Wood, Mary Wood, Panina Wood, Andrew B. Williams, Abigail Williams, James Townsend, Susan Townsend, Carlos Stevens, Jane Stevens, Amelia Stevens, and Rebecca Ann Marshal.

Fourth Company: Olive A. Smith, John Cole, Charlotte Cole, Galen Cole, Lucinda Cole, Lucy Ann Cole, Moses Whitaker, Alice Whitaker, John Stoker, Jane Stoker, Cynthia Shepherd, Caleb G. Edwards, James M. Butler, Lorenzo D. Butler, Sarah Jane Goff, John W. Stoker, Sarah Stoker, Catharine McCall, Elizabeth Foutz, and Susan Miller.

Fifth Company: Alfred B. Lambson, Melissa Jane Lambson, Worthy

Clark, Lydia Clark, Jonathan S. Wells, Margaret Wells, William W. Patten, Betsey Patten, Thomas Dunn, Harriet Dunn, Gideon D. Wood, Hannah Wood, Charles Robbins, Mary Jane Robbins, Alfred Randall, Emeret L. Randall, Samuel B. Merrill, Elizabeth Merrill, John Lawrence, Thomas Matthews, Mercy Katy Matthews, Ebenezer Hanks, Jane Hanks, Charles Barnum, Philip Klingensmith, Hannah Klingensmith, Shadrack Driggs, Eliza Driggs, Justice Morse, Nancy Morse, Philemon C. Merrill, Cyrena E. Merrill, Thomas Weir, Elizabeth Weir, Gad Sprague, Sally Sprague, William D. Morton, Anna Maria Morton, Emily P. Merrill, Elizabeth Taylor, Horace Fish, Hannah Fish, Julia Fish, William Somerville, John Edgar, Ann Edgar, James Burgess, Mary Thompson, William W. Rust, Mary Rust, Mary N. Darrow, Elias Langdon, Sarah Langdon, James Eastman, Clarissa Eastman, Henry J. Doremus, Harriet Doremus, Dorr P. Curtis, Catharine/Adelia Curtis, and James Kibby.

—Summary of information compiled by the Temple Index Bureau, *Nauvoo Temple Endowment Register: 10 December 1845 to 8 February 1846*. Editors' note: According to the register, Elizabeth Barnum, Anna Cole, Elizabeth Daley, and Rhoda Lawrence were washed and anointed on this date and therefore probably received through the veil.

....

Second anointings performed on this date:

Thomas Grover, Caroline (Nickerson) Grover, Hannah (Tupper) Grover, and Lodeska (Tupper) Grover, anointed by Parley P. Pratt; Lewis D. Wilson and Nancy (Waggoner) Wilson, anointed by William Snow; William Miller, Phoebe (Scott) Miller, and Lucretia (Johnson) Miller, anointed by Orson Hyde; Henry G. Sherwood, Jane (McManagal) Sherwood, and Marcia (Abbott) Sherwood, anointed by Parley P. Pratt; David D. Yearsley and Mary Ann (Hoopes) Yearsley, anointed by Orson Hyde; John Pack, Julia (Ives) Pack, Ruth (Mosher) Pack, Eliza (Graham) Pack, Mary Jane (Wilker) Pack, and Nancy (Broothe) Pack, anointed by Parley P. Pratt; Jacob Gates, Mary (Snow) Gates, and Elizabeth (Hutchings) Gates, anointed by Orson Hyde; Isaac Chase, Phebe (Ogden) Chase, and Rosanna (Whipple) Chase, anointed by Parley P. Pratt; Elvira (Teeples) Rockwood to Albert P. Rockwood for time and Joseph Smith (deceased) for eternity, anointed by [not given]; Angeline (Hutchinson) Horne to Albert P. Rockwood for time and Moses Horne (deceased) for eternity, anointed by [not given]; Clarissa (Chase) Young, Susan (Snively) Young,

Ellen (Ackland) Young, Mary Ann (Clark) Young, and Martha (Bowke) Young to Brigham Young, anointed by Heber C. Kimball; and Hannahette (Snively) Pratt to Parley P. Pratt, anointed by Orson Hyde.

—Summarized from "Book of Anointings."

Sealings for the living performed on this date:

Robert E. Baird to Hannah Everhart McCullough; Elias Bassett to Matilda Salter; Rufus Beach to Mary Catharine Aber and Eliza Jane Fosdick; George Washington Bratton to Mary Palmer Graves; Vernon Hamond Bruce to Mercy Ann Simons; David Marks Burbank to Abigail Blodget; Harrison Burgess to Sophia Minerva Foster; Isaac Chase to Phoebe Ogden and Rozina Whipple; Aaron Cheney to Sarah Griffith; Hayden Wells Church to Sarah Ann Arterbury; Joseph Clements to Deborah Ann Price; Joseph Wellington Coolidge to Elizabeth Buchanan, Mary Ann Buchanan, and Elizabeth Jane Tuttle; Libbeus Thaddeus Coons to Mary Ann Williamson; Howard Coray to Martha Jane Knowlton; Alfred Cordon to Emma Parker; Benjamin Covey to Elmira Mack, Diana Cowles, Phebe Cowles, and Elizabeth Skinner; Jonathan Crosby to Caroline Barnes; John Dalton to Rebecca Turner Crammer; Silas Stillman Davis to Lucretia Wells; Jabez Durfee to Magdalena Pickle; Addison Everett to Orpha Mariah Redfield; John Solomon Fullmer to Olive Amanda Smith; Jacob Gates to Mary Minerva Snow and Elizabeth Caroline Hutchins; William Gray to Catherine B. Pruce; Thomas Green to Mary Ann Gibson; Joseph Jackson to Nancy Ann Clough; Huntington Johnson to Jemima Davis; Asahel Albert Lathrop to Jane Peacock and Hannah Peacock; Lyman Leonard to Abigail Calkins; John Lytle to Christiana Whitney; Willard Glover McMullin to Mary Richards; Hiram Mace to Elizabeth Armstrong; John Harrison Mikesell to Maragaret J. Nelson; John Pack to Julia Ives, Nancy Aurelia Boothe, Eliza Jane Graham, and Ruth Mosher; Calvin Crane Pendleton to Salley Ann Seavey; John President Porter to Nancy Rich; Parley Parker Pratt to Hannahette Snively; Thomas Ricketts Rich to Henrietta Peck; Albert Perry Rockwood to Alvira Wheeler Teeples; Ellis Mendenhall Sanders to Rachel Broom Roberts; Joseph Smith Schofield to Clarissa Aurilla Terry; Henry Garlic Sherwood to Marcia Abbott and Jane McManagal; Charles Shumway to Julia Ann Hooker and Louisa Minnerly; Nicholas Thomas Silcock to Jane Heath; Chauncy Griswold Webb to Eliza Jane Churchill and Elizabeth Lydia Taft; Edward Milo Webb to Caroline Amelia Owens; Silas Wilcox to

Margaret Belinda Allen; David Dutton Yearsley to Mary Ann Hoops; and Brigham Young to Clarissa Chase Ross, Susannah Snively, Ellen Rockwood, Mary Ann Clark, and Martha Bowker.

—Summarized from the Book of Living Sealings.

....

Sealings for the dead performed on this date:

Caroline Whiting (Caroline Eliza Nickerson, proxy) to Thomas Grover, Brigham Young officiating; Harmon Jackson Akes (George Washington Langley, proxy) to Martha Foster, Brigham Young officiating; Zillah Welland (Martha Collins, proxy) to Job Vassal Barnum, Brigham Young officiating; Edmund Durfee (Jabez Durfee, proxy) to Laura Pickett, Brigham Young officiating; Electra Cranson (Laura Durfee, proxy) to Jabez Durfee, Brigham Young officiating;[20] Lydia Van Blaricon (Abigail Blodget, proxy) to David Marks Burbank, Brigham Young officiating; Cinthia Jackson (Jane Peacock, proxy) to Asahel Albert Lathrop, Heber C. Kimball officiating; Moses Horne (Albert Perry Rockwood, proxy) to Angeline Hodgkins, Brigham Young officiating;[21] and Sarah Pierce and Margaret Connley (Mary Gibson, proxy) to Thomas Greene, Brigham Young officiating.

—Summarized from the Book of Proxy Sealings.

Thursday, January 22, 1846

William Hyde was anointed a King and a Priest unto the Most High in the Church of Jesus Christ of Latter Day Saints and to all Israel And Elizabeth Hyde was also anointed a Queen and Priestess unto her husband (William Hyde) in Room No. 4 commencing at 10 Minutes past 2 and ending at 30 minutes past 2 P.M. in the presence of Daniel Spencer, Lorenzo Snow, George Miller, Peter Haws, David Fullmer, D[avid]. Yearsley, William Huntington, James Allred, W[illiam]. W. Phelps, Henry J Sherwood, [and] J[oseph] W Coolidge[;] Elder Orson Hyde officiated.

—"Book of Anointings."

....

Willard Richards born Jun[e] 24 1804 [in] Hopkinton Middlesex Mass[achusetts]— & Jenn[e]tte Richards, (was born Aug[ust] 21—1817.

20. Laura and Jabez Durfee were also sealed for time on this occasion.

21. Angeline Hodgkins was also sealed to Albert Rockwood for time.

Walkerford Chaidgley Lancashire England deceased) were sealed Husband & wife for time & all Eternity[,] Amelia Elizabeth Peirson acting [as] proxy for & in behalf of the (deceased) who died at Nauvoo; July 9th 1845[.] Done in [the] presance of Heber Chase Kimble Orson Hyde & J[ohn]. D. Lee[;] Pres[ident]. B[righam]. Young officiating at the Alt[a]r done at 5 minutes to 9. evening—

Jennette Richards was Sealed to Willard as his wife for time and all Eternity & with him attended to all the ordinances pertaining to the House of the Lord—to & including the washing of feet [as] in the days of Pres[ident]. Joseph Smith Jr the first Prophet of the Church of the Last days[.]

—Book of Proxy Sealings.

....

35 m[inutes]. p[ast]. 8. p.m.

[See pages 454-60 for excerpted portion.]

—Seventies Record, Book B.

....

At nine oclock a.m. I [Thomas Bullock] went to the Temple with L[ucy]. C. C[layton]. who went thro[ugh]' the ordinances of washing and anointing. Received into the Cel[estial]. Room by Levi Hancock. I saw Pres[ident]. B[righam]. Young who shook me by the hand very cordially. He told me to take my wife [Henrietta] and L[ucy]. C[layton]. tomorrow evening at dusk to receive their second anointings and sealing. His words were as the Lord whispering peace to my Soul. I feel very happy for the blessings and privileges that I am receiving at the hands of the Lord. May I ever have the same Spirit within me, and then I shall always feel well.

—Thomas Bullock, Diary.

....

On the 22nd of January we [William and Elizabeth Hyde] received our second anointing, on which day my Father and Mother [Heman and Polly Hyde] also received theirs.

—William Hyde, Diary, L. Tom Perry Special Collections,
Harold B. Lee Library, Brigham Young University, Provo, Utah.

....

Visited the Temple with Wealthy [Richards.] she was sealed to me by the Prophet B[righam]. Young and then we repaired to the High Priests room where we were Anointed King and Queen Priest and Priestes to

[Washings and anointings for Thursday, January 22, 1846]

Female Department List 1. com[pany]. at 50 min p[ast]. 8

Dorothy Moon born Feb 9, 1804	Jane Sharp born Apl. 27, 1813
Hannah Moon " May 29, 1802	Agness Hill " Mar 4, 1800
Ann Burch " Nov. 1, 1804	Mary Hunt " May 15, 1796
Jane Burch " Dec. 21, 1802	Lydia Potter " June 11, 1802
Drusilla Hendricks " Feb. 8, 1810	Isabella Thompson " Jan 10, 1819
Eliza Burton " Apl. 8, 1810	Hannah C. Mumford " Apl. 1, 1808
Rachel Kingsly " July 6, 1805	Sarah Ann Casper " Oct. 31, 1822
Mary C. Rolph " May 25, 1824	Hannah Garner " Nov. 19, 1808
Catharine Foy " Oct. 18, 1808	Elizabeth Brashen " Oct. 24, 1790
Eleonor Cragun " Nov. 11, 1896	Louisa M. Sprague " Nov. 24, 1813
Juliatta Griffith " Apl. 14, 1806	Eliza Lake " Apl. 1, 1825
Lucy Alice Wheeler " Apl. 3, 1810	Margaret Hardman " Aug 2, 1805

Washed and anointed by Mirilla Johnson, Lydia Granger, Agness Smith, Julia Pack, Nancy Winchester, Phebe Miller, Sarah Davis, Ellen A Rockwood, Clarissa Chase, Lucinda Harris. Fin. at 16 min p. 10.

Male Department List 1 com. 15 min to 9 A.M.

Seventies		Seventies	
	1 Alexander Hill born Mar. 1, 1811		7 James Sharp born Apl. 15, 1812
"	2 Hunt " Mar. 9, 1792	"	8 Richard Hardman " May 4, 1807
"	3 Richard D. Sprague " Mar. 2, 1807	"	9 Joseph Thompson " Oct. 1, 1814
"	4 John S. Rolph " Aug 21, 1820	"	10 W. Bates " Feb 16, 1827
"	5 William W. Casper " Mar. 12, 1828	"	11 Edward J. Mumford " June 27, 1807

"	6 James Gragun " July 26, 1814	"	12 John S. White " Feb 16, 1814

January 22

H. Priests		H. Priests	
	1 Michael Rank born Jan. 22, 1792		Alanson Pettingill born ~~Nov 5, 1803~~ ^Mar 16,1801^
"	2 Levi Bracken " Mar. 11, 1792	"	6 Daniel Burch " Nov 5, 1803
"	3 Thomas B. Fay " Dec. 30, 1802	"	7 William Garner " Mar. 8, 1807
	4 Eleazar King, Senr " Oct. 11, 1784		

Washed by P. G. Sessions and L. A. Shirtliff. Anointed by Samuel Moore and Noah Rogers — Fin 25 Min to 10.

Male Department List 2, com. 15 min to 10

Seventies			
	13 Edmund Nelson born Jan 16, 1815		8 Samuel J. Winger born Dec 7, 1782
"	14 David B. Davis " Jan 15, 1823	"	9 Wm Henrie " Sep. 11, 1799
"	15 Jonathon O. Durfee " Aug 31, 1807	"	10 John Smith " Feb 13, 1799
"	16 Matthew Mansfield " Oct 25, 1810	"	11 John Moon " July 2, 1804
"	17 George W. Bean " Apl. 1, 1831	"	12 Hugh Moon " Aug 5, 1813
"	18 Elijah Allen " Feb. 7, 1826	Elders	George Stringham " Mar. 16, 1791
H. Priest			
	~~19~~ John Smith " Feb. 13, 1799	"	Wm Middleton " May 24, 1810
~~Sev~~	20 Frederick Wright " Jan 22, 1817		

Washed by P. G. Sessions, L. A. Shurtliff. Anointed by Samuel Moore, and Noah Rogers. Fin. 5. min p. 12. m.

Note Richard Hardman on List 1 was ordained Seventy by Israel Barlow. Frederick Wright on List 2 was ordained Elder by B. L. Clapp.

Female Department List 2. com. 5. min p. 11 A.M.

Ann Kelsall June 19, 1819	Margaret Buckwalter born Nov. 12, 1825
Harriet Emaline Barney Oct 13, 1810	Sarah Buckwalter " Nov. 12, 1825
Caroline F. Davis born Oct 3, 1825	Eleanor Jane Davis " Nov 21, 1824
Mary Duke " Sep. 1, 1805	Eliza Jane Stringham " Mar. 20, 1823
Mary Ann Mansfield " Dec 30, 1805	Sarah Lurena Baily " Dec. 3, 1826
Myra Henrie " Nov 1, 1803	Mary Middleton " July 24, 1795
Polly Stringham " Apl. 3, 1803	Meranda Elliott " Dec. 16, 1810
Laura Reynolds " Apl. 3, 1803	Elizabeth Pulsipher " Nov. 5, 1772
Sarah Smith " May 19, 1806	Joanna Dexter " Jan. 15, 1830
Vienna Sherer " June 10, 1787	Mary Cannon " Sep. 30, 1810
Jemima Huff " Apl. 2, 1780	Vina Hollister " Dec. 19, 1799
Laura Ann Loss " July 20, 1822	Jane Gulley " May 16, 1820
	Lucy Caroline Clayton " Mar. 21, 1820

Washed and anointed by Lydia Granger, Agness Smith, Nancy Winchester, Lucinda Harris, Jane Ann Green, Anna Harmon, Phebe Angel, Sarah Davis, Clarissa Chase, Lucinda Allen, Ellen Rockwood. Finished at 15. min past 12. m

Male Department. List 3 com 15 min p. one

Seventies		Seventies	
	19 Ezra Parish born May 4, 1804		Joseph Davis born Dec 12, 1826
"	20 William R Parrish " July 29, 1816	"	28 James A. Tyler " Sep 22, 1824
"	21 James Proctor " ~~June~~ ^Oct^ 5, 1804	"	29 Rufus Patrick " Sep 4, 1818
"	22 Thomas McLaland " Mar. 28, 1819	"	30 Benjamin Chapman " Nov 11, 1811
"	23 Jesse C. Braley " Apl. 20 1810	"	31 George G Johnston " Aug 11, 1815
"	24 John Worthen " July 22, 1817	"	32 George Norvill " June 30, 1800

"	25 James Grovet " Oct. 28, 1817	H. Priests	Thomas Evans " Oct. 4, 1796
"	26 Lewis Gaulter " Oct. 28, 1817		

Washed by P. G. Sessions & L. A. Shurtliff. Anointed by Samuel Moore and Noah Rogers. — James Grovet was ordained a seventy by Randolph Alexander.

Finished at 7 min p 2 P.M.

Female Department. List 3, com. 24 min p. 1 P.M.

Mary Parsons born Apl. 7, 1810	Catharine Nauvil age unknown
Elizabeth Evans " Apl 25, 1796	Elizabeth Coleman born 1820
Elizabeth Camer " Dec. 21, 1801	Elizabeth McLellen " August 1824
Lettice Proctor " 1802	Sarah B. Davis " Apl. 15, 1827
Mary Dickens " Apl. 30, 1830	Elmedia Harmon " Dec. 31, 1829
Eleanor Tuttle " Dec. 11, 1800	Nancy Buchanan " Feb 25, 1791
Catharine Thomas " Feb. 16, 1794	Harriet Golter " Feb. 8, 1824
Julia Ann Durphy " Nov. 19, 1822	Henrietta Whitney " Dec 25, 1821
Jane Eldridge " Nov. 3, 1803	Mary Worthen " July 27, 1796
Sarah S. Johnston " Apl. 22, 1820	Hannah Worthen " July 22, 1816
Susannah Parrish " Sep. 17, 1802	Charlotte Tyler " Mar. 19, 1823
Elvira Parrish " July 17, 1815	Marion Bishop " Nov. 14, 1829
Achsah S. E. Patrick " Dec. 20, 1818	Sarah Mackly " Dec. 8, 1801
Clarissa Fosdick " Aug 15, 1799	Rachel Braley " Apl. 1, 1829
Maria Fosdick " Apl. 7, 1825	Ann Grocott " Mar 27, 1823

Washed by Lucinda Harris, Julia Pack, Jane Ann Green, Julia Stone, Agness Smith, Phebe Angel, Clarissa Chase, Nancy Winchester, Sarah Smith, Ann Whitney, Lucinda Allen, Ellen Rockwood. Finished at 3 P.M.

Female Department List 4. com. 35 min p. 3.

Susan Miller born Jan. 25, 1812	Sarah Jane Goff born Mar 22, 1831
Catharine McAll " May 18, 1828	Anna Cole " Mar 18, 1812
Cynthia Shephard " Feb. 9, 1819	Alice Whitaker " Jan. 28, 1821
Elizabeth Foutz " Sep. 25, 1827	Olive A. Smith " Sep. 15, 1825
Jane Stoker " Feb. 24, 1810	Sarah Stoker " May 26, 1806

Washed by Caroline Crosby, Jane Ann Green Lucinda Harris, Lydia Granger, Nancy Winchester, Phebe Miller, Elizabeth Barlow, Merilla Johnson. Finished at 4 P.M.

Thursday evening January 22nd Male Department List 4

Seventies		Seventies
"	James Lambson born July 20, 1820	John Hardman born Jan. 6, 1813
"	33 Levi Graybill " Mar. 12, 1818	39 Richard Thorn " June 18, 1825
"	34 Ebenezer Sanders " Sep. 19, 1818	40 William Swapp " Aug. 1820
"	35 Lewis Hulse " Feb. 7 1805	41 Sydney A Hanks " Aug 17, 1820
"	36 Wesley Rose " Mar. 23, 1821	42 James German " Mar. 26, 1813

Washed by G. Sessions and L. A. Shirtliff. Anointed by Samuel Moore and Noah Rogers. Fin. 6. min to 5.

Female Department List 4 com. 20 min p 4 P. M.

Abigail Abbot born Apl. 26, 1829	Elizabeth Boveer born Apl. 6, 1831
Sarah Holister " Feb. 7, 1827	Mary Hardman " Nov. 1, 1819
Hannah Conklin " Jan. 25, 1806	Patience Graybill " Nov. 25, 1824
Jemima Losee " Sep. 3, 1823	Anna Sanders " Aug 16, 1818
Harriet Anna Thorn " Jan. 21, 1826	Cynthia Cloyd " Jan. 28, 1816
Charity Pierce " Oct. 4, 1811	Rachel Jyrmin " Jun 5, 1810

Washed and anointed by Nancy Winchester, Sarah Smith, Agness Smith, Julia Pack, Anna Harmon, Julia Stove, Sophronia Harmon. Finished at 20 min p. 5. P.M.

List 5. Male Department, List 5, commenced at 8 P.M.

Seventies		Seventies	
	Freeman P. Richards born Dec. 29, 1816		Lorenzo W. Roundy born June 18, 1819
"	44 John W. Berry " Dec. 17, 1822	"	54 Francis Lee " June 26, 1811
"	45 David Moore " Jan. 20, 1819	"	55 Danford Atwood " Feb 25, 1824
"	46 James McFate " Apl. 19, 1804	"	56 Thomas Derby " Mar. 10, 1812
"	47 Ira J. Willow " Jan. 21, 1812	"	57 Simmons Curtis " Mar. 26, 1818
"	48 George Moore " July 3, 1820	"	58 David Holman " July 15, 1808
"	49 Samuel S. Thornton " Dec. 3, 1817	"	59 George Wilson " Dec. 28, 1807
"	50 Joseph King " Nov. 25, 1815	"	60 Edward Pew " Aug. 28, 1824
"	51 John Boyce " Feb. 20, 1815	"	61 Jesse Snyder " Apl. 12, 1825
"	52 William W. Lane " Aug 29, 1797	"	62 Chester Snyder " June 10, 1815

Washed by Milo Andrews and William Cahoon. Anointed by Edson Barney, Harrison Burgess, and William Cahoon. Finished at 6 min to 7 P.M. John W. Berry, Ira G. Willes, and Edward Pugh were ordained seventies — Harrison Burgess, B. L. Clapp, and Samuel Moore officiated.

List 5 Female Department com. at

Mahala King born Nov. 18, 1823	Amelia Berry born Jan. 24, 1804
Lucy F. McFate " Sep. 23, 1820	Nancy Jane Berry " June 19, 1828
Mary Allen Moor " Dec. 4, 1822	Martha Derby " Feb. 10, 1818
Jane Vail Lee " Sep. 30, 1815	Mariah Lane " Jan. 5, 1806
Harriet Jane Thornton " June 4, 1830	Harriet Thornton " June 11, 1791

Susan Moor [born] Feb 5, 1820	Rebecca Atwood [born] Oct. 2, 1816
Jerusha Burdick " Jan. 25, 1816	Cynthia Baggs " Apl. 20, 1800
Catharine Burdick " Oct. 3, 1824	Elizabeth Tidwell " Jan. 20, 1804
Adaline Roundy " Mar. 24, 1822	Sarah Frazier " Jan. 24, 1810
Mary Ann Boyce " Nov. 4, 1821	Emeline Curtis " Mar. 1, 1820
Eliza Holman " Mar. 5, 1819	Eleanor Richards " June 19, 1818
Catharine Snider " June 1, 1811	Catherine Snider 2nd " Apl. 21, 1827

Washed and anointed by Sophia M. Burgess, Julia Stone, Sarah Smith, Electa Whitesides, Lettice Barney, Hannah Wood, Nancy Cahoon, Jane Richards, and Jane Ann Green. Finished at 40 min p. 8 P.M.

—Seventies Record, Book B, oversized portion, January 22, 1846.

the most high God for Time and through out all Eternity by P[arley]. P. Pratt as mouth[.]

—Phinheas Richards, Diary, LDS Archives.

....

One hundred and ninety-eight persons received ordinances in the Temple.

—"Manuscript History of Brigham Young," in *History of the Church,* 7:572.

....

Nauvoo temple endowments performed on this date for:

First Company: Lucy Alice Wheeler, James Sharp, Jane Sharp, Joseph Thompson, Isabella Thompson, Rachel Kingsley, Richard D. Sprague, Louisa Maria Sprague, Julietta Cravath, Drusilla Hendricks, William W. Casper, Sarah Ann Casper, Dorothy Moon, Alexander Hunt, Mary Hunt, Alexander Hill Jr., Agnes Hill, Richard Hardman, Margaret Hardman, Hannah Moon, John S. Rolph, Mary A. Rolph, Eleazer King Sr., Lydia Potter, Thomas B. Foy, Harriet Foy, Levi Bracken, Michael Rank, Jane Rank, Edward T. Mumford, Hannah C. Mumford, Eliza Burton, Joseph W. Bates, William Garner, Hannah Garner, Alanson Pettingill, Daniel Burch, Ann Burch, John S. White, Eliza Lake, James Cragun, Eleaner Cragun, Jane Hall, and Sarah Longstroth.

Second Company: Sarah Buckwalter, William Middleton, Laura Ann Loss, Mary Middleton, Harriet Emeline Barney, Sarah Bailey, Miranda Elliott, Lucy Caroline Clayton, Samuel T. Winegar, Rhoda Winegar, Jemima Hough, Jonathan O. Duke, Mary Duke, Eleanor Jane Davis, David V. Davis, Caroline Davis, Rachel Middleton, John Moon, Eliza Jane Stringham, Margaret Buckwalter, George Stringham, Mary A. Cannon, Viny Hollister, George Dexter, Joanna Dexter, Polly Stringham, Elizabeth Pulsipher, Vienna Shearer, Laura Reynolds, William Henrie, Myra Henrie, Jane Gully, Hugh Moon, Matthew Mansfield, Sarah Smith, Edmund Kelsaw, Anna Kelsaw, Mary Ann Mansfield, John Smith, George S. Colmere, Frederick Wright, Elijah Allen, and George W. Bean.

Third Company: William R. Parish, Alvira Lucena Parish, Thomas Evans, Mary Parsons, Almeda Harmon, James A. Tyler, Jane Eldridge, Elizabeth Evans, Ezra Parish, Rufus Patrick, Clarissa Fosdick, Maria Fosdick, George G. Johnston, Sarah S. Johnston, Charlotte Tyler, Mary Ion Bishop, Jesse C. Braley, Susannah Parish, Rachel Maria/Lodema Braley, Achsah S. E. Patrick, Lewis Gaulter, Harriet Gaulter, James Grocott, Ann

Grocott, Catharine Thomas, James Proctor, Letitia Proctor, Benjamin Chapman, Elizabeth Canner, Julia Ann Durfee, Henrietta Whitney, George Norvil, Catharine Norvil, Sarah Mackley, John Worthen, Hannah Worthen, Mary Worthen, Joseph Davis, Elizabeth Coleman, Nancy Buchanan, Eleanor Tuttle, Mary Dickens, and Sarah B. Davis.

Fourth Company: Sidney A. Hanks, Abigail Abbott, Elizabeth Bovee, William Swap, Sarah Ann Hollister, Elizabeth Swap, Levi Graybill, Patience Graybill, James Lawson, Hannah Graybill, John Hardman, Mary Hardman, Wesley Rose, Maria Rose, Cynthia Clyde, Lewis Hulse, Anna Landers, James Jerman, Charity Pierce, Jemima Losee, Ebenezer Landers, Harriet Anna Thorn, Richard Thorn, and Rachel Jerman.

Fifth Company: David Holman, Eliza Holman, George Moore, Mary E. Moore, John Boice, Mary Ann Boice, Jerusha Burdick, Catharine Burdick, Truman P. Richards, Eleanor Richards, Lorenzo W. Roundy, William W. Lane, Maria Lane, Adaline Roundy, David Moore, Susan Moore, Chester Snyder, Catharine Snyder, Thomas Derby, Martha Derby, Jesse Snyder, Catharine D. Snyder, Samuel S. Thornton, Harriet Jane Thornton, Harriet Thornton, George Wilson, Elizabeth Tidwell, Edward Pugh, Cynthia Baggs, Sarah Frazier, John W. Berry, Nancy Jane Berry, James McFate, Lucy T. McFate, Danford Atwood, Rebecca Atwood, Francis Lee, Jane Vail Lee, Ira J. Willis, Armilla Berry, Joseph King, Mahala King, Simon Curtis, and Emeline Curtis.

—Summary of information compiled by the Temple Index Bureau, *Nauvoo Temple Endowment Register: 10 December 1845 to 8 February 1846.* Editors' note: According to the register, Sarah Bovee, Benjamin Bracken, Elizabeth Bracken, and Rachel Inman were washed and anointed on this date and therefore probably received through the veil.

Second anointings performed on this date:

Harrison Burgess and Sophia (Foster) Burgess, anointed by Heber C. Kimball; Heman Hyde and Polly (Tilton) Hyde, anointed by Orson Hyde; Phinehas Richards and Wealthy (Dewey) Richards, anointed by Parley P. Pratt; William Hyde and Elizabeth (Bullard) Hyde, anointed by Orson Hyde; Mary (Pierce) Kimball and Margaret (Pierce) Young to Heber C. Kimball, anointed by Orson Hyde; Cornelius P. Lott, Permelia (Darrow) Lott, Rebecca (Fausett) Lott, and Charity (Dickinson) Lott, anointed by Parley P. Pratt; Elizabeth ([Durfee] Davis) Smith to Cornelius P. Lott for time and Joseph Smith (deceased) for eternity, anointed by Parley P. Pratt; Shadrach Roundy and Patsy (Quimby) Roundy, anointed by Isaac Morley; Hannah (Libby) Morley, Nancy (Black) Morley, and Harriet (Cox) Morley to Isaac Morley, anointed by Daniel Spencer; Joseph A. Kelting and Minerva (Woods) Kelting, anointed by Parley P. Pratt; Mary Ann (Turner) Miller to William Miller, anointed by George Miller; and Winslow Farr, Olive (Freeman) Farr, Roxanna (Porter) Farr, Almeda (Randall) Farr, and Adelia (Clemens) Farr, anointed by Parley P. Pratt.

—Summarized from "Book of Anointings."

....

Sealings for the living performed on this date:

Reddin Alexander Allred to Julia Ann Bates; Reddick Newton Allred to Lucy Hoyt; Erastus Bingham to Lucinda Gates; Mathias M. Bovee to Waitstill Hill; Luman Hopkins Calkins to Mehitable Russell; Barnet Cole to Phebe Van Alstyne; Simmons [Simmon] Philander Curtis to Emeline Buchanan; Joshua Davis to Susan Ann Cole; Jonathan Oldham Duke to Mary Elois Stone; Simeon Adams Dunn to Margaret Snyder; Edward Peas Duzette [Dunzell] to Eliza Ann [Elizabeth] Cowen; Winslow Farr to Olive Hovey Freeman, Almina [Almena] Randall, Adelia Maria Clemens, and Roxanna Porter; William Fossett to Matilda Butcher; Peter Fullmer to Susannah Cerfers; William McGee Fausett to Elizabeth Bukie [Boshard]; Ebenezer Joseph Hanks to Jane Wells Cooper; John Harvey [Havry] to Eliza Averett; David Jones to Mercy Ayers; Archibald Kerr to Nancy Felwood Frost; John Morris King to Sally Ann Jewell [Fewell]; Cornelius Peter Lott to Pamelia Darrow, Narcissus Rebecca Faucett, and Charity Dickinson; Andrew Lytle to Hannah Hull; William Warner Major to Sarah Coles; Joseph Mecham Jr. to Hannah L. Tyler and Elizabeth Ann Bovee; Isaac Morley to Nancy Ann Bach, Harriet Lucinda Cox, Hannah Knight Libby, and Eleanor Mills; Alexander Neibaur to Ellen Breakell; John DeGroot Oakley to Mary McCormall Patterson; Stephen Perry to Rhoby Edwards; Chauncy Warriner Porter to Emma [Amy] Sumner; Phinehas Richards to Wealthy Dewey; Willard Richards to Amelia Elizabeth Pierson and Sarah Longstroth; Daniel Russell to Harriet Elizabeth Seymour; William Harrison Sagers to Olive Amanda Wheaton and Sarah Lorene Bailey; George Stringham to Polly Hendrickson; William Stringham to Eliza Lake and Jemima Young; Jonathan Taylor to Martha Price; Jacob Weiler to Anna Maria Malin; Brigham Young to Mary Harvey Pierce; and Phinehas Howe Young to Sarah Ann Hollister.

—Summarized from the Book of Living Sealings.

Sealings for the dead performed on this date:

Zina Taylor (Martha Pierce, proxy) to Jonathan Taylor, Heber C. Kimball officiating; Joseph Smith (Cornelius P. Lott, proxy) to Elizabeth (Davis) Durfee, Brigham Young officiating;[22] Adaline Rawson (Margaret Snyder, proxy) to Simeon A. Dunn, Heber C. Kimball officiating; Esther Knight and Polly Knight (Eliza Lake, proxy) to William Stringham, Brigham Young officiating; Sally Chase (Harriet Elizabeth Seymour, proxy) to Daniel Russell, Brigham Young officiating; Eunice McDearman (Mehittable Russell, proxy) to Luman H. Calkins, Brigham Young officiating; Isaac F. Freeman (Winslow Farr, proxy) to Roxanna Porter, Brigham Young officiating; Lydia Farr (Roxanna Porter, proxy) to Winslow Farr, Brigham Young officiating; Joseph Smith (George Washington Harris, proxy) to Lucinda (Pendleton) Harris, Brigham Young officiating;[23] Jennetta Richards (Amelia Elizabeth Peirson, proxy) to Willard Richards, Brigham Young officiating; and Morris Whitesides (Brigham Young, proxy) to Margaret Pierce, Heber C. Kimball officiating.

—Summarized from the Book of Proxy Sealings.

Friday, January 23, 1846

List 1 Friday morning, January 23d Male Department, 7 to 9

[See pages 465-66 for excerpted portion.]

Friday morning January 23d House of the Lord. Present of the quorum of the Twelve [apostles] Pres[iden]t. B[righam]. Young, H[eber]. C. Kimball, P[arley]. P. Pratt, Orson Hyde and John Taylor ^and Amasa Lyman^. Nothing of importance occurring, except the great press of business of giving endowments. One man by the name of Millburn who is not in the church, but works every tenth day on the Temple came to receive an endowment, in order as he told a confidential friend to find out what was going on there, that he might reveal it to the world. Of course he did not get admission. The Celestial room is immensely thronged with persons waiting to receive the higher ordinances of endowment.

Female Department commenced at 15 min[utes] to 12.

[See pages 466-67 for excerpted portion.]

John Parker, Jesse Lambson, ^and^ Henry Jolley, were ordained High

22. Elizabeth Durfee was also sealed to Cornelius Lott for time.

23. Lucinda and George Harris were also sealed for time on this occasion.

[Washings and anointings for Friday, January 23, 1846]

Seventies		H. Priests	
	1 Moses Deming born Mar. 16, 1804		John Tyson born July 12, 1772
"	2 Daniel McArthur " Apl. 8, 1820	"	2 Levi Osgood " May 19, 1773
"	3 Charles P. Cunningham " June 10, 1794	"	~~3 Daniel E. McArthur~~ "
"	4 John Thomas " Dec. 10, 1822	"	3 Thomas Richmond " Dec. 21, 1804
"	5 Sidney Roberts " Aug. 28, 1809	"	4 William Rickmore " May 14, 1799
"	6 Telemachus Rogers " Jan. 1, 1816	"	5 John Carter " Oct. 6 1816
"	7 Dustin Amy " Oct. 24, 1801	"	6 Willard Woodstock " Apl. 29, 1800
"	8 John Wait " May 17, 1813	"	7 Ira Ames " Sep. 22, 1804
"	9 John Gheen " Dec. 14, 1806		

Washed by Samuel Moore and Simeon A. Dunn. Anointed by Israel Barlow.

" 10 William C. Smoot " Jan 30, 1828

" 11 William Box " Nov. 24, 1804

Miles Anderson and Abraham O. Smoot. — William C. Smoot and William Box were ordained seventies by A. O. Smoot, Randolph Alexander and Edson Barney — Thomas Richmond was ordained High Priest by Abraham O. Smoot. Finished at 13 min. to 10.

List 1 Female department com. at 9 A.M.

Sarah Ann Roberts born May 23, 1810	Sarah Cunningham Jan 20, 1801
Margaret White " Apl. 9, 1800	Eliza Rogers " Apl. 1, 1823
Matilda E. McArthur " May 1, 1820	Elizabeth Richmond " Oct. 2, 1805
Olive Box " Jan. 28, 1805	Christana Richmond " June 12, 1808
Clara Lake " Dec. 12, 1808	Patience Asgood " Nov. 11, 1787

Susan I. Jonas [born] Aug. 3, 1820
Anna Perry " May 24, 1816
Mary Gheen " July 20, 1813
Elizabeth Ann Edwards " Apl. 14, 1819
Semantha Woodstock " June 24 1806

Leonora Amy [born] June 25, 1811
Elizabeth Carter " July 1, 1813
Mariah Deming " Nov. 10, 1814
Sarah Ames " May 6, 1814
Malinda Tyson " [illegible]

Washed and Anointed by Sophia M. Burgess, Mary E. Harris, Jane [illegible] Mary M. Cahoon, Louisa Clark [line illegible]

. . . .

[Washings and anointings for Friday, January 23, 1846—second excerpt]

Amy C. Aldridge born June 30, 1804
Susannah Stilman " June 4, 1796
Hannah Marsh " Feb 22, 1797
Almira Furgason " Feb. 25, 1807
Sarah Ripley " Dec. 12, 1801
Rosena Chandler " Aug. 2, 1819
Fanny Chandler " Dec. 19, 1822
Belinda Wylon " April 21, 1823
Mary Ann Leaver " June 21, 1810
Sarah Chandler " Apl. 30, 1782
Mary A. Savage " Mar. 30, 1823
Ruth Lambson " Sep 12, 1792
Sarah Patrick " Feb. 19, 1790
Mary Ramsbottom " July 15, 1826

Amelia M. Robinson born Aug 4, 1826
Eliza B. Perry " Oct. 5, 1826
Sidney Foot " Jan. 24, 1829
Nancy Wilkins " Mar. 5, 1811
Mary H. Parker " Sep. 8, 1825
Ellen Douglass " Nov. 4, 1806
Sarah Crandle " Mar 4, 1825
Elizabeth Owen " Feb. 7, 1798
Mary Ann Lamoreaux " May 15, 1815
Lucy Alred " Mar. 26, 1824
Barbara Jolly " Apl 7, 1799
Rosannah McIntire " May 20, 1810
Agness Moss " Aug 4 1792

Washed and anointed by Mary S. Horn, Phebe Miller, Lydia Granger, Sarah Smith, Nancy Cahoon, Jane A. Green. Hester A. E. Brown, Louisa Clark, Leonora Taylor, and Mary Ann Young. Finished at 1. p.m.

List 2 Male Department. commenced at 25 to 12

Seventies		Seventies	
"	12 William L. McIntyre " Aug 29, 1809		William C. Perry born Jan. 26, 1812
"	13 John G. Wilkins " July 28, 1800	"	21 David Savage " July 25, 1812
"	14 Isaac Furguson " Sep. 4 1810"22		Thomas Moss " Feb. 12, 1808
"	15 John Parker Jr. " Feb. 14, 1812	H. Priests	8 Alanson Ripley " Jan 8, 1798
"	16 Spicer W. Crandall " Dec. 30, 1821	"	9 John Parker " 1774
"	17 Redick N. Alred " Feb. 21, 1822	"	10 Jesse Lambson " Dec. 20, 1787
"	18 Warren Foot " Aug 10, 1817	"	11 David B. Lamoraux " Sept. 18, 1819
"	19 Samuel Leaver " Apl. 13, 1809	"	12 Henry Jolly " Aug. 26, 1789

Washed by Samuel Moore and Simeon A. Dunn. Anointed by Israel Barlow and Milo Andrews.

—Seventies Record, Book B, oversized portions, January 23, 1846.

Priests by A[braham]. O. Smoot and Edward P. Duzett. — Spencer W. Crandall was ordained [a] Seventy by [blank.]

Friday evening January 23d House of the Lord. Brother Reuben Miller who was appointed to gather up a company to emigrate West, out of the Branches of the church in Ottaway [Ottawa] and vicinity, returned to Nauvoo, and reported this day to the Twelve [apostles], that one James J. Strang[24] had been among the branches in that vicinity, and by professing to have received ^a^ revelation from God constituting him the visible head of the church — to have received plates, Urim and Thummum[— claimed authority above that of the Quorum of the Twelve Apostles] & had led many of the people astray.

G[eorge]. A. Smith of the Twelve [apostles] entered the Celestial room at 3 P.M. Orson Pratt at ½ p[ast]. 3.

List 3 Male Department commenced at 2 P.M.

[See pages 469-70 for excerpted portion.]

—Seventies Record, Book B.

....

At dusk I [Thomas Bullock], Henrietta [Bullock] and Lucy [Clayton] went to the Temple, dressed, sat in the Cel[estial]. Room, and shook hands with B[righam]. Young. H[eber]. C. Kimball. O[rson]. Hyde, P[arley]. P. Pratt, [and] A[masa]. Lyman. Went into the President's room when I and [the] two others were sealed up to eternal life, thro[ugh]' time to come forth in the morn of the resurrection, and thro' all eternity. Were sealed up against all sin except the sin against the Holy Ghost and the shedding of innocent blood by A[masa]. Lyman. I praise the Lord for this great manifestation of his love and mercy towards me and grant that the happiness which I now enjoy may last for all eternity. And may my whole soul continually praise his holy name. Amen.[25] Afterwards we staid till

---

24. James J. Strang (1813-56) joined the LDS church in February 1844 and claimed succession to Joseph Smith after the latter was killed four months later. After Strang's excommunication in August 1844, he founded colonies at Voree, Wisconsin, and Beaver Island, Michigan, and was crowned king of his theocracy in 1850. In 1856 he was shot by one of his followers; upon his death, most of those who had joined with him affiliated themselves with the Reorganized Church of Jesus Christ of Latter Day Saints (later Community of Christ), organized four years later. Today, about 200 people identify themselves as Strangites.

25. As none of the Bullocks is listed in "A Book of Anointing" as having received the second anointing, this ceremony must have been an eternal marriage sealing only.

[Washings and anointings for Friday, January 23, 1846—third excerpt]

Seventies			
"	22 Willard Darrow born June 25, 1819		Millen Atwood born May 24, 1817
"	23 James Wareham " July 2, 1813		32 John S. Deavenport " Feb. 25, 1816
"	24 Chauncey Peck " July 29, 1816		33 Avin M. Stoddard " Sept. 1, 1825
"	25 Samuel L. Paine " Sept. 1, 1808		34 Levi Young " Jan. 1, 1830
"	26 Robert A. Russell " Mar. 12, 1812		35 Isum Flynn " Mar 10, 1826
"	27 Francis C. Case " June 17, 1813		36 Zadok K. Judd " Oct. 15, 1827
"	28 William A. Hickman " Apl. 16, 1815		37 Egbert Elsworth " June 4, 1816
"	29 Erastus Gee " July 29, 1828	High Priests	William Wilsey " May 18, 1797
"	30 Edwin Rushton " June 1, 1824	Elder	2 Chauncey Turner " May 19, 1800
"	31 John M. Freeman " Nov. 20, 1823		3 Joseph D. Lane " May 3, 1788
			4 Ira J. Dibble " May 23, 1820

Washed by Charles Bird and Samuel Moore. Anointed by P. G. Sessions and L. A. Shirtliff

Ordinations

Willard Darrow, Robert A. Russell, Levi Young, and Isum Flyn were ordained by Joseph Young, Edson Barney, Levi Hancock and Israel Barlow. Finished at 17 minutes p. 3. P.M.

Female Department. commenced at 10 min p. 2.

Harriet Wareham born May 22, 1818	Eliza Thomas born Mar. 4, 1824
Emily Waterman " Dec. 1826	Nancy Lane " July 31, 1795
Margaret B. Russel " Oct. 3, 1811	Mary Paine " Oct. 5, 1816
Theisa Bowley " Oct. 7, 1828	Hannah F. Turner " Jan. 18, 1805
Cynthia Leffingwell " Jan. 5, 1832	Mary Ann Turner " Mar. 30, 1827

Amanda M. Gee [born] Jan. 5, 1823
Susan E. Gee " Jan 31, 1828
Catharine Wilsey " Dec. 28, 1803
Anne Huston " May 8, 1821
Mary Ann Gilmore " Aug. 12, 1824
Olive Electa Elsworth " July 2, 1822
Amanda McHorton " Aug. 3, 1830
Mary Ann Rushton " Apl. 23, 1823
Mary Less Gee born Dec. 31, 1796

Mariah Peck [born] Jan. 2, 1821
Elizabeth Dunn " July 4, 1828
Mary Ann Case " June 11, 1812
Flora C. Gleeson " Aug 2, 1819
Sarah Hickman " Sep. 11, 1829
Lucretia A. Dibble " June 23, [illegible]
Amy Gardner " Aug 14, 1801
Lettice Rushton " Dec. 8, 1784

were washed and anointed in the House of the Lord; by Lydia Granger, Jane A. Green, Ann Whitney, Sarah Smith, Nancy Cahoon, Hester Brown, Sophronia Harmon, Phebe Miller, Merilla Johnson. Finished at 40 min p. 3.

—Seventies Record, Book B, oversized portion, January 23, 1846.

midnight rejoicing to the sound of music with songs of praise. Pres[ident]. Young addressed the assembly and H[eber]. C. Kimball offered up prayer to our Heavenly Father—especially for those who had made covenants that night.

—Thomas Bullock, Diary.

....

At 1 [o'clock I] went to a council in the Temple with the Twelve [apostles], Bishops &c ... Evening with [Newel K.] Whitney dividing goods purchased by [Erastus] Snow. R[euben]. Miller reports that [James] Strang is making heavy breaches in the church, and drawing many after him. In one place 30 families have left the church and gone with him. It is also rumored that many of the saints here are full of Strangism and talking [is] had in his favor. Among the rest are John Gaylord and W[illia]m. A. Sangor who are openly advocating his rights to the presidency. I [William Clayton] read a copy of a letter perporting to be wrote by Pres[iden]t. Joseph Smith on the 18th June 1844 in which he appoints Strang as his successor. The letter is a base forgery and is well calculated to deceive the simple minded and unfaithful.It is also rumored that many are dissatisfied because the Twelve & some others are going West without taking the whole Church. This is a matter of impossibility and the saints have no cause for complaint. Amongst the rest are many of the Temple hands who are complaining much. The arrangements are made by which the whole church can go *comfortably,* but it is necessary that some men should go beforehand to prepare a place for the rest and the Twelve & some others have to go to save their lives for there are plans laid for their destruction.

—William Clayton, Diary.

....

[W]e [Joseph Fielding, Hannah Fielding, and Mary Ann Peake] were sealed in the Temple by Heber C Kimball and on the same day we were also anointed by Parley P. Pratt[.]

—Joseph Fielding, Diary, LDS Archives.

....

Jane Snyder & myself were made husband & wife by the ordinances of Priesthood in the Lords House ^by H[eber]. C. Kimball^ & also were anointed King & Queen, Priest & Priestess, by P[arley]. P. Pratt Phin[e]as Richards, [and] Lorenzo Snow[.]

—Franklin D. Richards, Diary.

I received with Artimesia [Beaman] and Minerva [White] the sealings & further endowments.

The Spirit, Power and wisdom of God reigned continually in the Temple and all felt satisfied ~~that~~ during the two months we occupied it in the endowments of the Saints, ~~that~~ we were amply paid for all our labour in building it.

—Erastus Snow, Diary, LDS Archives.

....

One hundred and twenty-eight persons received ordinances in the Temple. I continued administering at the altar.

—"Manuscript History of Brigham Young," in *History of the Church,* 7:573, and *Manuscript History of Brigham Young,* p. 18.

....

Nauvoo temple endowments performed on this date for:

First Company: Samantha Woodstock, Susan J. Jones, Jefferson Edmonds, Elizabeth Ann Edmonds, Thomas Richmond, Elizabeth Ann Richmond, Telemachus Rogers, Eliza Rogers, Mary Gheen, John Gheen, Charles Cunningham, Sarah Cunningham, Daniel D. McArthur, Matilda C. McArthur, Sidney Roberts, Sarah Ann Roberts, John Wait, Willard Woodstock, Margaret White, Dustin Amy, Leonora Amy, Levi Osgood, Patience Osgood, Melinda Tyson, John Tyson, Ira Ames, Sarah Ames, William Box, Olive Box, William Bickmore, Christeen Bickmore, Moses Deming, Maria Deming, Clara Lake, John Thomas, John Carter, Elizabeth R. Carter, Anna Perry, and William C./Atkinson Smoot.

Second Company: Amy C. Aldridge, Reddick N. Allred, Amelia M. Robinson, Lucy Allred, Thomas Moss, Sarah Ripley, Agnes Moss, Mary Ramsbottom, David Savage, Elizabeth Owen, Alanson Ripley, Mary A. Savage, John G. Wilkins, Nancy Wilkins, Almira Ferguson, Mary H. Parker, Jesse Lampson, Ruth Lampson, John Parker, William C. Perry, Eliza B. Perry, Sarah Chandler, Isaac Ferguson, Samuel Leaver, Mary Ann Leaver, Hannah Marah, John Parker, Ellen Douglass, David B. Lamoreaux, Belinda Wyborn, Sarah Patrick, Mary Ann Lamoreaux, Susanna Stillson, Warren Foot, Sidney Foot, Henry Jolly, Barbara Jolly, Lovina Chandler, William L. McIntyre, Rowena Chandler, Spicer W. Crandall, Lucinda McIntyre, and Sarah Crandall.

Third Company: Samuel L. Paine Jr., Mary Paine, Robert A. Russell, Eliza Thomas, Ruth Hess, Margaret B. Russell, William Wilsey, Harriet Wareham, James Wareham, Chauncey Turner, Hannah F. Turner, Mary

Ann Turner, Catharine Wilsey, Edwin Rushton, Mary Ann Rushton, Lettice Rushton, Anne Huston, Chauncey Peck, Erastus S. Gee, Maria Peck, William A. Hickman, Sarah/Elizabeth Hickman, Francis C. Case, Mary Ann Case, Amanda M. Gee, Olive A. Ellsworth, Susan E. Gee, Egbert Ellsworth, John M. Freeman, Theresa Bowley, Flora C. Gleason, Joseph T. Lane, Mary Ann Gilman, Ira T. Dibble, Lucretia A. Dibble, Willard Darrow, Emily Waterman, Elizabeth Dunn, Amy Gardner, Isum Flynn, Cynthia Leffingwell, Millen Atwood, Amanda M. Hartson, John S. Davenport, Arvin M. Stoddard, Levi Young, Zadoc K. Judd, and Nancy Lane.

—Summary of information compiled by the Temple Index Bureau, *Nauvoo Temple Endowment Register: 10 December 1845 to 8 February 1846.*

....

Second anointings performed on this date:

Erastus Snow, Artimesia (Beaman) Snow, and Minerva (White) Snow, anointed by Parley P. Pratt; Joseph Bates Noble, Mary (Beaman) Noble, and Mary Ann (Washburn) Noble, anointed by George Miller; Franklin D. Richards and Jane (Snyder) Richards, anointed by Parley P. Pratt; William Weeks and Caroline (Allen) Weeks, anointed by George Miller; Joseph Fielding, Hannah (Greenwood) Fielding, and Mary Ann (Peck) Fielding, anointed by Parley P. Pratt; Mercy R. (Fielding) Thompson to John Taylor for time and Robert B. Thompson (deceased) for eternity (John Taylor, proxy), anointed by Parley P. Pratt; Mary (Ramsbottom) Taylor to John Taylor, anointed by Parley P. Pratt; and John Scott, Elizabeth (Menery) Scott, and Mary (Pugh) Scott, anointed by George Miller.

—Summarized from "Book of Anointings."

....

Sealings for the living performed on this date:

James Tillman S. Allred to Eliza Bridget Manwaring; William Moore Allred to Orissa Angelia Bates; Josiah Arnold to Elizabeth Bliss; John Boylston to Sarah Vanthranham Van Wagoner; Thomas Bullock to Henrietta Rushton, and Lucy Caroline Clayton; Eli Chase to Olive Hills; Stephen Chase to Orryanna Rowe; Peter Clinton to Melissa Diantha Snow; Frederick Cook to Sarah Elizabeth Davis; William Spencer Covert to Mary Cartright; Charles Root Dana to Margaret Kennedy and Emily Waterman; Howard Egan to A. Tamson Parshley and Nancy A. Redding; Joseph Fielding to Hannah Greenwood and Mary Ann Peake [Peck];

George Davison Grant to Elizabeth Wilson; Harvey Green to Jane Ann Rich; Richard Harrison to Mary Ann Whitaker; Benjamin Jones to Anna Stout; Abel Lamb to Almira Merrill; George Mayer [Meyer] to Ann Yost; William Miller to Mary Ann Turner; Ezra Oakley to Elizabeth DeGroot; James Olive to Sina [Sinia] Martin; Joseph Bates Noble Sr. to Mary Adeline Beman, Sarah B. Alley, and Mary Ann Washburn; John Parker to Ellen Briggs Douglas; Thomas Bryant Parker to Martha Ann Nelson; Albert Petty to Catherine Petty; Franklin D. Richards to Jane Snyder; Sidney Roberts to Sarah Ann Rowell; William Rowley to Mary Ann Maddox; Henry Royle to Matilda Braddock; John Scott to Elizabeth Menery and Mary Pew [Pugh]; Peter Shirts to Margaret Cameron; Charles Smith to Sarah Price; Erastus Snow to Artimesia Beman [Beaman] and Minerva White; William Symons to Helenora Graham; John Taylor to Mary Rainsbottom; and John Weinel to Alice Daniels.

—Summarized from the Book of Living Sealings.

Sealings for the dead performed on this date:

Elizabeth Clarke (Matilda Braddock, proxy) to Henry Royle, Heber C. Kimball officiating; Hannah Moorcroft (Mary Ann Maddox, proxy) to William Rowley, Heber C. Kimball officiating; Sarah Pichard (Jane Ann Rich, proxy) to Harvey Green, Heber C. Kimball officiating; Elizabeth Lewis (Melissa D. Snow, proxy) to Peter Clinton, Heber C. Kimball officiating; Cardelia Jane Clark (Matilda Caroline Fuller, proxy) to Daniel Duncan McArthur, Amasa M. Lyman officiating; Martha McDuffee (Elizabeth Bliss, proxy) to Josiah Arnold, Amasa M. Lyman officiating; Robert B. Thompson (John Taylor, proxy) to Mercy Rachel Fielding, Heber C. Kimball officiating;[26] Lydia Hadlock (Anna Stout, proxy) to Benjamin Jones, Amasa M. Lyman officiating; Nathaniel Thomas (Charles R. Dana, proxy) to Susan Luce, Brigham Young officiating;[27] and Asenath Marvin [?] (Martha Jones, proxy) to John Harrington, Brigham Young officiating.

—Summarized from the Book of Proxy Sealings.

Saturday, January 24, 1846

I [Brigham Young] attended a general meeting of the official members of the church held in the 2nd story of the Temple which I had or-

26. Mercy Fielding was also sealed to John Taylor for time.

27. Susan Luce was also sealed to Charles Dana for time.

dered for the purpose of arrainging the affairs of the church prior to our exit from this place— The meeting having been organized [i.e., called to order] previous to my coming by A[lmon]. W. Babbit & C[harles]. C. Rich[,] whom I sent [ahead] for that purpose[,] O[rson]. Pratt was nominated to take the chair & D[avid]. Candland Clerk of this meeting[, which] carried by unamious consent of the assembly[.] the object of the meeting[, to endorse the selection of trustees for the church,] had also been stated [prior to my arrival.] but in order that entire satisfaction should be produced I arose & said I wish the Brethren to understand correctly the design of appointing those Trustees— we do not intend dropping the present Trustees but we [will] appoint 5 more to act in concert with Bishop [Newel K.] Whitney & [George] Miller & take charge of the church as well as [of] individual property & this we do for the accommodation & convenance of those that are obliged to leave for safety[,] also to have them (the p[roposed]. Trustees) take the place of Bishop Whitney & Miller in their absence that the work of the Lord may continue here[,] that is[,] the finishing of the Temple & Nauvoo House & the disposing of Property & fitting of the Saints & sending them on after us[.] but to return as regard [to] the old Trustees (Whitney & Miller) I will never give them a quit claim or Suffer them to resign theire commission by my consent—Where ever we go we want them with us & they shall be the Trustees wherever we go but it is wisdom to take the course that we are proposing to you[.] the old Bishops will leave soon in all probbity & it is advisable to appoint & leave some good substantial eficient men to act for & in behalf of the church & people[.] I want Br[others]. Whitney & Miller here while we are [here.] I will [now] Speak [of our] designs relative to our journey West[.] we intend to start a company of young men & some few Families perhaps within a few weeks[.] this company will go untill we can find a good location beyond the borders of the united states. & there stop & put in a sumer crop that we me [sic] may have something to subsist upon & there remain until we Shall—can make further discoveries— We have been forced to take this stept & that too by Men that holds the Keys of power[.] I find no fault with the Law or constitution under which we live[;] it is good enough[,] but I despise the abuse of those Laws—God! Men & Angels abhor it. I hope to find a place, where no self righteous Neighbors can say that we are obnoxious to them— I exhort you not to be self important— we have covenants to remove the Poor that are worthy[.] this we will do[,] God being our helper[, if we] walk Humbly before the Lord[.] be upright & sustain yourselves & learn that you are engaged in an important move[.] If any should want to stay Let them do it Pause & should any want to go with us that are not members let them have the prevelege & bid them welcome for I consider every man that is a true republican as Bone of my Bone of my Bone & flesh! of my flesh & if any one wishes to follow Sidney [Rigdon] W[illia]m Smith J[ames]. J. Strang I say go away & [we] will all cut them off from the church & let them take their course for salvation[.] I know where the Power of the Priesthood lies[.] But now I will drop the subject of the out laws & refer to the enemy of all righteousness who seek[s] our downfall[.] he has sent [a] bogus Factory [to our city] & [is] lying [about the] cir- ~~cumstes~~ [circumstances of its founding and, through the] medium [of counterfeit coin] through[out] the country [and] by [spreading the] wholesale [untruth] that we [are the ones] making Spurious Coin & exchanging it by waggon loads as Land office money & a thousand other lies[,] all of which I pronounce to be a base fabricated lie[;] Nevertheless we may have to suffer repeated wrongs in consiquence of those falsehoods that are & will be circulated about us[.] but my Faith is that God! Rule[s] the elements & the Prince & Power of the air will be Stayed while the Lord will fight our battles[.] as in the days of Moses we will see deli~~b=~~ [v]erance brought to pass although there may be blood shed frequently[.] still this must needs be that the scriptures might be fulfil[le]d[.] it is but a smawel [small] mat[t]er for a saint to lay his Life down[.] if he is only prepared to receive his change when he takes his exit from this world[,] he goes into the Society of disembodied Spirits & there become[s] one of those that wait the reserction of the body[.] if Humility and Faithfulness has characterized your live you will find your state much better than the present[.] I say the time will come & many of you shall see it when the purposes the Lord will be carried out. upon the Heads of those who has committed ungodly deeds upon his Saints[.] they will not be permitted to run at large as they now do[,] neither will you be permited to use the Name of the deity in vain as you have in [past] times done[.] the more knowledge that you will have the less inclination you will have to diveation from the law of God[.] this Nation is fearful that we will turn the world upside down. & accomplish wonderful things in the Land & in fact[,] they have reason to fear[,] for their Kings & Noblem[e]n & the wise among them have been confounded by th[os]e in our Ministerial Body— [T]hough confounded[,] it is hard to convince them of the Truth—

[W]hen we leave here[,] fear & Terror seezis them lest when we leave them that we will convert the savages of the Forest & [they] say that we [should make our intentions regarding the Indians clear, whether we] shall not teach them the principles of civilization & demestical usages or not. I say we will & further we would yet bring Salvation to this Nation if they would cease their hostitilites & repent[.] The Lord has said, that he would fight our Battles & if this Nation shall still continue to be actuated towards [us] with a persecuting spirit[,] vengence shall come from the Lord & not from me upon this Nation until they shal be uterly wasted[.] but I intend to preach & do all the good that I can[.] I was informed this morning that some persons were advocating the folly & nonsense of J[ames]. J. Strang[.] Now if they wish to follow him let them go. they are at liberty to [do] as they please[.] I want no person to follow us contrary to theirr wishes[.] thierfore let no one go off & say that they are in danger of their lives amongst us because that we differ in opinion[.] this is not so[.] Mr. J[ames]. Strang represent[s] Jos[eph] Smith as the Stone & Shepherd of Israel of & that he Strang is his Sucsessor in office—this is certainly an obserd idea & comes in contast with Joseph's views relative to the matter— (he Jos[eph]) Says in the Book of Doctrine & covenants & so does the scriptures that christ is the shepherd & stone of Israel & not Jos[eph] nor Strang. However I will not consume time to talking such nonsense[;] it is not worth the Short Jorney of a mans Horse[.] yet there are those that tire on the way & wish to rest to rest [sic][.] they think that they have gone far Enough. but those that endure to the End I think will get the crown[.] When the time comes [for] our Pioneers to start then there will be no ces[s]ation of gathering for we must gather up the House of Israel & every man will have his Penny for his services—let there be no feelings about this matter should you not be first[.] we are laying a Foundation for you all that will bring you all up in rememberence before the Lord—in his own due time & none of you will be neglected—I have one request to make of all the Saints that expect to emigrate with us & that is that they do just as they are asked by their leaders with thire property & means[—] they [who] are apointed to arrainge that matter. & if you will do this thing I tell you now there shall never be a lack in this church[.] we want the captains of (100) to borrow or raise out of their $1,000 out of their companies[.] remember that from the head you are nourished[.] if any man can say that he has been wronged out of his Money by the bishop let him speak & it shall be restored to him again[.] but I know that is not so[.]

Keep your money in circulation & you will do good & will be blesst in so doeing[.] retain it when the poor are crying for bread & it will prove a curse to you[.] be honorable in all your dealings promp & pun[c]tual to pay all your debts & restore confidence & let promptiness & punctuality be the Standard with you & the very God of Peace will pour out blessings upon [us] that [you] cannot have room enough to receive[.]

The chairman then arose & proceeded to the nominations of the Trustee[s.] at this junction A[lmon]. W. Babbitt pro[po]sed to me that we drop. J[acob]. B. Backenstos one of the proposed committe[e] & take an other (not by objection however) & let a part of the committe act as Trustees for the Nauvoo House[,] upon which I spoke a few words more[.] we intind to finish the Temple & the Nauvoo House as far as putting on the Roof & putting in the windows & we shall drop all Political opperattions & church government after (we the 12 [apostles] leaves here)[.] by so doing we can preserve our public buildings from the torch[.] I propose that all the saints will lay down their property & for the building the Temple & the Nauvoo House & help the poor away such as must go in the first company—[For] Temple Trustees & [of the] Nauvoo House I then nominated Almon W. Babbitt[,] Joseph L— Haywood & John S. Fulmer [to] be the Trustees for the Temple & Henry M. Miller & John M. Bernhisel be the Trustees & committe for the Nauvoo House[.] carried without a desenting vote[.] on motion the meeting adjourned at. 2. P.M. after which I assended the stairs which led up into the celestial departments[,] cal[l]ed at the Dining room[,] & took some refreshments— then repaired to room No. 1. where I continued at the Alt[a]r till near midnight.

—Brigham Young, Diary.

....

Harison Burgess, Lucius N. Scovil, Isaac Allred, David D. Yeardsley, Harvey Green and Samuel Richards met in room No 9, to consecrate oil. Twenty bottles were consecrated; Harrison Burgess being mouth. After which they prayed for the Twelve [apostles], Brother Woodruff, Brother Pratt in the South Sea Islands and the saints in general, with [i.e., including] brothers Lyman Wight, [James] Emmet and their companies[.] L[ucius]. N. Scovil lead in prayer.

List 1 Male Department commenced at 20 [minutes] to 9

[See pages 479-83 for excerpted portion.]

This afternoon, a meeting was held in the 2nd Story of the Temple. The object of the meeting was to elect trustees to supply the places of the

[Washings and anointings for Saturday, January 24, 1846]

Seventies		Seventies	
	1 Joseph Taylor born June 4, 1825		12 Gilbert Morse born Sep. 20, 1815
"	2 Thomas Dobson " Feb. 8, 1819	"	13 David Brown " Oct. 2, 1822
"	3 Thomas C. [illegible] " Aug 25, 1820	"	14 John D. Huntington " Feb. 11, 1827
"	4 Pleasant G. Taylor " Feb. 8, 1827	"	15 John Brown " Aug 25, 1819
"	5 John Anderson " Mar. 9, 1796	"	16 Francis Brown " Nov 2, 1827
"	6 Jacob E. Terry " July 4, 1805	"	17 Thomas Pierce " Aug 25, 1819
"	7 Samuel R. Aiken " Oct. 28, 1803	H. Priest	1 Samuel Bringhurst " Dec. 21, 1812
"	8 William S. Smith " Dec. 1804	"	2 William Niswanger " May 11, 1796
"	9 John S. Lott " Mar. 22, 1826	Seventy	18 Carlos G. Murray " Mar. 12, 1829
"	10 John R. Murdock " Sep 13, 1826	"	19 Eli H. Pierce " July 29, 1827
"	11 Jordon J. Hendrickson " Jan. 8, 1809	Elder	1 James Mendenhall " July 25, 1810

were washed ~~and anointed~~ by Edward P. Duzett and Chandler Holbrook. Anointed by Simeon A. Dunn and Samuel Moore.

Ordinations

John D. Huntington, Thomas Pierce, were ordained Seventies by Joseph Young and Randolph Alexander. William Niswanger and Samuel Bringhurst were ordained High Priests by William Huntington and Peter Haws. Finished by 5. m. to 10.

List 1 Female Department commenced at 10 A.M.

Francis Hendrixon born May 8, 1809	Francis Kelly born Dec. 6, 1768
Mary Mariah Terry " May 5, 1813	Amanda Jane Ivie " May 12, 1824
Mary Taylor " Feb 4 1826	Sarah K. B. Dobson " Aug 24, 1823
Mary Niswanger " Aug 22, 1811	Almira Lott " Dec. 15, 1830
Eliza Mendenhall " Mar 8, 1811	Cynthia Ann Morse " Nov. 19, 1823

Minerva Stowell [born] Apl. 23, 1824	Melissa Lott [born] Jan 9, 1824
Pamelia Jane Lott " Oct. 2, 1832	Mary Lott " [illegible]
Eleanor Bringhurst born Dec 25, 1816	Lydia Anderson born July 21, 1792
Mary Thompson " Aug. 5, 1823	Hannah Holbrook " July 18, 1806
Catherine Barton " Nov. 9, 1805	Mary Parker " July 9, 1829
Mary Caul " Mar. 27, 1812	Naomi Murray " July 9, 1830

were washed and anointed by Lydia Granger, Mary J. Horn, Hester A. E. Brown, Nancy Cahoon, Elizabeth Durphy and Unice Holbrook.

List 2 commenced at 11 15/60 Male Department

Seventies		Sev.	
	20 Reuben Strong born Apl. 20, 1820		29 Weeden V. Yakes born Apl. 5, 1810
"	21 Benjamin Willis " Mar. 29, 1792	H. Priests	3 John Burscough " Dec. 25, 1795
"	22 William K. Rice " Oct. 27, 1822	"	4 Calvin Beebe " July 1, 1800
"	23 James Rhodeback " May 22, 1807	"	5 Absalom Perkins " Nov. 22, 1797
"	24 Levi Lightfoot " Mar. 13, 1816	"	6 Edmund Durfee " Sept. 4, 1814
"	25 William L. Perkins " June 18, 1819	"	7 Daniel Sanger " Sept. 17, 1782
"	26 Daniel Allen " Dec. 9, 1804	Elders	2 Daniel P. Clark " Sept. 29, 1824
"	27 Jeremiah Carpenter " Aug. 29, 1807		were washed by Chandler Holbrook and Edward Duzett
"	28 Peter Fife " Apl. 5, 1806		

List 2 In the Female Department, commenced washing at 11 45/60

Susan Ann Lightfoot born Nov. 15, 1814	Mary Sanger born Dec 31, 1783
Mary Ann Allen " June 11, 1813	Harriet A. Brown " Feb 11, 1828
Jane Bauscow " Nov. 17, 1790	Mary Brown " Apl. 14, 1829

Eliza A. Hakes " Nov. 2, 1803	Sarah Very " May 19, 1788
Hannah E Strong " Jan. 26, 1825	Jane Fisher " Sep 22, 1792
Rachel Drollinger " June 14, 1798	Caroline Durphy " Aug 12, 1821
Mary Ann Perkins " Feb. 10, 1823	Doreas Brown " Aug 20, 1792
Subruit Beebe " May 17, 1800	Nancy Perkins " May 1, 1792
Lucy W. Rice " Feb. 23, 1824	Hannah Willis " Apl. 15, 1802
Sarah Ann Willis " Feb. 4, 1820	Mary Brown " June 2, 1806
Sarah M. Clark " Dec. 10, 1825	Phebe Rhodeback " June 25, 1811
Susan Carpenter " Apl. 11, 1814	Ann Longstroth " Aug. 3, 1796
Nancy Longstroth " Apl. 15, 1828	

were washed and anointed by Mary S. Horn, Unice Holbrook, Hester A. E. Brown, Nancy Cahoon, Sophronia Harmon and Elizabeth Durphy. Finished at 15 p. 1 P.M.

List 3 In the Female [sic] Department

commenced washing and anointing the following persons, commencing at 5 p. 2

Seventies

	Levan Simmons born Aug. 1, 1812	Johan Thornton born May [illegible]
"	31 Joseph Woodward " Mar. 16, 1816	36 Ezra Strong " [illegible]
"	32 Charles A. Terry " Nov. 10, 1820	37 Walter M. Edwards " Apl 20 [illegible]
"	33 George D. Van Beck " Feb 9 1815	38 Samuel Keele " [illegible]
"	34 Horace Thornton " Jan 12, 1810	39 Joseph G. Hall [illegible]

Saturday evening January 24th 1846

Seventies	Elder
Horace M. Alexander born Feb 15, 1812	Thomas Bingham born July 19, 1824

[Seventies]	Otis L. Terry [born] Mar. 12, 1818	[Elder]	John Smith [born] Sep 22, 1832
"	James Rollin " June 30, 1798	"	Amaziah Hamden " July 26, 1789
"	Thomas Forsyth " Sep 20, 1813		

were washed ~~and~~ by Edward P Duzett and Chandler Holbrook. Anointed by Simeon A. Dunn and Samuel Moore.

Ordinations.

James Bingham and Amaziah Hamden were ordained to the office of Elder by President Benjamin L. Clapp. Fin. at 5. to 3. P.M.

In the Female Department commenced at 15 p. 2

List 3

Catherine Seibel born Dec 24, 1814	Susannah Mohr born May 15, 1791
Nancy W. Ott " Aug. 27, 1822	Margaret Woodward " July 27, 1817
Philinda S. Terry " July 8, 1819	Harriet Simmons " Mar 30, 1821
Isabella Begg " Nov. 1785	Fanny M. Terry " July 8, 1825
Mariah L. Bingham " June 23, 1828	Adaline E. Banbuk " Apl. 28, 1819
Sarah Morris " Nov. 6, 1810	Sarah Colburn " Dec. 31, 1810
Susannah Thornton Apl. 21, 1814	Nancy Alexander " Dec. 8, 1819
Sarah Hillman " Aug. 24, 1797	Mercy Rollin " Apl. 4, 1806
Mariah Strong " Feb. 18, 1824	Elizabeth Taylor " Mar. 31, 1809
Sarah Moore " July 29, 1803	Sally Adams " May 29, 1825
Isabella Forsyth " Mar. 17, 1819	Mahala G. Edwards " Nov. 12, 1821
Delaney Hall " Apl. 12, 1818	

were washed and Anointed by Mary J. Horn, Mary Smith, Unice Holbrook, Nancy Cahoon, Elizabeth Coolidge and Elizabeth Durphy. Finished at 20 p. 3.

In the Male Department commencing at 20 p. 4 P.M.

Seventies		Seventies	
	Thomas McKenzie Sep 29, 1869		~~Christopher Williamson~~
"	Thomas Steed " Dec 13, 1826	Seventies	Guy C. Wilson born Aug 31, 1801
"	William Mathews " June 16, 1826	"	Nelson Merkley " Nov 11, 1829
"	Ephraim M. Thomas " Apl. 6, 1803	"	David E. Bunnel " June 25, 1809
"	Whitford G. Wilson " June 4, 1799	"	John B. Atchison " Jan. 19, 1823
"	Littlejohn Utley " Feb. 18, 1806	Elder	Christopher Williamson " Mar 7, 1789

were washed ~~and anointed~~ by Perrigrine Sessions, and Joseph Holbrook. Anointed by Simeon A. Dunn and Samuel Moore. 5 P.M.

In the Female Department commencing at 30 M. p. 4

Abigail Williams born Feb. 23, 1799	Ann R. Gould born Feb. 10, 1818
Mary McKenzie " Apl. 29, 1818	Mary Wilson " Nov. 15, 1805
Jane Steed " Aug. 15, 1826	Elizabeth Utley " June 31, 1809
Elizabeth Wilson " Sep. 26, 1803	Sarah Rummel " Sep. 19, 1810
Roxena Repsher " May 20, 1805	Rachel Ann Sherman " Feb 8, 1812
Melinda Atchinson " Mar. 31, 1823	Eliza [illegible] " [illegible]

[remainder of page illegible] Horn, Nancy Cahoon, Elizabeth Cooledge, Hester A. E. Brown, Sophronia Harmon, Unice Holbrook and Elizabeth Durphy. Finished at 10 m. to 5.

—Seventies Record, Book B, oversized portion, January 24, 1846.

trustees of the Church and the Nauvoo House. Almon Babbit, Joseph L. Haywood, and [blank] were elected ~~to~~ as Trustees in trust for the Temple &c. J[ohn]. M. Bernhisel and William Miller were appointed Trustees of the Nauvoo House Association.[28]

—Seventies Record, Book B.

....

[O]ur 4 Children were washed, anointed and Sealed to Jos[ep]h & Hannah Fielding And we (Joseph & Hannah) were sealed to Hyrum Smith for time and Eternity by elders B[righam] Young & H[eber]. C. Kimball[.]

—Joseph Fielding, Diary, LDS Archives.

....

During this time in the winter of [18]45 and [18]46 not withstanding my sickness I went into the Temple in Nauvoo and received my endowment by washing and anointing and was sealed to my wife Sophia for time and all eternity, and afterwards we [were] annointed the second time a king and queen in the Kingdom of God which annointing [end of line.]

—Noah Packard, "Autobiography," LDS Archives.

....

One hundred and fifty-one persons received ordinances in the Temple. I [Brigham Young] attended a general meeting of the official members of the church held in the second story of the Temple, for the purpose of arranging the business affairs of the church prior to our exit from this place.

The meeting being organized previous to my arrival[,] Elder Orson Pratt was appointed chairman.

I explained to the brethren the object of appointing trustees, and informed them that the trustees would act in concert with Bishops [Newel K.] Whitney and [George] Miller while they remained here; and that when the Twelve [apostles] left the bishops would accompany them, and that the trustees now appointed would carry on the finishing of the Temple and the Nauvoo House, also dispose of our property, fit out the saints and send them westward. It is wisdom to take this course that we may have efficient men to act for and in behalf of the church and people. I

28. The Nauvoo House was to be a hotel for visitors to Nauvoo, and although the Nauvoo House Association was formed to help secure donations and investments, the project was officially instigated and sanctioned by the church. Like the temple, it was abandoned when the Saints left Nauvoo in early 1846.

want Bishops Whitney and Miller here while we are here, and when we go, they will go with us.

We intend to start a company of young men and some few families perhaps within a few weeks. This company will travel until they can find a good location beyond the settlements, and there stop and put in a summer crop, that we may have something to subsist upon, and a portion of us remain there until we can make further discoveries.

We are forced to this policy by those who are in authority. I find no fault with the Constitution or laws of our country, they are good enough. It is the abuse of those laws which I despise, and which God, good men and angels abhor.

I hope we will find a place, where no self-righteous neighbors can say that we are obnoxious to them; I exhort you brethren not to be self-important. We have covenanted to remove the poor that are worthy, and this we intend to do, God being our helper. Let us walk humbly before the Lord, be upright and sustain yourselves and realize that we are engaged in a great and important movement. If any want to go with us that are not members of the church bid them welcome; for I look upon every man that is a true republican as bone of my bone and flesh of my flesh; and if any wish to follow Sidney Rigdon or J[ames]. J. Strang I say let them go; we will cut them off from the church, and let them take their own course for salvation.

I know where the power of the priesthood lies and I know that the enemy of all righteousness seeks our downfall, but God is our preserver.

A set of bogus-makers who recently commenced operations in this city, who are determined to counterfeit coin here by wagonloads and make it pass upon the community as land office money; [they] are determined to be revenged upon us, because we would not permit them to pursue their wicked business in Nauvoo, they have scattered through the country circulating their bogus money and spreading lies and every species of falsehood, saying that we are engaged in bogus-making in order thereby to conceal their crimes, and screen themselves from observation and punishment, and at the same time be avenged upon us for not consenting to the establishment of their bogus mints at Nauvoo.

Nevertheless, we may have to suffer repeated wrongs in consequence of those falsehoods that are and which will be circulated about us; but my faith is that God will rule the elements, and the Prince and power of the air will be stayed, and the Lord will fight our battles, as in the days of Moses;

and we will see the deliverance brought to pass. Although, there may be bloodshed frequently, still this must needs be that the scriptures may be fulfilled.

It is but a small matter for us to lay down our lives if we are prepared for the change; when we take our exit from this world we go into the society of disembodied spirits, and there become one of those who await the resurrection of the body: if humility and faithfulness has characterized our lives, our condition will be much better than the present. This nation is fearful that we will turn the world upside down and accomplish wonderful things in the land: our elders have confounded the wise men if they have not converted them. The nation are afraid that we will convert the savages of the forest; we will teach them and all with whom we may have intercourse, and further we will yet bring salvation to this nation if they will cease their hostilities against us, and repent of their sins. The Lord has said he would fight our battles, and if this nation still continues to be actuated towards us with a persecuting spirit, vengeance shall come from the Lord upon them, until they shall be utterly wasted; but I intend to preach and do all the good that I can.

When the time comes to start westward we will continue to gather, until Israel is gathered; let there be no feelings about who shall go first; those who go first will lay a foundation for those who shall come after, and none will be neglected in their time.

I have one request to make of all the saints that expect to emigrate with us, that they be subject to their leaders, with their property and means, and if this is done I can say there never will be a lack in the church. If any man can say that he has been wronged out of his money by the bishops, let him speak and it shall be restored to him again; but I am aware it is not so. Keep your money in circulation and it will enable you to do good and you will be blessed in so doing; retain your money when the poor around you are crying for bread and it will prove a curse to you. Be honorable in all your dealings, prompt and punctual to pay all your debts and restore confidence, let promptness and punctuality be the standard with you and the God of peace will pour out blessings upon you that there shall not be room enough to receive them.

We intend to finish the Temple and the Nauvoo House, as far as putting on the roof and putting in the windows are concerned, and we shall drop all political operations and church government, and by so doing we may preserve our public buildings from the torch. I propose that all the saints lay down their property to be used in building the Temple, the Nauvoo House and helping the poor away, such as must go in the first company.

I nominated Almon W. Babbitt, Joseph L. Heywood, and John S. Fullmer, trustees for the building of the Temple and Henry W. Miller and John M. Bernhisel, trustees or committee for the building of the Nauvoo House, which nominations were seconded and carried without a dissenting voice.

Two p.m., on motion, the meeting adjourned, after which I ascended the stairs—called at the dining room and partook of some refreshment, then repaired to room No. 1 where I continued administering at the altar until midnight.

—"Manuscript History of Brigham Young,"
in *History of the Church,* 7:573-76.

Nauvoo temple endowments performed on this date for:

First Company: Catharine Barton, Hannah Holbrook, Mary Call, Thomas McLelland, Elizabeth McLelland, Thomas C. Ivie, Amanda J. Ivie, Jacob E. Terry, Mary Maria Terry, Lydia Anderson, John Anderson, Thomas Dobson, Pamela Jane Lott, Almira Henrietta Lott, Melissa Lott, Mary Lott, Sarah Dobson, Samuel Bringhurst, Eleanor Bringhurst, Jordan P. Hendrickson, Frances Kelly, Frances Hendrickson, James Mendenhall, Eliza Mendenhall, Mary Thompson, Mary Taylor, Joseph Taylor, Minerva Stowell, William Niswanger, Mary Niswanger, Gilbert Morse, Cynthia Ann Morse, William S. Smith, Daniel Brown, Naomi Murray, Samuel R. Aiken, John S. Lott, Mary Parker, Pleasant Green Taylor, Eli Harvey Pierce, John Brown, John R. Murdock, Francis Brown, Thomas Pierce, Carlos G. Murray, and John D. Huntington.

Second Company: No names recorded; however, the following were washed and anointed and were therefore probably received through the veil on this date: Daniel Allen, Mary Ann Allen, Calvin Beebe, Submit Beebe, Dorcus Brown, Harriet A. Brown, Mary Brown, Jane Burscough, John Burscough, Jeremiah Carpenter, Susan Carpenter, Daniel P. Clark, Sarah M. Clark, Rachel Drollinger, Edmond Durfee, Caroline Durphy, Peter Fife, Jane Fisher, Eliza A. Hakes, Weeden V. Hakes, Levi Lightfoot, Susan Ann Lightfoot, Ann Longstroth, Nancy Longstroth, Absalom Perkins, Mary Ann Perkins, Nancy Perkins, William L. Perkins, Lucy W. Rice, William K. Rice, James Rodeback, Phebe Rodeback, David Sanger,

Mary Sanger, Hannah F. Strong, Reuben Strong, Sarah Very, Benjamin Willis, Hannah Willis, and Sarah Ann Willis..

Third Company: Thomas Thornton, John Smith, Susan C. Thornton, Ezra Strong Jr., James Rollins, Sarah Hillman, Elizabeth Taylor, Otis L. Terry, Mariah Strong, Mercy Rollins, Leven Simmons, Walter M. Edwards, Mahala G. Edwards, Sarah Morris, John Thornton, Sarah Colburn, George D. VanBeek, Isabella Begg, Amariah Harnden, Samuel Keele, Nancy Ott, Joseph Woodward, Catharine Seibel, Susanna Mohr, Adaline VanBeek, Margaret Woodward, Philinda S. Terry, Harriet Simmons, Charles A. Terry, Susanna Thornton, Joseph John Hall, Sarah Moore, Delaney Hall, Horace M. Alexander, Fanny M. Terry, Sarah Adams, Caroline M. Keele, Isabella Forsyth, Nancy Alexander, Thomas Forsyth, Maria Louisa Bingham, and Thomas Bingham.

Fourth Company: Thomas McKenzie, Mary McKenzie, William Matthews, Jane Steed, David E. Bunnel, Elizabeth Utley, Little John Utley, Sally Bunnel, John Atchisen, Eliza Murdock, Roxena Repsher, Whitford G. Wilson, Mary Wilson, Ephraim M. Sherman, Rachel Ann Sherman, Christopher Williams, Abigail Williams, Guy C. Wilson, Melinda Atchison, Nelson Merkley, Elizabeth Wilson, Thomas Steed, Mary Forsyth, and Ann R. Gould.

—Summary of information compiled by the Temple Index Bureau, *Nauvoo Temple Endowment Register: 10 December 1845 to 8 February 1846.*

....

Second anointings performed on this date:

Lorenzo Snow, Mary (Goddard) Snow, Charlotte (Squires) Snow, Sarah Ann (Prichard) Snow, and Harriet (Squires) Snow, anointed by Parley P. Pratt; Jesse P. Harmon and Anne (Barns) Harmon, anointed by Orson Hyde; John Herrington and Martha (Jones) Herrington, anointed by Parley P. Pratt; Almon W. Babbitt and Mary (Tulley) Babbitt, anointed by Orson Hyde; Dulcena D. (Johnson) Sherman to Almon W. Babbit for time and Lyman R. Sherman (deceased) for eternity, anointed by [not given]; John Smith, Julia (Hills) Smith, Asenath (Hurlburt) Smith, and Rebecca Smith, anointed by Parley P. Pratt; Lucien R. Foster and Anna Maria (Still) Foster, anointed by Orson Hyde; William Snow and Sarah (Sally) (Adams) Snow, anointed by Orson Hyde; Noah Packard and Sophia (Bundy) Packard, anointed by Winslow Farr; William Huntington, Mary (Johnson) Huntington, and Mary Ann (Armstrong) Huntington, anointed by George Miller; and Willard Richards and Amelia Elizabeth (Pierson) Richards, anointed by Brigham Young.

—Summarized from "Book of Anointings."

....

Sealings for the living performed on this date:

Randolph Alexander to Myrza Nix; Albern Allen to Marcia [Mariah] Allen; John Watson Bell to Ann Fish; Thomas Colburn to Sarah Bower; Almon Whiting Babbitt to Mary Tulley and Julia Ann Johnson; John Bair to Lucinda [Belinda] Tyler Owen; Ethan Barrows to Lorena Covey [Corey]; Ariah Coates Brower [Brewer] to Margaret Elizabeth Hussey; Anson Call to Mary Flint; Graham Coltrin to Harriet Hechman; Libbeus Thaddeus Coons to Elizabeth Maria Dixon; Charles Dalton to Mary Elizabeth Warner; Cyrus Daniels to Frances Amelia Turley; Augustus Alvin Farnham to Mary Jane Pottle; Warren Foote [Foot] to Artemisia Sidney Myers; Thomas B. Forsyth to Isabella Donald; Lucian Rose Foster to Anna Maria Still; James Harvey Glines to Elizabeth Ann Myers; Joseph Levi Graybill to Patience Smith; Henry Grow to Mary Moyer; Hector Caleb Haight to Julia Van Orden; Isaac Chauncy Haight to Eliza Ann Snyder; Clark Hallett to Ann Rosorry Gould and Phebe Bray; Jesse Pierce Harman [Harmon] to Anne Barnes [Parris]; Samuel Heath to Jane Haynes; George Washington Hickerson [Heckerson] to Sarah Woolsey; John Herrington to Martha Jones; Joseph Horne to Mary Isabella Hale; William Huntington to Mary Anne Armstrong and Mary Johnson; Shepherd Pierce Hutchings to Lucinda Clark; Eli Brazee Kelsey to Mary Forsyth and Jane Waite; Stephen Longstroth to Ann Gill; Daniel Duncan McArthur to Matilda Caroline Fuller; William McBride to Elizabeth H. Voram; Christopher Merkley to Sarah Davis and Minerva Stowell; Charles Wetherby Patten to Peggy Campbell and Caroline Pope; Jacob Peart to Elizabeth Haldon; Absalom Perkins to Nancy Martin; William Gant Perkins to Dicey Ray; Charles Shreeve Peterson to Mary Ann Patten; James Bertwistle Proctor to Letitia Clayton; Return Jackson Redding to Martha Maria Hurlbutt and Jane Fidelia Whiting; Daniel Mayhope Repsher to Hannah Walton; Samuel Whitney Richards to Mary Haskins Parker; Willard Richards to Nanny Longstroth; Rowland Shannon to Lucretia Marsh; Ranson Shepard to Mary Ann Goodwin; Frances Smith to Isabella Ray Bond; John Smith to Julia Hills, Asenath Hurlburt, and Rebecca Smith; William Snow to Sarah [Sally] Adams; Eller Stoker to Margaret Judd; Robert Stone to Julia Treby; Ezra Strong to Maria Louisa Beard;

John Thomas to Eliza J. Dunn; James Tomlinson to Sarah Berry; Bradley Barlow Wilson to Agnes Hunter; Whitford Gill Wilson to Mary Sheehand; and Thomas Woolsey to Mary Burrell.

—Summarized from the Book of Living Sealings.

....

Sealings for the dead performed on this date:

Ann B. Dennis (Mary Ann Patten, proxy) to Charles S. Peterson, Amasa M. Lyman officiating; Alice Bevill (Sarah Berry, proxy) to James Tomlinson, Amasa M. Lyman officiating; Lyman R. Sherman (Almon W. Babbit, proxy) to Dulcena D. Johnson, Heber C. Kimball officiating;[29] Joseph Smith (Almon W. Babbit, proxy) to Maria Lawrence, Heber C. Kimball officiating;[30] Mayhew Hillman (Libbeus T. Coons, proxy) to Sarah King, Brigham Young officiating;[31] Harriet Eliza Burr and Mary Ann Graham (Anna Maria Still, proxy) to Lucien R. Foster, Amasa M. Lyman officiating; Anna Norwood (Harriet Hechman, proxy) to Graham Coltrin, Amasa M. Lyman officiating; Laura Trask (Martha M. Hurlburt, proxy) to Jackson Redding, Amasa M. Lyman officiating; Sarah Cartright and Mary Maria Smith (Julia Treby, proxy) to Robert Stone, Amasa M. Lyman officiating; and Abby Jane Smith (Caroline Calkins, proxy) to John Harvey Tippets, Heber C. Kimball officiating.

—Summarized from the Book of Proxy Sealings.

Sunday, January 25, 1846

[A]t 10 in the morning I [Brigham Young] with a number of the 12 [apostles]. & others assembled in the Celestial Room of the Temple where I attended to the Sacred ordinances of Sealing by adoption—and also anoint[e]d Willard Richards & wife[.] the spirit of allmighty god attended the administration & filled our hearts to overflowing & many wept for joy that [they] were adopted into my Family—we continued in the Temple in attending to those ordinances until near Night—when I went home & spent the night[.]

—Brigham Young, Diary.

....

Parley P. Pratt conversed with some brethren, in the Celestial Room

29. Dulcena Johnson was also sealed to Almon Babbit for time.

30. Maria Lawrence was also sealed to Almon Babbit for time.

31. Sarah King was also sealed to Libbeus Coons for time.

of the Temple (Attic Story) on the subject of authority and Priesthood, to the following purpose: He said that in case the Quorum of the Twelve [apostles] should by any means become disorganized, that the Seventies held the Jurisdiction and authority of Presidency of the church in all the World ~~were~~ wherever it might be found. That the High Priest's duty would be the same as it is now, they would have to attend to their affairs; but the authority of Presidency over the whole church belonged to the Seventies; and if all the Seventies were killed off except one seventy, that Seventy would not only possess the right, but would be in duty bound to stand in their place as the First Presidency of the Church. He said that Joseph Smith the prophet undertook to establish this idea in the minds of the brethren in Kirtland, but the jealousies that began to arise in the minds of the High Priests prevented [him] from doing so[.] he therefore, left the matter undecided. He further stated, that the difference between the authority of the Seventies and High Priests was this: the High Priests possessed the High Priesthood, but the Seventies possessed the High Priesthood and the *Apostleship* which was the the [sic] highest power on the earth or in the Church[.] A man might be a prophet and seer and not be in the church or even be baptized; and Joseph himself was a prophet Seer, and Revelator before he was even baptized or had any Priesthood whatever; but having proved faithful in the thing that was committed to his charge; God sent John the Baptist to ordain him a priest after the order of Aaron and having been faithful to this latter trust, the Almighty sent Peter, James a[n]d John unto him in due time and ordained him and [sic] Apostle and first Elder in the Church which was the highest authority of all. During this conversation, there were present, Charles Wesley Wandell, Isaac Allred, and some others of the Presidency of the Seventies David Candland also. And J[oh]n M. Bernhisel and another of the High Priests, were also present. Heber C. Kimball also preached the same thing to the public congregation the same forenoon.

—Seventies Record, Book B.

....

[A]t 11 AM in the house of the Lord a convention of the leading members[.]

—John D. Lee, Diary.

....

Prepared for the Temple at 10. I, Henrietta [Bullock] and Lucy [Bullock] went. Called at bro[ther] W[illia]m. Clayton's and on to the Temple.

Dressed and at a little after 3 we were adopted into the family of Dr. Willard Richards who was anointed K[ing] of [his] K[ingdom] and a K[ing] and P[riest] to the most high God. Whomsoever he blesses shall be blessed and who he curses shall be cursed. It was a solemn time. A many were sealed up. Brigham [Young] kissed all his children.

—Thomas Bullock, Diary.

....

At ten oclock I [Willard Richards] went to the Temple & after some ordinances of a[n]ointing &c the following were adopted into my family viz.

Ellen Partington—[born in] Preston Lancashire England[,] Sept[ember]. 14. 1834[.]
Stephen Longstroth [born in] Langcliffe Yorkshire England[.]
Ann Longstroth [born in] Arncliffe do do [ditto.]
Thomas Bullock [born in] Leek Straffordshire d[itt]o[,] Dec[embe]r. 23, 1816[.]
Henrietta Bullock d[itt]o d[itt]o d[itt]o Feb[ruary]. 13. 1817[.]
Lucy Caroline Bullock [born in] Farrington Lancashire d[itt]o[,] March 21, 1820[.]
Wilmer Benjamin Benson [born in] Lynchouse London d[itt]o[,] Feb[ruary]. 13, 1814[.]
Ann Elizabeth Fox King [born in] Stornley Glo[u]cestershire d[itt]o[,] Feb[ruary] 17. 1815[.]
George Darling Watt [born in] Manchester Lancashire d[itt]o[,] Jan[uary] 16. 1816[.]
Mary Matt Walton d[itt]o d[itt]o 1811
Peter Muir Fife

—Willard Richards, Diary.

....

We went to the Temple and anointed our children, George Albert and Bathsheba to the birthright and they were sealed to us upon the altar by Presidents Brigham Young, Heber C. Kimball and Bishop George Miller, and a great many others.[32] We were sealed to father [John Smith] in the same manner.

—George A. Smith, "History of George Albert Smith."

32. This may mark the first such sealing of children to their own parents in the Nauvoo temple. "Although adoptions were performed there for nearly a month," Gordon Irving writes (p. 295), "the forced departure of the Church leaders from

I [Brigham Young] attended to [the] ordinances in the Temple.

—"Manuscript History of Brigham Young,"
in *History of the Church,* 7:576.

....

Sealings for the living performed on this date:

Clarence Merrill to Bathsheba Kate Smith; George Miller to Elizabeth Bouton and Sophia Wallace; Joshua Lewis Miller to Elizabeth Ann Anderson; and George Darling Watt to Mary Gregson.

—Summarized from the Book of Living Sealings.

....

Adoptions performed on this date:

To Joseph and Hannah Fielding: Heber Fielding, Joseph Fielding, Rachel Fielding, and Ellen Fielding, sealed by Heber C. Kimball: "The birthright of the sexes being upon Heber and Rachel, they were sealed to their parents above written, in the Holy Order at the Altar &c, &c."; to Heber C. and Vilate Kimball: William Ellis Murray, Mary Murray, James Davenport, Angelia Phelps, William Pitt, Cornelia Melvina Divine, Harmon Burgess, Sophria Minerva Burgess, James Smithies, Nancy Knowles, Charles Wesley Hubbard, Mary Ann Bosworth, Joseph Grafton Hovey, Martha Ann Webster, William A. King, Mosea Cushing, David Candland, and Sarah Susan Divine (all sealed by Brigham Young), and Mary Ann Candland, George White Pitkin, and Amanda Pitkin (all sealed by Amasa M. Lyman on January 28), and Jesse Henry Nichols, Edward Martin, and Alice Martin (all sealed by Brigham Young on February 1): "These persons were all adopted and sealed to Heber Chase Kimball and Vilate Kimball as their children by the usual covenant and ordinances of adoption at the Altar" (January 25) and "Adopted and sealed the same as the above" (February 1); to George and Mary Catherine Miller: Joshua Lewis Miller, Mary Catherine Miller, Elizabeth Virginia Miller, Elizabeth Ann Miller, Lewis Elijah Anderson, and Henry C. Boyle; to George Miller and Sophia Miller: William Leyland, Eliza Leyland, Sophia Leyland, and Sarah Leyland; to George Miller and Elizabeth Miller: Lewis Miller, Harrison Miller, Charles Miller, Ruth Ann Miller, and Mary Jane Miller, sealed by

---

Nauvoo prevented the general membership from being adopted or having their own children sealed to them" ("The Law of Adoption: One Phase of the Development of the Mormon Concept of Salvation, 1830-1900," *BYU Studies* 14 [Spring 1974]: 291-314). Sealings of children not born under the covenant (i.e., to parents already sealed to each other before a child's birth) are administered in LDS temples today.

Brigham Young: "The above named persons were all sealed up unto their parents and to George Miler and [Mary] Catherine Miller, whose names stand at the head of this list. The natural children to their parents and the adopted children to their adopted parents, with the full ceremony of washing and anointing, clothing &c. with the usual covenant at the Alter and were sealed up unto eternal life and unto their parents for time and for all eternity &c."; and to Brigham Young and Miriam Young (Mary Ann Young, proxy): Albert Perry Rockwood, Nancy Haven Rockwood, John D. Lee, Aggatha Lee, George Davidson Grant, Elizabeth Grant, Joshua Sawyer Holman, Rebecca Whitcomb Holman, Truman Osborn Angel, Polly Angel, William Weeks, Caroline Weeks, Jacob Flinn Hutchinson, Constantia Hutchinson, Leslie Lyme, and Elspith Lyme, sealed by Heber C. Kimball.

Summarized from "Sealings and Adoptions."

Monday, January 26, 1846

[A]t 9— I went into the Temple & commenced the ordinances of Sealings & anointings in different apartments that were set apart for that purpose—the washing & anointings in the first departments I suspended to the morrow—that hands that labored might have one[.]

—Brigham Young, Diary.

[W]ent to the Temple with Ruth [Moon Clayton], Margaret [Moon] and Diantha [Farr]. We waited till about 8 o clock before we could be waited on. We then dressed and went into room No 1 and were sealed to each other on the alt[a]r by Pres[iden]t. B[righam]. Young. Afterwards in No 2 We received our anointing by H[eber]. C. Kimball and a number of others. And afterwards Heber blessed us. I [William Clayton] then took Ruth and Diantha home but Margaret tarried till morning.

—William Clayton, Diary.

Nine a.m., I [Brigham Young] went to the Temple and commenced the ordinances in the different departments which were set apart for the purpose; the washing and anointing was suspended until tomorrow.

—"Manuscript History of Brigham Young," in *History of the Church,* 7:576.

Second anointings performed on this date:

George D. Grant, Elizabeth (Wilson) Grant, and Margaret (Redd) Grant, anointed by Parley P. Pratt; Lorenzo Dow Young, Harriet (Wheeler) Young, and Susan (Ashby) Young, anointed by George Miller; Desdemona C. Fullmer to Ezra T. Benson for time and Joseph Smith (deceased) for eternity, anointed by George Miller; Benjamin L. Clapp and Ann (Thomas) Clapp, anointed by George Miller; Willard Richards, Sarah (Longstroth) Richards, and Nancy (Longstroth) Richards, anointed by Parley P. Pratt; Joseph W. Coolidge, Elizabeth (Buchannon) Coolidge, Mary Ann (Buchannon) Coolidge, Elizabeth Jane (Tuttle) Coolidge, and Rebecca (Atwood) Coolidge, anointed by [not given]; Willard Snow, Malvina (Harvey) Snow, and Susan (Harvey) Snow, anointed by Orson Pratt; Newel K. Whitney, Olive (Bishop) Whitney, Henrietta (Keyes) Whitney, Abigail (Pond) Whitney, Emmeline (Harris) Whitney, Anna [Anne] (Huston) Whitney, Elizabeth (Pone) Whitney, and Elizabeth (Moore) Whitney, anointed by Orson Pratt; Heber C. Kimball, Harriett (Sanders) Kimball, and Mary Ellen (Harris) Kimball, anointed by Brigham Young; Martha (McBride) Knight, Sylvia P. Sessions, and Sarah P. Lawrence to Heber C. Kimball for time and Joseph Smith (deceased) for eternity, anointed by Brigham Young; George Miller, Elizabeth (Bouton) Miller, and Sophia (Leyland) Miller, anointed by Parley P. Pratt; Joseph Rich and Nancy (O'Neal) Rich, anointed by Parley P. Pratt; Harvey Green and Jane Ann (Rich) Green, anointed by Parley P. Pratt; William Clayton, Ruth (Moon) Clayton, Margaret (Moon) Clayton, and Diantha (Farr) Clayton, anointed by Heber C. Kimball; and George A. Smith, Lucy (Meserve) Smith, Nancy (Clements) Smith, Zilpah (Stark) Smith, Sarah Ann (Libby) Smith, and Hannah (Libby) Smith, anointed by Heber C. Kimball.

—Summarized from "Book of Anointings."

....

Sealings for the living performed on this date:

William Aldridge to Margaret Van Blarcum; Jonathon Beckelshymer to Susanna Kinsey; John Benbow to Jane Holmes and Agnes Taylor; Wilmer Benjamin Benson to Ann Elizabeth Fox; Benjamin Lynn Clapp to Ann Brigham [Bingham] Thomas; William Ogelby Clark to Julia Ruhamah Appleby; William Clayton to Diantha Farr, Margaret Moon, and Ruth Moon; Joseph Wellington Coolidge to Rebecca Atwood; Joel Drury to Tirzah Winters; John Eldridge to Cynthia Ann Howlett; Edward Meeks Fuller to Hannah Elizabeth Eldridge; Thomas Eldridge Fuller to Sally Libby McArthur; John Groesbeck to Margaret King; Peter Haws to Mary Quaid and Sarah Morris; James Houston to Margaret Crawford; William Jenkins to Eliza Phelps; Frederick Kesler to Emeline Parker; Heber Chase Kimball to Mary Ellen Harris Able, and Harriet [Helga] Sanders; Joseph Corrodon Kingsbury to Dorcas Adelia Moore and Louisa Loenza Alcina Pond; Moses Martin to Julia Priscilla Smith; Amasa Mason Lyman to Caroline Eliza [Ely] Partridge; David Nelson to Mary Thompson Miller; Jared Porter to Abiah Franklin; William Pugh to Caroline Fidelia Calkins; Joseph Rich to Nancy O'Neal; Telemachus Rogers to Eliza Watton; George Albert Smith to Nancy Clement, Lucy Meserve Smith, Zelpha Start, Hannah Maria Libby, Sarah Ann Libby, and for time only, Agnes Coolbrith Smith; Samuel Snyder to Henrietta M. Stockwell; Preston Thomas to Sarah Ann Jane Morehead; William Thompson to Sarah Bell [perhaps Jan. 27]; John Harvey Tippets to Caroline Fidelia Calkins; Newell Kimball Whitney to Olive Maria Bishop, Elizabeth Mahala Moore, Elizabeth Almera Pond, Abigail August Pond, Emmeline Blanch Woodward, and Anne Houston; Brigham Young to Vilate Clarissa Decker and Rebecca W. Greenlief Holman; and Lorenzo Dow Young to Harriet Page Wheeler and Susan Ann Ashby.

—Summarized from the Book of Living Sealings.

....

Sealings for the dead performed on this date:

Mary Ann Lattermore (Eliza Watton, proxy) to Telemachus Rogers, Amasa M. Lyman officiating; Charles Brown (Loren Babbit, proxy) to Mary Aray [officiator not given];[33] Joseph Smith (Ezra T. Benson, proxy) to Desdemona Fullmer, Brigham Young officiating;[34] Agnes Hume and Elizabeth Van Blarcum (Sophia Coleman, proxy) to William Aldridge, Brigham Young officiating; Aziel Stevens (William Aldridge, proxy) to Sophia Coleman, Brigham Young officiating;[35] Alonzo W. N. Whitney (Newel K. Whitney, proxy) to Henrietta Keys, Heber C. Kimball officiating;[36] Caroline Whitney (Dorcas A. Moore, proxy) to Joseph C. Kingsbury, Brigham Young officiating; and Joseph Smith (Heber C. Kimball,

33. Mary Aray was also sealed to Loren Babbit for time. This entry is crossed out in the original "Book of [Proxy] Sealings."

34. Desdemona Fullmer was also sealed to Ezra T. Benson for time.

35. Sophia Coleman was also sealed to William Aldridge for time.

36. Henrietta Keys was also sealed to Newel K. Whitney for time.

proxy) to Martha (McBride) Knight, Sylvia P. (Sessions) Lyon, and Sarah Lawrence, Amasa M. Lyman officiating.[37]

—Summarized from the Book of Proxy Sealings.

....

Adoptions performed on this date:

Brigham Young sealed to Hyrum Smith (Heber C. Kimball, proxy) and Jerusha Barden Smith (Mary Fielding Smith as proxy) the following: John Smith, Joseph Fielding Smith, Jerusha Smith, Sarah Smith, and Martha Ann Smith ("The birthright belongs to John Smith. Joseph Fielding Smith and Martha Ann Smith are Hyrum and Mary Smith's children, Joseph Fielding holding the birthright in that branch of the family. These being natural children were sealed to their parents by the usual ordinance of Sealing at the Alter"), and Joseph Fielding, Hannah Greenwood Fielding, Robert Blashell Thompson (John Taylor, proxy), Mercy Rachel Thompson, Howard Coray, Martha Jane Coray, James Lawson, Charles Smith, and Sarah Smith ("These persons were adopted unto their parents above written by the usual ceremony in full, at the Alter &c. &c. ... The adoption of Howard and Martha J. Coray to Hyrum Smith cancelled by Pres[iden]t. [Wilford] Woodruff 18 Dec[ember] 1893. G[eorge]. Reynolds, Recorder"); to Robert B. Thompson (John Taylor, proxy) and Mercy Rachel Thompson: William Jenkins and Eliza Jenkins, sealed by Heber C. Kimball ("Bro[ther] and Sister Jenkins were adopted and sealed unto R[obert]. B. Thompson and M[ercy]. R. Thompson at the alter &c."); and to Newel K. and Elizabeth Ann Whitney: Joseph C. Kingsbury, Dorcas Adelia More Kingsbury, and Loenza Alcina Pond.

—Summarized from "Sealings and Adoptions."

Tuesday, January 27, 1846

[M]orning[,] the washing commenced in both departments[.] the Sealings were attend[ed] to [to]day by myself [Brigham Young] Heber C. Kimball and A[masa]. Lyman—the 2nd anointings was likewise carried on in Room No[.s] 2 & 4[,] O[rson]. Hyde P[arley]. P. Pratt [and] O[rson] Pratt officiating in No[.s] 2 & 4[.] G[eorge]. A. Smith & W[illard]. Richards are absent on account of sickness— about noon Bro[ther].

37. Martha Knight, Sylvia Lyon, and Sarah Lawrence were also sealed to Heber C. Kimball for time.

Benj[amin]. Mcegensis & Lady called me. I took my clerk J[ohn]. D. Lee & we repaired to the North vestry where I had an interview with the 2 forementioned Persons setting forth to them the Law of god relative to his case ... I return[e]d back to the Temple & assumed my labors—which lasted to 10. o.clock [in the] eve[ning,] after which I went to A[lbert]. P. Rockwood & spent a few hours then went back to the Temple & spent the Night[.]

—Brigham Young, Diary.

....

[A]t 10 o'clock A.M. the following persons namely, Isaac Allred, Harrison Burgess, William Hyde, Samuel W. Richards, Chandler Holbrook, and Lorin Farr, met in room No. 9, and consecrated 15 bottles of oil. Harrison Burgess officiating.

This morning many were turned away from want of oil.

List 1 In the Male Department commencing at 10 m[inutes]. to 10 A.M.

[See pages 499-502 for excerpted portion.]

Ordinations

John Milburn was ordained a Seventy by Miles Andrus and Samuel Moore. Finished at 30 [minutes] p[ast]. 5. [p.m.]

—Seventies Record, Book B.

....

One hundred and twenty-six persons received ordinances.

Elders Heber C. Kimball, Orson Hyde, Parley P. Pratt, Orson Pratt, Amasa Lyman, and I [Brigham Young] officiated in the higher ordinances. Elders George A. Smith and Willard Richards were absent, being sick. ...

I officiated at the altar until 10 p.m. and remained in the Temple all night.

—"Manuscript History of Brigham Young,"
in *History of the Church,* 7:576-77.

....

Nauvoo temple endowments performed on this date for:

First Company: Rebecca Williams, Ezra G. Williams, Alexander Hay, Janette Hay, Henry Swank, Anna Swank, Robert Stewart, Nancy Stewart, Elizabeth Arrowsmith, Elias Harmar, Charlotte R. Harmar, George B. Gardner, Elizabeth D. Gardner, Hiram N. Byington, Ann Sanford, Thomas Booth, Sarah Byington, Mary Booth, Sophia Jewitt, Peter Boyce, Olive Boyce, James Sweeney, Lewellin Mantle, Catharine Mantle, Matthew McEwen, Mary McEwen, Thomas D. Casper, Rachel Caspar, Truman

[Washings and anointings for Tuesday, January 27, 1846]

Seventies		Seventies	
	1 Richard Shelden born Nov 24, 1806		12 Lewelin Mantle born Aug 21, 1808
	2 Robert Stewart " June 27, 1807	"	13 Peter Boyce " June 8, 1805
	3 Matthew McEwen " 1814		14 Hiram V. Byington " Aug 19, 1800
	4 Alexander Key " Aug. 3, 1808		15 Tueman Gilbert " May 30, 1799
	5 Artemus W. Holton " Mar. 13, 1809		16 Ezra G. Williams " Nov. 17, 1823
	6 Abner Bell " Jan. 26, 1812	H. Priests	1 Sweank Henry " July 5, 1776
	7 Thomas Booth " Mar. 22, 1819		2 John Lamson " June 20, 1806
	8 William Thompson " 1821		3 James Sweeny " Aug. 12, 1807
	9 George B. Gardner " Apl. 4, 1813		4 Thomas Crooks " 1791
	10 Thomas D. Casper " Dec. 27, 1809	Elder	1 Thomas H. Park " Aug 30, 1803
	11 Elias Harner " Nov. 25, 1811		

were washed by Joseph Horn and Alfred Brown. Anointed by Welcome Chapman, P. G. Sessions and Hiram Dayton. Finished at 11 A.M.

List 1 In the Female Department commencing at 10 A.M.

Anna born Sep. 1782	Mary Crooks born Sep 1802
Mary Booth " May 29, 1821	Rachel Cooper " Oct 17, 1816
Elizabeth Arrowsmith " Sep. 4, 1819	Charlotte R. Harmer " Sep. 8, 1818
Elizabeth D. Gardner " Feb. 28, 1814	Huldah Park " July 22, 1805
Catherine Mantle " Oct. 29, 1815	Ann Sanford " May 2, 1770
Rebecca Raimond " Nov. 13, 1792	Nancy Bell " Dec. 16, 1812
Janette Kay " Sep. 14, 1813	Sarah Byington " May 3, 1808
Sarah Thompson " April 9, 1809	Rebecca Williams " Aug 3, 1798

Mary McEwan [born] April 1812	Lodema Sheldon [born] Jan. 11, 1826
Olive Boyce " Aug. 21, 1808	Nancy Gilbert " Aug 12, 1808
Sophia Jewett " Feb. 1, 1822	Stewart " Nov. 4, 1836

were washed and anointed by Mary J. Horn, Nancy Cahoon, Lydia Granger, Agness Taylor, Unice Holbrook, Elizabeth Cooledge, Hester A. E. Brown, Louisa [illegible] and Zeruah Godard.

Tuesday evening January

List 2 In the Female Department commencing at 45 p. 1,

Mary Richardson born May 5, 1829	Mariah B. Stoddard born Apl. 12, 1832
Lucy Jane Leonard " Oct. 9, 1825	Ingabor Johnson " Jan. 1818
Hannah Doll " Oct. 1792	Clarinda Allen " Aug. 10, 1802
Sarah Collins " Aug 23, 1802	Martha Young " Nov. 6, 1812
Lydia Alcock " Oct. 31, 1829	Jane Marsden " Aug 25, 1814
Lydia Knapp " May 3, 1805	Sarah Harris " Apl. 11, 1785
Mary Ann Price " Mar. 14, 1791	Rachel Blackburn " Jan. 27, 1821
Mary Rockwell " July 27, 1826	Mary Jenkins " Jan 19, 1818
Sarah G. Richards " Dec. 26, 1802	Emma S. Smith " Apl. 18, 1819
Elizabeth Rogers " Dec. 1815	Adaline H. Manchester " Oct. 18, 1819
Margaret Ann Hammond " Jan. 19, 1809	

were washed and anointed by Mary Elizabeth Horn, Unice Holbrook, Louisa Clark, Sopronia Harmon, Zeruah Godard, Elizabeth Cooledge, Nancy Cahoon, Hester A. E. Brown. Finished at 45 min p. 2.

List 2 In the Male Department, commencing at

Seventies		~~Seventies~~^H. Priests^
	Maude Madison born Sept 29, 1812	Joseph Dunlap born Apl. 15, 1799
"	18 Lars Olson " Sept 29, 180	75 Shur Olson " July 1818

"	19 Ira Thomason " June 16, 182		56 Chauncey S Calkins " Jan. 2, 1799
"	20 Jonas Saby " Jan. 1827		7 Andrew Doll " Apl. 14, 1788
"	21 [illegible] Johnson " Nov. 11, 1807		8 John Stevens " Apl. 6, 1785
"	22 Seven Jacobs " Nov. 25, 1822		9 Levi Richards " Apl. 14, 1799
"	23 Ever Aftedahl " May 1, 1823	Seventies	27 Ola Johnson " May 17, 1816
"	24 Hervey Saby " June, 1793	"	28 Yence Jacobs " Mar. 15, 1814
"	25 Asa Manchester " Sept 15 1809	"	29 Canute Peterson " May 13, 1824
"	26 Edward O. Haymond " Mar. 8, 1802	"	30 William Marsden " Mar. 15, 1814
			31 Zephaniah J. Warner " Aug 30, 1801
			32 William Jenkins " Oct. 23, 1818
		Elders	2 Moses C. Leonard " July 26, 1827
			3 Andrew L. Allen " Nov. 27, 1794

The Ten above named persons were ordained Seventies by Joseph Young and J. M. Grant, previous to their receiving their washing & anointing. Were washed by Joseph Horn and Alfred Brown. Anointed by Charles Bird and Welcome Chapman.

Finished at 2 ½ P.M.

In the Female department commencing at 45 m. p. 3,

Aidah Clements born Dec. 24, 1801	Barbara Miller born Mar 27, 1800
Mary Carpenter " Sep 10, 1810	Hannah Baven " Oct. 20, 1797
Martha Weaver " July 8, 1804	Anna Mariah Baven " Oct 10, 1828
Elizabeth Draper " Feb. 25, 1806	Mary Bateman " May 18, 1800
Mary Brown " Jan. 9, 1818	Elizabeth Pugmire " Feb 22 [illegible]
Mary King " May 11, 1816	Esther Forsyth " [illegible]
Amanda Curtis born Sept 30, 1822	Almira Curtis born Sep. 8, 1815
Mary Archer " Apl. 4, 1798	Catherine Barker " Aug. 12, 1804

Betsey McBride [born] Jan. 6, 1802	Lovina C. Milburn [born] Mar. 18, 1824
Abigail McBride " Jan. 29, 1770	Jerusha Ann Richardson " May 15, 1818
Mary Bybee " Oct. 27, 1809	Rheuanna Card " Jan 20, 1794

were washed and anointed by Nancy Cahoon, Unice Holbrook, Louisa Clark, Hester A. E. Brown, Mary Isabella Horn, Zeruah Godard and Sophronia ~~Godard~~ Harmon Finished at

In the Male department, commencing at 20 to 5

Seventies		High Priest	
	33 John B. Carpenter born May 20, 1810		John W. Archer born Dec. 21, 1794
"	34 Enoch M. King " May 1, 1821	" "	William Draper " Apl. 24, 1807
"	35 David R. Miller " Dec. 13, 1793	Elders	4 John Miller " Aug. 31, 1818
"	36 Archibald Forsyth " Aug 10, 1812	"	5 Peter Mc Coy " Nov. 29, 1792
"	37 Robert Brown " Feb. 1, 1818		
"	38 James Bearon " Apl. 2, 1789		
"	39 John W. Curtis " Aug 11, 1820		
"	40 Albert Bybee " Nov. 4, 1810		
"	41 Thomas Bateman " Sep 17, 1808		
"	42 David A Curtis " Aug 11, 1820		
"	43 Thomas Parker " 1807		
"	44 John Milburn " Mar. 6, 1812		
"	45 Jonathan Pugmire Jr Dec 7, 1823		

were washed by Joseph Horn and Alfred Brown. Anointed by Charles Bird and Welcome Chapman.

—Seventies Record, Book B, oversized portion, January 27, 1846.

Gilbert, Artemus W. Holton, Thomas H. Park, Nancy Gilbert, Huldah Park, Abner Bell, Nancy Bell, Rebecka Raymond, John Lawson, Thomas Crooks, Mary Crooks, Richard D. Sheldon, Lodema Sheldon, William Thompson, and Sarah Thompson.

Second Company: Chauncey Calkins, Sarah Calkins, William Marsden, Jane Marsden, Andrew Dahl, Joseph Dunlap, Sarah Harris, Mary Ann Price, Hannah Dall, Zephaniah J. Warren, Levi Richards, Sarah Richards, Mary Richardson, Maria Stoddard, John Stevens, Rachel Blackburn, Eli Johnson, Mary Rockwell, Edward O. Haymond, Ingabor Johnson, Lydia Alcock, Emma Sarah Smith, Asa Manchester, Adaline H. Manchester, William Jenkins, Martha Young, Margaret Ann Haymond, Made Madison, Mary Jenkins, Andrew L. Allen, Lydia Knapp, Shure Olsen, Ola Johnson, Lucy Jane Leonard, Ever Afterdahl, Yance Jacobs, Clarinda Allen, Scwen Jacobs, Lars Olsen, Canute Peterson, Henry Sabey, Ira Thomason, Jonas Sabey, Moses C. Leonard, and Elizabeth Rogers.

Third Company: David Curtis, Amanda Curtis, Jerusha/Ann Richardson, David R. Miller, Barbara Miller, Alfred Bybee, Abigail McBride, Peter McCoy, Betsey McBride, Enoch M. King, Mary King, William Draper Jr., Mary Bybee, Robert Brown, Mary Brown, Elizabeth Draper, John B. Carpenter, Mary Carpenter, James Beavan, Catharine Barker, John Milborn, Hannah Beavan, Rheuama Card, Hannah Maria Beavan, Lovina Milburn, Thomas Bateman, Martha Weaver, Mary Bateman, Jonathan Pugmire Jr., Elizabeth Pugmire, Aidah Clements, Archibald Forsyth, Esther Forsyth, John W. Archer, Mary Archer, John W. Curtis, and Almira Curtis.

—Summary of information compiled by the Temple Index Bureau, *Nauvoo Temple Endowment Register: 10 December 1845 to 8 February 1846.* Editors' note: According to the register, Thomas Barker and John Miller were washed and anointed and therefore also probably received through the veil.

....

Second anointings performed on this date:

Moses Martin and Julia (Smith) Martin, anointed by William Huntington; John Eldridge and Cynthia Ann (Howett) Eldridge, anointed by William W. Phelps; James Brown and Esther (Jones) Brown, anointed by Ezra T. Benson; Peter Haws, Mary (Quaid) Haws, and Sarah (Morris) Haws, anointed by Ezra T. Benson; William W. Major and Sarah (Coles) Major, anointed by Parley P. Pratt; Samuel Rolfe and Elizabeth (Hathaway) Rolfe, anointed by Ezra T. Benson; William Felshaw and Mary

(Gilbert) Felshaw, anointed by Isaac Morley; Elijah Fordham and Anna (Chaffell) Fordham, anointed by Ezra T. Benson; Frederick W. Cox, Emmeline (Whiting) Cox, and Jemima (Losee) Cox, anointed by Parley P. Pratt; Cordelia C. Morley to Frederick W. Cox for time and Joseph Smith (deceased) for eternity, anointed by Parley P. Pratt; Levi Richards, Sarah Ann (Griffith), and Persis (Goddall) Richards, anointed by George Miller; Isaac Morley and Betsy (Pinkham) Morley, anointed by George Miller; Charles Shumway, Julia Ann (Hooker) Shumway, and Louisa (Minnerly) Shumway, anointed by Parley P. Pratt; and Willard Richards and Mary (Thompson) Richards, anointed by [not given].

—Summarized from "Book of Anointings."

....

Sealings for the living performed on this date:

James Bean to Elizabeth Lewis; Abner Bell to Nancy Garwood; William Blackhurst to Margaret Stephenson and Jane Hamilton; Edmund Bosley to Ann Kelley; William Brown Jr. to Phebe Narcissia Odell; Chauncey Ira Calkins to Sarah Kellogg; Thomas Carrico [Carico] to Betsey Baker; Ezra Chase to Tirza Wells; Isaac Chase to Rebecca Pierce; Hiram Bradley Clawson to Ellen Curtis Spencer; Frederick Walter Cox to Emiline Sally Whiting and Jamima Losee; Hiram Dayton to Sophia Lance; Freeborn DeMill to Anna Knight; Horace Sunderland Eldridge to Betsey Ann Chase; Andrew Dill to Euphanah Young; Almon Linus Fulmer Sr. to Sarah Ann Follett; Jonathan Harriman Hale to Olive Boynton; James Hendricks to Drusilla Dorris [Davis]; Alexander Hill Jr. to Agnes Hood; Chandler Holbrook to Eunice Dunning; Alvin Horr to Sarah Davis; John Houston to Christiana Ettleman; Eleas Johnson to Isabella Abraham; Easton Kelsey to Abigail Finch; John Kay to Ellen Cockcroft and Susannah Roberts; Enoch Marvin King to Mary Bigg Ware; Thomas Rice King to Matilda Robison; William McCleary to Sophronia Smith; William Patterson McIntire to Anna Patterson; Albert Merrill to Margaret Ann Richardson; Reuben G. Miller to Rhoda Ann Letts and Orice Burnham; George Washington Oman to Malvina Graham Dickey; William Cornwall Patten to Jane Crouse; David Pettigrew to Elizabeth Alden; Levi Richards to Sarah Griffith and Persis Goodall; Willard Richards to Mary Thompson, and Jane Hall; Jeremiah Robey to Ruth Tucker; Thomas Rodgers to Aurelia Spencer; James Sloan to Mary Magill; Alfred Alexander Smith to Ann Austin; Chauncey Turner to Hannah Franklin Redfield; Edwin Whiting to Elizabeth Partridge Tillotson, Almira Mehitable Meacham, and Mary Elizabeth Cox; David Wilding to Alice Atkinson; Benjamin Willis to Hannah Himilwright; Daniel Wood to Mary Snider and Panina Cotton; and Jacob Zundell to Sarah Forstner.

—Summarized from the Book of Living Sealings.

....

Sealings for the dead performed on this date:

Mary Raymond (Betsy Baker, proxy) to Thomas Carrico, Amasa M. Lyman officiating; Julia Wells (Tizrah [Wells] Chase, proxy) to Ezra Chase, Amasa M. Lyman officiating; Hyrum Smith (Reuben Miller, proxy) to Louisa Sanger, Amasa M. Lyman officiating;[38] John Stephenson (William Blackhurst, proxy) to Catherine Brimford, Amasa M. Lyman officiating;[39] Hannah Barns (Sophia W. Sanborn, proxy) to Gad Yale, Heber C. Kimball officiating; Joseph Smith (Gad Yale, proxy) to Sophia W. Sanborn, Heber C. Kimball officiating;[40] Joseph Smith (Frederick W. Cox, proxy) to Cordelia C. Morley, Amasa M. Lyman officiating;[41] Harriet Clarke and Lucinda Marsh (Sarah Davis, proxy) to Alvin Horr, Amasa M. Lyman officiating; Mary Ann Chase (Betsy Ann Chase, proxy) to Horace S. Eldridge, Amasa M. Lyman officiating; Nathan Pinkham (Isaac Morley, proxy) to Betsy Bradford, Amasa M. Lyman officiating;[42] Elizabeth Haldin (Phebe Robson, proxy) to Jacob Peart, Amasa M. Lyman officiating; John Thompson (Jacob Peart, proxy) to Phebe Robson, Amasa M. Lyman officiating;[43] Elizabeth Copper and Julia Ann Bench (Jane Crouse, proxy) to William C. Patton, Amasa M. Lyman officiating; and Amasa Card (John Bair, proxy) to Jerusha Ann Richardson, Brigham Young officiating.[44]

—Summarized from the Book of Proxy Sealings.

....

Adoptions performed on this date:

To Orson and Catherine Curtis Spencer: Howard Orson Spencer, George Boardsman Spencer, Ellen Curtis Spencer, Aurella Reed Spencer, Catherine Curtis Spencer, and Lucy Curtis Spencer, sealed by Brigham

38. Louisa Sanger was also sealed to Reuben Miller for time.

39. Catherine Brimford was also sealed to William Blackhurst for time.

40. Sophia Sanborn was also sealed to Gad Yale for time.

41. Cordelia Morley was also sealed to Frederick Cox for time.

42. Betsy Bradford was also sealed to Isaac Morley for time.

43. Phebe Robson was also sealed to Jacob Peart for time.

44. Jerusha Ann Richardson was also sealed to John Bair for time.

Young: "These were sealed to their parents with the usual covenants, blessings and ordinances, &c. at the Alter in the usual manner."

—Summarized from "Sealings and Adoptions."

Wednesday, January 28, 1846

I spent [Wednesday] officiating at the Holy Alt[a]r for most of the time—through the day—at ½ after 9—at Night the opperations of the day closed—I staied over Night in the Temple[,] the evening being remarkably—Rainy.

—Brigham Young, Diary.

....

List 1 In the Male Department, the administration of the ordinances commenced at 9 minutes to 9 a.m. When [line ends]

[See pages 507-508 for excerpted portion.]

H[arrison]. Burgess as Elohim, Noah Rogers as Jehovah, Simeon A. Dunn as Michael, Willard Snow as Peter, Luman Shurtliff as James, Joseph Horn as John, William Hyde as the Serpent and Isaac Alred as Prompter. Commenced at the vail at [blank]

At 9 o'clock, Benjamin L. Clapp, William Hyde, Samuel W. Richards, Simeon Carter, Harvey Green, Joseph Horn, and Harrison Burgess met in the Attic story of the Temple room No. 9 and consecrated 18 bottles of oil.

List 2 In the ~~Fe~~male department commencing at 4 [minutes] p[ast]. 11 [.am.]

[See pages 508-12 for excerpted portion.]

This afternoon Brother [Moses] Sanders arrived with olive oil (two barrels) to be used in the endowments. the money with which the oil was bought was raised by the *Seventies only.*

—Seventies Record, Book B.

....

[O]n [the] 28th or 29th [of] Jan[uary]. 1846 I [Joseph C. Kingsbury] received my Second Anointing with my two wives, under the hands of Pres[ident]. Orson Pratt in the North East Room in the upper part of the Temple in the City of Nauvoo.

—"History of Joseph C. Kingsbury," Special Collections,
Marriott Library, University of Utah, Salt Lake City.

[Washings and anointings for Wednesday, January 28, 1846]

Seventies		Seventies	
	1 Louis R. Chaffin born Dec 3, 1808		11 Hyrum D. Buys born Oct. 18, 1802
"	2 Henry Moore " Aug 6, 1802		12 Thomas Elliot " Apl. 15, 1810
"	3 Jacob L. Workman " July 7, 1812		13 Noah Packard " Apl. 24, 1821
"	4 Edward Cuthbert " Jan. 15, 1815		14 Orrin Packard " Dec. 25, 1822
"	5 Andrew Burnham " May 19, 1808		15 Henry Packard " May 26, 1825
"	6 John A. McIntosh " Apl. 14, 1806		16 Adam Long " Mar. 11, 1802
"	7 Benjamin F. Pendleton " Mar. 13, 1818		17 Henry J. Young " Nov. 13, 1798
"	8 Andrew A. Timmons " May 4, 1798	H. Priests	1 Arnold Stevens " Aug 24, 1802
"	9 William A. Follett " Dec. 12, 1825		2 Milton Kelly " Nov 12, 1807
"	10 Morgan Thomas " Dec. 7, 1826		

were washed by Loren Farr and Leslie Lyme. Anointed by Edward G. Dusett and P. G. Sessions. Finished at 10 A.M.

In the Female department commencing at 15 p. 8

Malinda Kelly born Oct 16, 1815	Linette Elliot born Sep 27, 1819
Nancy Timmons " July 18, 1818	Christiana Long " July 24, 1799
Nancy A. MacIntosh " Feb. 14, 1825	Temperance Young " May 23, 1811
Philinda A. Loss " Nov 23, 1806	Cornelia Moor " Feb 15, 1803
Sarah M Chaffin " June 2, 1815	Elizabeth Buys " Feb 10, 1815
Lavina Pendleton " Nov. 17, 1820	Harriet R. Burnham " Jan 26, 1818
Susan Cuthbert " Mar. 18, 1819	Nancy M. Follett " July 20, 1824
Mary Ann Fausett " May 17, 1831	Nancy Workman " Jan. 12, 1801
Esther P. Packard " Sep. 6, 1824	Sophia A. Packard " Oct. 1, 1828

Sarah Granger [born] Mar. 5, 1793 — Hannah Henderson [born] May 12, 1818
Sarah Harmon " Oct 21, 1786

were washed and anointed by Mary J. Horn, Nancy Cahoon, Cynthia Ann Eldredge, Zeruah Goddard, Lucina Sessions, Lydia Granger, Eda Rogers, and Myrza Alexander. Finished at 30 m. p. 9 A.M.

. . . .

[Washings and anointings for Wednesday, January 28, 1846—second excerpt]

Seventies		Seventies	
	18 Silas Nowell born Jan. 20, 1798		30 William Hawks born Nov. 3, 1799
	19 Elijah Haws " Nov. 9, 1806		31 Garret W. Mikesell " M
	20 Richard Hewett " Sep. 22, 1794		32 Charles Kimball " Jan. 20, 1824
	21 Elijah N. Freeman " Apl. 17, 1822		33 Geurnsey Brown " Nov. 8, 1824
	22 Philo Johnson " Dec. 6, 1814	H. Priests	Thomas Jones " Apl. 5, 1811
	23 John Pickels " Mar. 8, 1822		4 Jacob Degaw " July 15, 1811
	24 Lyman S. Hutchings " July 3, 1828		5 Gustavus A Perry " Jan. 4, 1797
	25 Joseph Kelly " Feb. 4, 1806	Elder	1 Samuel McMurtry " Feb 8, 1797
	26 Francis Burch " 1808		2 Alexander Mills " Dec. 23, 1801
	27 George C. Wilson " Aug 23, 1800		3 James Cowley " 1804
	28 Albert Tyler " Nov. 15, 1826		4 George Babcock " Apl. 27, 1792
	29 George W. ~~Taylor~~ Fowler " June 23, 1821		

were washed by Leslie Lyme and Loren Farr. Anointed by E. P. Duzett and P. G. Sessions. Finished at 25 min to 1. H. Burgess as Elohiem, Noah Rogers as Jehovah, Simeon A. Dunn as Michael, William Hyde as Peter, L. A. Shirtliff as James, Joseph Horn as John. Levi Hancock as Serpent and [illegible]

Wednesday evening January 28, 1845.

List 2 In the Female department commencing at 11—

Elizabeth Wilson born July 13, 1805	Mary Freeman born Apl 1, 1820
Elizabeth Cowley " 1804	Ann Mills " Sep. 8, 1820
Nancy Nowell " Feb. 28, 1805	Mary Ann Jones " Oct. 25, 1815
Nancy Houd " Dec. 30, 1800	Julia McMurtree " July 9, 1812
Lucy Young " June 8, 1813	Catherine Haws " Sep. 15, 1808
Ruth Mikesell " Jan 9, 1811	Margaret Hawk " Dec. 23, 1803
Amanda Babcock " Feb. 14, 1806	Asenath Babcock " June 2, 1826
Betsey Fowler " July 19, 1819	Elizabeth Birch " Mar. 22, 1810
Jerusha Hewitt " Dec. 16, 1800	Unice Perry " July 8, 1794
Abia Hawkins " Jan. 6, 1828	Sophia Degraw " Aug. 26, 1814
Sarah M. Johnson " Feb. 10, 1812	Abigail Grey " Mar 25, 1795
Sally Allred " Nov. 25, 1794	Eliza Gray " Nov. 4, 1824

Washed and anointed by Mary Ann Young, Nancy Cahoon, Mary J. Horn, Lidia Granger, Eda Rogers, and Lucina Sessions. Finished 35 p. 12.

List 3 In the Female Department commencing at 35 p. 1

Laura W. Merrill born Dec. 21, 1810	Sylvia Vanfleet born Aug. 4, 1819
Rhoda Stodard " Sep. 29, 1830	Mary Clark " Mar. 16, 1797
Sarah Thorn " June 14, 1809	Lorena Thorn " Apl. 16, 1814
Margaret Bateman " July 21, 1794	Harriet St. John " Nov. 7, 1829
Polly Smith " Sep. 29, 1817	Elizabeth F. Harmison " Apl. 20, 1820
Julia Ann Maylor " Feb. 12, 1826	Achsa M. Thompson " Nov. 6, 1824

Jane Holmes [born] Oct. 6, 1797	Elizabeth Armstrong [born] June 16, 1811
Martha Bennett " June 9, 1817	Elizabeth Smith " June 1, 1826
Isabella Leach " Dec. 1820	Mary Chipman " Apl. 25, 1813
Clarissa Marsh " July 1, 1832	Sarah Blezard " Mar. 15, 1815
Josina Glasgow " Apl. 19, 1812	

were washed and anointed by Phebe Chase, Mary J. Horn, Nancy Cahoon, Cynthia Ann Eldridge, Rusina Sessions, Lucinda Harris, Eda Rogers and Myzra Alexander. Finished at 40 minites past 2 P.M.

List 3 In the Male Department commencing at 25 to 3

Seventies		Seventies	
	34 Samuel Glasgow born Feb. 6, 1822		44 James Myler born Feb. 3, 1822
"	35 Lucullus P Thompson " Dec 31, 1822	"	45 Joseph Bateman " Sep. 4, 1802
"	36 Austin S. Merrill " Sep. 25, 1802	"	46 Joseph Armstrong " Apl. 27, 1812
"	37 Cyprian Marsh " July 16, 1813	"	47 Thomas S. Smith " Apl. 3, 1818
"	38 John H. Bleazard " Feb. 22, 1803	"	48 Silas Smith " June 6, 1822
"	39 Joseph Thorn " Dec. 22, 1811	"	49 Hiram Bennet " Mar. 1, 1823
"	40 Judson Stodard " Apl. 13, 1823	"	50 Francis Holmes " July 5, 1815
"	41 Harmon J. Chipman " Sep. 11, 1812	H. Priests	6 John Clark " Nov. 12, 1790
"	7 Joseph Cole " Feb. 6, 1808		
"	42 James Harmison " Feb. 20, 1820	Elders	5 Asahel Thorn " Feb. 6, 1808
"	43 James Leach " May 8, 1818		Josephus W. Northrup " Aug 3, 1826
	[last line illegible]		

were washed by Samuel Richards and Edward P Duzett. Anointed by William F. Cahoon and Leslie L. Young. Fin. at 25 to 4

Ordinations

James Harmison and Thomas S. Smith were ordained Seventies by Charles Bird and Samuel Moore.

List 4 In the Male Department commencing at 15 to 5.

Seventies		Seventies	
	51 David Garner jr. born Jan. 30, 1818		William Johnson born Sep 22, 1811
"	52 Alvin S. Stewart " Apl. 18, 1819	"	62 Richard Hampton " Aug. 22, 1819
"	53 John Myers " Feb. 6, 1814	"	63 Nelson McCarty " Sep. 22, 1813
"	54 John McLaughlin " May 31, 1806	"	64 John Reynolds " Nov. 9, 1806
"	55 Abel Butterfield " Dec. 31, 1812	"	65 Joseph Code " Mar 21, 1818
"	56 Samuel McBride " Aug. 25, 1789	Elders	8 Charles Hopkins " Feb. 20, 1810
"	57 John Steele " Mar. 21, 1821	"	9 Edwin S. Little " Jan. 22, 1817
"	58 John McBride " Jan. 5, 1788	"	10 Arvin Allen Avery " Oct. 27, 1812
"	59 Uriah B. Powell " July 11, 1809	"	11 Pulaski Cahoon " Sep. 18, 1820

were washed by P. G. Sessions and Leslie L. Young. Anointed by Lorin Farr and Charles Bird. Finished at 6 P.M.

Pulaski Cahoon was ordained Elder by William Cahoon and Saml. Moore.

List 4 In the Female department commencing at 40 p. 4

Mariah Avery born Sep. 19, 1815	Caroline Bullard May 19, 1816
Lucinda Clark " Apl. 18, 1824	Minerva Edon June 5, 1810
Lydia Hopkins " June 21, 1798	Julia Ann Mitchell " Feb. 19, 1828
Elizabeth Ann Holliday	Phebe Reynolds " Jan. 10, 1813
Sarah Powel " Mar. 29, 1816	Mary Jane McCarty " Apl. 11, 1819
Harriet Little " Mar. 13, 1806	Jane Mercer " June 11, 1824
Eliza Johnson " June 16, 1809	Catherine Steele " Nov. 1818

Caroline Butterfield [born] June 1, 1810	Lemira McBride [born] June 29, 1793
Sara Mc Laughlin " Feb. 7, 1822	Louisa Cahoon " Apl. 1, 1823
Camera Stewart " Oct. 31, 1824	Caroline Kempton " Dec 31 1821
Sarah Meyers " Aug 5, 1822	Martha Horsman " Apl. 16, 1782

were washed and anointed by Mary Smith, Lucina Sessions, Nancy Cahoon, Sophronia Harmon, Zeruah Godard, Eda Rogers, Cynthia Ann Eldridge, Jane Ann Green and Myrza Alexander. Fin at 50 M. p. 5.

—Seventies Record, Book B, oversized portions, January 28, 1846.

One hundred and seventy-two persons received ordinances in the Temple.

Nine-thirty p.m., the labors of the day closed. I [Brigham Young] remained in the Temple.

—"Manuscript History of Brigham Young,"
in *History of the Church,* 7:577.

....

Nauvoo temple endowments performed on this date for:

First Company: Edward Cuthbert, Susan Cuthbert, Henry Moore, Cornelia Moore, Orrin Packard, Philinda A. Loss, William A. Follet, Nancy M. Follet, Henry Young, Temperance Young, Sarah Harmon, Andrew A. Timmons, Nancy Timmons, John A. McIntosh, Nancy A. McIntosh, Adam Long, Christiana Long, Hanna Henderson, Benjamin F. Pendleton, Sarah Granger, Nancy Workman, Arnold Stevens, Lavina Pendelton, Louis R. Chaffin, Jacob L. Workman, Sarah M. Chaffin, Milton Kelly, Hyram D. Buys, Amanda Kelly, Elizabeth Buys, Ithamar Elliot, Linetta Elliot, Andrew Burnham, Harriet R. Burnham, Noah Packard Jr., Henry Packard, Esther P. Packard, Sophia A. Packard, Morgan Thomas, and Mary Ann Fausett.

Second Company: Alexander Mills, Lucy P. Young, Philo Johnson, Sarah Maria Johnson, Ann Mills, Sally Allred, James Cowley, Isabella Cowley, George Babcock, Abigail Gray, Amanda Babcock, Eliza Gray, Aseneth Babcock, Frances Burch, Elizabeth Burch, Thomas Jones, Nancy Howd, Mary Ann Jones, Gustavus A. Perry, Eunice Perry, George C. Wilson, Elizabeth Wilson, Silas Nowell, Nancy Nowell, Elijah N. Freeman, Mary Freeman, Richard Hewitt, Jerusha Hewitt, Garrett W. Mikesell, Ruth Mikesell, Joseph Kelly, Lucy Stanton, Samuel McMurtrie, Julia McMurtrie, Abiah Hawkins, Jacob Degraw, Sophia Degraw, Elijah Haws, Catharine Haws, William Hawk, Margaret Hawk, George W. Fowler, Betsey Fowler, Albert Tyler, Lyman S. Hutchings, Guernsey Brown, John Pickels, and Charles Kimball.

Third Company: John Clark, Mary Clark, Thomas S. Smith, Polly Smith, Francis Holmes, Jane Holmes, Asahel Thorn, Sarah Thorn, Austin S. Merrill, Laura W. Merrill, John H. Blazard, Sarah Blazard, Joseph Thorn, Harriet St. John, Lorena Thorn, Alanson Van Fleet, Sylvia Van Fleet, Harmon J. Chipman, Mary Chipman, Joseph Armstrong, Elizabeth Armstrong, James Myler, Julia Ann Myler, Silas Smith, Elizabeth Smith, James Harmison, Elizabeth/Fanny Harmison, Hiram Bennet, Martha Bennet,

Joseph Bateman, Samuel Glasgow, Josina Glasgow, Cyprian Marsh, Clarissa Marsh, Lucullus P. Thompson, Achsah Thompson, James Leach, Isabella Leach, Judson L. Stoddard, Rhoda Stoddard, Josephus W. Northrup, Joseph Code, and Margaret Bateman.

Fourth Company: John Reynolds, Phebe Reynolds, Abel Butterfield, Caroline Butterfield, Arvin A. Avery, Fanny Maria Avery, Minerva Eaton, Pulaski S. Cahoon, Elizabeth Holliday, Louisa Cahoon, Edwin S. Little, Julia Mitchell, Harriet A. Little, Richard Kempton, Caroline Kempton, David Garner Jr., Martha Horsman, Charles Hopkins, John Myers, Lydia Hopkins, Samuel McBride, Caroline Bullard, Sarah Myers, Nelson McCarty, Lemira McBride, Mary Jane McCarty, John Steele, Catharine Steele, William Johnson, Eliza Johnson, Alvin Stewart, Camera Stewart, Lucinda Clark, John McGlaughlin, Sarah McGlaughlin, Uriah B. Powell, Sarah Powell, Jane Mercer, Hartley Mercer, John McBride, and Joseph Code.

—Summary of information compiled by the Temple Index Bureau, *Nauvoo Temple Endowment Register: 10 December 1845 to 8 February 1846.* Editors' note: According to the register, Roxy Ann Mooman was washed and anointed on this date and therefore also probably received through the veil.

....

Second anointings performed on this date:

Randsom Sheppard and Mary (Goodwin) Sheppard, anointed by George Miller; Stephen H. Gooddard and Zeriah (Roby) Goddard, anointed by George Miller; Edison Barney and Lettis (Ballou) Barney, anointed by Parley P. Pratt; Agnes M. (Coolbrith) Smith to Don Carlos Smith (deceased; George A. Smith, proxy), anointed by Parley P. Pratt; Israel Barlow, Elizabeth (Haven) Barlow, and Elizabeth (Barton) Barlow), anointed by George Miller; Samuel Bent, Elizabeth (Burgess) Bent, Anna (Hartshorne) Bent, and Asenath (Slafter) Bent, anointed by [not given]; Hirum Spencer and Emily (Thompson) Spencer, anointed by Parley P. Pratt; Milo Andrus and Abigail (Daley) Andrus, anointed by Orson Spencer; James Taylor and Agnes Taylor, anointed by John Taylor; Lyman Leonard and Abigail (Calkins) Leonard, anointed by Orson Spencer; Brigham Young, Phebe (Morton) Young, Nabby (Works) Young, Cynthia (Weston) Young, Jemina Young, and Lucy P. Young, anointed by John Taylor; James Allred and Sally (Warren) Allred, anointed by John Taylor; William D. Huntington and Caroline (Clark) Huntington, anointed by Parley P. Pratt; Amasa M. Lyman and Laura (Reed) Lyman, anointed by

Orson Pratt; Aaron Johnson and Jane (Scott) Johnson, anointed by Orson Pratt; and Joseph C. Kingsbury, Dorcas (Moore) Kingsbury, and Lorenza (Pond) Kingsbury, anointed by Orson Pratt.

—Summarized from "Book of Anointings."

....

Sealings for the living performed on this date:

Milo Andrus to Abigail Jane Daley; Isaac Ashton to Abigail White; Daniel Bailey to Sarah Kindrick Currier; Israel Barlow to Elizabeth Barton; Edson Barney to Lillis Ballou [Batton]; Joseph Bateman to Margaret Turner; Thomas Bateman to Mary Street; Samuel Bent to Anna Hartshorne, Elizabeth Burgess and Asenath Slater; Ezra Bickford to Abigail Hartford; Alfred Brown to Hester Ann Eliza Merritt; Samuel Webster Brown to Lydia Maria [Mariah] Lathrop; John Burrclough to Jane Harrison; James Morgan Butler to Catherine McCall; William Farrington Cahoon to Nancy Maranda Gibbs and Mary [Casson] Douglas; John Button Carpenter to Mary Fisk; William Fourtsburg Carter to Sarah York; Thomas Durbin Caspar to Allison Rachel; Lewis Rice Chaffin to Sarah Maria Cossit; Jesse Wentworth Crosby to Hannah Elida Baldwin; Dorr Purdy Curtis to Catherine Adelia Haight; Edward Cuthbert to Susan McGee; Amos Davis to Mary Jane Scott; David Davis to Caroline Frances Angel; Henry John Doremus to Harriet Fairbanks; William Draper Jr. to Elizabeth Staker; Joseph Eaton to Minerva Sagers; Elisha Franklin Edwards to Mariah Elizabeth Duzett [Dugett]; Samuel Eggleston to Lauranna Burgess; Jacob Foutz to Margaret Mann; John Streetor Gleason to Desdemona Chase, Elisha Hurd Groves, and Lucy [Sally] Simmons; Ephraim Knowlton Hanks to Harriet Amelia [Little] Decker; Nelson Hanson to Merilla Terry; James Harmison to Elizabeth Fanny Brownell; Elijah Haws to Catherine Floyd Pease; Aaron Johnson to Jane Scott; Milton Kelly to Malinda Allison; Edwin Sabiski Little to Harriet Amelia Decker; John Loveless to Rachel Mahala Anderson; Elijah Malin to Catherine Essex; William Manhard to Jane Gates; David McCall to Margaret Bell; Marcellus McKown to Susan Ann Lamereaux; Hartley Mercer to Jane Sly; Austin Shepherd Merrill to Laura Wylder Harris; Joseph Stacy Murdock to Eunice Sweet; Levi North to Arminta Howard; Ezekiel Peck to Electa Buck; Parley Parker Pratt to Sarah Houston; Leonard Lake Randall to Maria Louisa Warren and Mary Jane Brooks; William Redfield to Mary Ann Scott; George Christian Riser to Christiana Kull; Chandler Rogers to Amanda Hollister; John Henry Rumel to Eliza Gray; William

Swapp to Elizabeth Hill; Urban Van Stewart to Lydia Gage Jacobs; John Joshua Tanner to Rebecca Archibald Smith; Nathan Tanner to Rachel Winter Smith; Sidney Tanner to Louisa Conlee; John Harvey Tippets to Nancy Calkins; Charles Blanchard Thompson to Elizabeth Yincks [Jencks] and Catherine Ann Houck; Lorin Walker to Lovina Smith; Charles Wesley Wandell to Mary Pratt Brown; Ira Enos West to Charlotte Amelia Van Orden; Edson Whipple to Lovina Gass; Jeremiah Willey to Samantha Call; George Clinton Wilson to Elizabeth Kinney; Alvin Winegar to Mary Judd; Thomas Woolsey to Julia Ann Mitchell and Elizabeth Ann Holdaway; Brigham Young to Phebe Morton Angel, Abigail [Libby] Works, Cynthia Porter, and Jemima Angel; and Phineas Howe Young to Lucy Pearce Cowdery and Phebe [Phoebe] Clark.

—Summarized from the Book of Living Sealings.

....

Sealings for the dead performed on this date:

Harriet Cooper (Lydia M. Lathrop, proxy) to Samuel Brown, Amasa M. Lyman officiating; Robert P. Wilson (William Carmichael, proxy) to Mary Clark, Amasa M. Lyman officiating;[45] John Hollister (Samuel Bent, proxy) to Vina Clearwater, Brigham Young officiating;[46] Don Carlos Smith (George A. Smith, proxy) to Agnes M. Coolbrith, Brigham Young officiating;[47] Phebe Weston (Susan Ann Lamereaux, proxy) to Marcellus McKown, Amasa M. Lyman officiating; William Allred (James Allred, proxy) to Sally Warren, Heber C. Kimball officiating;[48] Harriet P. Partridge (Caroline E. Partridge, proxy) and Easter Gleason (Louisa M. [Tanner] Lyman, proxy) to Amasa M. Lyman, Heber C. Kimball officiating; Hannah Pressey and Bathsheba Stevens (Samantha Call, proxy) to Jeremiah Willey, Brigham Young officiating; and Edward Weaver (William Draper, proxy) to Martha Raymer, Heber C. Kimball officiating.[49]

—Summarized from the Book of Proxy Sealings.

....

Adoptions performed on this date:

Anson Mathews to Samuel and Mary Bent (Lethis Palmer Bent,

45. Mary Clark was also sealed to William Carmichael for time.
46. Vina Clearwater was also sealed to Samuel Bent for time.
47. Agnes Coolbrith was also sealed to George A. Smith for time.
48. Sally Warren was also sealed to James Allred for time.
49. Martha Raymer was also sealed to William Draper for time.

proxy): "Anson Mathews was adopted and sealed to Samuel and Mary Bent in the usual manner, &c."; to Howard and Martha Jane Coray: Howard Coray and Martha Jane Coray: "These children were sealed to their parents by the usual ordinances and covenant at the Altar &c."; to David and Mary Ann Candland: Sarah Emily Candland "by the usual ordinances &c."; to Willard and Jennetta Richards (Amelia Elizabeth Richards, proxy), Heber John Richards, Rhoda Ann Jennette Richards, Ellen Partington, Stephen Longstreet, Ann Longstreet, Thomas Bullock, Henrietta Bullock, Lucy Caroline Bullock, Willmer Benjamin Benson, Ann Elizabeth Fox, George Darling Watt, Mary Watt, and Peter Muir, sealed by Brigham Young: "These persons were all adopted and sealed to Willard and Jennette Richards — Amelia Elizabeth Richards acting at the Alter for Jennette deceased"; to John and Clarissa Smith: George Albert Smith, John Lyman Smith, Caroline Smith, Thomas Callister, Bathsheba Wilson Smith, Augusta Bowen Smith, and Helen Mar Clark Callister, sealed by Brigham Young: "The above named children having all received their Endowments were Sealed to their parents John and Clarissa Smith at the Alter, mutually entering into [a] covenant, the Parents and children covenanting together according to the order were all sealed (both natural and adopted) to them for time and all eternity to bear their name and be numbered with them in their inheritance and Kingdoms which may be given and also sealed unto eternal life &c on condition of keeping their covenants made on this sacred alter. In the east room in the presence of an assembly ... The above sealing of B[athsheba]. W[ilson]. Smith to John Smith was cancelled by Pres[iden]t. W[ilford]. Woodruff, 16 March 1896. Geo[rge]. Reynolds, recorder"; to George Albert and Bathsheba Smith: George Albert Smith and Bathsheba Smith, sealed by Brigham Young: "According to the Holy Order—as [directed by] Pres[iden]ts [Brigham] Young & [Heber C.] Kimball"; and to Hyrum Smith (Heber C. Kimball, proxy) and Jerusha B. Smith (Mary F. Smith, proxy): Lovina Smith Walker, Lorin Walker, Charles Wesley Wandall, and Mary Brown Wandall, sealed by Brigham Young: "Lovina is Hyrum's eldest living daughter, and holds the birthright for her own sex, but was present when the other children were sealed &c. Lorin Walker — her husband was adopted in the usual manner &c. These [Charles and Mary Wandall] were adopted to Hyrum and Jerusha Smith in the usual order &c. &c."

—Summarized from "Sealings and Adoptions."

Thursday, January 29, 1846

I continued the work of the endowment in the temple in connection with my Brethren the 12 [apostles] & such others; as we appointed & set apart to assist us ... we now ask God our Heavenly Father to exert his Power in our deliverance that we may be preserved—to establish Truth upon all the face of the Earth[.]

—Brigham Young, Diary.

....

[See pages 519-23 for the Seventies Record for this date.]

....

I [Brigham Young] continued giving endowments in the Temple in connection with my brethren of the Twelve [apostles] and others. One hundred and thirty-three persons received ordinances. ...

We ask God our Heavenly Father to exert his power in our deliverance that we may be preserved to establish truth upon all the face of the earth.

—"Manuscript History of Brigham Young," in *History of the Church,* 7:577; and *Manuscript History of Brigham Young,* p. 24.

....

Nauvoo temple endowments performed on this date for:

First Company: Luther Reed, Charity Reed, Christian Houtz, Susan Houtz, Samuel Thompson, Patience Childs, Benjamin Loss, Sally Loss, Albert Pease, Olive Pease, David Norris, Sarah Louisa Norris, John Carling, Ann Carling, William Greenalgh, Mary Greenalgh, Increase Van Deuzen, Maria Van Deuzen,[50] Samuel Kelly, Eleanor Kelly, David Cluff Sr., Betsey Cluff, James Jepson, Eleanor Jepson, John W. Hess, Emeline Hess, Alexander M. Shoemaker, Margaret Shoemaker, Samuel H. Alexander, Mary Alexander, Robert C. Moore, Keziah Orcutt, Richard H. Withnell, Elizabeth Withnell, Levi Allred, Abigail Allred, Asahel G. Talcott, and Joseph Parker.

Second Company: Alexander Clough, Julia Clough, Michael B. Welton, Keziah Welton, Nathaniel Childs, Sarah Lancaster, Almond M. Williams, Susan Jordan, Amos Tubs, Zilpha B. Williams, George Edwards, Catharine

50. For the published account of their experience in the temple, see Increase McGee Van Deusen and Maria Van Deusen, *Mormon Endowment, A Secret Drama, or Conspiracy in the Nauvoo Temple, in 1846; in Which Process Mr. & Mrs. McGhee, (the Authors of this Work,) Were Made King and Queen* (Syracuse, NY: N. M. D. Lathrop, Printer, 1847), 3-9.

[Washings and anointings for Thursday, January 29, 1846]

List 1 In the Male department beginning at 30 p. 8 A.M.

Seventies		Seventies	
	1 Luther Reed born Aug 11, 1797		11 David Norris born Aug. 10, 1800
"	2 Levi Allred " Dec. 16, 1800	"	12 Increase Vandeusen " May 25, 1810
"	3 Albert Pease " Mar. 16, 1809	"	13 John W. Hess " Aug. 24, 1824
"	4 James Japson " June 24, 1816	"	14 Samuel Thompson " Mar. 30, 1810
"	5 William Greenhalgh " July 29, 1811	"	15 John Carling " Sep. 11, 1800
"	6 David Cluff " June 20, 1795	"	16 Asahel Talcott " July 28, 1812
"	8 Samuel H. Alexander " July 12, 1822	H. Priests	1 Benjamin Loss " May 4, 1783
"	9 Robert C. Moore " May 4, 1821	Elders	1 Richard H. Withnell " Apl. 28, 1805
"	10 Samuel Kelly " Oct. 29, 1792		2 Alexander M. Shoemaker " July 8, 1813
		"	3 Christian Horitz " July 16, 1805

were washed and ~~an~~ by Madison D. Hamilton and M. M. Sanders, Anointed by Samuel Moore, John Eldridge and Darwin Chase. Finished at 5 min. to 10 A. M.

In the Female department commenced at 9 A.M.

Mary Greenalsh born	Eleonar E. Kelly born Apl. 28, 1793
Margaret Shoemaker "	Charity Reed " Mar 9, 1801
Mariah Vandeusen " Aug 12, 1824	Ann Carlinges " 1806
Olive Pease " Nov. 5, 1797	Hezekiah Orcutt " Mar. 17, 1797
Abigail Allred " Sep. 11., 1804	Mary Alexander " Dec. 11, 1818
Eleonar Jepson " July 4, 1816	Susan Hautz " June 17, 1812
Sarah L. Norris " Aug. 5, 1805	Elizabeth Withead " Sep. 13, 1806

Sally Loss [born] July 9, 1776	Patience D. Childs [born] Sep. 27, 1827
Emaline Hess " Aug 4, 1824	Betsey Cluff " July 10, 1805

were washed and anointed by Lydia Granger, Zeruah Godard, Eda Rogers, Mary J. Horn, Myrza Alexander, Caroline Huntington Susan A. Chapman, Martha S. Haven and Caroline Bird. Finished at 15 minutes p. 10 AM

F. Richards, William Snow, Willard Snow, O. Spencer, J. Holman, Zebedee Coltrin and George Miller met in room No 9 and consecrated 26 bottles of oil, [illegible] consecrated 6 Bottles.

List 2 In the Male department commencing at 15 p. 11

Sev		Sev	
	16 Almond M. Williams born Jan 11, 1807		26 Amos B. Moore born Dec. 13, 1828
"	17 Abraham Stevens " Dec. 3, 1818	"	27 William Young " Aug 28, 1806
"	18 Edmund R. Butler " Apl. 28, 1822	"	28 Jedediah S. Woodward " July 10, 1806
"	19 Eli Lee " July 11, 1816	"	29 Nathaniel Childs " June 16, 1789
"	20 Levi Thornton " May 19, 1819	"	30 Alexander Clough " Jan. 13, 1822
"	21 Orman Houghton " Oct. 1, 1806	"	31 Myron N. Crandall " Aug 17, 1818
"	22 Matthew Moore jr. " July 7, 1820	H. Priests	2 Amos Tubs " Jan. 22, 1790
"	23 George Edwards " Mar. 22, 1810	"	3 Naum M. Stove " Apl. 2, 1801
"	24 Henry L. Cook " July 8, 1803	Elders	4 Nelson Allen " Sep. 28, 1802
"	25 M. B. Welton " Aug. 13, 1794	"	5 David Norton " Oct. 26, 1795

were washed by Madison D. Hamilton and M. M. Sanders Anointed by Samuel Moore and John Eldridge. Finished at 12.

Ordinations

Nelson Allen was ordained Elder by John Eldridge and S. Moore. Amos Tubs was ordained High Priest by George Miller, Albert P. Rockwood and Samuel Moore.

List 2 In the Female department commencing at 50 p. 10.

Catharine Fuller born May 20, 1820	Sarah Moore born June 6, 1820
Tryphenia Crandall " Apl. 4, 1819	Christena Stevens " June 24, 1818
Ann Edwards " July 13, 1803	Sarah Sagers " Feb. 16, 1789
Lydia Butler " Oct. 19, 1830	Elizabeth C. Lee " Feb. 28, 1822
Sarah Lancaster " June 28, 1771	Leah Young " Dec. 1, 1810
Eliza Thorn " June 26, 1820	Margaret Stoe " Sep 9, 1811
Lovinia Cook " Oct. 22, 1803	Zilpha B. Williams " Oct. 25, 1815
Sarah Lytle " May 10, 1774	Elizabeth Norton " Aug 9, 1801
Sarah Lancaster " Mar 23, 1806	Keziah Welton " Nov 9, 1820
Lucia Allen " Dec. 17, 1810	Emily Woodward " Jan. 1, 1805
Julia M. Clough " Jan 16, 1817	Susan Jordan " Apl. 14, 1789
Mary Houghton " Nov 15, 1831	

were washed and anointed by Mary Smith, Louisa Clark, Zeruah ~~Clark~~ Goddard, Lydia Granger, Eda Rogers, Susan A. Chapman, Lucina Sessions, Caroline Huntingdon, Martha S. Haven, Cynthia A. Eldridge, and Nancy Rockwood. Finished at 50 p. 11 A.M.

List 3 In the Male department commencing at 30 p. 1.

Sev		Sev	
	32 Lorenzo H. Hatch born Jan. 4, 1826		37 Jonathan Pugmire born Mar 28, 1799
"	33 Albert Dunham " May 23, 1828	"	38 Joshua Davis " Dec. 23, 1820
"	34 Mose A. D. Morse " Mar. 14, 1801	"	39 Joseph Huff " Apl 24, 1818
"	35 [illegible] Clark " Nov. 1805	"	40 William Bateman " Apl 23, 1824
"	36 [illegible] L. Bliss " Aug 1, 1805	"	41 Oden Jacobs " Dec. 1 [illegible]

Seventies			High Priests
	42 Hiram Murdock born Sep 4, 1823		4 Alva West born June 21, 1795
"	43 Spencer W Whitblank " Oct. 22, 1824	Elders	6 Simeon Andrews " Sep 16, 1798
"	44 William H. Clawson " Nov. 6, 1825		
"	45 Richard Wolsey " Aug. 28, 1808		
"	46 Peter G. Meesic		

were washed ~~and~~ by Madison D. Hambleton and M. M. Sanders. Anointed by Samuel Moore and Leslie L. Young. Finished at 20 m. p. 2 P.M.

Ordained William Bateman, Oden Jacobs, and William H. Clawson Seventies — Andrew Moore, and Samuel Moore officiating.

List 3 In the Female department commencing at 10 p. 1

Susan Ann Davis born June 1829	Lillice Clark born Feb. 22, 1820
Fanny Eliza Green " Jan. 17, 1821	Mariah Louisa Roberts " Nov. 11, 1829
Lydia Ann Trumbel " Apl. 8, 1819	Hannah Woolsey " Jan. 7, 1823
Elizabeth Pugmire " Oct. 15, 1800	Mary Ann Bliss " Mar. 23, 1811
Hannah E. Fuller " Feb. 24, 1827	Jane Morse " Nov. 11, 1805
Evaline Griffith " June 22, 1825	Martha E. Berry " Nov. 22, 1826
Sally West " Oct 19, 1800	Louisa Jane Berry " Dec. 1, 1828
Dorcas Andrews " May 26, 1801	Amelia H. Berry " Jan. 17, 1830
Elizabeth Cheney " June 7, 1814	Mary Jane Huff " Oct. 4, 1820
Sarah Bateman " Mar. 21, 1824	Jane Mathews " May 12, 1829

were washed and anointed by Mary J. Horn, Louisa Clark, Cynthia A. Eldridge, Clarissa Hancock, Altamira Shirtliff, Jane Ann Green, Eda Rogers, Lucina Sessions. Fin at 10 p. 2.

List 4 In the Male department commencing at [?]

Seventies		Seventies
	47 Thomas S. Williams born Jan. 2, 1826	53 David Frederick born Sep. 15, 1801
"	48 Jonathan F. Parker " July 26, 1817	54 James M. Wait " Apl. 6, 1811
"	49 Levi L. Skinner " Oct 27, 1819	55 Henry Parker " Sept. 26, 1807
"	50 Samuel Musick " Mar 23, 1804	56 Isaac Shepherd " Sep. 2, 1806
"	51 William R. Orton " Mar. 19, 1802	
"	52 James Barnes " Feb. 10, 1815	

were washed by Madison D. Hambleton and M. M. Sanders. Anointed by Samuel Moore and Leslie L. Young.

Ordinations

Levi S. Skinner was ordained Seventy by Samuel Moore, Darwin Chase, and Wilkinson Hewitt. Finished at 6 P.M.

List 4 In the Female Department commencing at 10 p. 3

Rachel Henderson born Sep. 15, 1822	Louisa Eddy born Mar 8, 1812
Alvina M. Williams " July 25, 1826	Angeline A Packer " Jan. 8, 1820
Charlotte Barnes " July 1819	Catharine Skinner " Dec. 4, 1810
Rebecca Warden " July 14, 1807	Elizabeth Musick " July 15, 1809
Sophronia Wait " Sep. 13, 1816	Rebecca Musick " July 5, 1830
Nancy Parker born May 22, 1816	Harriet Rank born Aug 24, 1825
Sarah Shepard " Dec. 30, 1807	Clarissa Higbee " Oct. 1, 1829
Jane Rank " Aug. 23, 1828	

were washed and anointed by Nancy Cahoon, Eda Rogers, Altimita Shirtliff, Susan A Chapman, and Caroline Huntington, and Nancy H. Rockwood. 10 p. 4.

—Seventies Record, Book B, January 29, 1846.

Walker, William Young, Sarah Lancaster, Jedediah Woodard, Emily Woodard, Edmund R. Butler, Ann Edwards, Levi Thornton, Lydia M. Butler, Amos B. Moore, Leah Young, Ornan Houghton, Mary Houghton, Nelson Allen, Lucia Allen, Eli Lee, Elizabeth Lee, Abraham Stevens, Christina Stevens, David Norton, Elizabeth Norton, Nahum M. Stow, Margaret Stow, Matthew Moore Jr., Sarah Moore, Myron N. Crandall, Tryphena Crandall, Henry Cook, Lovina Cook, Eliza Thorn, Sarah Lytle, and Sarah Sagers.

Third Company: Joshua Davis, Susan A. Davis, Simeon Andrews, Dorcas Andrews, John Clark, Lillias Clark, Richard Woolsey, Hannah Woolsey, Jonathan Pugmire, Elizabeth Pugmire, Lorenzo H. Hatch, Hannah E. Fuller, Alva West, Sally West, Jane Mathers, Hiram Murdock, Anna Eliza Green, Elizabeth Cheney, Oden Jacobs, Louisa Jane Berry, Martha Elizabeth Berry, Armelia H. Berry, William Bateman, Sarah Bateman, Lydia Ann Trumbull, Moses A. D. Morse, Jane Morse, Robert S. Bliss, Marrian Bliss, Maria Louisa Roberts, Spencer W. Wiltbank, Eveline Griffith, Joseph Huff, Mary Jane Huff, Peter Mesic, Albert Dunbar, and William H. Clawson.

Fourth Company: James M. Wait, Sophronia Wait, Henry Parker, Nancy Parker, Levi Skinner, Catharine Skinner, Thomas S. Williams, Albina M. Williams, Jonathan Packer, Angelina A. Packer, David Frederick, Rachel Henderson, William R. Orton, Rebecca Orton, Isaac Shepard, Sarah Shepard, James Barns, Charlotte Barns, Samuel Musick, Elizabeth Musick, James Rank, Harriet Rank, Rebecca Ann Musick, Clarissa Higbee, and Eliza Bowley.

—Summary of information compiled by the Temple Index Bureau, *Nauvoo Temple Endowment Register: 10 December 1845 to 8 February 1846.* Editors' note: According to the register, Louisa Eddy was washed and anointed and therefore also probably received through the veil on this date.

....

Second anointings performed on this date:

Charles W. Wandell and Mary (Brown) Wandell, anointed by Parley P. Pratt; Nathan Tanner and Rachel (Smith) Tanner, anointed by George Miller; James Pace and Lucinda (Strickland) Pace, anointed by George Miller; Daniel Duncan McArthur, Susan (McKeen) McArthur, and Cynthia (Nichols) McArthur, anointed by Parley P. Pratt; William F. Cahoon, Nancy (Gibbs) Cahoon, and Mary (Casson) Cahoon, anointed by Parley

P. Pratt; John M. Lytle and Christina (Whitney) Lytle, anointed by George Miller; Andrew Lytle and Hannah (Hull) Lytle, anointed by George Miller; John J. Tanner and Rebecca (Smith) Tanner, anointed by George Miller; Edward Hunter, Ann (Stanley) Hunter, Laura (Shimer) Hunter, and Susanna (Wann) Hunter, anointed by George Miller; and Sidney Tanner and Louisa (Conlee) Tanner, anointed by George Miller.

—Summarized from "Book of Anointings."

....

Sealings for the living performed on this date:

Alvah Alexander to Phoebe Houston; John Fletcher Atwood to Sarah Ann Woods; Thomas Bateman to Mary Street [Sheet]; William Bateman to Sarah Lavendar; Anson Matthews Bent to Mary Emery; Charles Bird to Mary Ann Kennedy; Abram Dodge Boynton to Hannah Maria Burbank; Daniel Brown to Harriet St. John; Andrew Burnham to Harriet Ruhamah Kimball; John Lowe Butler to Sarah Lancaster; Isaac Decker to Fanny Eliza Green and Maria Louisa Roberts; David Bue Dille to Harriet Lucretia Welch; Oliver Hunt Dudley to Mary Ann Robinson; William Felshaw to Elizabeth Cheney; John Fido to Lydia Pullin; Elijah Knapp Fuller to Catherine Walker; Dwight Harding to Phebe Holbrook; Jeremiah Hatch to Louisa Pool Alexander; Archibald Newell Hill to Isabella Hood; Charles Hopkins to Lydia Okie; Christian Houtz to Susannah Pauling; Joseph Huff to Mary Jane Losee; Alexander Hunt to Mary Beard; Oliver Hunt to Mary Ann Robinson; Edward Hunter to Ann Stanley, Laura Lovina Kaufman Shimer, and Susanna Wann; Dimick Baker Huntington to Fanny Mariah Allen; William Dresser Huntington to Ann Maginn; James Jepson to Eleanor [Eleana] Nightingale; Thomas Kington to Margaret Pisel; Henry Earl Lamoreaux to Harriet Price; John Doyle Lee to Martha Perry; Levi Loveland to Hannah Pease; Edward Martin to Alice Clayton; Duncan McArthur to Cynthia Nickols; James Madison Morehead to Elizabeth Turner Thomas; Josiah Moulton Jr. to Hannah Symonds; Stephen Nixon to Harriet Rushton; William Reed Orton to Rebecca Hessy; Jonathan Taylor Packer to Angelene Avilda Chaplin; Samuel Parker to Delaney Shafer; Alfred Randall to Emerett Louisa Davis; William Richey to Margaret Ann Adair; William Wommack Riley to Charity Sasnett; Noah Rogers to Eda Hollister; David Sanger Jr. to Mary Palmer; William Alonzo Sanger to Mary Miles; Luman Andrus Shurtliff to Altamire Gaylord; Gardner [Gardiner] Snow to Sarah Sawyer Hastings; Thomas Spiers to Mary Cochran; Richard Demont Sprague to Louisa

Maria Rose; Alvin Franklin Stewart to Camera Owen; Allen Tally to Catherine Blair; Allen Taylor to Sarah Lovisa Allred; Edward Tuttle to Catherine Vanever Geyer; Little John Utley to Elizabeth Ruthledge; and Edward Milo Webb to Jane Mathers.

—Summarized from the Book of Living Sealings.

....

Sealings for the dead performed on this date:

Eunice B. Gaylord (Altamaria Gaylord, proxy) to Luman A. Shurtliff, Amasa M. Lyman officiating; Anna Steel (Lydia Okie, proxy) to Charles Hopkins, Amasa M. Lyman officiating; James Casson (William F. Cahoon, proxy) to Mary Wilson, Amasa M. Lyman officiating;[51] Hannah Pitt (Margaret Pisel, proxy) to Thomas Kington, Amasa M. Lyman officiating; Harriet Loomis (Catharine Walker, proxy) to Elijah K. Fuller, Amasa M. Lyman officiating; Hyrum Smith (Edward Tuttle, proxy) to Susan Ivers, Heber C. Kimball officiating;[52] and Nancy Ridge (Margaret Adair, proxy) to William Richey, Heber C. Kimball officiating.

—Summarized from the Book of Proxy Sealings.

Friday, January 30, 1846

[A]t 10. o. clock I entered the Temple where I confined my Servises through the day in attending to the sealings & anointings at 20 minets [minutes] past 7—eve[ning]—the work stoped in [the] Sealing department[.]

—Brigham Young, Diary.

....

[See pages 527-32 for the Seventies Record for this date.]

....

One hundred and seventy-two persons received the ordinances of endowment.

Nine a.m., the vane was put upon the tower of the Temple.

The weather is stormy, yet not cold. At ten a.m., I [Brigham Young] entered the Temple where I labored until evening.

—"Manuscript History of Brigham Young,"
in *History of the Church,* 7:577-78.

---

51. Mary Wilson was also sealed to William Cahoon for time.

52. Susan Ivers was also sealed to Edward Tuttle for time.

[Washings and anointings for Friday, January 30, 1846]

List 1 In the Male department commencing at 10 Min p. 8. A.M.

Sev		Sev	
	1 Lorenzo D. Hickey born Feb. 15, 1819		11 Parmenas H. Woodworth b. June 30, 1806
"	2 James Harle " Sep. 18, 1826		12 Jacob Lance " Aug 15, 1816
"	3 William Myres " Feb. 9, 1809		13 James H. Heath " Mar. 26, 1814
"	4 Calvin Reed " Oct. 18, 1821		14 George B. Teeples " Mar. 26, 1814
"	5 Robert Plunket " Dec. 23, 1800		15 Ransford Coalby " Jan. 1, 1820
"	6 Wilson Lund " Feb. 9, 1815		16 William J. Phelps " Oct. 14, 1817
"	7 Silas Willman " Feb. 27, 1820		17 John Horlick " Aug. 25, 1809
"	8 Hiram B. Chase " Mar. 14, 1823	Elders	1 Seth Palmer " Feb. 22, 1824
"	9 John A Casper " Feb. 9, 1823	"	2 Ira S. Miles " Dec. 25, 1808
"	10 Ira Hillman " Apl. 30, 1827	"	3 Sanford Bingham " May 3, 1821

were washed by Alexander Whiteside and Andrew Moore. Anointed by Randolph Alexander and David P. Rainey. Finished at 15 p. 9.

Ordinations

Ira Hillman was ordained Seventy by Samuel Moore and Steven Godard.

List 1 In the Female department commencing at 8 A.M.

Mary Reed born May 15, 1821	Mariah Heath born Nov. 29, 1824
Ann Hickey " Jan. 20, 1814	Mary Mariah Chase " Mar. 29, 1825
Electa P. Hillman " May 1, 1823	Marilla Woodworth " Jan. 20, 1807
Sarah Plunket " May 1, 1823	Mary Jane Lance " Sep. 1, 1828
Mary C. Coury " July 7, 1822	Rebecca Casper " Jan. 1, 1808

Zeruah Myres [born] Mar. 25, 1817	Nancy Henderson [born] ~~May 11 1829~~ ^Jan 13, 1828^
Elizabeth Horlick " Sep. 22, 1814	Abigail Henderson " May 11, 1829
Eliza Lund " Oct. 11, 1821	Lucy Haile " Nov. 22, 1825
Jane Hamer " Apl. 14, 1802	Clarissa Pulsipher " Mar. 14, 1799
Emily Woolsey " Jan. 4, 1830	

were washed and anointed by Clarissa Hancock, Caroline Huntington, Zeruah Goddard, Jane Ann Green, C. A. Eldredge, N. Cahoon, C. Hamilton, L. Sessions, Nancy Rockwood.

List 2 In the Male department commencing at 10 A.M.

Seventies		Sev	
	18 Abraham S. Workman born Sep. 18, 1822		John Heslem born May 31, 1826
"	19 William Steele " Jan 9, 1806	"	23 William Earl " Apl. 19, 1830
"	20 Edward L. Page " Dec. 23, 1819	"	24 Levi Thomas " July 28, [illegible]
"	21 John Worsley " Feb 2, 1812		25 Israel J Clark " Dec [illegible]
Sev.		H. Priests	
	26 Samuel Bell born Feb. 2, 1814		1 David Evans born Oct. 27, 1804
"	27 Morgan L. Gardner " Aug 19, 1808		2 James Graham " Oct. 11, 1804
"	28 John Riley " Feb. 6, 1795		3 Robert Gibson " Nov. 11, 1787
"	29 William Turpin " Jan. 18, 1811		4 Thomas Hamilton " Apl. 20, 1785
"	30 Ezra Factout " Dec. 24, 1801	Elders	4 Joseph ^William^ Richards " May 25, 1829
"	31 Jacob Woolsey " Aug 22, 1781		5 David Smith "

were washed ~~and anointed~~ by Alexander Whiteside, and Andrew Moore. Anointed by Randolph Alexander and David P. Rainey. Fin. at 10. p 11.

Ordinations

Thomas Hamilton was ordained High Priest by Ezra T. Benson and Phinehas Richards — Abraham L. Workman was washed and Anointed only.

List 2 In the Female department commencing at 55 p 9

Mary Graham born Apl. 18, 1804	Sarah Worseley born Oct. 26, 1816
Elizabeth A. Clark " Mar. 13, 1822	Eliza Woolsey " Mar. 14, 1813
Henrietta Williams " Sep. 26, 1826	Catherine J. Page " Feb. 8, 1816
Ellen Wilding " Apl. 8, 1822	Sarah Mills " Mar. 1, 1828
Sarah Earl " Feb 16, 1796	Elizabeth Turpin " May 24, 1815
Martha Workman " Sep. 8, 1824	Ellen M. Bolton " Feb. 27, 1823
Jemima Bell " Dec. 9, 1818	Martha Haslem " July 1, 1826
Mary Thomas " Apl. 15, 1813	Elizabeth Smith " Jan. 23, 1825
Polly Ann Childs " July 20, 1823	Angeline Richardson " Nov. 25, 1815
Esther Gibson " April 1779	Elizabeth Riley " May 6, 18
Margaret Steele	Abigail Hamilton

were washed and anointed by Mary H. Richards, Martha S Haven, Clarissa Hancock, Altemira Shirtliff, Margaret M. Rainey, Eda Rogers, Anna Harmon, and Susan A. Chapman. Finished at 50. p. 10

List 3 In the Male department commencing at 20 m. to 1

Sev.

	32 Asa P. Waldo born Apl. 6, 1823	43 Thomas Allman " May 30, 1819
"	33 Howard Thomas " Dec. 6, 1814	44 Job. Hall " Aug. 16, 1820
"	34 James E. Daniels " Feb. 8, 1825	45 Charles Hall " Feb. 5, 1823
"	35 Andrew J. Workman " July 15, 1824	46 Richard Moon " June 25, 1805

[Seventies] 36 Turner H. Moore [born] July 24, 1817
" 37 Jacob Strong " Oct. 9, 1799
" 38 Erastus Bingham " Sep. 30, 1822
" 39 Daniel P. Foster " July 16, 1815
" 40 Rufus Allen " Mar. 22, 1814
" 41 William Boss " June 15, 1827
" 42 Adison Smith " Aug. 7, 1814

47 Henry Moon [born] Mar 29, 1819
48 Hiram Falk " July 22, 1810
49 William Martin " Oct. 11, 1811
50 Benager Brooks " Feb. 2, 1812
51 William Moon " Aug 17, 1807

were washed by Alexander Whitesides and Andrew Moore. Anointed by Randolph Alexander and David Rainey. Finished at 15 min to 2. P.M. Friday, January 30, 1846.

List 3 In the Female department commencing at 20 p. 12

Eliza Moon born Feb. 10, 1816
Lydia Moon " Oct. 9, 1811
Ann Moon " Mar. 1, 1811
Sarah Strong " Sep. 1, 1816
Olive H. Bingham " Jan. 8, 1820
Margaret Foster " Feb. 18, 1812
Jane Alman " Mar. 12, 1815
Ruth Tyler " Feb. 25, 1820
Obedience Boss " Feb. 28, 1797
Elizabeth Daniels " Mar 8, 1799

Sarah Martin born Sep 12, 1812
Martha Moulton " June 11, 1798
Josephine Garnand " July 22, 1796
Clarissa Jones " July 6, 1815
Isabella Lamoreaux " Mar. 28, 1808
Relief Cram " Jan. 17, 1820
Minerva Brooks " Oct. 2, 1818
Asenath P. Allen " June 20, 1818
Rachel Moore " July 4, 1814
Mariah Faulk " June 9, 1815

were washed and anointed by Martha Jane Farnham, Eliza Ann Felt, Altemira Shirtliff, Nancy Cahoon, Jane Ann Green. Fin. at 25. p. 1.

List 4 In the Male department commencing at 25 m. to 3.

Sev	52 Ebenezer C. Richardson born Aug 7, 1815	Sev	64 John Griffiths born Jan 20, 1815
"	53 Jesse H. Atherton " Dec. 7, 1823	"	65 John Ellison " May 23, 1818
"	54 Ithamar Sprague " Sep. 18, 1807	"	66 Alexander S. Stanley " May 12, 1800
"	55 Agrippa Cooper " Dec. 18, 1814	"	67 George Morris " Aug. 23, 1817
"	56 Peter H. Goodwin " Mar. 14, 1819	"	68 Oliver G. Workman " Jan. 7, 1828
"	57 Azariah Tuttle " Apl. 20, 1818	"	69 Hiram Mott " Nov. 7, 1799
"	58 Daniel Fisher " Oct. 12, 1817	"	70 Ɉ Thomas Jaap " Jan. 22, 1808
"	59 Alfred S. Hadden " Jan. 13, 1813	"	71 Henry Russel " Oct. 7, 1827
"	60 John Mills " July 24, 1804	"	72 Alexander Allen " Aug. 1801
"	61 Thomas J. Brandon " Mar. 5, 1806	H. Priests	6 Emer Harris " May 29, 1781
"	62 George Nixon " Aug. 16, 1818	"	7 John Evans " May 9, 1790
"	63 Hugh ^H.^ Cole " Sep. 17, 1808	"	8 Hezekiah Sprague " Nov. 10, 1775

~~64~~ were washed by Alexander Whiteside and Andrew Moore.

Anointed by David Rainey and Leslie L. Young. Finished at 30 p. 3.

List 4 In the Female Department commencing at 55 p. 2 P.M.

Elizabeth Mart born Nov 7, 1804	Ann Griffiths born Oct. 5, 1813
Nancy Brown " May 29, 1792	Jane Mills " Apl. 13, 1808
Martha Cooper " Mar. 9, 1816	Hannah Mariah Morris " Mar. 13, 1823
Louisa Aldridge " Apl. 9, 1809	Abigail Sprague " July 8, 1773
Allice Ellisson " Nov. 25, 1820	Elizabeth Sprague " June 28, 1819
Julia Ann Hadden " Aug. 9, 1813	Mary Jane Eighmen " Nov. 25, 1828
Elizabeth Stanley " Mar. 25, 1782	Femey Nixon " Feb. 9, 1818

Ann Tuttle [born] Dec. 2, 1820	Philanda Stanley [born] Aug 1, 1814
Mary Evans " May 7, 1780	Susannah Cole " Feb. 11, 1808
Hannah Lane [?] " June 18, 1807	Jane Allen " [illegible]

Friday Evening, January 30, 1846

Sophronia Morris born Feb 28, 1810	Jane Jaap born Mar. 12, 1798
Mary Ann Fisher " July 17, 1820	Parma Harris " Nov. 12, 1792
Elizabeth Jane Moorman " June 10, 1823	Maria E. Mart " July 22, 1823

were washed and anointed by Eda Rogers, Altemira Shirtliff, Electa Whitesides, Ann Harmon, Chelmicia Hamilton, Martha S. Horn, Mary Jane Farnham, Margaret M. Raney, Eliza Ann Felt and Mary H. Parker. Finished at 4 oc P.M.

In the evening, after the day's work was finished, those worked in the Endowments, assembled in the Celestial room and spent about 1½ hour in singing and prayer; after which each one retired to their respective apartments for the night. Charles W. Wandell Smith.

—Seventies Record, Book B, January 30, 1846.

Nauvoo temple endowments performed on this date for:

First Company: William Myers, Zeruah Myers, William J. Phelps, Calvin Reed, Mary Reed, Jacob Lance, Lorenzo D. Hickey, Mary Jane Lance, Ann Hickey, Hiram B. Chase, Mary C. Corey, Mary M. Chase, John A. Caspar, Silas Hillman, Electa Hillman, Rebecca Caspar, Ira S. Miles, Nancy Henderson, James Haile, Lucy Haile, Seth Palmer, Abigail Henderson, Wilson Lund, Eliza Lund, George B. Teeples, Jane Hamer, Parmenas N. Woodworth, Marilla Woodworth, Robert Plunket, Sarah Plunket, James H. Heath, Huldah Maria Heath, John Horlick, Elizabeth Horlick, Ira S. Hillman, Clarissa Pulsipher, Ransford Colby, Sanford Bingham, and Emily Woolsey.

Second Company: William Steele, Margaret Steele, Jacob C. Woolsey, Eliza Woolsey, Joseph W. Richards, Catharine J. Page, Thomas Hamilton, Abigail Hamilton, Edward Lang, Ellen M. Bolton, James Graham, Mary Graham, David Evans, Sarah Mills, Morgan L. Gardner, Nancy M. Gardner, Ezra Faitout, Robert Gibson, Esther Gibson, Levi Thomas, Mary Thomas, William Earl, Sarah Earl, Samuel Bell, Jemima Bell, Daniel Smith, Elizabeth Jane Smith, Israel Justus Clark, Elizabeth A. Clark, John Riley, Elizabeth Riley, Henrietta Williams, Ellen Wilding, John Worsley, Sarah Worsley, William Turpin, Elizabeth Turpin, Angeline Richardson, Polly Ann Childs, John Haslam, and Martha Haslam.

Third Company: Daniel Tyler, Ruth Tyler, William Moon, Ann Moon, Isabella Lamoreaux, Daniel Perry Foster, Maryette Foster, Jacob Strong, Martha Moulton, Clarissa Jones, Sarah Strong, Hiram Falk, Maria Falk, Relief Cram, Benajah Brooks, Minerva Brooks, Richard Moon, Eliza Moon, Asa Perry Waldo, Thomas Allman, Jane Allman, Rufus Allen, Asenath Allen, Erastus Bingham, Olive H. Bingham, William Martin, Sarah Martin, Andrew J. Workman, Lydia Moon, Henry Moon, Josephine Garner, Job Hall, Obedience Boss, Tanner H. Moore, Rachel Moore, James E. Daniels, Charles Hall, Elizabeth Daniels, Hayward Thomas, Addison Smith, and Willis Boss.

Fourth Company: Daniel Fisher, Louisa Aldridge, Ebenezer C. Richardson, Mary Ann Fisher, George Morris, Mary Jane Eighmey, Azariah Tuttle, Hannah Maria Morris, John Griffiths, Ann Griffiths, Hugh H. Cole, Ann Tuttle, Susanna Cole, Emor Harris, Parna Harris, Hannah Grove, Elizabeth Jane Moorman, Nancy Brown, Sophronia Norris, Hiram Mott, Elizabeth Mott, Alexander S. Stanley, Philinda Stanley, John Ellison, Alice Ellison, Elizabeth Stanley, Hezekiah Sprague, Abigail

Sprague, George Nixon, Fanny Nixon, John Mills, Jesse H. Atherton, Maria Emeline Mott, John Evans, Mary Evans, Thomas Jasp, Jane Jasp, Thomas J. Brandon, Alexander Allen, Jane Mills, Oliver G. Workman, Jane Allen, Agrippa Cooper, Martha Cooper, Alfred S. Hadden, Julia Ann Hadden, Ithamar Sprague, Elizabeth Sprague, Henry Russell, and Peter H. Goodwin.

—Summary of information compiled by the Temple Index Bureau, *Nauvoo Temple Endowment Register: 10 December 1845 to 8 February 1846.* Editors' note: According to the register, Abraham S. Workman and Martha Workman were washed and anointed and therefore also probably received through the veil.

....

Second anointings performed on this date:

Elisha Averett and Sarah (Witt) Averett; Elisha H. Groves and Lucy (Simmons) Groves; Stephen Winchester and Nancy (Chase) Winchester; Sarah (Smith) Haws to Peter Haws for time and Joshua Smith (deceased; Peter Haws, proxy) for eternity; Isaac Higbee, Eliza (Darling) Higbee, and Charlotte (Carter) Higbee; Charles Bird and Mercy Ann (Kennedy) Bird; Polly (Miller) Bent to Samuel Bent for time and Hyrum Smith (deceased) for eternity; James Whitehead and Jane (Marshall) Whitehead; Titus Billings and Diantha (Morley) Billings; Clark L. Whitney, Rhoda Ann (Ballard) Whitney, Adeline (Ballard) Whitney, and Nancy (Richardson) Whitney; John Taylor, Sarah (Coleman) Taylor, and Ann (Hughlings) Taylor; Mary (Fielding) Smith and Lydia (Dibble) Granger to John Taylor for time and Hyrum Smith (deceased) for eternity; and William Anderson and Emmeline (Stewart) Anderson.

—Summarized from the "Book of Anointings"; no officiators listed for this date.

....

Sealings for the living performed on this date:

George Alley to Mary Symonds; Miles Anderson to Elizabeth Anderson and Nancy Pace; William Anderson Jr. to Emeline Tilton Stewart; Arvin Allen Avery to Francis Marie Babbitt; Ephraim Badger to Harriet Snow Farr; John Williams Berry to Nancy Jane Bass; Titus Billings to Diantha Morley; Pulaski Stephen Cahoon to Louisa Leopold; John Austin Caspar to Rebecca Highbarger; Vincent M. Conrad to Electa Cotton Bradway; George Dexter to Joanna Vance Gilliam; Nathaniel Henry Felt to Eliza Anne Preston; Lewis Gaulter to Harriet Eliza Morgan; Emer

Harris to Parma Chapel; Alpheus Peter Haws to Adaline Dunn; Aaron Freeman Farr to Persis Atherton; Elijah Norman Freeman to Mary Bingham; William Adams Hickman to Sarah Elizabeth Luce; William Hainey Hickenlooper to Sarah Hawkins; Michael Jacobs to Emily Sophia Lathrop; Jerome Bonaparte Kempton to Maria Williamson; John Leek [Leeks] to Sarah Carter; Wilson Lund to Eliza Ann Brace; Asa Manchester to Adaline Hopy Burnham; Stephen Markham to Hannah Hogaboom and Prudence Fenner; Warren Markham to Catherine Ann Jones; Priddy Meeks to Sarah Mahurin; Ira S. Miles to Mary Kilburn Bent; Joseph Mount to Elizabeth Bassack; Samuel Moore to Eunice Sibley Bliss; William Derrick Morton to Anna Maria Houck; Jonathan Pugmire to Elizabeth Barns; John Social Rolph [Ralph] to Mary Ann Russell; Ithamar Sprague to Elizabeth Goodner; Isaac Shepard to Sarah Lackore; Erastus Snow to Axy [Achsah] White; Andrew Jackson Stewart to Eunice Peas Quimby; John Taylor to Sarah Thorton Coleman and Ann Hughlings Pitchforth; Clark Lyman Whitney to Adeline Elizabeth Ballard, Rhoda Ann Ballard, and Nancy Richardson; Jeremiah Willey to Sarah Ann Ward; Stephen Winchester to Nancy Case; Jonathan Calkins Wright to Rebecca Wheeler; and Brigham Young to Augusta Adams and Elizabeth [Betsy] Fairchild.

—Summarized from the Book of Living Sealings.

....

Sealings for the dead performed on this date:

Mary Bartlett (Sarah Mahurin, proxy) to Priddy Meeks, Amasa M. Lyman officiating; Gideon H. Carter (Isaac Higbee, proxy) to Charlotte Woods, Brigham Young officiating;[53] Joshua Smith (Peter Haws, proxy) to Sarah Baldwin, Brigham Young officiating;[54] Hyrum Smith (Samuel Bent, proxy) to Polly Miller, Brigham Young officiating;[55] Julia Ann Burnham (Adaline H. Burnham, proxy) to Asa Manchester, Amasa M. Lyman officiating; Hyrum Smith (John Taylor, proxy) to Lydia Dibble, Brigham Young officiating;[56] and Louisa W. White (Minerva W. Snow, proxy) to Erastus Snow, Brigham Young officiating.

—Summarized from the Book of Proxy Sealings.

53. Charlotte Woods was also sealed to Isaac Higbee for time.

54. Sarah Baldwin was also sealed to Peter Haws for time.

55. Polly Miller was also sealed to Samuel Bent for time.

56. Lydia Dibble was also sealed to John Taylor for time.

Adoptions performed on this date:

Agnes Charlotte Smith and Josephine Donna Smith to Don Carlos Smith (George Albert Smith, proxy) and Agnes Moulton Smith, sealed by Brigham Young.

—Summarized from "Sealings and Adoptions."

Saturday, January 31, 1846

[A]t 19 minets past 11[,] I [Brigham Young] came into the Temple[. T]he work in the sealing department had not commenced as yet[.] ...[57] [The] dilligence [in other departments] to redeem if possible the fleeting moments that we had suffered to pass by [had transpired] without being improved [upon] in this department—the work in the other department was in lively opperation[.] yesterday I had some conversation with Rubin Miller of Norway—he being considerably bewildered by [James] Strang['s] new—fangled Revelation—[which] rendered him [Miller] almost devoid of Reason[,] although [he was] apparently honest in what he was doing & said that the word of the Lord would be decidedly satisfactorily to him[,] where upon I said thus saith the Lord unto Reuben Miller through Brigham Young that Strang is a wicked & corrupt man & that his revelations are as false as he is—therefore turn away from his folly & never let it be said of Reuben Miller that he ever was led away & entangled by such nonsense[.] Thus saying I left him[,] my time being to[o] precious to be spent in hearing and even talking about—such trash—

... Amasa Lyman came into the Temple being quite Feeble[.] Bro[ther]. H[eber]. C. Kimball administered to him—[and] he apparently seemed much relieved— [A]t 39 minits past 10 o-clock—evening—when after calling the House [temple] to gather[,] Bro[ther] C[harles]. C. Rich Supplicating the Throne of grace by prayer—I then with Bro[ther]. H[eber]. C. Kimball & F[ranklin]. D. Richards retired to my Room No. 1 & Slept in silent repose till 7 in the morning when I arose & washed & changed clothes & walked out into the cook Room & took some refreshments[.] at 11 in the morning I attended a Publick meeting in the 2nd story of the Temple—Elder O[rson]. Pratt & myself addressed the meeting[.] at the close of our remarks one Moses A. Smith an Apostate from our Faith arose and claimed the liberty of defending or rather investigat[ing] what he called Strangism & after holding his [Strang's] claims to the

57. The writing is difficult here: "whomever commenced with unweariness"?

Presidency forth to the assembly[,] which was that Jo[seph Smith] gave him (Strang) the Keys & rights of Presidency over the church by a letter directed to him from Jo[seph] Smith previous to his Martyrdom & so on—all of which was a simple fabricating thing—without the least shadow of evidence to sustain all his position[,] Bro[ther]. O[rson]. Hyde & myself then arose [and] gave Strangism an entire blowing up & also excluded W. A. Smith & Samuel C. Shaw from the church and also an action was taken upon J[ames]. J. Strang & Aaron Smith who had been cut off Previously for attempting to palm of[f] a deception upon the church by his Pretended Revelation[,] all of which was Sanctioned by a hearty Amen[.] The meeting closed at 3 O clock [in the] evening[.] I Then walked up into the atic story of the Temple & took some refreshments[,] after which I walked into the celestial Room where I in company with my wife remained assisting to individual needs for [the purpose of] attending to the adoption of persons into my Family[,] the alt[a]r having been placed into the celestial Room the better to See it [and for] the conven[i]ance of all present[.] at candle light the ordinances of adoption commenced & ended at 33 minets past 8 in the evening[,] during which time about 65 persons who were [present were] adopted to Elder H[eber]. C. Kimball A[masa]. Lyman, & to myself—48 of that No were adopted into my family February 1st 1846[.]

—Brigham Young, Diary.

....

[See pages 538-44 for the Seventies Record for this date.]

....

I went to the Temple at 10 with Sisters Rhoda Richards, Amelia Elizabeth Richards & Jane Hall.

—Willard Richards, Diary.

....

Two hundred and thirty-three persons received ordinances.

About noon, Brother Amasa Lyman came into the Temple being quite feeble; Elder H[eber]. C. Kimball administered to him.

The labors in the Temple came to a close at 10:39 p.m. I [Brigham Young] called the house to order and Elder Charles C. Rich prayed and we retired to rest.

—"Manuscript History of Brigham Young," in *History of the Church,* 7:578.

[Washings and anointings for Saturday, January 31, 1846]

List 1 In the Male department, commencing at 8. A.M.

Seventies		Sev.	
	1 Richard Steele born Feb 14, 1818		12 Chester Southworth born May 7, 1793
"	2 Cyriel E. Brown " June 1818	"	13 Thomas Noakes " Apl. 18, 1791
"	3 John Dixon " July 26, 1818	"	14 George W. Voorheese " June 4, 1816
"	4 Nathaniel P. Warden " Apl. 9, 1826	"	15 William Parsons " Mar. 7, 1808
"	5 James Palmer " Aug. 6, 1820	"	16 Benjamin Hendrix " May 4, 1809
"	6 Joseph Dodd " Aug. 15, 1811	"	17 William Edwards " May 16, 1810
"	7 William Hetherington " Nov. 23, 1793		18 Elisha Wilcox " Oct. 24, 1809
"	8 James Bennett " Oct. 10, 1810	"	19 John Preece " Nov. 26, 1810
"	9 Isaac Butterfield " Aug 11, 1816	"	20 Jackson Goodale " Apl. 28, 1816
"	10 James Carroll " June 14, 1796	"	21 (Mosiah Hancock " Apl. 9, 1834 washed and anointed only)
"	11 Thomas Corbitt " Apl. 9, 1807	"	22 Charles Drown " Dec 28, 1814

All the rest were washed by Royal Barney and Andrew Lytle. Anointed by Alfred Brown and Bradford W. Elliot. — Finished at 9. A.M.

List 1 In the Female department commencing at 8 A.M.

Mary Ann Palmer born Aug. 6, 1815	Ann Corbet born Mar 2, 1805
Mary Ann Steele " Aug. 15, 1823	Elizabeth Pries " June 14, 1828
Elizabeth Brown " Aug 3, 1818	Catherine Hendrix " Aug. 21, 1804
Mary " Aug. 11, 1811	Ellen Bennett " May 14, 1816
Ann Warden age unknown	Mariah Goodale " Jan 23, 1823

Ann Voorheese " Jan 30,	Elizabeth Edwards " 1804
Emma Noakes " Oct. 25, 1789	Lucinda L. Loss " Feb. 17, 1823
Adaline Johnson " May 21, 1830	Hannah Carroll " Oct. 1802
Jane Hetherington " Aug. 18, 1806	Mary Parsons " Sep. 28, 1813
Anna Wilcox " Sep. 12,	Mary King " June 22, 1825
Mary Dunn " Nov. 2, 1833	

were washed and anointed by Mary K. Richards, Zeruah Goddard, Unice E. Holbrook, Martha S. Haven [illegible] Saturday January 31, 1846.

List 2 In the Male department commencing at

Sev		Sev	
	22 John Laird born Oct. 25, 1809		31 Christopher Hayton born Mar. 8, 1822
"	23 James Cowlays " Dec. 2, 1829		32 John Holden " Sep 27, 1821
"	24 Edmund Robins " Feb. 27, 1828		33 John H. Bullard " Nov. 30, 1825
"	25 Sandford Jacobs " Aug. 16, 1810		34 Charles Rhodebach " June 8, 1811
"	26 Samuel Thomas " July 2, 1803		35 Charles Kinsey " June 18, 1818
	^Henry Standage^		
"	27 ~~Pleasant Ewell~~ " Feb. 26, 1811		36 Alexander W. Calender " Apl. 1, 1822
"	28 Jerome Bishop " May 28, 1811		37 William Wood " Feb 3, 1823
"	29 Thomas Brown " Jan. 12, 1821		38 Henry Slam " June 3, 1808
"	30 Josiah F. Martin " Dec. 15, 1815		39 George Johnson " Oct. 19, 1817
Elder	1 Pleasant Ewel " Aug 2, 1788		40 William Fawcett " Dec. 13, 1814

were washed ~~and anointed~~ by Royal Barney and Andrew Lytle. anointed by Charles Bird, Miles Andrews, Alfred Brown and Jesse P. Harmon.

List 2 In the Female department commencing at 50 p. 10.

Charlotte Ballard born June 3, 1827	Mary Brown born Aug 17, 1821
Lucy C. Harwood " Mar. 26, 1812	Susan Burton " Dec 17, 1821
Lucinda M. Calender " May 6, 1809	Mary Shaw " July 20, 1830
Laura Bishop " Feb 20, 1813	Nancy Shaw " Mar 16, 1805
Ann Forest Kinsey " Aug. 16, 1810	Ellen Holden " Aug 10, 1823
Ann Fargher " Feb. 19, 1819	Louisa Brown " May 13, 1816
Jane Fawsett " Nov 4, 1814	Susanna Jacobs " Jan 4, 1812
Jane Rhodeback " Mar. 28, 1811	Mary Ann Hall " Mar. 13, 1828
Sarah Johnson " July 29, 1820	Elizabeth Kendle " May 20, 1815
Sabra Vorhees " Mar. 10, 1773	Henrietta D. Thomas " Apl. 14, 1810
Eliza Bebee " Jan. 12, 1792	Sophronia A. Standage " Jan. 13, 1821
Irena Flack " Oct. 18, 1826	Eleanor Lemmons " Dec. 22, 1817
Mary Corbet " Nov. 25, 1815	Dolly Newton " June 30, 1784

were washed and anointed by Sarah B. Barney, Sarah Horr, Chelmecia Hamilton, Susan Green. Eunice Holbrook, Hester A. E. Brown and Zeruah Goddard. Finished at 55 min. p. 11 A.M. C W Wandell Smith, clerk

List 3 In the Male department commencing at 5 m. p. 1 P.M.

Sev.

	42 James D. Davis born Aug. 8, 1801		49 George Rhodes born Oct. 5, 1815
"	43 Jeremiah Root " Jan. 18, 1802	"	50 George W. Brandot " Oct. 20, 1809
"	44 Zachariah Hardy " Mar. 20, 1799	"	51 Francis M. William " Apl. 29, 1824
"	45 Steling Davis " Aug. 8, 1822	"	52 Orem S. Griffith " Oct 28, 1820
"	46 Walter Mc^C^Allester " 1814	"	53 John M. Lytle " Feb 25, 1829

"	47 Simon Dike " Sep. 16, 1814	"	54 William H. Carsson " Jan. 8, 1818
"	48 Hiram [illegible] " Dec 18, 1816	"	55 Lewis Harmen " [illegible]

Saturday Evening January 31, 1846.

Sev		Elders	
	56 William Daley born Oct. 9, 1809		1 George Davidson born Apl. 6, 1809
"	57 Thomas Frazier " June 1, 1827	"	2 William Jones " Feb. 12, 1799
"	58 William J. Jenkins " Dec. 11, 1816	"	3 Joseph H. Tippetts " June 4 1814
"	59 William Hall " 1800		
"	~~60 Joseph H. Tippets~~ " June 4, 1814		
"	60 Hugh Walker " Apl. 15, 1790		
"	61 John McDonald " Jan 1797		

were washed by Royal Barney, and Andrew Lytle. Anointed by Chandler Holbrook, Alfred Brown, and John Lytle. Finished at —

List 3 In the Female Department commencing at 1 P.M.

Emaline Root born July 22, 1812	Mariah Davis born Dec 16, 1822
Hannah Jenkins " Feb. 19, 1820	Rozanna Davis " Nov. 30, 1808
Ruth Bostwick " Apl. 15, 1806	Nancy Davidson " Dec. 5, 1805
Jane Hall " Aug. 11, 1810	Mary Jane Lytle " Aug. 6, 1831
Mary Ann Dyke " Feb. 22, 1822	Jane Frazier " Jan. 1799
Rachel McDonald " Apl 1 1806	Mary Fawney " Mar 23, 1790
Harriet Card " Aug. 23, 1820	Curilla Carson " Oct. 22, 1818
Elizabeth Harvey " July 20, 1824	Elizabeth McFate " Oct. 28, 1829
Martha Jane Williams " Dec. 10, 1829	Elsie Walker " Aug. 27, 1812

Epsy Jane Williams [born] Jan. 10, 1831	Amanda M. Tippets [born] Sep. 11, 1821
Mary Ann Daley " Feb. 20, 1818	Eliza Hardy " July 25, 1807
Isabella McAlister " Feb. 1815	Elizabeth Jones " Mar. 22, 1803
Mary E. Jones " Mar 17, 1828	

were washed and anointed by Eunice Holbrook, Hester A. E. Brown, Sarah M. Barney, Almira Tafts, Chelmicia Hamilton, Elvira Teeples, Sarah Horn, Zeruah Goddard.

List 4 In the Male department commencing at

Sev		Sev	
	62 Nathaniel W. Packer born Jan 2, 1811		73 Eliezer King Jr. born Dec 1, 1811
"	63 Josephus Hatch " July 2, 1801	"	74 John G. Hardy " May 11, 1811
"	64 William Adams " Feb. 23, 1822	"	75 Peter C. Vrooman " Dec. 28, 1822
"	65 John Wood " 1804	"	76 Abraham Hunsaker " Nov. 23, 1812
"	66 Andrew Henry	"	77 Noah J. Gymon " June 30, 1819
"	67 George W. Slad " Dec. 15, 1816	"	78 John Pulsipher " July 17, 1827
"	68 Joseph^hua^ Holden " Jan. 7, 1800	"	79 Joseph Coon " Jan 24, 1805
"	69 James Porter " Aug. 4, 1805	"	80 Nathan Steward " Apl. 9, 1807
"	70 William E. Horner " Mar 2, 1807	H. Priests	2 James Jones " Mar. 14, 1794
"	71 Daniel McIntosh " Aug. 12, 1820	Elders	4 Lemuel Herrick " Mar. 13, 1792
"	72 Charles Pulsipher " Apl. 20, 1830		

were washed by Royal Barney, and Andrew Lytle. Anointed by Bradford Elliot, and Alfred Brown

List 4 In the Female department commencing at 20 p. 3

Elizabeth Packer born Dec. 6, 1820	Elizabeth Hardy born Nov. 21, 1814
Mary Ann Adams " Oct 22, 1820	[illegible] " Feb 8, 1825

Mary Jones " Aug. 7, 1800	[illegible] " Dec. 16, 1810

Saturday Evening January 31, 1846.

Elizabeth Porter born Feb 20, 1800	Elizabeth McIntosh born June 23, 1824
Rose Wood " Mar. 1811	Sarah Squire " Sep 14, 1810
Melinda Hatch " Feb. 20, 1806	Margaret Henry age unknown
Eliza Hunsaker " Mar 5, 1817	Nancy Horner " Mar. 19, 1805
Harriet Colflesh " Feb. 24, 1824	Mary C. King " Nov. 19, 1818
Lydia Moon " Sep. 4, 1826	Margaret Guymon " Feb. 28, 1821
Mary Holden " Jan 7, 1803	Jane Slade " Feb. 20, 1825
Mary Ann Rock " Mar. 4, 1822	Lucy Herrick " Dec. 14, 1827
Eliza Ann Coon " Feb. 15, 1811	

were washed and anointed by Chelmicia Hamilton, Alvira Wheeler, Hester A. E. Brown, Sarah B. Barney, Almira Tufts, Sarah Horr and Eunice Holbrook. 30 p. 4

List 5 In the Male department commencing at 30 p 5 P.M.

Sev.		High Priests	
	George Crowther born July 1, 1811		3 James Dunn born Sep. 26, 1788
"	82 Jacob D. Buram " Oct. 1, 1820	"	4 Joseph Barrow " Nov. 4, 1797
"	83 John Barrow " Dec. 19, 1819	"	5 Samuel Swanner " Apl. 21, 1811
"	84 Joseph Barrow jr. " Feb. 25, 1824	"	6 Henry Ettleman " Sep. 6, 1798
"	85 Thomas P. Kerr " Mar. 14, 1816	"	7 John Cleminson " Dec. 28, 1798
"	86 Edward Larkey " June 17, 1811	Elders	5 Thomas Orr " Dec. 18, 1802
"	87 Lewis Thompson " Jan. 7, 1811		6 Silas G. Simmonds " Nov. 26, 1810
"	88 John Robison " Feb. 22, 1811		7 Sylvanus Caukins Dec. 30, 1823

[Seventies] 89 John Barton [born] June 22, 1808
" 90 Oliver N. Harmon " Oct. 18, 1826
" 91 Edwin Harley " Jan. 13, 1819

[Elders] 8 Leonard E. Harrington Jan. 27, 1816
9 Michael Yeomans Dec. 29, 1807

were washed by Royal Barney and and Andrew Lytle. Anointed by Alfred Brown Bradford Elliot. Finished at [?]

List 5 In the Female department commencing at 20 p. 5

Mary Thompson born May 29, 1820
Susanah Barton " Mar. 16, 1814
Nancy Larkey " Dec. 4, 1812
Hannah B. Kerr " Oct 2, 1819
Margaret Harley " Jan 13, 1823
Christiana Ettleman " Aug. 31, 1802
Lydia Cleminson " July 11, 1811
Mary Cleminson " Apl. 23, 1823
Elizabeth Heward " Mar 27, 1795
Elizabeth Simmons " Jan 19, 1817
Mary Ann Bullock " Sep. 19, 1829
Didama Clark " Dec 21, 1782
Lois Harrison " Mar. 25, 1824
Huldah [illegible] " Feb 24, 1827

Sarah Crowther born Sep 20, 1812
Thurza Harley " Dec. 18, 1820
Rachel Swanner " Sep. 12, 1803
Cynthia Yeamans " Oct. 10, 1811
Mary Robinson " Oct. 12, 1801
Mariah Barrow " Sep. 11, 1811
Anna Barrow " Dec. 19, 1825
Sarah Lincoln " Apl 3, 1800
Mary E. Burnham " Feb 20, 1828
Lucinda Harmon " Mar. 16, 1829
Adaline M. Woodward " Dec. 6, [illegible]
Elizabeth Ann Dunn " Sep 20, [illegible]
Catharine Orr " Sep [illegible]

were washed and anointed by Mary H[illegible] Chelmicia Hamilton [illegible] Sarah B. Barney [illegible]

—Seventies Record, Book B, January 31, 1846.

Nauvoo temple endowments performed on this date for:

First Company: Thomas Noakes, Emma Noakes, G[eorge]. W. Voorheese, Ann Voorheese, James Carroll, Hannah Carroll, Elisha Wilcox, Anna Wilcox, Isaac Butterfield, Adaline Johnson, William Parsons, Mary Parsons, James Palmer, Mary Ann Palmer, Chester Southworth, Mary Southworth, William Hetherington, Jane Hetherington, Joseph Dodd, Margaret Dodd, Cyrill E. Brown, Elizabeth Brown, William Edwards, Elizabeth Edwards, Benjamin Hendrix, Mary Jane King, Catharine Hendrix, Thomas Corbitt, Ann Corbitt, Richard Steele, Mary Ann Steele, John Dixon, Lucinda L. Loss, James Bennet, Ellen Bennet, John Preece, Elizabeth Preece, Jackson Goodale, Maria Goodale, Nathaniel P. Worden, and Ann Morton.

Second Company: Henry Standage, Sophronia A. Standage, John Holden, Ellen Holden, Christopher Layton, Ann Fargher, Edmund Robbins, Eleanor Lemmons, Sanford Jacobs, Mary Corbitt, Pleasant Ewel, Dolly Newton, Susanna Jacobs, Sabra Voorhes, William Fawcett, Jane Fawcett, Eliza Beebe, John Laird, Charles Drown, Louisa Drown, Charles Kensey, Ann Forrest Kensey, Jerome Bishop, Lucy Bishop, Henry Shaw, Nancy Shaw, Lucinda P. Callender, Samuel Thomas, Henrietta D. Thomas, Lucy C. Harwood, John H. Ballard, Sarah Johnson, Susan Burton, Mary Shaw, Thomas Brown, Mary Brown, Charles Rodaback, Jane Rodaback, Belinda Newel, Harriet Atwood Newel, Josiah F. Martin, Abigail Griffith, Elizabeth Kendall, William Wood, George Johnson, Mary Ann Hall, Alexander W. Callender, Ann Eliza Mann, Matthias Cowley, Irena Flack, and Charlotte Ballard.

Third Company: Jane Frazier, Orrin L. Griffith, Polly Ann Workman, George W. Branden, Mary Forney, Simon Dike, Mary Ann Dike, Lewis Harvey, Elizabeth Harvey, Joseph H. Tippets, Amanda Malvina Tippets, William Jones, Elizabeth Jones, Ruth Bostwick, Hugh Walker, Elsie Walker, George Davidson, Nancy Davidson, Walter McAlister, Isabella McAlister, Jeremiah Root, Emeline Root, James D. Davis, Roxana Davis, Sterling Davis, Maria Davis, William J. Jenkins, Hanna Jenkins, John McDonald, Rachel McDonald, Mary Elizabeth Jones, William Daley, Mary Ann Daley, Zachariah Hardy, Eliza Hardy, Thomas Frazier, Epsy Jane Williams, John M. Lytle, Elizabeth McFate, William Hall,[58] Harriet Card, Jane

58. Six years later William Hall wrote and published a criticism of Mormonism, including his experience in the Nauvoo temple: *The Abominations of Mormonism Exposed; Containing Many Facts and Doctrines Concerning That Singular People During Seven Years' Membership with Them: From 1840-1847* (Cincinnati: For the Author by I. Hart & Co. 1852), 45-50.

Hall, William Carson, Corilla Carson, Francis M. Williams, Martha Jane Williams, George Rhodes, and Hiram Bostwick.

Fourth Company: Eleazer King Jr., Mary Caroline King, Abraham Hunsaker, Eliza Hunsaker, James Porter, Elizabeth Porter, Nathan W. Packer, Elizabeth Packer, Daniel McIntosh, Elizabeth McIntosh, Noah T. Guymon, Margaret Guymon, William E. Horner, Nancy Horner, Peter C. Vrooman, Louisa Vrooman, John G. Hardy, Elizabeth Hardy, Andrew Hendry, Margaret Hendry, William Adams, Mary Ann Adams, John Wood, Rose Wood, James Jones, Mary Jones, Sarah Squires, Mary Ann Rock, Harriet W. Colflesh, Lydia Moon, Nathan Steward, Sarah Steward, Lucy Herrick, Joshua Holden, Mary Holden, Josephus Hatch, Melinda Hatch, Lemuel Herrick, Joseph Coon, Eliza Ann Coon, George W. Slade, Jane E. Slade, John Pulsipher, and Charles Pulsipher.

Fifth Company: Henry Ettleman, Christiana Ettleman, James Dunn, Elizabeth A. Dunn, George Crowther, Sarah Crowther, John Barton, Susanna Barton, Samuel Swanner, Rachel Swanner, Michael Yeamans, Cynthia Yeamans, Thomas P. Kerr, Hannah B. Kerr, Elizabeth Heward, Sarah Lincoln, Jacob D. Burnham, Mary C. Burnham, Mary C. Burnham, Edward Larkey, Nancy Larkey, Lewis Thompson, Mary Thompson, Mary Ann Bullock, Thomas Orr, Catharine Orr, Joseph Barrow, Maria Barrow, Leonard Herrington, Louise Herrington, John Barrow, Silas G. Simmonds, Elizabeth Simmonds, John Robinson, Mary Robinson, Sylvanus Calkins, Adaline M. Woodworth, John Clemenson, Lydia Cleminson, Edwin Harley, Thirza Harley, Margaret Harley, Mary Clemenson, Joseph Barrow, Hannah Barrow, Diadama Clark, Huldah E. Frost, Olive N. Harmon, and Lucinda Harmon.

—Summary of information compiled by the Temple Index Bureau, *Nauvoo Temple Endowment Register: 10 December 1845 to 8 February 1846.* Editors' note: According to the register, Mary Dunn, Mosiah Hancock, and Mary Jane Lytle were washed and anointed and therefore also probably received through the veil on this date.

....

Second anointings performed on this date:

Isaac Allred and Mary (Calvert) Allred, anointed by Orson Pratt; Lucius N. Scovil and Alice (Hurst) Scovil, anointed by Parley P. Pratt; Willard Richards and Jane (Hall) Richards, anointed by Parley P. Pratt; Rhoda Richards to Brigham Young for time and Joseph Smith (deceased) for eternity, anointed by Parley P. Pratt; Jeremiah Willey, Samantha (Call) Willey, and Sarah (Sanders) Willey, anointed by Parley P. Pratt; Levi Stewart, Malinda (Howard) Stewart, and Charita (Holdaway) Stewart, anointed by Ezra T. Benson; Jacob Foutz and Lucinda (Loss) Foutz, anointed by Ezra T. Benson; William Burton and Elizabeth (Oates) Burton, anointed by Orson Pratt; Augusta Farnham and Mary Jane (Pottle) Farnham, anointed by Orson Pratt; Philo Dibble and Hannah (Dubois) Dibble, anointed by Orson Pratt; Evan M. Greene and Susan (Kent) Green, anointed by Parley P. Pratt; and Mary Elizabeth (Nelson) Greene to John P. Greene (Brigham Young, proxy), anointed by Parley P. Pratt.

—Summarized from "Book of Anointings."

....

Sealings for the living performed on this date:

Buckley Burnham Anderson to Sally Maria Cutler; Simeon Andrews to Dorcas Millikin; Amos [Amasa] Babcock to Mary Ann Archer; Harmon [Herman] Daggett Bayles [Bayliss] to Juliette Horman; James Bennett to Ellen Pincock; Jacob G. Bigler to Amy Lorett Chase; John Bowen to Ann Lanbough; Isaac Seal Brown to Lydia Miller; William Burton to Elizabeth Oates; Cyrus Culver Canfield to Louisa Jones and Clarissa Lora Jones; Albert Carrington to Rhoda Maria Woods and Mary Ann Rock; Welcome Chapman to Susan Amelia Risley; John Clark to Mary Noddings; George Colemere [Coleman] to Rachel Burgess; William James Conner to Jane Charnock; Thadeus Cutler to Lemira Scott; James Davis Sr. to Elizabeth Sykes; Osmign Merritt Deuel to Mary Whiting; James Duane Davis to Roxanna Davis; Edmond Durfee Jr. to Caroline Eliza Clark; Simeon Dyke to Mary Ann Forney; Joseph Teasdale Egbert to Mary Caroline Allred; William Adam Empey to Mary Ann Morgan; John Erick Forsgreen to Mary Ann Hunt; Jacob Foutz to Lucinda Loretta Loss; George Robert Grant to Mary Dorsey Barney; Evan Melbourne Greene to Susan Kent; Charles Henry Hales to Julia Ann Lockwood; Stephen Hales Jr. to Eveline Lydia Carter; Zachariah Hardy to Eliza Phillbrook [Philbrook]; Benjamin Hendrix to Catherine Lobdell; Wilkinson Hewitt to Sarah Ann Robinson; John Currie Hill to Margaret Gardner Bryce; Jacob Hofheins to Mary Ann Elizabeth Stevenson; James Jones to Mary Ann Partridge; John Lawrence to Rhoda Sanford; Christopher Layton to Mary Mathews; John D. Lee to Polly Ann Workman; Samuel Leaver to Mary Ann Harlett; Lyman O. Littlefield to Adeline Hamblin; Waldo Littlefield to Mary Leah Thompson and Sarah

Mary Thompson; Chester Loveland to Fanny Call; James M. McFate to Lucy Thompson Lisk; David Manhard to Mary Jane Swasey; Matthew Mansfield to Mary Ann Harris; Thomas McLelland to Elizabeth Murphy; William Moss to Elizabeth Cottom; Henry Mower Sr. to Mary Amick; Nathan Williams Packer to Elizabeth Taylor; Aaron Rager [Roger] to Rebecca Haines; David Pinkney Rainey [Rainy] to Margaret Minerva Andrews; Tunis Rappleye to Louisa Elizabeth Cutler; Luther Read to Charity Buel; Franklin Dewey Richards to Elizabeth McFate; Joseph Lee Robinson to Susan McCord; Lorenzo Wesley Roundy to Adeline Whiting; Lucius Nelson Scovil to Alice Hurst; Almon Worthy Sherman to Lois Huntington Cutler; Isaac Shepherd to Sarah Lackore; Abraham Stevens to Christina Zimmerman; Jacob Stoker to Catherine Burcham; Thomas Tanner to Ruth Fox Tanner; Jacob Err Terry to Mary Maria Riley; Thomas Travis to Mary Derbyshire; Daniel Tyler to Ruth Welton; George Washington Voorheese to Ann Sumner; John Wardrobe to Lucy McIntosh; Alexander Williams to Isabella Gill and Jane Ortrey; Almond McCumber Williams to Zilpha Baker Cilley; and John Zundel to Anna Christiana Lautenschlager.

—Summarized from the Book of Living Sealings.

....

Sealings for the dead performed on this date:

Joseph Smith (Brigham Young, proxy) to Rhoda Richards, Heber C. Kimball officiating;[59] Laura Snow (Alice Hurst, proxy) to Lucius N. Scovil, Heber C. Kimball officiating; Mary Pole (Mary Noddings, proxy) to John Clark, Heber C. Kimball officiating; Jane Smalley (Mary Derbyshire, proxy) to Thomas Travis, Heber C. Kimball officiating; Henry A. Bauermaister (John Zundel, proxy) to Hannah Barbara Rickin, Heber C. Kimball officiating;[60] Artemisia Kilburn (Mary Jane Swasey, proxy) to David Manhard, Brigham Young officiating; Mary Ann Boggess (Amy Lorett Chase, proxy) to Jacob G. Bigler, Brigham Young officiating; Sarah Newell and Betsy Miller (Sarah Searcy, proxy) to John Hopwood Blazard, Brigham Young officiating;[61] John P. Greene (Brigham Young, proxy) to Rhoda Young (Mary Eliza Nelson, proxy), Heber C. Kimball officiating;[62] Betsy Bradbury (Dorcas Milliken, proxy) to Simeon Andrews, He-

59. Rhoda Richards was also sealed to Brigham Young for time.

60. Hannah Barbara Rickin was also sealed to John Zundel for time.

61. This entry is crossed out in the original "Book of [Proxy] Sealings."

62. Mary Eliza Nelson was also sealed to Brigham Young for time.

ber C. Kimball officiating; Catherine Brown (Mary Maria Riley, proxy) to Jacob E. Terry, Heber C. Kimball officiating; and Elizabeth Williams (Lucy T. Lisk, proxy) to James McFate, Heber C. Kimball officiating.

—Summarized from the Book of Proxy Sealings.

....

Adoptions performed on this date:

To Alpheus and Lois Cutler: Thaddeus Cutler, William Lathrop Cutler, Benjamin Franklin Cutler, Lois Huntington Cutler, Louisa Elisabeth Cutler, Sally Maria Cutler, Clarissa Crissy Cutler, Emily Track Cutler, Almon Worthy Sherman, Buckley Burnham Anderson, Lenira Scott, and Margaret Melvina Bouck: "These were sealed and adopted and sealed to their Parents Alpheus and Lois Cutler with the usual rites and ceremonies at the Altar &c. F[ranklin]. D. Richards, clerk"; and to Daniel Spencer and Mary Spencer (as proxy): Claudius Victor Spencer, Gilbert Henry van Schoonhoven, and Mary Leone Spencer, sealed by Brigham Young.

—Summarized from "Sealings and Adoptions."

Sunday, February 1, 1846

This day a number of persons met at my Fathers [house, that of Joseph Knight Sr.,] for the purpose of a family interview and to understand each others feelings, as Father had been called upon to go the following day to the temple to receive his sealing and anointing[.] my Step Mother [Phoebe (Crosby) Peck Knight] refused to be sealed to my Father[.] I [Newel Knight] took some pains to get the family to gather that we might all know each others feelings and understand the cause of my Fathers and Mothers separation[.] I arose and made a statement of my feelings and intentions [and] allso showed the neccesity of such a separation being fully understood by all parties[. I] first called upon Father to [state] his feelings[.] he said he loved and respected Phebe but she was not satisfied to abide with him and he had agreed to let her go[.] I asked her the cause of her dissatisfaction[.] She said she respected the old gentleman [and] believed he was a good man[, that] he had ever been kind to her[,] and as a good man she respected him but [she] did not love and honor him as her head and bosom companion and for this reason alone she was not satisfied to abide wit[h] my Father[.] then [I] told them all I wanted them to express their feelings towards me[.] I did not know at the time why my feelings were thus impressed that I should be this particular but the sequel will show[. My] Mother [stepmother] said she had no feelings against me[.] she believed my motives and intentions had ever been good towards her self and family [and] said she could find no fault with me and that the above reason alone was all she had for not abideing wit[h] my Father[.] I told her that reason ought to make her free yet if she was satisfied to abide with my Father I should have no objections [and] as such I should honor and respect her [as my mother,] but as her feelings were to leave I should say amen and still respect her and wishe her well [but no longer recognize a family bond.] [T]he children Henrietta [Peck] Rich[,] Hezekiah [Peck,] and Sarah Peck were present[.] they said they [had] not ought against me[.] we agreed to close our interview by prayer asking the blessings of God upon each other in the presence of Ezekiel and Electa Peck[,] Thomas Rich and wife[,] and Fathers family[.] my wife went home in company with uncle and aunt Peck[.] I took my horse and buggy and went 4 miles out on the prairie to get my oldest sister Anna [(Knight) DeMille] to go to the temple with my Father and act as proxy for my Mother [Polly (Peck) Knight] whose remains were the first of [the] Saints the earth opened and [prepared] he[r] bosom to receive in Jackson Co[unty] M[issouri in August 1831].

—Newel Knight, Diary, quoted in Lyndon W. Cook, compiler, *Nauvoo Marriages: Proxy Sealings, 1843-1846* (Provo, UT: Grandin Book, 2004), pp. xx-xxi.

....

I labored in the Temple the last 8 working days Annointing in the High Priests Room. learnt the ordnance of the washing & anointing of feet for burial.

—Phinehas Richards, Diary, LDS Archives.

....

Public meeting in the second story of the Temple. Elder Orson Pratt and myself [Brigham Young] addressed the meeting.

After meeting, I returned to the attic and partook of some refreshments.

Elder Heber C. Kimball, Amasa Lyman, and I administered at the altar.

—"Manuscript History of Brigham Young," in *History of the Church,* 7:578.

Second anointings performed on this date:

Parley P. Pratt and Belinda (Marden) Pratt.

—Summarized from "Book of Anointings," officiator not mentioned.

....

Sealings for the living performed on this date:

Daniel Duncan McArthur to Matilda C. Fuller; and Horace Ephraim Roberts to Harriet McEvers [McEvens].

—Summarized from the Book of Living Sealings.

....

Adoptions performed on this date:

To Amasa M. and Maria Louisa Lyman: Francis Marion Lyman, Matilda Lyman, Ruth Adelia Lyman, David Frederick, John Sheeter Gleason, and Desdemona Gleason, sealed by Brigham Young: "Were adopted and Sealed to their Parents with the usual ceremony at the Alter &c."; to Newel K. and Elizabeth Ann Whitney: Spencer Walton Welsbank, Thomas Moor, and Mahala Dorcas Higby; to Brigham Young and Miriam Young (Mary Ann Young, proxy): Elisha Averett, Sarah Ann Averett, Elijah Averett, Cherrizada Averett, John Harvey, Eliza Harvey, Jesse Charles Braley, Jeremiah Willey, Sammantha Willey, Alexander Williams, Isabella Williams, William Warren Major, Sarah Major, Stephen Hezekiah Goddard, Zemiah Norwood Goddard, Moses Martin Sanders, Amanda Armstrong Sanders, George R. Grant, Mary Dorsey Grant, Samuel Lindsey Sprague, Mary Woodward Sprague, Chandler Holbrook, Eunice Holbrook, Samuel Gully, Ovanda Gully, Harmon Daggott Bayless, Juliet Bayless, Simson Adams Dunn, Margaret Dunn, Israel Barlow, Elizabeth Haven Barlow, Samuel Brown, Lydia Maria Brown, Philo Dibble, Hannah Ann Dibble, Joseph Busby, Ann Cady Busby, Curtis Edwin Bolton, Rebecca Bunker, John Lytle, Christiana Lytle, James Boyd Woodward, and Mary Ellen de la Montague, sealed by Heber C. Kimball; and to Heber C. and Vilate Kimball: Jesse Pierce Harmon, Anna Harmon, John Brick Forsgren, Mary Ann Forsgren, Hans Christian Hanson, Peter Olson Hansen, Howard Egan, Abraham Palmer, Patience Deliah Palmer, Alvah Lewis Tippets, and Caroline Tippets, sealed by Brigham Young: "These persons were adopted and sealed to Heber C. Kimball and Vilate Kimball in the usual manner at the Alter &c."

—Summarized from "Sealings and Adoptions."

Monday, February 2, 1846

[W]e suspended the work in the Sealing department for the purpose of bringing up the record[s] which were yet in the rear—The washings & anointings were continued with all Possible Speed in the other departments ... The sun was near down when the meeting adjourned— we then returned to our labours in the Temple & continued the[re] till near 9. oclock[.] before leaving I gave instructions to my Clerks not to stop until the record of the endowments are brought up so that nothing may escape the Notice as for the want [of] recording in a legible & intelegable [manner]— Then to let the work of sealings & anointings [continue] & if any one wants to be sealed [in the meantime] & we have the time to attend to it—let them make out the records themselves & that will be their way[.]

—Brigham Young, Diary.

....

This morning the vestry and the reception rooms of the House are litterally cramed with applicants for Endowments. At about 20 minutes past 8 A.M. the administration of the ordinances [began] in the

List 1 Male department when

[See pages 553-560 for excerpted portion.]

In the evening, after labor, the workhands and others assembled in the celestial room and danced before the Lord about 1 hour, when all activity ceased [?] Note Bena, for several evenings past, the hands have assembled in the Celestial room and sung and prayed.

—Seventies Record, Book B.

....

Monday morning [I] took my sister Anna [(Knight) DeMille] to the temple to meet my Father [Joseph Knight Sr.] according to previous agreement[.] when Father came Phebe [(Crosby) Peck Knight] was with him [and] said she wanted to talk with some of the Twelve [apostles.] I went to attend to [the] usual labor in the temple until we were called in to council by our President who stated [to] us that the Spirit dictated that it was time to commence our intended move into the wilderness and soon bring our labors to a close in the temple[,] to which the Council all agreed[. A]bout the time this Council closed[,] one of the Twelve came to me and said that Phebe had concluded to be sealed to Father provided my oppression to her could cease[.] she told them ^the Twelve^ she was willing to be ruled by the Old gentelmen but not by his children[.] I replied I

[Washings and anointings for Monday, February 2, 1846]

Seventies		Seventies	
	1 Jesse Pierson born 1813		11 James Jeffs born Sep. 1, 1816
"	2 John Harper " Mar. 9, 1812	"	12 Barnett Rigby " Aug. 16, 1815
"	3 Benjamin R Heeles " Jan 3, 1815	"	13 Elmer Chaney " May 16, 1825
"	4 Elijah Elmer " Apl. 13, 1810	"	14 Hugh McKenney " Dec. 20, 1803
"	5 Ebenezer M. Kimball " Sep. 9, 1811	"	15 David Callett " Dec. 12, 1808
"	6 Samuel M. Horn " June 26, 1824	"	16 Hiram Olmsted " Nov. 22, 1827
"	7 John Lambert " Jan. 23, 1820	"	17 Charles W. Dalton " July 10, 1826
"	8 Dewitt Tyler " Aug. 4, 1828	"	18 Henry Dalton " 1825
"	9 William Payne " Jan. 4, 1816	"	19 Joseph Curtis " Dec. 24, 1818
"	10 John F. Stocking " Apl. 24, 1806	Elder	1 Peter Maughan " May 7, 1811
"	20 John Borrowman " May 13, 1816		
"	21 Joseph Hancock " Mar. 18, 1799		

were washed by Albert Merrill and Benjamin Mitchell. Anointed by Dana Jacobs and Elisha Edwards. Finished at

Ordinations

Jesse Pierson and Joseph Hancock were ordained Seventies by Levi Hancock, Charles Shumway, Jesse Haven, and Darwin Chase.

List 21 In the Female department commencing at "

Mary Ann Maughan born Mar 10, 1817	Patience Lambert born Oct. 25 1786
Melancy S. Kimball " Mar. 11, 1813	Catherine Payne " Dec. 4, 1821
Eliza Tyler " Dec. 7, 1823	Eliza Hibbard " Apl. 26, 1796
Esther Collet " Oct. 14, 1814	Margaret Harper " Feb. 12, 1814

Harriet Stocking [born] Sep. 6, 1814	Mary Clift [born] June 16, 1815
Hannah Cheney " May 1811	Mary Almer " Jan. 1810
Sarah Ann McKinney " Sep. 27, 1803	Elnora L. Berry " June 8, 1822
Jane Howe " Mar. 12, 1830	Jane Hulse " Apl. 9, 1816
Ann Jeffs " Jan. 13, 1815	Sally Ann Curtis " Mar. 6, 1824
Ann Rigby " June 4, 1816	Speedy Hancock " Dec. 21, 1795
Mary Ann Pierson " Mar. 2, 1815	Eliza Clift " July 2, 1813

were washed and Anointed by Julia Ann Shumway, Myrza Alexander, Mary E. Frost, Mariah E. Edwards, Chelmicia Hamilton, Sarah B. Barney, Zeruah Goddard, Lucina Sessions, and Altemicia Shirtliff.

List 2 In the Male Department. commencing at 25 p. 10

Seventies		Seventies	
	22 Alfred Kenney born Nov. 17, 1810		28 Henry Overly born July 12, 1818
"	23 Moses Curtis " May 8, 1816	"	29 Robert Wright " Feb. 10, 1815
"	24 Samuel Smith " May 22, 1818	"	30 Samuel Suffycool " June 15, 1806
"	25 Freeman Tupper " Sep. 13, 1821	"	31 Jesse McCarrol " Jan. 8, 1793
"	26 Abraham Hoover " June 25, 1802	"	32 Caleb C. Baldwin " June 3, 1817
"	27 Solomon G. McIntosh " Aug. 28, 1813	"	33 [illegible] " Apl. 2, 1799

Monday February 2nd, 1846.

Sev		Elder	
	34 Dorminicus Ellmore born May 25, 1819		3 David Wood born July 6, 1799
"	35 Elisha Smith " July 15, 1798		4 Samuel Parrish " Sep. 30, 1778
H. Priests	1 Enoch King Senr " Jan 22, 1770		5 Batholomew Mahoney " Oct. 1802
Elder	2 Gemal Hildreth " Dec. 10, 1807		6 Jacob Baum " Apl. 5, 1794

were washed ~~and~~ by Albert Merrill and Burr Frost. Anointed by Elisha Edwards and Dana Jacobs.

List 2 In the Female department commencing at 30 p. 10.

Mary Ann Mahoney born June 18, 1803	Rebel Hanney born Mar. 14, 1816
Mary Ann Smith " June 17, 1811	Agness Baum " Oct. 6, 1793
Sally King " Nov. 17, 1781	Aurelia Curtis " Sep. 20, 1820
Susan Tupper " Dec. 18, 1828	Julia Hampton " Nov. 18, 1811
Louisa Hildreth " Mar. 22, 1806	Fanny Parish " Oct. 28, 1795
Elizabeth Suffacole " Mar 11, 1805	Mary Hoover " Aug. 1, 1809
Ann Wright " Nov. 28, 1819	Catherine Wood " Dec. 4, 1797
Amanda Simmons " Oct. 30, 1805	Mary McIntosh " Feb. 6, 1813
Rebecca Smith " Dec. 5, 1815	Martha Almore " June 21, 1814
Mary Mackarrel " 1793	Ann Eliza Baldwin " Aug. 15, 1819
Rebecca Overly " Jan 29, 1821	

were washed and anointed by Julia Ann Shumway, Ellen Kay, Chelmicia Hamilton, Sarah B. Barney, Margaret Ann Merrill, Zeruah Goddard, Myrza Alexander, and Cynthia Ann Eldridge. Finished at 20 minutes past 11 A.M.

List 3 In the Male department commencing at 20. to 1.

Sev.		Sev.	
	36 Oliver Stratton born June 24, 1818		48 Russel T. Baldwin born May 18, 1815
"	37 James Woodward " July 23, 1823	"	49 George Allen " Aug. 16, 1801
"	38 Wilson Keirnes " Nov. 30, 1824	"	50 Edward Stevenson " May 1, 1821
"	39 Marcus B. Thorp " June 12, 1822	"	51 Alonzo Reed " Nov 24, 1816
"	40 Thomas Mackey " July 23, 1810	"	52 W. B. Marshall " Nov. 7, 1819
"	41 Nathan D. Porter " July 10, 1820	Elders	7 Lyman Homiston " Sep. 27, 1778

[Seventies]	42 William Cook " Sep. 2, 1822	[Elders]	8 John Cox " Sep. 5, 1803
"	43 M. H. Braninger " Dec. 18, 1810	"	9 William S. Hathaway " Feb. 26, 1800
"	44 Mirick W. Reed " Dec. 13, 1812	"	10 Eric Glines " Oct. 5, 1822
"	45 Lorenzo Babcock " Dec. 22, 1822	"	11 Joseph Clark " May 15, 1792
"	46 Henry Fairbanks " Dec. 3, 1826	"	12 Isaiah Hamblin " June 20, 1790
"	47 William Smith " Jan. 22, 1810		

were washed by Albert Merrill and John Kay. Anointed by James Townsend and Samuel Moore.

Ordination

Isaiah Hamblin was ordained Elder by Randolph Alexander & P G. Sessions.

List 3 In the Female department commencing at 50 p. 12

Mary McGhan born Dec. 28, 1827	Delight Parker born Sep. 9, 1820
Nancy A. Stevenson " Aug 8, 1826	Ann Allen " Feb. 27, [illegible]

Monday February 2, 1846. 50 min p. 12.

Sarah Cook born Apl. 29, 1818	Phebe Ann Reed born June 1, 1810
Elizabeth Kiernes " Sep. 17, 1795	Mary E. Reed " Apl. 22, 1822
Harriet Thallon " Feb. 6, 1826	Mary Hard " May 4, 1793
Eunice M. Baldwin " May 29, 1821	Ann Mackey " Sep. 18, 1799
Mary [illegible] " 1804	Elizabeth Shiffer " Jan. 12, 1829
Elizabeth Beard " June 7, 1820	Lovina Woods " Apl. 24, 1811
Clara Homiston " Oct 28, 1796	Mary Bruninger " Oct. 15, 1814
Nancy Woodard " Mar. 8, 1820	[illegible] Clark " Feb. 14, 1820
Sarah Box " July 22, 1808	Mary Ann Babcock " Feb. 14, 1826
Daphne Hamblin " Aug 27, 1797	

were washed and Anointed by Altemira Shirtliff, Mary E. Frost, Zeruah Goddard, Julia Ann Shumway, Susan Townsend, Lucina Sessions, and Lovina Mitchel.

List 4 In the Male department commencing at [blank]

Sev			
	53 Austin Grant born Dec. 30, 1808		65 Henry Davis born Feb. 25, 1804
"	54 John Wood " Aug. 25, 1818	"	66 Levi Tofield " Dec. 18, 1803
"	55 John Cunningham " May 10, 1818	"	67 William Tubbs " Jan. 25, 1824
"	56 Joseph Griffiths " Jan. 17, 1816	"	68 Russel G. Brownell " July 11, 1818
"	57 John Bright " Oct. 1, 1811	"	69 John J. Mowery " Oct. 18, 1827
"	58 Samuel Payne " July 24 1814	"	70 Philo Allen " Jan. 3, 1818
"	59 William Smith " Aug 11, 1825	"	71 Jeremiah Leavitt " May 30, 1796
"	60 James C. Williams " Feb. 23, 1814	H. Priests	2 Joseph Price " July 11, 1794
"	61 James Park " Jan 181		3 William Gould " May 17, 1808
"	62 Norman S. Williams " Aug. 27, 1820	Elder	13 John Newman " 1802
"	63 Charles B. Hamock " Dec. 21, 1823	"	14 Nelson W. Whipple " July 11, 1819
"	64 Moses A. Vince " Oct. 29, 1809	"	15 Jeremiah Bingham " June 15, 1806

were washed by Burr Frost and David Jacobs. Anointed by Albert Merrill and Elisha Edwards. Finished at —

Ordinations

Austin Grant, William Smith, Henry Davis, and Levi Fifield, were ordained Seventies by Prests. J. G. Grant, and Levi Hancock.

List 4 In the Female department commencing at 50 p. 2

Larinda Williams born May 3, 1816	Susan Jane Whipple born Mar 9, 1828
Sarah Bright " May 1800	Sarah Levet " Sep. 5, 1798

Mary Jane Loub [born] Jan. 11, 1831	Ann Griffith [born] Apl. 18, 1819
Elizabeth Huntsman " Aug. 10, 1777	Ann Roxy Grant " Mar. 16, 1820
Mary Clark " Nov. 25, 1804	Sarah Jane Grant " Oct. 4, 1810
Patsey Reynolds " Feb 30 [sic], 1829	Elizabeth Jane Davis " Sep. 17, 1831
Susan Cunningham " Mar. 11, 1829	Rachel Davis " Oct. 13, 1810
Alsigna Easton " Sep. 7, 1824	Polly Ann Clothier " Apl. 23, 1829
Ann Newman " Aug. 30, 1796	[illegible] " Oct 1, 1811

Monday February 2, 1846.

Lucy Hawks born Feb. 27, 1829	Clarissa Phelps born June 10, 1817
Dalia Pine " Jan. 1, 1794	Elizabeth Deem " Dec. 11, 1778
Caroline A. Stanton " June 3, 1830	Sally Ann Gould " July 25, 1812
Mary Payne " July 16, 1815	Margaret Calhoun " Aug. 16, 1825
Harriet Stanton " May 31, 1827	Ann Wood " Oct. 6, 1821

were washed and anointed by Altemia Shirtliff, Zilpha Jacobs, Chelmicia Hamilton, Susan Townsend, Cynthia Ann Elridge, Lovina Mitchel, Louisa Clark, Mariah E. Edwards, and Margaret Ann Merrill. 4 P.M.

List 5 In the Male department commencing at 25. p. 5. P.M.

Sev		Sev	
	72 Florillo B. Morris born Feb. 14, 1829		85 George Beach born Mar. 8, 1817
"	73 James Mowery " Nov. 26, 1828	"	86 Robert Watts " Sep. 5, 1801
"	74 John Marriott " Mar. 6, 1827	"	87 Isaac H. Brown " July 28, 1819
"	75 James M. McGaw " Aug 27, 1823	"	88 George W. Hancock " Mar. 8, 1826
"	76 Arnold Potter " Jan 11, 1804	"	89 Robert Telford " Jan 8, 1826
"	77 Charles Green " July 4, 1802	"	90 Harvey Tidwell " Nov. 29, 1823

"	78 Robert Campbell " Jan. 21, 1825	"	91 Edward Knapp " June 3, 1823
"	79 James Robins " Jan. 19, 1818	H. Priests	4 William Wixom " Feb. 27, 1786
"	80 John Harding " Nov. 28, 1811	Elders	16 Luther Barney " Sept. 8, 1806
"	81 John Gibbs " Jan. 3, 1812	"	17 John Kelley " Oct. 9, 1795
"	82 Robert Williams " Sep. 14, 1815	"	18 John M. Clark " Jan. 4, 1823
"	83 William Dally " Mar. 2, 1822	"	19 Albert Clark " Mar. 1, 1824
"	84 Edward Robinson " Oct. 16, 1807	"	20 Thomas M. Helsey " Dec. 9, 1825

Washed by Burr Frost and Dana Jacobs. Anointed by John Kay and Madison D. Hamilton.

Ordinations.

Isaac H. Brown was ordained a Seventy and William Wixom was ordained a High Priest by Samuel Moore, Darwin Chase, and Allen G. Stout.

*Florilla B. Morris, James Mowery, and Harvey Tidwell were washed and anointed only.

List 5 In the Female Department commencing at 25 p. 5

Elizabeth Watts born Dec. 8, 1815	Fanny A. Decker born Apl. 24, 1830
Tryphena Brimhall " Mar. 4, 1822	Laura Stowell " July 7, 1825
Mary Ann Greathouse " Nov. 4, 1827	Mercy Ann Meginess " Dec. 8, 1821
Mahala Dudley " June 15, 1822	Elizabeth Robbins " Mar. 19, 1818
Cynthia Mariah Beech " Dec 1816	Elizabeth Markham " Feb 9, 1830
Mary Jane Barney " May 29, 1823	Mary Harden " Feb. 15, 1815
Ann Dunham Williams " Dec. 25, 1819	Ann Robinson " Nov. 1810
Sarah Gibbs " Jan. 7, 1787	Parcy A. Goddard " Jan 13, 1787
Margaret Nixon " Oct. 19, 1782	Emma Eliza Grant " [illegible]
[illegible] ^Jean Campbell^ " Apl. 3, 1825	Melissa Knapp " [illegible]

[line illegible]

Elizabeth Kelly [born] Apl. 1797	Susannah Marriot [born] Jan. 30, 1821
Elizabeth Potter " Nov 2, 1821	Anna Telford " Nov. 22, 1827
Deana Kelsey " Aug. 8, 1827	

were washed and anointed by Louisa Clark, Susan Townsend, Mary E. Frost, Chelimicia Hamilton, Lucina Sessions, Zilpha Jacobs, Sarah B. Barney and Zeruah Goddard. 20 p. 6

—Seventies Record, Book B, February 2, 1846.

had never oppressed her neither did I wish to rule or oppress her but if they were agreed I should not hinder their union but the reader can better judge than I describe my feelings on hearing the above statement after what transpired yesterday[.] suffice to say they were sealed and received their anointing.

—Newel Knight, Diary, quoted in Lyndon W. Cook, compiler, *Nauvoo Marriages: Proxy Sealings, 1843-1846* (Provo, UT: Grandin Book Company, 2004), p. xxi.

[On the] Second day of February [1846] Mary Jain Laub my Wife Recieved her Washing and Anointing in the house of the Lord & her Endewment. this I [can confirm because I] am present this day in the house of the Lord in Nauvoo at this time while I wright.

—George Laub, Diary, LDS Archives.

[R]eturned about 10—soon Brigham Young & Heber Kimball came in & we continued in Council till 1 or 2 oclock ... in the course of Council we walked out in the garden examined the Trees &c & after returning in my office made such enquiries of the Lord as ~~the~~ our circumstances & the circumstances of the Saints [required] & [we] received satisfactory answers[.]

—Willard Richards, Diary.

Went with my wife [Louisa Stout] to the Temple to be Sealed but there was no sealing going on to day. ... [I later] went up to the Temple & saw Br[other] [Heber C.] Kimball who told us that we might bring our wives to the Temple to night and have them Sealed which we did & came home at 9½ o'clock.

—Hosea Stout, Diary, in *On the Mormon Frontier: The Diary of Hosea Stout, 1844-1861,* edited by Juanita Brooks (Salt Lake City: University of Utah Press/Utah State Historical Society, 1964).

Two hundred and thirty-four persons received ordinances.

Ten a.m., the Twelve [apostles], Trustees and a few others met in council, to ascertain the feelings of the brethren that were expecting to start westward. We agreed that it was imperatively necessary to start as soon as possible. I [Brigham Young] counseled the brethren to procure boats and hold them in readiness to convey our wagons and teams over the river, and let everything for the journey be in readiness, that when a family is called to go, everything necessary may be put into the wagon within four hours, at least, for if we are here many days, our way will be hedged up. Our enemies have resolved to intercept us whenever we start. I should like to push on as far as possible before they are aware of our movements. In order to have this counsel circulated, I sent messengers to notify the captains of hundreds and fifties to meet at 4 p.m. at Father [Alpheus] Cutlers'.

At four o'clock, I met with the captains of hundreds and fifties, and laid my counsel before them, to which they all consented, and dispersed to carry it into execution.

I received letters from England and the eastern states.

At sundown, I returned to the Temple and continued there until 9 p.m. Before leaving I gave instructions to my clerks not to stop recording until the records of the endowments were finished.

Elder H[eber]. C. Kimball and I went to Willard Richards' office, where we remained in council with him. In the course of our council we walked out into the garden, and examined his grove of chestnut trees, and his wife, Jennetta's grave, and after returning to the office made inquiries of the Lord as to our circumstances and the circumstances of the saints and received satisfactory answers. Retired about 1 a.m.

—"Manuscript History of Brigham Young,"
in *History of the Church,* 7:578-79.

Nauvoo temple endowments performed on this date for:

First Company: William Payne, Catharine Payne, Ebenezer M. Kimball, Melaney S. Kimball, Dewitt Tyler, Eliza Tyler, John Harper, Margaret Harper, John Lambert, Patience Lambert, Harry Dolton, Eliza Hebard, Jesse Pierson, Mary Ann Pierson, Eliza Clift, Mary Ann Clift, James Jeffs, Ann Jeffs, Joseph Hancock, Speedy Hancock, Elam Cheney, Anna Cheney, Barnet Rigby, Ann Rigby, Joseph Curtis, Sally Ann Curtis, Peter Maughan, Mary Ann Maughan, John J. Stocking, Harriet Stocking, Daniel Collet, Esther Collet, Hugh McKinney, Sarah Ann McKinney, Elijah Elmore, Mary Elmore, Benjamin R. Hulse, Jane Hulse, Samuel Milton Howe, Jane Howe, Charles W. Dolton, John Borrowman, Hiram Olmstead, and Eleanora L. Berry.

Second Company: Samuel Suffycool, Elizabeth Suffycool, Freeman Tupper, Susan Tupper, Samuel Parriah, Fanny Parriah, Alfred Kinney,

Relief Kinney, Jesse McCarroll, Mary McCarroll, Abraham Hoover, Mary Hoover, Jehiel Hildreth, Louisa Hildreth, Caleb C. Baldwin, Ann Eliza Baldwin, Enoch King Sr., Sally King, David Wood, Catharine Wood, Bartholomew Mahoney, Mary Ann Mahoney, Henry H. Overly, Rebecca Overly, Samuel Smith, Mary Ann Smith, Julia Hampton, Moses Curtis, Amelia Curtis, Jacob Baum, Robert Wright, Agnes Baum, William B. Simmons, Ann Wright, Amanda Simmons, Rebecca Smith, Elisha Smith, Dominicus Elmore, Martha Elmore, Solomon P. McIntosh, and Mary McIntosh.

Third Company: Michael H. Branninger, Mary Branninger, Thomas McKee, Ann McKee, Isaiah Hamblin, Daphne Hamblin, Alonzo Reed, Mary E. Reed, John Cox, Sarah Cox, Lyman Homiston, Clara Homiston, William Cook, Sarah Cook, Joseph Clark, Susanna Clark, William S. Hathaway, Mary Hard, Elizabeth Beard, Russel P. Baldwin, Eunice Baldwin, Marcus B. Thorp, Mary McGhan, Delight Parker, Lorenzo Babcock, Emma Ann Babcock, James Woodward, Nancy Woodward, George Allen, Ann Allen, Oliver Stratton, William Smith, Rebecca Smith, Mirick W. Reed, Phebe Ann Reed, Elizabeth Thorn, Lavina Woods, Wilson Keirnes, Elizabeth Keirnes, Edward Stevenson, Nancy A. Stevenson, Henry Fairbanks, Washington B. Marshall, Nathan D. Porter, and Eric Glines.

Fourth Company: John Cunningham, Susan Cunningham, Elsina Eastern, Polly Ann Clothier, Levi Fifield, Elizabeth Huntsman, Mary Jane Laub, Margaret Calhoon, Roxey Ann Grant, Austin Grant, Sarah Jane Grant, Philo Allen, Elizabeth Deem, Lucy Hox, John Bright, Sarah Bright, Mary Clark, Lorinda Williams, Patsy Reynolds, James C. Williams, William Gould, Sally Ann Gould, Jeremiah Bingham, Clarissa E. Phelps, John Newman, Ann Newman, Charles Hancock, Harriet Stanton, Samuel Payne, Mary Payne, Elizabeth Jane Davis, Joseph Griffith, Joseph Pine, Adelia Pine, John Wood, Ann Wood, Nelson W. Whipple, Susan Jane Whipple, William Tubs, Caroline Stanton, Jeremiah Leavett Sr., Sarah Levit, Henry Davis, Rachel Davis, Lucy Foot, Norman S. Williams, Russel G. Brownell, James Bark, William Smith, Moses A. Vance, and John Thomas.

Fifth Company: Edward W. Knap, Laura Stowel, Edward Robinson, Malissa Charlotte Knap, Thomas M. Kelsey, Ann Robinson, William Nixon, Margaret Nixon, Diana Kelsey, Robert Campbell, Ivan Scobie, Isaac Brown, Percy Amanda Goddard, John Gibbs, Sarah Gibbs, Robert Williams, Ann Dunham, Robert Watts, Elizabeth Watts, Charles Green,

Ema Eliza Green, George Beach, Synthia Maria Beach, John Hardin, Mary Hardin, James Robins, Elizabeth Robins, Luther Barney, Lucinda Jane Barney, John Kelly, Mary E. Kelly, James E. McGaw, Mary Ann Greathouse, John Marriott, Susanna Marriott, Mercy Ann Meginess, Mahala Dudley, John Milton Clark, Trifenia Brimhall, George W. Hancock, Arnold Potter, Elizabeth Potter, Albert Clark, Fanny Decker, Robert Telford, Anna Telford, William Dally, and Elizabeth Barker.

—Summary of information compiled by the Temple Index Bureau, *Nauvoo Temple Endowment Register: 10 December 1845 to 8 February 1846.* Editors' note: According to the register, Florillo B. Morris, James Mowery, and Harvey Tidwell were washed and anointed and therefore also probably received through the veil on this date.

....

Second anointings performed on this date:

Thomas Burdick and Anna (Higby) Burdick, anointed by Orson Pratt; Alvah L. Tippetts and Caroline (Beard) Tippetts, anointed by Parley P. Pratt; William D. Huntington and Anna (Maginn) Huntington, anointed by Parley P. Pratt; Samuel Williams and Ruth (Bishop) Williams, anointed by Orson Pratt; Joseph Knight Sr. and Phebe (Crosby) Knight, anointed by Parley P. Pratt; Peregrine Sessions and Lucinda (Call) Sessions, anointed by Orson Pratt; Heber C. Kimball, Clarissa (Cutler) Kimball, Emily (Cutler) Kimball, Anna (Gheen) Kimball, and Amanda (Gheen) Kimball, anointed by Parley P. Pratt; Ezra Chase and (Elizabeth Hills?) Chase, anointed by Willard Snow; to Brigham Young for time and Joseph Smith (deceased) for eternity: Augusta A. Cobb, Zina D. H. (Huntington) Jacobs, and Amanda Barnes, anointed by John Taylor; Randolph Alexander and Myrza (Nix) Alexander, anointed by [not given]; William W. Phelps, Laura (Stowell) Phelps, and Elizabeth (Dunn) Phelps, anointed by [not given]; John Taylor and Mary (Utley) Taylor, anointed by Brigham Young; and Chandler Holbrook and Eunice (Dunning) Holbrook, anointed by John Taylor.

—Summarized from "Book of Anointings."

....

Sealings for the living performed on this date:

Charles Allen to Eliza Tibbits; Thomas Burdick to Anna Higley; Elam Cheney Sr. to Hannah Compton; Raymond Clark to Louisa Gill; George Washington Hancock to Betsy Jane Fackrell; Jesse D. Hunter to

Lydia Ann Edmunds [Edmonds]; Jesse Divine Hunter to Kiziah [Keziah] Brown; George Given Johnston to Mahaley Dudley; Joseph Knight Sr. to Phebe [Polly] Crosby; Heber Chase Kimball to Amanda Trimble Gheen, Emily Trask Cutler, and Clarissa Crissy Cutler; John Marriott [Marryott] to Susannah Folks; William Wines Phelps to Laura Stowell and Elizabeth Dunn; and Hosea Stout to Louisa Taylor, Lucretia Fisher, and Marinda Bennett.

—Summarized from the Book of Living Sealings.

....

Sealings for the dead performed on this date:

Polly Peck (Phebe Crosby, proxy) to Joseph Knight, Brigham Young officiating; William A. Gheen (Ellis M. Sanders, proxy) to Easter Ann Pierce, Heber C. Kimball officiating;[63] Joseph Smith (Brigham Young, proxy) to Zina Diantha Huntington, Heber C. Kimball officiating: "Henry B. Jacobs [Zina Jacobs's civil husband] expressed his willingness that it should be so in the presence of these witnesses";[64] Luther Sweat (John Loveless, proxy) to Sally Elmer, Brigham Young officiating;[65] and Samantha Peck (Louisa Taylor, proxy) to Hosea Stout, Heber C. Kimball officiating.

—Summarized from the Book of Proxy Sealings.

....

Adoptions performed on this date:

To Brigham and Augusta Adams Young: James Graham, Mary Graham, Isaac Morley, Lucy Morley, Robert Pierce, and Hannah Pierce, sealed by Heber C. Kimball.

—Summarized from "Sealings and Adoptions."

Tuesday, February 3, 1846

Notwithstanding I gave out word that we would not attend to these matters—yet the House [temple] was thronged all the day. The anxiety are so great that the Brethren would have us stay here & continue the endowments until our way will be Hedged up & our enemies intercept us—but I tell you Brethren that it will not do—this is not the last Temple that we will build—in this house we have been payed well if we were to

63. Easter Ann Pierce was also sealed to Ellis Sanders for time.

64. Zina Diantha Huntington was also sealed to Brigham Young for time.

65. Sally Elmer was also sealed to John Loveless for time.

receive no more—& I tell that there will be double the anxiety manifest to build the next that there was to Ericte [erect] this—then be satisfied—I am going to load up my waggon & be away from this place immediately— I walked off some little distance from the Temple soposing the crowd would disperse— but on returning to the Temple again—I found the House thronged to overflowing[.] looking upon the multitude & knowing the anxiety of the Brethren—that were thirsting & hungering for the word—we commenced sealing & anointing & continued & continued [sic] also the washings Night & Day—putting through from 2[00] to 300 Persons within 24 hours & spent the night.

—Brigham Young, Diary.

....

John Milton Bernhisel [born] June 23 1799 Tyrone. Cumberland Co[unty]. Pennsylvania this day came to the sacred Alt[a]r in the upper room of the "House of the Lord" founded by Pres[iden]t. Joseph Smith (martyred) the Prophet Seer & Revelator to the church and there upon gave himself to Pres[iden]t. Joseph Smith (martyred) to become his son by the law of adoption and to become a legal heir to all the blessings bestowed upon Joseph Smith pertaining to exaltations even unto the eternal Godhead with a solemn covenant to observe all the rights & ordinances pertaining to the new & everlasting covenant as far as now is or shall hereafter be made known unto him[;] done in the presence of Patriarch John Smith, Pres[ident]. Brigham Young Heber C. Kimball, Amasa Lyman, O[rson]. Hyde & George A. Smith at 4 O.clock P.M.

—Book of Proxy Sealings.

....

List 1 In the Male department commencing at 8. A.M.

[See pages 567-75 for excerpted portion.]

The rooms of the Temple were thronged all day, and in the evening the crowd was very great. About 3 o'clock A.M. president B[righam]. Young requested the people to withdraw, as it would be impossible to administer the ordinances to them. After which Hellen Kimball was given in marriage to George Whitney. Pres[iden]t [Heber C.] Kimball sent for a barrel of wine, and the work hands partook freely of it. The music was then called for and the remainder of the night was spent in festivity. Charles W. Wandell Smith Clerk

★ Enoch B. Tripp and David Sessions Jr. were ordained Seventies by

[Washings and anointings for Tuesday, February 3, 1846]

Seventies

	1 Nathan C. ~~Derby~~ ^Tenney^ born July 28, 1817		12 Emery Barrus born Apl. 8, 1809
"	2 Gordon E. Deuel " July 21, 1821		13 John G. Herr " June 18, 1799
"	3 Ephraim Hawks " Mar. 21, 1827		14 William Green " Dec. 17, 1811
"	4 Ethan Pettit " Jan. 11, 1810		15 ~~William Green~~ Nathaniel Jones " Oct. 13, 1822
"	5 Wiley B. Corbitt " April 2, 1808		16 Nathan Lewis " Mar. 28, 1808
"	6 Nathaniel Frampton " Mar. 5, 1798		17 Frederick Farney " Oct. 9
"	7 Orson G. Beach " May 30, 1808		18 Laban Morrill " Dec. 8, 1815
"	8 ~~John Cairns~~ ^Willis^ Boren " Mar. 11, 1796		19 Walker Smith " July 28, 1823
"	9 Seth Rigby " Apl. 23, 1820	H. Priests	1 Henry Steven " July 31, 1811
"	10 Charles Merrell " Oct. 13, 1811		2 John Cairns " Oct 21, 1808
"	11 Jefferson Dimick " Dec 2, 1805		

were washed by Jonathan Crosby, and Alonzo Barrow. Anointed by Zenos H. Gurley and Samuel Mulliner.

List 1 In the Female department commencing at 45 p 7

Marinda Corbet born Aug. 11, 1825	Margaret Pettit born Apl. 15, 1815
Laura Ann Frampton " Dec. 11, 1813	Elizabeth King " Feb. 25, 1777
Mary Ann Dimick " Oct. 3, 1810	Mary Davis " Feb. 2, 1814
Huldah F. Barrus " Apl. 16, 1816	Olive Tenney " Feb. 18, 1819
Almira G. Kairns " June 3, 1815	Sarah Merrill " Feb. 18, 1819
Harriet Green " Apl. 17, 1813	Matilda Stevens " July 31, 1819
Permelia Morrill " Aug. 20, 1821	Margaret Rigby " Jan. 31, 1822
Clara Ann Farney " Sep. 1819	Mary Boren " Sep. 6, 1784
Margaret Herr " Apl. 25 1811	Rebecca Lewis " Aug. 9, 1813

Lucinda Beach [born] Mar. 26, 1802	Rebecca M. Jones [born] Feb 16, 1826
Ann Deuel " June 13, 1826	Laura Atley " Jan. 24, 1815

Were washed and anointed by Caroline Crosby, Myrza Alexander, Permelia Dayton, Sophia Land, Rahamah Derby, Catherine Mulliner, Zeruah Goddard, Susan A. Chapman. 55 minutes p. 8. A.M.

Tuesday, February 3d 1846.

List 2 In the Male department commencing at 10 A.M.

Sev		H. Priests	
	20 Henry Nelson born Sep. 6, 1826		3 Horace Ransom born July 15, 1799
"	21 Nicolas W. Empy " Dec. 14, 181		14 William G. Bennet " July 22, 1790
"	22 William C. Calkins " Feb 1, 1807		5 Henry Zabrisky " Aug 11, 1788
"	23 David Bernel " June 16, 1803		6 John Coomer " Nov. 11, 1764
"	24 John M. Wakeley " Dec. 26, 1820	Elders	1 James Whaley " Nov. 30, 1797
"	25 Orson Tyler " Jan 10, 1821		2 Henry Shafer " Apl. 3, 1789
"	26 Peter Nicko " Nov. 5, 1800		3 Henry Appleton " Sept. 1,
"	27 Charles Perrin Apl. 26, 1812		4 Reuben P. Hartwell " Nov. 2, 1808
"	28 John Spicer " Dec. 4, 1816		Mart~~ah~~^in^ Potter " Aug 10, 1790
"	29 Benjamin Hawkins " July 7, 1805		Rodney Badger " Feb. 4, 1824
"	30 ~~Reuben S Hartwell~~		Jacob Vansteenburgh " Dec. 14, 1805
	^William Sweat^ " ~~Nov 2, 1808~~ July 7, 1805		
"	31 James M. Hemmick " Nov. 7, 1822		

were washed by Jonathan Crosby and Alonzo Le Baron. Anointed by Zenos H. Gurley and Samuel Mulliner.

List 2 In the Female department commencing at 45 p. 9.

Nancy Sabrisky born Mar. 14, 1801	Polly Wakely born Apl. 29, 1820
Anna Potter " May 22, 1795	Vienna Vansteenbrough " July 13, 1810

Lucinda A. Hartwell " July 29, 1809	Elizabeth Cummer " age unknown
Mary Ann Cleveland " Oct. 17, 1802	Elizabeth Stevenson " Aug 11, 1792
Mary Nicoll " Feb. 22, 1825	Mariah Empy " June 24, 1816
Rene Tyler " Apl. 1, 1824	Joanna Bennet " July 22, 1803
Abigail Whaley " Sep. 22, 1825	Jane Nelson " Dec. 1824
Elizabeth Bennet " Nov. 4, 1792	Mary Appleton " Sep. 24, 1791
Hannah Perrin " Dec 24, 1812	Elizabeth Rawson " Oct. 18, 1807
Sylva Ann Calkin " Jan 15, 1818	Eve Sheffer " May 8, 1789
Anna Spicer " Dec. 30, 1817	Lucy Swett " Dec. 28, 1810

were washed and anointed by Lucina Sessions, Lovina Mitchel, Sophia Lance, Caroline Crosby, Zeruah Goddard, Susan A. Chapman, and Catherine Mulliner. Finished at 40 minutes past 10 A.M.

List 3 In the Male department commencing at 12 M.

Sev.		Sev.	
	32 ~~Alfred Bell~~ ^Thomas Tarbet^ born Oct. 10, 1813		40 William M Wall born Sep. 30, 1822
	33 Henry Mower " Nov. 22, 1824		41 William W. Willis " Aug. 16, 1811
	34 John Gould " May 11, 1808		42 ~~Mar~~ Ally D. Boren " Mar. 6, 1818
	35 Lewis Zabrisby " Sep. 17, 1817		43 Coleman Boren " Oct. 14, 1808
	36 John Ruston " May 20, 1821		44 Abel M. Sargeant " Feb. 27, 1799
	37 William P. Vance " Oct. 22, 1822	H. Priests	7 Alfred Bell " Aug 16, 1794
	38 Cole W. Lyons " Sep. 21, 1818		Arthur S. Smith " Jan 30, 1809
	39 John Wheeler " Feb. 3, 1802		Andrew B. Rose " [illegible]

Tuesday February 3d. 1846.

H Priests 10 Justis A Seeley born Nov. 17, 1779

Elders 8 Athe Meeks " Nov 16, 1820

[Elders] 9 Joshua A Thomas [born] Dec. 21, 1818
" 10 Dolphus Babcock " Feb 23, 1800
" 11 Lyeon Cragun " Aug. 13
" 12 David Young " June 18, 1772

The foregoing persons were washed by Jonathan Crosby and Alonzo LeBarron. Anointed by Zenos H. Gurley and Samuel Mulliner. Finished at 1 P.M.

List 3 In the Female Department commencing at 12 m.

Susan Skreghan [?] born July 11, 1829
Margaret Wilcox " Jan. 11, 1790
Jerusha Babcock " June 30, 1804
Mary Ann Knighten " July 22, 1811
Aby Gould " Mar. 23, 1811
Mary Zabrisky " Sep. 5, 1821
Nancy Wall " Aug 23, 1823
Margaret Vance " Nov. 29, 1820
Susan Mower " May 3, 1821
Elizabeth Rose " July 9, 1789
Elizabeth Smith " Jan. 1, 1814
Hetty Seely " Oct. 12, 1780
Margaret Willis " Aug. 15, 1812

Martha L. Bell born Apl. 7, 1807
Loretta L. Scovill " Jan 17, 1832
Margaret Rushton " July 28, 1822
Adaline M. Boren " Nov. 21, 1823
Malinda Boren " Nov. 9, 1812
Eleonar R. Turbot " Jan. 23, 1819
Elizabeth Young " Oct. 17, 1783
Mary Young " Nov. 10, 1818
Tabitha Cragun " Mar. 5, 1830
Sarah Lyons " Oct. 9, 1819
Martha Wheeler " Dec. 3, 1808
Theodaska Willis " Sep. 27, 1818

were washed and anointed by Margaret M Raney, Caroline Crosby, Sophia Lance, Permelia Dayton, Zeruah Goddard, Lucina Sessions, Julia P. Martin, and Susan A. Chapman. Finished at 1 o'clock P.M.

List 4 In the Male Department commencing at 2 P.M.

Sev

	45 Robert Crookston born Sep. 21, 1821		55 Stephen Chipman born Aug. 8, 1805
"	46 John Ackerly " Dec 25, 1812		56 Barnabas L Adams " ~~Aug~~ ^May^ 28, 1812
"	47 Joshua F. Holman " Aug. 22, 1825		57 Rufus P Stewart " Feb. 26, 1811
"	48 John Holman " Oct. 18, 1828		58 Thomas M. Eude " May 6, 1819
			~~Nel M Sargent~~
"	49 Samuel Brown " Nov. 14, 1801	H. Priests	11 John S. Martin " Mar. 15, 1801
"	50 Marel Wheeler " Nov. 14, 1827	Elders	13 George Tiffany " May 14, 1808
"	51 John Dutson " Sep. 28, 1825		14 Byron Bybee " Feb. 25, 1799
"	52 William H. Forsyth " Oct. 14, 1839		15 Merit Rockwell " Apl. 30, 1825
"	53 William King " Apl. 21, 1822		16 Horace Rockwell " Apl. 30, 1825
"	54 William S. Seelye " May 18, 1812		17 Lewis Lane " Dec. 10, 1825

were washed by Jonathan Crosby and Alonzo LeBarron. Anointed by Zenos H. Gurley and Darwin Chase.

List 4 In the Female Department commencing at

Polly Braley born June 10, 1826	Betsey Bybee born Jan. 20, 1811
Almira Tiffany " June 13, 1811	Jane Mitchel " June 12, 1777
Amanda M. A. Hammond " May 6, 1828	Eliza Pace " Apl. 8, 1806

Tuesday February 3d, 1846.

Nancy Carter born Feb. 8, 1826	Abigail Gray born Nov. 19, 1826
Drucilla Seymour " Feb. 1, 1826	Almeda Hawkins born Nov. 22, 1803
Matilda Martin " Feb. 6, 1807	Susannah Wallace " Dec. 12, 1818
Jane Ackerley " Feb. 17, 1828	Lovina Brown " Jan. 5, 1808
Beulah Chipman " Feb. 18, 1826	Elizabeth Seelye " Sep. 4, 1815

Sinah Chipman [born] Sep. 13, 1822	Laura E. King [born] Aug. 25, 1826
Olive Wheelock " July 16, 1812	Jane Dutson " Mar 10, 1821
Margaret Shaslam " Apl. 2, 1783	Orrilla Tippits " Jan. 27, 1803
Elizabeth Dana " Apl. 10, 1826	Harriet Chandler " June 4, 1789
Mary Dixon " Apl. 11, 1804	Amanda M. Forsyth " May 20, 1826

were washed and anointed by Sarah Smith, Nancy Cahoon, Permelia Dayton, Julia T. Martin, Sylvia Lance, Elvira Teeples, and Susan A. Chapman, and Sister Green.

List 5 In the Male department commencing at 4 P.M.

Sev		Sev	
	59 Melvin Ross born Oct. 12, 1812		70 John Grier born Feb. 8, 1815
"	60 William Childs " July 6, 1819	"	71 John C. Kelley " Aug. 26, 1819
"	61 John Evans " May 29, 1822	"	72 Elihu B. Adams " Jan. 14, 1822
"	62 Judson Johnson " July 14, 1826	"	73 Riley Houffh ^Hough^ " Aug. 7, 1821
"	63 John W. Norton Nov. 6, 1820	H. Priests	12 Moses Daily ^ley^ " Apl. 16, 1791
"	64 John Gray " May 24, 1820	"	75 13 John Fore " May 3, 1790
"	65 Albert Miner " Mar. 31, 1809	"	14 76 John Reed " Oct. 12, 1784
"	66 William Coll " May 22, 1817	"	15 77 Isaac Davis " Feb. 20, 1783
"	67 James Bird " May 18, 1812	"	16 78 Elisher Whiting " Dec. 17, 1785
"	68 Benjamin Gray " Feb. 2, 1829	Elders	18 Henry Kearns " Jan. 18, 1830

were washed by Jonathan Crosby and Alonzo LeBarron. Anointed by William O. Clark, Samuel Richards, Darwin Chase and Zenos H. Gurley.

List 5 In the Female Department commencing at 45. p. 3

Rebbecca Hammer born Aug 20, 1827	Sarah Toalman born Jan 21, 1832

Almira Daley " Nov. 21, 1801	Eliza S. Lincoln " Sep. 9, 1829
Edith Davis " Mar. 16, 1894	Elizabeth Rowe " Aug. 2, 1813
Ruth Wellington " Mar 11, 1809	Abigail Buchanan " Jan 9, 1802
Rachel H. Brewer " Sep. 5, 1808	Electa Crane " Sep. 8, 1812
Mary Doll (or Bell) " Dec. 2, 1802	Phebe L. Jackson " Jan. 17, 1817
Sedenia Hough " June 30, 1824	Elizabeth Gray " Aug 15, 1822
Sally Whiting " Oct. 29, 1786	Margaret Bird " July 14, 1812
Tamina Miner " Mar. 6, 1813	Nancy S. Cole " Dec. 18, 1830
Mary Evans " Jan. 1, 1823	Rebecca Ross " age unknown
Susanna Slater " Oct. 9, 1816	Sally Childs " [illegible]

were washed and anointed by [illegible]

Tuesday, February 3d 1846.

List 6 In the Male Department commencing at 6 P.M.

Sev		Seventies	
"	74 Burrice Griffin born Dec. 18, 1812		87 Thomas Harran born May 1, 1810
"	75 Justus W. Seelye " Jan 31, 1815	"	88 Joseph W. Adams " Dec. 1, 1823
"	76 Barnabas Merrifield " June 2, 1816	"	89 John Rose " Dec. 25, 1807
"	77 Justin G. Merrill " Feb. 18, 1806	"	90 Henry Wilcox " Feb. 14, 1822
"	78 Daniel Shearer " Aug. 30, 1791	"	91 James C. Earl " Mar. 27, 1822
"	79 John Willes " Jan 4, 1827	H. Priests	17 Samuel Merrill " Sep. 24, 1785
"	80 Nicolas Runyan " Aug. 27, 1810	Elders	20 William Ford Jr. " Oct. 17, 1820
"	81 Isaac Harrison " Nov. 2, 1815	"	21 Samuel Thompson " Feb. 14, 1812
"	82 Amos W. Harmon " Oct. 30, 1829	"	22 Samuel Conrad " Sep. 10, 1803

[Seventies]	83 John G. Adams [born] Mar. 9, 1826	[Elders]	23 James J. McKnight [born] Nov. 20, 1818
"	84 William H. Deuel " Jan 1, 1812	"	24 John F. Guthrie " Feb. 22, 1821
"	85 Joseph H. Murphy " Jan. 25, 1814	"	25 Benjamin Baker " Mar. 26, 1796
"	86 James D. Scott " Feb 3, 1818		

were washed by Jonathan Crosby and Edson Barney. Anointed by Zenos H. Gurley, Darwin Chase, Jackson Goodale and Joseph Hovey.

Amos W. Harmon was ordained a Seventy by Levi Hancock.

List 6 In the Female Department commencing at 3 p. 5

Sara Wilcox born Dec. 17, 1820
Mary Conrad " Jan. 23, 1808
Anna Spencer " Jan. 27, 1830
Matilda Kelley " Aug. 13, 1817
Emily Abbot " Sep. 19, 1827
Charilla Abbott " Sep. 19, 1827
Sally Ann Griffins " Mar. 16, 1811
Ann Kerren " Nov. 1, 1815
Eliza Deuel " Oct. 14, 1819
Abigail Baker " Mar. 26, 1801
Martha Nelson " June 20, 1825
Minerva Rose " Dec. 11, 1815
Sarah Murphy " Nov. 25, 1825
Mary Scott " Dec. 8, 1822
Eunice Brown " Mar. 4, 1808
Serena Merrifield " May 15, 1824

Amanda Sherwin born Mar. 24, 1802
Mary Hemingway " Jan. 24, 1810
Clarissa Jane Seely " Oct. 1, 1821
Roxy Keller " Nov. 12, 1810
Sabina Ann Harrison " Feb 8, 1819
Phebe Merrill " Apl. 22, 1787
Sarah Lindsey " Sep. 10, 1809
Delana Ford " Feb. 1, 1821
Charlotte Felshaw " Nov. 28, 1826
Emily Runyan " June 29, 1815
Mary Hill " Sep. 20, 1807
Bathia Fordham " June 2, 1825
Sarah Mulliner " Oct. 25, 1817
Cammilla Merrill " Oct. 5, 1815
Elizabeth Thompson " May 23, 1811

were washed and anointed by Lydia Granger, Caroline Crosby, Sophia Lance, Permelia Dayton, Mary M. Felshaw, Elvira Teeples, Zeruah Goddard, Catherine Mulliner, Louisa Clark and Sarah M Kimball. Also was washed and anointed the following persons, viz.

Mary Cheese born [illegible]

Catherine Phelps " [illegible]

Finished at 55 p.

Tuesday February 3d. 1846.

List 7 In the Male department, commencing at 9 P.M.

Sev		H. Priest	
	92 Enoch B. Tripp born May 23, 1823		18 Windsor T. Lyon " Feb. 8, 1809
"	93 David Sessions Jr. " May 9, 1823	Elders	26 Joseph H. Woolsey " Jan. 10, 1828
"	94 Joseph W. Young " Jan. 12, 1829	"	27 David W. Adams " Mar. 5, 1797
"	95 John Richards " May 16, 1805 were washed by George Grant and		

* Welcome Chapman. Anointed by Perrigreen Sessions and Jackson Goodale.

List 7 In the Female Department commencing at 9 P.M.

Temperance Adams Aug 29, 1796

Sarah Shelton August 26, 1824

155 Julia Felshaw " June 27,

were washed and anointed by Anna Harmon, Sarah Jane Everett, Catherine Mulliner and Mary M. Felshaw.

—Seventies Record, Book B, February 3, 1846.

George Grant and Perrigreen Sessions — Windsor P Lyons, was ordained a Hi[g]h Priest by Dimick Huntington.

—Seventies Record, Book B.

....

The next week we were to work in the temple and father [Heber C.] Kimball called on me to go home and get my wife and also James Smith and wife to be sealed to our wives. We did this. We were conducted into another department and received our Second Anointing. This was a source of knowledge to us and it was a great consolation that we were counted worthy before our Father in Heaven to receive that which we did receive.

—Joseph Hovey, Autobiography, p. 34, LDS Archives.

....

Notwithstanding that I [Brigham Young] had announced that we would not attend to the administration of the ordinances, the House of the Lord was thronged all day, the anxiety being so great to receive, as if the brethren would have us stay here and continue the endowments until our way would be hedged up, and our enemies would intercept us. But I informed the brethren that this was not wise, and that we should build more Temples, and have further opportunities to receive the blessings of the Lord, as soon as the saints were prepared to receive them. In this Temple we have been abundantly rewarded, if we receive no more. I also informed the brethren that I was going to get my wagons started and be off. I walked some distance from the Temple supposing the crowd would disperse, but on returning I found the house filled to overflowing.

Looking upon the multitude and knowing their anxiety, as they were thirsting and hungering for the word, we continued at work diligently in the House of the Lord.

Two hundred and ninety-five persons received ordinances.

... I stayed at home until 6 p.m. I went to the Temple and returned p.m. again in an hour, busy preparing for my journey to the west.

—"Manuscript History of Brigham Young,"
in *History of the Church,* 7:579-80.

....

Nauvoo temple endowments performed on this date for:

First Company: Ethan Pettit, Margaret Pettit, Laban Warren, Pamelia Drury, Frederick Fauncy, Clara Ann Fauncy, Orson G. Beach, Lucinda

Beach, Jefferson Dimick, Mary Ann Dimick, John P. Herr, Margaret Herr, Charles Merrell, Mary Davis, Nathan C. Tenney, Olive Strong, Elizabeth King, Sarah Merrill, Henry Stevens, John Cairns, Matilda Stevens, Almira J. Cairns, Willis Boren, Mary Boren, Henry Ackley, Wyley B. Corbitt, Merinda Corbitt, Ann Deuel, Gordon E. Deuel, Margaret Rigby, Emery Barries, Huldah A. Barries, Laury Ann Frampton, Nathaniel V. Jones, Rebecca Maria Jones, Harriet Green, Seth Rigby, Rebecca Lewis, William Green, Nathan Lewis, Walter Smith, Mannasseh/Ephraim Hanks, and Nathaniel Frampton.

Second Company: Nicolas W. Empy, Mariah Empy, James Whaley, Nancy Zabrisky, Henry Zabrisky, Lucy Swett, James Madison Hammick, Mary Nicol, William Swett, Lucinda/Almedia Hartwell, William C. Calkins, Sylvia Calkins, Henry Shaffer, Eve Shaffer, Jacob Vansteenburgh, Vianna Vansteenburgh, John Spicer, Anna Spicer, John Coomer, Elizabeth Coomer, William J. Bennett, Abigail Whaley, Henry Appleton, Elizabeth Bennet, Reuben T. Hartwell, Mary Appleton, Henry Nelson, Mary Ann Cleveland, Horace Rawson, Elizabeth Rawson, Martin Potter, Amy Potter, Jane Nelson, Orson Tyler, Rene Tyler, Charles Perrin, Mary Perrin, David Bennett, Juana Bennett, John N. Wakely, Polly Wakely, Rodney Badger, Elizabeth Stevenson, Benjamin Hawkins, and Nicol Peter.

Third Company: Arthur Mix, William W. Willis, Margaret Willis, Justice A. Seely, Hetty Seely, John Gould, Aby Gould, Mary Knighton, Arthur Sydney Smith, Lara Leavett Scovil, Elizabeth Smith, Margaret Vance, Andrew Rose, Elizabeth Rose, John Rushton, Margaret Rushton, Thomas Tarbot, Elna Tarbot, Albert Bell, Simeon Cragun, Martha G. Bell, William P. Vance, Margaret Wheelcox, Susan Prekin, Henry Mower Jr., Syria Sheal, Ganum Lians, Melinda Boren, Susan Mower, David Young, Sarah Lyons, Elizabeth Young, Coleman Boren, Mary V. Young, Allyn D. Boren, Adaline M. Boren, William M. Wall, Nancy Wall, John Wheeler, Martha Wheeler, Dolphus Babcock, Theodosia Willis, Joshua Thomas, Mary Zabrisky, Lewis C. Zabrisky, and Abel Morgan Sargent.

Fourth Company: John Akerly, Jane Akerly, Orrilla Tippets, Lewis Lane, Joshus Franklin Holman, Harriette Chantley, Nancy Carter, John Holman, William King, Lara Elizabeth King, Mary Dixon, George Tiffany, Almiah Tiffany, Rufus T. Stewart, Olive Wheelcock, Drusilla/Sargent Seymour, William S. Seelye, Elizabeth Seelye, Barnabas L. Adams, Stephen Chipman, Susanna Wallace, Belah Chipman, Merit Rockwell,

Amanda/Melvina Hammond, John S. Martin, Matilda Martin, Samuel Brown, Lovina Brown, Merrel Wheeler, Almedia Hawkins, Robert Crookston, Eliza Pace, Jane Mitchel, Thomas H. Ewell, Margaret Sheblin, Sana Chipman, Abigail Gray, Horace Rockwell, Elizabeth Denny, Byrum Bybee, Betsey Bybee, John Dutson, Molly Brailley, William Forsyth, Amanda Forsyth, Jane Dutson, Edith Davis, Isaac Davis, Phebe Jackson and Sedelia Hough.

Fifth Company: Riley Hough, Barbara Kairns, Mary Bell, Moses Daley, Almira Daley, Susannah Slater, John Evans, Mary Evans, Henry Kairns, Margaret Cureten, Albert Miner, Tamma Miner, James Bird, Margaret Bird, Elizabeth Gray, John Grier, Sarah Tolman, John Gray, Nancy Serepta Cole, William B. Cole, Judson Tolman, John Fox, Mary Fox, John W. Norton, Rebecca Hammer, Rebecca Ross, Melvin Ross, Elizabeth Rowe, John L. Cally, George A. Loyd, Electa Gray, Rachel Brewer, Henry Wheeler, Sophia Dayton, Elisha Whiting Jr., Sally Whiting, Sarah Childs, William Childs, Benjamin Gray, Abigail Buchanan, Elihu B. Adams, Ruth Wellington, and Eliza T. Lincon.

Sixth Company: Mary Scott, Roxy Keller, James D. Scott, Anna Spencer, Charlotte Felshaw, Barnabas Merrifield, Mary Hemmingway, Serena Merrifield, James C. Earl, Phebe Merrill, Samuel Conrad, Samuel Merrill, Mary Conrad, Charilla Abbot, Sabina A. Harrison, John Rose, Emily Abott, Matilda Kelley, Mary Cheese, Catharine Philips, Amos W. Harmon, Bathia Fordham, Mary Hill, Burrier Griffin, Minerva Rose, Sarah Sally/Ann Griffin, John G. Adams, Amanda Sherwin, James Brown, Unice Brown, Sarah Linsey, Camilla Merrill, Justin J. Merrill, Delaney Ford, William Ford Jr., Abigail Baker, Daniel Shearer, Ann Kerren, Benjamin Baker, Eliza Deuel, William Henry Deuel, Isaac Harrison, Justus W. Seeley, James J. McKnight, Martha Nelson, Nicolas Runyen, Sarah Wilcox, Thomas Kerren, Emily Runyan, Joseph H. Murphy, Sarah Murphy, Henry Wheelcox, Clarissa Jane Seely, Elizabeth Thompson, Samuel Thompson, John T. Guthrie, John Willis, and Joseph W. Adams.

Seventh Company: John Richards, Windsor P. Lyons, Enoch B. Tripp, David W. Adams, Temperance Adams, Joseph W. Young, David Sessions Jr., Julia Felshaw, Joseph Hiram Woolsey, and Sarah Shelton.

—Summary of information compiled by the Temple Index Bureau, *Nauvoo Temple Endowment Register: 10 December 1845 to 8 February 1846.* Editors' note: According to the register, John Reed was washed and anointed and therefore also probably received through the veil on this date.

Second anointings performed on this date:

Daniel Carn and Margaret (Moses) Carn, anointed by William Snow; Calvin C. Pendleton and Sally Ann (Seavey) Pendleton, anointed by Parley P. Pratt; Joseph G. Hovey and Martha Ann (Webster) Hovey, anointed by William Smith; George Pack (deceased, no proxy given) and Phylotte (Green) Pack, anointed by [not given]; James Smithes and Mary (Knowles) Smithes, anointed by Parley P. Pratt; Abraham Palmer and Patience (Pierce) Palmer, anointed by Winslow Farr; Joseph L. Heywood and Serepta Maria (Blodgett) Heywood, anointed by William Snow; Theodore Turley, Frances (Kimberly) Turley, Sarah (Clift) Turley, Eliza (Clift) Turley, and Mary (Clift) Turley, anointed by William Snow; William E. Murray, Mary (Spring) Murray, and Eliza (Cravath) Murray, anointed by Parley P. Pratt; Alpheus Cutler, Margaret (Carr) Cutler, Abigail (Carr) Cutler, Sally (Cox) Cutler, Disey (McCall) Cutler, and Henrietta C. (Miller) Cutler, anointed by [not given]; Heber C. Kimball, Laura (Pitkin) Kimball, Abigail (Pitkin) Kimball, Ruth (Reese) Kimball, Angelina Kimball, Ruth (Crozier) Kimball, Sophrona (Harmon) Kimball, and Christeen (Golden) Kimball, anointed by Parley P. Pratt; Nancy Maria Winchester to Heber C. Kimball for time and Joseph Smith (deceased) for eternity, anointed by Parley P. Pratt; John S. Fullmer, Mary Ann (Price) Fullmer, and Olive (Smith) Fullmer, anointed by Parley P. Pratt; James Allred and Elizabeth (Patrick) Allred, anointed by Parley P. Pratt; and Raymond Clark and Louisa (Gill) Clark, anointed by Ezra T. Benson.

—Summarized from "Book of Anointings."

....

Sealings for the living performed on this date:

Arza Matson Adams to Sabina Clark; William Anderson to Druzilla Sargant; Nathaniel Ashby to Susanna Hammond; John Milton Bernhisel to Catherine Barker [Burgess] and Elizabeth Barker; Daniel Carn to Margaret Moses; John Alpheus Cutler to Margaret Carr, Disey Caroline McCall, and Henrietta Clarinda Miller; Amos Cox to Philena Morley and Cordelia Calista Morley; James Davenport to Almira Phelps; Elijah Fordham to Clarissa Fosdick [on this date or February 6]; Peter Joseph Fory to Elizabeth Fory; William A. Garner to Sarah Workman, and Elizabeth Ann Dunn; James Graham to Mary Butler and Orilla Crandall; Jesse Haven to Martha Spring Hall; Jonathan Harriman Holmes to Marietta Carter; Lorenzo H. Hatch to Hannah Elizabeth Fuller; Joseph Leland Heywood to Sarepta Maria Blodgett; Joseph Grafton Hovey to Martha Ann Webster; Elias Hutchings to Sally [Sarah] Cox; Benjamin Franklin Johnson to Melissa Bloomfield LeBaron, Mary Ann Hale, and Flora Clarinda Washburn Gleason; Joel Hills Johnson to Susan Bryant and Lucinda Alsine Bascom; Daniel Kent to Nancy Young; Heber Chase Kimball to Christeen Golden, Hulda Barnes, Theresa Arathusa Morley, Sophrona Melinda Harmon, Ruth L. Pierce, Laura Pitkin, Ruth Amelia Reese, and Sarah Stiles; Truman Leonard Jr. to Ortentia [Ortensia] White; Leslie Lyme to Elizabeth Wirvender; Samuel Miles Sr. to Prudence Marks; Hyram Washington Mikesell to Ann Augusta Scott; William Ellis Murray to Ellen Sarvis and Mary Spring; John Davis Parker to Harriet Sherwood, Almeda Sophia Roundy, and Samantha Roundy; William Waterman Phelps to Lydia Caroline Brewster; Charles Coulson Rich to Emeline Grover; Thomas Pearson [Parson] to Catherine Spickernagle; Joseph White Pierce to Amanda Mary Heath; William Pitt to Cornelia Melvina Devine; Sanford Porter to Nancy Arrita Warriner; John Reynolds to Phebe Ramsey; James Henry Rollins to Eveline Walker; William Stewart Seely to Elizabeth DeHart; James Smithies to Nancy Ann Knowles; James Chauncey Snow to Eliza Ann Carter; Charles Blancher Thompson to Catherine Ann Hank; Elbridge Tufts to Elmira Pinkin; Theodore Turley to Mary Clift and Eliza Clift; Chauncey Whiting to Editha Ann Morley; William Wesley Willis to Margaret Jane Willis; Lewis Dunbar Wilson to Patsy Minerva Reynolds; and Brigham Young to Amelia Alice Cooper, Mary Ellen de la Montague, Abigail Harback, and Mary Ann Turley.

—Summarized from the Book of Living Sealings.

....

Sealings for the dead performed on this date:

George Pack (John Pack, proxy) to Phylotte Green, Heber C. Kimball officiating; Ann Pixley Johnson (Susan Bryant) to Joel Hills Johnson, Brigham Young officiating; Sophia Meirs and Catherine Forsyth (Elizabeth Fory, proxy) to Peter Joseph Fory, Heber C. Kimball officiating; Elizabeth Jenks (Catherine Ann Thompson, proxy) to Charles B. Thompson, Amasa M. Lyman officiating; Hellen Davis Murray (Mary Spring, proxy) to William E. Murray, Brigham Young officiating; Austin Cravath (William E. Murray, proxy) to Eliza Doty Fairfield, Brigham Young officiating;[66] Caroline Smith (Cornelia M. Devine, proxy) to William Pitt,

66. Eliza Fairfield was also sealed to William Murray for time.

Amasa M. Lyman officiating; William Taylor (James Allred, proxy) to Elizabeth Patrick, Amasa M. Lyman officiating;[67] John M. Bernhisel to Joseph Smith "to become his son" [no proxy given; no officiator given]; Joseph Smith (Heber C. Kimball, proxy) to Nancy Maria Winchester, Brigham Young officiating;[68] Sally Simonds (Prudence Marks, proxy) to Samuel Miles Sr., Brigham Young officiating; Jonathan Hampton (Brigham Young, proxy) to Julia Foster, Amasa M. Lyman officiating;[69] Joseph Smith (Brigham Young, proxy) to Eliza Roxy Snow, Heber C. Kimball officiating;[70] Maria Chase (Clarissa Chase Young, proxy) to Brigham Young, Heber C. Kimball officiating; Joseph Smith (Heber C. Kimball, proxy) to Mary Ann Houston, Amasa M. Lyman officiating;[71] James Mulholland (Heber C. Kimball, proxy) to Sarah (Scott Mulholland) Smith, Amasa M. Lyman officiating;[72] Marietta Carter (Elvira A. Cowles, proxy) to Jonathan H. Holmes, Brigham Young officiating; and Joseph Smith (Jonathan H. Holmes, proxy) to Elvira A. Cowles, Brigham Young officiating.[73]

—Summarized from the Book of Proxy Sealings.

....

Adoptions performed on this date:

To Isaac and Lucy Morley: Isaac Morley Jr., Joseph Steward Allen, Chancey Whiting, Aaron Cox, Philena Morley, Lucy Diantha Morley, Eaitha Ann Morley, [and] Cordelia Celestia Morley, ~~and Theresa Arathusa Morley~~ sealed by Brigham Young: "These were all sealed up unto their parents with the usual ceremony at the alter &c. Cordelia Celestia Morley had been sealed to Pres[ident]. Joseph Smith, Pres[iden]t. B[righam]. Young his proxy, at the alter and Theresa Arathusa Morley had also been sealed to Heber C. Kimball about 35 minutes before the adoption and sealing of their father's family, but they were sealed to their parents and then by them given respectively to Joseph and Heber by mutual consent &c."

—Summarized from "Sealings and Adoptions."

---

67. Elizabeth Patrick was sealed to James Allred for time.
68. Nancy Maria Winchester was also sealed to Heber C. Kimball for time.
69. Julia Foster was also sealed to Brigham Young for time.
70. Eliza Snow was also sealed to Brigham Young for time.
71. Mary Ann Huston was also sealed to Heber C. Kimball for time.
72. Sarah Smith was also sealed to Heber C. Kimball for time.
73. Elvira Cowles was also sealed to Jonathan Holmes for time.

Wednesday, February 4, 1846

I [Brigham Young] continued loading up my wagons, preparatory to starting west.

—"Manuscript History of Brigham Young," in *History of the Church,* 7:580.

....

Second anointings performed on this date:

Helen Mar Kimball to Horace K. Whitney for time and Joseph Smith (deceased) for eternity, anointed by Heber C. Kimball; Mary Ann Huston and Prescindia (Huntington) Buell to Heber C. Kimball for time and Joseph Smith (deceased) for eternity, anointed by Isaac Morley; James Hendricks and Priscilla (Davis) Hendricks, anointed by Charles C. Rich; Flora Ann Woodworth to Joseph Smith (deceased), anointed by [not given]; John Benbow, Jane (Holmes) Benbow, and Agnes (Taylor) Benbow, anointed by John Taylor; Elvira Ann (Cowles) Holmes to Jonathan H. Holmes for time and Joseph Smith (deceased) for eternity, anointed by Isaac Morley; Samuel Whitney and Catherine (Davis) Whitney, anointed by Zebedee Coltrin; and Hezekiah Peck, Martha (Long) Peck, and Mary (Bell) Peck, anointed by Orson Spencer.

—Summarized from "Book of Anointings."

....

Sealings for the living performed on this date:

Jonathan Allen to Charlotte Hatch; Joseph Steward Allen to Lucy Diantha Morley, Nancy Jane Putman, and Mary Lemon; Simon Cooker Dalton to Elnora Lucretia Warner; Lysander Gee to Amanda Melvina Sagers; Daniel S. Jackson to Phebe Lawrence Cowderey; Alva Keller to Roxey Lucina Elliot; Heber Chase Kimball to Mary Ann Shefflin; Joseph Knight Jr. to Betsey Covert; Thomas Moore to Mahala Dorcas E. Higley; Robert Pierce to Hannah Harvey; Stillman Pond to Maria Louisa Davis; Judson Lyman Stoddard to Rhoda Chase; and Lyman Stoddard to Ruth Wright.

—Summarized from The Book of Living Sealings.

....

Sealings for the dead performed on this date:

Joseph Smith (Horace K. Whitney, proxy) to Helen M. Kimball, Brigham Young officiating;[74] Elizabeth Ford Sykes (Helen M. Kimball,

74. Helen Kimball was also sealed to Horace Whitney for time.

proxy) to Horace K. Whitney, Brigham Young officiating; James Bell (Hezekiah Peck, proxy) to Mary Lemon, Brigham Young officiating;[75] Elizabeth Bell (Mary Bell, proxy) to Hezekiah Peck, Brigham Young officiating; Joseph Smith (Heber C. Kimball, proxy) to Presendia L. Huntington, Amasa M. Lyman officiating;[76] Almira Whittemore (Maria Louisa Davis, proxy) to Stillman Pond, Amasa M. Lyman officiating; and Sarah Kenworthy (Hannah Foxhall Lee, proxy) to Richard Woolsey, Amasa M. Lyman officiating.

—Summarized from the Book of Proxy Sealings.

....

Adoptions performed on this date:

To John and Leonora Taylor: Richard Ballantyne, Jane Benbow, John Benbow, Agnes Benbow, Joseph Horne, Mary Isabella Horne, Stephen Hales, Charles Lambert, Mary Alice Cannon, William Symmonds, Helenora Symmonds, William Rowbey, Mary Ann Rowbey, Thomas Danville, Mary Peters, Thomas Hall, Ann Hughs, Samuel Bringhurst, Eleanor Beitler Breisler, Ariah Coats Brower, Margaret Eliza Brower, William Blackhurst, Mary Blackhurst, Samuel Langdon Payne, Mary Belknap, and George Cannon: "These were all Sealed and adopted to Bro[ther] and Sister Taylor, at the Alter with the usual ordinance and ceremony ... The adoption of Mary Isabella Horne to Elder John Taylor was cancelled 21 Sept[ember]. 1893, she having been sealed to her parents in the Logan Temple. George Reynolds, Recorder. ... The foregoing adoptions to President John Taylor of Mary Alice Cannon and George Q. Cannon were, by request of the latter, cancelled by Pres[iden]t. Woodruff, 14 Oct[ober]. 1893[?]; and Mary Alice and George Q. Cannon were the next day sealed to their parents in the Logan Temple. Geo[rge]. Reynolds, Recorder."

—Summarized from "Sealings and Adoptions."

Thursday, February 5, 1846

Now Amasia Lyman being autherised to adopt & Sea[l,] So on the 5th day of Febr[uar]y, 1846, I [George Laub] & My Wife with many others ware adopted to J[ohn]. D. Lee family. This adoption is to Link the chain of the priesthood in Such a way that can not be broken only by

75. Mary Lemon was also sealed to James Bell for time.

76. Presendia Huntington was also sealed to Heber C. Kimball for time.

braking Covanants, for they are made before God, Angels and the present Witness. We covanent together for him to be a father unto those who are Seald to him, to do unto them as he would to his own Children, & to counsil them in rituousness & to teach them all the principles of Salvation & to share unto them of all the blessings to comfert. These & all that are calculated to make them happy both in time & Eternity. This was done at the alt[a]r according to the pattern of the ordinance.

Sealing of Mar[r]iag[e]. Now on the Same date, on the 5th of Februry, 1846, My wife Mary Jane was Sealed to me a wife for time & Eternity, to be my companion & comfert & to fill up the measure of our creation, & we was sealed up unto Eternal Lives, to come fourth in the Morning of the first Resurection & nothing to prevent, only the Sin against the Holy Ghost, which is Sheading Inocent blood or the concerting there unto. Now when we was sealed in this order, J[ohn]. D. Lee Embraced us in his arms & blessed us in the name of the Lord that we Should become mighty upon the Earth & our names to be honerable in all generations.

—George Laub, Diary, in "George Laub's Nauvoo Journal," edited by Eugene England, *Brigham Young University Studies* 18 (Winter 1978): 165-66.

....

Law of Adaption [sic?] tended on the 5th of February 1846[,] I [George Laub] and my wife Mary Jane with many others was Adopted into John D Lee's family. th[u]s I took upon myself the Name of Lee in this manner[:] George Laub Lee & my wifes Name Mary Jane Laub Lee[.] this order of Adaption will [be] like the chain of the Prieshood in such a way that it cannot be seperated[. It is done] by covenanting before god Angels and the Present witnesses[, whereby] we covenant together for him to be as father unto those who are sealed to him to doo unto them as he would unto his own children and to councell them in rituousness and to teach them all the Principles of Salvation and to share unto them of all the Blessings[,] to comfort these and all [other things] that are calculated to make them happy both in time and in Eternity. Now we also did covenant on our side to do all the good for his upbuilding and happyness Both in time & Eternity[.] this was done in the hous of the Lord across the alt[a]r as was Prepared for this Purpos of ordinances [having to do with the] Sealing of Marriages.

Now on the same date on the 5th of February 1846 My Wife Marry

Jane was sealed to me as wife for time and Eternity to be my companion and comforter and to fill up the measure of our creation. and we was sealed up unto Eternal Life. to come fourth in the morning of the first resurection. only the sining aganst the holy Ghost which is the sheding of inocent blood or consenting to the same. Now when we was sealed to this order together with the promises given unto us by the Power and spirit of the Lord[,] Father Lee[,] being filed with the spirit[,] Embraced us in his arms and bless[ed] us in the name of the Lord, that we should become mighty upon the Earth &c our names to be honerable in all generations.

—George Laub, Diary (expanded version), LDS Archives.

....

J[ohn]. D. Lee's family Adoption. Feb[ruary] 5, [18]46[,] ½ past 8 [in the] eve[ning]. John D Lee Young was born Sept[ember] the 6 1812 — Town of Kas Kas Kis [Kaskaskia] Randolph County Ill[inoi]s. Aggatha Ann Lee Young was born Jan[uary] 18 1814 [in] Lincoln K[entuck]y.—

1 Georg Laub was born Oct[ober] 5-1819 [in] Lancaster Co[unty]. State [of] Penn[sylvania].— &c adopted

2 Mary Jan Maginess [wife of George Laub] was born Jan[uary] 11. 1830 [in] Lancaster Co[unty]. Penn[sylvania].— adopted

3 Horace Burr Owens — born June 23-1819— [in] Me[r]c[e]r—& Mercer Co[unty]. — Penn[sylvania]. Adopted

4 Sally Ann Lane [wife of Horace Owens] — born Feb[ruary] 21-1829— [in] Barren Co[unty]. K[entuck]y — adopted—

5 James Pace [born] Jan[uary] 15th 1811 [in Mu]rfreesboro Rutherford Co[unty]. — Tenn[essee]. — adopted—

6 Luncinda Gibson ^Pace^ Strickland [wife of James Pace] born Jan[uary] 16 1805 [in] Aberville Destrich South Carolina — adopted

7 W[illia]m Pace [born] July 3d 1806 [in] Clark Co[unty] Georg[ia] — adop[t]ed —

8 Margaret ^Pace^ Nichols [wife of William Pace] — [born] May 30 1808 [in] Logan Co[unty]— K[entuck]y — adopted —

9 Levi North — [born] July 17-1817 — [in] White co[unty]. State of Ill[inoi]s — adopted —

10 Arminta [Howard] North [wife of Levi North] — [born] Feb[ruary] 15 1819 — Madison co[unty] Tory — Ill[inoi]s — adopted —

11 Benjamin Meginnis [McGinniss] — [born] May 3-1803 [in]

Lancaster co[unty]. — Penn[sylvania]. Adopted

12 Sarah ^Maginnes^ Johnson [wife of Benjamin McGinniss] — [born] Sept[ember]. 4 1802 [in] Chester Co[unty]. Penn[sylvania]. — adopted —

13 Levi Loveland [born] Feb[ruary] 20 1816 [in] Madison Geauga Co[unty]. Ohio — adopted

14 Hanna [Pease] Loveland [wife of Levi Loveland] — [born] Mar[ch] 23 1814 in Handen Geauga co[unty]. Ohio — adopted

15 Chester Loveland — [born] Dec[ember] 30 1912 [in] Madison Geauga co[unty]. Ohio — adopted

16 Fanny Loveland [wife of Chester Loveland] — [born] May 11 1815 [in] Fairfax — Franklin N[ew]. Y[ork]. — adopted

17 Richard Woosley [Woolsey] — born Aug[ust] 28 1808 [in] Jes[sa]m[i]n[e] co[unty]. K[entuck]y — adopted —

18 Hannah Foxall [wife of Richard Woolsey] — [born] Jan[uary] 7 1824 — [in] Herriford shire En[glan]d — adopted —

19 James Woosley [Woolsey] born Marc[h] 2d 1822 — [in] K[entuck]y —

20 Lovina Patterson [born] Jan[uary] 9, 1824 [in] N[ew]. Y[ork]. [wife of James Woolsey]

21 Jos[eph]. Hiram Woosley [Woolsey] [born] Jan[uary] 10-1828 — [in] Jackson c[ounty]. Indiana adopted

22 Oliver Gaulter Workman — [born] Jan[uary] 7-1828 [in] Levingston — Monro[e] co[unty]. — Tenn[essee]. — adopted —

[All] were sealed & adopted to the above br[other] & sis[ter] [John D.] Lee ^Young^ by the usual ordinance at the Altar by Amasa Lyman in the presence of William Felshaw & Elijah Fordham at [blank][77] ...

—"John D. Lee's Family—Adoption," LDS Archives.

....

Second anointings performed on this date:

Miles Romney and Elizabeth (Gaskell) Romney, anointed by William W. Phelps.

—Summarized from "Book of Anointings."

---

77. Joseph F. Smith, in "Sealings and Adoptions," 803, noted: "Divorces: John Doyle Lee and Nancy Bean, his wife, desolved Matrimony, Feb[ruary] 25, 1848[;] John Doyle Lee and Allen Weeks + 3 wives desolved Covenants Apr[il]. 19 1848[;] John Doyle Lee and Levi North + wife desolved Covenants Apr[il]. 19 1848." Weeks's adoption apparently occurred on another date. Lee married his first plural wife, Nancy Bean, on February 5, 1845 (see Juanita Brooks, *John Doyle Lee: Zealot, Pioneer Builder, Scapegoat* [1961; Salt Lake City: Howe Brothers, 1984], 65-66, 379-81).

Sealings for the living performed on this date:

Able Lamb to Mary Maria Sanberg Peterson; George Laub to Mary Jane Maginness; Chester Loveland to Rose Ann Winter; Richard Woolsey to Hannah Foxhall; Benjamin Meginness to Sarah Johnston and Mary [Mercy] Ann Brooks; James Hopkins Woolsey to Lovina Patterson; and Richard Woolsey to Sarah Kenworthy.

—Summarized from the Book of Living Sealings.

....

Sealing for the dead performed on this date:

Sarah Kenworthy (Hannah Foxhall Lee, proxy) to Richard Woolsey, Amasa M. Lyman officiating.

—Summarized from the Book of Proxy Sealings.

Friday, February 6, 1846

The [news] having arrived that the Twelve [apostles] and a large company with them are about starting for the West, such is the hurry and hustle of getting away, that for the last ~~s~~ two days no Endowments have been [done?]; But this morning the doors are opened again for this purpose, and the crowd is greater than ever, such is the anxiety of the people to get their blessings in this house.

[See pages 588-602 for excerpted portion.]

—Seventies Record, Book B.

....

I went in the temple at Nauvoo and received my washings and anointings, it being at the closing of giving endowments. There was a great crowd—near five hundred passed through their ordinances in the last twenty-four hours—but I felt greatly blessed for the opportunity of receiving the little I did, for it gave me keys of knowledge for me to improve upon until I could get more.

—"The Life of Joseph Holbrook, Written by His Own Hand," LDS Archives.

....

[An adoption ceremony was held involving the following:]

Willard Richards [born] June 24. 1804 [in] Hopkinton Middlesex Co[unty]. Mass[achusetts]:

[Washings and anointings for Friday, February 6, 1846]

List 1 In the Male Department commencing at 5 ½ A.M.

Seventies		Sev	
	1 Zachariah Martin born Sep. 29, 1822		15 Lorenzo Pettit born July 26, 1825
"	2 Frances T. Whitney " Mar. 24, 1805	"	16 Samuel White " Apl. 8, 1822
"	3 Francis Boggs " May 17, 1807	"	17 Lorenzo D. Driggs " Mar 14, 1722
"	4 Alpheus C. Ellsworth " Apl. 15, 1812	"	18 William H. Barger " Jan. 3, 1812
"	5 Stephen P. Meechum " Mar. 12, 1797	"	19 Charles Haslem " Apl. 15, 1821
"	6 Samuel Barnes " ~~May 2~~ ^Apl 27^, 1806	"	20 Lewis Dalrymple " Oct. 8, 1809
"	7 Lewis Hardy " Oct. 17, 1803	"	21 George Allen " May 23, 1810
"	8 Lewis Barney " Sep 8, 1808	H. Priests	1 Isaac Cooper " Feb. 9, 1807
"	9 Asa C. Earl " May 2, 1810	"	2 John ~~Williams~~ Reed " Oct. 12, 1793
"	10 Robert Harris " Dec. 16, 1808	"	3 Ezra Strong " July 18, 1826
"	11 Oley Hagar " June 1, 1813	Elders	1 John B. Williams " June 13, 1826
"	12 Christian Hager " July 8, 1823		2 Fletcher Strong " July 18, 1826
"	13 Hans Hager " July 8, 1823		3 Sterling Driggs " Feb. 12, 1817
"	14 Richards Pettit " Aug 8, 1822		

were washed ~~and an~~ by Leslie L. Young and Lorenzo Clark. Anointed by Jesse P. Harmon and Moses M. Sanders and Levi W. Hancock. ~~to 20 p. 7~~ ^20 p. 7^ A.M.

List 1 In the Female Department commencing at ½ p. 5.

Harriet Eliza Ellsworth Oct. 1, 1814	Elvina Boggs born Mar. 3, 1816
Nancy Catherine Martin born May 14, 1827	Hannah Pack " Nov. 5, 1816
Lodemia Barnet " Apl. 21, 1810	Phebe Hardy " June 2, 1810

Elizabeth Barney " July 30, 1808	Nancy Earl " Nov. 4, 1815
Margaret Hayer " Oct. 1, 1812	Hannah Mariah Herris " June 10, 1817
Ferreby Barger " Sep 17, 1818	Catherine Pettit " Oct. 16, 1822
Jerusha Dalrymple " June 28, 1800	Susanna Pettit " July 25, 1828
Clarissa Williams " Sep. 26, 1820	Mary Cooper " Feb. 16, 1814
Rebecca White " May 30, 1818	Malinda Driggs " Sep. 20, 1825
Mary Carpenter " Dec. 26, 1819	Caroline Webb " Aug. 15, 1821
Nancy Allen " July 19, 1811	

were washed and anointed by Mary D Grant, Hannah Repshor, Louisa Clark, Roxanna Kepher, Lydia Granger, Abigail Abbot and Clarissa Hancock. 20 p. 7.

Friday February 6, 1846

List 2 In the Male department commencing at 9 A.M.

Sev		Seventies	
	22 Edward Corless born Mar. 14, 1804		34 John Congers born Apl. 25, 1814
Elder	4 Garrett Groesbeck " Feb. 1, 1795	"	35 Francis W. Pomery " Feb. 22, 1822
Sev	23 Columbus Bindick " Aug. 22, 1826	"	36 Hiram B. Clawson " Nov. 7, 1826
"	24 William S. Bachelor " age unknown	"	37 John R. Clawson " Dec. 23, 1829
"	25 Robert Callins " Dec. 2, 1822	"	38 Robert Burton " Apl. 29, 1826
"	26 John Huntington " Oct. 17, 1824	"	39 William Cook " Apl. 17, 1814
"	27 James ~~Mc~~ ^W.^ Hill " Jan 19, 1809	"	40 Oliver Higgins " Aug. 17, 1819
"	28 Henry Manhard " Nov. 12, 1824	Elder	5 Benjamin Gardner " Aug. 9, 1800
"	29 Samuel Worthen " Dec. 21, 1825	"	6 Joseph Dudley " July 8, 1825
"	30 James R. Allred " Jan. 28, 1827	"	7 Thomas Tidwell " July 8, 1825

[Seventies]	31 Thomas R. Burns [born] Aug. 18, 1824	[Elders]	8 William Head [born] June 29, 1824
"	32 David Rogers " May 27, 1823	"	9 Samuel R. Aiken " Jan. 7, 1827
"	33 Mark Rogers " Feb. 21, 1830		

were washed ~~and~~ anointed by Lorenzo Clark, and Edward M. Webb. Anointed by Leslie Lyme Young and Moses M. Sanders.

Ordinations

Wiliam L. Bachelor and Oliver Higgins were ordained Seventies by L. W. Hancock and Rufus Beach. Thomas Tidwell and William Head were ordained Elders by Zebedee Coltrin and Noah Rogers.

List 2 In the Female department commencing at 18 to 9

Mary Mosely born Sep 6, 1812	Catherine Corless born Dec. 12, 1816
Huldah Bachelor " June 24, 1823	Elizabeth Burton " Sep. 17, 1822
^Fanny^ Manhard " Mar. 11, 1823	Phebe Hancock " June 7, 1810
Esther Halam " Feb. 9, 1783	Elizabeth Atchison " 1830
Sarah Worthing " Sep. 14, 1823	Mary Huntington " May 4, 1817
Elizabeth Cook " Dec. 3, 1814	Mercy Groesbeck " Mar. 13, 1820
Priscilla Congers " Dec. 11, 1825	Mary Collins " Nov. 7, 1819
Sarah Dudley " Mar. 14, 1816	Electa Gardner " Mar 5, 1811
Mary Jackson " Jan 23, 1777	Susanna Myres " Sep 22, 1810
Mary Ann Tuttle " June 5, 1830	Julia Ann Hickenlooper Nov. 6, 1811
Martha Ann Tuttle " June 8, 1830	Allmantha Goddard " May 31, 1830
Irene N. H. Pomeroy " Nov. 1, 1825	Sarah L. Harmon " May 17, 1830
Harriet M. Simpson " Jan. 26, 1824	Sarah Johnson " 1870
Sylena Higgins " Apl. 25, 1826	Lucy Burdick " May 10, 1827

were washed and anointed by Clarissa Hancock, Hannah Repsher, Zeruah Goddard, Roxanna Repsher, Sally Ann King, Bulah Ann Clark, Demistia Walker, Lydia Granger and Mariah Bond.

Friday February 6, 1846.

List 3 In the Male Department commencing at

Sev.		Sev.	
	41 Lorenzo Booth born Oct. 13, 1808		54 Harley Mowry born Aug 9, 1822
"	42 John W. Bailey " Apl. 18, 1816		55 Homer Duncan " Dec. 7, 1815
"	43 Alonzo F. King " Aug 26, 1819	"	56 William K. Pieshall " Aug. 25, 1802
"	44 Cyrus Eddy " June 18, 1804	"	57 William Evans " Mar. 11, 1818
"	45 Furman Mulford " July 21, 1812	"	58 James Sewell " 1807
"	46 Elijah Clifford " age not known	"	59 Thomas Maybern " June 7, 1824
"	47 Joseph Hardy " Apl. 27, 1808	H. Priests	4 Nathan Stoker " Nov. 28, 1805
"	48 Robert M. King " June 11, 1829	"	5 Lincoln Thayre " Oct. 13, 1777
"	49 William Farrar " Jan. 26, 1821	"	6 Hirum Winder " Apl. 5, 1805
"	50 Lucius Richards [?] " Feb. 24, 1817	Elders	10 Henry Jennings " Aug 6, 1812
"	51 Mahlon [?] Johnson " Aug. 2, 1803	"	11 Joseph Fisher " Nov. 25, 1801
"	52 James Dunn " June 6, 1810	"	12 Leonard Shushler " Dec. 7, 1797
"	53 Samuel Driggs " Feb. 15, 1820	"	13 Nathaniel Winship " July 9, 1822

were washed by Lorenzo Clark and Edward W. Webb. Anointed by Leslie Lyme Young and Moses M. Sanders.

List 3 In the Female Department commencing at 30 p. 10

Lois Stevens born Mar. 10, 1811	Catherine Mehring born Nov. 19, 1824
Elizabeth McElroy " Jan. 25, 1819	Amanda Jennings " Mar. 20, 1816
Lucy Thorndyke Hardy " Feb. 9, 1812	Chloe Thayer " Oct. 19, 1771

Celinda Vankosen [born] May 16, 1811
Margaret Shussler " Mar. 8, 1807
Parthema Booth " June 23, 1811
Sarah Dunn " Oct. 23, 1819
Jane Staker " July 23, 1810
Evaline Fisher " Dec. 25, 1805
Elizabeth Matilda Fring " Mar. 11, 1811
Mary Ann Johnson " Dec. 15, 1808
Mary Mumfred " May 22, 1816
Lucy Matilda Johnson " Dec. 15, 1808
Aseneth Robinson " Nov. 14, 1827
Hortensia Merchant [born] Mar. 30, 1824
Fanny Jane House " Aug. 13, 1826
Mehitable Duty " Sep. 5, 1796
Martha Binley " Dec. 14, 1814
Lydia Burgess " Mar. 15, 1822
Elizabeth Ann Diggs " Nov. 30, 1822
Cynthia Hampshire " Mar 16, 1831
Jane Evans " Dec. 17, 1817
Mary Lameraux " Jan 29, 1829
Margetta Stowe " Oct. 3, 1831
Rebecca Winter " Dec. 16, 1801

were washed and anointed by Clarissa Hancock, Mary Ann Bird, Roxena Repsher, Zeruah Goddard, Mary Ann Nickerson, Margaret Dana, Lydia Granger, and Buleah Clark. 10 ½ A.M.

List 4 In the Male department commencing at 45 p 12

Sev	
	60 Franklin R. Tower born July 26, 1815
"	61 Pardon Webb " Dec. 26, 1818
"	62 James Robinson " Aug. 27, 1826
"	63 James Hawkins " Mar. 17, 1818
"	64 Abraham Coon " Apl. 2, 1810
"	65 Thomas C. D. Hamell " Feb. 22, 1814
"	66 Edward Hunter Jr. " Mar. 5, 1826

Sev	
	67 Horace Evans born Sep 5, 1810
"	68 George Foster " Feb. 8, 1807
"	69 Philander J. Perry " Sep. 29, 1821
"	70 George Whitaker " Mar. 18, 1820
"	71 Wm S. Chomplin " Apl. 16, 1794
"	72 Wm C. Andrews " Feb. 23, 1820
"	73 John R. Frink " Aug 8, 1829

Friday February 6, 1846

Sev		Sev
74 John R. Frink born Aug. 8, 1829		84 John Snalham born Nov. 15, 1813
75 David P. Barnes " Jan. 15, 1809		85 Richard Ralphs " 1813
76 Thomas W. Smith " Dec 23, 1815		86 James Bird " Dec. 22, 1823
77 John Moward " Oct. 11, 1826	H. Priests	7 David M. Hard " Oct. 22, 1823
78 Peter McFarlane " May 1, 1810	"	8 Elam Mecham Jr. " Oct 9, 1799
79 Alphonzo E. Miles " Apl. 5, 1813	"	9 William Milam " Mar 18, 1799
80 John D. Murdock " July 28, 1825	"	10 William M. Parker " Apl. 28, 1793
81 Richard Brazier " Dec. 6, 1793	Elders	14 Jacob Bigler " June 9, 1793
82 Norman B. Shearer " Apl. 10, 1821	"	15 Isaac A. Bogue " Dec. 14, 1822
83 Joseph Outhouse " Mar. 20, 1820	"	16 David C. Roundy " Jan. 5, 1827
		17 John Gribble " Aug. 10, 1788

were washed ~~by~~ by Lorenzo Clark & Edward M. ~~Wooley~~ Webb. Anointed by L. L. Young and Moses M. Sanders.

Ordinations

William C. Andrews, John R. Frink, John Moward were ordained Seventies by Rufus Beach. — Jacob Bigler was ordained ~~by~~ Elder by Charles Bird.

List 4 In the Female Department commencing at 20 to 1

Sally Barnes born Mar. 7, 1812	Mary Ann Hunter born Dec. 15, 1825
Mary Jane Gee " Apl. 29, 1812	Mary Champlin " Jan 27, 1794
Candace Evans " Jan 13, 1820	Almira Mecham " Aug ~~17~~ ^21^ 1796
Jane Bird " Dec. 25, 1808	Mary Jane Murdock " Aug 3, 1832
Ruth Jane Giles " June 2, 1812	Margaret McDougal " Dec. 2, 1781

Sarah Howell [born] Jan. 15, 1815	Fanny Mirick [born] Aug. 11, 1831
Julia Ann Razey " Nov. 20, 1823	Sarah Hawkins " Apl. 4, 1818
Clarissa Jane Webb " Aug. 19, 1825	Sarah Peacock " Mar. 16, 1828
Eveline P. Robinson " Dec. 19, 1827	Francis Snalam " Sep. 11, 1805
Tireshe Cregen " Apl. 28, 1825	Mary Ralphs " Jan 8, 1820
Delliah Andrews " May 30, 1820	Elizabeth Milam " Feb 20, 1815
Sarah Brazier " Feb 24, 1783	Sarah Ann Smith " Oct. 28, 1825
Hannah P. Palmer " Nov. 30, 1780	Sarah Ann Perry " May 28, 1822
Elizabeth Yarbrough " Dec. 23, 1808	Mary Waterman " Mar 3, 1825
Christina Shearer " May 21, 1815	Francis Yarborough " March 1825
Lucina A. Woolsey " Jan. 1, 1832	Louisa Miles " Mar 19, 1826
Hannah Parker " Aug. 11, 1785	

were washed and anointed by Mary Ann Nickerson, Jemima C. Mead, Sally Ann King, Margaret Dana, Mary Ann Bird, Mary K. Felshaw, Abigail Abbot, and Bulah Ann Clark.

Friday February 6, 1846

List 5 In the Male department commencing at 3 Oclock

Sev		Sev	
	87 John F. Renault born Jun 8, 1812		108 Thos. M Taggart born — 1808
"	88 Oliver Hayer " Mar. 2, 1802	"	109 Absolam Pennington " Mar. 12, 1798
"	89 James Dean Miller " Aug. 25, 1806	"	110 Robert Pixton " Feb 27 1819
"	90 Andrew Hayer " June 17 1826	"	111 Edwin Cadwell " July 7 1810
"	91 Orson Hayer " June 17 1826	"	112 George Simon Dalton " Sept. 7 1828
"	92 Christian Lurant " [illegible] 1830	H. Priests	Lance Hayer " Oct. 1, 1784

"	93 Tharson Simpson " Dec. 11, 1808	"	Oley Luraas " Dec 26 1803
"	94 James Dacke " Mar. 16, 1806	"	Wm Woodland " Nov 26 1889
"	95 John Miller " Feb. 19, 1820	"	Benj. Andrews " Oct. 6 1792
"	96 Robert Wells " Sept. 24, 1815	Elders	18 Wm H Edwards " June 13 1821
"	97 Thos. McCann " May 1, 1816	"	19 Frederick Connington " July 1 1821
"	98 Joseph Bostock " Nov. 21, 1820	"	20 Aroet L. Hale " May 18 1828
"	99 Hubert Hill Foster " Jan 24 1827	"	21 Edwin Peck " July 24 1828
"	100 Moses A. Jones " Mar 18 1825	"	22 Thos. Foster " July 22 1790
"	101 Josiah Lobdel Deforest " Aug 9, 1820	"	23 Asa Barton " Dec 3 1802
"	102 Joel Edmonds " Apr. 14 1799	"	24 John Hammond " July 22 1795
"	103 Peter Spur " Feb. 25 1823	"	25 Henry Malvin Potter " Feb 18 1817
"	104 Peter Ofton " Dec. 18, 1821	"	26 Joseph Shelly " Sept 8 1802
"	105 Henry Boley " Apr. 14 1795	"	27 Horace Burdick " Nov 7 1831
"	106 John W. Lesley " Feb 1 1812	"	28 Abraham Bond " Apr 4 1789
"	107 John R. Walker " May 12 1804		

were washed by Cyrus A. Allred and E M Webb. Anointed by Leslie Lyme Young and Moses M. Sanders Young ½ p. 4

Ordinations

Frederick Connington was ordained an Elder by Horace Owens. Henry Malvin Potter and Horace Burdick were ordained Elders by J. M King

List 5 In the ~~M~~ Female Department commencing at 10 p. 3

Polly Bond born Apl. 19, 1788	Mary Bennett born Dec. 9, 1786
Lo^u^isa Hammond " Oct. 5, 1790	Elizabeth Reeves " Dec. 6, 1790

Elizabeth Edwards [born] Aug 30, 1790
Melissa Bennett " Dec. 27, 1829
Rebecca Cunningham " May 8, 1820
Betsey Free " Jan. 30,
Hannah Carilla Free " June 9, 1829
Sarah McCain " Mar. 26, 1818
Elizabeth W. Madison " Dec. 22, 1799
Jane Miller " Oct. 8, 1821
Polly Colson Shelby born Aug. 19, 1814
Eliza Spurr " Jan. 1, 1823
Mary Deforest " July 16, 1816
Phillis M. Taggart " Aug 29, 1810
Lucretia Burdick " Mar. 1829
Rhoda Andrews " Sep 9, 1810
Barbara Jolee " Oct. 10, 1792
Nancy Walker " Oct. 7, 1815
Catherine Woodland " June 7, 1788
Mary Barton " Mar. 16, 1823
Ann Luras " July 1823
Betsey Patten " Sep. 29, 1813

Elizabeth Ann Frazier [born] Jan 22, 1825
Elizabeth Pixton " Feb 8, 1820
Elizabeth Lesley " Nov. 5, 1813
Polly Foster Dec 11, 1791
Eliza Edwards " Aug 31, 1826
Olive Wells " July 4, 1830
Jane Dock " Mar 15, 1808
Lydia Rafferty " Aug 22, 1795
Sarah Often born July 27, 1822
Isabella Miller " July 26, 1811
Elizabeth Hager " Oct 25, 1829
Olena Heyer " Sep. 16, 1820
Statira Beach " Aug 17, 1821
Mariah Jeffries " Nov. 16, 1807
Agness Thompson " Mar 14, 1820
Martha Renault " Dec. 29, 1807
Eliza Edmunds " Nov. 18, 1802
Julia Heyer " Apl. 1, 1820
Mary Simpson " May 13, 1818
Lucretia Burdick " Apl. 4, 1829

were washed and anointed by Clarissa Hancock, Zeruah Goddard, Mary Carpenter, Loisa Clark, Lucy Hatfield, Mary Colrin, Sarah B. Barney, Margaret M. Raney, Mary H Felshaw, Mary Ann Bird, Pamelia M. Robinson, and Elizabeth Caroline Hutchinson.

List 6 In the Male Department commencing at 6 oclock P.M.

Sev		Sev	
	113 Anthony Stratton born Jan 11 1824		127 George Patrick born Sept. 17 1826
"	114 C. S. Dalton " Apr. 3 1824	"	128 Hugh Patrick " Feb. 28 1822
"	115 Israel Herriman " June 13 1813	"	129 John Patrick " July 17 1802
"	116 Conrad Stealy " Jan 1 1812	Elders	29 James McDaniel " July 17 1802
"	117 Ransom R Potter " Mar 4 1807	"	30 Abraham Nelson " June 15 1783
"	118 Thos. Morris " Oct 15 1799	"	32 James C. Nelson " June 15 1793
"	119 Abraham Losee " Sept 6 1814	"	33 Wm Jennings " June 16 1814
"	120 Ephraim Cheney " May 1 1796	"	34 Wm Ainscaugh " Mar 18 1818
"	121 David Burrows " 1802	"	35 Ransom Tidwell " Dec 22 1825
"	122 Moses Dayton " Feb. 12 1832	"	36 Richard Brazier " Nov 12, 1822
"	123 Ansora Shumway " June 30 1823	"	37 Anson B Shumway " Aug 8 1821
"	124 Wm Williams " Feb 5 1819	"	38 John McMurray " Mar 9 1788
"	125 Isaac M Steward " Feb 23 1816	"	39 Wm Ralphs " May 16 1816
"	126 James Kippen " Feb 19 1819	"	40 Philip Packard " Mar 7 1776
		"	41 John Killpatrick " Sep 27 1783

were washed by Horace Owens and Lorenzo Clark Anointed by Hiram Dayton and Leslie Lyme Young.

Ordinations

Abraham Nelson was ordained an Elder by Darwin Chase.

Friday February 6 1846

List 6 Female Department commencing at 6 oclock

Mary Cole born Aug [illegible] Deborah Jennings born Jan 11, 1817

Sophronia Drake [born] Nov 20 [illegible]
Rebecca [illegible] " [illegible]
Mary [illegible] " July 17 1797
Lovina [illegible] " [illegible]
[illegible] " Aug 17 1810
[illegible] " Dec 3 1821
Elizabeth Frazier " Oct 29 1827
Sarah [illegible] " July 3 1800
Matilda E. [illegible] " Dec. 4, 1823
Sarah [illegible] " Sept 13 1804
Sarah McDaniel " Nov 13 1800
Sarah Plum " May 30 1830
Elenor Packard " May 3 1782
Lydia Losee " June 6 1798
Amanda B Colborn " Dec 29 1826
Eleanor Kingsley " July 8 1820

Mary Stowell [born] Sept 15 1798
Flora Kingsley " May 27 1827
Isabella Kippen " 1818
Harriet Phelps " April 7 1832
[illegible] Murray " May 6 1801
Elizabeth Ralphs " Mar 3 1818
Sabra Herriman " Mar 2 1827
Matilda J. Steward " Oct 19 1820
Emiline Potter " May 18 1823
Sarah Husbands " June 28 1826
Flora Drake " July 11 1817
Elizabeth Shumway " Aug 12 1827
Leanda E. Shumway " Aug 25 1827
Catharine Hendricks " Aug 2 1838
Hannah Stealy " July 31, 1806

were washed and annointed by Abagail Abbott, Susan Ann King, Mary Ann Nickerson, Maria Fosdick Chelmicia Hamilton Mary Coltrin Almira Dailey Sarah B. Barney Zeruah Godard.

List 7 In the Male department commencing at ~~p~~ past ^½ past 8^ PM

Seventies		Sev	
	130 Henry Call born Sep 10 1808		147 John Howard born Apr 7 1803
"	131 Carter Graham " July 8 [illegible]	"	148 Hiram Blackmore " June 15 1804
"	132 Benj. Ashby " Dec 19 1828	"	149 Geo. Hickenlooper " Aug 8 1826

"	133 Robt. B Stewart " Aug 1 1817	"	150 Milcher Oyaler " Jan 14 1814
"	134 Nathaniel S. Harris " Mar. 9 1829	"	151 Andrew Hawkes " Sept 26 1827
"	135 John C. Smith " Sep 18 1821	"	152 John O. Angus " Nov 17 1822
"	136 John W Thorp " Mar. 14 1819	"	153 Wiley H. Holden " June 22 1820
"	137 John Pyper " June 17 1820	"	154 Seth Dodge " Apr 22 1821
"	138 Alexander [illegible] Oct 1 1823	"	155 Thos. Rogers " July 5 1826
"	139 John Edmunton " July 23 1821	"	156 Robt. Hill Jr. " Oct 12 1816
"	140 Charles Kenedy " July 1 1807	"	157 Wm H. Bishop " Sep 11 1821
"	141 Robert Kelly " Dec 25 1825	"	158 Wm R R Stowell " Sep 22 1822
"	142 John Johnson " Dec 1826	"	159 James Holmes " Dec 25 1827
"	143 John Proctor " Mar 5 1819	"	160 John S Wait " Aug 29 1806
"	144 George Snow " Sept 7 1821	"	161 Abner Chase " May 18 1813
"	145 Franklin Beach " July 26, 1819	"	162 Amos S. Chase " Dec. 18 1820
"	146 Wm Burrows " Nov 6 1828	H. P.	15 Joseph Holbrook " Jan 15 1816

Friday February 6, 1846

Elder		H. P.	
	42 John Rowley born Oct 15 1799		16 Philip Garner born Oct 12 1808
"	43 John Westfall " Sept 26 1818	"	17 Wm Crutchlew " July 8 1809
"	44 Udney H. Jacob " Apr 24, 1781	"	18 Robt. Hill Sen " Apr 17 1788

were annointed by Leslie Lyme Young & M. M. Sanders Young & were washed by Lorenzo Clark & Edward M. Webb. 10 oclock PM

Feb 6, Female Department commenced ½ p. 11 PM
List 7

Nancy M Smith born
Madalene Gardner " Oct 12 1830
Sophia Crooks " Oct 6 1828
Eliza Kelly " Aug 4 1830
Jane Rogers " Mar 5 1829
Elizabeth Oyaler " Sept 12 1813
Ann Proctor " Apr 8, 1813
Mary McLain " July 17 1792
Lydia M. Rolph " Dec 26 1822
Agigail Holden " Feb 25 1818
Hannah Stoell " May 10, 1830
Amanda Wilson " Sept 17 1828
Eliza Bishop " Feb 8 1819
Elizabeth Ashby " May 17 1832
Lovina Dodge " Apr. 11 1822
Elsie P. Jacob " May 13, 1831
Sarah Smith " Oct 24 1828
Clarissa Blackman " Sep. 3, 1804

Nancy Ann Mackley born Sept 13 1828
Margaret Stewart " Oct 30 18
Martha Orson " Mar 12 1803
Matilda Stowell " Sept 24, 1827
Abigail Chase " June 22, 1822
Eliza Graham " Mar 4, 1812
Elizabeth Mackley " Aug 16, 1825
Mary Ann Call " Oct. 18. 1816
Melana Pulsipher " Jan 9, 1828
Martha Shoop " Nov. 20, 1825
Huldah E. Kenedy " Apl. 4, 1817
Margaret G. Clark " Aug 4, 1812
Martha Jane Edmuston " Sep. 1828
Mary Snow " Aug 18, 1828
Elizabeth Heward " Nov. 17, 1814
Agness Richards " June 6, 1808
Mary Garner " 1813
Melinda Westfall " 1829

were washed and anointed by Mary Ann Nickerson, Chelmicia Hamilton, Maria Fosdick, Philinda C. Keeler, Louisa Clark, and Peggy Patten.

List 8 In the Male Department commencing at ½ past 11 P.M

The following named persons were washed and anointed, but on account of the carelessness of L. Gee the clerk in the reception room, it is impossible to state what authority or priesthood they held except in a few instances, and that from memory. C. W. Wandle Smith, clerk.

	Warren Foot born Sep. 22, 1811		Thomas Boardman " Oct. 15, 1811
Sev.	Henry W. Brizzier " May 1, 1826	Sev	William Neely " Aug. 29, 1830
	William Gibbs " Jan. 11, 1821	"	Levi N. Hendall " Apl. 19, 1822
Sev.	Lewis Zigler " June 24, 1817		William Smith " Feb 1814
"	Benjamin Leland " July 4, 1819	Sev	James Pullin " May 17, 1822
"	John Topham " Aug 21, 1825	"	Lewis Neeley " Oct. 4, 1806
Elder	45 Ira Oviatt " Dec 8, 1804		Robert Linford " Dec 25, 1805
Sev	Edward Starr " Feb 27, 1817		John Stevens " Mar 31 [illegible]

Friday February 6, 1846

	Sev	
Cyrus Sandford born Dec. 16, 1813		Jacob R. Butterfield born Feb. 17, 1816
Edward Davis " Nov. 5, 1827	"	Walker Gardner " July 5, 1826
William A Simmons " June 28, 1826	"	James Daily " Mar. 26, 1815
Charles Ford " Nov. 4, 1807	"	Harrison Lever " Sep. 17, 1820
F. G. Davis " Aug. 2, 1806	"	William Barnett " June 24, 1831
Charles Stewart " May 14, 1814	"	Lewis H. Miller " Aug. 30, 1827
John H. Reed " Dec. 12, 1815		193 Samuel A Wilson " Mar. 21, 1819

were washed by Horace Owens and Cyrus A. Mead. Anointed by Leslie Lyme Young and Moses M Sanders. 10 p. 12

List 8 In the Female Department commencing at 40 p. 11 P.M.

Eliza Gibbs born Apl. 14, 1813
Elizabeth Neeley " Apl. 4, 1810
Sarah Ann Stewart " Feb 6, 1820
Mary Emeline Pendleton " Mar. 1, 1816
Alice Pullen " July 31, 1818
Sarah Jane Barnes " Mar. 1808
Almira Prentiss " Sep. 24, 1820
Nancy Rice " Mar. 4, 1776
Sylvia Almira Sandford " Mar 11, 1815
Elizabeth Leland " Mar 7, 1828
Martha Simmons " Jan. 1, 1828
Ann Linford " May 10, 1802
Mary [illegible] " Oct 13 1803
Sarah [illegible] " Apr. 19, 1804
Catherine [illegible] " June 16 1821

Ann Smith born Mar 6, 1817
Sophronia Reed " Mar. 29, 1817
Martha Wilcox " Jan. 23, 1820
Elizabeth Zigler " June 7, 1827
Sarah Leonard " Mar. 8, 1788
Anna Ford " Oct. 13, 1810
Jane Bordman " Apl. 31, 1824
Amanda Ann Clark " May 5, 1824
Ann Davis " Feb 16, 1814
Elizabeth Daley " Mar. 29, 1817
Elizabeth Stevens " May 9, 1813
Ruth Abraler " Sept 25 1818
Mary Lance " Oct 5 1754
Dorcas Sevire " Aug 15 1823
Kindness A. Canes " Sept 13 1830

were washed and annointed by Mary J. Sanderson, Philinda [illegible] Mary H. Felshaw, Clemicia Hamilton, Unice Holbrook, Peggy Patten Mary [illegible] and Mary D. Frost.

—Seventies Record, Book B, oversized portion, February 6, 1846.

Susanna Lee [Liptrot] [born] May 19. 1809 [in] Pendleton Clithero Lancashire Eng[land]:
Ann Reed [born] March 5. 1794 [in] Bedford Bedfordshire England
William Kay [born] April 1. 1811 [in] Chaidgley Lancashire d[itt]o
Mary Watters [born] August 25. 1819 [in] A[l]frick Worcestershire d[itt]o
William Kay and Mary Kay were adopted into the family of Willard Richards.

—Willard Richards, Diary.

....

Five hundred and twelve persons received the first ordinances of endowment in the Temple.

—"Manuscript History of Brigham Young," in *History of the Church,* 7:580.

....

Nauvoo temple endowments performed on this date for:

First Company: Lewis S. Dalrymple, Jerusha Dalrymple, Asa E. Earl, Nancy Earl, George W. Allen, Nancy Allen, Stephen P Meechum, Nancy Catharine Martin, Zachariah Martin, Hannah Draper, John Reed, Avalina Boggs, Francis Boggs, Francis T. Whitney, Caroline Webb, Ezra Strong, Mary Carpenter, Alpheus C. Ellsworth, Harriet/Eliza Ellsworth, John B. Williams, Clarissa Williams, Lewis Barney, Lucy Ann Pettit, Lorenzo Pettit, Lodemia Barnett, Samuel Barnett, Elizabeth Barney, Richard Pettit, Catherine Pettit, Robert Harris, Hannah M. Harris, Samuel White, Rebeckah White, Isaac Cooper, Martha Cooper, Ole Hayer, Margaret Hayer, Lorenzo D. Driggs, Melinda Driggs, William H. Barger, Ferraby Barger, Lewis Hardy, Phebe Hardy, Charles Haslden, Fletcher Strong, Christian Hayer, Hans Hayer, and Sterling Driggs.

Second Company: Francis M. Pomeroy, Irene Pomeroy, William S. Bachelor, Huldah Bachelor, Sarah Johnson, Alamantha Goddard, Catherine Corless, Edward Corless, Hester Hallam, John Huntington, Phebe Hancock, Mary Huntington, Benjamin Gardner, Electa Gardner, Mary Jackson, Oliver Higgins, Sylvia Higgins, John Coners, Priscilla Coners, James W. Hills, Mary Moseley, Garret Groesbeck, Mercy Crosby, Fanny Mahhart, Samuel Worthen, Sarah Worthen, Joseph Dudley, Sarah Dudley, William Head, Elizabeth Atchison, Sarah L. Harmon, Samuel R. Aiken Jr., Mary Ann Tuttle, William Cook, Elizabeth Cook, Robert Burton, Elizabeth Burton, Robert Collins, Mary Collins, Thomas R. Burns, Martha Ann

Tuttle, Hiram B. Clawson, Susannah Myers, Julian Hickenlooper, John R. Clawson, Lucy Burdick, James R. Allred, Harriet M. Simpson, Columbus Burdick, Thomas Tidwell, David Rodgers, and Mark Rodgers.

Third Company: James Dunn, Sarah Dunn, Simeon Thayne, Chloe Thayne, Margaret Shusler, Alonzo F. King, Elizabeth M. King, Mary Driggs, Martha Bindlay, John W. Bindlay, Celinda Van Hosen, Leonard Shussler, Harley Mowry, Mehitable Duty, Samuel Driggs, Hortensia Merchants, Lucius Merchants, Lydia W. Burgess, Jane Evans, Lois Stevens, Cyrus Eddy, Cynthia Hampshire, John Gibble, Marcetta Rowe, Mary Lamoreaux, Henry Jennings, Lucy Matilda Johnson, Amanda Jennings, Nathan Staker, Jane Staker, Fanny Jane Adams, William Evans, Lucy Thorndyke Hardy, Joseph Hardy, Mary Ann Johnson, Mahlon Johnson, Mary Mulford, Furman Mulford, Jemima Powell, William K. Parshall, Eveline Fisher, James Powell, Arsenath R. Duncan, Homer Duncan, Rebecca Winters, Joseph Fisher, Catherine E. Merhing, Elijah Clifford, Elizabeth McElroy, Hiram Winter, Parthena Boothe, Lorenzo Booth, William Farrar, Robert M. King, Nathaniel Winship, and Thomas Mayberry.

Fourth Company: John Murdock, Mary Jane Murdock, Fanny Merrick, Sarah Ann Perry, Sarah Brazier, Richard Brazier, Philander/Jackson Perry, James Bird, Jane Bird, Peter McFarlane, William M. Parker, Hannah Parker, Hannah Palmer, Jacob Bigler, Clarissa Jane Webb, Pardon Webb, Sarah Howell, Louisa Miles, William Milam, Margaret McDougal, Alphonso Edwin Miles, Ruth Jane Childes, George Foster, Christine Shearer, Norman B. Shearer, Sarah Ann Smith, Thomas W. Smith, Mary Ann Hunter, Edward Hunter Jr., Elizabeth Milam, Horace Evans, Candace Evans, Thomas Charles/Davis Howell, Almira Meekham, Elam Meekham, William S. Champlin, Mary Champlin, James Hawkins, Sarah Hawkins, Abraham Coon, Frances Yarbrough, Frances Nallam, William Cornwall Andrew, Sarah Peacock, James Robinson, Delila Andrews, Mary Jane Gee, John Smolham, Mary Ralphs, Sally Barnes, David P. Barnes, Lucinda Wolsey, Richard Ralphs, George Whitaker, Eveline P. Robinson, David M. Hard, Mary Waterman, Tyeritia Cragon, Julia Ann Rizey, John Mower, Isaac A. Bogue, Franklin R. Tower, Joseph Outhouse, John R. Frink, and Jared C. Roundy.

Fifth Company: Joseph Bostick, Agness Thompson, Thomas McCann, Nancy Walker, John R. Walker, Janet Miller, Elizabeth Edwards, Sarah McCann, James Dack, Eliza Edmonds, Ole Lurus, Anna Lurus, Maria Jeffries, John Miller, Elizabeth/Welch Madison, Sarah Ofton, William

Holliday Edwards, Eliza Edmonds, Peter Ofton, Lydia Raffety, Phillis McTaggart, Sally Shelly Colson, Joel Edmonds, Mary DeForest, Thomas McTaggart, Elizabeth Lassey, Josiah Lobdel DeForest, Polly Foster, Joseph Shelly, Eliza Spurr, Thomas Foster, Elizabeth Pixton, Larce Hayer, Amelia Caldwell, Peter Spurr, Rebecca Cunnington, Edwin Cadwell, Mary Bennett, Frederick Connington, Catharine Woodland, John Wilton Sealley, Robert Pixton, Benjamin Andrews, Rhoda Andrews, Robert Wells, Olive Wells, Elizabeth Reeves, John Hammond, Melissa Bennett, John Francis Reynolds, Martha Reynolds, Austin Hazen, Lovisa Hammond, Herbert Hill Foster, Elizabeth Hazen, Abraham Bond, Polly Bond, Barbary Boley, Henry Boley, Mary Simpson, Thorson Simpson, Elizabeth Ann Frasure, Lucretia Burdick, Asa Barton, Olivea Hayer, William Woodland, Mary Barton, James Dean Miller, Isabella Miller, Aroet Lucius Hale, Betsey Free, Henry M. Patten, Betsey Patten, Andrew Hayer, Rebecca Hess, Moses Ayres Jones, Hannah Carrilla Free, Oliver Hayer, Statira Beach, Absolom Pennington Free, Edwin Peck, George Simon Dolten, Christian Luras, and Horace Burdick.

Sixth Company: Ephraim Cheney, Harriet Cheney, Amanda Dover Colburn, Thadeas Alvord, Loanda Eliza Shumway, Matilda Jane Steward, Isaac M. Steward, Sarah Husbands, James Kippen, Matilda E. Owens, William Williams, Lovina Susan Riggs, Mary Williams, Lydia Losee, Conrad Staly, Isabella Kappin, Mary Cole, Hannah Staley, James McDonald, Mary Aimscough, Sarah McDonald, Flora Drake, William Aimscough, Sophronia Drake, Elizabeth Ralphs, William Ralphs, Elizabeth Shumway, Alanson Burt Shumway, Sarah Plumb, Emeline Potter, John McMurray, Mary McMurray, Abraham Nelson, Sarah Nelson, Richard Brazier Jr., Elizabeth Brazier, Ransom Robert Potter, Anthony Stratton, Elenor Packard, Philip Packard, Israel Herriman, Sabira Herriman, Harriet W. Phelps, James Nelson, Thomas Morris, Mary Stephens Stowell, Aurora Shumway, David Burrows, Sarah Burrows, Rebecca Nelson, Abraham Losee, Flora Kingsley, Elenor Kingsley, Henry Simon Dalten, William Jennings, Deborah Jennings, John Kirkpatrick Sr., Ransom Tidwell, Catharine Hendrix, and Moses Dayton.

Seventh Company: John C. L. Smith, Sarah Smith, Amanda Wilson, Huldah Elvira Canada, Jane Rogers, William Crutchlow, Ann Proctor, Belana Pulsipher, Nancy Mason Smith, Charles Kennedy, Agness Richards, John Proctor, Ann Hill, Joseph Holbrook, Anna Holbrook, Huldah Dans, Mary Snow, Robert Hill Sr., George Snow, Margaret Clark, Udney

H. Jacobs, Elizabeth Heward, John Hayward, Martha Shupe, John W. Shupe, Jane Edmundston, Melchee Oyaler, Elizabeth Oyaler, Thomas Rogers, Martha Orsor, John Edmundston, Clarissa Blackman, Eliza Bishop, Abigail Holden, William H. Bishop, Hiram Blackman, Philip Garner, Mary Garner, Wiley H. Holden, Mary McLain, Carter Graham, Eliza Graham, Elsie Jacob, Andrew Fawks, Matilda Stowell, John Pyper, Magdalena Gardner, Alexander Gardner, Sophia Crooks, John Angus, Margaret Steward, Franklin Beach, Abigail Chase, Robert B. Steward, Elizabeth Kelly, Amos S. Chase, Melinda Westfall, George Patrick, Hannah Stowell, William R. R. Stowell, Elizabeth Mackley, Abner Chase, Hugh Patrick, Mary Ann Mackley, George Hickenlooper, John Westfall, Robert Kelly, Lovina Dodge, Seth Dodge, Mary Ann Call, John Wait, Harvey Call, Lydia M. Rolph, John Johnson, John Rowley, Robert Hill, Elizabeth Ashby, John Patrick, James Holmes, Benjamin Ashby, Nathaniel S. Norris, and William Burrows.

Eighth Company: Elizabeth Stevens, John Stevens, Sarah Weston, James Dailey, Kindness N. Hence, Charles Stewart, Sarah Ann Stewart, Samuel A. Wheelcoxe, Martha Wheelcoxe, Ira Oviatt, Ruth Oviatt, William Smith, Ann Smith, Lewis Neeley, Isabelle Dailey, Sarah Lennert, Cyrus Sandford, William Gibbs, Nancy Rice, Edward Starr, Eliza Gibbs, Robert Linford, Elizabeth Neeley, John H. Reed, Silva Elmona Sandfort, Joseph T. Pendleton, Mary Ann M. Pendleton, Warren Post, Amanda A. Starr, Franklin J. Davis, Sophronia Reed, Ann Linford, Samuel Lance, Ann Davis, Harrison Severe, Dorcas Severe, Mary Lance, Sarah Jane Barnes, William Pope, Elizabeth Seeler, Lewis Seeler, Mary Biddlecom, William Neeley, Almia Prendis, Anna Ford, Charles Ford, Catharine Pope, Thomas Boardman, Jane Boardman, James Pullin, Alas Pullin, Alexander Molliner, Elizabeth Leland, Benjamin Leland, Martha Simmons, Levy N. Kendell, Jacob K. Butterfield, William A. Simmons, Henry W. Braicee, William Barnett, Walter E. Gardner, John Topham, Orrin McKown, Edward H. Davis, and Lewis H. Miller.

—Summary of information compiled by the Temple Index Bureau, *Nauvoo Temple Endowment Register: 10 December 1845 to 8 February 1846.*

....

Second anointings performed on this date:

Lewis D. Wilson and Patsy (Reynolds) Wilson, anointed by William W. Phelps; John D. Parker and Almeda (Roundy) Parker, anointed by

William Snow; William Pitt and Cornelia (Divine) Pitt, anointed by William W. Phelps; Wandle Mace and Margaret (Merklee) Mace, anointed by William W. Phelps; Brigham Young, Mary Ann (Turley) Young, Abigail (Harbach) Young, and Cecilia (Cooper) Young, anointed by John Taylor; Eliza R. Snow to Joseph Smith (deceased) for eternity, anointed by John Taylor; Elijah Fordham and Clarissa (Brooks) Fordham, anointed by John Taylor; Heber C. Kimball, Theresa (Morley) Kimball, Hulda (Barnes) Kimball, Sarah (Stiles) Kimball, anointed by John Taylor; Daniel M. Repshire and Hannah (Walton) Repshire, anointed by Zebedee Coltrin; and Simeon A. Dunn and Margaret (Snyder) Dunn, anointed by Zebedee Coltrin.

—Summarized from "Book of Anointings."

....

Sealings for the living performed on this date:

Lorin Whiting Babbitt to Almira [Elmira] Castle and Mary Aray; James Bevan to Hannah Jones; Erastus Bingham Jr. to Olive Hovey Freeman; Curtis Edwin Bolton to Rebecca Bunker and Ellen Merritt; Benjamin Boyce to Susanna C. Judd; Benjamin Brown to Polly Thompson; Charles Brown to Mary Arey; Lorenzo Brown to Frances Crosby; Harrison Burgess to Amanda Melvina [Maria] Hammond; James Burgess to Lydia Stiles Wyman; John Mathias Burk [Burn] to Abigail Fellows, and Keziah [Keturah] Van Benthuysen; Samuel Burton to Hannah Shipley; Hiram Norton Byington to Sarah Holkins; Ezra Thompson Clark to Mary Stevenson; Raymond Clark to Elizabeth Andrews and Mary Carpenter; Robert Collins to Mary Jane Mayberry; Joseph W. Coolidge to Rozilla Milla Carter; George Crowther to Sarah Dugard; David Avery Curtis to Amanda Ann Starr; Enos Curtis to Ruth Franklin; William Luce Davis to America Jane Overlin; Walter M. Edwards to Mahala Garner Green; Bradford White Elliot to Ann Eliza Dunlap; Samuel Ensign to Mary Everet Jordan [Gordon]; Lucian R. Foster to Maria Fosdick; Burr Frost to Mary Elizabeth Potter; Nathan Fulton to Phylena Hasting; John Gheen to Mary Willard and Margaret McCullough; William Gibbs to Eliza Dana; Truman Gillett to Fidelia Teal; Stephen Hezekiah Goddard to Alamantha Goddard; George Davis Grant to Elizabeth DuBois; Ephraim Green to Fidelia Thompson; Joseph John Hall to Delany Oller; Madison Daniel Hambleton to Chelnicia Smith; Solomon Hancock to Phebe Adams; Jesse P. Harmon to Margaret Allen; Daniel Hendrix to Louisa Lester; Wilkinson Hewitt to Julia Ann Jacques; Edward Hunter to Mary Ann Whitesides;

George Given Johnston to Sarah Sophia Johnson; Thomas Smith Johnson to Patience Thornton; Daniel Hutchinson Keeler to Philinda Clark Eldredge Merrick; Joseph Andrew Kelting to Lucy Matilda Johnson; John Kempton to Hannah Bradford; Heber Chase Kimball to Alice Buchanan, Sarah Shuler Buckwalter, Rebecca Swain Williams, Harriet Hereford, and Nancy Maria Mason Smith; Enoch Marion King to Mary Bigg Ware; Joseph King to Mahala Carter; Benjamin R. Lamb to Elizabeth DuBois; Andrew Losey Lamoreaux to Isabelle Wilson; Wright Lancaster to Sarah Bryant; Tarleton Lewis to Melinda Gimblin; Henry Manhard to Fanny Richardson; Matthew McEwen to Mary Smith; Eliphas Marsh to Hannah Hustead; Cyrus Alamson Mead to Jemima Clement Forbs; William Meeks to Mary Elizabeth Rhodes; Moses Worthen Mecham to Elvira Berby [Derby]; John Aylor Mikesell to Katherine Mikesell; John Mills to Elizabeth Hall; Edward Thompson Mumford to Hannah Cann Crosby; Levi Newton Myrick to Philinda Clark Eldridge; Levi Stillman Nickerson to Mary Ann Lyman; Zadoc Parker to Miriam Parker; William W. Patten to Betsey Darrow; Andrew H. Perkins to Jemima Wilson; William Job Perkins to Martha R. Perkins; Ute Perkins to Ann [Anna] Warren; Alanson Pettingill to Susanna Goddard Young; Lorenzo Pettit to Lucy Ann Merrill; Robert Pixton to Elizabeth Cooper; Francis Martin Pomeroy to Irene Ursula Haskell; William Monroe Pope to Catherine McBride; Uriah Burk Powell to Sarah Moore; Samuel Maxwell Price to Abi Salina Burk; David Harvy Redfield to Fanny M. McAtherton; Willard Richards to Ann Reed Braddock and Susanna Lee [Liptrot] Walker; James Robinson to Amelia Marie Aldrich; David White Rogers to Martha Collins [Calkins]; Perrigrine Sessions to Julia Ann Kilgore, Mary Call, and Lucina Call; Asahel Smith to Elizabeth Schellenger; Elias Smith to Lucy Brown; Ezra Strong to Olive Lowell; Elizur Goodrich Terrill to Eliza Crosby; Theodore Turley to Ruth Jane Giles; George Day Vanbeck to Adaline Elvira Hunck; Phares Wells to Maria McLane; Robert Wells to Olive Wells; John Alexander Whitesides to Electa Eleanor Sherman; Samuel Whitney to Catherine Davis Wilson; John Benjamin Williams to Clarissa Harding; David Wood to Catherine Crites; Daniel Wood to Nancy Ann Boice; Edwin Dilworth Woolley to Mary Wickersham, Louisa Chapin Gordon, and Ellen Wilding; Stephen Winchester to Caroline Fulton; Brigham Young to Clarissa Blake; John Young Jr. to Louise Jones; and Joseph Young to Mary Ann Huntley Gurnsey.

—Summarized from the Book of Living Sealings.

Sealings for the dead performed on this date:

Joseph Smith (Parley P. Pratt, proxy) to Mary Ann Frost, Heber C. Kimball officiating;[78] John Sanderson Twist (Brigham Young, proxy) to Naamah Kendal (Jenkins) Carter [no officiator given][79]; and Oliver Walker (Brigham Young, proxy) to Nancy Cressy.[80]

—Summarized from "Sealings and Adoptions."

....

Adoptions performed on this date:

To Winslow and Olive Hovey Farr: Aaron Freeman Farr, Harris Farr, Olive Hovey Farr, Ephraim Badger, Harriet Badger, Ebenezer Marshall Kimball, Melancy Sweet Blakey, Lucius Marchants, Hortensia Patrick, Sarah Bowen, and Amanda Bowen Colbourn: "These persons were all adopted into the family of Winslow Farr, 6 Feb[ruary]. 1846, 9 p.m."; and to Brigham and Augusta Adams Young: James Graham, Mary Graham, Isaac Morley, Lucy Morley, Robert Pierce, and Hannah Pierce, sealed by Heber C. Kimball.

—Summarized from "Sealings and Adoptions."

Saturday, February 7, 1846

[See pages 610-13 for the Seventies Record for this date.]

....

The endowments were continued in the evening [February 6]. I [Norton Jacob] again repaired to the House of the Lord with my father, Udney, my wife Emily, my daughter Elsie P., and Miss Matilda Stoel. In the course of the night my father, daughter, and Miss Matilda received their washing and anointing, and about 11 o'clock I with my wife Emily, received my second anointing and was ordained a King and Priest unto God in room no. 4.

—"Life of Norton Jacob," typescript, L. Tom Perry Special Collections, Harold B. Lee Library, Brigham Young University, Provo, Utah.

....

I [George A. Smith] went to the Temple with Bathsheba. Upwards of

78. Mary Ann Frost was also sealed to Parley P. Pratt for time.
79. Naamah Carter was also sealed to Brigham Young for time.
80. Nancy Cressy was also sealed to Brigham Young for time.

[Washings and anointings]

List 1 Saturday February 7th 1846. commenced at 15 m. past 7.

Male department

Sev		Sev.	
	1 John Milton Born Jan 30 1815		9 Elisha Mabery born Apr 4 1827
"	2 Charles Dicken " June 21, 1824	"	10 James R. Cutler " Feb 1 1828
"	3 Edward Wilcox " Dec 18 1819	"	11 Edward Dailey " Mar 24, 1826
"	4 Duncan Casper " Dec. 8, 1825	"	12 Saml. K. Gifford " Nov. 11 1821
"	5 Norman Sharp " Sep 16 1808	"	13 Saml Burgess " July 8 1820
"	6 James K. Baldwin " Jan 23 1826	"	14 Joseph Brunelle " Nov 15, 1827
"	7 John Hadson " Jan 10 1809	H. P.	1 Thos Burgess " Dec 21 1787
"	8 Moses Corey " Apr 30 1824	Elders	1 John Marks [?] "

Saturday February 7th 1846

Elders		Elders	
	2 Augustus Stowell born Mar 24, 1829		Thorit Peck born May 30 1826
	3 Allumbee Lemon " Mar 2 1823		

were washed by Horace Owens & Geo C. Riser, and were Annointed by Leslie Lyme Young & M M Sanders Young.

Ordinations

John Moiels was ordained an Elder by Leslie Lyme Young Augustus Stowel Ordained an [blank] by Darious Chase. Charles Decker ordained a Seventy by L. Gee and Thos Burgess was ordained a High Priest by Anson Call. Finished 10 Minutes to 3 A.M.

Female Department

List 1st

Ann Corey born July 21 1830 Martha Powers born Mar 21 1824

Lucy McKown " Dec 20 1830	Matilda Casper " Dec 31 1820
Margaret Brunel " July 6 1831	Losa Geer " Dec 6 1836
Martha Sharp " Sept 24 1828	Avarille Casper " Nov 26 1789
Priscilla Snider " Feb 2 1806	Mary Ann Burgess " Mar 29 1781
Rachael Fryman " May 27 1832	

were washed and annointed by Chelmecia Hamilton, Peggy Patten, Philinda ~~Patten~~ C Kesler Mary Ann Nickerson Jane Rogers, Mary Deforest and Mary Coltrin.

Male Department commenced at 10 p 9. A.M.

List 2

Sev		Sev.	
"	15 Richard Griffiths born Feb. 9, 1811		31 Hiram Hoyt born June 8, 1812
"	16 Wm Ormsby " July 25 1796	"	32 Timothy S Hoyt " Mar. 4, 1818
"	17 Peter Williams " Jan 15 1811	"	33 Charles Chase " Nov. 23, 1813
"	18 Edward Gabbot " Feb 1803	"	34 Alfred B. Child " Nov. 15, 1796
"	19 Levi W Montague " Oct 12 1806	"	35 Alfred A. Taylor " Feb. 22, 1823
"	20 Mark Hall " Oct. 25, 1824	"	36 William Coons " May 17, 1818
"	21 Edward Bunker " Aug. 1, 1822	"	37 Henry Smith " May 2, 1828
"	22 John Husband " Apl. 5, 1792	"	38 John Leonard " Dec 5, 1831
"	23 Amos Northop " Feb 2, 1820	"	39 Philo T. Farnsworth " Jan 24, 1826
"	24 William Smith " July 10, 1824	"	40 David B. Haight " Oct 18, 1807
"	25 Anthony Myers " Aug. 19, 1811	"	41 A. P. Chesley " Oct 22, 1814
"	26 Frederick J. Rushton " Feb 1806	H. Priest	2 James A. Smith " Dec 6 1787
"	27 William Casto " Feb 18, 1816	Elders	5 Wm Gribble " Aug 15 18[?]
"	28 Thomas Ralphs " July 22, 1819	"	6 William Spears " May [?] 1793

[Seventies]	29 Harmon Cutler [born] July 15, 1799	[Seventies]	7 Alanson Smith [born] Aug [?] 18[?]
"	30 Cyrus Wingate " Jan 22, 1815	"	8 Lee Bybee " [illegible]

Saturday, February 7, 1846.

Elders

9 Simon Bailey born Nov 28, 1816	were washed by Daniel D. Hunt and
10 Reuben Attwood " May 25, 1797	Levi Nickerson
11 John Egbert " July 12, 1778	Anointed by Andrew Moore, and
12 John Shore " June 30, 1790	John M. Chitister 5 to 10 a.m.
13 Charles Bonney " Mar 23,	

List 2 In the Female Department commencing at 10 to 9

Eleanor Parsons born July 18, 1802	Mary A. Haight born Jan 18 1830
May E Consay " Nov. 3, 1810	Elvira Stevens " Mar 17 1852
Sarah Gabbot " Feb 7 1811	Janette Spears " Mar 10 1811
Hannah Pullin " July 14, 1811	Harriet Williams " Sept 13 1808
Mary Wilsey " Oct 7 1825	Sophia Smith " Aug 5 1809
Luticha Smith " June 13 1824	Huldah S Gribble " June 28 1823
Susan Egbert " Aug 10 1786	Eliza Child " Oct 31 1822
Leeann Bybee " Mar 29 1800	Huldah Wilcox " Jan 22 1781
Elenor Myres " Oct 6, 1823	Mary A Northrup " March 1 1824
Lucy Atwood " Oct. 8, 1786	Catherine Head " Aug 10 1792
Polly Child " Mar 30 1798	Malinda Wood " Nov 18 1823
Elizabeth Williams " April 1814	Clarissa Haight " Jan 31 1815
Jane Rushton " Apr 8 1808	Rochelina Casto " June 7 1818

Sarah Hoyt " Sept 22 1807
Deborah Barney " Sept 22 1808
Lucy Ann W Cutter " Apr 6 1817
Margaret Smith " Apr 18 1791
Phebe Husbands " July 30, 1831
Susanna Dunn " Jan 4 1831
Catharine Wright " Mar 12 1820
Polly Shaw " Jan 11 1790
Susan S Chase " June 25 1811
Mary Griffiths " May 1810

were washed and annointed by Mary Carpenter & Sarah M Johnson Mary Deforest Elizabeth Hutchen Caroline Crosby Louisa Clark Sarah B. Barney Mary Coltrin & Lucy Hatfield finished 10 to 10

List 3 In the Male Department commenced 15 to 12

Sev
Thos. Bradbury born Dec 17, 1827
E. D. White " Mar. 30, 1816
John O. W " May 16,1799
Wm Holmson " July 6, 1802
Wm I Robinson " Dec. 20, 1818
J. R. Blanchard " Jan 18, 1795
Albert B. Griffin " Feb. 28 1809
John Cochron " July 23 1824
John Lowell " Mar. 65 1812
Israel Hay " April [?] 1828
Samuel Alger " Feb 14 1786
Eld Henry M McArthur " [illegible] 1829

Sev
Elisha Hoops born Oct 13 1813
Henry Morton " June 17 1821
John W Follett " Oct 26 1819
John Porter " Dec 18 1815
Perry Oman " July 27 1823
M. [?] Spencer " May 6 1804
Thos Crompton " Nov 9 1804
Eld F. Knapp born Feb 24 1806
Sev Peter Rabins " Apr 27 1817
Orsage Tromer " June 23 1805
Thomas D. [illegible] " Apr 20 1812

—Seventies Record, Book B, February 7, 1846.

six hundred received the ordinance of first anointment of the Priesthood, this being the last day for administering them, for the present.

—George A. Smith, "History of George Albert Smith."

....

According to G[eorge]. A. Smith's Journal upwards of six hundred received the ordinances: One hundred and twenty-six of which were reported in the Seventies Record.

—"Manuscript History of Brigham Young," in *History of the Church,* 7:580.

....

Nauvoo temple endowments performed on this date for:

First Company: Samuel K. Gifford, James K. Baldwin, Edward Davis, Lucy McKown, Mary Ann Burgess, Martha Powers, John M. Powers, Thomas Burgess, Martha Jane Sharp, John Hodson, Thorit Peck, Edward Wilcox, Eliza Mosier, Edward Daley, Matilda Casper, Denton S. Casper, Margaret Brunell, Moses Corey, Allum Bee Lemmon, Ann Corey, Norman Sharp, John Miles, Percilla Snyder, Joseph Brunell, Avarilla Casper, James Royal Cutler, Augustus Stowel, Laura Geen, Charles Decker, Rachael Neyman, Elisha Mallorey, and Samuel Burgess.

Second Company: John Egbert, Susan Egbert, Lee Bybee, Leanah Bybee, Lucy Atwood, Charles Williams, Harriet Williams, Reuben Atwood, Huldah Wilcox, Richard Griffith, Mary Griffith, Malinda Wood, Charles Barney, Debrah Barney, Peter Williams, Elizabeth Williams, David B. Haight, Clarissa Haight, Frederick James Rushton, Sarah Rushton, Amos Lothrop, Mary Adelia Northrup, Alfred Bosworth Child, Polly Child, Edward Gabbot, Sarah Gabbot, John Shaw, Polly Shaw, William Smith, Lotitia Smith, Harmon Cutler, Lucy Ann Cutler, Elansine Smith, Sophia Smith, Charles Alvin Chase, Susan Sterns Chase, Alexander P. Chesley, Eliza Chesley, William Gribble, Huldah Sophia Gribble, Cyrus Winget, Hannah Pullin, Anthony Myers, Catharine Winget, James S. Smith, Catharine Head, Levi W. Montague, Elenor Myers, Janette Broom, William Spiers, Alvira Stevens, John Husbands, Phebe Husbands, Hiram Hoyt, Sarah Hoyt, Margaret Smith, William Ormsby, Mary Wilsey, Simon Bailey, Eleanor Parsons, Mark Hall, Mary Elizabeth Corsey, William Casto, Racheline Casto, Edward Bunker, Mary Adelia Haight, Timothy S. Hoyt, Susanna Dunn, Thomas Ralphs, John Leonard, William Coons, Alfred A. Taylor, Philo/Taylor Farnsworth, and Henry Smith.

Third Company: Perry Owman, Hannah Oman, Rosetta Glazier,

Shepherd Glazier, Margaret Blanchard, John R. Blanchard, Sarah Ann Knapp, Flewellin Knapp, Mary Vail Morse, Younger McCaslin, Caroline Orcutt, John Mitchell, Eunice P. Eaton, Halmagh J. Van Wagoner, Harriet A. Van Wagoner, Eunice McRae, Ezra Thompson, Amanda Thompson, Amelia Spencer, Mathias Spencer, Polly Chandler, Edmund Nelson, Sarah Bigler, Jane Nelson, Orange Warner, Delilah Warner, Thomas Crompton, Amity Johnston, Betsey Crompton, John Cochran, Marietta Cochran, Erasmus Darwin White, Eliza White, John O. Waterman, Jane Waterman, Thomas Callahan, Lucinda Callahan, Thomas Bradbury, Elizabeth Bradbury, William Robinson, Elizabeth Robinson, Peter Robinson, Mary Haywood, Samuel Alger, Clarissa Alger, Selina H. Robinson, Joseph Mecham, Malinda Mecham, Joseph Fairbanks, Polly Fairbanks, Albert B. Griffin, Abigail Griffin, Elisha Hoopes, Elizabeth Hoopes, Rufus King, Elizabeth Fidelia King, Israel Hoyt, Sarah Haskell, William J. Robinson, Rachel Robinson, Henry Morton, Mary Ann Jamison, Elisha Voorhes, Nancy Voorhes, John W. Follet, Susanna Bayles, John Porter, Ann Matson, John Lovell, Elizabeth/Melvina Huffaker, David Moss, Talitha Morris, Henry M. McArthur, Rhoda Luxton, and Aseneth Hubbard.

Fourth Company: Lorenssa Spaulding, Helen Nelson, Nehemiah Harmon, Margaret Blaisdel, Aurelia Harmon, Janette Blaisdell, Isaac Nelson, Thirza Angelina Nay, Almira Stoker, John Gailey, Mary Winkless, Thomas Winkless, Paulina Snyder, Edward M. Green, Susanna Green, John Nay, Ann Gailey, William Smith, Hannah Smith, Henry Snyder, Matilda Reeves, John Mayberry, Alonzo Pierce, Esther Pierce, Samuel Smith, Maria Smith, John Topham, Jane Topham, Richard Carter, Rebecca Dew, George P. Hicks, Martha Hicks, Thomas Dew, Hannah Carter, William B. Coffin, Abigail Coffin, Alonzo P. Raymond, Clarinda Raymond, Richard B. Payne, Lurena Payne, William Topham, Sarah Topham, William Ford, Hannah Ford, James Herron, Catharine Herron, Edwin Holden, Angeline Holden, Nathan Davis, Martha Campbell, Richard S. Doty, Anna Zemmer, Samuel Meecham, Margaret Doty, Ezra H. Curtis, Sarah Meecham, James Farrer, Ursula Curtis, Jacob Frazier, James P. Pettigrew, Price W. Nelson, Sanford Porter Jr., Augustus Dodge, and Abijah Reed.

Fifth Company: Thomas Clark, Charlotte Clark, Andrew Baston, Emma Turner Baston, George Bradley, Betsey Bradley, Zemira Deafare, Jane Wait, David Ellsworth, Catharine Ellsworth, James Fife, Margaret Fife, Francis Duff, Mary Duff, Prudence Hooks, William R. Terry, Mary A.

Terry, Robert L. Gott, Sarah Gott, Jessee Hitchcock, Nancy Hitchcock, Robert Owens, Catharine Ann Owens, Lyman Curtis, Charlotte Curtis, Julius Lathrop, Ruth Ann E. Lathrop, Salsbury B. Davis, Ruth Davis, George Brafet, Amy Draper, Benjamin Ellsworth, Jane Lyndsay, David Abel, Ann Abel, Joel Parriah, Anne Ellsworth, John Almond, Christiana Almond, John Riggs, Ann Braffett, Hiram C. Jacobs, Jane Riggs, Caroline Jacobs, Elenor Skinner, Horace B. Skinner, Elizabeth Richards, Silas Richards, Elizabeth McMillan, James McMillan, Balinda Jane Webb, Elenor Langden, James Wesley Webb, John Durfee, Sarah Ann Durfee, Sarah Holden, Archibald Campbell, Mary Moore, Lorenzo Moore, Mahala Strong, Osias Strong, Elizabeth Babit, Sarah Brown, Henry Sanford, Nancy M. Sanford, Daniel Bulard, Elizabeth Bullard, Elizabeth Newman, Johnathan Newman, Isaac C. Niles, Conrad Clyman, Elizabeth Clyman, Warner Hoakes, Jane Baldwin, William Stoker, Ahser Baldwin, Andrew J. Moore, John A. Hunt, Henry P. Richards, and Jesse Johnson.

Sixth Company: John Welch, Annis Springer, George W. Springer, Rebecca S. Colmere, Peter John Western, Eliza Welch, Asa Davis, Emily Mace, Thomas Bishop, John Mace, Sally Davis, Lucia Ann Bishop, Francis Pullin, Sabrina King, George E. King, Lorance Gardner, Daniel W. Gardner, Rhoda Potter, George Hogan, Margaret Hogan, Hylan Davis, Sophia Davis, David Smith, Phebe Smith, Samuel G. Clark, Melissa Coe, John Winn, Christiana Winn, George Curtis, Mary Jane Andrus, Solomon N. Conley, Melinda Miles, Eve Conley, Owen Coles, Calista Conant, Esther Benion, William Engus, Milley Yarbrough, Ruell Perris, Abigail W. Spear, John Benion, Huldah Cole, Alfred W. Childs, Amanda S. Childs, William Weston, Dorothy Weston, Charles Raymond, Catharine Raymond, Thomas Cottam, Adelia Lambert, Robert Boyd, Margaret Caster, Thore Thurston, Lodicia Thurston, Israel Mott, Lydia Parish, Hobbart Pendleton, Phebe Pratt, Hugh Lytle, Christinia Lytle, William S. Lish, Ferocinia Lish, Henry Hills, Mary Hills, John S. Woodbury, Rebecca W. Chaplin, and Helen S. Pratt.

Seventh Company: William Cameron, Asaph Blanchard, Jane Cameron, George Wardel, Fanny Wardell, Ruben Hoton, Elizabeth Hoton, Frances Robins, Thomas Harrington, William Allen, Margaret Harrington, Joseph Hill, Ann Young, Edward Ockey, Eliza Ockey, Charles McGary, Charlotte McGary, James Bailey, Mariah Hudson, William D. Johnston, Sally Plumb, William J. Lavens, Polly Lavens, Matthew Casto, Catharine Folett, Joseph Billington, Martha Billington, John Hamer, Nancy Hamer, Thomas Peterson, Mary Peterson, Elizabeth Allen, Martin Miller, Mary Miller, Mary Clark, Joseph Pulling, Nancy Clark, John Garner,

Mary Ann O. Garner, Anna Bishop, Sarah B. Allen, Ezra Allen, Elizabeth Hannah, George W. Johnston, Mariah Jane Johnston, German Elsworth, Spedy Elsworth, John Cole, Charlotte Cole, Heber Johnston, Sally Johnston, William Millgate, Hannah Millgate, John Gaylord, Lucinda Gaylord, George Coleman, Mary Coleman, James H. Aldrich, Naham Holden, John Sigler, and John K. Crosby.

Eighth Company: John McAuley, John Wickel, Leah Brandon, Elcitae Ford, Stephen Cooper, Lucy Ann McClenahan, Robert McClenahan, Julian Houghas, Goodman Houghas, Thomas Nelson, Mary Nelson, John Morrison, Sarah Morrison, Mary Ann Wich, James Bullock, Foster Curtis, Celia D. Bulk, Elijah Leonard, Sabre Tuttle, John Henry Tuttle, Isabel Alcos, Charles Lurus, William Smith, Anna Smith, Mary Wickel, James Guyman, Maryann Guyman, Elizabeth Luras, David Wilson, Mary Wilkinson, Augustas Richards, Juliann Burton, Judith Mellows, John Mellows, Thomas J. King, Rebecka King, Abigail Hitchcock, Samuel Pollock, Nancy Hammers, Henry Kingsley, Horace Thornton, Mahitable Thornton, Marcus H. Lemons, Cleopatra Lemons, John Chelley, Elizabeth Pickles, Benjamin Taylor, Mary Taylor, Elijah Mehring, John W. Dyer, James Loveless, T. W. Treat, Walter Barney, and Jeptha Condit.

Ninth Company:[81] William Mooney, Eliza A. Mooney, Triphenia Follet, William Strong, Lucy P. Dow, James H. Woodland, Louisa Whitaker, Chester Andrews, Mary Andrews, Dennison L. Harris, Ruth Kelly, Nelson R. Johnson, Lavinna Johnson, William T. Follett, Harriet Lamb, Nancy Nowel, Gilbert Bickmoore, Martha A. Bagly, Luther T. Tuttle, Sally R. Whitlock, Eliza A. Bickmoore, Daniel Giffern, Lewis Philips, Benjamin K. Bullock, William Woodland, G. W. Myres, Newel W. Blackman, Lucian Barney, Maximin H. B. Orcher, Noble N. Daniels, Henry Barley, James Young, Abraham Hendrickson, Matthew Willcox, Joseph McMerry, James McMerry, Joseph A. Peck, and Joseph Rank.

—Summary of information compiled by the Temple Index Bureau, *Nauvoo Temple Endowment Register: 10 December 1845 to 8 February 1846.*

....

Second anointings performed on this date:

Hyrum Dayton, Permelia (Bundy) Dayton, and Sophia (Lance) Dayton, anointed by [not given]; Mary Ann (Frost) Pratt to Joseph Smith (de-

81. Members of this company were probably received through the veil early on February 8, 1846.

ceased) for eternity, anointed by Zebedee Coltrin; Joseph A. Kelting and Lucy (Johnson) Kelting, anointed by Willard Snow; Jesse P. Harmon and Margaret (Allen) Harmon, anointed by Willard Snow; Ashal Smith and Elizabeth (Schellenger) Smith, anointed by Zebedee Coltrin; Edwin D. Woolley and Mary (Wickersham) Woolley, anointed by Willard Snow; Peter Fullmer and Susannah (Cefers) Fullmer, anointed by Zebedee Coltrin; Nathan Fulton (deceased) and Phylena (Hastings) Fulton, anointed by Zebedee Coltrin; Benjamin Brown and Sarah (Mumford) Brown, anointed by Willard Snow; Lewis Robbins, [no spouse identified], anointed by Willard Snow; Thomas Pearson and Catherine (Spickernagle) Pearson, anointed by Zebedee Coltrin; Royal Barney and Sarah (Esterbrooks) Barney, anointed by Willard Snow; Norton Jacob and Emily (Heaton) Jacob, anointed by Zebedee Coltrin; Jesse Baker and Sarah (Hawks) Baker, anointed by [not given]; John M. Burk and Keziah (Van Benthusen) Burk, anointed by [not given]; Enos Curtis and Ruth (Franklin) Curtis, anointed by [not given]; Solomon Hancock and Phebe (Adams) Hancock, anointed by [not given]; Elias Smith and Lucy (Brown) Smith, anointed by [not given].

—Summarized from "Book of Anointings."

....

Sealings for the living performed on this date:

Jesse Baker to Sarah Hawkes [Hanks]; Royale Barney Jr. to Sarah Bowen Esterbrook; Richard Bennett to Mary Bell; Israel Calkins Jr. to Lavina Wheeler; Alfred Bosworth Child to Polly Barber; Charles Chrisman to Mary G. Pearson; William Lathrop Cutler to Abigail Eliza Chase; David DeVo to Delia Toby; Zemira Draper to Amy Terry; Hiram Falk to Sybil Maria Smith; Lorin Farr to Nancy Bailey Chase; Winslow Farr to Amanda Bower Colburn; William Felshaw to Charlotte Walters; Josiah Wolcott Fleming to Nancy Bigler and Nancy Henderson; John Gailey to Ann Graves; John Gaylord Jr. to Lucinda Bagg; William Greenwood to Alice Houghton; Albert Bailey Griffin to Abigail Varney; Ole [Oley] Hayer [Hagar] to Margaret Anderson; Caleb Haight to Sarah Aldridge; Jefferson Hunt to Celia Mounts and Martha [Matilda Jane] Nease; William Kay to Mary Twimberrow Wattis Bennett; Joseph Kelly to Matilda Hull and Abiah Huchins; Eli Brazee Kelsey to Jane Caldwell; Hazen Kimball to Derinda Clark; Heber Chase Kimball to Charlotte Chase, Abigail Buchanan, Ruth Wellington, and Elizabeth Hereford; Flewellin Knapp to Sarah Ann Stickney; John Doyle Lee to Talitha [Delethea]

Morris; Cornelius Peter Lott to Jane Roger; John P. McEwan to Amanda Melvina Higbee; Moses Worthen Mecham to Elvira Derby; William Miller to Emeline Potter; James Newberry to Elizabeth Haskins; James Buchannan Porter to Elizabeth Slaughterback; Alonzo Pearce Raymond to Clarissa Clark; William Warner Player to Zillah Sanders; William Rufus Rogers Stowell to Hannah Topham; George Albert Smith to Susannah Ogden Bigler; Samuel Stratton Thornton to Harriet Jane Hickenlooper; John Topham to Jane Thornton; George Wardle to Fannie Rushton; James Wesley Webb to Balinda Jane Webb; Allen Weeks to Sarah Jane Bennett, Melissa Bennett, and Mary Bell; Joseph West to Lucinda Burton; Charles Hamilton Williams to Harriet Baldwin; Stephen Winchester Jr. to Mary Pierson; Thomas Winkless to Mary Palmer; David Dutten Yearsley to Harriet W. Dilworth Caulfish; and Brigham Young to Diana Severence Chase.

—Summarized from the Book of Living Sealings.

....

Sealings for the dead performed on this date:

John Buckwalter (Heber C. Kimball, proxy) to Sara Schuler;[82] and Frederick Granger Williams (Heber C. Kimball, proxy) to Rebecca Swain.[83]

—Summarized from "Sealings and Adoptions."

Sunday, February 8, 1846

10 minutes past 1 P.M. Nauvoo, Hancock Ill[inois]. President B[righam]. Young, H[eber]. C. Kimball, P[arley]. P. Pratt, N[ewel]. K. Whitney, Willard Richards, Amasa M. Lyman, John Taylor, Geo[rge]. A. Smith, Orson Hyde, kneeled at the Alt[a]r and President Brigham Young led in prayer according to the Holy Order, asking for the Holy Spirit to rest upon all those who had received their endowments. Gave thanks for the privileges which they had enjoyed in the Temple, ~~gave thanks~~ and asked for the privilege of returning and dedicating the other rooms of the Temple in the Lords own due time, that the records of the Temple might be preserved, that the Temple might not be polluted, that the walls of [the] Nauvoo House might be preserved, and completed, and that the records

82. Sara Schuler was also sealed to Heber C. Kimball for time.

83. Rebecca Swain was also sealed to Heber C. Kimball for time.

of the Nauvoo House might be preserved, and many other ~~things~~ excellent, needful things,

That the weather might be favorable for the Journey, that those who go might be able to find provisions, that teams and means may be provided for all the Saints to go in due time and that the temple may be completed and dedicated to the name of the Lord.

—Minutes of the Quorum of the Twelve Apostles, LDS Archives.

....

[A]t 9 oclock A.M. the Endowments were stopped in the House of the Lord & the veils were taken down—the People were then called out into the grove West of the Temple where wee were addressed by Presid[e]nt Joseph Young who is president of all the seventies, there being thirty-two quorums.

—"Life of Norton Jacob," typescript, L. Tom Perry Special Collections, Harold B. Lee Library, Brigham Young University, Provo, Utah.

....

[A]t 10 I went up the Temple—in council and returned about 1 or 2.

—Willard Richards, Diary.

....

[It] was this day [on which were] performed the last ordinances which were performed in the Lords House in Nauvoo & the closing prayer made at the Alt[a]r by the 12[.] I dissected the Alter carried the records to Pres[ident] B[righam]. Youngs & saw them carefully deposited for the Journey[.]

—Franklin D. Richards, Diary.

....

This Evening [I was] in a social meeting in the Temple[, and after] retiring to a private room[,] Sister Mary Vail Morse was sealed to me by Pres[ident] B[righam]. Young in [the] presence of H[eber]. C. Kimball and Sarah Ann Sanders. Although [there was opposition to this marriage,] Wealthy [Richards] being opposed, yet says Br[other] Kimball[,] dont let a woman take your crown[,] Bro[ther]. Richards.

—Phinehas Richards, Diary, LDS Archives.

....

Met in council with the Twelve [apostles] in the south east corner room, No. 1, in the upper story of the Temple. Kneeling around the altar we dedicated the building to the Most High and asked His blessing on our intended move to the West, and asked Him to enable us some day to finish the lower part of the Temple, and dedicated it to him and asked him to preserve the building as a monument to Joseph Smith. We then left it.

—George A. Smith, "History of George Albert Smith."

....

I [Brigham Young] met with the Council of the Twelve [Apostles] in the southeast corner room of the attic of the Temple. We knelt around the altar, and dedicated the building to the Most High. We asked his blessing upon our intended move to the west: also asked him to enable us some day to finish the Temple, and dedicate it to him, and we would leave it in his hands to do as he pleased; and to preserve the building as a monument to Joseph Smith. We asked the Lord to accept the labors of his servants in this land.[84] We then left the Temple.

—"Manuscript History of Brigham Young,"
in *History of the Church,* 7:580.

....

Sealings for the living performed on this date:

Stephen Joseph Abbott to Abigail Smith; John Milton Bernhisel to Permelia Darrow Smith and, for time, Melissa Lott Smith; James Brown to Abigail Abbott; Parley Parker Pratt to Phoebe Sopher; and Lewis Robbins to Frances Smith.

—Summarized from the Book of Living Sealings.[85]

....

Among the sealings for the dead performed on this date:

Joseph Smith (John M. Bernhisel, proxy) to Melissa Lott and Permelia Darrow, Brigham Young officiating.[86]

—Summarized from "Sealings and Adoptions."

---

84. This dedicatory prayer would be followed by another pronounced by Joseph Young on April 30, 1846, and a public dedication held from May 1 to May 3, 1846, at which Apostle Orson Hyde officiated. Most of the Saints had already started the trek across Iowa by the time the public dedication was held.

85. The following two sealings occurred on February 9, 1846: Edward Bunker to Emily Abbott and Freeman Nickerson to Hulda Chapman, according to the Book of Living Sealings.

86. Melissa Lott and Permelia Darrow were also sealed to John Bernhisel for time.

INDEX

Note: *Only the names of the men and women appearing most frequently or most prominently in this book are indexed. Ellipses are used to signal that some entries below appear on almost every page of the book and that such pages will not be specified separately thereafter. Discrepancies or variations in the spellings of proper names are indicated within square brackets.*